Mar

Marketing Research

Fourth Edition

Peter M. Chisnall

McGRAW-HILL BOOK COMPANY

London · New York · St Louis · San Francisco · Auckland
Bogotá · Caracas · Lisbon · Madrid
Mexico · Milan · Montreal · New Delhi · Panama · Paris · San Juan
São Paulo · Singapore · Sydney · Tokyo · Toronto

Published by
McGRAW-HILL Book Company Europe
Shoppenhangers Road, Maidenhead, Berkshire, SL6 2QL, England
Telephone 01628 23432
Fax 01628 770224

British Library Cataloguing in Publication Data

Chisnall, Peter M. (Peter Michael),
Marketing research. – 4th ed
I. Title
658.83

ISBN 0-07-707429-7

Library of Congress Cataloging-in-Publication Data

Chisnall, Peter M.
Marketing research/Peter M. Chisnall. – 4th ed.
    p.   cm. – (The McGraw-Hill marketing series)
Includes bibliographical references and index.
ISBN 0-07-707429-7
1. Marketing research.   I. Title.   II. Series.
HF5415.2.C48   1992
658.8'3 – dc20   91-42207 CIP

5 CUP 95

Typeset by Computape (Pickering) Ltd, North Yorkshire,
and printed and bound in Great Britain at the University Press, Cambridge

Printed on permanent paper in compliance with ISO Standard 9706

CONTENTS

PREFACE TO THE FOURTH EDITION

When this fourth edition is published, this book will have run for nearly twenty years, during which time it has been widely adopted as a standard text on marketing research for business degree and diploma courses in many institutions. I hope that this new edition, which has been thoroughly revised and updated, will continue to be useful to lecturers and students.

As before, the text is in four parts, and follows, systematically, from the evolution of marketing research to basic methodologies and specific applications. In particular, the development of electronic systems of data capture and the now widespread use of computer-assisted interviewing techniques are discussed at some length. The complexities of advertising research and the range of geodemographic analytical services are also given special attention. Research approaches in international marketing and qualitative research techniques have, likewise, been extended.

I am grateful to all those leading marketing researchers who have readily provided me with extensive and up-to-date information about their services. Their professional co-operation has been generously given and, at the undeniable risk of omitting some, I acknowledge, in random order the following: Nigel Newson-Smith of BARB, Joan Montgomerie of CAC, Linda Prior of Gallup, Celia Jones of Research Services, Janet Mayhew of JICNARS, Linda Hawkins of IPC, Linda McHugh of AGB, Tim Hunter-Henderson of Capital Radio, Greg Vaughan of RMS, Lionel Gordon of IFT, David Brennan of Tyne-Tees TV, Gill Troop of TVS TV, Professor Matthias Steinmann, Peter Meneer of BBC Research, Kathering Passerieu of the Harris Research Centre, Tim Grey of *Radio Times*, Michael Roe of Research International, Jack Paramore of JWT, Susannah Quick of BMRB, Elaine Jewell of DTI, Sheena Evans of Stats MR, Mic Rogers of NOP, Sharon Simms of Nielsen, Vivien Merles of Granada TV, Marion Crichton of Taylor Nelson, and David Taylor of JICPAS.

Once again, my thanks are given to the editorial staff of McGraw-Hill for their ever friendly and professional help, and to Mrs Mary Mason of Dublin Business School who, with her customary efficiency, produced the typescript.

This edition is dedicated to Charles and Georgina, whose reading preferences will certainly not yet include this book.

GENERAL INTRODUCTION

ROLE AND DEVELOPMENT OF MARKETING RESEARCH

1.1 INTRODUCTION

At one time, businesses were small, customers were few, and markets were mostly local. Suppliers and customers were in almost daily, close personal, contact; bargaining was done face-to-face; the market place was the hub of economic and social life.

Businesses were run not by corporate executives but by people who were similar to those whose custom they sought to attract. They shared the same culture – often they were kinsfolk – and communication was direct and resonant with cultural values.

With large-scale industrialization and vastly improved methods of transport and communication, entrepreneurs looked further afield for customers to buy their products. Today, technologies are dispersed over the world; new centres of production have been set up for motor cars, electronic equipment, and many other products that were once viewed as the prerogative of the Western developed countries.

Inevitably, the gap between producer and final consumer has widened: some firms are in danger of losing touch with the actual needs of their customers, particularly if they are thousands of miles away.

The management of the commercial, industrial, and many other kinds of organization which make up the mixed and advanced economies of countries like Britain seems to grow increasingly difficult as each year passes. Without valid and reliable information, management decision making would soon degenerate into some crazy game of chance. Hence, a systematic approach to the task of management is increasingly important in today's complex environment. One of the prime functions of management is to make decisions; marketing decisions are peculiarly difficult to make and their effects are felt throughout a business and, indeed, entire industries, as in the case of the British motor cycle industry whose products were once world-famous and are now no more.

Good information is the raw material used by management in deciding a company's policy and day-to-day operations. As the widely read text[1] *In Search of Excellence* showed, keeping 'close to customers', one of the critical factors identified during research, helped to make the American companies surveyed outstandingly successful over many years.

In a sellers' market, such as existed a few years after the Second World War, almost every kind of product was in short supply and manufacturers and distributors had little difficulty in securing satisfactory sales figures. With the rebuilding of industry in devastated Europe and the greater availability of raw materials from across the world, a buyers' market re-emerged (when customers were able, once again, to exercise personal preferences in the selection of products); it became evident that producers would have to study their markets and make sure that their products satisfied the specific needs of customers. Artificial restrictions on trading, such as rationing and shortage of raw materials, no longer influenced business and personal buying behaviour, which became for more critical.

Marketing as a separate business, identifiable, management function evolved from the business philosophy that recognized the importance of the customer; to be successful in the new competitive atmosphere, the needs of the customer had to be satisfied. This re-orientation of business activities demanded a more analytical and systematic approach, founded on an assessment of customer requirements, with the objective of maximizing net profits by providing customers with products and services that really fulfilled their particular needs.

This point was well expressed in a PEP[2] Report which was published some years ago:

> The essence of marketing is that a firm will make what it can sell, rather than sell what it can make. Marketing therefore requires an assessment of consumer needs through market research and the orientation of all the firm's activities towards the satisfaction of those needs. . . . The key technique of marketing is that of market research. Information about a firm's market and its customers is collected and analysed in order to determine who buys the firm's products, why, when, and under what circumstances. On the basis of this analysis a marketing policy is evolved.

Identification of customer needs entails, therefore, some systematic investigation into markets, either those currently being supplied or new market areas of potential interest. This is the role of marketing research, which is the foundation of sound marketing strategies and their associated tactics.

Without reliable data, management cannot be expected to plan and execute all the many activities necessary for the production and distribution of a range of products involving, perhaps, many months or even years of expensive development.

Marketing research is not a substitute for management decision; it is an aid to making better decisions by providing additional information relative to specific marketing problems.

> It is both wasteful and dangerous to 'under-research' to the extent that results are blurred and inconclusive. . . . It is equally a waste of good research if the facts are not applicable to the problem – or if they are not applied to the problem. Marketing research does not take the place of judgement. But by reducing the area in which judgement has to operate it simultaneously reduces the chance of error.[3]

Managerial experience and judgement are, of course, important ingredients of decision making, but they should be reinforced and expanded by objective data from systematic field investigations. This disciplined approach should appeal particularly to those working in technical and industrial markets, where rigorous standards of performance are demanded from the products and services developed.

As already observed, marketing problems tend to become more complex with the growth of sophisticated business organizations, whose customers are becoming increasingly demanding of their suppliers.

It is sound business practice that marketing policies should be founded on carefully planned research; this is possible only by applying the systematic approach of research methodology used in other areas of investigation.

Today management decisions frequently carry considerable risks, and it is clearly prudent for management to do everything possible to minimize these. Marketing research is a fact-finding process, logical and essential for successful marketing, and adaptable to the requirements of firms and other types of organizations that aim to attract the support of customers, clients, patrons, patients, or donors. To survive, every organization has to be able to offer acceptable goods and services which satisfy the identified needs of specific kinds of people, industries, and firms.

'Value in exchange' lies at the root of business and personal negotiations; perceived value is not necessarily dependent on objective assessment; people buy with their hearts as well as their heads. Motivations may be myriad; attractive new values can be built into products to make them stand out from their competitors. The concept of the augmented product and the nature of buying behaviour has been considered at some length in another text.[4]

1.2 DISCRIMINATION IN DATA

Although marketing research is indeed a valuable management tool, managers should not expect too much from it. For instance, the data collected may be of exceptional quality but the wrong decisions may be taken, perhaps because the data have been misinterpreted and/or wrong prognoses have been made. The fact that techniques such as marketing research may reduce the extent of risk in management decisions does not absolve managers from exercising skill, judgement, and initiative. The interpretation of the data in a marketing research report may give rise to different opinions which may be hotly argued. According to the requirements of the research brief, researchers may be asked to interpret as well as present the data collected from market surveys (see Chapter 16).

In many organizations often there is no shortage of information: the trouble is that it is frequently the wrong kind of information – excessive, irrelevant, incompatible, and also outdated. Relatively simple but up-to-date market information is more useful to management than sophisticated analyses which have lost most of their value because of excessive delay in collection and presentation. Discrimination should be exercised in the selection of data; sheer abundance leads merely to computerized confusion. Before seeking information, marketing management should discipline its search by defining with care the nature of the problem with which it is faced. Too frequently, managers appear to be trying to solve problems which they have not sufficiently identified and then blithely expect marketing researchers to pull the chestnuts out of the fire for them.

1.3 DEFINITION OF MARKETING RESEARCH

There have been several attempts to define marketing research, and some confusion has been caused by the term 'market research' being rather freely used to describe the full range of activities properly covered by marketing research.

Although the term 'market research' is now largely used as a synonym for 'marketing research', there was originally a distinct difference between the scope of the activities they covered. The responsibilities of market research, as noted later, extend comprehensively, whereas marketing research is limited to finding out information about the market for a particular product. It is this rather narrow view of research that has inhibited management from taking full advantage of the opportunities which the systematic study of the market can offer. To restrict market investigation merely to surveying, deprives management of vital contributions which can be made by researchers studying the marketing problems of an organization as a whole.

Marketing, as a specialized function of management, is generally interpreted today as including all those activities concerned with the development, production, and distribution of products to identifiable markets, where they will provide satisfaction to those who buy them. Marketing research is, therefore, far ranging in its enquiries; it covers product development, identifying the market, and suitable methods of selling, distribution, promotion, and sales/ service facilities. In fact, every aspect of business activity from the 'idea stage' to eventual consumer satisfaction. As indicated in Chapter 15, marketing research is by no means restricted to profit-motivated business activities. It has very useful applications in, for example, the development of charities, public sector leisure, and cultural services, etc. The wide responsibilities of marketing research are reflected in the definition given years ago by the American Marketing Association:[5] 'The systematic gathering, recording, and analysing of data about problems relating to the marketing of goods and services'.

The above definition was echoed in the British Institute of Management's definition[6] which was published in 1962: 'The objective gathering, recording, and analysing of all facts about problems relating to the transfer and sales of goods and services from producer to consumer',

In reviewing the AMA's definition, Kotler[7] commented that while the major activities of marketing research are clearly stated, its objectives are less well articulated. He offered the following definition which emphasizes the purpose of marketing research, viz., to help management make better decisions: '... systematic problem analysis, model building and fact-finding for the purposes of improved decision making and control in the marketing of goods and services'.

A further definition of marketing research has been offered by the Market Research Society, the leading British professional body for those using survey techniques for market, social, and economic research: 'Market research is the means used by those who provide goods and services to keep themselves in touch with the needs and wants of those who buy and use those goods and services'.

Another definition of marketing research, specifically related to industrial products, has been made by the Industrial Marketing Research Association (IMRA)[8] as follows: 'The systematic objective, and exhaustive search for and study of facts relevant to any problem in the field of industrial marketing'.

These definitions have much in common: market or marketing research is essentially about the disciplined collection and evaluation of specific data in order to help suppliers to understand their customers' needs better. From this fuller appreciation, which is likely to include economic, psychological, sociological, and cultural information, marketers are able to develop raw products and services, and also improve existing ones. Decision making necessarily involves some element of risk: market research data should be used to reduce, and control to some degree, the parameters of risk surrounding particular marketing proposals. (See Chapter 16 for Bayesian's approach in evaluation of marketing research.)

Buzzell,[9] writing in the *Harvard Business Review*, has expressed concern that the term 'research' had ever been adopted to describe the activities of data collection and evaluation for marketing decisions. He felt that this term was inappropriate for what essentially is some distance removed from pure academic research such as that conducted in a research laboratory under controlled conditions. Instead, he suggested that the function of marketing research was more analogous to military intelligence which had the duty of obtaining 'complete, accurate, and current information' for the development of strategic plans.

Marketing research should be viewed as a form of applied research that, while imposing on its practitioners the rigours and discipline of scientific enquiry, has a pragmatic purpose. Without this scientific orientation, marketing research would have little validity; it would deteriorate into subjective and biased assessments of market behaviour. Hence, an objective posture and systematic methods of enquiry are vital constituents of marketing research. It has been observed that marketing research is scientific in the sense that 'science may be at least partly defined in terms of the attitude of disinterest and impersonality one must take toward the outcomes of scientific investigation ... science deals with the unembroidered fact rather than with opinion and belief'.[10]

1.4 EVOLUTION OF MARKETING RESEARCH

The developmental stages of marketing research occurred in the United States, where marketing, as a distinct function of management, also originated. Lazer[11] identifies five stages in this developmental process spanning the following intervals, although some degree of overlap probably occurred.

1. Pre-1905: application of research to marketing problems.
2. 1905–19: organized approaches to market information.
3. 1919–30: structuring the marketing research discipline.
4. 1930–45: solidification and refinement of marketing research.
5. 1945–73: restructuring and the modern era of marketing research

The earliest recorded application of marketing research is generally agreed,[11–13] to have occurred within Lazer's first period and refers to a pioneer American advertising agency, N. W. Ayer & Son, which, in 1879, conducted a market survey into grain production throughout the United States so that the agency could develop an advertising schedule for its clients, the Nichols-Shephard Company, manufacturers of agricultural machinery. By modern standards, this survey was rudimentary, but it was important in opening up a new approach to marketing problems.

Between 1895 and 1897, Professor Harlow Gale of the University of Minnesota used mail questionnaires in an opinion survey on advertising. In 1901, Professor Walter Dill Scott, Director of the Psychological Laboratory at North Western University, Chicago, was engaged in experimental research on advertising, for the Agate Club of Chicago; in 1903 his notable text, *The Psychology of Advertising* was published. Other pioneer researchers around the time were J. George Frederick and R. O. Eastman, and Professor E. J. Hagerty of Ohio State, whose work principally involved relatively simple descriptive analyses of markets or of attitudes and opinions about advertising. An example of the unsophisticated techniques adopted by such early market researchers is given by Ferber.[14] In the 1870s, 'John Jacob Astor is said to have employed an artist to sketch hats in the park to help him determine the fashions of women's hats'.

During the next period (1905–19) marketing research was to assume a more significant role in business activities. J. George Frederick founded the Business Course, a market research survey organization, in 1908. In 1911, R. O. Eastman, Advertising Manager for the Kellogg Company, is reported[11, 13] to have undertaken what was probably the first systematic readership survey. Eastman's success led him to found his own research firm, Eastman Research Bureau, in 1916. Among his early clients was the General Electric Company, which commissioned him to investigate the public awareness of its trademark 'Mazda'.

Also in 1911, the Bureau of Business research was established at the Harvard Graduate School of Business under the influence of A. W. Shaw and Paul T. Cherington. The first project 'was a study of operating expenses of retail shoe stores'[11] from which a standard classification was developed.

Charles Coolidge Parlin, Manager of the Commercial Research Division of the Curtis Publishing Company, is generally acknowledged to be the founder of the modern principles and practice of marketing research. Parlin vigorously tackled the problem of acquiring systematic data and 'immediately started to produce marketing studies of a kind never before produced in the United States'.[12] He produced an impressive survey of the farm implement market and, in the next year, 1912, he published a comprehensive textile study and from this developed estimates of department stores' sales in cities with populations of 54 000 and over. Parlin's personality, plus the publicity given by the Curtis Publishing company 'gave his work a stature which assures him a prior and important place in the development of market research'.[13] Parlin's status earned him the popular title of the father of market research; he even predicted, as early as 1914, that eventually there would be only five or six automobile manufacturers in the United States.

Another important figure during this period was Dr Paul Nystrom who, in 1915, became Manager of Commercial Research for the US Rubber Company. Nystrom was influenced by Parlin, as also was L. D. H. Weld who, in 1917, undertook market research for Swift & Co.

In 1916, *The Chicago Tribune* published a market study of Chicago households. 'Although the questionnaire used was primitive and biasing by today's standards, and although there is no indication of concern over sampling techniques, it is likely that the techniques were not extemporized'.[13] Such a carefully qualified appraisal reflects the parlous nature of emergent marketing research; nevertheless, it provided 'a benchmark in the development of marketing research.'[11]

During this period of growth, marketing research techniques were gradually being systematized, while in management literature the role of marketing research began to be noted, particularly in connection with advertising, as typified by Daniel Starch's *Principles of Advertising – A Systematic Syllabus* (1910), and *Advertising: Its Principles, Practice and Technique* (1914). Paul Nystrom published *Retail Selling and Store Management* (1913), and *Economics of Retailing* (1915). In 1916 A. W. Shaw's *An Approach to Business Problems* appeared, in which he characterized markets as being made up of strata or segments, identifiable by various behavioural, economic, and physical attributes such as attitudes, demographic analyses, etc. Although the title does not denote marketing research, 'over half the book was directed to the analysis of problems of distribution'.[11] Over this era, papers also appeared in American psychological journals.

The third period of the development of marketing research covered the years 1919–30, and it was during this time that marketing research became more rigorous and disciplined in practice.

C. S. Duncan published *Commercial Research* in 1919; this text was significant in discussing with some expertise the fundamental principles of marketing research. This was followed in 1921 by Percival White who published *Market Analysis: Its Principles and Methods* in which he advocated the use of surveys in market analyses. The same author published *Sales Quotas* in 1929, a text concerned with marketing research applications to the problems of sales management.

George Gallup, whose name has now become virtually synonymous with public opinion polling across the world, conducted, in 1928, the first recorded study of reader interest in a newspaper. His 'recognition' techniques are still practised today in advertising research studies. Another pioneer who concentrated on advertisement measurement was Dr Daniel Starch who founded his Readership Survey Organization in 1931, using a system of 'Starch Scores' to indicate the relative recall of advertisements in journals.

The American Market Research Council was founded in 1926, and in some leading American universities greater attention began to be given to market data gathered by means of surveys. It is of interest to note that the term 'market research' was 'first listed as a subject heading in the American Index of Publications in 1926/1927'.[12]

Strong impetus was given to the adoption of business surveys when the United States Department of Commerce launched, in 1927, an important study into the methods of wholesale and retail distribution. This project was under the direction of Wroe Alderson who attained considerable fame for his market research studies.

Other significant official patronage occurred with the 1929 Census of Distribution, which set the seal on the systematic study of business activities in the United States.

From the early 1900s survey techniques were also being developed in Britain, and although the mainspring of activities originated in the United States, some advances were made which had considerable effect on survey methodology. Bowley [15] used systematic sampling techniques in his famous survey of working-class conditions in Reading during 1911; in 1924, H. G. Lyell founded the first independent market research firm in the UK, and Unilever was said[12] to be active in consumer research during 1920–24.

Even earlier, Booth [16] had made a massive and pioneer social enquiry: *Labour and the Life of the People of London* over the period 1886–1902. His historic survey attempted to measure working-class conditions by a system of eight classifications; four below and four above the poverty line; information was gathered from large-scale interviewing. Rowntree[17] was to continue this social investigation in his notable series of surveys commencing with *Poverty: A Study of Town Life* in 1902.

In the 1930s, Tom Harrison founded Mass Observation, which pioneered observational methods in British social studies. This mode of research had its roots in anthropology and was influenced by contemporary anthropologists like Malinowski who stressed the valuable contributions of participant observation. Harrison's organization has now become a byword in Britain for public opinion polling.

Survey practice in the UK during the first 30 years or so of the twentieth century stemmed, therefore, from social investigations stimulated mostly by pioneering social reformers who were disturbed by the distressing living conditions of the working classes. Without reliable facts, their arguments could be distorted or ignored by those who held political and industrial power.

Lazer's fourth period (1930–45) witnessed the extension and strong entrenchment of marketing research practice. The American Marketing Association appointed a Committee on Marketing Research Techniques; its findings,[18] published in 1937, covered the wide spectrum of marketing research responsibilities. Further texts [19] extended this discussion and firmly planted marketing research as a modern business technique.

In Britain, the British Broadcasting Corporation founded the Listener Research Department (later known as Audience Research when television was introduced) in 1936. Probably the most significant event in British survey history occurred in 1941 when the Government Social Survey started operations. Over the years it has exercised 'unquestionable influence in raising the standard of survey methods and in persuading policy makers in government to pay attention to survey results.'[20] The Survey has been responsible for a very diverse range of enquiries on behalf of government departments. Since 1970 it has been part of the Office of Population Censuses and Surveys.

The Market Research Society, the British professional body that has contributed significantly to raising the standards of survey practice, was formed in 1947. From a modest start – only 20 people were reported [21] to have agreed to found the Society – market research has grown consistently and 'if normal commercial criteria are applied [it] can be considered to be one of the major growth industries since the early 1950s'.[21]

The final phase of Lazer's model (1945–73) is typified as a period of restructuring, refinement of techniques, and 'interdisciplinary convergence'.[11]

Sampling theory and research designs were significantly improved; the testing of hypotheses and multi-variate analyses received growing attention. Non-parametrics and a wide array of other statistical techniques were introduced.

Psychological concepts and techniques were increasingly being borrowed in order to study consumer behaviour. Motivation research became almost a fetish of the early 1950s. Joyce[22] has commented that 'psychology has influenced market research on a large scale at least twice. The first period was in the 40s or perhaps earlier with the importation of common-sense psychology into the business'; the second period was 'the middle and late 50s when there was a wholesale introduction of methods from a number of psychological fields, and the growth of attitude and motivation research'. Joyce perceived market research as 'now to have begun a more stable and sensible relationship with psychology'.

A new armoury of attitudinal measuring techniques became popular in marketing research. These included Guttman's cumulative scaling. Osgood's semantic differential procedures, and Kelly's personal construct theory. Emphasis was increasingly on studying people's behaviour as consumers of a wide range of products and services. Various models or theories were developed, which could be evaluated by using data collected from marketing research surveys.

Concepts such as opinion leadership, social class, family structure, group behaviour, life style, and cultural values added complexity to research designs. Quantitative assessments were viewed as inadequate; a demand was growing for 'depth and insight' which the behavioural sciences claimed to give. Qualitative research became a vogue which tended to outpace its validity and, in time, a more mature and somewhat less uncritical use of qualitative research techniques resulted.

In 1959, *Commentary*, the official journal of the Market Research Society was founded in the UK; the title was subsequently altered to the *Journal of the Market Research Society*, which has now a high reputation in management and academic circles. In 1964, the American Marketing Association founded the *Journal of Marketing Research*. These journals reflect the status now given to marketing research.

From the relatively crude and elementary methodologies practised by the pioneer social and commercial investigators, marketing research has approached the level of a profession. It has responded[21] to two important pressures: external and internal. The former relates to the changing and more complex needs of marketers for reliable data; the latter refers to the consistent improvements which have characterized the practice of marketing research. Today, sophisticated methods of collecting, processing, and evaluating data have transformed the whole process of survey investigation. 'Management science, operations research, systems engineering, econometrics, and computer science contributions have resulted in more scientific marketing research approaches, more timely, applicable information, and improved market decision making.'[11] Whether, in fact, decision making itself is superior to that exercised by earlier generations of businessmen is not easily checked. Perhaps it should be said that the raw material, i.e., information, of decision making is more readily available, but it would be naïve to accept that this automatically leads to better decision making. Elaborate data are not to be confused with effective guidance; as observed already, marketing research data require expert interpretation.

A special report by Mintel,[23] published in 1990, stated that the market research industry was being technology driven because of growing pressure from: (i) clients demanding increased levels of sophistication and speed from market research agencies; (ii) increasingly fast-moving consumer markets and the need for constant monitoring; and (iii) growing difficulties of recruiting and keeping face-to-face interviewers (see Chapter 7).

1.5 SOURCES OF MARKETING RESEARCH THEORY AND PRACTICE

It will be evident from earlier discussion that marketing research has borrowed liberally from other disciplines; this is not surprising because research methodologies and techniques have application over many fields of study. Like other emerging disciplines, marketing research theory has been developed by creative adaptation rather than blind adoption.

The extent to which marketing theory has been built on borrowed concepts was noted some years ago by the Marketing Science Institute of America. 'Historically, most sciences started by borrowing their conceptual approach and general theoretical ideas from other sciences. Our current state of marketing theory is no different.' However, the MSIA warned against the wholesale importation of methodologies from other areas of study.

Marketing investigations should be undertaken with 'scientific care and conceptual honesty'.[24] Discrimination, as noted earlier, had not always been practised in the development of marketing research. While it is true that most sciences often use techniques that originated outside their particular province, indiscriminate adoption tends to impede progress. Joyce[22] has observed that:

Market research is not a practice or study isolated from other practices or studies. It has drawn freely from certain expert academic fields and will no doubt continue to do so. Further, market research organisations make use of people with expert, specialist training – especially from those fields known broadly as 'the social sciences' – both as staff members and consultants.

As a discipline matures, the standards of its research should rise; these will depend significantly on the research methodologies and instruments that are in use.

Marketing research focuses on human and organizational behaviour and consumption habits. Buying behaviour is merely one element of human behaviour, and so it may be postulated that some of the theories and findings from the behavioural sciences make a relevant contribution towards understanding patterns of consumption. That curious, rational abstraction, economic man, which early classical economic theory projected, is now discarded and is regarded as an inadequate model of consumption. Rationality, even in industrial purchasing situations, is by no means the sole or dominant influence.

Because buying behaviour is complex and is affected by many variables – economic, psychological, sociological, cultural, and demographic – the approach by marketing researchers should be subtle and well designed. The interaction, for example, of economic and social factors may produce degrees of conflict. Cultural inhibitions may frustrate the introduction or diffusion of new products, such as dehydrated foods or contraceptives.

People seek what may be termed syntheses of benefits from the goods and services they consume. Benefits are often more than physical; even relatively fundamental needs such as food or clothing have become complex and sophisticated in modern advanced communities. On the simple foundation of nourishment, basically provided by food, people have built a highly elaborate edifice of needs that have been termed 'psychogenic' and are derived from psychology, sociology, aesthetics, etc. Choice has proliferated in response to the sophisticated behaviour of relatively affluent consumers. Those at the lowest level of subsistence in an undeveloped country eat eagerly and whenever they can; they do not have to be cajoled by advertising to try new experiences in foods. Their expectations and horizons are limited.

Psychology, as noted earlier, made its impact increasingly felt in marketing research during the fifth phase of Lazer's model (1945–73).[11] Psychological theories have enabled market researchers to develop hypotheses about buying behaviour, and to apply some of the techniques of psychological investigation to obtain a deeper understanding of marketing problems. Learning theory, for example, has been utilized in studies of advertising effectiveness.[25,26] Psychological techniques have been linked with mathematical models and applied to learning behaviour related to the phenomenon of brand switching.[27–29]

The emphasis on building comprehensive models of buying behaviour has increased; qualitative assessments are now acknowledged to be vital components of marketing research designs. At the same time, the exaggerated claims of some psychological applications in research practice have been discredited, particularly those introduced from clinical psychology involving various kinds of projective techniques. Motivation research, based on Freudian psychology, has attracted particularly strong criticism. The subjectivity of such research methods, the selection and size of the samples involved, lack of quantitative analyses, and the generalizations that have been delivered, have caused considerable controversy about the validity of the resultant findings.

Over recent years, there has been a swing away from relying solely on these clinical methods of psychological enquiry into buying behaviour. Market researchers tend to make more use of methods like group discussions to guide in the development of new product concepts, advertising copy, etc. The use of groups, particularly during the exploratory stages of marketing research, will probably become a permanent feature of research methodology, since they offer a speedy and economical method of obtaining qualitative information 'which is often substantiated when quantification is carried out',[21] using multi-variate statistical techniques.

Sociology has been influential in marketing research strategies. Social class gradings have been widely adopted by marketing researchers, particularly in advanced economies such as the US and the UK

Apart from social classifications, sociology has also introduced into marketing research studies concepts such as social mobility, life cycle, opinion leadership, diffusion of innovations, household behaviour, etc.[30-42] These concepts have added immense depth and value to marketing research enquiries.

Cultural anthropology has also contributed to the development of marketing research, by focusing enquiries on environmental influences which affect patterns of consumption. The cultural values of a society are not abstract notions; they find expression in the products and services that are demanded; the acceptance of new products may be very dependent on cultural norms.

Cultural values have particular impact on export marketing strategies. Within national cultures, sub-cultures are often present with distinctive needs. The status of women in society tends to vary over cultures; these differences are particularly marked between advanced industrial communities and less developed countries. Such cultural differences have accounted for the difficulties in selling, for example, labour-saving domestic equipment.

Cultural studies have been founded on work by Horney,[43] Riesman,[44] and Mead.[45]

Horne *et al* [21] have observed that the 'fundamental discipline' of marketing research is statistics, in particular the law of probability. The sampling procedures used in marketing research were developed, therefore, from the concept of probability which is the core of sampling theory.

From statistics, marketing research has taken the theory of sampling; without sampling methodology, marketing research could never have originated. But the process has not been one-way, for marketing research practitioners have developed sophisticated sampling techniques, as in the case of multi-stage sampling, where 'clustering' techniques have resulted from demands for controlling the costs of commercial surveys.

Statistical theory has also contributed to the practice of marketing research through the application of techniques concerned with the acceptance or rejection of specific hypotheses. Lazer,[11] as seen earlier, commented that the period 1945–73 had witnessed a refinement of techniques which had become more widely applied in order to improve the standards of research practice. Complex statistical computations became feasible with the introduction of computer packages such as Statistical Package for the Social Sciences (SPSS).

Another aspect of statistics, which has been helpful in developing marketing research as a science, emanates from the design of experiments towards which Fisher made a notable contribution. Green and Tull[46] noted that R. G. Fisher is to be 'credited with formulating rigorous statements regarding inferences to be drawn from sample observations. He defined the "null" hypothesis as an assertion about the real world whose validity was to be tested'.

Experimental techniques have been used in marketing research to test, for example, the relative efficiencies of advertising copy, packaging, pricing, etc.

Economics has also played a part in establishing marketing research as a management technique. Many of the early practitioners of marketing research were economists. It might be expected, therefore, that during the developmental stages of marketing research, economic analyses received substantial attention. 'Descriptive' economics related, for example, to the structure of industries, general background economic data, and the identification of trends in business and industry provided the essential framework of market research reports. These were valuable contributions which enabled marketing researchers to guide clients on the formulation of business policy. But Joyce[22] has observed critically that in the field of 'theoretical' economics, the contributions have been disappointing. 'If we take the study of the simplest, most basic economic relationships and occurrences – the theory of consumer choice – we find that the traditional theory is of little use or relevance to us.' The chief reason, as observed earlier, is the naïve assumption by earlier classical economic theorists that man is a rational or economic being who maximizes his utility or expected utility in all purchase considerations. The weakness in earlier versions of the principle of utility lay in a misunderstanding of basic human behaviour. These misconceptions have been largely corrected through the influence of the behavioural sciences like sociology and psychology; consumer choice studies would now be considered inadequate if the parameters were perceived to be solely economic.

The theory and practice of marketing research have drawn freely, therefore, from diverse academic disciplines. They have enriched the emerging discipline of marketing, of which marketing research is a core element. This process of selective borrowing, adaptation, and synthesis has transformed the entire nature and scope of marketing research investigations. Marketing research can never be a pure scientific activity; it 'is an applied field rather like engineering – which involves knowledge of metallurgy, electronics, mathematics, etc., but which has a technique and methodology of its own'.[22]

1.6 SCOPE OF MARKETING RESEARCH

The area of marketing decisions is wide; it covers product design, pricing, distribution, and promotion. It acknowledges the fact that there are many variables affecting marketing activities which cannot be controlled by suppliers to a market. These environmental variables, such as the demographic structure of the population, economic conditions, legal restrictions, competitors' activities, and the shifting tastes dictated by fashion, cause marketing decisions to be complex and difficult to make.

Every organization must make marketing decisions of some kind. Frequently these involve large capital expenditure on the building and equipping of a new plant. Marketing decisions may result in the redirection of the resources of a business into entirely new markets, or in exploiting new technologies which have been developed by research laboratories. Also, as noted earlier, decisions may relate to the provision of specific cultural and leisure services by public sector authorities; or, perhaps, to the development of new types of firms offering comprehensive house buying/selling services and legal services.

Sir Douglas Wass,[47] in his presidential address to the annual conference of the Market Research Society in 1990, commented that: 'Market Research enables producers of goods and services to design and deliver their products according to the informed preferences of the final consumer and so reduces the risk of costly production mistakes being made through poor market intelligence'. He also stressed that market research can help policy makers in both central and local government to design their programmes, 'in a way that takes into account the views of the consumers'. For example, social security beneficiaries might be surveyed to find out whether they would prefer cash payments to assistance in kind, as with subsidized travel or housing.

Statistical information can be gathered on the market in general, and also on particular segments that may be important, which will reveal the market standing of manufacturers relative to their competitors. Analysis indicates the general trend in that market, to be compared with the movement in specialized areas of the market, and to the sales trends of individual suppliers. The trend, evident in certain market segments, may be markedly different from the overall market movement. Market research attempts to isolate these phenomena and to explain the causes underlying them.

Information for marketing decision making may be broadly classified as: (i) strategic: (ii) tactical; and (iii) 'data bank'. The first type refers to information needed for strategic decisions, e.g., whether to enter a specific overseas market or to diversify into new markets; the second type relates to information for tactical decisions such as the planning of sales territories; the third type provides essential background knowledge about, for example, competitors' activities, market trends, VAT requirements, etc. Such information needs regular updating.

In practice, of course, these categories of information tend to become blurred, and companies often require a 'mix' of information.

Marketing management information has a two-way flow; from the organization to the environment (i.e., market), and from the environment to the organization; the principle of feedback is an essential element (see Fig. 1.1). In rapidly changing market conditions, it is imperative for management to have an up-to-date knowledge, to be aware of the entry of new, competitive products and services, and to be able to plan ahead for emerging trends in taste. Systematic enquiry is far preferable to hunch.

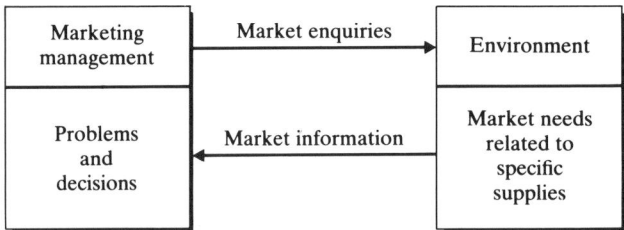

Fig. 1.1   Two-way flow of marketing information systems

1.7 MAIN DIVISIONS OF MARKETING RESEARCH

Marketing research, as noted when discussing formal definitions of this activity, should result in thorough and detailed knowledge about all aspects of the marketing of goods and services. The various subjects covered in a typical marketing research programme will now be outlined separately, although, of course, in actual surveys these rather arbitrary distinctions will tend to be subsumed in the overall research design. Further consideration of specific topics, such as promotion, occurs later in this text.

Product research

This is concerned with the design, development, and testing of new products, the improvement of existing products, and the forecasting of likely trends in consumers' preferences related to styling, product performance, quality of materials, etc. Comparative testing with competitive products should be undertaken to assess realistically the values of comparative goods, particularly as perceived by customers. Included in these evaluations will be pricing studies. Strengths and weaknesses need to be objectively identified across specific attributes, such as quality, shelf-life, ease of handling, pack acceptability, etc. The essence of marketing research is objectivity, so any attempt to fudge enquiries should be strongly resisted.

The product line should be examined to ensure that it is adequate to attract custom, but also it must be economic, so that marketing efforts are not being wastefully dispersed over too wide a range, some of which may not be making an effective contribution to overall profitability. The product mix should also be analysed, particularly with reference to competitive products, as mentioned earlier. With some products – both consumer and industrial – efficient after-sales servicing is influential in attracting sales; this function should be carefully assessed, particularly where technical products or durable consumer goods such as television sets or washing machines are concerned.

Over the past years, product design is an increasingly important influence in the buying of many types of goods. Research is needed to evaluate what customers expect in terms of product performance, visual appeal, comfort, etc. Expectations are dynamic; what pleased people a few years ago is unlikely to satisfy them today. Manufacturers and distributors cannot expect to compete successfully against global competition unless the products they make and stock perform at least equally and also look as attractive as those, for instance, which may be marketed by new suppliers from distant lands.

James Pilditch,[48] who has made a major contribution to the quality of British design, has observed that 'it is not uncommon for a manufacturer to be genuinely surprised and disappointed when something he has designed, and about which he is expert fails to sell'. He cites a manufacturer of high-powered engines used in military vehicles who developed an engine half the size of any other available in the market. Although an example of brilliant engineering, it failed to win customers, who continued to prefer competitors' bulkier products. It was then discovered that competing engines were easier to maintain, and this was more important than compact size.

Design adds value to products and contributes to the rising sales graph of a very wide range of products: cars, washing machines, machine tools, textile machinery, spin driers, home computers, etc. Electronics has had a profound effect on product design; equipment has been 'miniaturized' and generally made much more reliable, e.g., telephone exchange equipment. In some cases, design has been largely cosmetic and limited to restyling. Products should not only function well, they should also look good. As technological differences between products become smaller and more difficult to discern, design (in its total sense) becomes more important.

The increased volume of spending power today is largely controlled by women, or heavily influenced by them. By their nature, they are generally more sensitive to colour and fashion, and they have become accustomed to a wide choice of well-designed clothing. In the area of household products, kitchen equipment, and cars, women are now successfully demonstrating their desire for products that will satisfy them aesthetically as well as practically.

The growing importance of packaging as a buying influence necessitates research; packaging protects products but it can also be a powerful promotion tool. With many types of products sold in supermarkets, the appeal of the packaging is of immense importance. Unless research is undertaken before packaging is developed for specific kinds of products, serious problems may arise. If, for example, packs are not capable of standing firmly on shelves or of being stacked without difficulty, sales of such products are likely to be severely curtailed. Shelf-life, possible contamination, and ease of handling by consumers are other aspects to be researched. Labels should be well designed so that brands can readily be recognized; sudden, radical changes in typeface or general layout may annoy buyers or cause suspicion about the quality of the contents.

Profitable market segmentation strategies may be developed from product and packaging research, as was found with spray-on household polishes and traditional wax polishes. The tea market, for example, can be differentiated broadly by the intrinsic nature of the product (high-quality specialist blends versus relatively low - priced popular blends) and also by the style of packaging and product type (leaf tea versus 'bag' tea).

A creative product strategy which is a key input into the overall marketing strategy should aim to build a portfolio of products which will result in satisfactory development of a business.

Sales research

This involves a thorough examination of the selling activities of the company. This is usually made by sales outlets and/or sales territories, and preferably analysed so that direct comparisons can be made with published data. Information existing within the company should be fully utilized and matched with external data referring to the particular industry and its products. As observed already, the position of a company in its market should be checked in relation to its competitors; these should be identified and ranked in order of importance. If company sales are falling, the overall trend in the market should be checked, particular attention being given to those segments of the total market which may account for the company's main sales. Where it can be established that the total market is steady or improving in these significant areas, some urgent enquiries should be made to find out why company sales are not sharing this general trend. Research should aim to discover where these extra sales are being made – perhaps in outlets not adequately covered by the company sales plan. The effectiveness of the sales force should be examined; the distribution of territories, method of operation, system of remuneration, field supervision and training, all require careful analysis and assessment. Distribution plans should be compared for selling efficiency; if complete national coverage is desirable has this been accomplished at reasonable cost, or would alternative arrangements, e.g., through wholesalers, be more economical in certain areas? Is the sales force selling to those outlets that handle the majority share of the market? As an aid to realistic sales forecasting, research is recommended to ensure that estimates are based on sound knowledge of the factors likely to affect consumption in that market. This must take account of economic, political, and social developments and legislation in markets, whether in the UK or overseas.

Alternative methods of distribution may be examined and a feasibility study prepared for consideration by management. New outlets, such as vending machines, offer producers opportunities to expand their sales. Distribution research must constantly be alert to the needs of consumers, e.g., the growing importance of distribution centres serviced by adequate car-parking facilities.

Customer research

This covers investigations into buyer behaviour – studying the social, economic, and psychological influences affecting purchase decisions, whether these are taken at the consumer level, the trade distribution level, or in the industrial field (see specialist text[4]).

Reasons for preferences for certain brands, pack sizes, etc., of the products in a particular market will be examined. Attitudinal studies are valuable in distinguishing the appeals of competitive brands to certain types of users. The impact of the company's selling activities should be studied from the dealer and consumer angle; 'rationalization' of product lines can be interpreted unfavourably by customers and they may react by switching their purchases from other products made by the company to competitors. Consumer and dealer research is frequently planned jointly so that a useful cross-check can be made of the attitudes towards the company and its products. Unfavourable trade attitudes may be based on the failure of the company in the past to offer acceptable terms of trading, although the retailer may have no quarrel with the product range. Unfortunately, this may lead the retailer either to boycott those brands, or to give them merely nominal display in the stores. Deliveries may be another cause of dissatisfaction. Whatever complaints or prejudices exist, customer research is particularly useful in clearing them by pinpointing the causes which underly them. Manufacturers depend heavily for the success of their marketing operations on the goodwill and cooperation of distributors, and it is nothing more than sound common sense to make objective enquiries into the trading relationships that exist between producers and channels of distribution. It is useful to management to know how its particular company compared with other suppliers in that product field. This can be done by some form of rating applied to critical aspects, such as design, packaging, price, delivery, accounting procedure, sales representation, adequacy of product range, etc.

Consumer research, as far as retail products are concerned, includes consumer surveys to study the opinions and behaviour of ultimate users of the products. This may involve national enquiries using formal questionnaires with a sample carefully selected to be representative of the total population in that consumer class. It may also cover a series of 'depth interviews' to analyse the motivations of people in certain buying situations. A variety of techniques can be used, which are discussed later in this text. Over the years, a great deal of expertise has been accumulated in consumer marketing research, which has tended to attract attention because of its direct impact on members of the public.

Following the successful path of enquiry which led to the publication of the American text *In Search of Excellence*, which was noted at the onset of this chapter, two British authors produced *The Winning Streak*.[49] Like the US book, this text examined companies which had impressive corporate behaviour over several years. The British companies surveyed included Sainsbury's, the giant supermarket chain, and it was observed that Sir John Sainsbury 'had no doubt that keeping a close ear to the ground on changes of consumer taste and needs is a major reason why his company has survived healthily into the 1980s while virtually every other big name in the grocery business before World War Two has disappeared or been taken over'. Sainsbury's is dedicated to the collection and evaluation of market data covering general aspects of the economy, trends in food consumption, and socio-economic environmental changes. Trends are monitored and new sectors explored. Competitors' developments in terms of new stores, marketing strategies and prices are examined closely.

A study[50] of the current levels of usage of market research recorded in the *Journal of the Market Research Society* in October 1984, found that, in general, fast-moving consumer goods companies were more likely than industrial product companies to conduct marketing research. Of the former, 80 per cent undertook research, whereas only about 60 per cent of the latter do so; the principal reasons for not using marketing research were either that they felt that there was no need to assess their industrial markets, or that they already knew enough from first-hand experience. It was also found that a major obstacle to expansion into new markets was a 'genuine fear of the costs of marketing research' and a lack of belief in the benefits to be gained against the costs involved.

This research confirms that 'little seems to have changed' in the way UK companies conduct and use market research since the last major study published by Wills in 1971.

In 1986, the British Institute of Management[51] surveyed 12 leaders of British industry and 40 manufacturing companies. All said that good liaison with their customers was regarded as important; however, only a minority carried out thorough research to find out what their customers wanted. Only about one-quarter of respondent companies had actually researched product features that were regarded by them as vitally important and competitive.

Clearly, there is plenty of scope for well-devised marketing research in industrial and technical fields, and it is disconcerting that British industry in general is still reluctant to make use of this effective management tool. Specific aspects of industrial marketing research are considered in some detail in Chapter 12.

At times of recession, market research has a specially critical role to play: it can help in planning alternative strategies; it can indicate, for example, where more cost-effective methods of distribution could be adopted.

Marketing research can also help the service industries, such as tourism, hotels, banking, insurance, and the many other kinds of incorporeal production which provide the essential infrastructure of developed economies, as discussed in Chapter 14. As already noted, there are many ways in which marketing research can be useful in the design and administration of public sector services, such as those covering health and social welfare. Some examples of these applications are given later in this text and also in a specialist text[52] dealing with management of the National Health Service in the UK.

An imaginative use of market research occurred when the New Islington and Hackney Housing Association in London commissioned a leading research company to survey its tenants so that existing services and new housing design could be improved. This independent and objective approach resulted in findings that 'enabled the association to prove that tenants could not afford rent rises that would be the outcome of government-inspired privately-funded schemes'.[53] It was also discovered that noise was one of the biggest irritants to tenants; door-slamming, in particular, was identified as a nuisance – this was solved and tackled by the housing association. Other benefits to tenants resulted from the survey: for example, attention to security systems, heating improvements, and sound-proofing.

Customer research is particularly important in export marketing, which is assuming far greater significance in the overall marketing operations of companies manufacturing a wide range of products. Successful exporting is built on reliable and up-to-date information about the specific needs of customers. With competition on an international scale increasing in intensity, manufacturers need to be more aware than ever before of the factors that influence customers in their choice of products and of brands. The characteristic behaviour of buyers in the home market will generally be more familiar to manufacturers than that of buyers in overseas markets, especially where these are being entered for the first time (see Chapter 13).

Lack of market knowledge can have disastrous effects; Douglas and Craig[54] refer to the 'total failure' of the Renault Dauphine car in the United States, which was ill-suited to the demands of American highway driving.

International marketing has necessarily to be undertaken in a complex, heterogeneous environment: there are many opportunities for management to make mistakes, perhaps in the formulation of food products, design of equipment incorporating acceptable safety standards, methods of distribution, etc. Alternative strategies may include licensing arrangements, joint venture operations, establishment of subsidiary overseas companies, or some mix of these methods of extending sales overseas. Political and other cultural factors may, as discussed in Chapter 13, be significant influences in the selection of suitable marketing opportunities.

Pricing research

All businesses have to make decisions about the pricing of their goods and services. Pricing is one of the critical factors affecting business success. It is also one of the variables in the 'marketing mix' – those fundamental inputs into a business deal that have been termed the four P's (Product, Price, Place and Promotion). These inputs are necessarily interrelated and an effective blend is at the heart of successful marketing.

Pricing can (and should) be approached both analytically and creatively. Costs form the platform on which price is built and these must be known. But equally important is knowledge about the nature of demand, the level of competition, technological developments that may lead to substitute materials, etc.

Pricing can be used effectively to position a product relative to competitors' offerings. This suggests that some reliable information should be collected about competitive products specifically related to market segments. Price is an indicator of quality as well as an economic fact; products (and services) should be analysed for the *benefits* which they offer buyers, and, ideally, these should have been developed from objective knowledge of the *expectations* of certain types of buyers or users.

The sales of some products are highly sensitive to changes in price: as price falls, demand *tends* to rise, and vice versa; the extent of this movement is known as the elasticity of demand. The alternative, viz., inelastic demand, occurs when only small changes in demand follow from price alterations. Economists have developed sophisticated models of the relationships between price and demand; while theoretically impressive they often lack pragmatic value.

Market researchers may use various kinds of experimental designs to test price sensitivities (see Chapter 2: Causal studies and also Primary Data – experimentation). Most markets have price ranges for specific products; the skill lies in knowing, with a fair degree of certainty, the price (including trade discounts) that will attract favourable buying decisions. Too low a price will arouse suspicions about quality, continuity of supply, etc.; while too high a price (unless it is deliberately designed to 'skim' the market) may well result in insufficient levels of sales. It may be feasible to organize market tests involving price differentiation as well as other variations to the marketing mix (see Chapter 10).

Pioneer research into price sensitivities was undertaken by Gabor and Granger[55] who, extending from earlier work by Jean Stoetzel of the Sorbonne, developed 'buy-response' curves related to specific types of products. Their research approach has since been adopted by the Nottingham University Consumer Study Group, based on analyses of consumers' propensity to purchase new products.

Another pricing research methodology is practised by Research International[56] whose 'brand-price trade-off approach' involves groups of typical buyers who are asked to make a series of selections from a proposed new product (at different prices) presented in company with several competing brands. The results of these simulated shopping sessions are subject to conjoint analysis.

Special pricing research packages are offered by the leading market research firms.

Promotion research

This is concerned with testing and evaluating the effectiveness of the various methods used in promoting a company's products or services. These activities include exhibitions, public relations campaigns, merchandising aids such as show cards and point-of-sale stands, consumer and trade advertising, special promotional offers, etc. The variety of media available in most developed communities – television, press and magazine, cinema, radio, poster, exhibitions, etc. – and the wide choice of media within each of these classifications, make the task of selecting the most suitable media difficult in practice. So many variables affect purchasing decisions that only in very few cases can the real sales effectiveness of advertising be known with certainty.

In overseas markets, the availability of specific mass radio or television, should be carefully researched. The pattern of the mass media in the UK is by no means the same in other countries. Apart from technical considerations, cultural factors also influence the medium that is suitable for effective promotional purposes. Printed communications, for instance, are relevant to communities with high levels of literacy, but are ineffective in countries like Nigeria or Algeria (see Chapter 13) for widespread promotions.

Alternative and complementary forms of product promotion can be researched during the course of trade and consumer surveys. Many such surveys include questions on media habits, such as television viewing; magazine and newspaper readership; types of store at which purchases of particular products are made; brand recognition, and attitudes towards merchandising practices, e.g. 'special offers', 'banded packs', 'free gift vouchers, and trading stamps.

The most suitable methods of promoting products should be studied in detail. Present practice needs to be assessed for its effectiveness, and alternatives should be objectively considered. Where a company operates in more than one market, e.g., selling in bulk to the hotel and catering industries, and also in retail packs to the consumer through a network of stockists, separate promotional policies will be drawn up as the result of information collected through marketing research in these specialized sectors of the market.

Market research[57] by Elida Gibbs revealed that although Proctor and Gamble's 'Head and Shoulders' dominated the entire shampoo market in both the United States and Britain, there was need for a range of anti-dandruff shampoos – a special sector not yet exploited by the market leaders.

Elida Gibbs developed the 'All Clear' shampoo, test-marketed it, and launched it nationally in July 1979. The strategy included national TV advertising. Unfortunately, a strike by ITV staff soon after the initial launch forced a switch into press and radio. Despite this problem, an evaluation was made of the different media used in the 'All Clear' campaign, and the conclusion of the researchers was that the TV advertising campaign was the single most important factor in the successful launch of this product. It was noted that the television expenditure of £116 000 in late July was reflected in the 6 per cent brand share recorded in August, whereas this dropped immediately to 4 per cent when it became impossible to use television advertising. It was not until the resumption of this medium in January 1980 that 'All Clear' regained its 6 per cent brand share.

1.8 COMPLEXITY OF BUYING BEHAVIOUR

The complex pattern of buying influences affecting consumer purchasing is outlined in Fig. 1.2 and is discussed in some detail elsewhere.[4] Models of buying behaviour vary in complexity and orientation, and in dynamic market conditions these theoretical concepts need to be reviewed and updated.

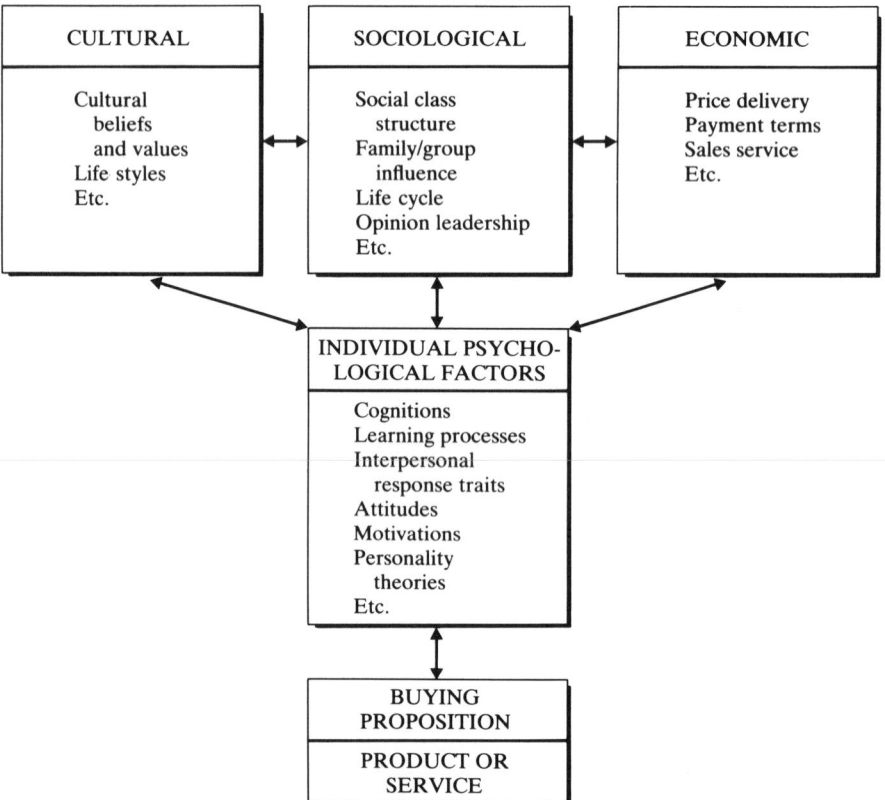

Fig. 1.2 The complex pattern of buying influences (*Source*: Chisnall, 1985)[4]

The multiple influences affecting buyer behaviour, as shown in Fig. 1.2, should be carefully considered when research proposals are being formulated. As noted earlier in this chapter, the interplay and significance of 'non-economic' factors demand that due attention should be given to these influences which, although often covert, may, nevertheless, spell success or failure in the marketing of goods and services.

1.9 SUMMARY

Marketing research aids decision making by providing management with specific kinds of information useful for strategic and tactical planning. The terms 'market research' and 'marketing research' are now used interchangeably to infer systematic, objective research into all the factors, such as product pricing, promotion and distribution, which contribute to the successful marketing of goods and services. This systematic analysis covers both quantitative and qualitative assessments of existing and prospective markets.

Research should be the foundation of marketing strategy; unfortunately it tends to be used less in industrial and technical fields where the need is often critical.

Market research techniques have evolved from relatively rudimentary social enquiries; the methodologies of other disciplines have been creatively adapted. But market research can never be purely scientific – it has the quality of an applied science, and must seek to offer pragmatic solutions without destroying its essential core, i.e., objectivity.

REFERENCES

1. Peters, Thomas J., and Robert H. Waterman, Jnr, *In Search of Excellence: Lessons from America's Best-Run Companies*, Harper & Row, New York, 1982.
2. Gater, Anthony, David Insull, Harold Lind, and Peter Seglow, 'Attitudes in British management', PEP Report, Pelican, London, 1965.
3. A. C. Nielsen, *The Nielsen Researcher*, A. C. Nielsen, Oxford, May–June 1969.
4. Chisnall, Peter M., *Marketing: A Behavioural Analysis*, McGraw-Hill, Maidenhead, 1985.
5. American Marketing Association, 'Report of the Definitions Committee', American Marketing Association, Chicago, 1961.
6. British Institute of Management, 'Survey of marketing research in Great Britain', Information Summary No. 97, British Institute of Management, London, January 1962.
7. Kotler, Philip, *Marketing Management: Analysis Planning and Control*, Prentice-Hall, New Jersey, 1967.
8. Industrial Marketing Research Association, 'Regulations', IMRA, Lichfield, 1969.
9. Buzzell, Robert D., 'Is marketing a science?', *Harvard Business Review*, January–February 1963.
10. Geldard, Frank A., *Fundamentals of Psychology*, Wiley, New York, 1963.
11. Lazer, W., 'Marketing research: Past accomplishments and potential future developments', *Journal of Market Research Society*, vol. 16, no. 3, 1974.
12. Bottomley, David T., 'The origin of marketing research', *Commentary*, vol. 13, spring 1964.
13. Lockley, Lawrence C., 'Notes on the history of marketing research', *Journal of Marketing*. vol. 14, no. 5, 1950.
14. Ferber, Robert, *Market Research*, McGraw-Hill, New York, 1949.
15. Bowley, A. L., and A. R. Burnett-Hurst, *Livelihood and Poverty: A Study in the Economic Conditions of Working-class Households in Northampton, Warrington, Stanley and Reading*, Bell, London, 1915.
16. Booth, C., *Labour and Life of the People of London*, Macmillan, London (17 vols, 1889–1902).
17. Rowntree, B. S., *Poverty: A Study of Town Life*, Longmans, London, 1902.
18. Wheeler, Ferdinand C., *The Technique of Marketing Research*, McGraw-Hill, New York, 1937.
19. Brown, Lyndon O., *Marketing Research and Analysis*, Ronald Ross, New York, 1937.
20. Moser, C. A., and G. Kalton, *Survey Methods in Social Investigation*, Heinemann, London, 1971.
21. Horne, Annette, Judith Morgan, and Joanna Page, 'Where do we go from here?', *Journal of Market Research Society*, vol. 16, no. 3, 1974.
22. Joyce, Timothy, 'The role of the expert in market research', Market Research Society, Summer School, July 1963.
23. Market Research, Special Report, Mintel, London EC1, 1990.
24. Halbert, Michael (Dir.), *The Meaning and Sources of Marketing Theory*, Marketing Science Institute, McGraw-Hill, New York, 1965.

25. Howard, John A., *Marketing Theory*, Allyn and Bacon, Boston, 1965.
26. Bayton, James A., 'Motivation, cognition, learning: Basic factors in consumer behaviour', *Journal of Marketing*, vol. 22, January 1958.
27. Estes, W. K., 'Individual behaviour in uncertain situations: An interpretation in terms of statistical association theory', in: *Decision Processes*, R. M. Thrall *et al.* (eds), Wiley, 1954.
28. Bush, Robert, and Frederick Mosteller, *Stochastic Models of Learning*, Wiley, 1955.
29. Kuehn, Alfred A., 'Consumer brand choice as a learning process', *Journal of Advertising Research*, vol. 2, December 1962.
30. Hyman, Herbert H., 'The psychology of status', *Archives of Psychology*, no. 269, 1942.
31. Hyman, Herbert M., 'Reflections on reference groups', *Public Opinion Quarterly*, autumn 1960.
32. Bourne, Francis S., 'Group influence in marketing and public relations', Rensis Likert and Samuel P. Hayes Jnr (eds), UNESCO, 1959.
33. Lazarsfeld, Paul F., Bernard Berelson, and Hazel Gaudet, *The People's Choice*, Columbia, New York, 1948.
34. Rogers, E. M., *Diffusion of Innovations*, The Free Press, New York, 1948.
35. Merton, R. K., *Social Theory and Social Structure*, The Free Press, New York, 1957.
36. Sheth, Jagdish, N., 'A review of buyer behaviour', *Management Science*, vol. 13, no. 12, August 1967.
37. Menzel, H., and E. Katz, 'Social relations and innovation in the medical profession: The epidemiology of a new drug', *Public Opinion quarterly*, winter 1955–56.
38. Asch, Solomon E., *Social Psychology*, Prentice-Hall, Englewood Cliffs, New Jersey, 1965.
39. Hill, Reuben, 'Patterns of decision-making and the accumulation of family assets', in: *Household Decision-Making*, Nelson, N. Foote (ed.), New York University Press, 1961.
40. Wells, W. D., and G. Gubar, 'Life-cycle concept in marketing research', *Journal of Marketing Research*. November 1966.
41. Field, J. G., 'The influence of household members on housewife purchases', Thomas Gold Medals Awards for Advertising Research, 1968, Thomson Organisation, London, November 1968.
42. Sampson, P., 'An examination of the concepts evoked by the suggestion of "other members of the household" influence over housewife purchases', Thomson Gold Medals Awards for Advertising Research, 1968, Thomson Organisation, London, November 1968.
43. Horney, Karen, *Our Inner Conflicts*, W. W. Norton, New York, 1945.
44. Riseman, David, *The Lonely Crowd*, Yale, New Haven, 1950.
45. Mead, Margaret, 'The application of anthropological techniques to cross-national communication', *Trans. New York Academy of Science, Series 11*, vol. 9, no. 4, February 1947.
46. Green, Paul E., and Donald S. Tull, *Research for Marketing Decisions*, Prentice-Hall, Englewood Cliffs, New Jersey, 1975.
47. Wass, Sir Douglas, Presidential Address to the Annual Conference of the Market Research Society, *MRS Newsletter*, May 1990.
48. Pilditch, James, 'Reputation and reality in design', *Industrial Marketing Digest*, vol. 5, no. 1, 1979.
49. Goldsmith, Walter, and David Clutterbuck, *The Winning Streak*, Weidenfeld and Nicolson, London, 1984.
50. Hooley, Graham J., and Christopher J. West, 'The untapped markets for marketing research', *Journal of the Market Research Society*, vol. 26, no. 4, October 1984.
51. Ovenden, Anthony, *Competitiveness in UK Manufacturing Industry*, BIM, Corby, Northants, 1986.
52. Chisnall, Pater M., 'Market research', in: *Management for Health Service Administrators*', David Allen and James A. Hughes (eds), Pitman, London, 1983.
53. Slingsby, Helen, 'House calls', *Financial Times*, 30 March 1990.
54. Douglas, Susan P., and C. Samuel Craig, *International Marketing Research*, Prentice-Hall, Englewood Cliffs, New Jersey, 1983.
55. Gabor, A., and C. Granger, *The Attitude of the Consumer to Prices in Pricing Strategy*, Staple Press, London, 1969.
56. Greenhaugh, Colin, 'Research for new product development', ex *Consumer Market Research Handbook* (3rd Edn), Robert Worcester and John Downham (eds.), ESOMAR, Amsterdam, 1986.
57. McWilliams, Gil, 'the case for "All Clear" shampoo', in: *Advertising Works*, Simon Broadbent (ed.), Holt, Rinehart and Winston, Eastbourne, 1981.

TWO

METHODOLOGIES OF MARKETING RESEARCH

In Chapter 1 it was observed that scientific research practice has influenced the development of marketing research and has encouraged high standards in surveys concerned with marketing activities in many spheres. To ensure the continued growth of marketing research as a valuable aid to management decision making, it is critical that the process of investigation is soundly based and organized in an efficient manner. This is helped by considering the marketing research process as a series of steps to be taken in gradually developing, planning, and executing research into specific problems.

2.1 DEVELOPING A RESEARCH DESIGN

A central part of research activity is to develop an effective research strategy or design. This will detail the most suitable methods of investigation, the nature of the research instruments, the sampling plan, and the types of data, i.e., quantitative or qualitative (or, ideally, both). A research design forms the framework of the entire research process: 'If it is a good design, it will ensure that the information obtained is relevant to the research problem and that it was collected by objective and economic procedures'.[1]

2.2 THREE TYPES OF RESEARCH DESIGN

Research designs can be classified in various ways; a widely used method identifies them broadly as: exploratory, descriptive, and causal.

Exploratory designs

Exploratory designs are concerned with identifying the real nature of research problems and, perhaps, of formulating relevant hypotheses for later tests. These initial steps should not be dismissed as of little consequence; the opposite, in fact, is nearer to reality, for exploratory research gives valuable insight, results in a firm grasp of the essential character and purpose of specific research surveys, and encourages the development of creative, alternative research strategies. As Douglas and Craig[2] emphasize: 'Rarely is one likely to be in a position to design a detailed research plan at the outset of a project'. Exploratory investigations provide guidance as to how the entire research programme (e.g., sampling methodology) should be devised.

In some cases, exploratory research based on published data (see later discussion of secondary data) may give adequate knowledge for particular marketing decisions to be made.

Descriptive studies

Descriptive studies, in contrast to exploratory research, stem from substantial prior knowledge of marketing variables. For this type of research to be productive, questions should be designed to secure specific kinds of information, related, perhaps, to product performance, market share, competitive strategies, distribution, etc.

Marketing research reports are largely descriptive; market demand, customer profile, economic and industrial phenomena, and other factors which characterize market behaviour are generally covered in quantitative and qualitative terms.

Causal studies

These attempt to identify factors which underlie market behaviour and to evaluate their relationships and interactions. For example, the extent, if any, of price elasticity of demand, or the degree to which advertising campaigns may influence sales.

The concept of causation needs to be approached with caution, and some understanding of the nature of causation would, no doubt, be helpful. Cause and effect relationships are notoriously difficult to deal with realistically and objectively; there is always the temptation to jump to conclusions, usually in support of a preconceived notion of how, for instance, the market behaves in specific situations.

Causation has two important aspects: (i) necessary condition and (ii) sufficient condition. It is accepted that an event can be regarded as the cause of another event if its occurrence is both the necessary and sufficient condition for the latter event to take place. 'A *necessary* condition means that the caused event cannot occur in the absence of the causative event. A *sufficient* condition means that the causative event is all that is needed to bring about the caused event. In other words, in a simple causative relationship, the two events *never* occur in isolation.'[3] This theory of basic and simple causative relationship does not, however, have much relevance to marketing problems which may, for example, be concerned with price reductions resulting in either increases, decreases or no effect at all upon sales, which themselves may change even if prices are unvaried. Environmental factors, such as fashion or consumer tastes, may contribute significantly to the perceived trend of sales.

Contributory cause has been defined as 'the occurrence of one event increasing the likelihood or probability of the occurrence of a second event'.[3]

A price reduction may attract business, i.e., increase the probability of buying, but if the lower price suggests to the buyer that the quality of the product has been debased, the probability of purchase will be likely to decrease instead of increase. In industrial markets, research[4] revealed that price reductions less than 1 per cent of competitors' prices caused virtually no changes in sources of supply, but cuts of 1–9 per cent resulted in about 40 per cent of buyers indicating that they would probably be prepared to change suppliers. However, where prices were reduced by over 10 per cent, only 14 per cent of buyers said they would be willing to switch to new sources; if prices are reduced too much, suspicions about quality tend to be aroused and fewer sales may result.

This probabilistic approach leads to experimentation in which, for instance, the results of two test markets are evaluated statistically. (See later section on experimentation.)

Three factors are likely to be useful in inferring causation: (i) *concomitant variation;* (ii) *time sequence of occurrence;* and (iii) *absence of other possible causal factors.*

Concomitant variation may be inferred where a marketing resource, such as advertising expenditure, is raised simultaneously across a number of market areas and sales in each are measured. If sales are high where extensive advertising occurs, but low sales are experienced where advertising expenditures are limited, it could be inferred (but *not* proved) that advertising causes sales to rise. Other tests might involve different elements of the marketing mix, e.g., packaging might be varied and sales measured in different territories or markets.

Time sequence of occurrence may also produce evidence of causation of some kind; one event must necessarily precede the other, otherwise it clearly cannot be said to cause the latter. If, for example, sales increases in specific test markets were not apparent until an improved discount structure was offered to distributors, then a causal relationship may be inferred.

Absence of other possible causal factors is most unlikely to happen in real-life business conditions; there is always the likelihood of some extraneous and hitherto unexpected factor to intrude into even the most carefully laid marketing plans. Simplistic interpretations of correlations are well-known hazards in forecasting. In theory, if every possible causative factor other than the particular one under focus was eliminated, then that factor could be accepted as the causative one. However desirable this may be, realism dictates that marketers have to exercise their skills in imperfect conditions and take every care in devising and interpreting market test operations. (See Section 2.8: Experimentation.)

2.3 SEQUENTIAL STAGES OF MARKETING RESEARCH

Five logical steps can be identified in the survey process; these apply irrespective of the nature of the market – consumer, industrial, or public service (see Fig. 2.1).

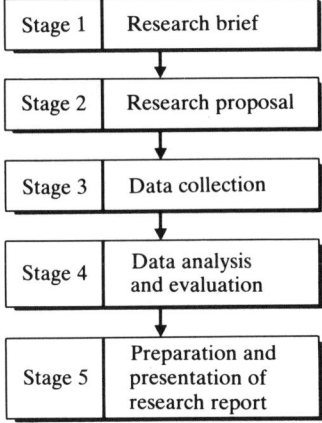

Fig. 2.1 Five sequential stages of marketing research

Stage 1: Research brief

This first stage is critical because it will decide the nature and direction of the entire research activity.

The marketing problem on which the survey is expected to focus should be clearly defined. Before this clear definition is possible, it may be necessary, as indicated earlier, to undertake some exploratory research into certain aspects of the client's business, e.g., the sales organization, methods of publicity, distribution arrangements, etc., in an attempt to pinpoint areas of significance to the enquiry. By consulting sales records, holding informal discussions with company executives and other staff, comparing published figures with company statistics, and generally checking through all those factors in the business that are likely to influence the situation as a whole, researchers gain a valuable insight into the client's business. Preparatory work of this nature, carried out conscientiously and objectively, is an essential element in the systematic study of marketing problems. After this preliminary study has been made researchers should be in a position to know whether it would be advisable for the clients to commission formal research into particular areas of their business activities, or if the present analysis provides adequate knowledge about their particular problem. The outcome will obviously depend on individual cases and their characteristics.

Both management and researchers should work closely together in this crucial task of developing survey objectives. For example, it is extremely important to define clearly the actual population to be surveyed. Unless the briefing is thorough – and an unbiased account of the firm and its problems is given by management – the resultant research objectives may be irrelevant and even counter-productive. The researcher should indicate the limitations of survey methodology; both parties should agree on the degree of accuracy required, the date by which the report is to be submitted, and the appropriate costs involved.

Assuming that additional research is thought to be necessary, clients and researchers must now agree on the exact terms of reference, including a statement of the problems that is unambiguous and directly useful as a guide during the research operations. This statement will discipline the whole process of research, concentrating activities and integrating them effectively in an overall planned scheme of investigation.

Stage 2: Research proposal

The second stage of research activity – the work plan – entails devising a research proposal which will describe the nature of the problem, the precise population involved, the principal factors affecting market behaviour, the methodologies to be adopted, and estimates of time and costs. This proposal should be agreed in detail before entering the next phase of research.

This stage of the research programme includes, for example, exploring and analysing relationships between variables that appear to be significant in the problem being surveyed. It may take some time before a satisfactory model can be built. Over a series of stages of development, through refining and clarifying the various factors in the problem, a useful model should emerge. The careful study involved in the search for facts and relationships will result in researchers having a thorough grasp and appreciation of all the facets of the research problem. This enables them to develop and select hypotheses that are appropriate to the research task. The objectives of the research have now been developed and refined into a series of working hypotheses which can be tested during the course of research. Ideally, a single hypothesis may emerge, the testing of which will adequately fulfil the research objectives. Some leading researchers[5] have commented:

> Essentially, therefore, working hypotheses arise as a result of a *a priori* thinking about the subject, preliminary investigation of available data and material (including related studies), or advice and counsel of experts or interested parties. Like the formulation of the problem, such hypotheses are most useful when expressed in precise, clearly defined terms.
>
> Occasionally, a problem will be encountered which won't need working hypotheses. This is particularly true of numerical estimation problems, such as, say, estimating the proportion of families covered by sickness insurance.

The objective of a survey might be concerned with evaluating the influence on sales of a proposed new style of packaging for a range of products. Before making this fundamental change in packaging, for example, from fibre-board cartons to blister packs, research is undertaken to test the hypothesis that sales are significantly affected by the type of packaging used. The extent of any increase in sales is carefully examined in view of probably additional costs in packaging. Information is, therefore, needed on the sales of products packaged in alternative forms. Data are collected over a series of test markets.

Designing research for international marketing is, of course, generally far more complex than for one country. 'The conduct of research in different countries implies much greater attention to defining the relative unit and level of analysis. . . . '[2] (Also see Chapter 13.)

Data for marketing research can be obtained by several methods; the research proposal will have submitted a general outline of the methodology. No research method is without bias; it is the task of professional researchers to eliminate, as far as possible, the intrusiveness of bias in surveys, which is likely to be controlled by a multi-technique approach. (See later discussion.)

Unfortunately, there are several sources of error in surveys. Samples, for example, may be defective; questions may be badly drafted or misunderstood; the interviewing process may lack objectivity; or the quality of the data may suffer from inappropriate coding.

The types of data required must be checked and considered in relation to the sources from which such information could be obtained. The methods of collecting the data must also be studied, and alternatives compared for their efficiency and likely value to the research.

Stage 3: Data collection

This stage will be a central part of the research activities. An effective sampling plan will have been devised in Stage 2, and the relative efficiencies of various methods of collecting data will have been evaluated. In this stage, the survey methodology has to be put into practice; since time constraints are inevitable, it would be advisable to plan operations on a time schedule.

Since so much of the efficiency of the complete research programme depends on reliable and valid data being gathered by researchers, activities during this stage of research should be carefully planned and executed, while control of field research should be in the hands of an experienced supervisor.

Stage 4: Data analysis and evaluation

The raw material of the research process, i.e., data, has to be processed by tabulation, analysis, and interpretation, so that the research findings can be communicated to clients and readily understood. This stage covers more than the mere mechanical handling of a mass of data. Significant relationships must be identified and discussed clearly and objectively in connection with the specific problems of the research. Data are expensive to collect and analyse; full value should be extracted from them.

According to the complexity and volume of the data collected, tabulations and analyses may range from hand processing through to sophisticated computer packages. But it is useless – if not decidedly dangerous – to apply sophisticated statistical tests to data that originate from an unsound research design. Unless care is taken at every stage of the survey process, the resultant information, masquerading as scientific, may be worth less than subjective opinion.

Stage 5: Preparation and presentation of final report

This last stage in the research process should be done thoroughly. During the preceding stage, researchers will be planning how to present their findings. Tables, graphs, and other diagrams may be developed from the processed data to illustrate the principal findings of the research.

Writing a marketing survey report involves professional skills in communication. Both the content and style of the report should satisfy the needs of specific clients. The format, printing, and binding of the report deserve considerable care; they help to make a report intelligible and effective. Whether researchers should interpret the research findings is open to debate, and is discussed later in this text. Some clients are content with the facts being reported, while others seek for the researchers' interpretation because it is likely that they will have acquired special insight into the business and its markets. The scope of researchers' responsibilities should, of course, be clarified in the research proposal.

2.4 CLASSIFICATION OF DATA

In the preceding section, the main processes of research methodology were outlined; in this section more detailed attention will be given to the main sources of data and the research instruments used.

There are *two generic classifications* of data on which research designs depend:

1. *Primary data:* data that have to be collected for the first time by either one or a blend of:
   (a) observation
   (b) experimentation
   (c) questionnaires
2. *Secondary data:* existing information that may be useful for the purposes of specific surveys. This may be available:
   (a) internally
   (b) externally

2.5 MAIN CATEGORIES OF RESEARCH TECHNIQUES

Both primary and secondary data will be discussed in some detail later in this chapter, but first of all, it would be worth while to reflect on the sad but true fact that the process of research is subject to many sources of bias. Every attempt should be made to reduce to the minimum, if not eradicate entirely, the intrusion of bias in research practice. With this point in mind it is advisable to note that two main categories of research techniques can be identified: *reactive* and *normative*. The former relates to survey situations where data originate from interaction between investigators and respondents as in interviews, questionnaires, or experiments. The latter techniques, also known as non-reactive measures, relate to surveys involving, for example, observation or library research, where there is no dependence on respondents directly to give information. It is recommended[6] that non-reactive measures, described as 'unobtrusive', should be more widely adopted by marketing researchers.

2.6 DESIRABILITY OF COMBINING SURVEY TECHNIQUES

The multi-technique approach to research underlies the desirability of using several different methods, which together make up a sound research strategy. It is not so much a question of which *method* is best as which *set* of methods is likely to result in an objective research programme.

A strong plea for the 'triangulation' of research methods has been made by Webb *et al.*,[6] who are particularly concerned with the limitations of research, especially reactive measurement errors: 'So long as one has only a single class of data collection, and that class is the questionnaire or interview, one has inadequate knowledge of the rival hypotheses grouped under the term reactive measurement effects'.

These potential sources of error, some stemming from an individual's awareness of being tested, others from the nature of the investigator, must be accounted for by some other class of measurement than the verbal self-report.

The obtrusiveness of reactive measures occurs in the social sciences, and it is important for marketing researchers to realize that it is often extremely difficult to eradicate the biases which can arise. A series of linked research operations can be helpful in revealing errors in measurement, the weaknesses of one survey method being compensated for by the particular strengths of an alternative method of investigation.

As observed earlier, no research method is without bias; the specific problems of bias associated with interviewing, questionnaires, and sampling techniques are discussed in some detail later in this text, when it will be apparent that the whole process of research is fraught with many dangers. These can be minimized, however, by intelligent planning in the early stages of designing a research strategy. Admittedly, it is difficult to eliminate entirely the effects of measurement on the subjects of an enquiry.

> The administration of IQ tests may alter an individual's future performance on tests of this type. Being subjected to socio-economic scales may alter respondents' behaviour by making them more conscious of their 'class' positions. The questions of election pollsters may stimulate a voter to take a stand on an issue.[7]

Where observation is used, people are often aware that they are being studied, and, as a result, may modify their behaviour in some way. In the opening scene of Shaw's play, *Pygmalion*, the behaviour of Eliza Doolittle is strongly influenced because she is aware of being observed by Professor Higgins.

Observation may also suffer from the observer's biases or expectations. The observer must be alert to the danger of seeing only those events which agree with his explicit or implicit hypotheses. Observation, to be of value to research, must be objective; observers should not allow themselves to become too involved, emotionally or socially, with those whom they are studying.

The selection and training of observers need to be undertaken with particular care. The reliability of individual observer's reports could be checked, of course, by comparing the reports of a series of identical events which have been observed by two or more observers. Bertrand Russell's witty comment on the study of animal behaviour well illustrates the problem of observer bias.

> One may say broadly that all the animals that have been carefully observed have behaved so as to confirm the philosophy in which the observer believed before his observation began. Nay, more, they have all displayed the national characteristics of the observer. Animals studied by Americans rush about frantically, with an incredible display of hustle and pep, and at last achieve the desired result by chance. Animals observed by the Germans sit still and think, and at last evolve the solutions out of their inner consciousness.[8]

The problem of maintaining objectivity arises particularly when participant observation takes place, i.e., the observer is disguised as a member of the society or group being studied, and must, to some extent, act out his role. While this type of hidden observation reduces considerably distorted behaviour by the group, it makes stringent demands on the observer, who needs special training for this work. Among the difficulties of operating this form of research is that of recording adequately what is being observed – obviously, overt note taking is out of the question. Participant observation may be particularly difficult in communities that are relatively 'closed', i.e., those which do not assimilate strangers easily, and the mere presence of a 'foreigner' may be sufficient reason for modifying the patterns of normal behaviour. In some cases, it may take a long time before the newcomer is accepted as a member of the group and is able to function usefully as an observer. In other cases, participant observation may have to be called off as impracticable. One of the best-known uses of participant observation in social studies was made by W. F. Whyte[9] in his study of American street-corner society. He lived for three-and-a-half years in a slum district in Boston as a member of various street-corner groups, though members of the group knew that he was studying their style of living.

The problem of reactive measures is pervasive and it increases the complexity of research. To reduce this form of bias, researchers have developed techniques which have been classified by Eugene J. Webb and his co-authors[6] as 'unobtrusive measures' or non-reactive research.

Unobtrusive measures allow research to be conducted without the subjects being aware of the process of investigation. Unobtrusive methods include the study of records of births, marriages, and deaths, of official publications of various kinds, company records of purchases and sales, etc. Physical evidence may offer valuable information, e.g., wear and tear on carpets in display areas, fingerprints on museum exhibits, time spent by people in various departments of a store or exhibition. Advertising exposure in a magazine was measured by a 'glue-seal record'. A small spot of glue, which would not reseal once it was broken, was inconspicuously placed close to the binding of the magazine so that it lightly held together each pair of pages in a specially prepared issue. Advertising exposure was assessed by noting whether or not the gum seals had been broken following reading of the magazine. This method was useful in checking the answers to more conventional enquiries, particularly since there is a tendency among respondents to direct questioning to claim viewing or reading habits that do not, in fact, coincide with their actual behaviour.

An interesting account[6] is given of a Chicago automobile dealer, who:

> ... estimates the popularity of different radio stations by having mechanics record the position of the dial in all cars brought in for service. More than 50 000 dials a year are checked, with less than 20 per cent duplication of dials. These data are then used to select radio stations to carry the dealer's advertising.

Webb[6] comments that the generalization of these findings is sound, provided the radio audience is typically the same as those who have their car serviced at the dealership, and that a significant number of cars have radios. Apparently, the American car dealer finds high correlation exists between radio audiences and the 'dial research' findings.

Apart from direct observation, unobtrusive measures may adopt 'contrived observation' including the use of what has been termed 'hidden hardware' operated by the investigator. This method may use one-way mirrors, tape recordings (unknown to those being tested), cine and still photography, etc.

Webb and his associates review some applications of covert research techniques, which range from the videotaping of audiences to concealed recording by a microphone hidden in a mock hearing aid. 'It works extremely well in inducing the subject to lean over and shout directly into the recording apparatus. The presence of a dangling cord does not inhibit response.'

They also mention various studies which have been undertaken to measure eye movement and pupil dilation, indicating the degree of interest shown by subjects in particular advertisements or products. Instruments for testing eye reactions are used in 'laboratory' advertising tests, when, of course, the techniques are generally apparent to the subjects. Webb adds that earlier research reported that Chinese jade dealers were aware of the importance of pupil dilation in expressing a potential buyer's interest in various stones offered to him; apparently, astute buyers wore dark glasses to counter this communication.

Alfred Politz,[10] the veteran American researcher, studied advertising exposure to posters on the outside of buses by means of movie cameras, specially arranged to film people looking towards the buses as they travelled the routes. This pioneer photographic survey technique was used successfully by Politz in Philadelphia in 1959, and in Chicago in 1964–65. It was adapted for research on London Transport bus advertising during 1966.[8,11]

The objectives of the London Transport research project were to derive estimates of the total number of people who were in a position to see advertisements on the outside of London Transport buses. Two separate but complementary surveys were involved; a Greater London survey which recorded time spent on roads that were also bus routes, and a photographic study in which people present on the bus routes were filmed and counted. The results of the first survey were related to the frequency with which the buses travelled the routes, and estimates of the number of 'opportunities to see' advertisements on the outside of buses were made. These estimates were then refined by using the photographic survey to produce estimates of 'full-face' viewing of the buses.

Since the details of this research are interesting, they are reported briefly here. A randomly selected sample of adults in the Greater London area was interviewed during June and July 1966, and information was obtained from 986 persons. Details of the pattern of journeys (both regular and casual) made by informants during a particular period of time, i.e., the seven days preceding the day of interview, were sought. Travel outside the bus route areas was regarded as irrelevant to the study, which was concerned with potential exposure to bus advertising.

The photographic survey covered the period March to September 1966, and involved a random sample of garages from which two or three vehicles per day were equipped with specially mounted cine cameras. These operated for two or three days per week, and a total of 40 000 photographs were taken. In practice, the researchers found that there were certain limitations to this technique because of the effect of shadows and the difficulty of identifying whether or not people were actually looking at the bus. It was only possible to classify people as 'full face' or otherwise.

Filming was intermittent: 11 frames at one-second intervals every two minutes. The average resultant count was then multiplied up to account for the whole hour.

The researchers report that the photographic survey was valuable in providing a cross-check on the results from more conventional research, i.e., interviewing. Because people happen to be within the area of a bus route, it does not necessarily follow that they will see the advertisements displayed on a bus.

The overall results of these two survey methods showed a statistical difference, which was, however, expected because the photographic survey included all individuals on the streets at the time of filming, whereas interviewing covered only residents of the Greater London area. The researchers 'were encouraged to find that agreement between the two methods was as good as it was', and they noted that London Transport advertising data were 'based mainly on the results of the interview survey, which, in fact, was a significantly lower estimate of advertising exposure'.

This interesting example of a dual method of investigation underlines the value of combining techniques in order to check data from one particular source and to give it greater acceptability.

In 1934, La Piere[12] studied the relationship between written statements and overt acts (behaviour) in a research on prejudice. He travelled throughout the US in company with a Chinese couple and visited 250 hotels and restaurants; they were refused service on only one occasion. Later, when questionnaires were sent to those same establishments, over 90 per cent said they would not accept Chinese customers. La Piere also sent identical questionnaires to a control group of 100 similar catering establishments, which had not been visited by his party, and the response was similar to his earlier finding. However, this particular research has attracted some criticisms, which are discussed elsewhere.[13]

There is need, therefore, for a more imaginative approach to research with a willingness to consider alternative and complementary methodological strategies. While 'questionnaires and interviews are probably the most flexible and generally useful devices we have for gathering information',[6] a more creative approach, using multi-measurement techniques, reduces the dangers of reactive effects. There is no standard strategy suitable for every research problem;

researchers must examine scrupulously and sensitively the requirements of individual enquiries. Research strategies should be designed to meet the identified needs of specific studies, bearing in mind the earlier comment that a sound research strategy is concerned not so much with what method is best as to what *set* of methods is most likely to result in objective findings.

The value of combining survey methods was advocated by the well-known American researcher, Stanley L. Payne,[14] some years ago:

> Still, it is only recently that our eyes have been opened to the fruitful idea of using the basic survey methods in combination. We may have been too blind from looking upon them as exclusive alternatives to observe that they might be applied as complementary parts of a single investigation ... sometimes a combination of all three methods (e.g., mail, telephone, personal interviews) may be used with the same respondents to produce results more efficiently than one method alone could do. What is wanted in survey design is an imaginative and flexible approach.

While contrived observation involving the use of 'hidden hardware' has methodological attractions, the increasing inventiveness of electronic apparatus in social research gives rise to the ethical implications involved in using them indiscriminately. In discussing such methods, Webb and associates, while recognizing the ethical issues which they raise: 'feel that this is a matter for separate consideration'. They do not feel able to pass judgement on the ethics of these complex issues, and invite 'thoughtful debate on these matters'.[6] The Market Research Society has specifically referred to this issue in its Code of Conduct to which members are expected to adhere.

Market research in countries where there are low levels of literacy, and where lists from which to draw samples are very unlikely to be available, demands considerable ingenuity in devising research instruments and tactics. 'Observational and projective techniques avoid some of the problems associated with survey techniques, since they do not impose any prestructured frame of reference on respondents. This may reflect the specific cultural referents of the researcher and hence be a potential source of bias.'[2]

2.7 PRIMARY DATA – OBSERVATION

This non-reactive research technique, widely used in scientific studies and often termed the 'classical method of investigation', has several applications in marketing research. It can be used alone or in conjunction with other forms of research to supplement the data collected. It is particularly useful in checking the validity of answers given in a questionnaire. For many reasons, people may not give completely accurate accounts of their actual behaviour; what they say they buy, or where they actually shop may not necessarily coincide with the answers given to an interviewer. Experienced researchers know well the inclinations of respondents to protect their egos, to project favourable images of themselves, and, even, on occasions to distort their reputed beliefs and behaviour in order to 'shock' those surveying them.

In Britain, as noted in Chapter 1, Tom Harrison popularized the use of observational techniques in social enquiries, and many of his studies have acquired the aura of pioneer investigations. However, it should be borne in mind that since those early days of market and social research, more elaborate and sophisticated alternative methods of collecting data have been developed and considerable expertise now exists in, for example, organizing non-directive discussion groups (see Chapter 8).

Observation, as indicated in the preceding section, may be either participative or non-participative. Participant observation would seem to have very limited application in marketing research.

In marketing research, *three methods of observation* are in general use: *audits, recording devices*, and *watching people's behaviour as buyers*.

Audits

The audit technique is exemplified by shop audit research as practised by Nielsen's, whereby physical checks of stocks of selected types of products are made every few weeks in order to estimate actual sales at certain outlets. Domestic consumer panels are operated by Audits of Great Britain Ltd, and other leading research companies (details are given in Chapter 9), including the auditing of home stocks of specific food products. Traffic counts are often taken in shopping centres and in stores to note the intensity and flow of traffic. This information is useful in locating display areas in strategic positions. Research on poster advertising is largely done by observing the amount and type of traffic that passes poster sites.

Recording devices

Recording devices used in observation include hidden movie cameras, and various kinds of counting meters, used in television research in the UK. In laboratory situations, devices like the psycho-galvanometer are often adopted to check reactions to selected types of advertisemment. This meter, by measuring the change in the electrical resistance in the palms of a subject's hands, registers the perspiratory rate, which is increased by excitement. The impact of a series of advertisements is checked against meter readings.

Of these sophisticated mechanical methods of observation, the tachistoscope is said to be the only device which is still popular but rarely used today without the additional information obtained from the inclusion of diagnostic questions in the questionnaire.[15] The tachistoscope is a device which allows a viewer a controlled, momentary glimpse (between $\frac{1}{200}$ and $\frac{1}{10}$ second) of, for example, a product pack or an advertisement. After this brief exposure, a respondent is asked what he saw. While this is an ingenious technique, the viewer is looking at the subject material in a contrived situation that is very different from the environment where shopping, for instance, takes place. Another disadvantage relates to cost, which limits the size of samples that can be exposed to this methodology.

Watching people's behaviour as buyers

Observational techniques were adopted to evaluate the use of car seat belts in the UK. Observers were sited at a representative number of points to note the proportions of drivers and front seat passengers who were wearing their seat belts. The researchers[16] reported that this research technique was the principal one used by the Central Office of Information to monitor the effectiveness of the advertising campaign urging motorists to use their seat belts. If straight questioning had been employed, it was recognized that the usage of seat belts would be overstated.

It was reported[17] that Honda observed the ways in which people loaded the boots of their cars and, as a result, redesigned the Honda Civic hatchback. The manufacturers of Philips shavers identify customers' needs partly through observing, through a two-way mirror, a recruited sample's typical shaving techniques.

Hidden movie cameras were used in research[1] to evaluate the amount of information that should be given on packaging labels by a manufacturer of frozen juice concentrates.

In a number of supermarkets, films were taken of consumers selecting frozen juice concentrates. Analysis of these films revealed that far more time was spent in carefully examining and in selecting brands than had previously been believed.

Personal observation by trained observers can be useful in many situations. Rival stores frequently check the special displays, prices, and merchandising techniques adopted by competitors. Observers can watch people's behaviour when they enter a particular department of a store;

how many walk round before settling down to consider specific styles or types of products; how important it is to shoppers to be able to handle goods, to feel their quality or weight; how many approach shop assistants for help, and how soon after entering the department; how carefully shoppers read labels, packaging, or 'guarantee cards' attached to products. All these (and more) can be checked and assessed for their importance as buying influences, and compared with answers received using questionnaires.

Observation of behaviour is rarely sufficient by itself; it yields information at a certain level, but it does not reveal hidden buying motives. When the technique is practised by skilled observers, it can be an economical method of acquiring additional knowledge about buying behaviour which may be unobtainable by other methods. Few people, for example, could accurately describe their customary shopping behaviour in detail, and the peculiarities of their behaviour may strongly influence their selection of products or brands of products.

Observers must be given clear instructions on the nature of the action or event which they are to observe. Detailed instructions should cover the time, place, and conditions involved to ensure that observations are likely to take place in representative situations. Traffic flow will obviously be affected by time; weather conditions may radically alter the normal pattern of buying behaviour. Observational data should be recorded on a specifically designed schedule to help in analysis and classification.

Apart from shoppers, the behaviour of shop assistants, for example, can be usefully observed. Do they appear biased towards a particular brand of product? Are they unwilling to demonstrate some item of domestic equipment? Do they appear to argue strongly with customers?

2.8 PRIMARY DATA – EXPERIMENTATION

In most fields of scientific enquiry, research is primarily centred around controlled experiments in which efforts are made to hold conditions constant, thus enabling the effects of a particular factor or variable to be studied and measured. Any change observed to have taken place in the test situation is measured, statistically checked by tests of significance, and, according to the results of these tests, the change may be held to be attributable to the intervention of the independent variable.

The ideal experimental conditions of laboratory testing are virtually impossible in the real-life conditions experienced in marketing. The environment in which commercial transactions take place is highly complex and many factors affecting product sales, e.g., competitors' activities, economic conditions, climatic changes, dealers' resistance, etc., cannot be controlled by the marketer. Marketing is deeply involved with human behaviour and with the reactions of people as consumers of a very wide range of goods and services. This involvement makes marketing experiments difficult to plan and execute, yet some attempt should be made to apply the principles of experimentation, as this is the only research method available for verifying cause and effect relationships in marketing studies. The marketing researcher has to be realistic in accepting the inevitable limitations of the marketing environment, and design his experiments so that the influence of the uncontrolled variables intrudes as little as possible in the research design. In overseas marketing, Douglas and Craig[2] emphasize the difficulty of designing an experiment that is comparable or equivalent in all respects in every country or socio-cultural environment.

The object of marketing experiments is to compare the responses to several alternatives in the marketing mix and to evaluate this information as a guide to management in deciding the most effective method of marketing specific products. Variations of product (flavour, colour); packaging (large packs, various kinds of packs); advertising (whether to advertise or not, what media to use); distribution arrangements (direct, appointed stockists, wholesale); price (price differentiation); sales force efficiency (sales training – formal/informal): these are some of the factors affecting marketing efficiency that could be subjected to experimentation.

Advertising experiments can be planned by using 'split-runs'; changing the style of advertisement in alternative editions or runs of a publication and checking the response, for example, to a coupon offer. The location of departments in stores can be experimentally changed and a check kept on sales. Display units may be placed in some stores (and not in others, which will be carefully chosen to act as 'controls') and comparative sales can be audited over a period of time.

Marketing experiments are often focused on short-term studies and this may possibly lead to wrong assumptions. The 'carry-over' effects of advertising, for example, may be significant from one selling period to another; for example, the case of the Du Pont advertising tests with 'Teflon' (Chapter 11). The time-lag before an idea is accepted may be considerable and acceptance may only occur after the promotion has finished. Where panels are used to evaluate the effects of advertising, the likelihood of 'carry-over' effects should be assessed. It may be advisable to extend testing beyond the actual period of advertising to ensure that the long-term effects are adequately measured.

The most popular use of experiments in marketing occurs with test marketing, which is discussed in some detail later. The techniques used in test marketing have improved considerably, although, of course, the environmental conditions of testing are still liable to be affected by unexpected interference, such as widespread labour redundancies in a test area. The experimental approach of test marketing is valuable in providing management with data collected in real-life conditions; the conclusions drawn from this research can be formally established as statistically significant or otherwise.

A model of the experimental method applied to marketing behaviour is shown in Fig. 2.2.

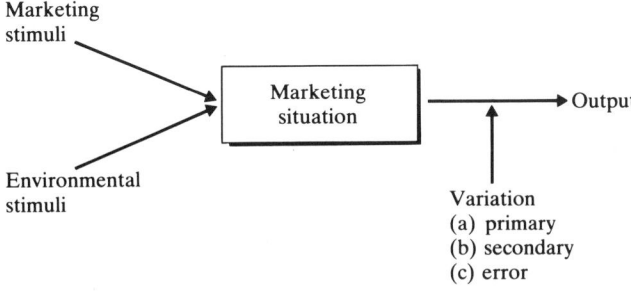

Fig. 2.2 Simplified model of experimental method in marketing.[18]

It will be seen that the model in Fig. 2.2 includes 'variation' which may be any of three types: (i) primary, (ii) secondary, or (iii) error. Primary variation refers to variation in the output caused by changes in the inputs, e.g., sales increasing because of price reductions. Secondary variation refers to variation in output resulting from changes in unidentified or exogenous variables, such as weather conditions. Error variation relates to variation in output caused by imperfect experimental conditions, e.g., measurement errors.

Figure 2.2 relates to a simplified market experiment; controls would be introduced to render the experiment more effective. Experimental designs vary considerably and may involve considerable complexity, e.g., before and after measurements, controls, multi-variate analysis, etc.

For example, 'control' areas are frequently introduced when checking the effect of marketing stimuli such as comparative promotion campaigns for a consumer product. The effects on sales in different areas of alternative forms of promotion (e.g., press advertising versus local radio) can be compared and contrasted with sales in a control area where no kind of promotion took place. It may be found that some common factor, such as the temperature, may be influential in sales trends, and, in fact, the effects of promotion could be minimal.

A more detailed account of nine principal types of errors which can affect experimental results will be found in Green and Tull[1] and also in Tull and Hawkins.[3] These are, briefly: pre-measurement; maturation; history; instrumentation; selection; mortality; interaction; reactive error; and measurement timing.

Over recent years, greater emphasis has been placed on quantifying marketing problems, and this has encouraged the development of an analytical approach, based on variables which are considered within the framework of a decision model.

Sophisticated experimental designs in marketing may be tested by the statistical techniques of analysis of variance or, perhaps, Latin square designs.[3, 19–22]

Experiments can range from the simple to the complex, as shown below.

Time series analysis

This could involve just one treatment and subsequent measurement, or, alternatively, several intermittent treatments over a period of time with individual measurements after each treatment. This type of experiment could cover measuring the effect of special displays staged with selected stores. In the first example, sales at these selected stores would be audited for a period before the displays, and also after the displays have been made. Designs can be formed with or without control groups, and with measurements both before and after the intervention of the variable, e.g., advertising, or merely after its introduction. These types can be summarized as follows:

1. *After-only design without control group*

$$X0 \quad X = \text{non-random group subject to variable.}$$
$$0 = \text{measurement after intervention of variable.}$$

This is a generally unsatisfactory experimental design as there is no measurement made *before* the variable intervened, and no basis exists for comparison.

2. *Before-after design without control group*

$$0_1 X 0_2$$

or   (multiple testing)

$$0_1 0_2 X 0_3 0_4$$

The difference between 0_2 and 0_1 indicates the influence of the variable tested.

This is the method applied in consumer panel testing. This is an improvement on 'after-only' designs, particularly when several measurements are taken. The absence of control groups reduces the general validity of this design.

3. *After-only design with control group*

$$(R) \; X0_1$$
$$(R) \; 0_2 \; \text{(control group)}$$

Both the test group and control group are randomly selected; the former is subjected to the effect of the variable being tested and the result is compared with the control group. No prior testing is undertaken, so comparisons with earlier situations cannot be made. In some cases, it may not be possible to measure before the test variable is applied, e.g., where a product had not been previously offered for sale. The design is suitable for testing the effectiveness of direct mail advertising, when mailing is directed only to the experimental group and the effectiveness is measured by the equation $(0_1 - 0_2$; as above).

4. *Before-after design with control group*

$$(R)\ 0_1 X 0_2$$
$$(R)\ 0_3 0_4\ (\text{control group})$$

Randomly selected groups control systematic errors. The experimental group and control group should possess similar characteristics in order to allow valid comparisons to be made.

The design can be extended to include several groups. It is useful for testing the effect of advertising in selected areas, although, of course, interpretation of the findings needs to be done with care. The control group is valuable because it is measured before and after the test applied to the other group, and, therefore, the likely effect of other factors during the time of the experiment will be reflected in the final measurement of the control group. This allows the effect of the test variable to be isolated more accurately in the test group comparison.

This type of experimental design is useful when sales data are being studied or in observational studies of consumers. If people are actually interviewed before an experiment, their subsequent behaviour may be affected and result in after measurements being non-typical. This could be minimized by using a more complicated (and more expensive) design involving two control groups, one of which is subjected to prior measurements as also is the corresponding experimental group.

Experimental design – multiple variables

The simple experiments considered so far have been concerned with single variables, such as the effect of advertising or point-of-sale display aids on sales. To restrict testing to only one experimental variable may be difficult in practice and also inefficient.

1. *Factorial designs:* these designs permit experiments involving combinations of observations of at least two variables to be tested simultaneously. This type of experiment could refer to a product offered for sale, at the same price, in several selected stores, and supported by varying combinations of display aids, special trade incentives, and display positions. The objective of the experiment is to identify the most profitable marketing mix.

   Sophisticated experimental designs can be tested by the technique of analysis of variance, as in the case of Du Pont[19] which used a factorial experiment on two different advertising media that were varied from very low to very high for each of the media. Twenty-seven markets, representing all possible combinations of the intensity test levels of the two media, were used.

2. *Latin square designs:* these are modified multi-variable designs, in that the interaction effects are usually assumed not to be significant. This simplifies the analysis, and reduces both time and cost.

   These more complicated experimental techniques are fairly popular in studying marketing problems. At the same time, it should be remembered that it is good design practice to select the simplest possible experimental design for the particular problem being studied. Statistical textbooks deal with multi-variable tests in detail.

Davis[23] has stressed that where the relative merits of two or more different 'treatments' are to be assessed (as with comparative tests), a control area is necessary to avoid wrong conclusions. This was illustrated when two experimental methods of promotion in separate areas resulted in sales increases of about 10 per cent. However, a control area in which no advertising took place, showed the same sales increase over the time of the experiment. Apparently, some other factor, perhaps climatic, was affecting sales. Without the control area, the wrong deductions might have been made.

A study[24] conducted in the supermarket section of a large discount store chain in Israel indicated how experimentation can help in designing efficient shelf display. A 4 × 4 Latin square design was used to examine the effect of the four types of display equipment on sales in four stores in successive time periods. Sales from this experiment were subject to analysis of variance and covariance. The results enabled the researchers to suggest specific locations for effective displays in these stores.

James Rothman[25] has helpfully given an illustration of a relatively simple Latin square design related to a store test on a product with a very high rate of sales over four stores during a one-week period. The labels A, B, C, and D represent the different stimuli, and these are arranged (see Fig. 2.3) so that each test stimulus is used once in every week and once in each store.

	Store 1	2	3	4
	A	B	C	D
	B	D	A	C
Week	D	C	B	A
	C	A	D	B

Fig. 2.3 Simple Latin square design for store promotion[25]

Rothman observes that more advanced versions of this basic experimental design can be used to control the sample across three or more dimensions.

Factorial design experiments can contribute to the development of a new product in which the formulation can be varied.[26] For example, a new hair dressing for men could be varied in terms of colour, perfume, and consistency. It would be both uneconomical and unwise to separate these elements for the purposes of product testing because of the possible interactions of these attributes. A factorial design could be devised that would allow, for example, two variations of each of the three elements (colour, perfume, and consistency) to be evaluated thus:

Colour	*Perfume*	*Consistency*
a	a	a
a	a	b
a	b	a
a	b	b
b	a	a
b	a	b
b	b	a
b	b	b

In this design, these three elements are considered over eight different products; the results of the test would be subject to analysis of variance to indicate which, if any, of the three variables significantly affected consumers' reactions to the product and whether any two or all three of the variables revealed an interaction effect.

The economy of adopting this type of experiment is typified by the fact that if a sample of 100 informants was taken and the three variables were tested separately, the total number of interviewees would need to be 300. By using a factorial design, 16 of the 28 possible pairings of test products would entail comparisons of the two variations of each of the three variables.

Hence, to obtain 100 reactions to each of these direct comparisons would require a total sample of fewer than 200 informants.

However, marketing experiments remain fairly expensive and their potential value should be estimated against the cost involved, and only proceeded with if it can be shown that the benefits they will bring to the business outweigh the costs incurred. This elementary principle tends to be overlooked at times, and it is as well to bear in mind that research in marketing entails management time and expense. The use of company resources in any area carries with it the responsibility of accounting for the profitable exploitation of them. Marketing researchers will find that the sound principle of accountability disciplines their efforts to advantage.

2.9 PRIMARY DATA – QUESTIONNAIRES

Most marketing investigations use some form of questionnaire, either postal or administered through personal interviewing, including telephone surveys.

The most commonly used type occurs in personal interviewing, where primary data can be directly collected from respondents in organizational and consumer markets. The amount of information obtainable from observation and experimentation is limited, whereas interviewing is flexible and capable of yielding a very wide range of valuable new data.

Questionnaires are the backbone of most surveys and require careful planning and execution. The objectives of the survey should always be carefully borne in mind when compiling questionnaires. (The detailed structure of questionnaires is considered in Chapter 6.)

Methods of enquiry

1. *Personal interviewing:* this involves trained interviewers working with a carefully selected sample of the population that is under survey. This method is widely used in marketing research. Interviewers must be specially selected, trained, and motivated; they are frequently the weak link in the chain of research. (The problems of interviewing and interviewers are studied in some detail later.)

   Face-to-face interviewing may take place in households, industrial, commercial, or public sector organizations, or, increasingly, in shopping malls. In the US, shopping mall interviewing started in the late 1960s and has grown significantly, so that by 1979 it became the most popular venue for face-to-face interviewing in marketing research.[27] Clearly, it would be unwise to generalize freely from the data obtained from such methodology. (Refer to the discussion on the principles of sample selection in Chapter 3.)

2. *Postal or mail surveys:* questionnaires are mailed to a sample of the population to be surveyed. This method is superficially attractive on account of its cheapness, but this should be related to the relatively low response rate unless the subject of research is of particular interest to the recipients of the questionnaire. Further, non-response is not a random process and those who do respond may not be representative of the population. The adequacy of the sample rests largely on the quality of the sampling list available; this may be incomplete or out of date. Observational data cannot be gathered by postal questionnaires, and this type of information frequently adds to the quality of the responses given in personal interviewing. There is no opportunity to probe or clarify answers that must be accepted as written.

3. *Telephone enquiries:* these are increasingly used in consumer surveys, and also popular in the industrial field. They are valuable in pilot-stage research and in forming sampling lists. Problems of using this method of research and new developments based on computer links, will be discussed later.

4. *Panel research:* this is particularly useful in tracing movements in buying behaviour over a

period of time. Several research bodies have regular panels which are concerned with providing information on family budgets, buying, entertainment habits, etc. Some danger exists from 'conditioning', i.e., that panel members, after a while, begin to behave in a non-typical fashion by becoming more self-conscious in their buying behaviour. Considerable expertise has been built up in the recruitment and management of consumer panels. (A general appreciation of this methodology occurs in Chapter 9.)

5. *Group interview technique:* this involves using psychological methods of enquiry by which free discussion of certain marketing problems is encouraged. (This area of investigation is considered in Chapter 8.)

6. *Special survey techniques:* these include shop audits, television measurement, shop laboratories, etc., which are discussed in some detail in Part Three of this text.

2.10 SECONDARY DATA – INTERNAL

The answers to many problems often lie within the files of an organization or in published material. But in many cases the only way of getting at the required facts is through a sample survey of a part or the whole population.[28]

Library or desk research, which has the attractive attribute of being non-reactive or unobtrusive, is an established method of collecting secondary data; it is economical, comparatively speedy, and can be undertaken with complete confidentiality. Only rarely is there no relevant information about a particular research problem; internal records or published records are often capable of giving remarkably useful information, and this may even be sufficient for the decisions that have to be made. This preliminary stage of research will help in developing the overall research strategy; it should always be undertaken before any further research is contemplated.

Many companies do not make full enough use of the information that is routinely collected. Internal records – production, costing, sales, and distribution – may be designed so that the information they contain is in a form useful for marketing research. Sales analysis should be designed to give information by markets, products, types of distributive outlet or industry, geographic area (home and overseas), characteristics of customers, such as heavy/medium/light buyers. Advertising expenditure should be carefully recorded and analysed by media, product type, and market. Other promotional expenses should also be available for market researchers to study. Some internal data may not be readily available and considerable checking of invoices may be necessary to establish product sales. If this is likely to be an extremely difficult task, some estimates may have to be made based on factory production figures for particular periods.

2.11 SECONDARY DATA – EXTERNAL

External sources of data include statistics and reports issued by governments, trade associations, and other reputable organizations. Research companies and advertising agencies frequently circulate useful information. Further information is obtainable from trade directories.

In the UK, the Government Statistical Service offers detailed data of great value to marketing researchers. Two very useful official publications are: *Guide to Official Statistics* (HMSO) and *Regional Statistics* (HMSO). The Central Statistical Office (CSO), Great George Street, London SW1, or The Business Statistics Office (BSO), Cardiff Road, Newport, Gwent, would give advice on the availability of statistical data for particular types of products and markets. The CSO also publishes annually a useful booklet *Government Statistics: A Brief Guide to Sources*, which lists the various ministries and departments (with telephone numbers) responsible for specific economic and social data, e.g., the *Annual Statistics in Retail Trades*, or the *Classified List of Manufacturing Businesses* – this publication, which is available in special regional and alphabetical analyses at reasonable cost – is useful in building up a specific industry mailing list or sampling frame (see Chapter 12).

Some other principal sources of official information

Annual Abstract of Statistics: provides information on population, housing, manufactured goods, etc.

Monthly Digest of Statistics: similar to above but published at monthly intervals.

Abstract of Regional Statistics: main statistics for Scotland.

Digest of Welsh Statistics: main statistics for Wales.

Economic Trends: monthly review of economic situation.

Social Trends: collection of key social statistics (yearly).

Digest of Health Statistics for England and Wales (yearly).

Agricultural Statistics: England and Wales (yearly).

Agricultural Statistics: Scotland (yearly).

Financial Statistics: key UK monetary and financial statistics (monthly).

Digest of Energy Statistics (yearly).

Highway Statistics (yearly).

Passenger Transport in Great Britain (yearly).

Housing and Construction Statistics (quarterly).

Monthly Bulletin of Construction Statistics.

Overseas Trade Statistics of the UK (monthly).

Family Expenditure Survey Reports (yearly).

National Income and Expenditure 'Blue Book' (yearly).

Census of Production: conducted since the beginning of this century at approximately five-yearly intervals.

Census of Population: full census every 10 years.

Annual Estimates of the Population of England and Wales and of Local Authority Areas (yearly).

Census of Distribution: last full-scale census in 1971 provided basic information on structure of retail areas of distribution; since 1976 superseded by annual sample enquiries.

Department of Employment Gazette (monthly).

Department of Trade and Industry: British Business (formerly *Trade & Industry*) (weekly).

Bill of Entry Service: Customs and Excise data.

Business Monitors: detailed information about many important industries in the UK.

Several of the official sources of data mentioned above are particularly significant in industrial and export marketing research, and they are referred to again in the relevant chapters.

Non-official sources of data

Non-official sources of data in the UK are plentiful and are published by trade associations, banks, academic institutions, the trade and professional press, and national newspapers, as well as survey reports by commercial research firms. Very useful guides are *Sources of UK Marketing Information* by Elizabeth Tupper and Gordon Wills (Benn, 1975), and, more briefly, *Principal Sources of Marketing Information* by Christine Hull (Times Newspapers). Another very comprehensive source of data was published in 1979 by John Wiley: *Where to Find Business Information* lists over 5000 main sources and comments on them in some detail.

Some specific sources of market data

National press:

The Economist; Financial Times; The Times; Daily Telegraph; Guardian; Sunday Times; Observer, etc.

Official publication:

British Business, formerly titled the *Trade and Industry Journal*, is published by the Department of Trade and Industry, and is a valuable source of information about industrial and commercial trends both at home and overseas. Also publishes industry reviews, statistical data, and news about trade fairs and overseas missions.

Trade press and technical:

Specialist journals cover almost every major industry and trade; some cater for highly specific segments. Typical examples are: *The Grocer; Chemist and Druggist; Packaging News; The Architect; Motor Trader; Applied Ergonomics; Footwear Weekly*. (Details can be found in *Willing's Press Guide* and *British Rate and Data Guide (BRAD)*.)

Subscription services:

Mintel Market Intelligence Reports, published monthly, with useful cumulated index at end of each new issue; mostly concerned with consumer products. Mintel also publishes a quarterly *Retail Intelligence* and some special major studies of various market sectors.

Mintel Digest 1992 monitors every UK national paper, selection of international papers, and over 100 trade journals.

ADMAP: monthly journal giving information and statistical data covering all advertising media with special thrice-yearly analyses of advertising expenditures by product categories and media.

Media Expenditure Analysis (MEAL): monitors advertising expenditure across all media and publishes detailed information related to product groups and individual advertisers.

The Economist Group, partly under the name The Economist Intelligence Unit (EIU), publishes, on a regular basis, reports on certain industrial sectors, e.g., the automotive industry, retail distribution, etc., as well as special reports on topics of current interest.

Retail Business and Marketing in Europe, published monthly, gives valuable coverage of specific aspects of markets; a series of printed indexes enable past data to be readily tracked and trends evaluated.

As a result of management buy-out in 1984, *The Corporate Intelligence Group* was formed; this publishes *ad hoc* surveys for clients, and also continuing surveys on off-highway equipment and industries in North America and West Europe.

Euromonitor publishes *Market Research Great Britain* (monthly) and *Market Research Europe* (bi-monthly); coverage given of up to 10 fairly specific topics per issue, e.g., mineral water or television market in Spain.

BLA Group publishes *Market Assessment* (bi-monthly) covering home, office and leisure market sectors in the UK; often useful for industrial market analysis.

Financial Times Business Information Service, established in 1971, provides a broadly based impartial business intelligence service covering all aspects of national and international industry and commerce. Detailed information can include brand shares, advertising expenditures, production, import, export, and sales figures for most industries. Demographic analyses of purchasing or usage patterns are available. Special project investigations can also be undertaken. The FT Business Information Service has close links with FINTEL, jointly owned by the FT and Extel to develop electronic information services; it is the major provider of business information on PRESTEL, the UK Post Office Viewdata system.

CBI Overseas Reports issued quarterly by Confederation of British Industries.

NEDO Reports: National Economic Development Office publishes reports on a range of industries.

Special financial analyses:

Extel Group publishes details of British and European companies.

Jordans Industrial and Financial Surveys. Although principally focusing on providing ratios for comparative purposes in particular market sectors, these reports also include useful overviews and reviews of specific industrial structures and trends.

ICC Business Ratio Reports also give specific information related to ratios of corporate efficiency.

Keynotes Reports cover about 200 consumer and industrial market sectors, giving market size and trends, financial data, industrial structure, etc. Recent press articles on these specific markets are listed.

Gower Press: valuable series of economic surveys covering several industries/markets.

Yearbooks and directories:

UK Kompass Register; Kelly's Directory of Manufacturers and Merchants; Dun and Bradstreet's Directories: *Guide to Key British Enterprises; International Market Guide; British Middle Market Directory; 'Who Owns Whom?'* Roskill.

Times Top 1000 lists major British-based companies.

Advertisers Annual (IPC) lists media, suppliers of advertising and promotional services, advertising agencies, and principal advertisers listed geographically.

Benn's Press Directory, in two volumes, gives details of printed media, e.g., regional newspapers.

BRAD (British Rate and DATA) (see Chapter 11).

Retail Directory (Newman) lists stores and other distributors' outlets.

Croner Publications give detailed and regularly up-dated business information covering commercial law, business strategy, EC data, etc.

Market Research Society Yearbook, published by the Market Research Society (MRS); this reference book contains a list of members, a detailed list of organizations providing market research services, and the Code of Conduct.

International Directory of Market Research Organisations, jointly sponsored by the MRS and the British Overseas Trade Board (BOTB); lists 1500 market research organizations in 67 countries, plus names and addresses of all major national market research associations.

TV audience reports: Available from individual television contractors and also specialist research agencies.

Professional institutions, etc.: Association of Market Survey Organisations (AMSO), Ince House, 60 Kenilworth Road, Leamington Spa, CV32 6JY.
(AMSO accounts for about two-thirds of all commercially-available UK research activities.)
British Institute of Management (BIM), Kingsway, London SW1.
Industrial Marketing Research Association (IMRA), 11 Bird Street, Lichfield, Staffordshire.
Chartered Institute of Marketing, Moor Hall, Cookham, Berkshire SL6 9QH.
Institute of Practitioners in Advertising (IPA), Belgrave Square, London SW1X 8QS.
Advertising Association, 21 Kings Road, Sloane Square, London SW3 4UP.
Market Research Society, 15 Northburgh Street, London EC1V 0AH.
Among its publications are *MRS Newsletter* and *MRS Survey* giving up-to-date information about market research courses and seminars, and also features on market research techniques and developments. The MRS also publishes a series of 'Committee Notes' providing information on survey procedures as well as useful hints on special local factors affecting market research in various countries throughout the world.
National Institute of Economic and Social Research, 2 Dean Tench Street, London SW1.
Barclays Bank Group, Economic Intelligence Unit, 54 Lombard Street, London EC3.
Lloyds Bank, Overseas Department, 5 Eastcheap, London EC3.
Association for Information Management (ASLIB), 26–27 Boswell Street, London WC1N 3JZ.
(Authoritative source of diverse range of information.)
In addition, some of the larger Chambers of Commerce, e.g., London, Birmingham, and Manchester, may be able to provide very useful data related to specific industries. Local authorities, particularly the larger ones, may also be able to provide industrial and commercial data for their areas. Another useful source could be organizations that promote industry in specific regions, New Town Development Corporations, etc.
Companies House may also be relevant for certain types of enquiries; some leading firms of stockbrokers may have undertaken research into specific industries.

Leading commercial libraries: City Business Library, London EC2.
Science Reference Library, Chancery Lane, London WC2.
Statistics and Market Intelligence Library, 1 Victoria Street, London SW1.

London Business School Library.
Manchester Business School Library.
Warwick, Lancaster Universities, etc.
Civic Commercial Libraries.

Overseas governments issue statistics and reports of use to marketing researchers. Some sources tend to be more reliable than others, and experienced researchers evaluate the information obtainable. Some of the larger research organizations, e.g., Nielsen or Gallup, have overseas companies or associates which can provide accurate data in specific market areas.

Exploitation of all relevant and reliable sources of data during desk research should be the first step in marketing research. In some cases the information resulting from persistent and patient desk research, as noted earlier, may be sufficient for management's needs.

On-line services:
Pergamon Infoline has over 20 databases covering marketing and sales prospecting, finance and credit checking, business intelligence and news, and British Trademarks and British Standards.

Kompass On-line, based on the well-known Kompass hard-copy directories, covers over 23 000 companies in Europe. It provides company name and address, telephone/telex numbers, description of business, number of employees; names executives, and, where feasible, sales figures.

Finsbury Data Services operate *Textline*, which offers abstracts from 80 British and European newspapers as well as a select number of marketing journals.

The Search and Advisory Service, The Patent Office, Hazlitt House, 45 Southampton Building, Chancery Lane, London WC2A 1AR.

Will undertake extensive, specialized searches in patent literature with national and international coverage. New product concepts can be checked against international technical trends and commercial developments.

On-line information may be numeric (as Prestel), bibliographic (as Pergamon Infoline), or a mix of these (like Data-Star). The wide use of desk-top micros has accelerated the growth of on-line data availability.

Teletext

Teletext is likely to become a useful method of conducting desk research.[29] Three alternative forms of Teletext exist in the UK: Ceefax (BBC); Oracle (IBA); and Prestel (British Telecom). The first two systems, which are one-way, use television as their transmission medium, whereas Prestel, which is two-way, uses the telephone network, and was developed from Viewdata technology (see Fig. 2.4).

In Chapter 6, an example of interactive home interviewing using Viewdata is given; Prestel is likely to attract more subscribers who will have access to a very wide range of information covering aspects of business and consumer activities. Hence, a subscriber could have quick access to desk research material that was up to date. In addition, because of the interactive nature of the system, users are able to transmit information, and market research organizations can interview subscribers.

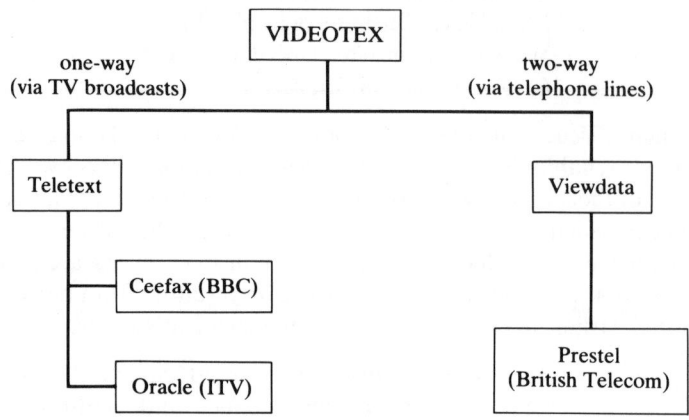

Fig. 2.4 Videotex network (UK)

2.12 SUMMARY

A central part of research activity is to develop an effective research strategy or design which details the most suitable methodology, sampling plan, and types of data to be collected. Five logical stages make up the survey process: brief, proposal, data collection, analysis and evaluation, and preparation and presentation of survey report. At every stage, professionalism is vital.

Two main types of data – primary and secondary: the former type could involve observation, experimentation, or questionnaires in order to collect *new* information about specific market problems: the latter type, known as desk or library research, involves collection of data that already exist – there are many sources of published information, from official or trade and industry sources. Every effort should be made to identify suitable secondary data that, in some cases, may provide adequate information for management.

A multi-technique approach stresses the desirability of combining survey techniques in order to reduce the bias inherent in one particular method, e.g., questionnaires. No research method is without bias of some kind, so a sound research strategy makes use of more than one technique in an effort to minimize bias: objectivity is the guiding principle of research.

REFERENCES

1. Green, Paul E., and Donald S. Tull, *Research for Marketing Decisions* (3rd Edn). Prentice-Hall, Englewood Cliffs, New Jersey, 1975.
2. Douglas, Susan P., and C. Samuel Craig, *International Marketing Research*, Prentice-Hall, Englewood Cliffs, New Jersey, 1983.
3. Tull, Donald S., and Del I. Hawkins, *Marketing Research*, Macmillan, New York, 1976.
4. Buckner, Hugh, *How British Industry Buys*, Hutchinson, London, 1967.
5. Ferber, Robert, and P. J. Verdoorn, *Research Methods in Economics and Business*, The Macmillan Company, Toronto, 1969.
6. Webb, Eugene J., Donald T. Cambell, Richard D. Schwartz, and Lee Sechrest, *Unobtrusive Measures – Nonreactive Research in the Social Sciences*, Rand McNally and Company, Chicago, 1966.
7. Burgess, Robert L., *Behavioural Sociology*, Don Bushell, Jnr (ed.), Columbia University Press, 1966.
8. Russell, Bertrand, *Philosophy*, Norton, New York, 1927.

9. Whyte, W. J., *Street-Corner Society: the Social Structure of an Italian Slum*, University of Chicago Press, 1943.
10. Politz, Alfred, 'A study of outside transit poster exposure', National Association of Transportation Advertising, 1959.
11. Day, D. J., and Jeniffer E. Dunn, 'Estimating the audience for advertising on the outside of London buses', *Applied Statistics*, vol. 18, no. 3, 1969.
12. La Piere, R. T., 'Attitudes vs. actions', *Social Forces*, vol. 13, 1934.
13. Chisnall, Peter M., *Marketing: A Behavioural Analysis*, McGraw-Hill, Maidenhead, 1985.
14. Payne, Stanley L., 'Combination of survey methods', *Journal of Marketing Research*, vol. 1, no. 2, May 1964.
15. Horne, Annette, Judith Morgan and Joanna Page, 'Where do we go from here?', *Journal of Market Research Society*, vol. 3, 1974.
16. Meneer, Peter, 'Retrospective data in survey research', *Journal of Market Research Society*, vol. 20, no. 3, July 1978.
17. Skapinker, Michael, 'Why people-watching is essential for product development', *Financial Times*, 2 February 1989.
18. Elliott, Ken, and Martin Christopher, *Research Methods in Marketing*, Holt, Rinehart & Winston, London, 1973.
19. Banks, Seymour, *Experimentation in Marketing*, McGraw-Hill, New York, 1965.
20. Hoofnagle, William S., 'Experimental designs in measuring the effectiveness of promotion', *Journal of Marketing Research*, vol. 11, May 1965.
21. Wallis, C. J., 'Research at retail level', in: *The Effective Use of Market Research*, Johan Aucamp (ed.), Staples Press, London, 1971.
22. Dominick, Bennett A., Jnr, 'Methods of research in marketing: Paper no. 2', Department of Agricultural Economics, Cornell University, June 1952.
23. Davis, John, 'Marketing, testing and experimentation', in: *Consumer Market Research Handbook*, Robert Worcester and John Downham (eds), Van Nostrand, Wokingham, 1978.
24. Wind, Yoram, Susan P. Douglas, and Aaron Ascoli, 'Experimentation as a tool for the retailer', *Market Research Society Journal*, vol. 13, no. 3, July 1971.
25. Rothman, James, 'Experimental designs and models', in: *Consumer Market Research Handbook*, Robert Worcester (ed.), McGraw-Hill, Maidenhead, 1972.
26. Collins, M., 'Product testing', in: *The Effective Use of Market Research*, Johan Aucamp (ed.), Staples Press, London, 1971.
27. Frankel, Martin R., 'Current research practices: general population surveying including geodemographics', *Journal of Market Research Society*, vol. 31, no. 4, October 1989.
28. Political and Economic Planning, 'Sample surveys – Part One', PEP Report, vol. 16, no. 313, Political and Economic Planning, London, May 1950.
29. Wills, P. A., 'Market research and the computer', Market Research Society Conference Papers, March 1980.

BASIC TECHNIQUES

THREE

INTRODUCTION TO SAMPLING

Sampling is one of the major tools of marketing research, which is concerned with collecting, analysing, and interpreting market data. It involves the study, in considerable detail, of relatively small numbers of informants taken from a larger group.

A good appreciation of the function and principal methods of sampling is particularly useful to market researchers, who need also to have a clear understanding of their reliability and limitations. It is useful, therefore, to define some of the terms used in sampling.

3.1 DEFINITIONS

1. *Population* (universe): this term is used in the statistical sense and refers to any group of people or objects which are similar in one or more ways, and which form the subject of study in a particular survey. Populations can consist of groups of inanimate objects, e.g., machine tools, as well as human populations, which may, in certain cases, refer to special sections of the general population of a country, such as those over the age of 18 and under 65. Before research is possible, the population to be surveyed must be clearly defined.

    Populations can be finite or infinite, e.g., the population of babies born in a year is finite, whereas all the possible outcomes of the tosses of a coin or rolls of a six-sided die form infinite populations, which are also known as theoretical or statistical populations.

    Populations have characteristics which can be estimated and classified according to the requirements of individual surveys. Attributes refer to particular characteristics that each sampling unit either does or does not possess, e.g., ownership of a colour television set; height six feet or over; left-handed; or blue-eyed. Measurement involves counting, or estimating, those members of the population having these attributes, so that this qualitative information is, in fact, quantified. It is then referred to as a variate or variable value. It can also involve calculating the extent or magnitude of some variable characteristic possessed by sample units, e.g., the average income of families in a certain area or the average weekly sales of canned soups in the Birmingham district.

2. *Census*: this occurs when a universe is examined in its entirety. This is unusual in commercial research, except where the universe is quite small and easily located, e.g., in some specialized industrial research. Most censuses are directed by governments and are

designed to provide vital information of trends in population, trade, and industry. Censuses are expensive, relatively slow, and comparatively rare.

3. *Sample*: this occurs when a number of sampling units (fewer than the aggregate) is drawn from a population and examined in some detail. This information is then considered as applying to the whole universe. It may, of course, be biased if the sample includes a high proportion of abnormal members of the population. A sample is a microcosm, of the population from which it is drawn. However, it cannot reflect a perfect image of that population; there will be some distortion, although attention to sound principles of sampling can keep this largely under control. Samples must, therefore, be representative of the populations from which they are drawn, so that valid conclusions about populations can be inferred.

4. *Elementary sampling units* (ESU): this refers to an individual element of the population to be sampled, e.g., a certain kind of person (socio-economic/age), or a particular type of retail store (a supermarket).

5. *Sampling frame*: this refers to lists, indexes, maps, or other records of a population from which a sample can be selected.

   In the UK, the Register of Electors is a convenient official frame for consumer surveys. The Postcode Address File (PAF) is increasingly used as a sampling frame in the UK.

6. *Statistic*: also known as 'estimator'; this refers to any quantity calculated from a sample to estimate a population parameter.

7. *Parameter*: this refers to the value of a variable (or attribute) calculated in the population, e.g., the average or mean (μ).

8. *Sampling variability* (experimental error): this refers to the fact that different samples drawn from a fixed population generally have different statistics, whereas population parameters for a given population do not change.

9. *Sampling distribution*: this refers to a frequency distribution based on a number of samples, e.g., 12 samples examined, their means calculated, and the 12 averages listed in a frequency distribution.

10. *Stratified sample*: this occurs when a sample is specially designed so that certain known characteristics in the population under survey are represented in certain proportions.

11. *Two broad types of sample*:
    (a) *Random* – 'probability': occurs where each element of a population from which the sample is chosen has a known (and non-zero) chance of being selected.
    (b) *Quota* – 'non-probability'; judgement; purposive: type of stratified sampling in which selection of sampling units within strata, e.g., age, sex, social group, is done by interviewers on a non-random basis, controlled to some extent by quotas allocated to the different strata.

12. *Sampling error* (systematic error): this refers to the difference between a sample estimate and the value of the population parameter obtained by a complete count or census.

13. *Sample cells*: these are formed when the strata of a sample are further divided, resulting in two or more subdivisions of the sample with common characteristics, e.g., population divided into two main strata by sex, further subdivided into specific age groups, 21 and over, and under 21. Four sample cells are thus formed. It is obvious that the number of cells increases rapidly as control bases are added.

	M	F
21 and over		
under 21		

14. *Statistical symbols and formulae*: these are most easily shown diagrammatically as Tables 3.1 and 3.2.

Table 3.1   Statistical symbols – outline summary

	Population parameter	Sample statistic	
Mean	μ	$\bar{x}$	Measure of location. Describes point around which scores in frequency distribution tend to cluster.
Variance	σ^2	s^2	Measure of dispersion. Measures distance or deviation of any score in a frequency distribution from the mean.
Standard deviation	σ	s	Square root of variance.

Note: Greek letters = description of populations. Roman letters = samples.

Table 3.2   Formulae

Statistic	Method
Mean $\bar{x}$	Add together scores in distribution and divide by number of scores: 52, 36, 26.

$$\text{Therefore } \bar{x} = \sum \frac{x}{n} = \frac{52 + 36 + 26}{3} = 38$$

| Variance s^2 | Calculate deviation of each value of distribution from mean ($\bar{x}$), add together the squares of deviations and divide by the number of values. |

$$\text{Therefore } s^2 = \sum \frac{(x - \bar{x})^2}{n}$$

Use $n - 1$, where $n < 25$.

It will be noted in these definitions that there are two types of error which may bias sample estimates:

(1) *Experimental error* arising from the differences in estimates that occur if repeated samples are taken from the same population. The degree of experimental error will be affected by the variability present in the population and by the size of the sample drawn from it.
(2) *Systematic error* arises from deficiencies in selection and measurement techniques, such as derives from an inefficient sampling frame or from a badly phrased questionnaire. In the former case, probability sampling minimizes this type of error.

3.2 ORIGIN OF SAMPLING

The sampling procedures used in marketing in the UK originated in social surveys that, as noted in Chapter 1, were pioneered many years ago by Bowley and others. By modern standards, much of this early research was statistically non-rigorous, though as far back as 1912 Bowley[1] used modern, practical sampling methods in his famous survey of working-class conditions in

Reading. His disciplined approach was to influence the methodology of social surveys, which became more systematic in the selection of samples.

Sampling was first used in the UK in a large-scale, official, field research conducted by the Ministry of Labour in 1937 into working-class expenditure.

As already noted, several opinion and marketing research organizations, among them the BBC Listener Research Department, developed in the 1930s, as sampling techniques improved and were accepted as good research practice.

Prominent among these research activities was the Social Survey founded, as observed in Chapter 1, in 1941. This was to make a decisive contribution to the standards of research, and over the years it has been responsible for very many enquiries on behalf of government departments. In 1949, samples of people from local authority waiting lists provided detailed information about their housing conditions, and it was possible to estimate the accuracy of local authority records in this area.[2] In the same year, the then Board of Trade asked the Social Survey to study the effects of experimental changes in rationing allowances for clothes and to state the extent to which clothes buying was limited by prices or shortage of coupons. As a result of this evidence, clothes rationing was eventually abolished.

Another notable example of sampling was in the National Farm Survey of England and Wales, published by HMSO in 1946. This showed the boundaries of every farm in considerable detail. The mass of information was analysed by means of a random sample taken from a total of nearly 300 000 records referring to holdings of five acres and over.

Sampling surveys also contribute to medical research. An early example occurred in 1946 when a survey of maternity services in the UK was made by the Royal College of Obstetricians and Gynaecologists and the Population Investigation Committee.[3] Existing information indicated that in order to obtain a reliable and complete picture: 'a direct approach had to be made to women who had recently borne children'. A sample was, therefore, chosen of all women who had given birth in the UK during a particular week in March 1946. This remarkable feat of surveying was achieved by using the services of medical officers of health and health visitors. As a result, 13 687 women out of a total of 15 130 who had given birth during that week were interviewed. Two years later, a follow-up study of the health and development of the children was made. Of the original sample of 13 687 babies, a sub-sample of 5380 was made at random. Despite the fact that nearly one-third of the families had moved, it was possible to follow them up through local authority medical services, and all but 37 were successfully interviewed.

Another notable use of sampling in medical science occurred in research into the relationship between lung cancer and smoking undertaken by Doll and Hill for the Medical Research Council. Patients were divided into two groups, those with lung carcinoma in a certain number of hospitals in England and Wales (1465 patients), and a 'control group., individually matched by personal characteristics, but who were suffering from other diseases. The findings were published in the *British Medical Journal* in 1950. They are a source of interest to statisticians studying the statistical significance of sample data. This research did not, in fact, provide statistical evidence of a relationship between smoking and lung cancer. The researchers, noting this rather inconclusive evidence, commented on the relatively small sample and also that the data were sufficiently reliable to show general trends.

The 1966 Population Census of the UK was, in fact, a 10 per cent sample enumeration based on the 1961 Census record as a main sampling frame. By means of a computer program, a qualified sample of 1 in 10 private dwellings was selected in England and Wales. In Scotland, the main sampling frame was the 1964–65 Valuation Roll for each of the cities and counties, supplemented by a list of dwellings coming into occupation for the first time between May 1964 and March 1966; a sample of 1 in 10 was again drawn.

In the US the Bureau of the Census selected a 5 per cent sample from the 1940 Population Census, and additional questions were asked of these respondents. This innovation led to the development of a 'Master Sample' by the Bureau of Agricultural Economics. In 1945, these two American bureaux cooperated in producing a 'Master Sample' covering the entire population.

Research studies of all kinds now make use of sampling, the techniques and applications of which have greatly improved. There is little doubt that a great deal of the acceptability that sampling now enjoys in academic and commercial research operations stems from the early pioneer work done by official survey organizations in both the US and the UK. Standards of research have greatly improved over the years, and it is interesting to note the strong development that took place during the Second World War when government enquiries were made, by means of sample surveys, into many different areas affecting the welfare of the community.

The fiasco of the *Literary Digest* poll in 1936 alerted researchers to the importance of sound methods of sampling, and today no reputable organization would be likely to select a sample with such a distinct bias (see Chapter 5).

Apart from national sampling surveys, the techniques of sampling extend internationally through the United Nations Statistical Office, which publishes survey reports on many topics.

3.3 THE THEORY OF SAMPLING

Sampling theory is concerned with the study of the relationships existing between a population and the samples drawn from it. Through the process of statistical inference, using probability theory, certain conclusions can be drawn about a population from a study of samples taken from it.

Ferber[4] has succinctly commented on the core of probability in sampling theory as follows:

> Probability is at the heart of all sampling theories. The very concept of sampling is based on the *probability* that one member will represent a group; on the *probability* that a number of members selected at random from a population will be so distributed as to provide a miniature representation of that population; on the *probability* that estimates drawn from this miniature will differ from the true population values only by a certain (measurable) amount attributable to the vagaries of sample selection.

Statistical sampling theory, based on the mathematics of probability, is particularly valuable in two ways:

1. *Estimation*: it allows estimates of population parameters, such as the population mean (μ) and variance (σ^2) to be made from sample statistics such as sample mean ($\bar{x}$), variance (s^2), etc.
2. *Hypothesis testing*: it enables certain probability statements, based on samples, about the characteristics of a population to be tested statistically. It involves the use of tests of significance that are important in the theory of decisions; for example, in determining whether the differences noted between two samples are the result of a chance variation or whether they are actually significant.

Estimation and hypothesis testing are distinct branches of statistical sampling theory, but they are related in that they both utilize the statistical measure known as the standard error. It will be seen later that the standard error is based on probability sampling techniques, and the conclusions drawn about populations studied by sample surveys are necessarily probability statements. The whole concept of sampling theory rests, therefore, on the fact that a sample has been chosen randomly, which implies that every member of the population from which the sample has been drawn has the same probability of being chosen for the sample.

Samples must be representative so that valid conclusions can be drawn about the populations they represent. Inevitably, some degree of distortion is likely, but this can largely be controlled through applying sound principles of sampling.

Estimates are continually being made of the distribution of age groups in a national population by studying a relatively small number of representative members, i.e., a sample. Production testing, traffic counts, etc., are all commonly used methods of estimating. Sampling estimates have been accepted practice in many areas for a long time; for example, tea tasting, wine tasting, handful of grain tests, and blood tests. The quality of the whole is judged by careful examination and testing of some small part. Often there is no alternative but to sample, as in the case of very large populations.

Sampling has many advantages; it saves money, time, and labour; it frequently enables data of high quality to be collected; and it provides data that could not be assembled by other means.

The overall cost of samples is lower than a complete investigation (census), though the cost per unit of study may be higher because of the need to employ skilled interviewers, administrative expenses incurred in sample design, etc.

Samples mean substantial savings in time and labour. Censuses takes many years to prepare for publication, whereas surveys can be published in a few months. In 1951, 1 per cent of schedules in the Census of Population were sampled for preliminary analysis, and summary findings were available in just over a year, which is considerably shorter than the time taken for the analysis of a complete census. Obviously, fewer staff are engaged in sample surveys than when complete censuses are taken. Labour economies also take place in the tabulation and processing of data.

Most censuses are directed by governments for purposes of estimating demographic trends, trade and industry developments, etc. They are expensive, relatively slow, and comparatively rare.

Because sample surveys investigate fewer cases, it is possible for them or provide more data, both quantitatively and qualitatively. In some instances, moreover, sampling may be the only possible method of collecting information. Blood counts are widely used and regarded as reliable in medical spheres; some industrial products are assessed by testing small samples of them to their utmost limits.

3.4 ESSENTIALS FOR SOUND ESTIMATORS

Estimation is concerned with finding food estimates of population parameters. There are certain criteria that determine good estimates:

1. *Lack of bias*: this occurs when the expected value of an estimate is equal to the population parameter. Otherwise, the estimate is 'biased', and the difference between the expected value and the population value is called the 'bias' or 'systematic error'. It is, of course, difficult to establish the value of the population parameter in actual practice and so it may not be possible to assess bias. Let (θ) = the expected value of the estimate and θ = value of parameter. Then $E(\theta) = \theta$ (where E = mathematical expectation). Basis in sample selection should be avoided in so far as it is possible, while particular care is needed in selecting the sample design. Random (or probability) sampling reduces the likelihood of bias.

   Bias can also result from sampling units being selected from a sampling frame or list that is incomplete, inaccurate, or inadequate. To select a sample of the general population from a telephone directory would obviously lead to bias.

   Bias also arises from non-response, either because some sampling units cannot be traced, or because, when contacted, they refuse to cooperate in the survey.

   The systematic errors or biases which may arise from any of these directions are not affected by increases in the size of samples. One of the cardinal concepts of sampling is representativeness, which means that a sample should adequately reflect, in the types of units it contains, the population it represents.

It should be noted that the present discussion of bias is restricted to sample selection. Unfortunately there are many other sources of bias in survey work, and these are considered in later chapters. Researchers must be constantly alert to the possibilities of bias at all stages of research operations. Everything possible must be done to avoid distortion. Sound techniques must be vigorously applied throughout the surveys.

2. *Consistency*: this means that a sample estimate, such as $\bar{x}$, approaches the population parameter (μ) that is to be estimated, as the sample size increases. This has been formally defined as:

$$P(\bar{x} \to \mu) \to 1 \text{ as } n \to \infty \text{ (or } N)$$

i.e., the probability that the sample average approaches the population average as n becomes larger and larger is 1. Hence, consistent estimators tend to approach the value of population parameters more exactly as sample size approaches infinity.

3. *Efficiency*: this involves the comparison between estimators and is stated in relative terms. Estimator θ_1 is more efficient than estimator θ_2 if the variance of the first expression is smaller than that of the second.

For example, it is known that the sample mean is an efficient estimate of the population mean, whereas the sample median is an inefficient estimate of it. It can further be said that of all statistics used to estimate the population mean, the sample mean gives the best or most efficient estimate.

$$\text{Var. } (\bar{x}) < \text{Var. (median)} < \text{Var. (mode)}$$

The measure of efficiency can be expressed by the ratio of the variances.

Table 3.3   Analysis of comparative properties of estimators

Parameter	Estimator	Unbiased	Consistent	Efficient
μ	$\bar{x}$	√	√	√
μ	median	√	√	×
μ	mode	√	√	×
σ^2	$s^2 = \frac{1}{n} \sum (x_1 - \bar{x})^2$	×	√	√
σ^2	$s^2 = \frac{1}{n-1} \sum (x_1 - \bar{x})^2$	√	√	√

Table 3.3 shows $\bar{x}$ and s^2 are most suitable for estimating population values.

3.5 CONFIDENCE INTERVALS

When sample values are used as estimates of population values, it is important to know how reliable these estimates are. How near, for example, is the sample mean $\bar{x}$ to the population mean μ, of which it is an estimate. The usefulness of a sample estimate will be increased if some indication can be given of the degree of reliability.

By using confidence limits, also known as fiducial limits, a sample estimate of a population parameter can be given which is likely to occur within a given interval. It is important to remember that confidence limits can be ascertained only if the sample has been randomly selected.

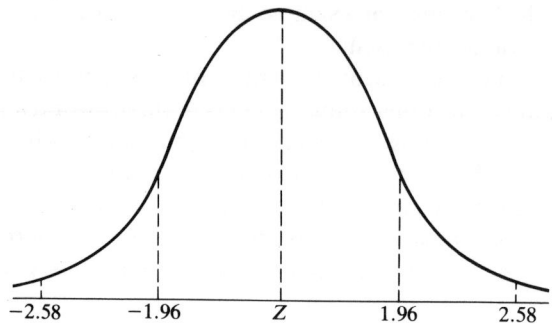

Fig. 3.1   Sample graph of population parameters

Confidence intervals or limits are used with the sampling distribution known as the normal distribution, which is discussed in some detail later in the text. Where the normal distribution applies to a sampling distribution, it is possible to estimate, for example, by $\bar{x}$ and to state to what degree of accuracy the estimate has been made. This can be stated in confidence intervals computed by confidence coefficients, as the following examples show:

95 per cent confidence interval, 1.96 confidence coefficient (Z value).

99 per cent confidence interval, 2.58 confidence coefficient (Z value).

If, therefore, the population variance (σ^2) is known, it is possible to calculate limits between which sample estimates are most likely to fall.

In Fig. 3.1:

95 per cent of the area of the normal curve lies between $Z \pm 1.96\sigma = 0.95$.

99 per cent of the area of the normal curve lies between $Z \pm 2.58\sigma = 0.99$.

Since the normal distribution has mean μ and variance σ^2, the sample mean will be calculated as follows:

95 per cent confidence: μ lies between $\bar{x} \pm 1.96\sigma/\sqrt{n}$

99 per cent confidence: μ lies between $\bar{x} \pm 2.58\sigma/\sqrt{n}$

Example   95 per cent confidence: from a sample of 100, the sample mean was found to be 40. If the population variance is 9, what is the confidence interval for this estimate, assuming the population to be normally distributed?

$$\bar{x} = 40, \sigma = \sqrt{9} = 3, n = 100, \mu = \bar{x} \pm 1.96\sigma/\sqrt{n} = 40 \pm 1.96 \cdot \tfrac{3}{10}$$

Hence, $\mu = 40 \pm 0.59$; therefore $(39.41 < \mu < 40.59)$.

Example   Let the data be the same as in the preceding example, but increase the sample size to 144.

$$\mu = \bar{x} \pm 1.96\sigma/\sqrt{n} = 40 \pm 1.96 \cdot \tfrac{3}{12}$$

Hence, $\mu = 40 \pm 0.49$; therefore $(39.51 < \mu < 40.49)$.

Comparing these two examples, it is evident that as the sample size is increased, the sampling error is decreased, and the confidence limits become narrower. This indicates that the precision of sample estimates improves as the size of samples for given populations increases.

The concept of a sampling error refers to the difference between a given sample estimate and the relevant population parameter. The concept of precision relates to the confidence interval for repeated samplings from a normal distribution, and is entirely a function of the size of the sample. The impact of precision on the sample size is discussed at some length in the section dealing with this factor.

The level of confidence with which a researcher wishes to give a population parameter will affect the limits of the confidence interval. If her wishes to state an estimate with high probability (99 per cent confidence), then the confidence interval will be wider than if he were content to give a lower probability (95 per cent confidence). A choice must be made between having a very narrow range within which the parameter will fall with lower probability, and a wider range but with higher probability.

Example   95 per cent confidence:

$$\bar{x} = 60 \; n = 225 \; \sigma^2 = 16$$

$$\mu = \bar{x} \pm 1.96\sigma/\sqrt{n}$$
$$= 60 \pm 1.96 \cdot \tfrac{4}{15}$$
$$= 60 \pm 0.52$$

Therefore, $(59.48 < \mu < 60.52)$

Example   99 per cent confidence:

$$\bar{x} = 60 \; n = 225 \; \sigma^2 = 16$$

$$\mu = \bar{x} \pm 2.58\sigma/\sqrt{n}$$
$$= 60 \pm 2.58 \cdot \tfrac{4}{15}$$
$$= 60 \pm 0.69$$

Therefore, $(59.31 \sqrt{} \mu < 60.69)$

These two examples, using similar data, indicate that higher probability is associated with greater tolerance in the estimated parameter limits.

3.6 SAMPLING FRAMES

Before a sample survey can be undertaken, it is vitally important to define closely the population that is to be sampled. This definition should be clearly understood and agreed by all those taking part in implementing the survey. Populations may be widespread and fairly general; for example, men and women in the age group 21 to 65, over the whole country. On the other hand, populations may be highly specific, as in the case of medical practitioners in the National Health Service, with surgeries within a 50-mile radius of Birmingham Town Hall.

Surveys may, therefore, cover many different subjects ranging from professional and technical enquiries to those concerned with social and commercial matters. If random sampling methods are to be used in these enquiries, the sample design, i.e, the method and planning of the sample, will be largely controlled by the type of sampling frames that are available. Where these are not available at once, the feasibility of constructing suitable frames should be considered. The quality of random sampling techniques rests largely on the selection of suitable sampling frames, and on their availability at the time of research.

There are five criteria[5] that are useful in evaluating sampling frames:

1. *Adequacy:* this means that a sample frame should cover the population to be surveyed and that it should do this adequately related to the purposes of the survey. If a random sample of people over pensionable age has to be drawn, it would be misleading to take as a sampling frame a list of those receiving retirement pensions.
2. *Completeness:* if the sampling frame does not include all those units of a population that should be included, the missing units will not have the opportunity of being selected and the resultant sample will be biased to this extent. This may be serious if those excluded happen to possess particular characteristics. It is frequently difficult to assess the completeness of a particular sampling frame, though some valuable research has been done by Gray and Corlett[6] on the Register of Electors.
3. *No duplication:* with some frames, it is possible for a unit to be entered more than once. If there is multiple entry, for example, as with some firms listed in telephone directories, and where the sampling frame is the directory, some weighting system may have to be applied to avoid bias.
4. *Accuracy:* many sampling lists, such as those covering dwellings or people, contain 'non-existent' units, owing to the dynamic nature of these populations. It is difficult to obtain an absolutely accurate, up-to-date frame in these circumstances, particularly when current lists are several months out of date, as in the case of the Register of Electors.
5. *Convenience:* this refers both to the accessibility of the list, and to the suitability of its arrangement for the purpose of sampling. Numbering of entries will obviously help when selecting sampling units. Lists should also be studied to see whether stratification of units is feasible.

No sampling frame is likely to satisfy all these exacting requirements, but they are useful standards by which to judge individual sampling frames. Existing frames should be identified and assessed for their suitability for particular kinds of research. In some cases, it may be necessary to build a sampling frame because existing lists are not suitable, though this rather tedious task should not be undertaken before carefully examining available frames. Compiling a special frame will, inevitably, delay the survey to some extent, but the delay may well be justified by the quality of the research findings.

Sampling frames are available covering general population characteristics in most advanced countries, but in some overseas countries it may not be possible to obtain reliable frames, and some quota system of sampling may have to be considered (see Chapter 13).

The particular problems of industrial marketing research are considered in some detail in Chapter 12.

Sources of national sampling frames in the UK

In the UK, there are two national address lists suitable for use as sampling frames: the Register of Electors, and the Postcode Address File (PAF). The former, as the title suggests, is a list of *individuals*, whereas the latter is a list of addresses – several individuals may, of course, reside at one address.

Register of Electors For samples of individuals, the Register of Electors is generally a useful frame. It is the duty of Electoral Registration Officers to compile a new register every October, (qualifying date 10 October) that is published the following 15 February, by which time it is already four months out of date. By the time it is due for replacement, it is 16 months old; this is a serious disadvantage in a dynamic population.

The register records electors for both Parliamentary and local government elections. Four categories of electors are entered: civilian Parliamentary electors; civilian local government electors; service voters; and persons who will attain the age of 18 years between the 17 February and the 15 February of the following year. To qualify for registration as a civilian Parliamentary elector, a person must be a British subject (Commonwealth citizens are British subjects) or citizen of the Irish Republic resident at the given address; must have reached the age of 18 years (except as qualified above); and must have been resident on the qualifying date in the area covered by that particular register.

Registered electors' names frequently appear in alphabetical order at their recorded addresses, but, apparently, this sequence is not always followed. It is usually possible to determine sex by the registered forename, but there is no clue to an individual's age. This could be a serious handicap if a particular age group is significant in the survey.

In rural areas, electors are generally listed in alphabetical order of surnames, further qualified by alphabetical forename where surnames are the same. This means that electors' names are not in address order, and where people of different names are living at the same address, they are recorded in different places in the register. It will be seen that this could cause problems if a sample of addresses was being extracted.

Registers are fairly easily available, both locally or centrally. The British Museum has a complete set, and copies of the entire register or part of it can be purchased from Electoral Registration Officers.

Moser[7] comments that at one time the register 'was greatly distrusted as a sampling frame, being thought incomplete and out of date'; it is widely used now because, since the Maintenance Register was discontinued, the Register of Electors has become the only national sampling frame of individuals available.

Experimental studies by Gray, Corlett, and Frankland in 1950, found it to be 'fairly reassuring as to its completeness and accuracy'. Deaths and removals are factors that influence the register's validity as a sampling frame. It has been estimated that about 12 per cent of electors are no longer at their registered address by the time that the register comes up for renewal. However, it has also been shown that about 70 per cent of these electors will be found to be living near their original address, and some effort to trace them will improve sampling. This was evident during the 1954 IPA Readership Survey of about 17 000 individuals; 2400 were found to have moved, and of these 1400 were traced to addresses covered by the survey and interviewed successfully.

It also appears that about 4 per cent of electors do not register, but it is considered that this relatively small loss is spread over all groups in the population and no bias is, therefore, likely. On the other hand, 'movers', estimated at about 5 per cent loss per month, contain a high proportion of under 30s, which results in some slight bias in the age distribution of the population remaining in the sample frame.

To use the register for sampling individuals, the sampling interval must be calculated; this is done by finding the ratio of the population and the sample. In a population of N size, with sample size n, the sampling interval will be N/n. Therefore, let $N = 500$ and $n = 50$, then the sampling interval is $500/50 = 10$. Any random number between 1 and 10 is chosen, say 3, and the series will then be 3, 13, 23, 33, etc. It is important that the population list should be randomly arranged.

It is more difficult to obtain a sample of households from the register, as the probability of selection is affected by the number of registered electors at any one address. Some system of weighting has to be devised to equalize probabilities. For example, addresses with four registered electors could be weighted $\frac{1}{4}$, and single-person addresses could receive a weighting of one. This method tends to be a bit troublesome in practice.

An alternative approach is to make a random selection of every nth individual, as outlined earlier, taking note of the address and the number of resident registered electors. This establishes the probability of selection of each household. A final sample is then drawn by selecting *every* address with one registered elector, every *second* address with two electors, every *third* address with three electors, and so on. The resulting sample of addresses will have equal probabilities.

Where it is not possible to construct sampling frames, some alternative method of sampling, such as quota, may have to be used. But it is often practicable to devise special frames, provided a reasonable amount of careful thought is given to the problems of particular surveys. Existing lists may have to be rearranged before they can be used for specific research purposes. It is advisable for researchers to acquire a good knowledge of the many specialist directories that could prove useful in constructing sampling frames. This applies particularly in the area of industrial and technical marketing research.

Researchers should, therefore, study the objectives of the survey, the population to be surveyed, the methods of sampling proposed, and relate these factors to the records available. Lists should be assessed for reliability, completeness, and adequacy, as already noted, and before using them as sampling frames, researchers should be satisfied that they will provide a sound foundation on which to construct the research project.

Postcode Address File (PAF)   Every address in the UK is post-coded; the system enables the Post Office to use mechanized sorting of mail.

The post code is a combination of up to seven alphabetical and numerical characters that define, in a unique way, four different levels of geographic unit, e.g., WA15 9AE.

The largest geographical unit, of which there are 120, is termed a post code area, e.g. WA, referring to Warrington. In turn, each area is subdivided into carefully chosen smaller geographical units known as districts (represented by 15 in the code quoted). These 2700 post code districts are next subdivided into post code sectors, of which there are 8900 in total (9 in quoted post code). Finally, the complete post code identifies one street, or part of a street, with the last two alpha characters (AE in above example, referring to an address in Hale, Altrincham) (see Fig. 3.2).

In the UK there are 1.5 million post codes covering 22 million addresses. Some very large users of mail (about 170 000) have their own unique post code, but, generally, there are approximately 15 addresses per post code.

Post codes can be used commercially in many ways, e.g., constructing sales territories and defining sales staff responsibilities; locating distribution depots; sales analyses; advertising responses, etc. The Marketing Department of the Post Office can supply details of specific services such as post coding address lists by computer, post code maps, and post code directories.

Fig. 3.2   Structure of UK post code

For the purposes of marketing research, the post code system offers an attractive sampling frame; it is a complete listing of UK locations that is developed through three stages, viz., post code area, district, sector, and final street location. (Stratification of samples is discussed in the next chapter.)

The Postcode Address File has been adopted by the Office of Population and Census, and by leading market research organization, such as Audits of Great Britain for its home audit surveys (see Chapter 9).

Specific applications of the PAF to marketing research may involve, for example, interviewing adults at selected post code addresses, or, perhaps, taking at random a number of post codes and proceeding to interview an agreed number and type of respondents. However, PAF does not, as noted earlier, indicate the number of people living at a specific listed address, so some further process of selection would be necessary for individual respondents. For example, individuals at any one selected address would be numbered and then a final selection made by a random process.

The problem of bias in drawing a sample from the telephone directory   Some interesting research on bias resulting from samples based on telephone directories was reported by David A. Leuthold and Raymond Scheele of the Public Opinion Survey Unit, University of Missouri, Columbia.[8]

These researchers conducted two state-wide surveys in Missouri in the autumn of 1968 ($N = 929$) and in the spring of 1969 ($N = 1924$). Enquiries revealed that about 10 per cent of respondents did not possess a telephone. This statistic indicated a sharp increase in telephone ownership from the 22 per cent who were not telephone subscribers reported for Missouri in the 1960 Census of Housing, and 'is somewhat similar' to the national trend in the US. Leuthold and Scheele[8] comment that 'those who live in rural areas or have a relatively low level of income are not as likely to have a telephone as those who live in urban areas or have higher incomes'. Although isolation and income frequently interact, income seems to be the more significant influence in telephone ownership.

Another source of bias was found to exist in unlisted telephones. Contrary to popular opinion, the incidence of unlisted numbers showed no correlation with income or occupation; in fact, those with average incomes and education were most frequently represented. Two particularly significant characteristics were discovered: one was being black; the other was being a city dweller. About 25 per cent of Missouri blacks reported that their telephones were unlisted compared with 10 per cent of telephones owned by whites. In large cities (over 500 000 population) in Missouri, almost one in five residential telephones was unlisted. The lowest proportions of unlisted telephones were found in rural areas.

Apartment dwellers, younger people, those divorced or separated, labour union members, and service workers such as policemen, tended to be comparatively highly represented among non-listed telephone users.

Some of the reasons for non-listing obtained from a consumer survey of housewives in St Louis city and county, were given as obscene or crank telephone calls, personal privacy, avoidance of salesmen. Blacks and elderly women were most likely to give the first reason quoted.

The researchers summarized this point by stating that samples based on telephone directories (in the area studied) 'will exclude one-third or more of the blacks, the separated and divorced, and service workers, and one-fourth of the large city-dwellers'.[8] They add, however, that samples based on telephone directories might be relatively unbiased for some specialized surveys, as their research indicated that 90 per cent or more of particular groups, such as professional workers or residents of medium-sized towns, were listed in telephone directories.

The problem of bias in drawing a sample from telephone directories is well illustrated by this carefully documented research.

In another study[9] in the US, concerned with radio listening habits, further evidence was obtained that survey samples based only on listed telephone entries can lead to distorted or biased results. Significant differences were found in radio listening habits as well as demographic characteristics. This research, undertaken in the metropolitan Toledo area, revealed that 16 per cent of the sample had unlisted telephone numbers.

Research[10] over the period 1970–74 found that non-listed telephones in the US were about 19 per cent; by 1978, this figure was reported[11] to be around 22 per cent. These were unevenly distributed with non-whites representing nearly twice the proportion of whites, and small counties having only about 9 per cent unlisted, compared with the five largest metropolitan areas with nearly 30 per cent. In 1984, the average unlisted/ex-directory level in the top 50 US markets was given[12] as 28 per cent, with Chicago at a staggering 48 per cent.

In the UK rental of domestic telephones has been largely restricted to the higher socio-economic classes, so that any attempt to sample the general population from telephone directories could lead to serious bias. Apart from social group bias, there is skewed distribution of domestic telephones over the country. However, home telephone rental has diffused rapidly; and British Telecom predicts that soon only about 10 per cent will be without telephones, so the degree of bias will by then be considerably reduced.

Unlisted numbers are estimated to be up to 20 per cent, either because people have asked to be 'ex-directory' (probably about 5 per cent), or because of removals or new installations since the last reprint of directories.

If sampling is restricted to the professional and business classes or other special occupations requiring domestic telephones, e.g., small business owners like plumbers, it would be acceptable to use telephone interviews in surveys.

It is conceded that 'comparatively little is known' about ex-directory telephone owners (XD's) in the UK, 'and the effects their exclusion from telephone surveys using directory based samples might have'.[13] Hence, the Market Research Development Fund – an autonomous working party of the Market Research Society – commissioned Wendy Sykes and Martin Collins to investigate the characteristics of XDs. An exhaustive study was made of 3100 respondents to the 1986 British Social Attitudes Survey. The major results were: 87 per cent of respondents were, or claimed to be telephone owners; 9 per cent of these were identified as ex-directory and 'little difference' was evident across socio-economic and age classifications, but there were 'noticeably higher' differences for London and some minority (generally *less* well off) groups. The findings of this report: 'Telephone Availability 1987', are instructive and emphasize the need for caution in using telephone surveys; the unlisted percentage is certainly markedly different from earlier estimates.

Random digit dialling   To overcome the problem of deficient sampling frames based on domestic telephone lists, the technique of random digit dialling (RDD) has been developed in the United States. From information supplied by the telephone company, researchers can generate telephone numbers by using a table of random numbers, so that any telephone number, whether listed in a directory or not, may then be dialled.

A health attitude survey[14] concerned with the 1976–77 swine influenza immunization campaign was conducted in Oakland County, Michigan, using RDD. It was reported that the cost and ease of administration of RDD and also its precision, made it 'an attractive survey research technique'.

The economies of RDD surveying were also noted by Klecka and Tuchfarber[15] who, in one case, found that fieldwork and sampling costs could be as low as 20–25 per cent of those incurred by personal interviewing. A survey using RDD replicated a survey based on a complex probability sample from a sampling frame from the 1970 Census. The resultant data were reported to offer strong empirical evidence that RDD surveys can effectively replicate those involving complex sampling designs and personal interviewing. The researchers also observed that when telephone interviewers are working from a central location, high standards of supervision are possible. In addition, interviews are not exposed to the hazards of visiting potentially unpleasant neighbourhoods that they might feel tempted to avoid in personal surveying.

Sudman[16] has suggested that RDD is most appropriate for surveys in large cities and conurbations where unlisted telephones are likely to be disproportionately high.

It is claimed[15] that telephone surveying using RDD techniques has gained general acceptance among American survey practitioners, who recognize it as a 'legitimate method for sampling public opinion'.

Further discussion of telephone survey methodology occurs in Chapter 6.

3.7 SUMMARY

Sampling is one of the major techniques underlying marketing research, whose sampling procedures originated in social surveys. Sampling theory is concerned with studying the relationships between a population and the samples drawn from it: probability is its heart, and it is particularly useful in (a) estimation, and (b) hypothesis testing.

Sampling frames are necessary for probability or random sampling; five criteria can be applied to evaluate the suitability of sampling frames: adequacy, completeness, no duplication, accuracy, and convenience. These exacting requirements are unlikely to be fully met, but they are useful standards. Two well-known national sampling frames are the Register of Electors and the Postcode Address File.

REFERENCES

1. Bowley, A. L., and A. R. Burnett-Hurst, *Livelihood and Poverty: A Study in the Economic Conditions of Working-class Households in Northampton, Warrington, Stanley and Reading*, Bell, London, 1915.
2. Political and Economic Planning, 'Sample surveys – Part One', PEP Report, vol. 16, no. 313, Political and Economic Planning, London, May 1950.
3. Political and Economic Planning, 'Sample surveys – Part Two', PEP Report, vol. 16, no. 314, Political and Economic Planning, London, June 1950.
4. Ferber, Robert, *Market Research*, McGraw-Hill, New York, 1949.
5. Yates, F., *Sampling Methods for Censuses and Surveys* (2nd Edn), Griffin, London, 1953.
6. Gray, P. G., and T. Corlett, 'Sampling for the Social Survey', *Journal of the Royal Statistical Society*, vol. 113, 1950.
7. Moser, C. A., *Survey Methods in Social Investigation*, Heinemann, London, 1969.
8. Leuthold, David A., and Raymond Scheele, 'Patterns of bias in samples based on telephone directories', *Public Opinion Quarterly*, vol. 35, summer 1971.
9. Roslow, Sydney, and Laurence Roslow, 'Unlisted phone subscribers are different', *Journal of Advertising Research*, vol. 12, no. 4, August 1972.
10. Glasser, Gerald J., and Gale, D. Metzer, 'National estimates of non-listed telephone households and their characteristics', *Journal of Marketing Research*, vol. 14, August 1975.
11. Groves, Robert, M., 'An empirical comparison of two telephone sample designs', *Journal of Marketing Research*, vol. 24, no. 4, November 1978.
12. Barnard, Philip, 'Research in the USA', *Journal of Market Research Society*, vol. 26, no. 4, October 1984.
13. McKenzie, John, 'Study of characteristics of ex-directory telephone owners', *MRS Newsletter*, December 1988.
14. Cummings, K. Michael, 'Random digit dialling: A sampling technique for telephone surveys', *Public Opinion Quarterly*, vol. 43, no. 2, summer 1979.
15. Klecka, William R., and Alfred J. Tuchfarber, 'Random digit dialling: A comparison to personal surveys', *Public Opinion Quarterly*, vol. 42, no. 1, spring 1978.
16. Sudman, Seymour, 'The use of telephone directories for survey sampling', *Journal of Marketing Research*, vol. 10, May 1973.

FOUR

TYPES OF SAMPLING

4.1 PROBABILITY SAMPLING (RANDOM SAMPLING)

Probability sampling, also known as random sampling, results in every sampling unit in a finite population having a calculable and non-zero probability of being selected in the sample. This means that the chance of a unit being included in a sample can be calculated. For example, if a sample of 500 people is to be chosen at random from a population of 50 000, each member of the population will have 1 chance in 100 of being selected in the sampling process.

Probability sampling has been widely adopted by leading research bodies because of its sound theoretical basis, which allows the legitimate use of the mathematics of probability. It is the only completely objective method of sampling populations. It is used almost exclusively by the Government Social Survey, and by the American Bureau of the Census. The results of random sampling are, therefore, statistically sounder; it is possible to calculate the standard error of the mean. Another advantage is that, because of the mechanical selection of those who are to be interviewed, the bias arising from interviewers interviewing only the most easily available informants is avoided.

The difficulties of random sampling should also be noted. In commercial practice, there are very few complete lists of a universe or population which are really satisfactory. National lists, such as the Register of Electors, quickly become out of date, and professional and trade directories vary greatly in their reliability. All are subject to printing delays.

Calls to obtain randomly selected informants may be widely scattered, causing considerable cost in time and money. The whole sample may suffer severe delay which will affect the usefulness of its findings. To overcome this delay, a larger interviewing staff could conceivably be employed, increasing costs yet again.

One of the principal drawbacks is the necessity of making 'call-backs', where the original call was not successful. It is important that randomly selected informants should be interviewed in order to maintain the statistical validity of the sample. Non-response is a serious source of bias (which is dealt with in Chapter 7) and every endeavour must be made to secure as many successful interviews as possible. Call-backs add to survey costs, but some proportion is inevitable in random sampling. Standard practice is to instruct interviewers to make up to three calls before abandoning the prospect of an interview. When this happens in rural areas, it increases travelling costs very considerably, apart from the probable physical difficulties of tracing some randomly chosen country dweller. Some system of substitution is often used after the third unsuccessful journey. Interviewers may well begin to lose interest in a survey which entails a great deal of repeat calling. Even after repeated calls have been made and the informant is eventually contacted, the interview may be refused.

As a result of these various drawbacks, random sampling tends to be fairly expensive, but like many other products and services, price by itself is no measure of comparison. The overwhelming view of experts is that the value of random sampling cannot be matched by other methods.

There are several forms of random sampling in general use which, to some considerable extent, overcome many of the disadvantages just discussed. These alternative forms are listed below and dealt with in some detail later.

1. Simple random
2. Systematic or quasi-random
3. Stratified random.
4. Cluster (including area)
5. Multi-stage
6. Replicated (interpenetrating)
7. Master
8. Multi-phase

There are other types which may occasionally be encountered, but the above cover most of the types of random sample commonly used. The section on sampling frames will be usefully referred to during the study of systematic (quasi-random) sampling.

Simple random sampling

This can be done by either the 'lottery method' or by using random tables. The essential purpose of random selection is to avoid subjective bias arising from a personal choice of sampling units.

In the lottery method, every unit of the population is identified by a numbered disc or slip. These are placed in an urn, well mixed, and then by chance selection, a quantity is withdrawn until the required sample size is achieved. After each selection, the disc is usually replaced in the urn to maintain the same probability of selection for all discs. But even this simple method can be subject to bias. An interesting study revealed that in one case a particular colour of counter was apparently more slippery than counters of other colours, resulting in biased selection.

The other method is to use a table of random numbers specially designed for sampling purposes. There are several well-known tables: Kendall and Babington Smith[1] (Table 4.1), for instance); Fisher and Yates; and the Rand Corporation's *A Million Random Digits*. Statistical textbooks generally include some random tables in their appendices. Every unit in the population must be numbered. Digits are selected from the random numbers table in any systematic way (horizontal, vertical, diagonal, etc.), and those units whose numbers coincide with the random digits are included in the sample population. Obviously, it is necessary to prepare a list of sampling frames beforehand.

Both methods ensure random selection because they do not rely on human judgement, but their practical use is largely restricted to small populations. If a national survey of the general population were to be planned, the difficulties inherent in either of these techniques would be apparent. Apart from the mechanics of selection, the resultant sample might well be so widely spread geographically that it would make interviewing difficult and expensive.

Table 4.1   Random sampling numbers

	1–4	5–8	9–12	13–16	17–20	21–24	25–28	29–32	33–36	37–40
					Fifteenth thousand					
1	12 67	73 29	44 54	12 73	97 48	79 91	20 20	17 31	83 20	85 66
2	06 24	89 57	11 27	43 03	14 29	84 52	86 13	51 70	65 88	60 88
3	29 15	84 77	17 86	64 87	06 55	36 44	92 58	64 91	94 48	64 65
4	49 56	97 93	91 59	41 21	98 03	70 95	31 99	74 45	67 94	47 79
5	50 77	60 28	58 75	70 96	70 07	60 66	05 95	58 39	20 25	96 89
6	00 31	32 48	23 12	31 08	51 06	23 44	26 43	56 34	78 65	50 80
7	01 67	45 57	55 98	93 69	07 81	62 35	22 03	89 22	54 94	83 31
8	24 00	48 34	15 45	34 50	02 37	43 57	36 13	76 71	95 40	34 10
9	77 52	60 27	64 16	06 83	38 73	51 32	62 85	24 58	54 29	64 56
10	36 29	93 93	10 00	51 34	81 26	13 53	26 29	16 94	19 01	40 45
11	94 82	03 96	49 78	32 61	17 78	70 12	91 69	69 99	62 75	16 50
12	23 12	21 19	67 27	86 47	43 25	25 05	76 17	50 55	70 32	83 36
13	77 58	90 38	66 53	45 85	13 93	00 65	30 59	39 44	86 75	90 73
14	92 37	51 97	83 78	12 70	41 42	01 72	10 48	88 95	05 24	44 21
15	28 93	48 44	13 02	49 32	07 95	26 47	67 70	72 71	08 47	26 18
16	09 68	01 98	80 27	49 78	56 67	49 22	13 66	61 33	53 18	36 03
17	61 73	92 33	89 48	20 42	32 33	79 37	68 88	44 59	35 17	97 61
18	82 35	37 33	53 42	52 04	16 54	08 25	48 89	57 87	59 89	96 76
19	39 20	77 72	55 19	66 58	57 91	38 43	67 97	52 66	45 29	74 67
20	51 90	71 05	82 38	37 40	94 52	24 09	35 44	37 33	35 20	65 89
21	97 49	53 79	17 25	02 65	77 70	88 45	53 51	63 30	89 66	42 03
22	73 18	91 38	25 82	29 71	56 89	86 74	68 58	75 36	93 13	33 31
23	17 79	34 97	25 89	01 17	67 92	62 25	54 70	52 88	28 05	61 17
24	97 27	26 86	17 67	59 56	95 07	49 05	70 06	70 35	21 35	26 18
25	56 06	63 00	07 40	65 87	09 49	70 34	67 02	33 39	04 40	01 51
					Sixteenth thousand					
	1–4	5–8	9–12	13–16	17–20	21–24	25–28	29–32	33–36	37–40
1	43 83	39 24	50 74	10 05	38 11	25 80	44 14	98 31	87 41	02 74
2	63 19	91 27	08 59	02 28	47 13	05 53	02 28	81 96	46 90	95 52
3	23 87	60 31	98 97	76 57	82 47	64 87	50 45	73 54	26 47	62 10
4	07 04	47 34	36 03	87 67	03 28	72 19	98 99	32 98	78 76	85 40
5	98 61	67 62	09 89	73 50	06 81	29 09	43 43	30 21	32 69	82 19
6	36 86	50 21	42 18	20 55	00 90	01 96	42 12	68 18	45 93	52 99
7	70 64	92 95	09 09	79 63	09 29	69 99	98 26	19 83	94 88	95 37
8	41 71	91 61	31 86	38 01	71 79	44 75	67 69	35 31	69 47	81 64
9	23 48	32 36	88 50	29 07	27 32	21 28	73 41	77 39	00 78	92 65
10	13 32	99 81	00 28	87 13	00 86	56 16	81 20	63 29	37 45	08 91
11	70 55	85 27	24 96	91 83	89 17	89 98	51 31	17 29	05 77	72 95
12	12 50	84 01	63 40	74 86	88 90	63 76	97 74	08 70	88 88	98 96
13	97 00	24 63	47 63	47 66	21 79	28 66	67 24	33 20	01 52	09 59
14	16 99	63 29	67 89	14 55	70 31	45 56	05 71	84 30	48 32	90 94
15	57 95	93 54	30 74	11 18	31 26	75 39	81 28	63 34	31 23	77 67
16	01 32	91 11	23 65	44 58	69 77	58 86	35 20	92 12	48 15	56 67
17	00 30	26 68	89 38	38 13	99 47	06 82	49 47	40 33	23 72	01 50
18	48 15	27 13	97 70	18 48	14 28	26 30	74 16	13 07	36 21	94 84

Table 4.1 (*cont.*)

	1–4	5–8	9–12	13–16	17–20	21–24	25–28	29–32	33–36	37–40
19	58 86	65 76	67 05	99 53	33 56	92 61	63 98	55 39	15 77	61 67
20	75 07	14 81	41 16	12 21	79 82	16 42	70 43	73 33	78 22	63 25
21	86 19	97 09	64 04	21 26	65 11	20 32	82 38	52 94	79 21	85 07
22	66 17	52 10	35 14	21 89	54 32	61 49	63 06	36 25	63 84	78 24
23	56 70	95 77	25 19	21 15	29 88	57 75	51 19	31 06	48 50	09 65
24	14 43	67 32	81 78	19 72	32 70	34 86	11 90	37 02	54 39	45 87
25	04 17	91 71	96 90	85 68	32 35	77 20	71 43	55 95	28 90	51 69

Seventeenth thousand

	1–4	5–8	9–12	13–16	17–20	21–24	25–28	29–32	33–36	37–40
1	34 51	16 59	02 45	39 71	72 53	96 32	81 60	47 92	90 09	27 20
2	20 23	36 13	23 12	60 71	99 12	65 55	07 97	09 60	52 61	88 14
3	76 68	10 33	58 10	16 70	54 96	94 81	99 37	12 66	99 93	88 34
4	80 82	10 98	00 30	85 07	67 55	92 50	59 19	75 25	71 38	54 26
5	42 25	41 73	49 19	52 51	57 28	37 83	26 76	88 64	78 20	15 67
6	26 46	28 74	47 63	13 67	03 78	71 82	02 10	39 66	92 35	62 25
7	68 99	45 26	07 70	50 41	79 30	29 91	54 35	27 54	85 51	81 24
8	87 31	65 32	41 62	04 03	22 04	51 76	64 73	39 26	29 39	81 71
9	06 14	44 15	83 78	99 51	20 01	30 27	97 05	62 64	35 74	06 00
10	38 47	56 59	19 55	74 36	52 90	49 97	05 57	70 89	40 26	11 91
11	89 13	92 60	35 31	05 13	64 38	43 52	24 87	06 54	87 66	67 47
12	15 51	88 78	45 84	46 06	67 48	21 82	94 35	63 00	67 03	67 10
13	70 02	74 26	04 96	41 76	11 84	98 33	32 35	39 41	39 51	84 00
14	57 77	07 06	55 97	19 69	53 37	37 39	70 87	73 75	28 96	25 75
15	51 07	68 68	36 99	06 42	23 74	15 56	86 28	30 87	48 08	53 48
16	89 21	03 65	84 88	85 72	22 08	63 78	95 56	69 91	69 67	21 43
17	24 31	92 71	55 69	02 45	14 91	48 47	34 58	54 12	00 70	22 82
18	00 33	45 41	03 23	97 65	49 67	75 63	74 02	13 24	92 66	69 21
19	59 56	56 08	10 14	68 21	06 51	25 66	16 28	01 07	87 16	51 42
20	57 34	54 02	75 26	66 35	52 72	19 95	20 38	98 40	37 26	20 36
21	72 97	03 22	47 61	64 15	99 32	89 71	31 92	41 63	24 36	76 75
22	08 94	07 60	27 12	26 06	60 20	37 87	56 54	59 88	44 11	38 06
23	00 78	97 34	17 57	07 84	19 25	27 56	11 92	26 76	99 52	97 52
24	89 38	07 16	20 25	37 78	52 85	90 75	35 07	97 12	39 78	37 47
25	52 58	28 43	32 38	41 74	88 13	90 58	05 47	50 21	95 25	42 01

Eighteenth thousand

	1–4	5–8	9–12	13–16	17–20	21–24	25–28	29–32	33–36	37–40
1	08 59	51 65	98 29	69 66	90 49	07 24	67 63	41 47	04 75	17 90
2	87 83	22 19	76 36	00 58	48 47	41 20	74 44	06 69	75 60	74 31
3	76 89	40 65	98 22	77 21	24 25	03 15	62 68	60 45	66 70	85 39
4	08 97	75 59	41 94	91 31	92 00	52 29	50 32	25 20	98 89	19 38
5	38 09	07 26	10 92	70 39	83 78	76 63	26 17	32 17	40 29	12 33
6	31 55	17 02	22 85	47 84	93 41	03 11	71 61	23 06	21 60	45 09
7	30 93	44 60	80 21	76 28	37 21	31 80	78 96	85 56	56 05	27 28
8	38 43	62 41	58 86	98 44	78 52	51 75	31 84	79 08	05 97	35 93
9	96 67	86 95	74 39	21 90	80 20	42 32	70 88	75 35	10 30	99 99
10	26 62	19 26	28 16	13 24	02 43	16 65	41 34	03 80	81 87	98 29

Table 4.1 (*cont.*)

	1–4	5–8	9–12	13–16	17–20	21–24	25–28	29–32	33–36	37–40
11	57 08	15 37	74 85	65 21	72 98	63 20	53 33	32 72	51 48	26 60
12	92 05	77 55	70 51	49 69	50 16	26 70	96 28	46 51	42 99	90 78
13	88 33	50 35	10 80	97 89	87 38	31 20	19 74	25 26	12 24	03 49
14	38 46	01 13	05 58	27 15	82 72	62 21	28 60	30 60	59 69	22 03
15	26 81	24 78	49 14	80 47	70 34	11 86	60 59	31 40	04 42	83 23
16	83 90	62 31	22 49	82 42	16 53	60 29	52 33	06 50	41 27	09 41
17	25 77	95 10	09 71	25 90	63 05	29 87	11 24	39 23	31 22	86 42
18	46 40	99 89	30 12	15 22	89 32	27 54	73 30	67 19	32 48	82 83
19	42 74	95 44	01 16	25 94	44 34	06 67	87 33	16 98	83 60	41 63
20	84 59	72 14	30 36	29 74	19 68	76 88	09 74	51 29	98 89	02 04
21	27 86	32 94	70 15	16 43	12 34	68 71	55 21	92 09	31 34	79 40
22	97 94	92 04	28 78	99 60	87 02	88 51	88 58	20 78	20 75	45 82
23	39 24	29 44	32 10	89 26	80 43	45 83	01 06	23 14	44 84	85 30
24	57 24	53 05	16 41	38 58	97 95	51 45	89 15	15 93	87 30	74 49
25	04 00	60 69	08 96	35 88	82 58	24 22	39 72	04 89	32 20	37 17

Reproduced from *Tracts for Computers*, no. xxiv, edited by E. S. Pearson.

Systematic or quasi-random sampling

This differs from simple random sampling in not giving equal probability of selection to all possible samples which could be taken from a population. The method is widely used in the UK and it offers: 'by far the most practical approximation to random sampling'.[2]

It depends on the existence of some sampling list or frame of the population under investigation. Polling records are frequently used; other lists, depending on the nature of the population, could include customer record cards, telephone directories, trade association lists, etc. It is argued that lists can be considered as being arranged more or less at random, and that they are usually compiled independently of the subject of the survey.

Quasi-random sampling involves calculating the sample interval, obtained by finding the ratio of the population to the sample, i.e., N/n, and rounding the result to the nearest interger. A random number is then chosen between one and the sampling interval. From this starting point, successive random points are chosen by adding the sampling interval to each succeeding number. Hence, the selection of one sample number is dependent on the selection of the previous one, and so strictly speaking they are not chosen by a truly random process. The initial number is, of course, randomly selected, but successive numbers are not independently chosen because the sampling interval predetermines them.

For example, in a survey covering a population of 10 000 people, it may be decided to take a sample of 250. The sampling interval will be 10 000/250 = 40, and the population list will be used as a sampling frame. A randomly selected number between 1 and 40 is chosen, say 4, and the series then becomes 4, 44, 84, etc., until the sample of 250 is achieved. Persons whose names coincide with these positions in the list are selected for interview.

The Social Survey used a card index as the sampling frame, when an investigation was made into the incidence of pneumoconiosis among ex-miners. This method has been used in other official surveys and is generally considered to be satisfactory except in those cases where population lists may be subject to some periodic arrangement. Before using lists, it is advisable to check on how they were compiled.

Stratified random sampling

This means that the population to be surveyed is divided into groups with similar attributes. In each group or stratum, the population is more nearly homogeneous than in the total population, and this contributes to the accuracy of the sampling process.

The population to be surveyed is carefully studied. This analysis may reveal bases for stratification which will help substantially in increasing the precision of the sample survey. The population of the UK, for example, is made up of men, women, and children of different age groups, social groups, and occupations. Individuals may well be influenced by these character-istics in their views on the subject of a survey, and it may, therefore, be possible to form strata which contain individuals of similar characteristics so that their opinions can be more accurately assessed. The number that should appear in each stratum should be based upon its proportion in the population.

Within these defined strata, random selection takes place, and provided this is done correctly, stratified random sampling tends to be more accurate than simple random sampling. Significant characteristics of the total population are represented adequately in the different strata of the sample population. A simple random sample *may*, in fact, result in the correct composition of sampling units from the various strata of a population, but this cannot be assumed in every case. Sampling errors resulting from simple random samples will be greater than from stratified random samples of the same size. This arises because, when a population is sampled by simple random methods, two sets of sampling errors have to be considered: those *within* each stratum and those *between* the various strata. For example, people in one particular socio-economic group may well have different views from those in another. In addition, there is likely to be some difference of opinion *within* each socio-economic group.

When stratified random sampling is used, the variation between strata is taken care of because the sample has already been divided into strata of suitable attributes corresponding to those significant in the total population. As noted earlier, the process of random selection only takes place after stratification, and, therefore, sampling errors can arise from only one source, i.e., from within strata. It follows that stratification is more effective where there is a high proportion of the total variation in a population accounted for by between strata variation. Strata should, therefore, be designed so that they differ significantly from each other, and the population within each stratum should be as homogeneous as possible. In this way, the benefits of stratification are fully exploited.

Stratification factors should be distinctly relevant to the survey, and this means that the population under survey should be closely examined relative to the objectives of the investi-gation. Factors eventually selected must be significant and useful. In many consumer surveys, stratification by age, sex, and socio-economic group is fairly routine practice, particularly when using quota sampling methods. Other special strata may be introduced to cover the particular needs of surveys, perhaps qualifying the ownership of product types.

Too many strata complicate the survey and make preparation and tabulation more difficult. Little is to be gained from adding strata that are not significant to the survey as a whole. Pilot surveys can help to identify population characteristics which may be suitable for stratifying samples.

There are two methods used to stratify samples: with uniform sampling fraction (propor-tionate) or with variable sampling fraction (optimal or disproportionate):

1. *Uniform sampling fraction* (proportionate): this occurs when equal proportions are sampled from each stratum. This may be necessary where there is little reliable information available about the population, and a researcher may assume that variation within individual groups of the population is relatively equal, though the strata may differ markedly in average values. For example, a researcher may assume that the average consumption of bread varies

substantially by family size, although the variance about the individual averages of the family strata would tend to be similar. By applying proportionate or uniform sampling fraction, the number of observations in the total sample is distributed among strata (family size) in proportion to the importance of each stratum in the population. This results in a rather more accurate sample than a simple random sample, because stratification has ensured that the various family sizes are already present in the sample.

2. *Variable sampling fraction* (disproportionate or optimal): however, it is more likely that both the mean and variance will differ significantly among strata in a population, and in these cases a variable sampling fraction is used in preparing a stratified sample. Larger proportions are taken from one stratum than from another according to the variability existing within strata. The more mixed or variable the population within particular strata, the more difficult it is to represent those strata by merely taking a uniform sample from them.

For·example, if a survey of chemists in the UK were planned to investigate selling prices of a range of toiletries or drugs, a sample population of 1000 might be considered, and it might be known that of these outlets, 40 per cent were owned by Boots. Within the stratum represented by Boots' stores, price variation is strictly limited, but in the remaining 60 per cent of the population there may be significant price variations among independent chemists. In such instances, disproportionate stratification would be suitable, because fewer examples of Boots' stores need to be sampled in order to give the overall picture of their stratum, while independents, on the other hand, require greater representation in the sample owing to the greater degree of variance existing within the different strata to which they belong. If it could be established beforehand that all Boots' stores observed the same selling prices for the products under survey, it would be feasible to represent this particular stratum by just one sampling unit. The vast majority of enquiries could be profitably concentrated on the 'independents' where it is believed that prices are subject to some fluctuation. Stratification by this method results in greater precision in the investigation of heterogeneous populations, and acknowledges the fact that some types of sampling units are more important than others in order to obtain valid survey findings.

Crisp[3] gives two interesting examples of this principle: an American advertiser who used television extensively was particularly interested in the media habits of inhabitants of rural areas and in other areas with relatively low television coverage. In these areas, the size of the sample was increased so that a detailed analysis could be made of these relatively minor sections of the national sample. The other case was of a major market beer study for a regional brewer where it was particularly important to obtain the preferences and attitudes of Negro beer drinkers. The size of the sample in those blocks in which more than half of the household heads were Negroes was, therefore, doubled so that the views of an adequate number of Negro respondents could be obtained.

The results for each stratum must be weighted by the size of that stratum to achieve a valid population mean or other measurement. This entails extra work, of course, and researchers need to assess whether the additional precision which results from using variable sampling fractions is worth while. Apart from the additional work entailed by weighting, it should be borne in mind that sampling errors may be increased.

Frequently, researchers lack sufficient knowledge of the relative variability in strata when surveys are being planned. Some guidance may possibly be forthcoming from earlier surveys covering similar populations. Failing this, a pilot survey is valuable in indicating the general structure of the population it is proposed to stratify. The approximate figures obtained will not, of course, be precise, but they serve to act as reasonable bases for stratification.

Neyman[4] has shown that for a sample of a given size, optimum distribution among strata is given by sampling each stratum with a sampling fraction proportional to the standard deviations

Table 4.2 Disproportionate sampling

Number of stores	Per cent of total grocery sales	Allocation of 100 sample stores
1000 cooperatives	15	15 shops
1000 multiples	50	50 shops
8000 independents	35	35 shops
Total 10 000	100	100

Source: Nielsen.

of the variable within the strata. Obviously this depends on knowing the standard deviations beforehand, and, as already observed, this is not generally the experience of survey planners. Disproportionate sampling is adopted by the A. C. Nielsen organization to cover enquiries involving, for example, 10 000 grocery outlets. In round figures, Nielsen estimates that 100 stores provide basic data to give an overall picture of the market.

Note that in Table 4.2 multiples account for 50 per cent of total sales, although they represent only 10 per cent of the total number of stores. Nielsen selects, therefore, 50 multiple stores (50 per cent of the total sample) for the audit. In the case of independents, only 35 are included in the sample because their proportion of total sales is 35 per cent, despite the fact that, in the example given, they total 8000 outlets. These examples illustrate the general principles which, in practice, are modified to take into account variations in turnover in each of the categories.

Cluster sampling

This form of probability sampling occurs when interviews are concentrated in a relatively small number of groups or clusters which are selected at random. Within these randomly selected areas of clusters, every unit is sampled. (Refer to discussion on post codes as sampling frames in Chapter 3.) For example, in a national survey of salesmen in a company, sales areas could be identified and a random selection taken of these. Of the areas chosen, every salesman would be interviewed.

This method of sampling is particularly useful where the populations under survey are widely dispersed, and it would be impracticable to take a simple random sample. Systematic sampling may not be possible because of the absence of a suitable sampling frame, and it could be expensive and cause delay to construct one.

In the US a method of cluster sampling known as area sampling is used in conjunction with maps. By map references, large areas can be divided into several small districts. Where, as frequently happens, census tracts or blocks are used, *all* the households in the selected areas would be surveyed, viz., one-stage sampling. However, if these areas are, first of all, sub-sampled and households are then surveyed, two-stage sampling occurs. This system has been used by the United States Bureau of the Census, when difficulties have been experienced with population listing.

Although cluster and area sampling are attractive in terms of time and cost, the drawback is that they tend to increase the size of the sampling error of a given sample size. Cluster samples may possibly miss complete sections of human populations, because they are not thoroughly mixed. Basically, the problem is whether or not the sampling units within the clusters are homogeneous, because, unfortunately for the researcher who intends to use cluster sampling, it has been found that clusters often include people with similar characteristics. Studies have shown that inhabitants of a particular district of a town tend to be more like each other than like people in other districts (see Chapter 11: ACORN segmentation). The dangers are obvious to researchers seeking representative samples. Clustered sampling can, therefore, miss whole sections of the community under survey. If relatively few clusters are taken, it can readily be seen that the resultant sample might be biased or non-representative of the population that it is intended to survey.

If, however, clusters are heterogeneous, i.e., they contain a good mixed population, then the sample which they make up is more likely to be representative. With this point in mind, researchers who plan to use cluster sampling should consider building up proposed samples from large numbers of small clusters. If relatively few large clusters are used to form samples, the sampling errors will be considerably greater than with the former method. In practice, a national sample in the UK would generally cover 2000 to 3000 sampling units spread over 80 to 100 first-stage units.

Multi-stage sampling

To attempt a national survey using simple random or systematic sampling methods would be extremely costly in both time and money. Where populations are widely dispersed, interviewing will be difficult, and the time taken to complete a survey will be considerably extended. In a dynamic market situation, this delay may affect the usefulness of the information collected.

Some alternative method of sampling national populations is obviously desirable, so that interviews can be concentrated in convenient areas. This, in fact, is the essence of multi-stage sampling which, as its name suggests, involves the process of selection at two or more successive stages. At each stage a sample (stratified or otherwise) is taken until the final sampling units are achieved. An added advantage of multi-stage sampling is that there is no need to have a sample frame covering the entire population.

For example, the first stage of a national sample survey would divide the country by standard regions as classified by the Registrar General. Each region would be allocated interviews on the basis of population. The second stage would involve selecting a sample of towns and rural districts, and then, in the third stage, a sample of individual respondents would be taken from the electoral registers of the second-stage area.

This process of sub-sampling of successive groups could be further refined so that administrative areas would be divided into wards, and then polling districts.

A four-stage sampling design of adults 18 years and over in private households in Britain (south of the Caledonian Canal) would, for instance, be as follows:

Stage 1   Parliamentary constituencies stratified by standard region, population density and percentage owner-occupation, and selected systematically with probability proportionate to size of electorate

$$\downarrow$$

Stage 2   Polling districts

$$\downarrow$$

Stage 3   Addresses chosen with probability proportionate to their number of listed electors

$$\downarrow$$

Stage 4   Individuals – one at each address (or household) chosen by a random selection procedure.

Where towns are being sampled, a system of sampling with probability proportional to size is customarily used. This means that irrespective of the size of the town in which he lives, every inhabitant in the towns being sampled has an equal chance of being selected for interview. If one town were to have five times as many inhabitants as another town, the individual members of the

Table 4.3   Probability of selection

Town	Population	Probability of selection	Size of sample for each town	Probability of selection for any individual within town	Overall probability of selection
x	50 000	5	200	200/50 000	(1/50)
y	25 000	2.5	200	200/25 000	(1/5)
z	10 000	1	200	200/10 000	(1/50)

population have five times more chance of being included in the sample selected at random than those living in the smaller town. Hence, to overcome this bias, the *same* number of second-stage units is selected from both towns, which results in the same probability of selection for all the inhabitants. This can be seen from Table 4.3.

The overall chance of being selected in town x, y, or z has been made equal by sampling with probability proportionate to size as shown in Table 4.3.

In the case of post codes (see Chapter 3) used as a sampling frame, the first stage would involve post code areas, followed by districts, sectors, and eventually complete post code locations (clusters of around 15 homes). Within districts and sectors, selection would be more with probability proportionate to the number of addresses each contained.

Cluster sampling

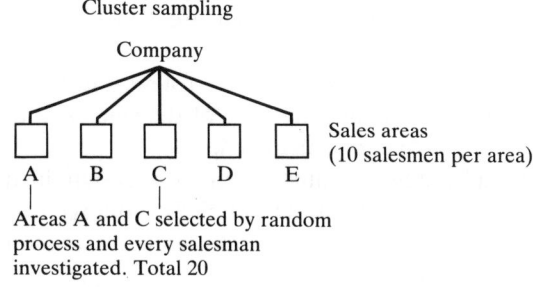

Areas A and C selected by random process and every salesman investigated. Total 20

Multi-stage sampling

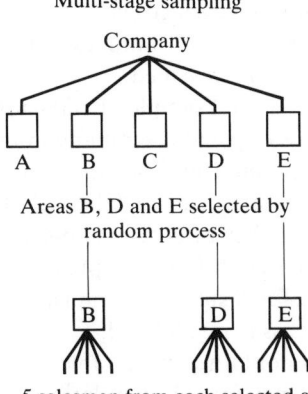

5 salesmen from each selected area chosen at random for investigation. Total 15

Fig. 4.1   Cluster sampling and multi-stage sampling

Cluster sampling and multi-stage sampling are closely related, though they have distinctive characteristics. Multi-stage sampling occurs where there is sub-sampling within the clusters selected at the first stage; where these clusters are individually sampled, cluster sampling takes place. A useful example in marketing is where it is planned to investigate the efficiency of a national sales force. Assuming that the company's organization includes selling areas, a random selection of these is made and every salesman in the chosen areas studied for sales efficiency. This is the clustered sample approach.

Alternatively, from the random sales areas, a random sample of salesmen within these areas could be selected for interview. This is a simple multi-stage technique which could, of course, be made more sophisticated by stratification. Sales areas, for example, could be included in the sample design.

Estimates based on these techniques are less reliable, on the whole, than those obtained from simple random samples of the same size. However, because of the economies inherent in their use – it is obviously much easier to complete interviews where respondents are clustered together than if they are widely scattered over the country – larger samples can be undertaken successfully, and this compensates to some extent for the relative reduction in their accuracy. Figure 4.1 shows comparative sample designs for a salesmen's efficiency survey.

Replicated sampling (interpenetrating sampling)

Instead of taking one large random sample from a universe, it is sometimes useful to divide the sample into a number of equal sub-samples, each being selected using the same method, at random from the population. Each of these sub-samples will be a self-contained miniature population. They are interpenetrating in that they are dispersed among each other as independently representing their common population.

This sampling procedure has been developed by Professor E. W. Deming[5] in his book *Sample Designs in Business Research*. He claims that one of the chief advantages of this method is the ease with which standard errors can be calculated.

Replicated sampling can be used with any basic sample design (including quota sampling) and is particularly valuable where the size of the sample is too large to permit survey results to be available quickly. The total sample can be split into representative sub-samples and one of these used to produce results ahead of the main survey.

Another major practical advantage lies in the valuable comparisons which can be made between different sub-samples, while some interesting controlled experimentation could be introduced. Possible sources of bias could be revealed as basically the sub-samples would be alike. Interviewer bias may be detected in some sub-samples, although, of course, systematic errors common to all interviewers would not be revealed.

In an investigation of 60 000 households a total sample of 1500 households might be planned. It is possible to take a systematic random sample at a sampling interval of 40, i.e., 60 000/1500 and select a starting random number between 1 and 40, successively choosing every fortieth household. By replicated sampling the total sample of 1500 households is divided into a number of sub-samples, chosen at random. The number of chosen sub-samples usually falls between 2 and 10, with higher numbers being more frequent. If, in this present example, 10 sub-samples are selected, each will contain 150 households. Each sub-sample must be a random sub-sample of the total sample, failing which the whole process is invalidated.

In the example just given, sub-samples contain a reasonable number of sampling units, i.e., 150 households, but there is a general tendency for sub-populations to be fairly small so that they are not really capable of being accurately examined in detail. Care should, therefore, be taken in using this sampling technique, for the whole purpose of sample surveys is to collect reliable information of a quality and quantity suitable for the agreed objectives.

Master samples

Where there is likely to be repeated sampling of a *static* population, it is useful to construct a master random sample from which sub-samples, chosen at random, can be taken as required. The sampling units should be relatively permanent or else the value of the method will decrease markedly with the passage of time. Human populations are dynamic because of natural causes and also because of removals to other areas, and so this type of population is unsuitable for master sampling. Dwelling lists are more stable, though even these are subject to considerable variation, particularly in towns where there is a large building programme.

In 1943, the American Bureau of Agricultural Economics started developing what was later to become known as the Master Sample of Agriculture. Two years later the Bureau of the Census cooperated in this venture, and the scope of the Master Sample was extended to the entire population. In 1954, there were further extensions to the Master Sample.

There would seem to be some attraction in having a national master sample of, say, dwellings in the UK, so that survey organizations could prepare individual enquiries conveniently. It certainly seems wasteful for so many researchers to be put to the trouble and expense of designing new samples when they might be able to draw, on payment of an agreed fee, useful sub-samples from a master sample.

Multi-phase sampling

Multi-stage and multi-phase sampling should not be confused. With the former method, distinct types of sampling units, e.g., towns, polling districts, wards, individuals, are sampled at different stages until a final sampling unit, e.g., individual, is defined. With multi-phase sampling techniques the *same* type of sampling unit is involved at each phase, but some units are asked to give more information than others. All of the samples are asked *some* of the questions, and a further sub-sample of the main sample is asked more detailed questions. For example, questioning all respondents on every aspect of a survey could be unnecessarily costly, and possibly result in loss of efficiency on the part of interviewers and reliability of answers on the part of informants. If some aspects of the survey are known to be fairly stable or relatively unimportant, they can be excluded from the general sample but included in the random sub-samples. In this way, not all respondents answer all the questions on the questionnaire, thus reducing costs.

This method was used by the Population Investigation Committee and the Scottish Council for Research in Education in a survey, during 1947, of the intelligence of 11-year-old pupils in Scotland. Group intelligence tests were administered to about 71 000 children. A sub-sample of 1120 children was selected by taking all those whose birthdays were on the first day of even-numbered months, and these were given more detailed and extensive tests. As a result of studying the scores from both the main sample and the sub-sample, an estimate of the 'intelligence quotients' of the whole group of 71 000 children was formed. It was reported that this multi-phase sampling proved most satisfactory. It is important to note that the ages and intelligence scores of the pupils in the sub-sample were 'closely similar'[6] to those in the main sample.

Multi-phase sampling won official recognition in the US when it was used in the population censuses of 1940 and 1950.

In addition to reducing costs, this method often permits the main sample to be used as a sampling frame for subsequent sub-samples. It may additionally provide information useful for stratification which will serve as a guide for optimal sampling fractions.

4.2 NON-PROBABILITY SAMPLING

There are two basic methods of sampling, probability and non-probability. With probability sampling – an American term introduced by Professor W. E. Deming to describe what is generally better known in the UK as random sampling – each unit of the population has a known chance of being included in the sample.

With non-probability sampling, individual units in the population do not have a chance of selection. Non-probability sampling is a type of stratified sample, sometimes referred to as 'judgement or purposive sampling', or expert choice. It occurs when selection of the sample is dependent on human judgement, and not on the rigorous application of probability theory. As Kalton[7] points out for instance, an educational researcher may choose a selection of schools in a city to give a cross-section of school types. But in practice, different experts rarely agree on what makes a 'representative' sample. The representativeness of such a sample is open, therefore, to some doubt. Subjective judgement, though sincere, cannot be said to be based on objective criteria.

There are occasions, however, when judgement samples may be useful:

> For example, an expert may select a sample of wheat off the top of a large pile to check its quality. It may be physically impossible to select a random sample from somewhere inside the pile. However, from long experience, the expert may know various facts about the wheat; perhaps, that it is usually of uniform quality. In this case, a small judgement sample selected from the top of the pile may be sufficient to provide the necessary information concerning the wheat.[8]

Other kinds of non-probability sampling have been variously described as haphazard, convenience, or accidental. These might refer to relatively indiscriminate methods of sampling such as street-corner interviewing, viewers responding to television programmes purporting to convey public opinion, etc. Clearly, it would be unacceptable to regard any such results as valid bases for making inferences about general populations.

Quota sampling

This is a form of judgement sampling in which the biases arising from the non-probability method of selection are controlled to some extent by stratification, weighting, and the setting of quotas for each stratum.

The population to be sampled is divided into sub-groups or strata according to the requirements of the survey, usually age, sex, and social class, though other classifications may be used. Too many sub-groups make survey work difficult and expensive. Quotas are set by researchers and interviewers are given allocations of specific types of informants. Selection of the actual informants is the responsibility of interviewers, and this can lead to bias, the degree of which 'cannot be objectively measured'.[8]

Quota sampling was widely used in the US during the 1930s and 1940s for a variety of surveys, but statisticians disliked the method and encouraged the use of probability sampling. A significant turning point occurred when the Bureau of Census selected a 5 per cent random sample from the population in the 1940 Census. With the development of random sampling techniques, researchers have grown more critical of the drawbacks of quota sampling.

In the UK the Government Social Survey occasionally used quota sampling methods in its early days, though for many years it has been using random techniques exclusively. There is still considerable controversy about the merits of the two methods, and opinion is sharply divided among those who would reject quota sampling entirely and others who are prepared to give it qualified approval. Provided certain precautions are taken, such as the careful selection and training of interviewers, the method may be useful for certain types of survey.

'In general, statisticians have criticised the method for its theoretical weakness, while market and opinion researchers have defended it for its cheapness and administrative convenience.'[2] It is, however, widely used by commercial researchers on grounds of cost, ease of administration and execution, and also because it appears to be quite adequate for many of the surveys which they are asked to undertake. In some cases, it may not be possible to draw a random sample, perhaps from lack of suitable sampling frames or because of the urgency with which information is needed in order to make some vital decision.

Further, it has been observed that as 'most market research is intended for decision-making and decisions are generally based upon comparisons rather than on absolute measurements. these comparisons seldom have to be very accurate. It is, in fact, usually difficult to find any reasonable system of weighting that would affect the decisions implied by a market research survey'.[9]

In establishing a quota sample, researchers must aim to achieve distribution over various sub-groups in proportion to their importance in the total population. (See later discussion of quota controls.) This means that researchers must study the universe to be sampled and analyse it into classifications covering basic characteristics useful for the purposes of the survey. To assist this task, researchers need to refer to published data, such as official censuses covering population, distribution, and production; reference could also be made to surveys published by the IPA and other professional organizations. The larger publishing houses also provide useful data.

The characteristics of the population which are considered significant will then be expressed as percentages in the following manner:

Let p = population; p_1 = units in population of certain characteristics; s = sample to be taken. Then, $p_1/p \times s$ = required number in sample stratum.

For example, if p is a population of 100 000, also p_1 represents 800 sampling units (e.g., people of a certain age) and s is a sample of 2000 which it is proposed to take, the equation becomes: $800/100\ 000 \times 2000 = 16$.

Other characteristics can be calculated in the same way, and quotas formed to cover the total sample. Interviewers are expected to obtain effective interviews within the controls set by the quota scheme.

Consumer surveys are frequently classified by geographical regions, urban/rural area, and size of town. Stratification is, therefore, used in both random and quota sampling, but in the former method the final sampling units are selected by random process, whereas in the latter instance, the selection of final sampling units is made by interviewers with variable success. In actual practice, it is difficult to stratify random samples on the bases of age, sex, and social groups, as available sampling lists are unlikely to include this type of information. Other stratifications may be made to meet the needs of special surveys, but it is unwise to increase strata too much, as interviewing will become more difficult; marital status, occupation, income, working wives, etc., are all frequently used. Care should be taken in deciding on strata, so that only those relevant to the problem being surveyed are included, though, of course, their relevance may not be apparent before the survey is done. In such cases, judgement and experience are valuable.

Classification by sex and age is not, on the whole, difficult in consumer surveys, and quota controls can be found from official sources. Social grouping, however, is notoriously difficult, both in setting the quotas and also in selecting suitable informants. (See later section socio-economic classifications.)

Random route or random walk

This is another type of non-probability sampling which is popular with some marketing research agencies. By this method, interviewers are instructed to start at specified points which are randomly chosen in each district and to call on households at set intervals. For example, clusters of streets could be chosen at random within the boundaries of selected wards; interviewers could be directed to approach the third house on the left side of a particular street, and then to continue their quota of calls according to the specific instructions given them. It has been observed by a leading British marketing researcher[10] that random routes or walks are open to even greater errors than a quota sample, tending to become virtually as expensive as a random sample.

Random location

This form of sampling is similar to random route sampling; interviewers are instructed to work in a highly specific, homogeneous area and to call at addresses until certain well-defined quotas are achieved, e.g., housewives of various age-groups, numbers of dependent children, etc.

BMRB: GRID sampling

The British Market Research Bureau (BMRB) has developed a method of sampling, called GRID, in order to eliminate the more unsatisfactory features of quota sampling without the costs and other constraints attached to strict probability methods.

Respondents are drawn from a small set of homogeneous streets, selected with probability proportional to population after stratification by their ACORN characteristics (see Chapter 11). Quotas are set in terms of characteristics relevant to the needs of particular sample surveys. Interviewers are instructed as to distribution, spacing, and timing of interviews.

A GRID-based sample takes as its universe all enumeration districts (150 households) in Great Britain. Each enumeration district as contained in the Census Reports of the Registrar General is stratified as follows:

1. Standard region.
2. Within standard region-by-ITV area.
3. Within strata (1) and (2) by ascending area of ACORN neighbourhood types.

The required number of enumeration districts are then selected with probability proportional to population.

GRID sampling differs principally from BMRB's traditional random location sampling technique at the final selection of streets stage. Random location sampling used, as its first stage of design, wards and parishes listed within ascending order of ACORN neighbourhood types, and, within these selected wards and parishes, streets were selected at random.

However, GRID sampling is a one-stage sample design and, as already observed, the universe is enumeration districts (150 households) listed within ascending order of ACORN neighbourhood types. This results in increased sensitivity of this technique and is caused by: (i) the cluster analysis performed on enumeration districts to determine ACORN neighbourhood types, and, (ii) the increased scope and sophistication of modern computer equipment.

BMRB states that the published literature on ACORN has indicated how apparently similar areas in terms of standard socio-economic classifications of populations differ considerably in their behaviour and GRID sampling technique allows BMRB to control and measure these differences at street level.

Sequential sampling

Instead of starting a research survey with a predetermined size of sample, sequential sampling involves gradually building up to a size where, as the result of a sequence of sampling, an acceptable level of knowledge has been gained from the research, perhaps related to the critical level of ownership of some specific product, or the circulation of a particular publication, believed to be around a certain percentage of households in an area. A series of interviews could follow, and the resultant data analysed, either simultaneously or at specific intervals of time, after which a decision would be made as to whether additional research was necessary, or whether to accept the information so far collected as indicative of the pattern of ownership, readership, etc.

The advantage of this method of sampling is noted [10] to lie in its economy – a relatively small sample can yield a sufficiently accurate result, and Douglas and Craig[11] believe that, in conjunction with computerized technology, sequential sampling is likely to become increasingly popular (see Chapter 6).

Specific problems of quota sampling

Research by Moser and Stuart[12] on the representativeness of quota sampling methods has shown them to be unrepresentative in two major factors, occupation and education. There was a definite tendency for interviewers to interview too high a proportion of better-educated people. This finding appears to confirm earlier views on the matter. In addition, there was some bias evident in the occupations of respondents obtained by quota methods, as a high proportion were 'in distribution, transport, the public service and building and road-making and a correspondingly small proportion of persons employed in manufacturing'. It is important to bear in mind that such bias is significant only if it is closely related to the subject of the study.

Another problem of quota sampling lies in the marked tendency for interviewers, even when experienced, to select distinctly different samples. This variability is not present in random sampling. It would seem that interviewers may, consciously or otherwise, avoid certain districts or types of people because of personal dislikes. Apparently, some serious bias could result as experiments have indicated that the composition of quota samples showed up to three times the variability of random samples of the same size. This point should be considered carefully when comparing the costs of the two forms of sampling; superficially the cost of quota sampling is between one-third and one-half that of random sampling.

Because quota sampling is frequently used in street interviewing, people who are out at the time of the survey are most likely to be sampled. Hence, the tendency noted earlier for a high proportion of non-factory workers to be interviewed. When home interviewing is conducted, only those women who are home at that particular time are available for interviews. Certain types of families, e.g., young mothers with babies, are more likely to be at home than 'working wives', whose children are probably at school. If the survey was interested in young mothers, then there would be no cause for anxiety about a biased sample. Quota sampling is, therefore, easily frustrated by the interviewers' pattern of work; at different times of the day samples of the same size may be quite dissimilar. It may also suffer from the bad spacing of calls, when interviewers fill up their quotas as quickly as possible by calling at the nearest house in a street, or several people are interviewed in the same factory or office when the sample is supposed to be well spread.

Admittedly, some of these dangers can be minimized by sound methods of controlling field staff. Reputable survey organizations are constantly trying to ensure that these sources of bias are eradicated as far as possible.

Quota sampling is particularly deficient in that it is impossible to estimate the sampling error in the estimates obtained, and so 'there is no way of evaluating the reliability of estimates based on samples constructed by arbitrary selection'.[13] This defect has caused statisticians to prefer the greater reliability of random techniques because the whole concept of sampling rests on the theory of probability. This principle is abandoned when quota sampling techniques are used. It is not legitimate, therefore, to apply the mathematics of probability to the results achieved by this process. Some researchers argue that quota sampling methods have so improved that it is in order to calculate the standard error on the same lines as for random sampling. This view, however, is not widely shared, and most survey organizations, particularly official ones, accept the statistical limitations of quota sampling. It is only fair to comment that Moser and Stuart,[12] after considerable research into the results of quota sampling, found this method gave fairly accurate results provided it was controlled by experts.

Advantages of quota sampling

Quota sampling has advantages as well as disadvantages. The former can be summarized as: speed, economy, and administrative simplicity.

First, the method allows investigators freedom to obtain interviews without unnecessary travelling. There is no need for call-backs, as in random sampling; this may be specially significant where information is urgently needed. Memories are not very reliable, in general, and quota sampling may be very effective in obtaining valid responses.

Each day BBC Audience Research surveys 1000 people about the previous day's programmes. This substantial task is shared among 60 part-time interviewers who undertake assignments involving periods of either two or three days. Between 'assignments' they remain members of an interviewers' 'pool', numbering about 700. Interviewers, who are carefully selected and trained, fulfil a quota of 18 interviews each day. There are 12 such sub-samples of 60 constituencies, such that over a period of a four-week month, the total number of sampling points is as high as 720.

Second, quota sampling is substantially less expensive than random sampling. But, as noted earlier, superficial costs should be related to reliability. Field costs are lower because there are no call-backs or elaborate systems of substitution. It is sometimes claimed that the problem of non-response does not arise with quota sampling. Unlike random sampling, there are no pre-selected informants who can refuse to answer questions; interviewers in quota samples merely have to obtain interviews to complete certain set quotas and they do not have to seek successful interviews with specific informants. While this is perfectly true, it does not state the case accurately: there is non-response with quota sampling in the sense that some people will not agree to be interviewed. Unless interviewers note such refusals, preferably with some description of the people concerned, the extent and type of non-response cannot be assessed. In both random and quota sampling, refusals occur. An experiment by Moser and Stuart[12] indicated a refusal rate of about 3 per cent for the former, and 8 per cent for the latter method.

Kalton[7] has alluded to the problem of non-response and the argument that quota sampling minimizes this. However, a quota sample interview may, in fact, 'substitute an alternative respondent for an unavailable or unwilling respondent. As a consequence, although a quota sample produces the required distribution across the quota controls, it under-represents persons who are difficult to contact or who are reluctant to participate in the survey'. It is these people who are less likely to be under-represented in a random sample because, as noted earlier in this chapter, interviewers must make several call-backs in an attempt to secure interviews with those who have been specified by random selection.

Third, quota sampling is administratively simple because it is independent of sampling frames. These may not always be available, and so the delay and expense of preparing special lists are avoided. In some overseas markets, for example, there are very sparse data available from which to build sampling lists, and in cases like these, quota sampling may be the only possible method of investigation.

In general, quota sampling is much more flexible than random sampling, and its advantages make it attractive, under certain conditions, to commercial researchers. Practical considerations may often be strong influences in survey work.

Quota controls

These have been developed to improve the quality of quota sampling. The technique involves identifying stratification factors which are important to the subject of the survey. Sample proportions of these factors are then used to structure a sample for interviewing purposes.

Each interviewer is given an allocation of specific characteristics of informants to be interviewed; for example, age, sex, and social class. Proportions of the various types within the sample reflect their actual distribution in the population.

Stratification, as already observed, is usually done by region and town size, as well as demographically. Special controls may be introduced to meet the needs of particular surveys; for example, occupation and industry.

There are two broad types of quota controls: independent and interrelated.

With independent quota controls, interviewers have a simple task, merely to obtain a number of interviews in certain specified strata which are not connected to each other. These could be related to sex, age, and social class independently as shown in Tables 4.4 and 4.5.

Table 4.4 Independent quota control

Sex		Age		Social class	
Sample	Total	Sample	Total	Sample	Total
Males	12	16–24	4	AB	3
		25–34	5		
Females	15	35–44	5	C	7
		45–64	9		
		65 +	4	DE	17
Total:	27	Total:	27	Total:	27

Simple examination of Table 4.4 will reveal the unsatisfactory nature of the control exercised over interviewers. In Table 4.4 the interviewer could conceivably fulfil the quota of 12 males entirely from one age group or from one social class. Similarly, if social class only is controlled, informants might be chosen from disproportionate age groups, perhaps all over the age of 45. In general, this system of quota control is unlikely to ensure that a representative sample is obtained.

The other method, interrelated quota control, is far more reliable. Interviewers are allocated specified samples, distributed systematically over stratification factors such as age, sex, and social group. This system is more generally used, and is illustrated in Table 4.5.

In this case it will be seen that a far greater measure of control is exercised on interviewers, who are handed quota sheets for particular assignments. This avoids some of the biases which could arise from the indiscriminate selection of informants.

Table 4.5   Interrelated quota control

	Sample		
Age	M	F	Total
Socio-economic group AB			
16–24	1	1	2
25–34	·	·	·
35–44	·	1	1
45–64	·	·	·
65 +	·	·	·
Socio-economic group C			
16–24	1	·	1
25–34	·	1	1
35–44	1	·	1
45–64	1	2	3
65 +	·	1	1
Socio-economic group DE			
16–24	·	1	1
25–34	3	·	3
35–44	2	1	3
45–64	2	4	6
65 +	1	3	4
Total	12	15	27

M = males, F = females.

4.3 SOCIO-ECONOMIC CLASSIFICATIONS

As mentioned earlier, socio-economic groupings are widely used in survey analyses, often in conjunction with other demographic criteria. Various systems of socio-economic classifications exist, and these will now be briefly reviewed.

Official socio-economic classifications

Available statistics relating to social classification are rather confusing, taken as a whole. The Registrar General's Census of Population recognizes five social groups, and 17 socio-economic groupings.

The five official social classes are as follows: I, II, III(N), III(M), IV, and V. It will be observed that Group III has been split between III(N) and III(M) (N = non-manual, and M = manual). This system was devised chiefly by a medical researcher, Dr T. H. C. Stevenson, and was first applied in 1913 to infant mortality statistics published by the Registrar General.

The 17 socio-economic groups have been based on the census recommendations of the Conference of European Statisticians and are as follows:

1. Employers and managers in central and local government, industry, and commerce (large establishments).
2. As above (small establishments).
3. Professional workers – self-employed.
4. Professional workers – employees.

5. Intermediate non-manual workers.
6. Junior non-manual workers.
7. Personal service workers.
8. Foremen and supervisors – manual.
9. Skilled manual workers.
10. Semi-skilled manual workers.
11. Unskilled manual workers.
12. Own account workers (other than professional).
13. Farmers – employer and manager.
14. Farmers – own account.
15. Agricultural workers.
16. Members of armed forces.
17. Indefinite.

The Official Classification of Occupations (1970) lists more than 20 000 separate occupational titles which are grouped into 223 occupational units. The official view is that each socio-economic grouping should contain people whose social, cultural, and recreational standards and behaviour are similar. However, because it is not practicable to ask direct questions about such matters in a population census, employment status and occupation are taken as guides when allocating people to socio-economic groups.

The Registrar General's social classification is the foundation of all official and sociological classification systems in Britain. Over time, some occupations have been regraded to reflect relative changes in the economic and social structure.

The General Household Survey This is an inter-departmental survey sponsored by the Central Statistical Office (CSO). It was introduced during 1973, and planned to be a continuous household survey covering a wide range of products. The socio-economic groupings used are based on the first 15 main classifications as defined by the Registrar General but these are 'collapsed' so that six classifications emerge. Table 4.6 indicates the coverage of these six categories related to the Registrar General's main classifications.

Table 4.6   Collapsed categories of Registrar General's socio-economic groupings as used in the General Household Survey

Collapsed categories	Percentage of population (approx.)	RG socio-economic groupings.
1. Professional	4.0	3, 4
2. Employees and managers	14.6	1, 2, 13
3. Intermediate and junior non-manual	20.0	5, 6
4. Skilled manual	33.4	8, 9, 12, 14
5. Semi-skilled and professional services	19.5	7, 10, 15
6. Unskilled manual/never worked	2.0	11

Source: General Household Survey, CSO.

The National Food Survey of the Ministry of Agriculture, Fisheries, and Food This groups households into eight classes based on the ascertained or estimated gross income of the head of the household, or of the principal earner in the household if the weekly income of the head is less than the amount defining the upper limit of the lowest income classification (D). These main groups are as follows: A1, A2, B, C, D, E1, E2 and OAP (Old Age Pensioners).

From the beginning of 1980, agricultural workers were assigned to an income group *entirely* on the basis of their income. They were formerly placed in Group C, even though their minimum weekly wage had sometimes been below the lower limit for that group.

The Family Expenditure Survey of the Department of Employment The occupational classification used in the report is based on the Registrar General's socio-economic groupings, but with these adjustments. The separate groups analysed are: professional and technical workers; clerical workers; shop assistants and manual workers; members of HM Forces are analysed separately. Where an individual has more than one job, the classification is related to the most remunerative occupation.

It will be observed, therefore, that while the socio-economic classifications adopted by various official investigations have distinct characteristics, the Registrar General's main groupings are largely utilized. In the case of the General Household Survey and the Family Expenditure Survey, however, certain adjustments are made to accommodate the needs of those particular enquiries. The type of information sought – its complexity and refinement – largely influences the structure of the socio-economic groupings which are used in individual surveys. Even where different groupings are in use, it is generally possible to compare these with related classifications and to obtain a reasonably adequate total appreciation of consumer activity in the area as covered by these surveys.

In addition to the survey classifications outlined above, the *Department of Employment* has a list of key occupations for statistical purposes which has 18 principal classifications as in Table 4.7.

Table 4.7 List of key occupations for statistical purposes as issued by Department of Employment

Group
I Managerial (general management)
II Professional and related supporting management and administration
III Professional and related in education, welfare and health
IV Literary, artistic and sports
V Professional and related in science, engineering, technology and similar fields
VI Managerial (excluding general management)
VII Clerical and related
VIII Selling
IX Security and protective service
X Catering, cleaning, hairdressing and other personal service
XI Farming, fishing, and related
XII Materials processing – excluding metal – hides, textiles, chemicals, food, drink and tobacco, wood, paper and board, rubber and plastics
XIII Making and repairing – excluding metal and electrical – glass, ceramics, printing, paper products, clothing, footwear, woodworking, rubber and plastics
XIV Processing, making, repairing and related – metal and electrical – iron, steel and other metals, engineering (including installation and maintenance) vehicles and shipbuilding
XV Painting, repetitive assembling, product inspecting, packaging and related
XVI Construction, mining and related not identified elsewhere
XVII Transport operating, materials moving and storing and related
XVIII Miscellaneous

Source: Department of Employment (HMSO).

These listed occupations are obviously different from the Registrar General's social class and socio-economic groups, but it is possible to segment the working population thus: non-manual (Groups I–X), and Manual Groups XI–XVIII) which could enable some basic comparisons to be made with the Registrar General's classifications.

The International Labour Office in Geneva issued, in 1969, an international standard classification of occupations with the major groups plus the armed forces (See Table 4.8).

Table 4.8 International standard classification of occupations

	Definitions of titles
Major group 0/1	Professional, technical and related workers
Major group 2	Administrative and managerial workers
Major group 3	Clerical and related workers
Major group 4	Sales workers
Major group 5	Service workers
Major group 6	Agricultural, animal husbandry and forestry workers, fishermen and hunters
Major group 7/8/9	Production and related workers, transport equipment operators and labourers
Major group X	Workers not classifiable by occupation
Armed forces	Members of the armed forces

Source: ILO, Geneva, 1969.

EC socio-economic classifications

Socio-economic status groups in the EC contain 14 classifications, as shown in Table 4.9.

Table 4.9 Socio-economic status groups of EC

Community code	Socio-economic status
1	Farmers
2	Other agricultural workers
3	Employers in industry, construction, trade, transport, and services
4	Own-account workers in industry, construction, trade, transport, and services
5	Employers and own-account workers in liberal and related professions
6	Managers, legislative officials and government administrators
7	Employees with liberal and related professions
8	Foremen and supervisors of manual workers (employees)
9	Skilled and semi-skilled manual workers (employees)
10	Labourers (employees)
11	Supervisors of clerical workers, sales workers and service staff; government executive officials
12	Clerical, sales, and service workers
13	Armed forces (regular members and persons on compulsory military service)
14	Economically active persons not elsewhere classified

Source: OPCS.

Most marketing research firms in Britain, which undertake enquiries in the EC countries, tend to use the British National Readership Survey socio-economic groupings as a basis for consumer analysis. In some cases the analysis is reduced to the three main socio-economic groupings: upper class, middle class, and lower class, corresponding to AB, C1C2, and DE.

In a multi-country consumer survey in the EC, Social Surveys (Gallup) used the classification of the occupation of the head of household as shown in Table 4.10.

Table 4.10   Gallup classification by occupation

Code	
1	Farmer/trawler owner, etc. (own account only).
2	Farm worker
3	Businessman, top manager
4	Executive; professional
5	Skilled tradesman, artisan, craftsman
6	Salaried, white-collar; junior executive
7	Worker
8	Student
9	Housekeeper
10	Unemployed; retired

Commercial socio-economic classifications

The National Readership Survey (NRS) classifies respondents over six groups (A, B, C1, C2, D, and E) according to the occupation of the head of the household. (Details and an evaluation of this classificatory system are given in Chapter 11.)

Gallup use four groups, classified as AV* (5 per cent of population); AV (upper middle class, 21 per cent of population); AV− (lower and middle working class, 59 per cent of population); Group D (very poor, 15 per cent of population).

Comparing official and commercial socio-economic classifications

It would clearly be immensely helpful if marketing research data could be related to official socio-economic groupings. The General Household Survey's six principal categories of socio-economic groupings (see Table 4.6), can fairly readily be related to the NRS socio-economic grades A–E. The cross-references given in the General Household Survey to the Registrar General's Census groupings should also assist marketing researchers.

The problem of analysing and presenting marketing research data so that official survey groupings could be adopted, has been discussed by the Head of Marketing Research at the Mirror Group of Newspapers.[14] He has suggested that since it seems unlikely that the OPCS would adopt the socio-economic groupings used by marketing researchers, the latter should consider analysing data by one or other official classifications in addition to 'traditional' analyses.

4.4 SUMMARY

There are two main types of sampling: probability (random), and non-probability (quota). Of these there are several variations, e.g., stratified random sampling.

Simple random sampling is rarely undertaken – systematic or quasi-random sampling, usually involving stratification of some kind, is more likely to be used.

Stratification may use either a uniform sampling fraction (proportionate), or a variable sampling fraction (disproportionate, or optimal).

Random sampling has been widely adopted by leading research bodies, e.g., the Government Social Survey, because of its sound theoretical basis which allows the legitimate use of statistical tests.

Non-probability sampling occurs when selection of a sample is dependent on human judgement and not on the rigorous application of probability theory. With suitably devised controls, this method of sampling may be very useful for certain types of enquiries; it may also be used in combination with random sampling techniques.

Various methods of socio-economic classification have been applied for setting quota controls: a popular one in marketing research is the A–E grouping used in the National Readership Survey. Official classifications of socio-economic groups stem from the Registrar General's Census reports which recognize five social groups and 17 socio-economic groups.

REFERENCES

1. Kendall, M. G., and B. Babington Smith, *Tables of Random Numbers, Tracts for Computers*, no. 24, Cambridge University Press, Cambridge, 1939.
2. Moser, C. A., *Survey Methods in Social Investigation*, Heinemann, London, 1969.
3. Crisp, Richard D., *Marketing Research*, McGraw-Hill, New York, 1957.
4. Neyman, J., 'On the two different aspects of the representative method; The method of stratified sampling and the method of purposive selection', *Journal of the Royal Statistical Society*, vol. 97, 1934.
5. Deming, W. E., *Sample Designs in Business Research*, Wiley, New York, 1960.
6. Political and Economic Planning, 'Sample surveys – Part Two', PEP Report, vol. 16, no. 314, Political and Economic Planning, London, June 1950.
7. Kalton, Graham, *Introduction to Survey Sampling*, Sage Publications, New York, 1984.
8. Yamane, Taro, *Elementary Sampling Theory*, Prentice-Hall, New York, 1967.
9. Rothman, James, and Dawn Mitchell, 'Statisticians can be creative too', *Journal of Market Research Society*, vol. 31, no. 4, October 1989.
10. Collins, Martin, 'Sampling', in: *Consumer Market Research Handbook* 1, Robert M. Worcester and John Downham (eds), Van Nostrand Reinhold, Wokingham, 1978.
11. Douglas, Susan P., and C. Samuel Craig, *International Marketing Research*, Prentice-Hall, Englewood Cliffs, New Jersey, 1983.
12. Moser, C. A. and A. Stuart, 'An experimental study of quota sampling', *Journal of the Royal Statistical Society*, vol. 116, 1953.
13. Ferber, Robert, *Statistical Techniques in Market Research*, McGraw-Hill, New York, 1949.
14. Allt, Brian, 'The future of social and economic classification', *Admap*, May 1979.

CHAPTER FIVE

CHARACTERISTICS OF SAMPLES

5.1 SAMPLE DESIGN

Sample design is an integral part of the total research design and contributes significantly to its integrity.

The success of research surveys rests largely on the quality of the sampling, and great care is needed at every stage in the development of suitable samples. Surveys are undertaken for many different reasons and differ also in their complexity. Sampling on a national scale is particularly complex, and most national random samples are of sophisticated design, mostly multi-stage stratified.

5.2 FACETS OF SAMPLING SURVEYS

The problems of sampling surveys can conveniently be considered under four headings: population, method, number of stages, and stratification of population.

Population

The first step in the design of a sample is to define as closely as possible the population to be covered by the enquiry. This is frequently done by demographic, geographic, and other characteristics such as professional or technical areas of interest. It is essential to define geographical areas so that there can be no misunderstanding, either during the course of the survey, or when the survey findings are being eventually studied. The importance of clear definitions can be appreciated by reference to a large metropolitan area such as London. To different authorities, this geographic description has particular significance, e.g., the City of London, Greater London, the Metropolitan London Police area, the Diocese of London, the London television area, etc. In the case of the term 'Birmingham area', this is sometimes intended to cover Coventry and also the Black Country, or to extend to include the residential towns of Sutton Coldfield and Solihull. It will be apparent, therefore, that the geographical boundaries of the survey should be closely defined and agreed by both researchers and their clients.

Age groups must also be well defined and relevant to the objectives of the survey. Other special characteristics must likewise be defined. If, for instance, the sample is to cover pensioners, it is important to define this class of persons. Is the receipt of a state old-age pension to be the criterion, or are people to be included who do not receive the old-age pension, or who may have retired from paid employment before the customary retirement age? If the sample is to take account specifically of young people's interests, is it important to include the armed forces in the survey?

Method

The next step is to decide whether a complete enumeration (census) is feasible or if a sample survey would be suitable. This decision will be affected by the constraints of time, finance, urgency, and staff availability.

Where random sampling techniques are to be used in selecting a sample, it is possible to calculate mathematically the size of sample required in order to give a desired level of precision in the results (see Section 5.3: Sample size).

Number of stages

The third step in sample design is concerned with the number of sampling stages. Most national random samples necessarily adopt some form of multi-stage sampling because of the practical limitations of surveys, namely, cost, administration, time, etc. At two or more successive stages a sample is taken by random selection (stratified or otherwise) until the final sampling units are achieved.

A four-stage sampling design could be distributed as follows:

Stage I   Administrative district
Stage II   Polling district (or electoral ward)
Stage III   Household
Stage IV   Individual

A two stage design could consist of:

Stage I   Administrative district
Stage II   Individual

Detailed consideration of multi-stage sampling is to be found in the section dealing with types of random sampling; it can briefly be said to consist of a series of sub-samples drawn from successive stages of the sampling process.

Stratification of population

The fourth step in sample design involves stratification of division of the population to be surveyed into groups with characteristics identified as relevant to the needs of the particular survey. Stratification, as noted in Chapter 4, is widely used in both random and quota sampling methods; commonly used strata in consumer surveys cover age, sex, and socio-economic grouping. In some cases, it may be necessary to undertake a pilot survey in order to establish suitable bases for stratification of a survey population.

In the section on stratified random sampling, it was noted that the number of strata chosen must be carefully controlled, as too many will complicate the survey. Samples can be stratified either by uniform sampling fraction (proportionate), or by variable sampling fraction (optimal or disproportionate). With the former type of allocation, each stratum is represented *pro rata* in the sample, say, 10 per cent of each stratum, calculated thus:

n = sample size, 100, and N = population size, 1000.

$$\text{Therefore } \frac{n}{N} = \frac{100}{1000} = 10 \text{ per cent (or 0.1).}$$

The number of actual sampling units from each stratum is dependent upon the size of that group in the population.

With variable sampling fraction, different proportions are sampled from each stratum: the method is specially useful where considerable variation occurs between strata, or when some strata contain only a small number of sampling units.

The standard error of a stratified random sample using a variable sampling fraction is less than that resulting from the use of a uniform sampling fraction, and both of them are superior to the standard error of a simple random sample. This can be shown as:

$$\text{SE} \geqslant \qquad \text{SE} \geqslant \qquad \text{SE}$$
$$\text{(RAN)} \qquad \text{ST/UNI} \qquad \text{ST/VAR}$$

When random sampling is adopted on a particular sample design, it is usually necessary to develop a suitable sampling frame unless, fortunately, one is already in existence. (See Section 3.6: Sampling frames.)

Quota controls must be planned in the case of quota (non-probability) sampling, and these should be relevant to the nature of specific surveys. The matter of sample size is difficult; a general guide is that sufficient cases must be sampled from each stratum to allow the population stratum value to be reasonably estimated.

In designing samples, cost must also be borne in mind, and some assessment should be made of the value of research information. Researchers should be prepared to evaluate the cost of research, and it may well be that an 'ideal' sampling plan is just not economically feasible. The information which management is seeking may, in fact, be adequately obtained by a less sophisticated sample design.

The cost of obtaining additional information could outweigh the benefits to be derived from it, and some critical control of research is obviously desirable. What should always be remembered is that extra information can usually be obtained, but the cost (not just 'direct' costs) will, at some stage, fail to bring in proportionate returns. The 'perfect' sampling plan may not always be the best from the company's viewpoint.

This view is confirmed by an early report issued by PEP[1] which commented that:

> The apparent high cost [of marketing research] must be set off against the results obtainable; if these obviously could not justify the expenditure, allowing for the normal 'trading risk' inherent in any estimate, then the survey should not be made. If the survey is likely to yield information on which major policy can be based – whether in manufacturing, in product design, in merchandising, or in advertising – then its likely cost will probably not appear too high. Many organisations spend large sums of money, often running well into six figures, on marketing and advertising, but fail to spend a thousand pounds or so to ensure that the hundred thousand or more is put to the best possible use.

It will be recalled that random sampling tends to be fairly expensive and it is certainly more costly than quota methods. Alternative sampling plans should be considered not just from the cost aspect, but also from the quality of the information they may be expected to supply. Researchers should offer clients an objective evaluation of alternative methods which could be suitable for the particular objectives of the survey. Inevitably, the technical aspects of sampling plans will be affected by factors, such as time, cost, and available interviewing staff, and some reasonable compromise may be necessary if the survey is to be put in hand. This does not mean that researchers should be forced into accepting conditions which would vitiate good research; it means merely that they, like other skilled technicians, must practise their expertise in the conditions which exist in today's markets.

5.3 SAMPLE SIZE

It is sometimes presumed that a sample should be based on some agreed percentage of the population from which it is taken. The view that there is a constant percentage, often thought to be around 10 per cent, which can be applied when sampling populations of all kinds and sizes, is quite wrong.

The size of a sample depends on the basic characteristics of the population, the type of information required from the survey, and, of course, the cost involved. Hence, samples may vary in size for several reasons. The application of an arbitrary percentage to populations in calculating size fails to acknowledge the individual requirements of different surveys.

If, in fact, a population had certain characteristics that were completely homogeneous throughout, a sample of one would be adequate to measure those particular attributes. On the other hand, where certain characteristics in a population display considerable heterogeneity, a large sample is needed in order to assess these attributes accurately.

Since surveys have different objectives, it is necessary, first of all, to distinguish clearly the aims of a particular survey so that the sample (including size) can be designed specifically to obtain the right quality and quantity of information. This means calculating beforehand the degree of accuracy required in the results of the survey. Some attributes may be more critical than others and the degree of precision over these should be known to the researcher. In some cases, it may be difficult for sponsors to state these critical limits, but they must be able to make some reasonable assessment to enable researchers to form a sampling design.

The sub-groups, or strata, into which the sample is to be broken down, should be relevant to the objectives of the survey, and researchers must then, working backwards from the smallest sub-group, gradually build up the size of the sample. The smallest sub-group must contain sufficient sampling units so that accurate and reliable estimates can be found of the population stratum. The significant characteristics of a population should be represented in the various strata of a sample in quantities large enough to allow valid interpretation.

It is accepted that the larger the size of the sample, the greater its precision or reliability, but there are constraints which practical researchers must acknowledge. These can be listed as time, staff, and cost. Increases in the size of a sample contribute some measure of greater precision, but, inevitably, increase the cost of the survey.

Careful thought should be given to the time constraint: urgency may not allow an extended survey, though the validity of research should not be sacrificed to expediency. Sponsors should be told what accuracy they can expect from a hastily done, fairly small, sample survey. It is then their responsibility whether or not to commission research. Cost and accuracy are closely linked with the time taken to complete a survey, and to some extent there is bound to be conflict. Fieldwork is relatively slow and expensive: it must be done thoroughly for there is no point in processing a lot of very doubtful material. Researchers may occasionally have to advise clients that the constraints placed on the survey are unreasonable, and would prevent them from undertaking valid research.

When the size of samples is being considered, it is well to bear in mind the non-response factor, some measure of which will be unavoidable. If a final sample of 3000 is planned, and non-response is estimated at 25 per cent, it would be prudent to inflate the original sample figure to 4000. While this preserves the number in the final sample – thus helping its precision – it does, not, of course, mitigate bias arising from non-response itself.

The error of the sample is inversely proportional to the square root of the sample size. For example, a sample of 8000 is only *twice* as accurate as a sample of 2000 (sample size is increased fourfold; the square root of 4 is 2). Therefore, to double the accuracy of a sample, it is necessary to increase its size four times.

Where distribution of a significant attribute in a population under survey is fairly even, i.e., about 50/50, a larger sample is necessary in order to evaluate that attribute with reasonable accuracy, than in a population with an uneven distribution of the critical characteristic.

Computing the size of a sample is, therefore, a complex process; the adequacy of a sample depends on its own numerical size rather than on its direct relationship to the size of the population being surveyed. Each survey should be carefully assessed, on the lines of this discussion, for its individual requirements.

Samples in the US range from 1500 to 2000 for national surveys, unless minority sub-sampling is involved when larger samples would be used. In the UK, national surveys of housewives' buying habits are frequently about 2000, and this figure is also relevant for Europe.

When random sampling techniques are to be used in a survey, it is possible to calculate mathematically the size of a sample designed to give a stated degree of precision in the survey findings. This is one of the most attractive features of probability sampling. It gives the findings of surveys sampled by this method a unique acceptance among professional researchers. Survey findings resulting from quota sampling cannot legitimately be interpreted with the same statistical precision.

To calculate the size of a sample to be taken by random selection, researchers must determine with what accuracy the results of the survey are needed. This can be stated as a confidence coefficient, i.e., it can be stated with a specified degree of certainty that the sample design will result in measurements within the tolerance which has been selected of the true value. Alternatively, it can be quoted as a level of significance.

For example, a level of confidence of 95 per cent (which implies a probability of .95) would result in a 5 per cent level of significance, while a 99 per cent confidence level (.99 probability) would result in a 1 per cent level of significance. These levels, incidentally, are most commonly used in practical research.

Sample values are estimators of the true population values, and it follows, for instance, that average values obtained from sampling procedures inevitably contain some measure of sampling error. The degree to which numerical data tend to be distributed about an average value (i.e., the mean, $\bar{x}$), is known as the dispersion or variation. A well-known and widely used measure of the variation of any distribution is termed the standard deviation (or its square, the variance).

The standard deviation of a sampling distribution is known as the standard error of the mean, sometimes referred to as $SE_{\bar{x}}$ (also shown as $s_{\bar{x}}$). From an examination of this statistic, an opinion can be formed of the precision and reliability of the sample estimate. As the number in the sample is increased, the standard error ($SE_{\bar{x}}$) becomes smaller. Hence, the larger the sample, the closer becomes the estimate of the population by the sample mean. This can be shown as

$$n \rightarrow N : \bar{x} \rightarrow \mu$$

Where: n = number in sample
N = number in population
$\bar{x}$ = sample average
μ = population average

If $SE_{\bar{x}}$ is very large, then the sample estimate of the population mean will vary greatly. Conversely, if $SE_{\bar{x}}$ is very small, then it can reasonably be assumed that the sample value is a good estimate of the population mean.

Some statistical texts tend to use 'sampling error' and 'standard error' as meaning the same statistic, but 'It seems preferable to use the former to describe the class of errors caused by sampling, and the latter (or sampling variance, as the case may be) from the actual measures'.[2]

It may be useful to recall some statistical notation at this stage:

	Population	Sample
Average or mean	μ	$\bar{x}$
Standard deviation	σ	s
Variance	σ^2	s^2

Note: Greek letters = population parameters
Italic letters = sample statistics.

Now, variance = σ^2, and the variance of a sampling distribution of $\bar{x}$ is σ^2/n. Standard deviation = $\sqrt{\sigma^2}$ or σ.

$$\text{Therefore, } SE_{\bar{x}} = \sqrt{\frac{\sigma^2}{n}} = \frac{\sigma}{\sqrt{n}}$$

By inverting the last formula ($SE^{\bar{x}} = \sigma/\sqrt{n}$), the value of n can be found, provided the standard deviation in the population is available, or, failing that, it is possible to use the standard deviation in the sample as a reasonable estimate of it. In addition, the size of the standard error tolerated must be known. Hence:

$$\text{Taking} \quad SE_{\bar{x}} = \frac{\sigma}{\sqrt{n}}$$

$$\text{Inverting it } \sqrt{n} = \frac{\sigma}{SE_{\bar{x}}}$$

$$\text{Therefore,} \quad n = \frac{\sigma^2}{SE^2_{\bar{x}}}$$

In marketing research, an estimate of the population proportion (or percentage) using a product or service is frequently made. The standard error of the proportion in a population can be obtained by the formula

$$\sqrt{\pi(1 - \pi)/n}$$

which can be estimated from the sample proportion p. The equation then becomes:

$$\sqrt{[p(1 - p)/n]}$$

$$\text{Therefore, } SE_p = \sqrt{\frac{p(1 - p)}{n}} \text{ or } \sqrt{\frac{pq}{n}}$$

Where: p = percentage of sample who have attribute under study
q = percentage of sample who do *not* have attribute under study
Sum of p and q is always 100 per cent

By inverting the formula

$$SE_p = \sqrt{pq/n}$$

$$\text{Therefore, } \sqrt{n} = \frac{\sqrt{pq}}{SE_p}$$

Hence, $n = \dfrac{pq}{SE_p^2}$

Both in calculating the standard error of the mean ($SE_{\bar{x}}$) and also in the standard error of the proportion (or percentage) (SE_p), it is necessary to have some estimate of σ and n respectively.

The formulae so far given relate, however, to simple random samples, but it has already been shown that practical marketing research usually involves more complicated random sampling techniques. Where, for example, stratification is used, these simple formulae are not strictly applicable. The alternatives are shown below:

Simple random sample

$$SE_{p(\text{ran})} = \sqrt{\frac{p(1-p)}{n}}$$

Stratified random sample (with uniform sampling fraction)

$$SE_{p(\text{st/uni})} = \sqrt{\frac{\Sigma n_i p_i (1-p)}{n^2}}$$

Where Σ = summation over all strata
n_i = sample number in ith stratum
p_i = proportion of sample in ith stratum possessing attribute defined in survey objectives
n = total sample size

Simple random sample

$$SE_{\bar{x}(\text{ran})} = \frac{\sigma}{\sqrt{n}}$$

Stratified random sample (with uniform sampling fraction)

$$SE_{\bar{x}(\text{st/uni})} = \sqrt{\frac{\Sigma n_i \sigma_i^2}{n^2}}$$

Example A stratified random sample was taken to ascertain people's attitudes to metrication. The sample consisted of 1000 people stratified by socio-economic groups, A-B, C, D-E, and a uniform sampling fraction was used.

Procedure:
1. Work out the proportion in favour of metrication for each social group.
2. Combine these proportions in a weighted average sum. Because a uniform sampling fraction is used, i.e., a constant percentage is taken from the population, the population numbers can be used as weights.

A town with an adult population of 10 000 was studied and a uniform sampling fraction of 10 per cent was applied to known social groups. The results are shown in Table 5.1.

Table 5.1   Stratified random sample

Population group	n_i	p_i	$n_i p_i$	q_i	$n_i p_i q_i$
A-B	150	0.8	120	0.2	24
C	650	0.7	455	0.3	136.5
D-E	200	0.3	60	0.7	42
	1000		635		202.5

$$\text{Estimate } \pi = p = \frac{\Sigma n_i p_i}{n} = \frac{635}{1000} = 0.635 \text{ or } 63.5 \text{ per cent}$$

$$\text{Estimate SE}_{p(\text{ran})} = \sqrt{\frac{p(1-p)}{n}} = \sqrt{\frac{0.635 \times 0.365}{1000}} = 0.0152$$

$$\text{Estimate SE}_{p(\text{st/uni})} = \sqrt{\frac{\Sigma n_i p_i(1-p)}{n^2}} = \sqrt{\frac{202.5}{1000^2}} = \frac{\sqrt{202.5}}{1000}$$

$$= 0.0142$$

It will be seen that stratification has resulted in some reduction in the standard error, therefore, the precision of the sample is improved.

Example A manufacturer is interested in the average sales values of a new line of merchandise which, it is believed, will be more acceptable to some types of customers than others. Sales to the public are made through three types of outlet: A, B, and C. The total number of outlets is 5000, made up as shown in Table 5.2.

Table 5.2 Types of outlet

Number of outlets	Average sales per period (£)	Sample	Standard deviation (£)
A 3000	20	75	6
B 1500	16	50	4
C 500	18	35	10

Table 5.3 Stratified random sample with variable sampling fraction

					Variable sampling fraction		
Type of outlet	population N_i	Sample average $\bar{x}_i$(£)	SD of sample s_i	$N_i\bar{x}_i$	Sample size n_i	$\frac{s_i^2}{n_i}$	$\frac{N_i^2 s_i^2}{}$
A	3000	20	6	60 000	75	0.48	4 320 000
B	1500	16	4	24 000	50	0.32	720 000
C	500	18	10	9 000	35	2.86	715 000
	5000			93 000	160		5 755 000

The mean turnover in population from the stratified random sample with variable sampling fraction, as shown in Table 5.3, is obtained by weighting means of different strata by strata populations.

$$\text{Estimate } \mu = \frac{\Sigma N_i \bar{x}_i}{N} = \frac{93\,000}{5000} = 18.6$$

$$\text{Estimate SE}_{\bar{x}(\text{st/var})} = \sqrt{\frac{\Sigma N_i^2 s_i^2 / n_i}{N^2}} = \sqrt{\frac{5\,755\,000}{5000^2}}$$

$$= \frac{\sqrt{5\,755\,000}}{5000} = 0.4797$$

This example is considered with a uniform sampling fraction in Table 5.4.

Table 5.4 Stratified random sample with uniform sampling fraction

Type of outlet	Population N_i	Sample $\bar{x}_i(\pounds)$	SD s_i	Uniform sampling fraction		
				Sample size n_i	$n_i\bar{x}_i$	$n_i s_i^2$
A	3000	20	6	60	1200	2160
B	1500	16	4	30	480	480
C	500	18	10	10	180	1000
	5000			100	1860	3640

Mean turnover obtained for population:

$$\text{Estimate } \mu = \frac{\Sigma n_i \bar{x}_i}{n} = \frac{1860}{100} = 18.6$$

$$\text{Estimate } \text{SE}_{\bar{x}(\text{st/uni})} = \sqrt{\frac{\Sigma n_i s_i^2}{n^2}} = \frac{\sqrt{3640}}{100} = 0.6034$$

On comparing the computed SE's, it will be seen that by using a variable fraction the sampling variance has been significantly reduced.

In these examples, the standard deviations of the strata have been quoted and so it has been possible to use the formulae. It has also been assumed that the proportion is quite well known and division into outlets has been possible.

Since the SE is now known, it is possible to calculate confidence intervals for the mean in the usual manner. To simplify operations, the finite population correction (f.p.c.) has been ignored in these examples (see later).

Examination of the formulae for the standard errors of stratified random samples shows that they involve far greater mathematical effort then simple random samples. The standard error for each stratum must be worked out individually, and the results for the strata combined into a weighted sum for the whole sample. This presupposes that the researcher knows a great deal about the population, or that he is able to form some reliable judgements.

In actual practice, researchers tend to avoid such complicated formulae in assessing standard errors by arguing that stratifcation of a random sample reduces the standard error, i.e., for a given sample size, the SE of a stratified random sample is less than the SE of a simple random sample. But a stratified sample is, often, also a clustered sample, and clustering tends to increase the SE. In view of all this, it is often assumed that these two tendencies roughly cancel each other out, and, therefore, it would be in order to calculate standard errors by the simple random sampling formulae. This view is not shared, however, by some leading authorities. Moser,[2] for example, has commented that available evidence suggests that stratification frequently results in little advantage, while clustering tends to increase considerably the size of standard errors.

Computing the desired size of sample is possible, within certain limitations, by mathematical processes, but, as noted earlier, other influences play an important part in deciding the eventual size and nature of the sample. In fact, Moser[2] has observed that for normal designs the proper estimation of a sample size may be quite complex and demand considerable knowledge or shrewd guesswork covering the population under survey.

An interesting reference to sampling errors was contained in the summary tables of the Sample

Census, 1966,[3] when it was stated that sampling errors consistent with the sample design (which was stratified) would be calculated and published later in the final statistical assessment of the census. Meanwhile:

> a rough indication of sampling error can be given on the assumption that the sample was a simple random sample of people, households or dwellings.
>
> If the sample figure for a particular category is less than a quarter of the whole sample population, as it is in most cases, then the 'standard error' of the sample figure is approximately its own square root.
>
> Using this approximation of standard error it can be stated that there is:
> a two-to-one chance that the error due to sampling for any figure is less than its square root;
> a twenty-to-one chance that the error due to sampling for any figure is less than twice its square root.
>
> For example, if in an area there are 625 widowed females in the sample, then the standard error of this figure is approximately $\sqrt{625}$ or 25. The estimate of widowed females in the total population is 6250 and there are odds of twenty-to-one that the correct population total lies within the range $(625 \pm 2 \times 25) \times 10$, or 5750 to 6750. It is important to remember that all such calculations must be made using the actual sample number, i.e., 625 and not the population estimate, i.e., 6250.

The official commentary also referred to the fact that relative sampling errors tended to decrease as the number of observations in the sample increased, as shown in Table 5.5.

Table 5.5   Relative sampling errors decrease as observations increase

Sample figure (a)	Twice the square root (b)	$\dfrac{(b)}{(a)} \times 100$ (c)
4	4	100
9	6	67
16	8	50
25	10	40
49	14	29
100	20	20
400	40	10
1600	80	5

It is interesting to observe from these figures that the rate of improvement in the sampling error is significant at first, but, as the absolute size of the sample is increased, decreasing returns are experienced. This phenomenon has been commented on earlier in this text, and it is apparent that, after a certain size of sample has been attained, additional large increases in size do not significantly improve the statistical precision of a given sample.

5.4 DESIGN FACTOR

Most surveys entail more complicated sampling methods than simple random sampling, and the overall effects of these complex sampling designs are expressed by the design factor ($\sqrt{\text{Deff}}$). This is 'the multiplier used to convert standard errors calculated by methods appropriate to simple random sampling into the true standard errors appropriate to the complex survey sample design being used'.[4] Hence, if the basic standard error is given as, say, 3 per cent, and the design factor is 2, the true standard error is $3 \times 2 = 6$ per cent.

In actual practice, knowing what the design factor is for a specific sampling scheme is not at all easy, so some simple and arbitrary guidelines have been proposed; for example, that *any* standard error should be multiplied by a factor of 1.5 when the sample is drawn by other than simple random method.

Collins[5] has observed that even the National Readership Survey, which has a particularly good sample design, has been estimated to have a design factor around 1.4, and many random samples have design factors of 2 or even more.

As already discussed, the quality of sample methodology profoundly influences the accuracy of sample statistics, and the design factor is important in evaluating survey data. For instance, a sample survey of 1500 indicated an estimate of 5 per cent for some proportion, with a simple standard error of about 1.8 per cent. A well-formulated sample, with a design factor of 1.4, has a real standard error of approximately 2 per cent, whereas a less efficient sample scheme with a design factor of 2 would have a real standard error of over 3.5 per cent.

When surveys are not based on random samples, significant problems arise in applying the design factor, and it has been suggested[6] that a well-devised quota sample could be taken as having the same accuracy as a simple random sample of half its size.

5.5 DESIGN EFFECT

Associated with the design factor is the design effect (Deff) which is defined as 'the ratio of the actual variance of a complex sample to the variance of a simple random sample of the same size'.[7] The latter type of sample, as noted earlier, generally serves as a useful basis for comparing the various versions of random sampling.

The following equations result:

$$\textit{Design effect (Deff)} = \frac{\text{Variance of complex sample}}{\text{Variance of equivalent-sized simple random sample}}$$

$$\textit{Design factor } (\sqrt{\text{Deff}}) = \frac{\text{Standard error (SE) of complex sample}}{\text{Standard error (SE) of equivalent-sized simple random sample}}$$

Applying the design effect to the two estimates of SE given in Table 5.1, the following equation results:

$$\text{Deff} = \frac{(.0142)^2}{(.0152)^2} = .873$$

Hence, the variance of the stratified random sample is seen to be about 13 per cent smaller than that of a simple random sample of the same size. To achieve the same precision, the size of the simple random sample (for the given example) would have to be $\frac{1000}{873} = 1145$.

5.6 NORMAL DISTRIBUTION*

Further discussion of the concept of the standard error will be helped by some consideration of the mathematical function known as the normal curve or distribution. This is one of several sampling distributions relating to sampling theory and is widely used in studying statistical data.

---

* Also known as Gaussian distribution, after Carl Gauss (1777–1855).

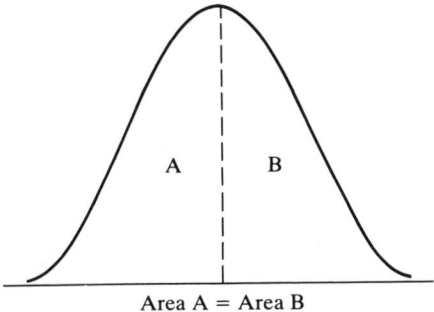

Area A = Area B

Fig. 5.1   Normal distribution graph

   The properties of the normal curve were first identified by scientists in the eighteenth century, when it was observed that repeated samplings of the same population showed remarkable regularity in their distributions. The sampling measurements formed a bell-shaped distribution, which was symmetrical and extending indefinitely in both directions. The curve comes closer and closer to the horizontal axis without ever touching it, no matter how far it is extended. In actual fact, there is no point in extending the curve very far, because the value of the measurements obtained would be negligible.
   Since there are equal frequencies in each half of a normal distribution (see Fig. 5.1), the mode, median, and mean are virtually the same for a frequency distribution which is approximately normal.

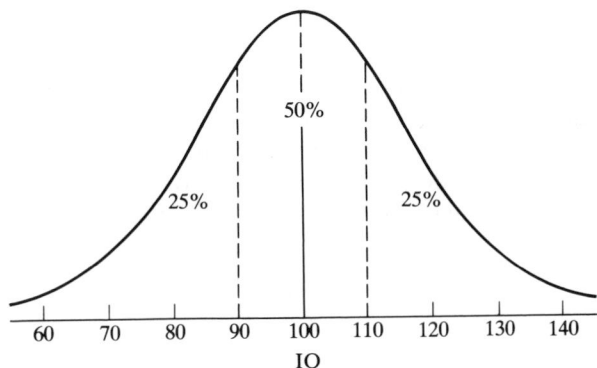

Fig. 5.2   Basic technique graph

   Many sampling distributions approximate to a normal curve, particularly, those involving measurement of human characteristics, such as height, weight, personality, intelligence, or muscular coordination. The symmetrical distribution of sampling characteristics allows researchers to make certain statements about the population under survey.
   As shown in Fig. 5.2, 50 per cent of IQ scores are within a narrow band; the other half is evenly distributed as indicated. If the middle range is divided at IQ 100, the population is divided into four groups of equal size.
   The normal distribution curves may differ in extent according to the distribution of particular attributes in the population. In simple occupations, there is less spread of ability than in complex occupations. For example, experienced production-line workers vary only comparatively slightly in their production figures, though random samples will reveal that certain individuals tend to be superior in performance. Where complex skills are applicable, the tendency is for the spread of ability to be greater as improvement in performance is evident over a longer period of time.

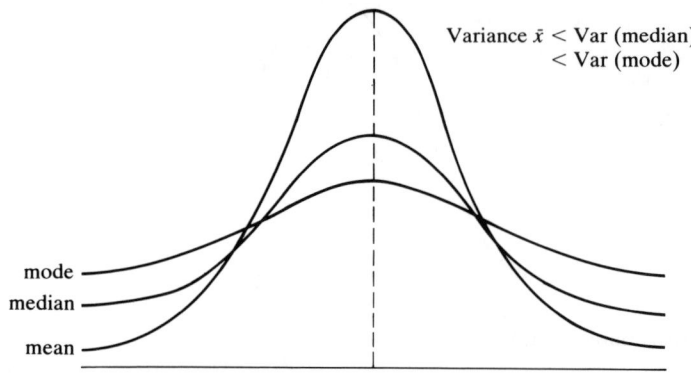

Fig. 5.3 Variance graph

The wider the spread of the distribution, the greater the variation between frequencies (see Fig. 5.3). The normal curve is always bell-shaped with a single peak, on either side of which there are equal frequencies. Normal frequency distributions are generally described numerically in two ways: central tendency and dispersion. The arithmetic mean or average is still the most widely used measure of central tendency, while the standard deviation is almost universally accepted as the measure of absolute dispersion of a distribution. It is important to note that because standard deviation measures dispersion in terms of the units sampled, it has limited use for comparative purposes. Because of this limitation, standard error, which is expressed as a percentage, is valuable.

The actual shape of the 'bell' of a normal curve is determined by the standard deviation of its distribution, and once the average and the standard deviation are known the complete distribution can be plotted. The sample average is not necessarily the same as the average for the population. The standard deviation is, therefore, useful in calculating the limits within which the population average occurs. Hence, the reliability of the sample average (or mean) of a frequency distribution depends upon the degree of dispersion about the average. Figure 5.4 illustrates the importance of the standard deviation in normal distributions.

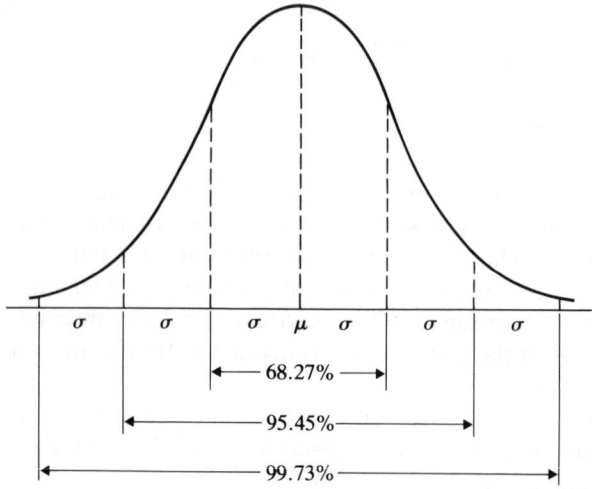

Fig. 5.4 Standard deviation graph

Figure 5.4 shows that if standard deviations (σ) are drawn at intervals of one standard deviation from the mean, the proportion of the area under the curve will be as follows:

Approximately 68 per cent of the units sampled will be within ± 1 SD of mean.
Approximately 95 per cent of the units sampled will be within ± 2 SD of mean.
Approximately 99 per cent of the units sampled will be within ± 3 SD of mean.

The areas contained by normal distributions are to be found in special Z scale tables in most statistical textbooks. Table 5.6 lists several values, of which the 95 per cent and 99 per cent confidence limits are the most frequently used in surveys.

Table 5.6   Values of confidence limits

Confidence level x/σ (per cent)	99.73	99	95.45	95	68.27
Z value	3.0	2.58	2.0	1.96	1.0

Hence, 95 per cent confidence interval for μ:

$$\bar{x} \pm 1.96 \frac{s}{\sqrt{n}}$$

99 per cent confidence interval for μ:

$$\bar{x} \pm 2.58 \frac{s}{\sqrt{n}}$$

(The figures 1.96 and 2.58 are often approximated to 2.0 and 3.0 respectively.)

Therefore, $\bar{x} \pm \dfrac{\sigma}{\sqrt{n}}$ covers 68 per cent of area under curve

$\bar{x} \pm \dfrac{2\sigma}{\sqrt{n}}$ covers 95 per cent of area under curve

$\bar{x} \pm \dfrac{3\sigma}{\sqrt{n}}$ covers 99 per cent of area under curve

Confidence intervals or limits for the mean of a normal distribution are useful in indicating the degree of accuracy which μ has been estimated by $\bar{x}$.

Example   From a sample of 100, $\bar{x}$ was found to be 50. If σ^2 is 16, what is the 95 per cent confidence interval for this estimate, assuming the population to be normally distributed?

$$\bar{x} = 50; \ \sigma = 4; \ n = 100$$

$$\bar{x} \pm 1.96 \frac{\sigma}{\sqrt{n}} = 50 \pm 1.96 \times \frac{4}{10} = 50 \pm 0.78$$

$$\text{Therefore, } 49.22 < \mu < 50.78$$

From the example just given, it will be appreciated that σ has to be known in order to calculate a confidence interval. In actual practice, σ is seldom known and it has to be estimated by using the sample standard deviation, s. Unless n is reasonably large (≥ 30), s will not provide a reasonable estimate of σ.

The Central Limit Theorem states that if n is large (≥ 30 observations), the theoretical sampling distribution of $\bar{x}$ can be approximated very closely with a normal curve, and it is in order to use confidence intervals and tests of significance, and to regard $s/\sqrt{n}$ as a good estimate of σ/n.

Hence, 95 per cent confidence interval for

$$\bar{x} - 1.96\,\frac{s}{\sqrt{n}} < \mu < \bar{x} + 1.96\,\frac{s}{\sqrt{n}}$$

99 per cent confidence interval for μ

$$\bar{x} - 2.58\,\frac{s}{\sqrt{n}} < \mu < \bar{x} + 2.58\,\frac{s}{n}$$

Example A population has a mean of 50 and a standard deviation of 20. State both the 95 per cent and 99 per cent confidence limits of the sample mean for a sample of 25.

$$\text{SE}_{\bar{x}} = \frac{s}{\sqrt{n}} = \frac{20}{\sqrt{25}} = 4$$

At 95 per cent confidence levels: $\bar{x} \pm 2\,\dfrac{s}{\sqrt{n}} = 50 \pm 2 \times 4$

Therefore, $\bar{x}$ will lie between 42 and 58

At 99 per cent confidence levels: $\bar{x} \pm 3\,\dfrac{s}{\sqrt{n}} = 50 \pm 3 \times 4$

Therefore, $\bar{x}$ will lie between 38 and 62

Example A population mean (μ) is 100 and $\text{SE}_{\bar{x}}$ is 20. Assuming that distribution is normal, what will be the 95 per cent confidence limits of sample means drawn from this population?

$\bar{x}$ is a good estimate of μ; 95 per cent confidence limit $= 1.96$ (or approx. 2)

Therefore, $100 \pm 2 \cdot \text{SE}_{\bar{x}} = 100 \pm 40$.

Therefore, $\bar{x}$ will lie between 60 and 140, at 95 per cent confidence level.

Example What size of sample, taken by random method, would be necessary to give a 0.95 probability that a sample mean of the productive output of a workshop group (> 30) would be within 2.0 points of the true mean? Assume $\sigma = 14$.

Since $0.95 = 95$ per cent confidence level $= 1.96$

$$\text{Therefore, } 1.96\,\frac{s}{\sqrt{n}} = 2.0$$

$$1.96 \times \frac{14}{\sqrt{n}} = 2.0$$

$$\frac{1.96 \times 14}{2} = \sqrt{n}$$

$$n = 188$$

An alternative formula which is often used for calculating the sample size of a simple random sample is:

$$n = \left(\frac{Z\hat{\sigma}}{E}\right)^2$$

Where: n = sample size

Z = Z-statistic corresponding to the desired confidence level (1.96 in above sample)

$\hat{\sigma}$ = the estimated value of the standard deviation of the population parameter (usually estimated from a pilot study/survey (14 in above example)

E = the maximum acceptable magnitude of error (2 in above example)

Example The average weight of 500 students is to be estimated to within a 4 lb tolerance, and the estimate is required to be 95 per cent reliable. Assume $\sigma = 12$. How large does the sample need to be?

$$\text{Therefore, } 1.96\,\frac{\sigma}{\sqrt{n}} = 4.0$$

$$\frac{1.96 \times 12}{4} = \sqrt{n}$$

$$5.88 = \sqrt{n}$$

$$n = 34.57, \text{ say, } 35.$$

Example What proportion of 4000 families in a certain suburban area of a large city own motorized lawnmowers? From a sample of 500 families, it appears that 50 had this gardening aid.

Hence, $p = 0.1$; $n = 500$.

$$SE_p = \sqrt{\frac{pq}{n}} = \sqrt{\frac{0.1 \times 0.09}{500}} = 0.0135$$

At a 95 per cent confidence level, i.e., taking two standard deviations, a sample probability of 10 per cent would be subject to ± 2.7 per cent, i.e., 0.0135×2.

Therefore, between 7.3 per cent and 12.7 per cent of the population would be owners of motorized lawnmowers (95 per cent confidence level) or between 292 and 508 families.

Example A sample survey of 1000 motorists found that 248 or 24.8 per cent had taken their cars overseas on holiday. What is the standard error of this percentage?

$$SE_p = \sqrt{\frac{pq}{n}} = \sqrt{\frac{24.8 \times 75.2}{500}} = 1.37$$

At a 68 per cent confidence level, sample value would lie in area 24.8 ± 1.37 per cent, or between 23.4 and 26.2 per cent.

At 95 per cent confidence level, sample value would lie in area $24.8 \pm 2 \times 1.37$ per cent, or between 22.1 and 27.5 per cent.

At 99 per cent confidence level, sample value would lie in area $24.8 \pm 3 \times 1.37$ per cent, or between 20.7 and 28.9 per cent.

From examination of the data now obtained, it may be thought that the range is far too wide and more precise measures are needed. By increasing the sample size the standard error will be reduced and, as a result, the range within which the sample value falls will be narrowed.

However, as indicated earlier in this text, the reduced error does not correspond directly to the size of the sample because the standard error is a square root. If the sample size is doubled, the standard error is not cut in half. As Table 5.7 shows, the sample size would have to be increased *four* times to reduce the standard error by half.

Table 5.7   Relation between sample size and standard error

Sample size	σ % (based on example)
1000	1.37
2000	0.97
4000	0.68
8000	0.48

Table 5.7 clearly indicates that substantial increases are necessary in sample size in order significantly to reduce sample standard errors. Field costs, of course, increase directly with larger samples, though other costs, e.g., tabulation, are not likely to increase proportionally. Practical researchers must carefully assess the needs of the survey against the costs of achieving specific precision in the sample results.

These calculations refer to samples chosen by random methods; non-probability sampling techniques cannot legitimately use these precision measures.

5.7 FINITE POPULATION CORRECTION

Before leaving the subject of standard errors, some mention should be made of the factor known as the finite population correction (f.p.c.). This is shown as $\sqrt{(N - n/N - 1)}$, there N = number of units in population and n = number of units in sample.

Where the population is very large relative to the sample, the f.p.c. approximates to unity and it can be omitted. As a general rule, the f.p.c. can be ignored in calculating the standard error if the sample does not exceed about 10 per cent of the population.

Hence, the formula $\text{SE}_{\bar{x}} = \sqrt{(\sigma^2/n)(N-n/N-1)}$ will be acceptable as $\text{SE}_{\bar{x}} = \sqrt{\sigma^2/n}$, which is generally used.

The adjustment factor contained in the expression $\sqrt{(N - n/N - 1)}$ is never greater than one, and it is, therefore, practicable to ignore it and use the simpler formula $(\sqrt{\sigma^2/n})$ assuming that sampling is being done from a very large population.

The following example illustrates that the f.p.c. can be omitted on these occasions:

Let sample = 100 (n) and population = 10 000 (N)

$$\text{Therefore, } \sqrt{\frac{N - n)}{N - 1}} = \sqrt{\frac{10\ 000 - 100}{10\ 000 - 1}} = 0.995$$

It is evident that this result is so near to one as to make an adjustment for population size serve no useful purpose.

5.8 *Z* VALUES

A normal curve with mean μ and standard deviation can be converted into a standard normal distribution by the formula:

$$z = (x - \mu)/\sigma$$

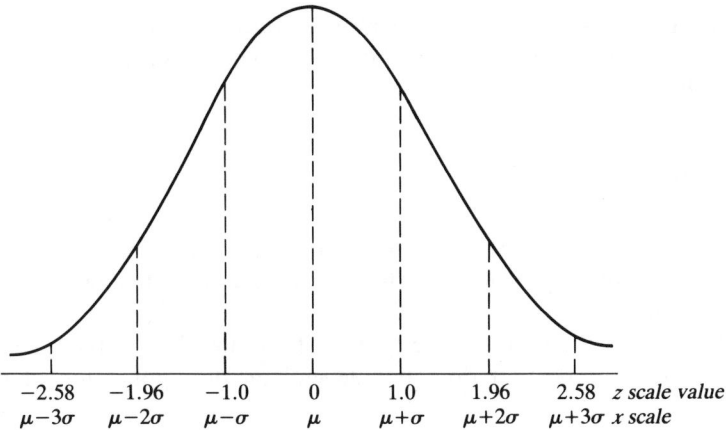

−2.58	−1.96	−1.0	0	1.0	1.96	2.58	*z scale value*
$\mu-3\sigma$	$\mu-2\sigma$	$\mu-\sigma$	μ	$\mu+\sigma$	$\mu+2\sigma$	$\mu+3\sigma$	*x scale*

Fig. 5.5 *Z* values graph

To determine an area under a normal curve whose mean and standard deviations are *not* 0 and 1, change *x*s to *z*s, and read off values from a normal curves area table, to be found in most statistical texts.

On referring to Fig. 5.5 showing *z* scale values and *x* scale, it will be seen that one standard deviation either side ($\pm$) of the mean (μ) has a *z* value of ± 1. The normal curve area between $z = -1$ and $z = +1$ (from standard normal curves tables) is $0.3413 + 0.3413 = 0.6826$. Hence, it follows that if a distribution can be approximated closely with a normal curve, approximately 68 per cent of cases fall within one standard deviation from the mean.

This should now be checked against the diagrams given earlier in the section on normal distribution; *z* values for two and three standard deviations can similarly be checked: these will be found to be approximately 95 per cent and 99 per cent, respectively.

5.9 SAMPLE SIZE DOES NOT GUARANTEE ACCCURACY

The American weekly magazine, *Literary Digest*, was accustomed to conduct an extensive mail poll of voters before national elections. In the last pre-election issue of the magazine, the state of the poll was reported according to the research.

In 1936, more than 10 million ballots were mailed, of which 2 350 176 were returned and included in the summary published on 31 October 1936. Of these, 55 per cent favoured Landon, and 41 per cent favoured Roosevelt.

In the actual election, Roosevelt polled 60 per cent of the votes cast. The difference between Roosevelt's proportion of the *Digest* poll votes and the actual percentage he obtained represented a 'sampling variation' of about 50 per cent.

Yet Gallup, using a sample of only a few thousand, had accurately predicted the election results.

The *Digest* sample was not proportional; it included too many upper-economic voters (telephone subscribers, car owners) and an inadequate representation of lower-level voters. The sampling lists used were telephone directories and similar lists biased towards upper-economic voters.

Non-response bias also existed, as only 20 per cent of mail ballots were returned, probably mostly from the more educated members of the sample.

The *Digest* sample was, therefore, biased in two ways: from an unsatisfactory sampling frame and also from non-response. One bias accentuated the other.

Although *Digest* forecasts had never been wrong for over 25 years, the 1936 predictions were hopelessly inaccurate. Unsound sampling methods may sometimes produce reasonably accurate data, but eventually they fail.

5.10   SUMMARY

Sample design is an integral and vital part of the overall research design. Four facets of sampling surveys are: definition of population; methodology; number of stages in sample design; stratification of population.

Sample size depends on the basic characteristics of the population, the type of information needed and, of course, the cost. It does not depend on the application of some arbitrary percentage.

The larger the sample, the greater its precision or reliability, but practical constraints such as time, staff, and cost affect marketing research in practice.

Sample values are estimators of true population values, and so the former inevitably contain some measure of sampling error; the degree to which numerical data are distributed about an average value is known as the dispersion or variation; a well-known and widely used measure is the standard deviation (or its square, the variance). The standard deviation, known as the standard error of the mean, indicates the precision and reliability of a sample estimate.

The design factor is important in evaluating the effect of sample design survey statistics.

The normal curve or distribution is one of several sampling distributions related to sampling theory and is widely used in studying statistical data.

REFERENCES

1. Political and Economic Planning, 'Sample surveys – Part One', PEP Report, vol. 16, no. 313, Political and Economic Planning, London, 1950.
2. Moser, C. A., and G. Kalton, *Survey Methods in Social Investigation*, Heinemann, 1971, London.
3. General Register Office, *Sample Census, 1966, Great Britain*, Summary Tables, HMSO.
4. Harris, P., 'The effect of clustering on costs and sampling errors of random samples', *Journal of Market Research Society*, vol. 19, no. 3, 1977.
5. Collins, Martin, 'Sampling' in *Consumer Market Research Handbook*, Robert Worcester and John Downham (eds), Van Nostrand Reinhold, Wokingham, 1978.
6. Koerner, Roy E., 'The design factor – an underutilised concept', *European Research*, vol. 8, no. 6, November 1980.
7. Kish, L., *Survey Sampling*, Wiley, New York, 1965.

SIX

QUESTIONNAIRES

6.1 INTRODUCTION

A questionnaire is a method of obtaining specific information about a defined problem so that the data, after analysis and interpretation, result in a better appreciation of the problem. It is an important element of the total research design, and its preparation and administration demand considerable professional expertise.

Survey questionnaires may be applied in several different ways: by personal interview, by telephone, by mail, or self-administered. A questionnaire form which has to be completed by an interviewer is often referred to as a schedule. The type of questionnaire obviously depends on the method of survey, and this will be dependent on the nature of the problem being investigated, the kind of population sampled, and the sample size.

The general form of questionnaires lies between two extremes. At one end of the continuum lies a highly structured questionnaire consisting of a series of formal questions designed to attract answers of limited response. Standardized questions are administered in the same way to all respondents. At the other extreme is the unstructured questionnaire where formal questions are replaced by a freer style of investigation. The interviewer encourages conversation to develop, during which respondents are invited to answer in their own words a series of open-ended questions, often phrased by the interviewer to suit individual respondents. The interviewer will have an 'interviewing guide', also known as a 'checklist', which outlines the sort of information to be collected, but the precise wording of questions is left to his discretion. This type of questioning calls for highly skilled interviewers.

In practice, surveys frequently mix the styles of questioning. However the questionnaire is formed, individual questions must be designed to attract respondents to give valid and reliable information about the subject of the enquiry, and to do this with the minimum distortion or bias.

Clearly, this cannot be done without a thorough background knowledge of the subject. Where the survey is to be undertaken by an outside organization, some preliminary study of the company and its products is necessary. It may then be possible to define the problems with which the survey has to deal and, therefore, the type and scope of questioning.

Some pilot survey work is advisable to assist in understanding the problems and difficulties of actual or potential users of the product or service. A series of informal discussions with selected individuals and groups should provide valuable background knowledge which could then be used in developing questions around certain subject areas, such as the extent and application of labour-saving appliances in the home. During the course of these unstructured interviews, ideas will emerge which may throw new light on the problems being surveyed, though the temptation to chase too many hares must be resisted.

The objectives of the survey should now be reviewed in the light of this additional information. It may be necessary to modify those originally projected so that they are feasible (see next section).

6.2 PLANNING THE QUESTIONNAIRE

In Chapter 2, the five stages of the marketing research survey process were described: the first stage, i.e., research brief, gives the essential guidance needed for development of the research proposal (2nd stage). At this stage, the overall plan of the research will be described, including an outline of the main areas of questioning. Researchers should discuss and agree with clients the proposed research strategy and satisfy them about, for example, the coverage of the questionnaire.

Five classes of information which are generally useful for marketing decisions have been identified[1] as follows:

1. *Facts and knowledge:* what are the present beliefs, perceptions, and depth of knowledge of the survey respondents about, for example, specific products, services, industries, or organizations?
2. *Opinions:* what are the existing attitudes towards products, etc., including an assessment of the strength with which these attitudes are held?
3. *Motives:* what underlies specific types of market behaviour, i.e., what motivates buyers of various kinds of products or services?
4. *Past behaviour:* what are the patterns of consumption of certain kinds or brands of products over specified time periods? Insight will be given into factors such as brand loyalty. Observational techniques, such as home audits, will help in verifying reported consumption behaviour.
5. *Future behaviour:* indications of possible future behaviour may be gleaned from sensitive questioning about, for instance, levels of satisfaction with existing products, nature of expectations, social habits, etc.

Included in this general approach would, of course, be an evaluation of the nature of buying behaviour which may be complex both in terms of the people involved (see Chapter 12 for discussion of industrial decision making) and also the sophisticated mix of motivations which could be influenced by economic, psychological, social, and cultural factors (see Chapter 1, Section 1.8: Complexity of buying behaviour).

6.3 QUESTION REQUIREMENTS

It has been seen that the questionnaire is a vital part of most surveys and great skill is needed to design an effective series of questions. Experts agree that there is no easy way to do this; it remains largely a matter of art rather than science. Fortunately, there are some general principles which can help in the design of questionnaires, though this essential tool of survey work can hardly be called a scientific instrument. At its best, it is a remarkably versatile method of gathering information about a wide variety of topics. Used with care and understanding, it can provide valuable data which, otherwise, would not be available.

Three conditions have been stated[2] as necessary for ensuring a true response to a question:

(i) respondents must be able to *understand* the question; (ii) they *must be able* to provide the information requested; and (iii) they *must be willing* to provide the information. If these simple but basic guidelines were observed, a great deal of the frustration experienced by researchers and respondents would be avoided.

Questions are the raw material of questionnaires, and on them depends the quality of the research. Some discussion of the factors which influence the construction of effective questions is, therefore, appropriate.

The frame of reference is important in determining what questions mean to respondents and how they will react to them. 'When drawing up a questionnaire we tend to forget how circumscribed our own experience is and we take for granted that whatever the word means to us it will mean to everyone else.'[3]

Questions should be phrased in simple language which can be easily understood by the particular respondents interviewed. There should be no attempt to impress respondents by the use of unusual words; the message in the question should be clearly understood in the meaning intended by the researcher. The language used should be within the common experience of all those who are being interviewed. Unilateral, for example, means one-sided, 'which for ordinary purposes is a more intelligible expression' and, the former word should 'be confined to the jargon of diplomacy and physiology, to which it belongs. . . . '[4]

Names of meals, for example, dinner or tea, may well mean different meal times for a sample taken from the general population of the country. For many topics, it has been discovered that the frame of reference is likely to be influenced by occupational groups, leading to professional or technical jargon which would not be understood in a general survey. The golden rule is to stay within the working vocabulary of the population which is being sampled, avoiding words which do not communicate the meaning of questions clearly and precisely.

The use of unfamiliar words should be avoided. It was reported,[5] although with some reservations, that when members of a small community in South Wales were asked: 'Who or what is devolution?', 10 per cent said he was Jeremiah's brother, 10 per cent that it was an aria from Elijah, 10 per cent thought it referred to the last book of the Bible, and the remainder said that he was a French prop forward. An imaginative if rather ill-informed 12-year-old schoolboy at a Shrewsbury school when asked for a definition of 'nostalgia', wrote: 'It is Welsh for "Goodnight".'[6]

Research[7] has shown that many words, though apparently in common use, are not properly understood by all who use them: 'incentive', 'proximity', and 'discrepancy' were known by half the population, while words like 'paradox' and 'chronological' were known by about one-fifth. Although, as Jean Morton-Williams[8] points out, context can aid understanding, often the reverse occurs and an unfamiliar word can make a whole sentence incomprehensible. Words should be selected carefully and used sparingly in questionnaire construction.

Questions should be specific; they should be related to particular aspects of the survey and ask for information in well-defined terms. Such enquiries as: 'Are you a regular user of product X?', or, 'Do you go to the pictures often?', can only produce a collection of very unreliable data. Researchers should take care to qualify questions so that respondents are quite clear in their minds about the nature of the information which is being sought. For example, questions about media habits should be carefully drafted. 'What newspapers have you read during this week?' might well include responses from those who:

(i)   actually bought the papers in question;
(ii) read someone else's paper;
(iii) read the specified papers in depth;
(iv) just skimmed quickly through the newspapers.

In addition, what time period is actually covered by 'this week'; is it intended to include, for example, the Sunday papers?

Questions should be economically worded; they should not ramble on as their length will merely confuse respondents. Complex questions should be broken down into a series of readily answerable short questions which focus attention on one specific, well-defined issue. For example, the following question: 'What do you think of the economic policies of this Government and how do you think they should be modified, if at all?', is likely to baffle most respondents who may decide to limit their response to the second part of the question. This type of question might well be split into two or more shorter enquiries confined to particular issues.

Third-party questions should be avoided if possible. It is better to ask people what they know from their own experience. Facts are to be preferred to opinions.

There is little use in taking uninformed opinion, or attitudes unrelated to experience, as firm guides to future action. Thus, the opinions of informants who have never lived in centrally heated houses, or have not used particular kinds of goods, are unlikely to be of use in deciding on long-term production plans. In such cases, firm information can be derived from sample surveys only by a process of observing the reaction of informants to changes which widen their experience in a particular direction, or which offer new opportunities.[9]

Writing about opinion polling, Harold Lind[10] remarked that a public sophisticated enough to recognize a pointless and frivolous question will be tempted to respond likewise. Market researchers should, therefore, be aware that respondents are also likely to give ill-considered answers to questions about consumption habits which they consider hypothetical or irrelevant.

It is often tempting to ask hypothetical questions, but the value of the responses they attract is small. Surveys should be concerned with collecting meaningful data, and prediction of likely behaviour is difficult enough without complicating it with information of dubious merit.

Questions should not place too much strain on the memories of respondents. Information should be sought within the ability of respondents to recall accurately. Where detailed information is required over a period of time, it is better to have some system by which respondents can actually record their expenditure or other behaviour, e.g., the diaries used by consumer panels.

The proximity to the event, the intensity of the stimulus, and the degree of association affect memory. Some events will be easily recalled over a long period of time; for example, the date of marriage, the birth of children, the purchase of the first car, or some personal accident. The memory of other events may soon fade, and a time limit should be written into questions about matters which have comparatively little personal significance; perhaps the price of some basic food like salt could be recalled soon after purchase, but it is doubtful if this could be done successfully in even a week's time.

Checklists to aid recall should be used with discretion, as they may introduce bias. Aided recall methods are used by BBC Audience Research interviewers, who help respondents, by reading out the listed programmes, to remember what programmes they may have heard.

Association is frequently used in advertising research in order to assist recall of particular advertisements. A magazine cover might be shown to respondents who are then asked if they have seen the issue and, if so, what advertisements they recall. Further questioning follows when particular advertisements are named, to test the impact of campaigns.

Lists of publications are often shown to respondents who are invited to say which they have read over the past week or month. (These periods need to be clearly defined.) Prestige bias often intrudes in the answers given.

6.4 BIAS IN QUESTIONS

Bias should be avoided in questions; this means that questions should be phrased carefully in order to avoid suggesting that certain answers are more acceptable than others. There is no generally agreed definition of a leading question.

Moser and Kalton[11] have defined it as one which by its content, structure, or wording, leads respondents in the direction of a certain kind of answer. Some American researchers[12] concluded, after studying many interviews, that in most uses of leading questions, the components or 'expectation' and 'premise' were present. The expectation component of a question occurs when an interviewer indicates the response which it is anticipated the respondent will give (or, alternatively, not give). The answer is of the closed (YES/NO) type, for example: 'You are 30 years old, aren't you?' Expectation can also arise through the interviewer's intonation, for example: 'Did you *agree* with this decision?' or 'Did *you* agree with this decision?' It is almost impossible to formulate a question that does not depend on some kind of premise or assumption. If the premise is incorrect, it is suggested that it is easier for the respondent to correct an open than a closed question, since the former allows the respondent to make a freer answer which modifies the influence of the premise.

There are 'leading' words and phrases, such as: 'You don't think ... do you?' which researchers should carefully avoid; these are usually more influential in attitudinal questions than factual questions. For instance, 'Nowadays most people think that corporal punishment in schools is wrong, do you?'

Bias may operate particularly with checklists or multi-choice questions. Tests have shown that when respondents were asked directly whether they read a particular low-prestige magazine, a larger proportion admitted readership than when the magazine was included in a checklist with high-prestige magazines. It was further discovered that the data from direct interviewing coincided closely with published circulation figures.

Respondents should not feel social pressure to answer in some particularly acceptable manner. This influence was felt in a survey undertaken some years ago to investigate readership of *Gone with the Wind*. To the question: 'Have you read this book?', an excessively high proportion of respondents said: 'Yes'. Obviously, those who had not read it were reluctant to say no. Rephrasing of the question to: 'Do you intend to read *Gone with the Wind*?' produced a more valid finding, as even those who would never read it could pretend that they would do so. But the people who had already read it did not fail to stress this point.[13]

In that excellent primer, *The Art of Asking Questions*, Payne[14] illustrated the influence of leading questions by his story of the snack-bar waiter in America who increased spectacularly the sale of eggs in milk shakes. He asked customers not whether they wanted an egg or not, but whether, in fact, they wanted one or two. While this was a good sales technique, it would, of course, be quite unsuitable for research.

Biased replies could also arise from the likelihood of respondents observing that earlier questions in a survey seemed to show interest in a particular brand, with the result that when later questions referred to products of that type, respondents may well be influenced to mention that particular brand.

Ferber[15] warns against using apparently harmless questions such as: 'Would you rather use Lux toilet soap than any other toilet soap?', since this would attract more favourable responses than if respondents were merely asked: 'What is your favourite toilet soap?'

6.5 QUESTION ORDER EFFECTS

Bias in questionnaires may also arise from the order in which certain questions are placed, and the importance of context effects has been studied by several researchers, including Schuman *et al.*[16] They focused on a pair of questions related to Communist and American reporters 'where the context effect has been shown to be both strong and stable over time'.

The Communist reporter item was: 'Do you think the United States should let Communist newspaper reporters from other countries come in here and send back to their papers the news as they see it?'

The American reporter item was: 'Do you think that a Communist country like Russia should let American newspaper reporters in and send back to America the news as they see it?'

Split ballot experiments (reversing the order of the question) in 1948 showed a highly significant question order effect; respondents were more likely to allow Communist reporters into the United States after answering the American reporter question; on the other hand, they were less likely to want American reporters admitted to a Communist country after having answered the Communist reporter question.

Replication in 1980 confirmed the 'sizeable order effect', and a new split ballot test in 1981 revealed that question order effects were still significant, even when the two items were separated by a series of 17 other unrelated questions. The researchers[16] suggest that 'at least in some cases, context effects are not necessarily a function of question contiguity in any simple sense, nor are they always reducible by the simple stratagem of dispensing items throughout a questionnaire'.

The effects of question order on survey responses were also studied in a random direct dialling telephone survey[17] of Kentucky households. In four non-overlapping sections, respondents were asked a series of questions on their attitudes towards energy, the economy, politics, and religion. Four question sequences were used: a general attitude question on each issue either preceded or followed a series of specific questions on each of the four issues.

Respondents expressed significantly greater interest in politics and religion when general questions on these matters followed specific questions. However, evaluations of the economic and energy issues were not significantly affected by the order of questions. It must appear that questions may vary in their susceptibility to order effects, and it is suggested that 'the more specific the content of a question and the more concrete the required response, the less susceptible the question is to order effects. Conversely, the more diffuse the question's content and the more vague the response required, the greater the possibility of these effects.'[17]

6.6 QUESTION SEQUENCE

Apart from government censuses, cooperation in surveys is voluntary and relies largely on the goodwill of informants. Some people, of course, will talk freely and at considerable length about any subject, particularly themselves, but willingness does not necessarily guarantee accuracy of observation. The purpose of survey questions is to obtain reliable data from as many members of the sample population as possible. There will, therefore, be respondents who are not always disposed to answer a series of questions, and special efforts must be made to encourage them to respond.

Some simple introduction should explain the nature of the survey and invite the respondent's cooperation. With personal interviewing, the interviewer may wish to reassure the respondent by showing a letter or card of authorization. There should be no attempt to coerce the respondent, as the quality of the responses will suffer in the unlikely event of an interview being granted. Tactful and courteous persuasion is far more likely to be successful, and this can be reinforced by quoting, perhaps, the first question in the survey.

This opening question should be as interesting as possible to the respondent and fairly easy to answer. Some researchers favour an opening question which builds up the respondent's confidence; it may not even be particularly significant to the survey. The value of the ensuing interview will depend largely on establishing effective *rapport* between respondent and interviewer, and so it is worth while to give the opening question some thought.

Succeeding questions should guide the respondent's thought in a logical progression from one topic to the next, each topic being explored before passing to its successor. This enables the respondent's mental processes to develop easily, and recall is facilitated. Past associations and memories are awakened by this steady, systematic approach.

Particular care is needed in planning the sequence of topics to avoid conditioning the respondent in his answers to later questions. To avoid this kind of bias, the 'funnel' technique is often used. This involves asking, first, the most general or unrestricted questions. In this way, the area of questioning is gradually restricted to precise objectives. The method is particularly useful for learning something about the respondent's frame of reference from earlier open questions. The smooth flow of questioning from the general to the more specific also builds up a good relationship between the interviewing parties.

In a survey[18] concerned with rheumatism remedies, respondents might be gradually 'funnelled' through a sequence of questions starting with health concerns, then on to rheumatic complaints; from there to methods of relieving rheumatism, and finally, to patent remedies for rheumatism.

An enquiry[19] into housewives' attitudes towards a semi-prepared foodstuff (cake-mix, instant coffee, etc.) which might be affected by 'guilt' feelings, could be started with a general discussion of household tasks (including use of various labour-saving devices), narrowed down to cooking, further focused down to labour-saving foods (e.g., tinned or frozen foods), then on to semi-prepared foods, and finally, to the subject of the survey, which might be cake-mix.

Another example of the funnelling technique in survey questioning occurred in a study[20] of attitudes to the noise of aircraft around Heathrow. Informants were asked a series of questions, starting with those of a fairly general nature so as to avoid biasing responses, and aimed to discover eventually their experience of and attitudes towards aircraft noise, e.g., 'What do you dislike about living around here?' 'If you could change just one thing about living round here, what would it be?' 'Have you ever thought of moving away from here?' 'Why?' 'What are the main kinds of noise you hear round here?'

Only after these sequential questions had been answered, was the subject of aircraft or aircraft noise mentioned. (The possibility of bias exists, however, in the wording of the first question, and this would have been improved by inserting 'if anything' after the word 'dislike'.)

The opposite technique known as 'inverted funnel' sequence is sometimes used; specific questions are asked first of all and then successively more general questions widen the area of enquiry. This obviously lacks the advantage of 'funnelling', but it is occasionally applied where the topics surveyed do not evoke strong feelings.

It may be necessary to discuss topics which are 'threatening' or 'taboo', about which respondents feel reluctant to answer questions. These sensitive areas of enquiry need to be handled with delicacy and skill, if valid responses are to be attracted. Questions of this nature should be deferred until the middle or towards the end of a questionnaire when goodwill has been firmly established. There is no point in forcing people to give information which they are reluctant to disclose, perhaps for reasons of social embarrassment, as the answers they will give are likely to be self-defensive and will not reflect their true opinions. Another good reason for deferring these questions is the risk that some respondents may abruptly discontinue interviews which include questions which they consider personally embarrassing. If these questions are placed near the end of an interview, the majority of information will already have been collected.

Indirect methods of questioning are sometimes helpful in securing information about subjects which are considered by respondents to threaten their self-esteem. Such threatening or taboo subjects might include enquiries into personal honesty; for example, 'fare dodging', or socially unpleasant habits such as litter dropping. Personal smoking and alcohol consumption may also inhibit people from giving factual answers to questions in these areas.

Experienced researchers acknowledge that, for personal defensive reasons, the consumption of alcohol and tobacco tends to be understated, while that of more 'approved' products such as soap, household cleaners, or toothpaste, will generally be inflated.

Other areas of enquiry, which may possibly be regarded by respondents as taboo or embarrassing, include racial prejudice or sexual behaviour. Prejudicial questions covering personal habits, race, religion, etc., and those involving prestige and pride should be treated with great care. With unstructured interviews, skilled interviewers are able to formulate questions on these subjects to suit individual respondents, whose likely reactions will already have been judged. This flexible approach is less likely to cause offence, though it should not be assumed that it will always result in accurate information.

Filter questions are useful in establishing whether respondents are users or non-users of products or services being surveyed. If the answers are in the affirmative, further questions may cover particular aspects of the problem, for example: 'Do you smoke?' YES/NO. Those who replied YES would be asked whether they smoke cigars, pipes, or cigarettes, and perhaps how much per day/week. Non-smokers would skip these further questions and go to the next question sequence.

Classification questions, i.e., those asking about age, sex, marital status, income, education, family size, etc., should normally be left to the end of the interview unless quota sampling is being used. It is necessary in the latter case to check the suitability of respondents in order to complete a representative sampling survey. Questions asking for personal information should be prefaced by a few introductory remarks, as respondents may well feel that it is unnecessary for interviewers to know so much about their personal background. They should be assured that the information will be treated confidentially, and that it will not result in their names and addresses being entered on some list of sales prospects.

Precise ages of respondents need not be sought, as age groups will normally be quite adequate. Respondents could be handed a card and asked to indicate their age group. Occupational classification is often difficult, and descriptions by respondents (particularly wives) are frequently subject to prestige distortion. Such descriptions as clerk, engineer, secretary, civil servant, or businessman need fuller qualification to be useful to the researcher.

Payne[14] instances the man who described himself as a 'bank director'; his actual duties were to 'direct' customers to the correct bank official.

A job applicant in the West Country described his last position as 'room director'. Later enquiries translated this impressive title into 'bouncer at a London club'.

A supermarket employee in Yorkshire who described himself as 'transport manager' was actually in charge of the trollies in the store.

This natural tendency of respondents to inflate the importance of their occupations can be checked by experienced interviewers who can tactfully probe and secure more accurate job descriptions.

Classification details supplied must be useful within the definitions of the survey. Housing, for example, should be defined precisely so that it can be correctly allocated in the survey analysis. Respondents should be guided for example, when they are counting the number of living rooms and bedrooms in their houses. Interviewers should qualify these descriptions so that the data collected during the survey are homogeneous. If a survey is interested in the number of bedrooms, it would confuse respondents to ask: 'How many rooms are there upstairs?' as they would probably include the bathroom and lavatory.

Researchers should understand that classification questions are not always welcomed by respondents. Unnecessary questions of a personal nature should not be asked; every question should be examined for its relevance to the objectives of the survey and excluded if there is no good reason for asking it.

At a seminar[21] organized by the Survey Control Unit of the Central Statistical Office, Peter Menneer criticized the use of questions involving meaningless concepts as, for instance, 'To what extent would you consider peanut butter as an alternative to jam?' Many people might not consider this in any way to be an alternative. He also warned against the use of double negatives like: 'Would you rather not use a non-medicated shampoo?' Ambiguity in questioning was also instanced by another researcher who quoted the question: 'How did you find your last job?', to which the statistician expected a response such as 'From the Labour Exchange', and who was disappointed to get the reply 'Very interesting and enjoyable'.

6.7 TYPES OF QUESTION

There are two main types of question which are commonly used in surveys: open-ended questions and closed questions.

Open-ended questions

An open-ended question, known also as 'free answer' or 'free response', calls for a response of more than a few words. The topic is established for the respondent, who is left to structure a reply as he sees fit. He has considerable freedom in phrasing his answer, which may be lengthy and detailed, and in his own words.

Interviewers are expected to record answers verbatim. There is the danger of interviewer bias intruding through inaccurate recording. An interviewer may, deliberately or otherwise, write down only part of the answer, and this selective recording may not adequately represent the full reply. Where answers are coded later, there is the real danger that some of the essential richness of the original responses will be lost. Frequently it is difficult to compress 'free answers' into a limited number of codings, though this handicap can be reduced by the experience gained during the piloting stage of the survey. This will have led to the drafting of principal classifications.

Open-ended questions are most likely to be used in the early stages of a study, when the unrestricted responses they attract are of value in giving researchers a general map of the area of survey. This can lead to the identification of significant aspects affecting the subject under survey, so that later stages of research can be designed to cover these factors.

In order to build up goodwill with the respondent, it is often advantageous to start a survey questionnaire with an open question. This will allow the respondent considerable latitude in forming his reply. A typical question might be: 'What do you like to do in your spare time?' Most people like to talk about their hobbies and spare-time interests, and will not be reluctant to tell an interviewer something about these activities. In doing so, they are more likely to form a favourable attitude towards the interviewer, and be more willing to answer the remainder of the questions.

Open questions are interesting because of the spontaneity and individual flavour of the replies, but questionnaire designers should not use them indiscriminately. Payne[14] warns: 'remember that the coding of thousands of verbatim replies adds up to a lot of work'. It might, therefore, be wise to see whether it is possible to convert open questions to some form of alternative choice questions.

In unstructured interviews where informal methods of enquiry are customary, open questions predominate. Skilled interviewers are responsible for phrasing questions in a style suitable for their particular audience, and also, of course, in agreement with the objectives of the survey. Interviewers should be briefed as to the extent to which they can probe for further information, to expand or clarify some statement in the open answer.

Additional information can be gathered by using either an 'extension' or an 'echo', related to preceding questions. An extension is a request for further information about something which the respondent has already said. An echo is an exact or nearly exact repetition of the respondent's words by the interviewer.

Questioning techniques to improve the quality of earlier responses include the 'summary', which, as the name suggests, summarizes the information already given by the respondent and asks implicitly or explicitly for confirmation or correction.

Another technique is the 'confrontation', which consists of asking a question that underlines an earlier inconsistency in the respondent's answers. Kinsey tended to use this method in his social surveys.

Payne[14] has suggested that when seemingly inconsistent replies occur, it may be possible to 'discover something' by confronting such respondents with their apparent inconsistencies.

Also popular is the use of 'repetition', which occurs when earlier questions are repeated if they are answered incompletely. They may also be repeated as a check on the accuracy of earlier responses.

These various types of antecedent question cannot easily be incorporated into a questionnaire because they depend on the kinds of responses which informants give. These, of course, will not be known in advance, though interviewers are sometimes allowed to deviate from scheduled questionnaires in certain circumstances. The Government Social Survey classifies questions as factual, opinion, and knowledge. Interviewers are allowed to repeat or explain factual questions and to ask for clarification of answers thought to be vague or ambiguous. Probing can be risky, and it should be done with care and sensitivity. Interviewers should not cause confusion by their questioning techniques. There should be no attempt to force people into certain categories of replies; they may not really know sufficient about the subject under survey to be able to give a definite answer. 'Don't know' may reflect genuine ignorance of the subject, disinterest, or even failure to understand the question. Experienced interviewers should attempt to judge why a respondent is content to give a 'don't know' answer.

The Government Social Survey allows no deviation from printed questions or opinion matters. Probing is likewise forbidden, but interviewers are allowed to repeat the question, if the answer is not clear, by asking a respondent to 'explain a little more fully what he "meant by that"'.

With knowledge questions, respondents should not be pressurized into giving substantive answers. They may not know exactly, and the duty of interviewers is not to inhibit them from saying 'Don't know' in such cases. The interviewers' responsibility is to obtain valid and reliable responses, and these may well include 'Don't know' on some occasions.

Closed questions

Closed questions call for responses which are strictly limited. The respondent is offered a choice of alternative replies from which he is expected to select an answer corresponding to his personal views on a particular subject.

Closed questions may be:

1. Simple alternative questions: these have only two choices of response. For example: YES/NO; GOOD/BAD.

   Respondents are divided into two sub-groups or categories affecting certain basic characteristics of the sample population, such as car ownership. Quantification is simple. These simple questions, sometimes referred to as dichotomous, are useful as filter questions, separating users from non-users, e.g., 'Did you buy product X last week?'

2. Multi-choice questions: these are an extension of simple alternative questions. Respondents are able to choose from a range of possible answers, which are designed to reflect different shades of opinion or variations in use of a product.

Careful pilot work is necessary in order to ensure that the alternatives offered in multi-choice questions provide sufficient scope for respondents to make valid answers. Alternatives must be mutually exclusive, so that respondents are able to differentiate between them without difficulty. Respondents can be shown a list of possible answers or interviewers can read them aloud. As bias can arise from the positioning of entries – extremes attract most attention – some system of randomizing the alternative answers over the sample should be considered. This was done during the IPA National Readership Survey (1954), when the order of periodicals within any one group, e.g., weeklies, was randomized to prevent biased presentation. For example, after establishing by the response given to a simple alternative question, that a respondent has bought a certain product, an interviewer might then ask for further information, such as 'In what kind of shop did you buy it?'

	Coding
Department Store	1
Furniture shop	2
Hardware shop	3
Grocery shop	4
Other (describe)	5

The appropriate code corresponding to the answer given by the respondent is ringed by the interviewer. Multiple answer lists generally include a coding ('Other') for unusual answers, which should be qualified by interviewers. Pre-coding of answers is very helpful when surveys reach the analysis stage.

Some researchers, as Oppenheim[3] notes, use the split-ballot technique in pilot work; the sample is divided into two or more equivalent parts with different answer sequences, so that it is possible to measure the ordinal bias and make allowances for it.

Checklists should be prepared from information gathered during piloting, and these should be as complete as possible. At the same time, respondents may well experience fatigue in reading carefully a lengthy list, and they may take the easy way out and select one or two entries just to close the interview.

Another difficulty with checklists is that entries on them may, in fact, suggest alternatives of which respondents had not previously thought.

An element of bias, may, therefore, affect their choice, particularly in readership surveys. Some respondents may be more inclined to tell interviewers that they read *The Times* than to admit that they are actually regular readers of a newspaper of lower standing. Some checks on this tendency are possible, and 'dummy' features are sometimes mentioned in questions. But even then human memory is fallible and tests have shown that people will state quite positively they recognize advertisements which have never gone beyond the proof stage.

Closed questions could lead to bias by 'forcing' respondents to choose between certain alternatives, but provided the piloting stage has been thorough this risk can be minimized.

There is some evidence[12] that respondents of low socio-economic status and education appear to prefer closed questions to open questions, since they can then answer questions which they do not fully understand without revealing their lack of understanding to interviewers. Survey planners should, therefore, take note of this potential source of bias, and design questionnaires which are likely to result in valid responses. This can depend on factors such as the respondent's degree of knowledge about the subject of the survey and the extent to which this can be established before formal interviewing takes place. Whether open or closed questions are appropriate is a matter to be judged in relation to the problems of specific surveys. In some situations, open questions may be preferable to closed questions; it is not possible to lay down general rules.

Some researchers have attempted to lay down guidelines on the effective use of open and closed questions. The general principle is to start the survey with open questions to encourage response and to obtain some background knowledge which will be useful in later stages of the survey. More specific questions (closed) follow, progressively narrowing down the field of enquiry.

This scheme is advocated by Gallup in his 'quintamensional plan of question design',[22] which outlines five steps in question formation. The first step is to find out whether the informant is either aware of or has thought about the issue under survey. This is followed by some open questions to attract his general feelings on the matter. The third step usually consists of multi-choice questions dealing with specific aspects; these, in turn, are followed by questions to discover the reasons for the particular views just given. The final stage is concerned with finding out how strongly these views are held.

Questions asking for further information – follow-up or 'Why?' questions – need to be handled with care or bias can easily creep in, perhaps from the different intonations given by interviewers to an apparently neutral question. Payne[14] has quoted the question: 'Why do you say that?', which is open to many interpretations according to the stress placed on each of the five words.

Single 'Why?' questions may often result in vague replies. It cannot be assumed that they will produce accurate information. Respondents may give all sorts of reasons why they performed a certain action, and the interviewer may well collect a bundle of useless material. For instance, people may be motivated to visit the theatre or cinema for diverse reasons: they really wanted to see the show; they were bored or had time on their hands in some strange town; they accompanied someone whose company was particularly valued; or they may have wanted to sit down somewhere and perhaps avoid the rain.

Drafting of 'Why?' questions needs to be approached, therefore, with care. For strong personal motives of self-esteem, prestige, or self-defence, respondents may not give reliable answers. They may rationalize their earlier behaviour, either consciously or otherwise, and so researchers may well question the validity of these types of question. Qualitative research methods, such as depth interviews, could be used to supplement the more formalized questioning techniques, and also to act as a useful means of checking the responses obtained from these formal methods. Qualitative research studies have shown that, in many cases, direct questioning is a fairly blunt tool to use in some delicate areas of investigation. Less direct methods may, through their more subtle and sensitive approach, reveal the true motivations of respondents.

6.8 PILOT TESTING

It is vitally important to make sure that the questionnaire is pilot-tested through all the stages of its development.

This may involve re-writing questions several times, changing their sequence or their style of composition, for example, constructing multi-choice questions from the answers received from earlier open-ended questions. This calls for patient attention to detail so that the questionnaire used in the final survey contains questions which are specific, clearly understandable, capable of being answered by the particular population sampled, and free from bias. Well-organized piloting reveals possible misinterpretations owing to ignorance or misunderstanding of questions, and indicates differences in the frames of reference between the researchers and respondents.

In one study,[23] the question: 'Do you like tomato juice?', was changed to: 'Do you like the taste of tomato juice?' Pre-testing revealed that considerable ambiguity surrounded the first phrasing. Some housewives liked the amount of vitamin C their children received from drinking tomato juice, whereas others liked the tenderizing effect that tomato juice has in cooking meat dishes, etc.

Another survey,[23] which was concerned with health care in America, also underlined the importance of testing carefully the phrasing of questions. Matched sets of respondents were given alternative forms of a question, resulting in significant differences in overall responses, as the following examples show:

1. 'Do you think anything should be done to make it easier
   for people to pay hospital or doctor bills?'   82 per cent 'YES'
2. 'Should' replaced by 'could'   77 per cent 'YES'
3. 'Should' replaced by 'might'   63 per cent 'YES'

Only one word was changed, but the alternatives had different connotations for respondents.

Perhaps one of the more amusing insights into the way in which questions are prone to subjective perception occurred in an investigation[24] concerned with respondents' interpretation of survey questions connected with the IPA National Readership Survey. An 82-year-old respondent who answered that 'young people' were not likely to be influenced by violence on television programmes, on subsequent questioning about the ages of the young people he had in mind, said: 'Oh, between 30 and 40'.

Pilot tests should be done under conditions which reflect in miniature the main survey. Respondents should be of the same socio-economic and age distribution as those in the main sample survey. They should be of similar educational achievement and possess any other characteristics which may be of significance in the specific sample; for example, leisure-boat owners. It would also be advisable for those conducting the pilot interviews to be representative of the level of competence likely to be exercised by the subsequent interviewing team. 'Average' interviewing performance will affect the ability of respondents to answer a questionnaire. A wrong impression might be gathered of the efficiency of a questionnaire, if only very experienced interviewers were used at the testing stages.

The arbitrary size of a pilot survey is often taken at about 10 per cent of the main survey, though this would obviously be affected by such factors as time, cost, and practicability.

The value of pilot tests lies in other areas of survey practice, apart from questionnaire construction. They are useful, for example, in testing the accuracy and reliability of sampling frames before extending their use to the main sample survey. They also indicate if extreme differences occur in some measured characteristic, such as the weekly expenditure on food or housing. If the variability is excessive, the results of pilot studies enable researchers to plan the final sample size so that it adequately reflects the population characteristics. With highly variable characteristics, the sample will need to be of a larger size than if there were little variation over significant characteristics. Another important use is in calculating the probable non-response rate from estimates of the results achieved in the piloting process. It might be feasible to vary slightly the sequence of some of the questions in part of the pilot survey, and compare results for effectiveness. Interviewers can also be compared for relative efficiency; they should be asked to report in some detail on respondents' reactions to the pilot questionnaires, and also to give their own estimation of the fieldwork. In addition, the pilot survey will indicate the time and cost involved, and if these are likely to be excessive, modifications may be made before the main survey is put into operation. In 1947, three years before the first complete Census of Distribution was taken, the Board of Trade (now the Department of Trade and Industry) undertook a pilot survey, which covered a few carefully selected areas and trades.

The pilot testing of questionnaires brings with it, therefore, many associated benefits apart from those directly concerned with the phrasing of questions. In the case of mail questionnaires, it is advisable to test not only the questions themselves but also the physical presentation of the survey. This covers such details as the type of paper (colour and texture), the layout of the questions (important for readability), the letter of introduction, and reply-paid facilities. It is important to do everything possible to make mail questionnaires pleasant in appearance and easy to complete. Respondents are influenced by these detailed aspects of presentation and researchers should plan to make their cooperation easy to win.

The length of questionnaires must also be carefully checked, particularly where surveys of a general nature are being planned. Although some respondents will not object to questionnaires of some length, there is evidence that fatigue sets in after a while, and affects the quality of responses. Moser[11] has commented that the length of a questionnaire must be presumed to affect the morale of both parties to the interview and this inevitably results in deterioration in the quality of the data collected. The law of diminishing returns appears to operate with questionnaires after a certain amount of time and effort have been expended. Piloting helps to estimate the likely effects, but no general principles can be laid down.

6.9 MAIL QUESTIONNAIRES

An alternative method of collecting information by questionnaire is to mail it to a list of potential informants (see Chapter 2).

Because of the impersonal nature of mail enquiries, the drafting of effective questions is more important than ever. These must be clearly worded and easily understandable; only one interpretation should be possible. The language in which they are phrased should be suitable for the sample population. In a general level survey, questions may be informally worded. Colloquialisms may help to attract genuine responses.

Open-ended questions must be strictly limited, for they are inclined to cause respondents some anxiety which may well result in rejection of the whole questionnaire. In general, only simple, straightforward questions can be asked which are capable of being answered relatively easily. Apart from special surveys covering professional and technical enquiries, questions should be limited in their field of enquiry and in the depth of knowledge required to answer them.

Questionnaires have to be self-contained, and this means that instructions have to be printed on them to guide respondents. These instructions must be clearly worded and appear next to the questions involved. Simple guides such as: 'Check the answer you prefer', or: 'If No, please go to question 4', should be used.

Where respondents are asked to detail, for example, the number of bedrooms in their house, questionnaire forms should give some simple definitions to ensure that answers are similarly based: 'In counting bedrooms, exclude toilet and bathroom'. The Family Census questionnaire of the Royal Commission on Population has to be filled in personally, though enumerators are allowed to assist where difficulties are experienced. It is a good example of a detailed enquiry with simple, well-positioned instructions.

Particular care is also needed in qualifying time intervals, such as 'week' or 'month'. In verbal enquiries, interviewers can qualify these and so avoid inaccuracies in response. These time intervals should be closely defined in relation to the objectives of the survey, and the questionnaire should state clearly what is meant by 'a week' or 'a month'. If enquiries are concerned with trading results, it would be ambiguous to ask for 'last month's sales'. Many firms have accounting periods that do not precisely coincide with calendar months. In any case, what is meant by 'sales'? Is this meant to refer to orders booked (and received) at head office, invoiced sales, or sales invoiced and paid for? This analytical probing could continue, of course, but it illustrates the need to make mail questionnaires capable of being answered accurately and easily without the intervention of investigators. Respondents appreciate questionnaires with clear instructions and definitions, and are inclined to cooperate more willingly in such enquiries.

Layout and printing are particularly important in mail questionnaires. Enquiry forms should look attractive; a poorly duplicated set of sheets will not impress recipients. Respondents should be approached in the right manner, and this relates to mail surveys just as much as to more personal methods of enquiry, such as interviewing.

The quality of paper, envelopes and printing should all be carefully considered. Layout should assist respondents to reply easily by inserting a cross or tick in appropriate 'boxes' against multi-choice questions. Coding is also helpful, and respondents can be invited to circle or underline the chosen answer. Whatever method is chosen, it is important to ensure that the instructions given are definite, otherwise analysis may be difficult.

Wherever possible, mail questionnaires should be individually addressed with the correct title, initials, and name accurately spelt. (This point is also discussed in Chapter 12.)

It is sound practice to include a covering letter with a mail questionnaire. The letter should outline the objectives of the survey and invite informants to respond by completing and returning the enclosed questionnaire. The letter should stress that information provided by respondents will be treated confidentially, and their names will not be revealed in any subsequent publication. As people may well wonder why they have received a questionnaire on a particular subject, some simple explanation of the method of sampling should be given.

The publishers of *Reader's Digest* are consistent and large users of mail surveys; every year they send out over half-a-million questionnaires. In their view, an accompanying letter is critical for an acceptable response rate.

> It must be constructed to induce the recipient to complete and return the questionnaire, and it has a lot of ground to cover in what should look like a short easy to read communication. It must seek to involve him, tell him why he has been selected, what's in it for him, and why it is important that everyone should reply. It should tell him that his information is either anonymous or confidential, strike a note of urgency and acknowledge that he is doing the sender a favour; tell him about the stamped reply envelope and thank him.[25]

Mail questionnaires have certain limitations, apart from the type of questions which can be asked. Answers must be accepted as written, without the benefit of additional explanations which interviewers could obtain by probing questions. In rare cases, it may be possible to check written answers by personal interviewing, but this would obviously add to the cost of the survey.

In general, mail questionnaires are not a suitable method of enquiry where sample populations are of low intelligence or poorly educated.

Because mail questionnaires can be read through completely before being answered, bias can result from knowing the overall structure of questioning when answering individual questions. With personal interviewing, the pattern of questioning is not immediately apparent, though a different type of bias may arise, namely, interviewer bias.

Responses to mail questionnaires may frequently represent the views of more than one person; this would be undesirable where the survey wanted the views of individuals. Some question-naires, particularly those dealing with technical matters, may profit, however, from being dealt with by specialists in functional areas. (This point is expanded in Chapter 12.)

Personal interviewing allows investigators to supplement the answers given by respondents by some qualitative assessment which adds to the value of the survey. These observational data are lacking in mail enquiries.

Mail questionnaires require some systematic follow-up to increase response to an acceptable level. Apart from official censuses, surveys are voluntary and researchers rely on the goodwill of informants. Follow-up reminders should be tactfully worded, bearing in mind the many quite valid reasons for non-response.

Good planning in the early stages of the survey is important in reducing likely non-response, but it would be unrealistic to expect a high response from a general mail questionnaire. Two reminder letters are often sent to non-respondents, usually at about 14-day intervals. It is advisable to include a copy of the questionnaire, as the original will probably have been mislaid. Research[26] on whether a questionnaire should be included in a follow-up to a mail survey indicated that, on balance, it was worth while to do so. In a mail survey[27] of the ethical perceptions held by advertising managers in the United States, a follow-up duplicate question-naire increased the response rate from 22 per cent to 32 per cent: 218 effective responses were achieved from a stratified sample of 687 advertising agency executives and advertising managers.

Returns from reminders typically decrease over time, and it is necessary to call off the search after some reasonable time has elapsed or the survey will never be completed. Time and cost are factors to keep well in mind. Each reminder will delay the results by several weeks, though this may not be as critical as the quality of the survey findings.

Bearing in mind that respondents and non-respondents may well differ in significant characteristics; for example, age, sex, social group, or location, it is advisable to check the replies attracted by reminder letters against those received from initial respondents. Some valuable clues may be revealed which will lead towards a better appreciation of the subject under survey.

Non-response is a critical limitation of mail surveys, an aspect which is considered at some length in Chapter 12. In general, the response rate tends to be substantially lower than when investigators are employed in surveys.

Although the loss in sample size from non-response must be considered, the problem is really the probability that non-respondents are significantly different in their opinions from respondents. They differ, obviously, in their behaviour towards the survey, but this may not be the only significant difference. The reasons for their lack of response will remain unknown, unless some special effort is made to check these, perhaps by telephoning or personally interviewing a sub-sample of non-respondents. It may be possible to send non-respondents a simpler form of questionnaire and ask them to give some salient features which will act as a guide in assessing the characteristics of non-respondents.

Response rates are closely linked to the type of population sampled, the subject of the survey, and its presentation. Sponsorship, where it can be revealed, may also encourage response. Professional sponsorship of a survey to a population sample which has particular interest in the subject surveyed, generally attracts high response. A survey of women graduates undertaken by PEP in 1954, had a 55 per cent response. A record 81 per cent response was reported by Gray and Corlett to a pilot survey of midwives sponsored by the Working Party on Midwives in 1950.

Controlled studies may be useful in indicating whether or not a particular method of mail enquiry improves response rates.

Some American researchers[28] reported that in an experiment for the Bureau of Census, two types of covering letter were used. One was short and authoritarian; the other, polite and tactful. The former attracted a slightly better response.

A US study[29] examined the effects of 'address personalization' on the response quality of a mailed questionnaire sent to subscribers of a large health maintenance organization in a major metropolitan area in the Mid-West. Of 2375 questionnaires mailed, 762 were returned, with four unusable, resulting in an overall response rate of 31.9 per cent. The hand-addressed group had a 32.6 per cent response, while the computer-generated label respondents had a 31.2 per cent response rate. However, statistical tests showed no significant difference existed, and the researchers suggested that computer-generated labels can continue to be used in mail surveys 'with little concern for negative effects'.

In the UK, valuable research on this matter has been done by Christopher Scott and reported in 'Research on mail surveys'.[30] He found that stamped, self-addressed envelopes produced a higher response rate than business reply envelopes. (Presumably, respondents felt that this reflected a more personal approach.) While the official sponsorship of the survey studied by Scott improved response rates, he reported that 'personalizing' the covering letter made no difference. He concluded that the more interested people are in the subject under survey, the better they will respond, even to quite lengthy questionnaires. A wave-like effect was noted in responses, and it was considered that informants who were particularly interested in the survey problem generally responded earlier.

It is interesting to note that Scott's observation related to social surveys involving individuals, and Dr F. T. Pearce has subsequently reported that correspondence with Scott has indicated that he would not necessarily expect industrial enquiries to reflect similar characteristics. 'The larger or more concerned company might well take longer to reply simply because the appropriate person to respond had to be found, figures to be collected, and so on.'[31]

Two experiments[32] to evaluate the effects of different postage combinations (first class, second class post, and business reply service) and speed of reply showed, for both national and regional samples of shoppers, that whereas the use of second instead of first class postage did not reduce levels of response, the use of business reply facilities resulted in a reduced number of returns compared with hand-stamped cards. Although second class post delayed the reception of the survey and the returns, the cost advantages were considered to outweigh these time-lags.

The findings of the research quoted above are related to a review by Linsky[33] of the research literature on stimulating response to mail questionnaires, who found that the following tactics were very effective:

1. Use of one or more follow-up postcards or letters, and especially reminders by telephone, registered mail, or special delivery letter.
2. Contact with respondents *before* questionnaire is mailed to them.
3. More 'high-powered' mailings, such as special delivery, are superior to ordinary mail, and hand-stamped envelopes are more effective than post-permit envelopes. (Note: compare Scott's report.)[30]
4. Small cash rewards or types of premiums.
5. Sponsoring organization and status of person signing letter accompanying questionnaire.

The use of incentives to boost return of mail surveys should be approached cautiously, otherwise bias may be caused. In the US it is noted that 'a newly minted quarter' is often used successfully with a letter having a postscript reading: 'The enclosed new coin is just a token of our appreciation. It may brighten the day of a child you know.'

Two studies[34] on the effects of including a non-monetary incentive in mail surveys were undertaken on a sample of the general public in the Netherlands and the results showed that an incentive, such as a ball-point pen, produced a higher initial response rate, but follow-ups reduced the effect of the incentive to a non-significant level.

An American study[35] investigated the effectiveness of two types of promised incentives in a mail survey: a personal cash payment ($1) versus a contribution to a charity of the respondent's choice. These two motivational appeals – egotistic and altruistic were made to three groups (each of 150) of Denver area residents. The overall response rate was 30.2 per cent, of which 41 per cent opted for the charity incentive, 26 per cent for no incentive at all.

In 1973, the *Financial Times*[36] launched the European Businessman Readership Survey and achieved a 54 per cent response rate for this mail survey. The survey, now sponsored by 25 newspapers and magazines and several leading advertising agencies, is sent to over 18 000 senior executives in 17 European countries and nearly 10 000 responded: 'try enclosing a crisp dollar bill with the questionnaire, along with the suggestion that they donate the money to charity'.[36]

There is evidence[37] that a higher response rate and lower costs are achieved by ensuring that questionnaires are designed so that they attract the interest of respondents; this may be effected by the content of the cover letter, the form of the questions (structured versus unstructured), the style of print, the use of cartoon characters or symbols in the margins of the questionnaire, or the features of the paper stock (e.g., colour, texture, weight, and scent). Clearly, a well-planned total scheme is necessary to make mail surveys productive, while the focus of the questionnaire on specific topics, for example, professional or personal interest is also of importance.

A mail survey[38] of 3104 American marketing executives involved a two-page questionnaire, equally distributed over white, blue, pink and yellow coloured paper. The covering letter and envelope were white. An overall effective response rate of 25.34 per cent resulted: the only significant difference was found to be between the colours pink and yellow. The researchers suggested that: 'One possible explanation ... is that the former is an action-oriented colour' compared with yellow. Apart from this observed significant difference, 'it appears that colour has little or no influence on response rates of mail questionnaires',[38] but the researchers also wisely suggested that because of the particular population surveyed 'who may have a level of sophistication not normally found with the general public',[38] additional research on more general population sectors would be advisable.

A UK survey[39] researched the relative merits of single-sided and double-sided printing of self-completion questionnaires, and a highly significant statistical difference was found. The former attracted 71 per cent response and the latter 63 per cent from a sample of residential telephone subscribers, although some extra stationery costs were necessarily involved.

The effect of respondent identification on response rates of mail surveys has been the subject of much debate over a long period of time, and some degree of ambivalence exists. A study[40] of 1500 policyholders of a large property and casualty insurance company in the United States focused on two randomly selected groups of insured clients over 65 years of age. One group received an insert with their most recent premium notice discussing reducing premiums and lowering rates for clients over 65 years old. A control group did not receive this insert with their premium notices. Both groups were sent identical questionnaires, except that the experimental group were asked several questions specific to the insert. Respondents were asked to return the questionnaires in pre-addressed, post-paid envelopes, and although they were not asked to identify themselves and keying was not used, provisions for a return address were included on the envelope.

Of the total sample, 66 per cent returned completed questionnaires and names and addresses were included on 890 envelopes (90 per cent of returned questionnaires). In this particular population, it appears that respondents to a mail survey are quite willing to identify themselves, presumably because of their commitment to the insurance company and the degree of trust which they have in that organization.

However, another US-based mail survey[41] – of 500 industrial accountants who were asked questions covering sensitive topics such as role conflict, job tension, and job satisfaction – revealed that anonymity was a significant influence in increasing response rates, a deadline by itself increased response rates, but not at significant levels, whereas a combination of these incentives was significant. The researchers suggest that anonymity seems to be 'especially appropriate' with respondents who are professionally responsive to this factor, and where the survey covers sensitive issues. They also believe that the use of a same-day deadline might be recommended with groups, such as accountants, who have 'an inherent respect and appreciation for deadlines'.

The setting of a deadline in a mail survey[42] of dentists for the American Bureau of Community Health Services resulted in an initial response rate 24 per cent higher from the four groups given a specific date for response. The cost of the follow-up on the remaining sample, including those who did not receive a deadline, was thus reduced by about one-quarter.

Linsky's[33] finding related to the effectiveness of telephone reminders in securing responses to mail surveys was also experienced in research[43] undertaken for AT&T. Because the survey mailing was local, telephone costs compared favourably with those normally incurred in printing, addressing, and mailing reminder postcards.

A study [44] of the factors affecting the response rates of international mail surveys concerned two surveys in 1971 into radio listening habits in Kenya and the Ivory Coast. General conclusions were that while techniques such as registration, personalization, and sending advance postcards may effectively increase response rates in international mail surveys, using more than one of these techniques in a single survey is not likely to be more productive than if only one were used. Of these techniques, registration was consistently more effective and, in addition, provided researchers with data on undelivered letters. If overall registration was too costly, it is suggested that part of the survey could use registered mail, and this would help to provide an estimate of actual return rate.

Research into the impact of asking for race information on a mail survey[45] of domestic telephone subscribers in the United States was conducted in race regions for the AT&T Company. In each geographic sector, a random sample of 300 telephone customers was selected and divided into a control and test group. Both groups received the same questionnaire, except that the test groups were also asked to describe their ethnic background as well as their demographic profile.

The mailing and follow-up procedures were developed from an earlier study [43] for AT&T. An overall response rate of 75 per cent was achieved; the test and control groups displayed, however, some regional variations, but these were not substantial. Hence, it was concluded that 'asking for race information produced neither positive nor negative effects on the response rate'.

By cross-tabulating refusal responses to the race questions with those to other personal demographic questions, such as age, sex, relationship to head of household, and income, it was found that 80 per cent of those who refused to answer the sex question also refused to answer the race question; similarly, 86 per cent of those who refused to give information on relationship to head of household, also refused to provide ethnic data. The researchers suggest that those who refused to provide race information had 'a more general refusal syndrome', and only a very small minority who cooperate in a mail survey are unwilling to be identified in terms of sex, age, relationship to head of household, and race. But the researchers point out that these results may not be fully applicable to other surveys; local telephone services are close to communities, and other parts of the questionnaire covered 'rather well-known and familiar' topics.

To conclude, mail questionnaires are useful where the sample population is widely scattered, or difficult to meet because of professional or other commitments. They are often considered to be particularly attractive in cost terms, but this assessment needs to be more critical. Costs should be more accurately compared against the quality of information obtainable by alternative methods of investigation. Costing should also be comprehensive if it is to be validly used: it should cover all the preparatory work involved in the survey. This is particularly significant in the testing of questionnaires. Mail questionnaires need to be tested several times because their questions must be absolutely clear to all who read them. Also to be considered are the costs of physical presentation (paper, printing, envelopes, postage) and also those arising from preparing, posting, and analysing reminders.

The real cost will eventually be governed by the rate of response, and it would, therefore, be unrealistic to cost out the operation solely on the number of enquiries sent out. It is the number of effective replies which is of vital interest in assessing the comparative costs of mail surveys.

Apart from financial costs, some opinion should be formed as to the time factor involved in mail surveys. This factor is often critical in management decisions, and mail questionnaires 'in general, cannot be regarded as a speedy method of gathering information if by speedy is understood a matter of weeks.[31]

Self-administered questionnaires

Mail surveys are, inevitably, self-administered and have to be completed without the guidance of interviewers. As noted earlier the content and design of the questionnaire is important if a high response rate is to be achieved. Respondents should be helped by clear instructions on how their responses should be recorded and what they should do, for instance, if their answer is either YES or NO to specific guidelines. ('Go to Question X', or 'OMIT next question if you answered "NO" to this question.')

Self-administered questionnaires are not a suitable method of research for heterogeneous populations which, as already observed, include those of low intelligence or poor education. Ognibene's[46] research involving a random sample of 176 men in the New York metropolitan area, confirmed that demographic differences tend to exist between respondents and non-respondents. The lower socio-economic groups responded least well. 'Education, occupation, and income levels of non-respondents are all significantly lower than those of respondents.' (The 117 non-respondents were followed up by telephone.) Ognibene concluded that 'education is probably the key demographic trait, because the other traits are derived from it to a large extent'. He suggested that with higher levels of education, people are more likely to be familiar with research and hence be more willing to cooperate in surveys.

As discussed earlier in this chapter, respondents of low socio-economic status and education have been observed by some researchers[12] to prefer, during personal interviews, closed questions to open questions, because they are then able to respond to questions which they do not fully understand and without revealing their ignorance. This potential source of bias should be borne in mind by researchers when designing self-administered questionnaires.

In some instances it may be possible to deliver questionnaires personally and invite cooperation in the survey, leaving respondents to complete questionnaires at a later time. This strategy would not be feasible with a very large and widely dispersed sample population, but it may be a practical and highly efficient method of attracting high response rates in clustered and relatively small samples which are homogeneous.

Sudman[47] has provided empirical evidence that self-administered questionnaires which were left with household respondents for completion after a lengthy personal interview, attracted high rates of effective response. Rates of response which ranged from 64 per cent to 89 per cent varied according to the characteristics of respondents and the method of return adopted.

An effective response rate of 77 per cent was achieved by Manchester Business School in a household survey[48] in which self-administered questionnaires were left after briefly informing residents of the nature of the research and arranging to pick up the completed surveys in one or two hours' time.

A newer type of self-administered questionnaire was reported in an article[49] in the *Journal of the Market Research Society* during 1978. Two matched samples of women were administered a questionnaire probing bathing habits; one set was interviewed by a conventional field interviewer, while the other group was faced with a computer-controlled television monitor which presented the questions, and a keyboard to be used for responses.

The two sets of resultant data were broadly similar, but there was a marginal tendency to give what might be construed as more 'frank' answers to the computer, and also a marginal tendency to adopt more extreme values of each scale in 'computer responses'. The researchers concluded that computer-administered questionnaires have a role to play in modern market research. (See section on computer-assisted telephone interviewing (CATI).)

6.10 TELEPHONE QUESTIONNAIRES

In Chapter 3 some of the problems facing researchers drawing samples of households from telephone directories were considered, and the technique of random digit dialling (RDD) was discussed. Further attention will now be given to the techniques, and limitations, of the telephone as a survey technique, while in Chapter 12 its particular applications in industrial market research will be reviewed.

The rapidly growing usage of telephone surveys in both consumer and industrial markets is already evident in the UK; during the 1980s, the Association of Market Survey Organizations' (AMSO) returns showed a volume growth of over 500 per cent, particularly related to CATI systems.

The problems and opportunities surrounding the use of the telephone in consumer surveys were the subject of a paper[50] given at the ESOMAR Hamburg Conference, 1974, when it was claimed that the telephone has greater potential as a technique of consumer research than is generally acknowledged. Also, researchers stated that the problems of sampling and other forms of bias are not 'as serious or ineradicable' as is commonly believed. In their view the advantages of using the telephone for consumer surveys outweigh, in many cases, the disadvantages.

The advantages of the telephone, briefly, are as follows:

1. It is convenient.
2. It is imperative.
3. It confers anonymity.
4. It attracts freer response.
5. It can be used at precise times.
6. It is easily controlled and supervised.

The disadvantages were classified as either 'prejudices' or 'serious'. Prejudices included the views that the telephone may be used only for short interviews or for structured interviews, or that it upsets people and that classification data cannot be collected. Such objections were discarded by these researchers for lack of supporting evidence. On the other hand, some real disadvantages were conceded, such as the fact that communication is limited to verbal exchanges – there can be no 'visual aids' to assist the process of questioning. Some inevitable problems arise with noisy and crossed lines and, in some cases, delays when one interviewer is dealing with several telephones.

It was observed that coincidental telephone surveying is a well-established, rapid, and low-cost technique in America. (Telephone subscribers are telephoned while a programme is on the air and asked if they are viewing or listening to it, etc.)

Where a representative sample is not 'a major issue', for example in qualitative pilot enquiries, the telephone was perceived not just to be quicker and cheaper but also better than face-to-face interviewing. The comparative ease of telephone surveying compared with the physical difficulties of locating and interviewing people face-to-face, should not obscure some of its drawbacks, e.g., there are no visual clues to assist the researcher; there is potential wastage because of unobtainable numbers or crossed lines; a growing problem of domestic telephone surveying lies in the increased adoption of answering machines and 'call-screening' equipment. These handicaps are already resulting in significant problems in telephone surveys in the United States.

The problems of acceptability facing telephone techniques in consumer surveys, in particular, were cogently expressed at another ESOMAR Conference.[51] 'Telephone interviewing finds itself in the same position now as ambitious women have experienced over the last few years: having been ignored for so long it has to prove itself better than personal interviewing before it is accepted as an equal.'

The significant advantages of telephone surveys were seen to rely on centralized telephoning where effective supervision ensured sampling accuracy and quality control, apart from the general factors of speed, flexibility, and the ability to conduct interviews at specific times. (See later discussion of central location telephone interviewing.)

In a survey[52] of New York residents, initial interviews were conducted in person, while follow-up data, involving complex attitudinal, perceptual and personal matters, were collected either by telephone or in person. The two methods of collecting follow-up data were studied and it was found that the quality of data collected by telephone was comparable in every way with that obtained by personal interviews.

It should be noted that in the New York survey[52] just quoted, and also in another research project,[53] which involved a telephone survey of Washington DC residents, a prior letter helped substantially the efficiency of the survey.

A comparability study[54] involving residential telephone subscribers in the UK found that for most of the characteristics examined, telephone interviews may have resulted in a small loss of accuracy compared with face-to-face interviewing, but there was no evidence of general bias.

However, a certain degree of 'up-grading' of type of dwelling and understatement of the age of the head of the household occurred.

Research has indicated the potentiality of this method of collecting data, particularly where respondents had prior notice of the intention to ask them to give information about a particular topic over the telephone. In one reported study,[55] telephone interviews with housewives before and after they had dealt with a new ice cream mix, gave valuable clues which enabled the product to be reformulated.

In 1986, the Market Research Society[56] set up a Telephone Research Working Party to develop a telephone survey version of the MRS Interviewer Identity Card Scheme for face-to-face interviewers, so that respondents could verify the authenticity of telephone enquiries. A Freephone Market Research Society facility enables telephone respondents to check the authenticity of a survey without cost to themselves.

Ford of Europe[57] tracks the acceptance of its products and ensures that its design and engineering staff know, almost immediately, exactly what new car buyers feel about their vehicles in the main European markets. This regular quality tracking study uses extensive and highly organized telephone surveys of new car buyers who had about 30 days' experience of their vehicles. Previously, mail surveys had been used, but it was found that, frequently, customers described faults inadequately, or their comments were too brief, vague, or over-generalized: telephone research led to more precise 'diagnosis'.

Telephone ownership of new (as distinct from used) cars is over 90 per cent in the principal European markets, so sample bias was clearly relatively small. The response rate was 'exceptionally good': if this is taken to mean the number of successfully completed interviews as a proportion of all eligible sample respondents, the achieved response rate is between 60 per cent and 80 per cent, according to the market segment and country surveyed. This 'strike rate' is particularly impressive, since average survey time has been 30 minutes.

It is important to note that Ford, working closely with a leading marketing research company, has developed effective telephone survey practice which, for instance, details how interviewers should approach respondents who are told how their names and addresses have been obtained, how the information will be used by Ford, what the expected time of the interview will be, and an assurance that there will be no sales follow-up of any kind.

The practice of telephone surveying compared with face-to-face interviewing of specific US populations in the 1970s was studied[58] by Herzog et al., and it was found that telephone surveys tended to under-represent older adults and those who did participate were disproportionately well educated. (Compare earlier discussion on mail surveys.) However, there 'was little evidence' to suggest that the responses of older people across a range of questions were different from other age groups. So, even though older respondents are under-represented and disproportionately well educated, their aggregate responses do not seem to suffer from systematic biases.

The marked advantages of using the telephone as a method of making personal interview appointments was noted in a health care survey[59] of the elderly in three survey sites in the United States. One random half sample in each site received a lead letter, followed by a telephone call to arrange a personal interview, while the other half sample were sent a lead letter, followed by a personal contact, but with no intervening telephone call. The first type of approach resulted in a 20 per cent saving in data collection costs with only a 1 per cent decrease in response rate. While this particular finding related to a specific sample, viz., 1260 Medicare eligible senior citizens, the researchers feel that, in general, telephone calls to make arrangements for personal interviewing hold 'great potential' in reducing data collection costs with little risk of increasing refusal rates.

An experiment was conducted[60] by the Center for Disease Control and the Opinion Research Corporation to determine the effectiveness of paying physicians monetary incentives to participate in a 20–30 minute telephone survey of influenza immunization. The research design included an introductory letter, guarantee of anonymity, promise of a copy of the report, and expressed willingness to interview the doctor by appointment either personally or by telephone. From a nationwide sample, 150 physicians from each of four main specialities were selected at random. These 600 doctors were then systematically distributed among three equal sub-samples, to which were allocated 'no incentive', $25, or $50 respectively.

Financial incentives appeared to be effective in increasing the response rate to a 25-minute telephone interview among private practice doctors from about 58 per cent ('no incentive') to nearly 70 per cent for the $25 incentive, and around 77 per cent for the higher incentive. How far such incentives could be offered before bias distorted survey findings would clearly be a matter for very careful consideration.

6.11 DEVELOPMENTS IN TELEPHONE SURVEYS

As observed already, the use of the telephone as an effective method of collecting marketing research data has been growing in the United Kingdom; this trend has been emphasized by the development of centralized telephone facilities, now operated by several market research companies and by the extension of electronic technology which has led to computer-assisted telephone interviewing (CATI), direct computer interviewing (DCI), and Viewdata.

Although a discussion of interviewing people in general takes place in Chapter 7, here we extend the present coverage of telephone surveying to include these developments.

Central location telephone interviewing

This system involves a number of interviewers who, from a central location, contact listed telephone subscribers and administer a paper questionnaire, which is then subject to the usual process of editing, coding, and key punching. BMRB, which operates the Telephone Market Research Bureau, has 40 CATI stations, staffed by interviewers working under close, direct supervision. With telephone surveys, it is possible to have very high quality unclustered sample designs; survey time is reduced significantly; all interviewers can be personally briefed; and the time and cost of telephone recalls is minimal. Of the BMRB's Target Group Index (TGI: see Chapter 11), 90 per cent are on the telephone and only 12 per cent have indicated that they will not participate in future research projects.

Central telephone interviewing facilities are now offered by about 100 research companies in the UK, and a detailed list,[61] produced by the Telephone Research Special Interest Group of the MRS, has been published, based on the 1988 *MRS Yearbook*. The Gallup Telephone Research Centre at Thame, Oxfordshire, operates 40 direct lines, and they view telephone surveying as one of the fastest growth areas in marketing research. It is seen to be a particularly ideal way of contacting opinion leaders and obtaining their views on a wide range of topics.

Another leading market research organization, AGB, has a subsidiary, Audience Selection and Telesales Ltd, which runs a 100-line telephone research unit in London and offers clients a full range of research services.

The geographical spread of the sample and the time taken, directly affect the costs of telephone surveying. In 1978, an experiment was conducted[51] in the London area to compare the costs of telephone and house-to-house personal interviewing (random route with 16 randomly selected starting addresses); exactly the same questionnaire was used. With 69 interviewer hours, 300 telephone interviews were achieved and 303 personal interviews with 109 interviewer hours; fieldwork costs per interview were – telephone, 60p, and personal, 74p. This study was limited to local call rates and covered only a very small sample, 'but it demonstrates that telephone interviewing can result in cost savings of around 20 per cent on the fieldwork element ... which, given that executive and analysis costs would be the same in both cases, would result in about a 10 per cent saving on the cost of the whole study'.[51]

However, long-distance dialling results in 'a very different story'. With careful planning of calls, telephone interviewing from a central location to various points across the country 'can cost about the same as door-to-door interviewing'.[51] But it is more expensive if day-time interviewing is required, or where longer questionnaires are involved.

Computer-assisted telephone interviewing (CATI)

This developing method of gathering survey data links computer technology and telecommunications, thus eliminating paper questionnaires. Questions are displayed on a monitor, and responses (pre-coded) are keyed by the interviewer directly into the computer. This direct entry method is termed 'simultaneous direct data entry' (SDDE).

Various CATI characteristics have been developed, but they all involve the same basic procedure: an interviewer is seated before a cathode ray tube terminal, reads the question on the screen to the telephoned respondent, and then records the response by means of the terminal's keyboard.[62]

CATI originated in the United States in the early 1970s, and developed from pioneer work undertaken by AT&T in the late 1960s. Since those early days, CATI systems have spread and are expected to grow significantly. Of the 2500 central telephone interviewing stations in the US 60 per cent were computer assisted in 1983.[63] In the UK, CATI has been slower to diffuse, because of general attitudes towards telephone surveying and, until fairly recently, the incomplete coverage of UK households by telephone.

The Market Research Society set up a working party in 1983 to examine the use and attitudes towards consumer telephone interviewing, and a register[64] of centralized telephone facilities was published; this showed that 19 UK research firms had CATI systems at that time.

British Telecom's Customer Attitude Research Survey (Telcare), costing an estimated £6 million, has significantly boosted CATI in the UK. From three Telcare regional centres specially developed by the research agencies involved, it is planned to complete about 4.5 million interviews by the time that their current three-year contracts expire in 1987. Both business and residential customers are covered by this comprehensive survey; summarized results are readily available for BT's management.

Marplan, a medium-sized UK market research company, now part of Research International, has a 50-line central location telephone facility called Hotline! which covers about 250 different surveys a year, including a large number of foreign language surveys to all parts of continental Europe (Euro Hotline!). Marplan's mainframe computer and CATI are both available to these specific surveys. (Also see Chapter 9 Section 9.6: Telephone panels.)

Distinct advantages associated with CATI are related to the measure of control exercised in the interviewing process: the computer is programmed so that the interview cannot proceed until a valid answer has been keyed in on the keyboard, so a question cannot be inadvertently omitted, or an answer given which is inconsistent with previous responses. Interviewer error is, therefore, eliminated, as also is the need (as with conventional interviewing) to write down replies on to a paper questionnaire which then has to be processed. CATI is also advantageous in that routings (sequence of questioning) are worked out automatically by the computer, and the next relevant question is automatically displayed on the VDU.

Although CATI can steer through quite complex sequences of questioning, it appears to be limited in its ability to handle open-ended questions.

The US Bureau of the Census[65] has studied the possible applications of CATI and concluded that the technology had great potential but, like other data collection methods, conferred specific benefits while also having certain disadvantages.

Its advantages and cost-effectiveness should be greatest in repeated surveys, and in carefully planned and thoroughly pre-tested surveys and censuses with large samples, the types of data collection which constitute the greater part of the Census Bureau's work. Its use in smaller one-time surveys and special applications presents more operational problems and less confidence of cost-effectiveness, although the experience of CATI agencies in the private sector suggests that such applications can also be handled in a cost-effective and timely manner.

The Census Bureau is continuing to test and develop this new interviewing technique.

A specific advantage of CATI is the immediacy of research responses; by sequential sampling techniques interim results of surveys can be readily obtained.[66] (See Chapter 4.)

Computer-assisted personal interviewing (CAPI)

This development of CATI has been pioneered in the UK by Research International. By means of lap-top computers, researchers conduct personal interviews and input data down the telephone. This dramatically reduces the time of the research process: 'Using the CAPI system, a Research International multinational client obtained the data on 500 interviews with US retailers within a week. In the past it would have taken five weeks'.[67]

An innovative application of CAPI occurs with a consumer-based fragrance data base operated by Sandpiper Fragrance Research International Ltd[68] across five countries (UK, USA, France, Germany, and Japan). Groups of consumers in these countries rate each fragrance on 70 attributes, such as 'strong, fruity, fresh, exotic, sharp, and clean', which are presented on computer screens set up in local houses. It is claimed that this method results 'in high quality data with low respondent fatigue; order effects are removed as attribute groups and individual attributes can be randomized'.[68] Stratified probability sampling is used to recruit women aged 16 + ; a minimum sample size per model is 500.

Direct computer interviewing (DCI)

In this system of data collection, the respondent interacts directly with the computer instead of through the medium of an interviewer. (See example given in Section 6.9: Self-administered questionnaires.)

Interactive personal input may be successful in encouraging respondents to give information which they may be unwilling to disclose to an interviewer.[49]

DCI has not been widely adopted either in the US or the UK. Both CATI and DCI share the same technology, but whereas professional interviewers are in charge of the former technique, in the latter case, respondents have to make the inputs themselves.

Some respondents may well feel unable to deal effectively with this new system, although an experimental study [69] by the English Tourist Board in 1981 showed that most respondents found DCI interesting and easy to use. However, older people and women tended to find VDUs and key-board inputs rather intimidating at first. The younger generation, who are exposed to computers at an early age, are likely to regard the DCI technique as conventional as traditional printed questionnaires.

Computer-assisted interviewing using home computers

Over recent years, several versions or derivations of CAPI have developed and some interesting experimental work has been undertaken.

The DISKQ survey method integrates the mail survey with the personal computer (PC). Diskettes programmed with a questionnaire are mailed to a sample of respondents 'who insert them in their PC disk drives, read and answer the questions on their PCs, and mail the diskettes, on which their responses have been recorded, back to the researcher'.

An experiment[70] compared DISKQ with a standard paper questionnaire, and although distinct reservations were made over the findings, the researchers felt that this comparatively new method of surveying may well follow the now acknowledged success of CATI.

The Sociometric Research Foundation[71] developed an interview programme for a home computer which was tested by a panel over a period of six months, and is now used for a consumers' panel by the Dutch Gallup Institute, NIPO.

6.12 INTERACTIVE TELEVISION POLLING (Also see Chapter 2)

In 1982 Granada Television[72] pioneered interactive techniques on television by commissioning AGB Cable and Viewdata to install special electronic equipment in the homes of 130 individuals in the North West ITV region. Viewdata technology enables a domestic television screen to be used, via the telephone, interactively with the television studio. This type of two-way communication is an established feature of cable television programmes in the United States, and allows audiences to take an active and direct part in quizzes, contests, etc.

Each of the 130 'Granada' households was equipped with a 9-inch black and white VDU portable Viewdata set with a built-in numeric key-board; these receivers constituted the 'Talkback' panel. During 'Granada Reports' programmes, the panel are asked direct questions live on air and select one of the possible answers from a pre-coded list shown on the Viewdata screen. Within three minutes, the panel's overall responses are presented in graphic form to the television audience. A typical question (and alternative responses) might be 'Do you think that looking after the baby is women's work?' (Yes; No; Not Sure).

Following these initial trials, AGB recruited, in 1983, a nationally representative panel of 500 who were equipped with the necessary hardware. Granada also extended its regional panel to about 270 homes, and by June 1983, had a national interactive panel of around 600 homes.

Apart from 'instant polling' on the popularity of television programmes, and social and political matters, Viewdata has been used in advertisement testing [73,74] by Beecham's, Cadbury-Schweppes, Sony, and Unilever. After viewing (at arranged times), respondents complete a questionnaire projected on their screens; results are analysed by AGB computer overnight, and given to clients the following day. 'What makes Talkback different from other ad testing systems is that respondents watch the commercials at home, in their normal environment, and that the results are available the next day.'[74] Of course, this technique, which is restricted to simple multi-choice responses, only allows a fairly superficial evaluation of advertisements to be made. Further discussion of advertising research occurs in Chapter 11.

6.13 HAND-HELD MARKET RESEARCH TERMINAL (MRT)

Ferranti Computer Systems has successfully developed a low-cost, hand-held data capture terminal specifically for marketing research surveys. It is battery operated (rechargeable) with a key-board for data entry and electronic storage which allows for direct feeding into a computer for processing.

The MRT 100 can transfer its stored data, in conjunction with a low-cost acoustic coupler or modem via a telephone line to a computer. Alternatively, the answer modules (which can store up to 3000 'multi-punch' answers) could easily be posted to a central office and transcribed there. Up to 12 answers can be recorded for multi-choice questions; answers are displayed as well as recorded.

The MRT 100 weighs only 1.5 kg, and its robust, weatherproof design makes it very suitable for outdoor surveying. Since launching the MRT in November 1984, Ferranti has had considerable success in selling both to dealers and direct to users, including RBL and NOP.

6.14 SUMMARY

Questionnaires are a vital element of the total market research design; they demand skill in composition.

Various methods of applying questionnaires are used: personal interviewing, telephone, mail (including self-administered).

Questionnaires should be carefully planned to cover the needs of specific research objectives. In devising questions, care must be taken to avoid bias, e.g., leading questions. A favoured sequence of questioning is known as 'funnelling': from the general to the specific.

Two main types of question are commonly used: open-ended and closed; the latter may be dichotomous (simple alternative) or multi-choice.

Pilot testing of questionnaires is imperative: this should be done with representative sub-samples.

Mail questionnaires must be self-contained and clearly worded; no interviewer will be present to assist respondents. The real costs should be based on the number of effective replies received; response rates tend to be low. Every aspect of mail survey presentation deserves special attention in order to boost responses.

Telephone surveys are growing in popularity with the rapid diffusion of telephones in UK households. Centralized location telephone interviewing is growing in both industrial and consumer surveys. CATI and DCI are newer developments linking computer technology and telecommunications, moving from a paper and pencil technology to an electronically based research approach.

Interactive television polling (Viewdata) has been successfully pioneered in the UK by Granada Television, and also used in advertisement testing.

REFERENCES

1. Barker, R. T., and A. B. Blankenship, 'The manager's guide to survey questionnaire evaluation', *Journal of Market Research Society*, vol. 17, no. 4, October 1975.
2. Ferber, R., and M. Hauck, 'A framework for dealing with response errors in consumer surveys', *Proceedings of the Fall Conference*, 1964, American Marketing Association.
3. Oppenheim, A. N., *Question Design and Attitude Measurement*, Heinemann, London, 1968.
4. Gowers, Sir Ernest, *Plain Words; A Guide to the Use of English*, HMSO, London, 1948.
5. 'Peterborough', *Daily Telegraph*, 27 November 1978.
6. 'Peterborough', *Daily Telegraph*, 18 December 1980.
7. Belson, W. A., *The Impact of Television*, Crosby Lockwood, London, 1967.
8. Morton-Williams, Jean, 'Questionnaire design', in: *Consumer Market Research Handbook* (2nd Edn), Robert Worcester and John Downham (eds), Van Nostrand Reinhold Company, Wokingham, 1978.
9. Political and Economic Planning, 'Sample surveys – Part One', PEP Report, vol. 16, no. 313, Political and Economic Planning, London, May 1950.
10. Lind, Harold, 'If you ask a silly question', *Daily Telegraph*, 21 September 1988.
11. Moser, C. A., and G. Kalton, *Survey Methods in Social Investigation*, Heinemann, London, 1971.
12. Richardson, S. A., Dohrenwend, and Klein, *Interviewing – Its Forms and Functions*, Cornell University, Basic Books, 1965.
13. Ferber, Robert, and P. J. Verdoorn, *Research Methods in Economics and Business*, The Macmillan Company, Canada, 1969.

14. Payne, S. L., *The Art of Asking Questions*, Princeton University Press, 1957.
15. Ferber, Robert, *Market Research*, William Hill, New York, 1949.
16. Schuman, Howard, Graham Kalton, and Jacob Ludwig, 'Context and contiguity in survey questionnaires', *Public Opinion Quarterly*, vol. 47, no. 1, spring 1983.
17. McFarland, Sam, 'Effects of question order on survey responses', *Public Opinion Quarterly*, vol. 45, no. 2, summer 1981.
18. Nolan, John, 'Behaviour and attitude research' in *The Effective Use of Market Research*, Johan Aucamp (ed.), Staples Press, London, 1971.
19. Henry, Harry, *Motivation Research*, Crosby Lockwood, London, 1963.
20. McKennell, A. C., 'Aircraft noise annoyance around London (Heathrow) Airport', Social Survey Report 337, Central Office of Information.
21. Brierley, P. W., 'Ask a silly question!', *Statistical News*, no. 30, August 1975.
22. Gallup, George, 'Qualitative measurement of public opinion. The quintamensional plan of question design', *Public Opinion Quarterly* II, American Institute of Public Opinion, 1947.
23. Green, Paul E., and Donald S. Tull, *Research for Marketing Decisions*, Prentice-Hall, New York, 1975.
24. Belson, William A., 'Respondent misunderstanding of survey questions', Survey Research Centre, LSE, Reprint Series 40, in *Polls* vol. 3, no. 4, 1968.
25. Whitley, Edward W., 'The case for postal research', *Journal of Market Research Society*', vol. 27, no. 1, 1985.
26. Heberlein, Thomas A., and Robert Baumgartner, 'Is a questionnaire necessary for a second mailing?', *Public Opinion Quarterly*, vol. 45, no. 1, spring 1981.
27. Ferrell, O. C., and Dean Krugman, 'Response patterns and the importance of the follow-up duplicate questionnaire in a mail survey of advertising managers', *European Research*, vol. 11, no. 4, October 1983.
28. University of Michigan, 'Field methods in sample interview surveys' in *The Interviewers' Manual*, Survey Research Center, University of Michigan, 1951.
29. Wunder, Gene C., and George W. Wynn, 'The effects of address personalization on mailed questionnaires response rate, time and quality', *Journal of Market Research Society*, vol. 30, no. 1, January 1988.
30. Scott, Christopher, 'Research on mail surveys', *Journal of the Royal Statistical Society*, vol. 24, 1961.
31. Industrial Marketing Research Association, *Postal Questionnaires*, G. R. Swain (ed.), Industrial Marketing Research Association, Lichfield, 1967.
32. Brook, Lindsay L., 'The effect of different postage combinations on response levels and speed of reply', *Journal of Market Research Society*, vol. 20, no. 4, 1978.
33. Linsky, Arnold S., 'Stimulating responses to mail questionnaires: A review', *Public Opinion Quarterly*, vol. 39, spring 1975.
34. Nederhof, Anton J., 'The effects of material incentives in mail surveys' (two studies), *Public Opinion Quarterly*, vol. 47, no. 1, spring 1983.
35. Robertson, Dan H., and Danny N. Bellenger, 'A new method of increasing mail survey responses: contributions to charity', *Journal of Marketing Research*, vol. 15, no. 4, November 1978.
36. Skapinker, Michael, 'The reading habits of Europe's managers', *Financial Times*, 3 April 1989.
37. Dommeyer, Curt J., 'Does response to an offer of mail survey results interact with questionnaire interest?', *Journal of Market Research*, vol. 27, no. 1, 1985.
38. Fullerton, Sam, and H. Robert Dodge, 'The impact of color on the response rates for mail questionnaires', in: *Developments in Marketing Science*, vol. 10, p. 413, 1988.
39. Hyett, G. P., and D. J. Farr, 'Postal questionnaires: Double-sided printing compared with single-sided printing', *European Research*, vol. 5, no. 3, May 1977.
40. Skinner, Steven J., and Terry L. Childers, 'Respondent identification in mail surveys', *Journal of Advertising Research*, vol. 20, no. 6, December 1980.
41. Futrell, Charles, and Richard T. Hise, 'The effects of anonymity and a same-day deadline on the response rate to mail surveys', *European Research*, October 1982.
42. Roberts, Robert E., 'Further evidence on using a deadline to stimulate responses to a mail survey', *Public Opinion Quarterly*, vol. 42, no. 3, autumn 1978.

43. Roscoe, A. Martin, Dorothy Lang, and Jagdish N. Sheth, 'Follow-up methods, questionnaire length, and market differences in mail surveys', *Journal of Marketing*, vol. 39, no. 2, April 1975.
44. Eisinger, Richard A., W. Peter Janicki, Robert L. Stevenson, and Wendel L. Thompson, 'Increasing returns in international mail surveys', *Public Opinion Quarterly*, vol. 38, no. 1, spring 1974.
45. Sheth, Jagdish, N., Arthur Le Claire, Jnr, and David Wachspress, 'Impact of asking race information in mail surveys', *Journal of Marketing*, vol. 44, winter 1980.
46. Ognibene, Peter, 'Traits affecting questionnaire response', *Journal of Advertising Research*, vol. 10, no. 3, June 1970.
47. Sudman, Seymour, *The Cost of Surveys*, Aldine Company, Chicago, 1967.
48. Chisnall, Peter M., 'Effecting a high response rate to self-administered household questionnaires', *European Research*, vol. 3, no. 4, July 1976.
49. O'Brien, Terry, and Valerie Dugdale, 'Questionnaire administration by computer', *Journal of Market Research Society*, vol. 20, no. 4, 1978.
50. Miln, D., and D. Stewart-Hunter, 'The telephone in consumer research', in: *The Challenges Facing Marketing Research: How do we Meet Them?*, ESOMAR Conference, Hamburg, September 1974.
51. Jarvis, Ian, 'Practical experience with central telephone interviewing' in *Value for Money in Market and Social Research*, ESOMAR Conference, Bristol, September 1978.
52. Rogers, Theresa F., 'Interviews by telephone and in person: Quality of responses and field performance', *Public Opinion Quarterly*, vol. 40, no. 1, spring 1976.
53. Dillman, Don, Jean Gorton Gallegos, and James H. Frey, 'Reducing refusal rates for telephone interviews', *Public Opinion Quarterly*, vol. 40, no. 1, spring 1976.
54. Hyett, G. P., and G. S. Morgan, 'Collection of data by telephone, and validation of factual data', *European Research*, July 1976.
55. Miln, David, 'Telephone research does work', *Marketing*, December 1976.
56. Deacon, Ruth, 'Telephone research matters', *MRS Newsletter*, November 1987.
57. Smith, R. P., and A. F. K. Watson, 'Product excellence on a complex product through telephone interviewing', *European Research*, January 1983.
58. Herzog, A. Regula, Willard L. Rodgers, and Richard A. Kulka, 'Interviewing older adults: A comparison of telephone and face-to-face modalities', *Public Opinion Quarterly*, vol. 47, no. 3, autumn 1983.
59. Bergsten, Jane Williams, Michael F. Weeks, and Fred A. Bryan, 'Effects of an advance telephone call in a personal interview survey', *Public Opinion Quarterly*, vol. 48, no. 4, 1984.
60. Gunn, Walter J., and Isabelle N. Rhodes, 'Physician response rates to a telephone survey: effects of monetary incentive level', *Public Opinion Quarterly*, vol. 45, no. 1, 1981.
61. Register of Central Telephone Interviewing Facilities, Telephone Research Special Interest Group, *MRS Newsletter*, December 1988.
62. Roshwalb, I., and L. Spector, 'New methods of telephone interviewing', 32nd ESOMAR Congress, September 1979.
63. Barnard, Philip, 'Research in the USA', *Journal of Market Research Society*, vol. 26, no. 4, October 1984.
64. Collins, M., 'Telephone interviewing in consumer surveys', *Market Research Society, Newsletter*, no. 11, October 1983.
65. Nicholls, William L. II, 'Development of CATI at the US Census Bureau', *Proceedings of the American Statistical Association Survey Methods Section*, Toronto, Canada, 1983.
66. Fry, Paul, 'The use of sequential sampling techniques (SST), in market research', *Market Research Society Conference Proceedings*, 1983.
67. Slingsby, Helen, 'A high street revolution', *Financial Times*, 30 September 1990.
68. Bigham, Jane, 'A new approach to international fragrance research', in: *Comparability Across Borders*. Seminar on International Marketing Research, ESOMAR, Amsterdam, November 1988.
69. Bartram, Mary M., and Antony E. C. Eastaugh, 'Let respondents speak for themselves!', Market Research Society Conference, 1981.
70. Higgins, C. A., T. P. Dimnik, and H. P. Greenwood, 'The DISKQ survey method', *Journal of Market Research Society*, vol. 29, no. 4, October 1987.
71. Saris, Willem E., and W. Marius de Pijper, 'Computer assisted interviewing using home computers', *European Research*, vol. 14, no. 3, July 1986.

72. Read, Susan, 'Interactive television: its role within a programme company', Market Research Society Conference, 1984.
73. Clemens, J., 'Ad testing via the TV screen', *AGB Newsletter*, 18 November 1983.
74. Douglas, Torin, 'Seeing the benefits of talking back about TV', *Marketing Week*, 25 November 1983.

SEVEN

INTERVIEWING

7.1 INTRODUCTION

In 1989, Mintel[1] commissioned a national survey of UK adults which showed that just under half of all adults had taken part in some form of market research during the past five years, while about two-thirds had been involved at some time or other. Those most likely are A–B social class, women, 35–44 age group, reflecting the importance of these types of people in the purchase of consumer goods and services.

With in-home research, face-to-face interviews continue to dominate; 27 per cent of the public having experienced this form of research during the past five years. It is also interesting to note Mintel's findings – that 60 per cent of adults found market research interviews enjoyable, and nearly 80 per cent felt that it was in their own interests to cooperate with market research interviewers because, as a result, they expected improvements to products and services. Over 85 per cent felt that market research companies treated their responses with complete confidentiality.

7.2 DEFINITION OF INTERVIEW

An interview has been defined as: 'a conversation directed to a definite purpose other than satisfaction in the conversation itself.[2] It is concerned with a purposeful exchange of meanings, and it is this interaction between the interviewer and the respondent which contributes so much to the success of the interview. This give and take and free exchange of communication lie at the root of a successful interview. The psychological atmosphere of an interview is at least as important as the mechanics of the interviewing process, for effective interviewing requires 'insight into the dynamics of interaction'.[3] If this interaction is treated with skill and sensitivity, the data collected during the interview will be accurate and, perhaps, unique. The quality of the interview depends largely on the interviewer developing a relationship with the respondent which will encourage good communication. This is a two-way process to which both interviewer and respondent subscribe in fulfilling their particular roles. The distinctive role of the interviewer is concerned with securing valid information about a particular problem which has been carefully defined in the objectives of the survey.

The interview must, therefore, be directed and controlled by the interviewer if it is to fulfil its essential function of a conversation with a purpose.[2] The techniques used should be those that are most likely to result in data which will satisfy these objectives. Flexibility is, therefore, an important attribute of the interviewing process, and there is no one ideal method which can be applied generally. There are some techniques which are more appropriate than others in particular cases; the success of the survey rests on the skill with which the interviews have been devised.

Where the information to be gathered from each respondent is of a similar kind, e.g., consumer buying habits, and it is planned to submit identical questions to all respondents, some form of standardized questionnaire can generally be constructed to be administered in the same way to all those taking part in the survey. This materially assists in the analysis and processing of data.

An alternative form of the standardized (or structured) interview replaces the formal questionnaire by allowing interviewers to vary the wording or sequence of questions in order to attract maximum response from individual informants. This method is discussed in Chapter 6.

It is particularly suitable where respondents are likely to be heterogeneous and the subject matter of the survey includes topics which are not customarily discussed freely. The interviewer is free to choose the most suitable timing for certain questions, though this places a greater responsibility on him, and also makes recording and analysis more difficult.

It is possible, of course, to combine 'schedule' and 'non-schedule' interviews effectively by treating simple factual details in a systematic manner and applying a more flexible approach to questions covering more sensitive areas of behaviour, or those which may be more vulnerable to language barriers.

The other general classification of interview, typified as non-standardized, does not attempt a systematic collection of the same classes of data from every respondent. There are many varieties of unstructured interviews, and they are often used as a preliminary to prepare the structure for more formalized techniques. In this way, the salient features of a problem can be identified, though valid comparisons of individual behaviour are not possible.

In Chapter 8, yet another type of interview, termed depth or focused interview, will be discussed. This kind of interview, which calls for special skills, is concerned with survey topics for which direct questioning would not be likely to result in valid information being given by respondents, perhaps for reasons of self-defence, or because they may rationalize their behaviour when answering 'straight' questions. This indirect approach to gathering 'sensitive' information could not be undertaken by the general level of survey interviewers. The method is also expensive and is, therefore, limited in its application.

7.3 FORMS OF INTERVIEW

Three forms of interview are commonly used:

1. *Limited response*: the informant is expected to respond to a series of questions, generally administered in a predetermined order. Closed questions tend to outnumber substantially open questions. As the description suggests, the scope of the informant's response is distinctly limited: the topic is closely defined and the respondent is expected to rely on a few words.
2. *Free response*: this method gives the respondent a great deal of freedom in answering questions arising from some general points of discussion made by the interviewer. Open questions are more general than closed questions, and the interviewer has the delicate task of encouraging the respondent to take an active part in the interview while, at the same time, keeping irrelevant discussion to a minimum.

3. *Defensive response*: the interviewer attempts to exert some pressure on the respondents over a range of topics, and the latter is expected to defend himself by refusing to be forced into any situation which is not really agreeable to him. There are few published examples of this type of interview, and it has been sharply criticized as being antithetical to well-established survey practice, namely, the establishment of a good relationship between respondent and interviewer. Kinsey, in his surveys of sexual behaviour, used the technique widely, and his respondents do not appear to have objected to his style of interviewing.

It may well be possible to incorporate more than one of these techniques in a particular interview, and some leading American researchers have commented that: 'There is need ... to question the widely held tacit assumption that an entire interview must embody the same general form of strategy'.[4]

7.4 INTERVIEWING TECHNIQUES ADJUSTED TO TYPES OF RESPONDENT

It has been noted that there are sensitive areas of enquiry which need skill and delicacy on the part of the interviewer in order to attract cooperation. These 'threatening' or 'taboo' subjects cover personal and intimate matters, which respondents may be reluctant to discuss openly, perhaps fearing that self-revelation *may* possibly disclose deviations from norms. To be successful in such cases, the interviewer must be able to adjust his technique to the needs of the respondent. He should, therefore, form some estimate of the personality of the person being interviewed. Admittedly, this is no easy task, for it is known that 'one of the most disconcerting sources of error in judging personality is the tendency for judgements on specific traits to be reflections of the interviewer's general impression of people.'[2]

This 'halo' effect, identified by Thorndike in 1920, was refined by Bingham (1939), who distinguished between the valid and invalid halo. The former refers to the tendency for ratings to reflect the actual correlation among themselves, e.g., there will probably be some relationship between 'emotional maturity' and 'dependability', since they are, in fact, correlated. 'Invalid halo refers to the excess of overlap beyond that to be expected due to correlation among the traits under consideration'.

Years ago, Walter Lippmann drew attention to the phenomenon termed 'stereotype'; that we frequently have 'pictures in our heads' of the supposed appearance of members of a given race, class, occupation, or social group. In 1926, Rice clearly showed the power of 'stereotypes' in affecting judgement, and Paterson (1930),[5] after careful study of this problem, stated that 'The impression that personality can be judged from physical appearance is a myth which stubbornly defies extinction'.

The classical study done by Sir Charles Goring, of the English prison service, at the beginning of this century, to disprove that there is a specific criminal type with recognizable physical stigmata, effectively disposed of this misleading assumption. However, Bingham and Moore suggest 'there may well be some connection between anatomy and physiology, with temperament and ability, but it is not obvious or readily observable'.[2]

It is as well for interviewers to bear in mind that this phenomenon may influence their relationship with respondents, and, to some extent, bias the interview. Because of the interpersonal nature of interviews, respondents also may form a stereotyped judgement of interviewers, and refuse to cooperate or respond unwillingly. The subtle influence of stereotypes may, therefore, extend to both parties in an interview.

Motivation within an interview can be either extrinsic or intrinsic. Extrinsic motivation occurs when a communication is made in order to influence, in some way, the person addressed. For example, the communicator may feel it worth while to give certain information in the hope or belief that it will lead to some desired change or action taking place. There is some expectancy of a 'pay-off' of some personal benefit. Intrinsic motivation depends more directly on the personal relationship between interviewer and respondent, who may feel disposed to talk freely about matters of interest even though the interview will not benefit him or her directly. This intrinsic motivation is at the heart of a good interview, and it again underlines the importance of the interviewer, who must be able to establish sound social relationships of goodwill and trust with those being interviewed. He or she should not attempt to 'score off' the respondent, arousing suspicions and encouraging the use of defensive tactics, such as suppression, rationalization, and repression. Lack of trust or confidence merely buries the repressed material deeper: 'direct probing or clever subterfuges more often than not merely increase motivation to keep repressed material hidden'.[2]

The fact that certain needs are repressed does not prevent them from influencing behaviour. Interviews make certain demands on informants; they should be encouraged to respond with a natural flow of information, and helped to overcome fears and inhibitions which may frustrate the purpose of the interview.

7.5 INTERVIEWERS

The interaction between those taking part in an interview is vital to the success of this method of obtaining information. Relations between the parties are complex, and are coloured by both conscious and unconscious reactions which can distort or, happily, attract communication.

Interviewers are active in the area of marketing research which frequently involves submitting questionnaires to carefully selected samples of a defined population. They are an important and essential link in the chain of research and their efficiency and reliability influence the whole structure of research. It is unfortunately evident that interviewers are one of the main sources of error in field research. Although some research has been done on interviewer selection and training methods, there does not appear to have been a great improvement on the unsatisfactory situation which Boyd and Westfall[6] reported in 1955. They recommended then that there should be systematic research on the development of criteria for selecting, training, and supervising interviewers. More recently, Moser[7] has indicated that the selection, training, and supervision of interviewers are closely bound up with response errors.

Selection of marketing research interviewers is a difficult task because it is frequently hard to assess the suitability of candidates. It would seem that there is no such person as a good 'interviewer-type' with definable characteristics. Interviewing is such a personal matter that some types of people seem to be better for some kinds of survey than for others, and to be able to establish *rapport* more easily with some respondents than with others. There appears to be a strong argument in favour of fitting interviewers to interviewing situations, and selecting applicants for their likely aptitude for specific areas of research. This means that selectors must have intimate knowledge of the nature of the surveys for which they are recruiting staff. An interviewer profile should be drawn up as a guide to the selection of candidates.

The selection process will probably be based on the scrutiny of application forms, which should give a useful indication of the ability of candidates to complete, accurately and neatly, detailed information. These background data will give personal details of value in forming a shortlist for interview. At the interview, some clerical tests could be set to assess the general suitability of the applicant to undertake fairly routine work. There is no general agreement on the value of intelligence and aptitude tests in the selection of interviewers, for some applicants appear to be able to pass such tests without ever being able to conduct a satisfactory interview.

The 'dummy-interview' technique, normally applied after the candidate has been initially selected, can be extremely effective in isolating good interviewers from those less suitable. It involves exposing interviewers to a series of interview situations which have been 'rigged', and in which informants are in collusion with the sponsors. 'Difficult' situations can be simulated to test and evaluate interviewers' reactions. The information they are able to collect is assessed against already known data. While this type of test is valuable, it tends to be costly in time and money, but it may well be worth while where investigations cover areas of critical importance.

In practice, interviewers seem to be selected in various ways, some more systematic than others. Leading research organizations tend to have more rigorous methods of selection. These methods are particularly effective with the Government Social Survey which employs about 200 part-time interviewers throughout the UK. The British Market Research Bureau (BMRB) has paid particular attention to the recruitment and training of interviewers; only 1 in 10 of those who apply to join BMRB's field force is eventually employed. A three-day general training programme involves market research theory and practice, including 'live' interviewing under supervision. BMRB's standard quality procedures entail regular field supevision of interviewers (10 per cent of assignments; also 5 per cent personal check of all surveys); the first day's work by each interviewer is 10 per cent checked by area office and errors immediately identified and rectified. Further checks occur during the editing and coding stages. The average interviewer has at least three years' BMRB interviewing experience; supervisors have an average of more than 10 years with the company.

It is interesting to note the BMRB pays interviewers by the (six-hour) day, *not* by completed interviews; and *not* by day subject to completion of a stipulated number of interviews.

Experienced researchers are concerned about the quality of interviewing in general. Selection processes often appear to be arbitrary and unrelated to the importance of the task. If marketing research is to develop improved techniques leading to greater validity and reliability, the role of the interviewer deserves serious consideration. Some of the biases with which 'the interview situation ... is fraught'[8] can be reduced, or even eradicated, by sound methods of selection.

A Working Party Report[9] of the Market Research Society gave guidance on factors such as age, personality type, speech, and education which were considered to be of primary importance for the selection of suitable interviewers.

A substantial proportion of market research interviewing is undertaken by women, mostly on a part-time basis. The Market Research Society Working Party Report[9] noted that women interviewers tend to be preferred for several reasons, among which are that: they are more suitable for interviewing housewives; they are available fairly readily; they have a natural aptitude for routine and repetitive work; they are equally acceptable to interviewees of both sexes; they are not so aggressive; and they are more likely to be invited into homes when fairly lengthy interviews are necessary. Joan MacFarlane-Smith[10] has observed that men who are available for part-time interviewing tend to be 'untypical and non-homogeneous', but that they are often preferred to women for industrial and technical interviewing and then usually on a full-time basis.

Effective selection needs to be followed by a systematic training. The character of this will vary according to the experience of the recruits and the nature of the work they are expected to do. Basically it should cover the general objectives of the survey, the survey methods, and the techniques of interviewing. Some practice sessions should be included, and it would be helpful to distribute a training handbook to new members of the research team. It is important that they have a clear understanding of the responsibility which interviewing bears to the success of the whole research operation.

As with selection methods, the techniques used in interviewer training vary considerably from formal short courses, which include supervised fieldwork and periodic assessment, down to virtually no actual training, survival being dependent on achieving an acceptable level of competence in the field. Again, the Government Social Survey has a well-organized training programme for interviewers; the BMRB's interview scheme has already been given in outline.

The value of experience to interviewers was the subject of research done by Durbin and Stuart[11] to assess the success of experienced professional and inexperienced student interviewers in *obtaining* interviews. The former were from the Government Social Survey and the British Institute of Public Opinion, and the latter from the London School of Economics. There was a striking difference in the 'success rates' (questionnaire wholly or partially completed) between the two classes of interviewers, though there was hardly any difference between GSS interviewers and BIPO interviewers. This is an interesting finding in view of the extra training undergone by GSS interviewers.

The effectiveness of short, intensive training courses against longer, more extensive courses, was studied by the American Bureau of the Census in 1951, and its findings were strongly qualified. It was conceded that shorter courses might, in fact, be adequate, provided they covered the essential features of interviewing.

Some training is obviously necessary, but the small amount of research which has been published does not provide an adequate basis on which to form valid judgement. Further research is desirable, and meanwhile practitioners should at least give their staff a thorough briefing on the objectives of the survey, so that they are able to appreciate the value of their contribution as interviewers.

Some system of field supervision is necessary in order to maintain the quality of interviewing. The BBC Audience Research Department and the Government Social Survey operate well-organized systems of supervision on a regional basis. The local supervisor is a valuable link in communication between head office and interviewing staff. Some systematic check, often 10 per cent of calls made by interviewers, should be the responsibility of the supervisor. Completed questionnaires should be scrutinized for inaccuracies or inconsistencies, and results obtained by individual interviewers compared to detect possible biases. If response rates are found to vary substantially, the supervisor should investigate the work of those interviewers who fail to achieve certain accepted standards. As in other areas of management, acceptable standards of achievement are laid down and deviations from norms are subjected to special investigation to establish the causes. The supervisor should not be content with mere 'policing' of the activities of interviewers. A vital part of the supervisory task is to motivate field staff by positive training methods, encouraging them to achieve better response rates, advising them on the inevitable problems which will arise, and generally building up morale in an occupation which, at times, exposes people to considerable frustration.

Morale is affected by working conditions, which include the type and level of payment. Pay rates are generally low for interviewers, and no doubt this contributes to the high labour turnover. Some professional surveys operate differential rates and interviewers are graded, as in the Government Social Survey which has four grades determining remuneration and type of work involved. Survey interviewing can be arduous, both physically and mentally; it calls for painstaking and conscientious attention to detail with an ability to assess the character of the respondent. Where informal interviewing takes place, the responsibility of the interviewer is considerable and great skill and background knowledge are demanded. The success of interviews depends so much on the quality of interviewing, that it would seem prudent to recruit the right type of applicant by offering attractive terms of payment and reasonable types of assignment.

In order to protect professional standards and to allay any possible fears experienced by members of the public approached for interviewing purposes, the Market Research Society, in 1981, introduced the MRS Interviewer Identity Card system. This well-devised scheme has the full support of the leading survey firms, and it forms part of the MRS Code of Conduct (see Chapters 14 and 16 for further discussion, and also refer to the MRS's initiative to protect the quality of telephone interviewing, as given in Chapter 6). The MRS Interviewer Identity Card (MRS IID Card) enables an individual member of the public to check the genuineness of the intended interview.

7.6 DUTIES OF INTERVIEWERS

Interviewers are responsible for collecting specific kinds of information that meet the objectives of particular surveys. Interviewers are a major influence on this process of communication which may relate to many different topics demanding, at times, expert knowledge as in highly technical enquiries. Aspects of this type of interviewing are discussed in Chapter 12. The majority of marketing research surveys, however, do not require interviewers to have knowledge in depth of the area of research. They should be given sufficient information about the subject of the survey and its objectives to enable them to do a worthwhile job of interviewing.

First duty of interviewers

The first duty of interviewers is to locate people who fulfil the requirements of the chosen method of sampling. With random samples respondents are pre-selected and interviewers are given lists of randomly selected persons who are to be interviewed. The responsibility of interviewers is limited to making effective contact with those listed. They will be given instructions on the problem of non-response, call-backs, etc. In quota sampling, interviewers have greater personal responsibility as they select respondents, within the limits of quota controls set by the researcher. This greater freedom is not without some danger to the quality of the survey findings, though it makes the task of interviewers rather less onerous.

Second duty of interviewers

The second responsibility of interviewers is to translate contacts into effective interviews. This may sometimes involve several call-backs in the case of random sampling, so interviewers need to be persistent and tactful. It is really quite surprising how willing people are to be interviewed, and after a preliminary warming-up period, how freely they are prepared to talk about a wide range of topics. Interviewers are frequently faced with the problem of limiting responses to the specific area of the survey. People's cooperation should not, however, be taken for granted. Interviewers should introduce themselves, briefly, perhaps by showing a card or letter of authorization, particularly when home interviews are planned. They should then outline the nature of the survey, the reasons why it is being done, and the method of sampling used. Very often people are curious to know why they, in particular, have been selected for interview, and interviewers should set aside any likely suspicions by giving a simple account of the technique used. In explaining the application of quota sampling methods, some tact is advisable as respondents may not necessarily agree with the interviewer's opinion of their social and economic grading; reference to specific personal details should, therefore, be avoided.

Interviewers should endeavour to build up empathy, which has been defined as: 'the ability of one individual to respond sensitively and imaginatively to another's feelings.[2] This is an essential prerequisite to successful interviewing.

Third duty of interviewers

The third duty of interviewers is to secure valid and reliable answers to questions, which may be formally presented in a structured interview or administered at the discretion of individual interviewers. The answers to questions provide the raw material which is processed into survey findings. It is, therefore, important that questions should be carefully worded and presented so that they lead to answers which give information useful to the objectives of the survey.

Some uniformity is obviously desirable in the course of a survey, and interviewers need to be trained to achieve comparable efficiency in handling questionnaires. Researchers have to remain alert to the dangers of interviewers changing the form of questions, even by just a word, or of elaborating standardized questions. In some cases interviewers are allowed to 'probe' and to follow up respondents' chance remarks, but these activities should be authorized before the survey takes place.

The wording, sequence, and presentation of questions fundamentally influence the responses given. Interviewers are human beings, subject to individual variations in behaviour, and they react in various ways to the circumstances of a particular interview. While researchers aim to achieve uniformity in the interviewing process, the risks of bias arising from interviewers' non-conformity cannot possibly be completely eradicated. The design of questionnaires should encourage positive reactions from interviewers rather than tempt them to change questions to satisfy their personal interpretations.

Fourth duty of interviewers

The fourth duty of interviewers concerns the recording of responses given during interviews. These must be accurately reflected in the opinions of those who were interviewed, and this calls for conscientious attention to detail with particular emphasis on objectivity. The sampling method chosen by the researchers must be faithfully adhered to, even if it results in some personal inconvenience, such as call-backs to secure interviews where random sampling is used. Interviewers experience fatigue, psychological as well as physical, and they need strong motivation to maintain consistently high standards of interviewing. Field supervision has an important role to play in the continued training and encouragement of interviewers to achieve these standards.

Interviewers also need to understand all the details of recording, such as the coding of answers and the use of some agreed pre-coding system. Coding should be consistent throughout the interviews, otherwise the survey findings will not be valid.

During their training, interviewers should be checked for their ability to record, in some detail, responses given to a series of set questions. Trainers should endeavour to identify individual biases which can be revealed by comparing data collected with known characteristics of the population.

In addition to completing question-and-answer sequences in questionnaires, interviewers should record useful observational data about respondents, such as their general reaction and behaviour during the interview. Comments like these add to the value of surveys.

Interviewer Quality Control Scheme (IQCS) This scheme is jointly run by the Market Research Society Quality Control, The Association of Market Survey Organizations, the Association of British Market Research Companies, the Association of Users of Research Agencies, and a number of companies in the UK. The 'basic philosophy of the IQCS is, firstly, that a properly trained and managed interviewer will do better work than one who is less well trained and managed ... The second strand ... is that clients have a right to know that certain standards of data validation are undertaken and documented'.[12] Survey organizations subscribing to this scheme are visited by quality control inspectors who audit their research operations with the common objective of maintaining and raising the standards of fieldwork. The IQCS has 'at its disposal a wide range of sanctions against those who do not "come up to scratch"'.[12]

7.7 CHARACTERISTICS OF INTERVIEWERS

The personality of the interviewer is crucial to the success of the interview. Interpersonal relationships are formed during the interviewing process and, as noted, the success of the interview depends so much on personal factors. These are difficult to isolate and apply indiscriminately in assessing the suitability or otherwise of individual interviewers.

However, Bingham and Moore,[2] as a result of their considerable studies in this area, have suggested that in order to be successful, an interviewer must be: 'fairly well put together himself'; capable of reacting empathically to the other person, unhampered by his own predispositions; and be widely read and extremely thoughtful about personality and its dynamics.

In fact, the successful interviewer appears to possess qualities which are not all that widely spread. People who are fortunate enough to have these endowments may not be able or willing to act as interviewers. Selection will have to be made from those who apply for this type of work. The successful applicants should be trained to become more aware of themselves, of the influence they have on others, and of the vital need for objectivity in all research activities.

High intelligence and education are not essential for general survey interviewing; the levels should be adequate for the specific tasks of individual surveys. As with other occupations of a repetitive nature, it would be unwise to employ people of too high a calibre on routine investigations, as they would soon experience boredom and probably leave the task uncompleted.

Research[13] at the Survey Methods Centre of City University Business School revealed that the following interviewer characteristics affected success in obtaining interviews: experience, training, and communication skills. The key to success was the flexibility of the interviewer, particularly when problems were encountered in interviewing.

7.8 INTERVIEWER EFFECT

This occurs when the influence of the interviewer on the respondent is such that it results in responses that do not accurately reflect the attitudes and opinions of the respondent. There are many sources of interviewer bias, some of which can be dealt with effectively by sound methods of selection, training, and supervision. Other biases may be more difficult to identify and may be largely covert. 'The possibility has long been recognized that two interviewers, asking questions of the same respondent, might obtain different answers.'[14] Despite the fact that features of a survey such as questionnaire design, common briefing of interviewees, or sampling arrangements may be identical, the interviewer effect persists.

Research on the influence of interviewers on survey information started when, as the result of careful scrutiny, unusual patterns in responses to survey questioning became evident. Classical research on the tendency for personality characteristics and attitudes to intrude in the interview was done by Stuart Rice.[15]

In 1914, the New York Commissioner of Public Charities ordered a study of the physical, mental, and social characteristics of 2000 destitute men, who applied for a night's rest at the municipal lodging house. They were interviewed systematically by trained social workers, each interview taking between 20 and 30 minutes and covering four pages of questions. When the results were carefully examined, it became apparent that there were consistent patterns in certain kinds of answers recorded by two of the interviewers, although these differed remarkably between the two investigators. One of the questions asked each man to give an explanation of his destitution, whereas the other interviewer attributed it more to social and economic conditions, such as hard times, lay-offs, etc.

What was even more interesting emerged when the explanations of the destitute men themselves were studied. They also attributed their miserable condition principally to excessive drinking on the one hand, and poor social environment on the other. In fact, they reflected the consistent biases of the interviewers.

It was subsequently discovered that the first interviewer was an ardent prohibitionist, and the other was a socialist. Both were well-trained, conscientious, and experienced investigators, probably unaware of how their attitudes were biasing results. Not only were *their* judgements biased, but the actual statements of the men interviewed appeared to have suffered contagion.

Other investigations[3] in this aspect of interviewer bias include enquiries undertaken by Cahalan, Tambulonis, and Verner (1947) into the interviews of more than 100 different interviewers. About three-quarters of the 51 interview questions showed significant differences in response, many in the direction of the interviewer's own opinions. In 1952, Ferber and Wales investigated a survey which had been made on prefabricated houses. It was found that the respondents of interviewers who liked such housing themselves were more favourable to prefabricated houses than were those interviewed by investigators who, themselves, disliked this type of housing.

Personality factors, such as age, sex, social group, and attitudes, seem, however, to be less influential than interviewers' expectations of the responses to the survey. Bias of this nature arises where interviewers expect respondents to show consistent attitudes throughout their answers, and in cases where later responses are rather vague and interviewers interpret them in the light of attitudes revealed by earlier answers. Interviewers may also interpret marginal answers according to the typical answers which they would expect from the kinds of person being interviewed. This 'stereotype' influence has already been noted, and the NORC studies found it significant.

Kahn and Cannell[3] emphasize that each person comes to an interview with many firmly fixed attitudes, personality characteristics, motives, and goals. Each participant has a 'constellation of characteristics' reflecting group memberships and group loyalties; these may well be potential sources of bias in the interviewing process.

If the two parties to an interview differ widely in their personality characteristics and experience, their attitudes and motivations are likely to be substantially different from one another. This will tend to make mutual understanding more difficult to achieve and could lead to bias. It has been suggested that interviewers should be matched closely to respondents in vital personal characteristics.

It is preferable in most cases to have women interview women and to have Negro interviewers where interviews are to be made in the homes of Negro respondents. Whether it is preferable to have men or women interview men is a point on which many research men disagree. The nature of the subject matter is one influence in a decision on that point.[16]

However, in a survey[17] to assess the demand for campaign medals after the Second World War, it was found that ex-servicemen, when interviewed by elderly women interviewers, indicated more definite interest in decoration than when they were interviewed by young women.

In a review of the problem of interviewer variability, Collins[14] has noted that within the panels of interviewers recruited by professional interviewing organizations, there is no evidence to suggest that one type of interviewer tends to obtain different answers from another, and that there is no reason to recommend that recruitment should be concentrated among women rather than men, or among the middle-aged rather than the young or the old; the question of training is vitally important.

In another paper,[18] Collins reported a carefully planned experiment for the OPCS over 32 electoral wards to evaluate the effects of (i) interviewer variabililty in asking the questions or in interpreting and recording responses, and (ii) the geographical clustering of interviews into electoral wards – each ward was covered by two interviewers. Overall, the two effects were found to be of similar scale, but while interviewer effects tended to be stronger for attitudinal items, sample design effects tended to be stronger for factual items.

In approaching the problem of area and interviewer variance, it was observed that these are, of course, radically different aspects of research methodology. 'The former is inescapable: only its effects can be moderated by the avoidance of excessive sample clustering. The latter can – at least in principle – be tackled through questionnaire design, pre-testing and interviewer instruction.'[18]

An extensive study[19] of interviewer variability was connected with the purchasing and attitudinal patterns of adults who regularly travel abroad from the UK. Interviewers were subjectively graded according to relative ability on a scale 10 (best) to 1 (poor); in practice the actual scores ranged from 3 to 9. In addition, interviewers were set quotas running from 10, 20, 30, to 40. The main findings were that interviewer grading is related to interview quality, while the effects of quota size on response levels 'remained uncertain'. It was recommended by the researchers that monitoring and play-back of the performance of individual interviewers should be done in order to maintain field morale and reduce overall variability.

A study[20] of interviewer effects in telephone surveys was based on data from 11 national CBS News/*New York Times* polls, taken during the 1980 American elections; 300 interviewers were involved. 'Some effects were found to exist, but they were generally quite small.' However, the fact that the interviewer load in telephone surveys is large, the cumulative effects of interviewer bias may be 'substantial'.

Several investigations, mostly in the United States, have been concerned with the effects of disparity in race between interviewer and interviewee in personal surveys. As Collins[14] has observed: 'The one interviewer characteristic that seems consistently to be important is that of race'. Most studies have focused on the effects on black respondents of being interviewed by white interviewers who constitute the majority of professional interviewing staff.

Weeks and Moore[21] have investigated the effects of interviewer ethnic origins involving non-black ethnic minorities; 1472 elementary school children from four districts: Miami (Cubans), El Paso (Chicanos), NE Arizona (native Americans), and San Francisco (Chinese), were surveyed by 101 interviewers (50 ethnics; 51 non-ethnics), who were carefully selected for their interviewing experience.

Twenty pairs of interviewers were randomly selected; each pair consisting of the interviewer who was not of the respondent's ethnic group and who did not speak the respondent's language and one interviewer who was of the same ethnic group and who did speak the respondent's language. From subsequent analysis, it was found that, as with black/white situations, a difference in ethnicity between interviewer and respondent did not appear to affect survey responses to non-sensitive questions. 'It should also be pointed out that in the survey as a whole the non-ethnic interviewers seemed to be at no disadvantage working with an ethnic sample *vis-à-vis* the ethnic interviewers, and actually outperformed the latter slightly on the basis of response rate and field costs.'

Another study[22] focused on the more unusual phenomenon of white respondents surveyed by black interviewers in metropolitan Detroit. Results indicated that white respondents were 'at least as susceptible to race-of-interviewer effects as black respondents, and they thus call into question earlier interpretations which focused entirely on asymmetrical racial deference'. Respondents of both cases appear anxious to avoid responses that might offend interviewers of the 'opposing' race, and tend to be franker with interviewers of their own race. 'Tentative evidence' suggests that the more educated whites are likely to have the strongest urge to appear tolerant and are, therefore, more inclined to emphasize liberal views when interviewed by blacks. Whether a comparable bias arises with educated black respondents and white interviewers seems to be uncertain.

An investigation[23] into whether race-of-interviewer effect is also present in telephone interviews was undertaken with a random sample of Alabama residents 18 years of age and older: 590 individuals were contacted of whom 548 answered the question asking their race. The results of this study were 'consistent with previous findings concerning a race-of-interviewer effect in other forms of surveying', viz., race of interviewer has little or no effect on non-racial questions; race of interviewer does have some effect on some, but not all racial questions; and on racial questions, respondents interviewed by an interviewer of another race were more 'deferential' to that race than are respondents interviewed by a member of their own race. The researchers, however, draw attention to the nature of the research location in which race is specially salient. In other situations these particular findings may not be applicable.

7.9 OTHER SOURCES OF BIAS

The MRS Working Party report[9] regarded the attitude of interviewers to the concept of market research to be a very important factor. 'If the applicant is not wholeheartedly in favour of it, or regards interviewing as an imposition on members of the public, she cannot be expected to carry out her work conscientiously.' Other possible sources of bias may emanate from political beliefs, or, perhaps, attitudes of a husband.

Bias can also arise from respondents who may be unwilling to give correct answers, perhaps from ignorance of the subject or difficulty in self-expression. They may also, consciously or unconsciously, not wish to give accurate answers, for various reasons, such as embarrassment, privacy, or personal dislike of disclosing information about their behaviour. There may also be genuine misunderstanding of questions, as in the experience of an American researcher[2] who interviewed textile workers on strike. He found that 'arbitration' had come to mean in the workers' vocabulary the same as 'surrender'. 'Are you in favour of arbitration?' was interpreted as 'Are you in favour of giving in completely to the employers?'

Respondents often tend to give the answer which they think interviewers want. The 'accommodating answer' is frequently attracted by a 'leading question', which had not been spotted when the questionnaire was designed. Crisp[16] reports that a question, such as: 'Have you seen this advertisement?' in which an advertisement is shown, has been proved to inflate positive replies by as much as three times over responses obtained by a less biased approach. (See Chapter 6, Section 6.4: Bias in questions.)

Sponsorship of surveys is not normally revealed to respondents as identification tends to influence their answers and may inhibit critical comment. Respondents may well feel inclined to look for clues in questions which will enable them to identify the sponsors, so particular care should be taken in drafting questionnaires. Unexpected events may also bias answers as respondents may mistakenly relate the sponsor of a survey with some news event concerning another organization.

A proposed survey on attitudes towards major airlines was postponed when one airline had the misfortune to make headlines as a result of two dramatic and fatal crashes within a two-week period.[16]

Interviewers may also be influenced by knowing the identity of sponsors, and it is generally considered unwise and unnecessary for names of brands of sponsors to be revealed. Bias could result from individual preferences for particular brands influencing interviewers. In cases where the survey is not handled by a research agency, it is advisable for the company involved to disguise its identity by some 'cover' name. In the case of mail surveys, 'cover' addresses also need to be used.

The place and time of interview may also bias response. Questions asked at an inconvenient time may well result in misunderstanding or attract a series of rapid replies designed to get rid of the interviewer as quickly as possible.

In such cases, it is better for the interviewer to ask for a more convenient appointment.

7.10 BIAS FROM NON-RESPONSE

Some degree of non-response is almost inevitable in surveys, and if this is large, survey findings are likely to be biased. The greater the proportion of non-respondents in the sample, the more serious the resulting bias. Research has shown that non-respondents often differ significantly in their opinions and behaviour from respondents; it would be unwise to assume that they do not.

Considerable consideration has been given to the problem of non-response. It is possible to keep it to a minimum by improving sample design and interviewing techniques.

A substantial proportion of non-respondents will obviously affect the size of the sample and, therefore, its precision or reliability. To reduce the effect of non-response bias, the final sample should be as near to the projected sample as possible. It is argued that if non-respondents *are* significantly different from respondents, merely substituting additional respondents will not solve the problem, although it will, of course, secure a final sample of adequate size.

In the case of random sampling, where fieldwork has shown a sampling frame to include units that do not, in fact, exist, e.g., demolished houses, deceased persons, etc., non-active units should be subtracted from the size of the sample before non-response rates are calculated. It would then be feasible to select substitutes for these non-existent units using a random technique.

With random samples, in particular, there will also be non-response owing to unsuitability, e.g., infirmity, language difficulties, etc., and interviewers must be instructed to substitute as appropriate.

Names selected randomly from the Electoral Register are bound to include some people who have moved. As already stated, the 1954 IPA Readership Survey of about 17 000 persons, found that 2400 had moved. Of these, 1400 had moved to an address covered by the survey and were traced successfully. Alternatively, it would be possible to substitute by sampling the new household in the place of the one that had moved. Investigation by Durbin and Stuart[24] showed that 10 per cent of an initial sample taken from the Electoral Register had moved address, the Register being 10 months out of date at the time of study.

The 'not at homes' may represent a fairly high proportion if common sense is not used by interviewers. Married women who work outside the home and those without children are less likely to be at home than those who do not go out to work or who have small children. American research[25] has found that the not-at-home rate varies considerably according to size of city, with the lowest rates in rural areas. Durbin and Stuart[24] reported that experienced interviewers had less difficulty (10.4 per cent) with 'not at homes' than less experienced colleagues (15.9 per cent). The same researchers also showed that when appointments were made, 71 per cent of second calls resulted in interviews, as against 40 per cent when none was made.

Some recalling is obviously necessary to bring non-response down to a minimum. The Government Social Survey stipulates a minimum of three calls (initial plus two call-backs). Other organizations usually request interviewers to make three calls, but extra cost is, inevitably, incurred, apart from lengthening the time of the survey.

Attempts have been made by some American statisticians, e.g., Politz and Simmons, to overcome the problem of call-backs by 'weighting' responses which had been obtained, but there does not appear to be any published evidence on the validity of the theory.

Bias can also arise from refusals to take part in a survey. Survey Research Centre (USA) interviewers,[6] who are highly trained, experience 2.4 per cent refusals on first calls, 4.1 per cent on second calls, steadily increasing to 10.6 per cent on sixth calls. Experienced interviewers were far more successful in securing interviews than those less experienced. In general, the refusal rate for surveys is remarkably low, and most interviewers experience difficulty in dissuading some people from talking at too great a length about the problem surveyed.

Non-response bias operates in many ways, and everything possible should be done to reduce it. Some knowledge, however slight, should be obtained about non-respondents. People who refuse to fill in a questionnaire may be persuaded to complete a postcard giving a few basic facts, which may help the survey planners to form some opinion of the nature of non-respondents.

It may be possible to compare the composition of the achieved sample with published data, in order to assess the extent and type of non-response bias.

Better training methods and increased motivation have been shown to improve the response rates achieved by interviewers. Respondents, also, have reacted favourably in an experiment reported by Ferber and Hauck.

A 90 per cent response was obtained from half of a sample receiving a long explanatory letter in advance, whereas only a 76 per cent response was obtained from those receiving a much shorter letter of explanation.[6]

Where interviewing takes place in factories, offices, colleges, and other institutions, some of the non-response factors which have been considered in some detail will not apply. Where quota sampling methods are used, non-response factors such as 'movers', 'not at homes', and 'refusals' can be modified by substitution.

Declining trends in survey response rates

Concern is being expressed by experienced researchers over the observable decline in long-term trends of survey response rates. Face-to-face interviews with the general public are more difficult to obtain; the National Readership Survey's (NRS – see Chapter 11) response rates have declined from just below 74 per cent in 1982 to 67 per cent in 1987, although a slight improvement was recorded in 1988. 'These results are very similar to most of the major surveys for which long-term trends are available.'[26] Problems of the inner cities have made their populations less inclined to be interviewed and have also affected the willingness of interviewers to work in these areas.

Leading research firms, such as Mintel, also feel concerned about the declining trend of survey response rates, particularly related to business and professional surveys, and suggest that the need for participation incentives will rise. GPs, for example, are already paid £30–£40 per interview. Clearly, to avoid further biases arising, it is critical that payments are not too generous.

7.11 SUMMARY

Interviewing is a core function of marketing research, and types of interview range from formal, unstructured interviews to informal discussions. Response can be limited, free, or defensive, and a creative interviewing approach would probably contain a mix of these tactics.

Successful interviewing depends significantly on the establishment of an effective relationship between interviewer and interviewee. There is a strong case for fitting interviewers to interviewing situations ('horses for courses').

Selection training, and motivation are essential elements for building up 'a productive interviewing team'. Interviewing tasks are as follows:

1. Locate respondents who fulfil requirements of specific samples.
2. Translate these contacts into effective interviews.
3. Secure valid and reliable responses.
4. Record survey responses accurately.

Interviewer effect occurs when the influence of the interviewer on the respondent results in responses that do not accurately reflect the respondent's attitudes and opinions. Research directors should pay special attention to the training and monitoring of interviewers in order to keep bias of this nature at a minimum level.

REFERENCES

1. Market Research, Special Report, Mintel, London, 1990.
2. Bingham, Walter Van Dyke, and Bruce Victor Moore, *How to Interview*, Harper, 1941.

3. Kahn, Robert L., and Charles F. Cannell, *The Dynamics of Interviewing*, Wiley, New York, 1957.

4. Richardson, S. A., Dohrenwend, and Klein, *Interviewing – Its Forms and Functions*, Cornell University, Basic Books, New York, 1965.

5. Patterson, D. G., *Physique and Intellect*, Appleton Century, New York, 1930.

6. Boyd, Harper W., Jnr, and Ralph Westfall, 'Interviewers as a source of error in surveys', *Journal of Marketing*, April 1955.

7. Moser, C. A., and G. Kalton, *Survey Methods in Social Investigation*, Heinemann, London, 1971.

8. Oppenheim, A. M., *Questionnaire Design and Attitude Measurement*, Heinemann, London, 1966.

9. Market Research Society, 'Fieldwork methods in general use', Working Party in Interviewing Methods: First Report, Market Research Society, London, 1968.

10. MacFarlane-Smith, Joan, *Interviewing in Market and Social Research*, Routledge and Kegan Paul, London, 1972.

11. Durbin, J., and A. Stuart, 'Differences in response rates of experienced and inexperienced interviewers', *Journal of Royal Statistical Society*, part II, 1951.

12. Harvey, John, 'Aims of Interviewer Quality Scheme', *MRS Newsletter* (Supplement), January 1988.

13. Collins, Martin, 'Responding to surveys', *ERSC Newsletter*, no. 62, June 1988.

14. Collins, Martin, 'Interviewer variability: A review of the problem', *Journal of Market Research Society*, vol. 22, no. 2, 1980.

15. Rice, Stuart, 'Contagious bias in the interview', *American Journal of Sociology*, vol. 35, 1929.

16. Crisp, Richard D., *Marketing Research*, McGraw-Hall, New York, 1957.

17. Wilkins, L. T., 'Prediction of the demand for campaign medals', The Social Survey, no. 109, 1949.

18. Collins, Martin, 'Interviewer and clustering effects in an attitude survey', *Journal of Market Research Society*, vol. 25, no. 1, 1983.

19. Bound, John, John Freeman, and John Mumford, 'The effect of the quality and quantity of interviewers on quality and quantity of data', ESOMAR, Monte Carlo, September 1980.

20. Tucker, Clyde, 'Interviewer effects on telephone surveys', *Public Opinion Quarterly*, vol. 47, no. 1, 1983.

21. Weeks, Michael, F., and R. Paul Moore, 'Ethnicity of interviewer effects on ethnic respondents', *Public Opinion Quarterly*, vol. 45, no. 2, 1981.

22. Hatchett, Shirley, and Howard Schuman, 'White respondents and race-of-interviewer effects', *Public Opinion Quarterly*, vol. 39, no. 4, winter 1975/76.

23. Cotter, Patrick R., Jeffrey Cohen, and Philip B. Coulter, 'Race of interviewer effects, in telephone interviews', *Public Opinion Quarterly*, vol. 46, no. 2, 1982.

24. Durbin, J., and A. Stuart, 'Callbacks and clustering in sample surveys: An experimental study', *Journal of the Royal Statistical Society*, vol. 117, 1954.

25. Mayer, Charles S., 'The interviewer and his environment', *Journal of Marketing Research*, November 1964.

26. Bowles, Tim, 'Data collection in the United Kingdom', *Journal of Market Research Society*, vol. 31, no. 4, October 1989.

EIGHT

QUALITATIVE RESEARCH AND ATTITUDE RESEARCH

8.1 INTRODUCTION

This chapter will deal first with qualitative research and then discuss attitude research, although, as observed later, distinctions are often blurred and some degree of overlap may be inevitable.

In Chapter 1, the development of marketing research over the past seven decades was reviewed, and Lazer's[1] five sequential stages in this evolutionary process were discussed. During the final phase of his model – covering the period 1945–73 – psychological concepts and techniques became influential in research methodology. A whole new armoury of attitude scales and projective techniques was borrowed from the behavioural sciences; a demand arose for depth and insight into consumers and their patterns of consumption.

In the middle and late 1950s, there was, as Joyce[2] noted, a 'wholesale introduction' of behavioural research techniques. This mushrooming activity was encouraged by an over-enthusiastic and at times rather naïve adoption of methodologies. Motivation research, in particular, attracted many disciples who, fascinated by its flamboyant claims, failed to discern the preposterous nature of some of its concepts and findings.

The early excitement generated by the indiscriminate importation of behavioural method-ologies has largely dissipated, and a more stable and realistic use is now made of these techniques in marketing research. This more mature approach has strengthened the theory and practice of marketing research, enabling it to develop creatively and make a significant contribution to marketing strategy.

This has led to a growing interest in improved methods of measuring the behaviour and attitudes of peoples as consumers of a wide range of goods and services. It became apparent that, when investigating people's feelings about some aspects of buying behaviour, a more subtle approach was needed than direct questioning. For many reasons, such as personal prestige or the pressures of social conformity, respondents may feel reluctant to express their true feelings when confronted with direct questions.

> In consumer research, it is rarely much use asking people why they bought a particular product or prefer one brand to another. They may not know. Even if they do, they are not always willing to say. Motives can be socially embarrassing. Moreover, people on the whole like to appear reasonable, both to themselves and to others, and direct questions are apt to elicit plausible but misleading answers.[3]

This greater awareness by marketing researchers of the importance of more subtle forms of investigation has encouraged experiments in the use of some of the techniques applied in psychology and sociology. Interest has centred particularly on the influence of attitudes on consumers' buying habits, and attempts have been made to measure more accurately the motivations, attitudes, and preferences of consumers.

The nature of attitudes and their effects on people's behaviour are fully discussed elsewhere,[4] and it has been noted in Chapter 1 that the variety and complexity of human behaviour, motivated by so many causes, may of which are not easy to identify, admittedly make the study of consumers difficult. In the process of satisfying their many needs, inherent and also acquired through learning and experience, people develop attitudes which influence their choice of products and brands. Cooper[5] has said 'we prefer to do things for their practical benefits and justify ourselves as rational and worthy, yet underlying this are deeper meanings . . . of which we may or may not be conscious'. The symbolic power of specific brands, for example, is often influential in buying decisions.

The particular experiences of individual consumers may include the satisfaction – or otherwise – which a brand of product gave them. These experiences will have contributed towards the attitudes which they hold, and it is likely that they will have discussed products with other consumers. In this way, attitudes tend to be acquired or modified. Personal influence is subtle, and studies have shown it to be very important in the purchase of foods, toiletries, clothing, and several other products. The diffusion of new products and the formation of favourable attitudes depend greatly on word-of-mouth recommendation. Opinion leadership has attracted considerable attention among marketing researchers; it is a subject which advertisers should not overlook. If products fail to live up to consumers' expectations, not only will repeat sales to those consumers be lost, but also the chances of selling to their friends and acquaintances will have been reduced.

A special committee[6] of the Market Research Society observed that qualitative research has 'long since extended from its original function of uncovering consumers' motivations to that of providing the constant conceptual link between consumer and decision maker in marketing and advertising development'. It was also noted that qualitative research is not 'scientific' in the way that some quantitative research based on statistical sampling theory and formal methods of interviewing may claim to be. As in some areas of enquiry covered by the behavioural sciences, where observational data lack precise measurement and replication, qualitative research, in general, may be perceived as lacking 'theoretical bona fides derived from any existing philosophy of science'. But it has to be admitted that the indubitable usefulness of qualitative research justifies its existence. Data may be rather inappropriately described as 'hard' or 'soft'; this does not necessarily endorse numeric data as being superior to non-numeric data: they are essentially complementary. As Colin McIver[7] observed: 'when it is affordable, a combination of qualitative and quantitative research is usually more informative than either by itself'. Of course, all data have to be interpreted and '. . . it is what the individual brings to the data that is important'.[6] Data of any type should result in *insight*; numeric data do not automatically result in that.

This view was also articulated by Crespi[8] in an interesting study of voting turnout in America. To many people, attitudinal data are more interesting than meaningful. Inherently soft, and incapable of providing a reliable theoretical base for understanding how and why people act as they do, attitude research has always attracted vocal critics. However, Crespi's research indicated that attitude measurement and theory, properly understood and undertaken, can provide a basis for predicting voting behaviour.

Cooper and Branthwaite[9] summarize the uses and rationales of qualitative research in a useful model given in Fig. 8.1.

The upper 'layers of response' are overt, communicable, deal with matters of which the respondent is aware, and can, though subject to the usual problems of bias, be elicited by structured interviews, e.g., brand awareness.

Further down the marked arrow, structured interviewing becomes increasingly difficult, and subject matter more likely to deal with 'private' feelings, irrationalities, 'illogical' behaviour, or repressed attitudes. Cooper and Branthwaite[9] observe that an essential feature of qualitative research is the level of trust developed between interviewer and respondents.

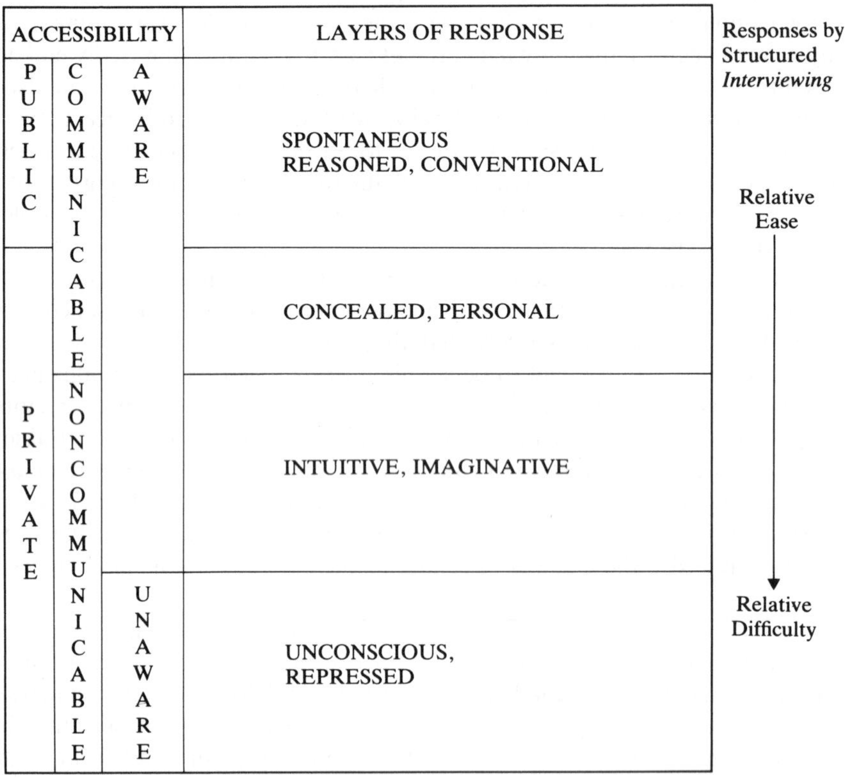

ACCESSIBILITY			LAYERS OF RESPONSE	Responses by Structured *Interviewing*
P U B L I C	C O M M U N I C A B L E	A W A R E	SPONTANEOUS REASONED, CONVENTIONAL	Relative Ease
P R I V A T E			CONCEALED, PERSONAL	
	N O N C O M M U N I C A B L E		INTUITIVE, IMAGINATIVE	
		U N A W A R E	UNCONSCIOUS, REPRESSED	Relative Difficulty

Fig. 8.1 Responses to interviewing[9]

The essence of qualitative research is that it is diagnostic; it seeks to discover what may account for certain kinds of behaviour; for example, brand loyalty. It seeks deeper understanding of factors, sometimes covert, which influence buying decisions. It is impressionistic rather than conclusive; it probes rather than counts. It observes and reflects on the complexity of human activities in satisfying many needs. Intrinsically, it is subjective. For its findings it cannot produce statistical evidence based on probability sampling. But for all its limitations, qualitative research is able to provide unique insights to inspire and guide the development of marketing strategy and tactics.

Sometimes, as the MRS study group notes,[6] marketers seek information that is too subtle and sophisticated to be derived from the structured, standardized techniques of quantitative research. They then seek for methods of enquiry that are unstructured, flexible, and oblique, such as non-directive group discussions, non-directive individual interviews, and projective techniques. Moser[10] observed that the chief recommendation for informal methods of enquiry is that they can 'dig deeper' and get a richer understanding than the formal interview.

Qualitative research has been a term rather freely used to describe several specific kinds of marketing research; for example, exploratory research, unstructured research, motivation research, depth interviewing, attitude and opinion research, etc.

Some of the techniques originally used in qualitative research were generally termed 'motivation research', but this classification is misleading, because since those early days the techniques have been applied to a variety of studies apart from buying motivation. Also, they do not represent the entire repertory of techniques available for researching motivation.[11]

Sampson[12] has warned that because qualitative research appears to be familiar to almost everybody, but really understood by relatively few, there is a danger that it could be presumed to lack subtlety and to require little skill. To the expert, however, the facts are just the reverse: it is a field of research calling for sophisticated and sensitive skills.

Qualitative research has grown significantly in Europe; in the UK it is estimated to represent 20 per cent of all market research,[13] and is the main research technique in marketing activities such as new product development (NPD), concept research and advertising pre-testing. Its growth has been accelerated, in particular, by the pressing need to understand more fully the dynamic opportunities offered by the enlarged European market.

In the US and also in the UK, several different kinds and functions of qualitative research have been classified:[13] (i) *exploratory research* – to generate language, and hypotheses for subsequent quantitative validation; (ii) *pre-testing research* – to check, sort and prioritize potential advertisement, pack, product concepts; (iii) *exploratory research*; and (iv) *everyday life research*.

The distinctive contributions of qualitative research are, therefore, both varied and valuable in marketing decision making. Modern information technologies have resulted in a veritable 'data deluge' on both sides of the Atlantic;[13] qualitative research in partnership with qualitative data, the warp and the weft, form the fabric of a creative research design.

8.2 TECHNIQUES OF QUALITATIVE RESEARCH

The basic techniques of this type of research are 'varied and eclectic';[13] they include depth interviews – either as individual unstructured interviews or as group discussions, focus groups, synectic groups, extended creativity groups (ECGs), sensitivity groups, brainstorming, Delphi role-playing, various kinds of projective techniques, etc. This imposing battery of qualitative research approaches has, as discussed earlier, attracted some critical views: Gerald de Groot,[14] for example, is distinctly unhappy about some of the assumptions and practices of qualitative research which, though fascinating, tend to drift away from its main purpose, viz., part of general market research which results in reliable, valid, and usable information.

Depth interviews

Basically, depth interviews are non-directive interviews in which the respondent is encouraged to talk about the subject rather than to answer yes or no to specific questions. Sometimes these interviews take place in groups, as people tend to be less inhibited in a group. The 'funnel' technique may be used – discussion at first on the broadest possible level; gradually narrowed down through progressively more restricted channels. The investigator has a list of points which the interview should cover and he guides conversation (without directly influencing by formal questioning), so that all the principal points are covered adequately.

It is open to some doubt how typical and representative of the total population some discussion groups actually are. Samples should be large enough to permit proper study of sub-groups, as has been noted earlier during discussion of more formal methods of marketing research.

Dichter draws participants for his group discussion from a panel of housewives and families recruited by his organization.

There is little general agreement on what constitutes a depth interview: in 1950 a committee of the American Marketing Association concluded that considerable confusion existed among practitioners, some of whom regarded depth interviewing as any kind of research that goes deeper than conventional fixed-answer questionnaires, while others stressed the 'interviewing' aspects of depth interviewing. By skilful use of 'probes' and other interviewing devices, the informant could be encouraged to respond in depth to the interviewer.

The AMA committee felt that market researchers should abandon the use of the term 'depth interviewing', and replace it with terminology of greater significance and agreement.

Depth interviewing is concerned with the study of one individual, whereas group depth interviewing studies the interaction of group membership on individual behaviour. It is this interaction – this free exchange of ideas, beliefs, and emotions – which helps to form the general opinion of people sharing common interests and responsibilities.

It has been reported[13] that group interviewing is the most prevalent form of qualitative research in both the US and the UK, but there has been a resurgence of interest in individual depth or 'one-on-one' interviews.

'A purchasing decision is frequently a social act in that the items are considered in the context of what others think of the product, and what others will think of *them* for having purchased it'.[15]

In the atmosphere of a group, individuals react to one another and the way in which they influence personal attitudes can be studied. Sharp criticism of individual beliefs is frequently aroused, and the discussion generated among the group by their shared interests tends to become extremely frank. Goldman cites the case of physicians, who are often difficult to interview alone and yet seem 'considerably more garrulous, frank, and at times argumentative when a group with other physicians'.[15]

The discussion leader, who should have psychological training, acts as a 'moderator' rather than as a formal interviewer. The group is encouraged to discuss freely the subject matter, while the moderator aims to keep the flow of conversation within the boundaries of the 'interviewing guide', which sets out the main areas of the subject to be covered. At the same time, the moderator should be sensitive to the value of remarks, which though not apparently directly relevant to the subject, may reveal interesting subconscious motivations.

This technique is widely used, but it is relatively expensive, as it entails interviews lasting from one to three hours and needs expert direction.

Group discussions depend for their success largely on the moderator who must establish the right 'atmosphere' by adjusting his behaviour to suit the type of group involved, so that maximum cooperation is attracted. His methods will vary according to the needs of the group: obviously, highly educated professional groups will react differently from, say, a group a working-class housewives.

Discussions are often recorded on tape, with the full knowledge of the audience, for later analysis. The use of portable tape recorders for individual depth interviews has attracted differing opinions. Sampson,[12] however, feels that the advantages outweigh the disadvantages. 'A friendly relaxed approach and manner, and the clear guarantee of anonymity by the interviewer can very quickly allay any suspicion and anxiety about the tape recorder on the part of the respondent'.

The analysis and interpretation of qualitative research, such as depth interviews, are demanding tasks: they require expert and objective attention. 'Content analysis' – defined by Berelson[16] as 'a research technique for the objective, systematic and quantitative description of the manifest content of communication' – may be used. Critics of qualitative research have suggested that some of the 'findings' of this method of enquiry are too greatly influenced by the individual analyst's training and background, with resultant subjectivity tending to bias analyses.

The group depth interview is particularly useful in the early stages of developing methods of enquiry into a particular problem, and in suggesting areas which questionnaires in a formal survey should cover. Between seven and nine people may be involved over a period of about 90 minutes; individual interviews, on the other hand, may take around 30–60 minutes.

Ciba-Geigy's agricultural division in the US uses several techniques in evaluating new products.[17] Following initial research work, Ciba-Geigy organizes what it terms a 'focus group' which is made up of actual growers who are likely to be users of the products from the company's agricultural division. For example, a group of avocado growers would be asked how they went about their work, problems encountered, such as insect pests, and the kinds of products which they use to meet their needs. From this focused discussion, Ciba-Geigy gathers valuable information for developing market concepts for the proposed new product. These developed concepts are likely to be subject to further focus groups and also survey interviews.

It is significant that Ciba-Geigy uses either an independent research organization or its own research service in order to preserve the objectivity of the research findings. Members of focus groups are screened by telephone to check on their eligibility. Groups are organized to cover topics of interest to farmers, doctors, teachers, housewives, or, in fact, any homogeneous group.

However, Ciba-Geigy, does not rely entirely on focus group evaluations; conventional test marketing is also adopted.

A special form of qualitative research known as ECGs (*extended creativity groups*) combined with depth interviews has been developed in consumer market research. Cooper and Lenton [18] reported a study of groups of medical general practitioners (usually about eight in each group representing high and low prescribers of drugs) over an extended period of time, of three to four hours or longer. A variety of releasing and projective techniques (see Projective techniques, page 160) were used. It was made clear to the GPs that the moderators (usually two per session) were not skilled in pharmacological/clinical matters, but wanted to know 'what really goes on'; they were, of course, skilled in handling these interviewing techniques.

Extended creativity groups were also used to explore the values, motives, and attitudes underlying voting behaviour and intention, and reported by Lunn *et al.*[19] at an ESOMAR Congress in 1983. Initially, in 1982, this research focused entirely on the Social Democrat Party (SDP), but it has since been extended to all the major political parties. The primary objective was to probe deeply into the appeal of the SDP; research was conducted, therefore, in two constituencies where voters could have the opportunity of voting either for SDP or its electoral partner, the Liberals. All respondents were aged between 30 and 50 years, and from C1, C2 socio-economic grades.

Findings – 'which should be treated as hypotheses and not as firmly established truths'[19] – indicated a segmentation of SDP voters at two levels: at the first level, there was a distinction between 'mainstream', 'liberal', and 'protest' voters. 'Mainstream' voters showed a strong positive commitment; 'liberal' voters appeared as radical thinkers, but without the commitment to join SDP; 'protest' voters were very different, and they were motivated to support the SDP chiefly to frighten the real party of their choice. 'This could be, in part, a manifestation of the tactical voting'. At the second level, 'mainstream' voters were differentiated as 'idealists' and 'depressives'; the first type were concerned about the decline of social values in Britain; the second type were more self-centred and were inclined to be jingoistic in their comments and feelings about life today.

The declining birth rate in the UK during the late 1970s and early 1980s has, among other matters, posed problems for army recruitment.[20] The traditional sources of many army recruits, the 'working classes' have also been affected by new sets of attitudes and job expectations. 'Marilyn' (Manning and Recruitment in the Lean Years of the Nineties) projected that the army needed a new communications strategy, and its advertising agency together with a marketing group were given the task of formulating one. The army was persuaded to fund some qualitative research in order to discover what young boys really thought about life in general, jobs, prospects, aspirations, etc. The discussion was wide ranging and did *not* directly focus on the army.

From these group interviews, the researchers were able to recommend a new approach to army recruitment advertising: three new TV commercials were aimed at changing the attitudes of this important age-group (under 20 years), and a tracking study made after the first two commercials was said to endorse the key findings of the researchers.

Researching ethnic tastes

Ethnic minorities account for about 5 per cent of the UK population; certain food products have an almost exclusively ethnic market, apart from exotic fruits and vegetables, such as panir and khoya in the Indian/Pakistan communities, and bean curd in the Chinese community.[21] But ethnic communities also buy some of the branded products marketed generally and marketers need to be aware of the cultural issues involved in advertising, etc.

> Any sensible advertiser should consider, if a black person is to appear in his advertising, how black people will react to it. It can be extremely difficult, and downright foolhardy, for a white person to speculate on this from behind a desk. Partly because black people appear so rarely in advertising, blacks often show extreme sensitivity to how they are depicted. They are likely to infer messages, intentions, prejudices and so on which, in fact, had never occurred to the advertiser or the agency.[21]

Group discussions and depth interviews are used successfully in ethnic minorities research in the UK.[21] It has, for example, ensured that labelling of ethnic foods provides adequate information to reassure prospective purchasers that the contents conform to their dietary laws.

Qualitative research has a special role in developing countries, particularly where there are no reliable sources of data available, and where cultural practices may significantly affect patterns of consumption.[22]

Projective techniques

Projective techniques use indirect methods of investigation, borrowed from clinical psychology, in order to obtain data that cannot be secured through more overt methods, e.g., direct questioning. They are also concerned with testing the hypotheses which have been constructed as a probable explanation of the causes underlying people's behaviour as consumers. These techniques are useful in giving respondents opportunities to express their attitudes without personal embarrassment or incrimination.

Oppenheim[23] has listed the following benefits from using projective techniques:

1. They can help to penetrate the barrier of awareness – people are frequently unaware of their own motives and attitudes.
2. The barriers of irrationality can be breached – people feel they must have 'rational' motivations for all purchases.
3. The barrier of inadmissibility may be broken – people are loath to admit to some kinds of 'non-ideal' behaviour.
4. The barrier of self-incrimination is penetrated – this is related to (3) and concerns kinds of beliefs, feelings, and behaviour that might lower other people's opinions of the person involved.
5. They can breach the barrier of politeness – where convention and actual politeness inhibit the expression of real feelings.

Projective techniques, according to Ernest Dichter[24] one of the progenitors of motivation research in the US, provide verbal or visual stimuli which, through their indirection and concealed intent, encourage respondents to reveal their unconscious feelings and attitudes without being aware that they are doing so.

These techniques include the following:

1. Third person test.
2. Word association test.
3. Sentence completion test.
4. Thematic apperception test.
5. Story completion test.
6. Rorschach ink blot test.
7. Psychodrama.
8. Cartoons (blank balloons).

1. Third person test A notable early example involving what is termed 'the third person' method, was the Mason Haire[25] instant coffee study in 1949 which was undertaken to determine the motivations of consumers towards instant coffee in general and the Nescafé product in particular.

When housewives were asked the direct question whether they liked instant coffee or not, most of those who rejected it gave as the reason the taste of this type of coffee. However, there was a suspicion that this was not the real reason and that there were hidden motives. Two shopping lists were prepared, identical except that one had Nescafé instant coffee and the other Maxwell House (drip-grind) coffee. Details of these shopping lists are given below:

Shopping list 1	*Shopping list 2*
1 ½ lb hamburger	1 ½ lb hamburger
2 loaves of Wonderbread	2 loaves of Wonderbread
Bunch of carrots	Bunch of carrots
1 can Rumford's baking powder	1 can Rumford's baking powder
1 lb Nescafé instant coffee	1 lb Maxwell House coffee (drip-grind)
2 cans Del Monte peaches	2 cans Del Monte peaches
5 lb potatoes	5 lb potatoes

A group of 100 respondents was asked to project themselves into the buying situation and characterize the woman who bought the groceries. The two lists were distributed (only one list to each person), each respondent being unaware of the existence of an alternative list. The findings revealed that the buyer of instant coffee was seen as lazier, less well organized, more spendthrift, and not as good a wife as the housewife using the conventional type of coffee.

Haire's research has been subject to considerable scrutiny over the years. Arndt[26] undertook a similar survey among Norwegian housewives in 1971 with some slight modifications to product brands: the baking powder was changed to 'Freia', and Nescafé was replaced Friele coffee. Because pilot research revealed criticism of the Haire shopping list for alleged lack of proportion in the quantities specified for the various items, some modifications were also made to quantities, e.g., carrots were increased from one to two bunches. The results indicated that 'instant coffee' housewife may have become associated with 'modernity and more intense involvement in the world around'.

In 1978, more fundamental evaluation of Mason Haire's research was made by James C. Anderson,[27] senior research psychologist of the marketing research division of Du Pont. He stated that most of the numerous studies had been content with replication and the question of the validity of Haire's research techniques was not adequately considered. What had not been evaluated before were the interactions of other products on the shopping lists with the two test products. Because this factor had been overlooked both by Mason Haire and by those who replicated his research, it was 'not possible to draw valid marketing conclusions about the perceived user characteristics [and] use of the technique for this purpose should be discouraged'.

This professional opinion reflects on the fragility of the research design underlying some projective techniques. In addition, changed attitudes towards the consumption of certain kinds of food have, as Sheth[28] pointed out some time age, rendered Mason Haire's original findings out of date. Not only have social taboos against instant coffee almost entirely disappeared, but starchy foods like potatoes are less favoured.

Another famous Mason Haire investigation[25] concerned a brewery company which made two kinds of beer: 'Regular', and 'Light' which was the more expensive. A survey had indicated that more than three times as many people drank 'Light' beer as those drinking the cheaper 'Regular' brew. In fact, for some years the company had been brewing and selling nine times as much 'Light' as 'Regular' beer. It was apparent that direct questioning had aroused defensive responses and had resulted in distorted replies in order to preserve the ego or self-esteem of those questioned.

Alfred E. Goldman[15] records an interesting group study of women shoppers, some of whom were strongly determined not to shop in one of the supermarkets in their neighbourhood, although they were unable to give clear reasons for this decision. They agreed that everything inside the store looked all right, and, in fact, the store at which they shopped was not as tidy as the other. Spontaneous remarks during a series of group discussions referred to a peculiar odour. There was general agreement that there was a 'bloody' or 'meaty' smell about the store, and that this had given rise to the vague impression of untidiness which they had associated with it. This information enabled the management to trace the cause of the offensive smell, and an improved drainage and air-extraction system was installed in the supermarket's meat processing room.

2. Word association test (sometimes called *free word association*)   This is probably the best known and oldest projective technique. The informant is given a single word and asked to say immediately what other words come into his mind. A series of words is fired at the respondent so that he is more likely to blurt out a meaningful response. For example, a spontaneous response to 'hot' is likely to be 'cold'; to 'library', 'books'.

Neutral words are mixed in a list of test words in order to overcome mental defensive tactics. Lists are carefully devised to reveal attitudes towards the subject under research.

Responses can be classified by the frequency with which a particular word is used as a response, the interval of time before response is made (hesitation), and by the total failure of some respondents to complete a sequence (blocking).

Hesitation occurs when a respondent takes more than three seconds to respond, and this indicates comparative emotional involvement in the particular word. Sometimes the stimulus word evokes such strong feelings that the respondent 'blocks' – he is unable to give any response.

Obviously, a stimulus word which has both a high hesitation rate and also a high 'blockage' rate, would not be suitable for an advertising message, as use of these words would result either in distortion or complete non-reception by the audience concerned.

There are many variants to this test ranging from one-word response to 'controlled' response, when selection is made, for example, from a given list of products to which respondents are asked to give brand names.

Household products like disinfectants or soap and foods, such as 'prepared meals', could be researched by this method.

Successive word association involves the respondent in supplying a chain of associations with the stimulus word. These links can be centred round samples of actual products, illustrations, or complete advertisements.

Word association tests are useful in selecting brand names, and for obtaining consumers' assessments of the relative qualities of a range of competitive goods. Tests could be staged before and after advertising and other promotions to measure the effectiveness of these on a selected panel of consumers.

3. Sentence completion tests   Word association and sentence completion tests are similar, and their value lies substantially in the spontaneity of the answers which they attract. People frequently reveal attitudes which they might otherwise be reluctant, or unable, to disclose consciously. Their responses can be tape-recorded and analysed for attitudinal meaning. In the case of sentence completion tests, respondents are asked to complete a short sentence and an analysis is made of the response. If the area of enquiry is sensitive, the series of sentences opens with a few innocuous sentences gradually 'funnelling' down to more difficult ones.

Typical sentences might be:

A mother who serves margarine to her family is . . .   Powdered coffee is popular because . . .
The food value of margarine is . . .   *or* The best flavoured coffee is . . .
The family using margarine instead of butter is . . .   Coffee that is easy to make is . . .
    People who drink coffee are . . .

The responses can be classified into approval (strong, general, qualified), neutral, disapproval (graded), thus revealing attitudes. Like word association tests, the respondent is subjected to some pressure in order to give spontaneous replies. It is possible for some individuals to 'rationalize' their replies, but, in general, the method is one of the most useful and reliable of the many projective techniques in use.

James M. Vicary[29] records that this test was useful where people would not openly express their anxieties and annoyance about increase airport noise near their homes. The depth and type of their hidden fears were revealed by a combination of sentence completion and word association tests.

4. Thematic apperception test (TAT)   The respondent is shown a series of pictures and asked to describe the situations shown, and what led up to those situations, and to give his idea of the outcome.

The most common form of TAT is the cartoon showing, perhaps, the simple outline of a woman at a cosmetic counter. The first cartoon might illustrate her standing near a display of cosmetics marked with a low price; the second cartoon shows her near a display of cosmetics clearly marked with a high price. Respondents are shown one of the cartoons (in random order) and asked to describe the person in the cartoon and also the quality of cosmetic involved.

Interpretation should be done by highly skilled specialists.

5. Story completion test   This is a logical development of the sentence completion test. Respondents are given the opening sentence (or sentences) describing a situation and are invited to continue the narrative. The way in which individuals develop a situation and complete the story will, it is considered, project their own psychological reactions. A marketing example could be concerned with studying women shoppers' attitudes towards trading stamps.

6. Rorschach ink blot test   This consists of a series of 10 standardized ink blot shapes, named after the Swiss psychiatrist who developed them for the study of psychopathology. These ink blots are shown to informants, who are invited to say what they see in them. It is claimed that what they see guides manufacturers in developing brands of their products to appeal to specific personality types.

This test does not have universal acceptance among psychologists.

7. Psychodrama   This psychological technique has had little application in motivation research, partly because of the difficulty of valid interpretation. People are asked to act a particular buying situation so that their responses can be studied. For example, the event could be typical behaviour when buying a pair of shoes.

8. Cartoons (blank balloons)   This type of test frequently involves a cartoon or sketch showing two people talking in a particular setting. The comments of one person are shown in a 'speech balloon'; the other person's 'balloon' is empty and the informant is asked to give the reply which he thinks fits the situation. Responses are limited to a few words.

Situations depicted can cover conversations between husband and wife, shop assistant and customer, teacher and pupil, etc. This 'third party' test is similar to sentence completion and is particularly useful as it allows people to be less inhibited in giving reactions to a situation than they might be if asked to describe their own reactions.

Associated with this type of test is the Rosenzweig's picture frustration test, originally developed for personality testing and later used for attitude studies. Cartoon characters are featured in frustrating circumstances in order to arouse the frustration-aggression aspects of the viewer's personality. The reactions of informants can be compared with those established in a set of 24 typical cartoon situations.

Cartoon tests have a variety of uses in testing marketing problems such as store service, packaging, trade-marks, etc.

8.3 CAN CONSUMER MARKETING RESEARCH DEVELOP NEW PRODUCTS

How far consumer marketing research can actually produce viable new product ideas is open to debate. One view is that it is an utter waste of time asking consumers, who often lack knowledge or imagination, about what new products they might like to see marketed.

The difficulty of understanding people's needs and their actual market behaviour is illustrated by *Fortune* (11 September 1978) of how Campbell's found that about 25 per cent of customers were concerned about salt in their diet. The company responded by introducing a line of salt-free soups which could be seasoned according to taste: they were a flop. What people say they want and what they will actually buy often fail to coincide. This task, it is argued, is best left to the 'experts' – technical and marketing staff already involved in that kind of business. The other view is that consumers are able to make valuable contributions to the development of new product concepts and they should certainly be consulted.

If the second thesis is accepted, the debate is then focused on the most effective method of researching consumers and gathering information useful in new product development.

8.4 PRINCIPAL METHODS OF RESEARCHING CONSUMER PRODUCTS

Some qualitative research techniques which could be used in developing ideas for new products include gap analysis, depth interviews, action studies, brainstorming, and synectics.

Gap analysis is concerned with identifying potential opportunities for new products from analysis of the positions (as perceived by consumers) or existing products and brands. (See the discussion on perceptual mapping in Chapter 15, page 351.) A simple perceptual model of the market, as viewed by the consumer, is constructed and research is then aimed at discovering 'unoccupied territory'.

A representative sample of consumers would be interviewed and a series of attitudinal measurements relevant to particular products would be collected. By means of multi-variate analysis techniques, the resultant data would be analysed and indications may be given of new product opportunities.

Depth interviews, as discussed earlier, may be used to discover people's covert feelings about, for example, day-to-day tasks such as housekeeping, cooking, laundry, etc. New product ideas may be sparked off during these interviews.

Action studies – case histories – in which very detailed studies of specific consumers' behaviour are made may provide useful guides to marketers. A panel of housewives may be asked to keep a detailed record ('diary') of their cooking habits – products bought, methods of usage, etc. These records may be used to assist recall in subsequent depth interviews. From these studies it may be possible to detect, for example, irritation with existing versions of products, and suggestions may be given about improved or wholly new product concepts.

Brainstorming is a method of group idea-generation which was developed by an advertising executive, Alex Osborn, in the late 1930s. In Osborn's[30] words the essence of brainstorming is 'to practise a conference technique by which a group attempts to find a solution for a specific problem by amassing all the ideas spontaneously contributed by its members'.

During the idea-generation stage, no judgement or evaluation is to be made; the process is intended to encourage *ideas*. Later, these will be subject to rigorous analysis; many are likely to be rejected, but some may well contain the elements of new product concepts.

Synectics 'is the study of processes leading to invention, with the end aim of solving practical problems, especially by a synectics group, a miscellaneous group of people of imagination and ability, but varied interests' *(Chambers, 20th Century Dictionary)*.

This technique is attributable to W. J. J. Gordon[31] who, in 1961, summarized the results of over a decade of research into creativity. He suggested that individual creativity was associated with certain psychological states. If these could be induced, the incidence of creative break-throughs might be increased. He collaborated with George Prince who developed this technique.

The synectics process aims to encourage people to view problems in a new light; to be willing to perceive how strange elements may be fitted into the framework of what is familiar or known. At the same time, people are stimulated to acquire a new way of looking at familiar objects or methods of operation; to break free from the limited perspectives imposed by familiarity.

As distinct from brainstorming, which Gordon felt was inclined to produce solutions before all aspects of a problem had been adequately developed, synectics was intended to give only a very broad indication of the problem so that creative thought would range freely.

One example of the application of this process involved designing a vapour-proof method of closing vapour-proof suits worn by workers who handled high-powered toxic fuels. Conventional devices such as zip, buttons, and snaps, were inadequate. Osborn would have described the problem in just this form to a brainstorming group. Gordon, on the other hand, would have kept the specific problem a secret and instead sparked off a discussion of the general notion 'closure'. This might lead to images of different closure mechanisms such as birds' nests, mouths, or thread. As the group exhausted the initial perspectives, Gordon would gradually interject facts that further defined the problem. The group then had new fields to discuss. Only when Gordon sensed that the group was close to a good solution would he describe the exact nature of the problem. Then the group would start to refine the solution. These sessions would last a minimum of three hours, and often longer, for Gordon believed that 'fatigue played an important role in unlocking ideas'.[32]

8.5 MODIFIED APPROACH TO QUALITATIVE RESEARCH

While acknowledging the general value of qualitative techniques, Peter Sampson[33] states that 'traditional techniques used in a conventional way provide very little of value in obtaining new product ideas *direct* from consumers'. He has introduced variations 'with the hope that these may effect an increase in useful data'.

Sampson's researches involved a 'traditional group' (B, C1, C2 housewives, all with young children) whose group discussions were concerned with the use of existing children's products generally and products especially given to their children. They were asked to suggest new products. Sampson found them 'singularly lacking in imagination', and very little of value came from the group discussions.

A second group were of both men and women from teenagers upwards and ranging over B, C1, and C2 social classes. They were recruited on their ability to give 'divergent' answers to a certain problem: 'How many uses can you think of for a housebrick?' Only those able to give a minimum of six unusual answers to this question were selected to take part in the group discussions which had three stages.

In the first stage, group members were asked to imagine they were children in considering children's food and drinks. The next stage involved subdividing the group and presenting each sub-group with the task of inventing a viable new product specifically for children; the types of product to be considered were specified as: a drink, a breakfast food, a spread, a dessert, a savoury, and a biscuit. The nine group members were divided into three groups of three to invent the first product, and re-shuffled to consider the remaining products. Hence, each person contributed to two sub-groups which focused on two products. The third stage consisted of evaluation by the panel of each proposed new product. The panel was arbitrarily divided into 'parents' and 'children'.

This modified synectics approach to generating new product ideas resulted in much more imaginative results; six potentially good product concepts resulted.

NOP Market Research, as reported by Sampson,[33] has experimented with brainstorming and synectic groups and believes that consumers may be able to create viable new products, although they are more likely to express new product ideas which can be developed further. To expect 'ready-made' products from such sessions would be unrealistic. The selection of groups and their 'guidance' during discussions are clearly important factors to success.

Marketing research clearly plays, or should play, a central role in the identification and profitable exploitation of new product ideas. This means that firms should constantly monitor the markets in which they operate (or plan to operate), so that trends and market gaps related to resources are identified. Creative flair is not to be frustrated, of course, but the basic analytical approach should be applied to the productive ideas of 'brainstorming' and other creative sessions.

Of course, marketing research itself cannot guarantee successful innovation. Data need interpretation and business decisions have still to be taken. Risk is always present – otherwise managers would largely be superfluous.

8.6 ATTITUDE RESEARCH

The measurement of behavioural factors such as attitudes and motivation has been attempted by researchers using a variety of techniques.

None is fully satisfactory, the ones that are the most reliable and valid from a technical viewpoint generally being the most difficult, and expensive, to apply. The selection of the 'best' technique in a particular situation is still a highly controversial question.[34]

In practice, researchers endeavour to measure attitudes by means of attitude scales and related techniques such as semantic differential scales. In addition, disguised methods involving projective techniques may also be used for studying motivation.

Two important factors are fundamental to all research activities including the measurement of attitudes, viz., *validity* and *reliability*. The former refers to the extent to which an attitude scale is free from both random and systematic error and measures what it is supposed to measure or what it is believed to be capable of measuring. The latter concerns the consistency of a method of measurement, i.e., that repeated measurements under the same conditions will give the same results.

The validity of a test rests on suitable external criteria being available – which is often not the case. Validity can be determined by any or all of these approaches:

1. *Content validity* established by the personal judgements of experts in the particular field.
2. *Predictive validity* involving matching test results against some external criterion; there appear to be few cases of this type of validation.
3. *Construct validity* by testing over 'known' groups or types of respondents who could reasonably be expected to hold certain attitudes which differ towards some defined object.

Reliability can be tested by the following methods:

1. *By repeating a given test* and comparing the two measurements (*test–re-test*). This is done by calculating the correlation between the results of the replicated and original tests.
2. *By comparing measurements* on two comparable forms of the same test (*equivalent forms*).
3. By the traditional method of *comparing measurements* on one half of the test with those noted on the other half, the result being expressed as a coefficient of correlation (*split-half*).

A certain type of attitude scale may possess the quality of reliability, but it may not be valid to use for a particular research project. Generally, it is easier to check the former than the latter attribute.

8.7 TYPES OF SCALES

Before considering specific scaling techniques it will be helpful to review briefly the principal types of scales which are in use. These can be classified as: nominal, ordinal, interval, and ratio.

Nominal

Nominal scales are the least sophisticated; they involve nothing more than simple classification by certain attributes which are then quantified. These may refer to population characteristics based on age or sex, or ownership of a specific consumer durable such as an automatic washing machine.

Ordinal

Ordinal scales, also called ranking scales, rank the objects which are being studied according to certain characteristics. Ranking is a technique which has been widely used for many years in psychology and sociology. While the rank order of a group of items according to some characteristic is indicated, no measure of the differences between the ranks is given. The 'distance' between two ranks may be substantial and yet another pair of ranks may have only a very slight difference between them. For example, the distance between ranking one and ranking two may be substantially different from that between ranking two and ranking three. Ranking is very widely used in grading people, products, and events. It is important to define clearly the attribute which is being ranked; this could refer to competitive products in terms of taste or freshness, or in evaluating shoppers' reactions to various types of grocery outlets (independent shop, 'symbol' shop, large company supermarket, etc). The method of 'paired comparisons' is sometimes used with ordinal scales. The objects to be ranked are considered two at a time, and all possible combinations of pairs are considered. This results in a steeply rising number of combinations as the number of objects increases, and because of this the method has rather limited usefulness. To illustrate this difficulty, paired comparison will be calculated for 5, 10, and 20 pairs, using the formula $\frac{1}{2}n(n-1)$ where n = number of objects to be ranked: A, B, C, D, E. This involves comparisons between:

A and B	B and C	C and D	D and E
A and C	B and D	C and E	
A and D	B and E		
A and E			

By formula $\frac{1}{2}n(n-1)$:

$$= \frac{5}{2} \times 4$$

$$= 10 \text{ (as shown independently in detail above)}$$

Taking 10 objects, by same formula:

$$= 5 \times 9$$
$$= 45$$

Taking 20 objects, by same formula:

$$= 10 \times 19$$
$$= 190$$

Statistical techniques which can be applied to ranked data are limited to positional measures which deal with *order*, e.g., median, quartile, percentile. Ranking or ordinal scales are, therefore, limited in the quality of the information which they can provide. Mere ranking of a group of items with regard to some attribute held in common, does not imply that the 'steps' between ranks are equal.

Interval

Interval scales (also known as 'cardinal') use equal units of measurement. This makes it possible to state not only the order of scale scores but also the distances between individual scores. The zero point is fixed arbitrarily and measurements are taken from it, as in a temperature scale. This limits the arithmetical calculations, since no value on the scale is a multiple of another. While the differences between pairs of scale positions, e.g., two and three and seven and eight, are identical, it is not correct to say that score eight has four times the strength of score two. This can be checked readily against temperature readings of 80°F and 20°F, taking the formula for converting Fahrenheit to Centigrade: $T_c = \frac{5}{9})T_f - 32$)

Therefore, 80°F = 26.6°C and 20°F = -6.6°C

If three competitive products were being assessed for buying preferences, the first might attain the highest score of, say, 8, the second score might be 4, and the lowest score 2. It cannot be said, however, that the first product is twice as much liked as the second one, because in an interval scale the zero point, as noted already, is fixed arbitrarily. But it is acceptable to report that the first product is clearly more favoured than the other two, and that the degree of buying preference between the first and second product is twice that existing between the second and third products.

Interval scales permit the use of statistical measures such as the arithmetic mean, standard deviation, correlation coefficient, and tests of significance.

Ratio

Ratio scales have fixed origin or zero points, which allow all arithmetical operations to be used. This means that, among other calculations, multiplication of scale points for comparison purposes is allowable. Ratio scales are found in the physical sciences, e.g., for measuring length or weight. Many marketing measurements, e.g., sales, market share, number of customers, etc., possess the properties of a ratio scale because in each instance a natural or absolute zero exists.

8.8 PRINCIPAL SCALING METHODS

Rating scales are those which measure by means of ordinal, interval, or ratio scales; they may be verbal, diagrammatic, or numerical. It is important to have a knowledge of the principal scaling methods and these are now considered in some detail.

Thurstone's equal-appearing intervals (differential scale)

This classic example of an interval scale entails elaborate preparation and involves sophisticated mathematical procedures. Because of these complications, the method tends to be little used in commercial practice.

In the late 1920s, Thurstone and Chave[35] published a series of scales relating specifically to measuring attitudes towards such matters as capital punishment, evolution, free trade, patriotism, war, censorship, etc. Thurstone scales can be adapted to measure attitudes towards any type of object, using the following procedure:

1. A large number of statements (favourable and unfavourable) relating to the survey subject is collected by the researcher.
2. These statements are independently assessed by a large* number of judges, who classify them in 11 groups, from 'most favourable' to 'least favourable'. The median values of each group are calculated.
3. Between 20 and 25 statements are finally selected, after discarding those which do not attract general support, as indicated by the interquartile range which measures the scatter of judgements.
4. These selected statements are presented, in random order, to respondents, who are asked to confirm all those statements with which they agree.
5. Respondents' total scores are calculated simply by taking the mean or median of the median values of all the statements which have been confirmed.

Critics of this method feel that the attitudes of those who judge the original collection of statements may bias the selection of those used in the test. Research into this problem does not appear to be conclusive, though Ballachey and colleagues[36] comment that 'the attitude of the judge will bias his judgements of items. However, in most cases this effect will be small. Only judges with extreme attitudes will show substantial distortion'.

It would seem that caution should be exercised in selecting judges who are most likely to be similar in their attitudes to the people eventually to be surveyed. Some researchers have speculated on whether Negro judges would be likely to produce the same scale measurements as white judges on a subject such as colour prejudice. Obviously, it would be unwise deliberately to include judges with extreme views about the matter under survey.

---

* This has varied considerably over reported studies. Between 100 and 150 statements and 40 and 60 judges have been involved, though with some tests as many as 300 judges have been used.

Empirical evidence has indicated that reliable scale values for statements can be obtained from a relatively small number of judges. In some of Thurstone's early experiments as many as 300 judges were used; later researchers have obtained reliable scale values with fewer than 50. Clearly, this affects the time and work involved in the preparation of Thurstone scales.

Likert summated ratings

Rensis Likert published 'A technique for the measurement of attitudes'[37] in 1932, in which he described a new method of attitude scaling known as Likert scales – a type of verbal rating scale. The following procedure is used:

1. A large number of statements relating to the particular object being surveyed is collected by the researcher.
2. These statements are then administered to a group of people representative of those whose attitudes are being studied, and they are asked to respond to each statement by indicating whether they:
    (a) strongly agree
    (b) agree
    (c) are uncertain
    (d) disagree
    (e) strongly disagree
3. These five categories are then scored, usually using 5, 4, 3, 2, 1, respectively, for favourable statements, and the reverse order for unfavourable statements.
4. Individual scores are achieved by totalling the item scores of each statement. This total can be compared with the maximum possible score. For example, a set of 12 statements carries a maximum possible score of 60 (5×12), and a minimum score of 12 (1×12). If an individual's total score amounts to 50, it would indicate a decidedly positive attitude to the survey problem.
5. Item analysis is now done to select the most discriminating items by computing for each item the correlation between item scores and the total of all item scores. Those with the highest correlations are retained for inclusion in the survey questionnaire. The number of items in a scale is arbitrary and is sometimes quite small.

Likert does not produce an interval scale, and it would not be correct to reach any conclusions about the meaning of the distances between scale positions. Respondents are merely ranked along a continuum relating to the study of a particular attitude. Scores achieved by individual respondents are only relative to other respondents' total scores. Moreover, it cannot be assumed that the mid-point on a Likert scale is necessarily the precise middle between the two extreme scores.

Likert scales are popular because they have been shown to have good reliability, are simpler to construct than Thurstone scales (with which they correlate favourably), and give rather better information about the *degree* of respondents' feelings. This allows respondents rather more freedom in expressing their views than restricting them to simple 'agree/disagree' endorsements as used in Thurstone scaling.

Example If Likert scaling is applied to advertising, the collected statements, ranging from positive to negative, could be scored as shown in Table 8.1. Statements which could be used are as follows (and other statements could be devised):

− 'Advertising increases the prices we have to pay for products.'
+ 'Advertising is an important source of information for consumers.'
+ 'Advertising makes an important contribution to modern living standards.'
− 'Advertising is socially undesirable and a wasteful use of resources.'

Table 8.1 Scoring of statements

Statements	Strongly agree	Agree	Uncertain	Disagree	Strongly disagree
'Positive' +	5	4	3	2	1
'Negative' −	1	2	3	4	5

Respondents are asked to indicate their reaction to each statement. High total scores reflect strongly favourable attitudes to advertising; lower total scores indicate unfavourable attitudes. However, it is important to note that a given total score may have different meanings because individual scores may, of course, be differently distributed.

Worcester[38] has observed that not only are Likert scales the most frequently used method of scaling, but they also tend to be most misused because of the relative ease with which they can be devised. While a Thurstone scale demands care in construction, a Likert scale can be constructed fairly easily. All the overworked research executive has to do is to 'think up a few contentious statements, add a Likert agree-disagree scale, and, hey presto, he has a ready-made questionnaire'.

Likert scales are easy for respondents to understand, but this strength is also a research weakness, for simple wording does not guarantee that perceptual differences will not arise. Is a scale position such as 'very dissatisfied' the precise negative of 'very satisfied'?

From a statistical appraisal of the relative precision of verbal scales, Worcester pleaded for care in the selection of words such as 'some', 'moderate', and 'considerable' to avoid misunderstandings.

Modifying adverbs should be used to balance side point statements as follows:

agree strongly		agree strongly
agree *slightly*		agree
	preferred	
neither agree		neither agree
nor	to:	nor
disagree		disagree
disagree *slightly*		disagree
disagree strongly		disagree strongly

In balanced 'agree-disagree' statements 'slightly' seems better than 'fairly' or 'quite', but in balanced 'satisfaction' scales, 'fairly' appears to be preferable. Another interesting insight from this research revealed that boxes indicating scale positions 'are not necessarily as "accurate" as some verbal tags'.

Guttman's scales (scalogram analysis)

Shortly before the Second World War, Louis Guttman and his associates[39] developed a method of cumulative scaling which attempted to define more accurately the neutral area of an attitude scale.

The method is rather complicated, but basically it is as follows:

1. Respondents are asked a series of attitude questions on the same subject and relating to the same dimension of that subject.
2. Intensity of feeling is registered by asking after each question: 'How strongly do you feel about this?'

Answers are classified by such intensities as: strongly agree, agree, undecided, disagree, strongly disagree. 'Favourable' statements are scored 4 to 0.

3. Each individual respondent's content score is computed, e.g., the maximum will be the number of statements times the highest intensity score. (If there are 7 statements and 4 is the highest score, $7 \times 4 = 28$; the range of possible scores will lie between 0 and 28.)

4. Scores of individual respondents are entered on a 'scalogram' board, which is a device designed to simplify the process against content scores, and the resulting curves are termed 'intensity curves'. The shape of these curves is of considerable value in indicating the distribution of attitudes in a given population. A flat-bottomed, U-shaped curve indicates a wide area of neutral attitudes, whereas a sharply angled curve downward and then rising steeply indicates that attitudes are held by two strongly contrasted groups.

Critics of Guttman scales have commented on the method of selecting the initial set of attitude statements, and it does seem that this selection of suitable statements was a matter of intuition and experience.

The fact that Guttman's method of scaling tackles the problem of the neutral region of attitude measurement makes it worth serious consideration by marketing researchers. As has already been seen, the other scaling techniques fail to deal with this region satisfactorily.

Apart from classifying responses from 'strongly agree' to 'strongly disagree', intensity of feeling can be conveyed graphically by a scale with divisions printed in various type sizes:

YES	YES	yes	no	NO	NO
SLOW	SLOW	slow	fast	FAST	FAST

A Guttman scale is similar to a Likert scale in that respondents express their agreement or otherwise with a series of statements about a specific subject. However, the distinctive difference between these types of scale arises because the Guttman technique is a cumulative scale, which means that statements are selected so that the responses to succeeding statements can be reasonably inferred from the response given to an earlier one. For example, a set of statements concerning company sales might be drafted as follows:

1. Group sales next quarter year will be considerably higher than this quarter.
2. Group sales next quarter will be higher than this quarter.
3. Group sales will show an improvement next quarter.
4. Group sales in the next quarter will be about the same or better than this quarter.

These statements are termed 'scalable', because if a respondent agrees with statement 1 it can be assumed that he will also agree with the succeeding ones. It is evident that this respondent has a more optimistic view of future business than another respondent whose agreement is confined to statement 4.

The survey concerned with evaluating people's awareness and attitudes to aircraft noise in the vicinity of Heathrow Airport used a Guttman scale (see Chapter 6, ref. 20) and this technique was also applied to investigate attitudes towards ball-point pens.[40] However, in this particular study, the researcher concluded that the complexity of the Guttman technique rendered it not particularly suitable for relatively simple problems in attitude research.

Semantic differential

This popular, diagrammatic scaling procedure was developed by Osgood *et al.*[41] of the Institute of Communications Research of the University of Illinois, to measure the connotative meaning of concepts. It rests on the assumption that the meaning of an object for an individual includes both the more obvious denotative meaning, which can readily be given, and also the connotative meanings which are frequently more subtle and difficult to describe. The semantic differential has been shown to be an easy method of quantifying the intensity and also the content of attitudes towards certain concepts.

The procedure is flexible, reasonably reliable, and much simpler to use than either Thurstone or Guttman scales. Basically, it usually consists of a number of seven-point rating scales that are bipolar with each extreme defined by an adjective or adjectival phrase. It is important that the bipolar terms used define accurately the difference between two extreme feelings. The words should be carefully chosen so that respondents are not confused.

Jean Morton-Williams[42] has commented that some researchers prefer five-point rather than seven-point semantic scales, because the former are easier for interviewers to explain and for informants to understand. From an inspection of answer patterns on seven-point scales, there appears to be a tendency for many respondents to restrict their answers to the extreme position and one other on each side of the mid-point.

Respondents are asked to rate each of a number of objects or concepts along a continuum. They should respond spontaneously as researchers seek first impressions, not studied answers.

As with Likert scales, the mid-point of a semantic differential may not coincide with the precise neutral region between two opposing attitudes. Further, it cannot be assumed that the seven points on the continuum are equally spaced.

Osgood developed 20 rating scales which have wide application:

active/passive	unsuccessful/successful
cruel/kind	important/unimportant
curved/straight	angular/rounded
masculine/feminine	calm/excitable
untimely/timely	false/true
savoury/tasteless	usual/unusual
hard/soft	colourless/colourful
new/old	slow/fast
good/bad	beautiful/ugly
weak/strong	wise/foolish

Scales have also been used successfully for marketing research investigations into consumer attitudes covering corporate image, product image, brand image, advertising image, etc. In these areas it is often difficult for consumers to articulate their feelings, and the semantic differential offers them a convenient and easily understood method of expressing themselves.

The mechanics of operating semantic differential scales are simple:

Fair	.X.	Unfair
Active	. .X.	Passive
Usual	. . .X. . . .	Unusual
Modern	. . . . .X. . .	Old fashioned

Respondents are asked to describe some particular concept along a seven-point scale by placing check mark (X) in the position which reflects their feelings. The seven positions could be shown as:

Extremely fair	Both	Slightly unfair
Very fair	fair and	Very unfair
Slightly fair	unfair	Extremely unfair

Weights are assigned to continuum positions, e.g., $3, 2, 1, 0, -1, -2, -3$ (this assumes equal intervals). Total ratings of individual respondents on the same scale can be combined and group mean scores computed which will give profiles for subjects along certain dimensions. Interesting comparisons can be made over time of attitudinal changes towards a company, its products, servicing arrangements and other important areas of activity.

Descriptive phrases instead of bipolar adjectives can be particularly effective in measuring the acceptability of certain features of a product or service. The 'image' which products acquire can be analysed, and the contribution made by individual features can be quantified. Competing brands can be subjected to the same test, and their profiles compared. Figure 8.2 relates to a fruit-flavoured 'soft' drink of which there are three well-known brands in popular demand.

Types of consumer can also be scaled and profiles established for different brands of products. This gives rather more qualitative information about consumers than the usual demographic breakdown. For example, housewives could be classified along a scale:

Careful shopper	Free and easy shopper
'Working' housewife	'Non-working' housewife
Likes to entertain friends	Likes a quiet life

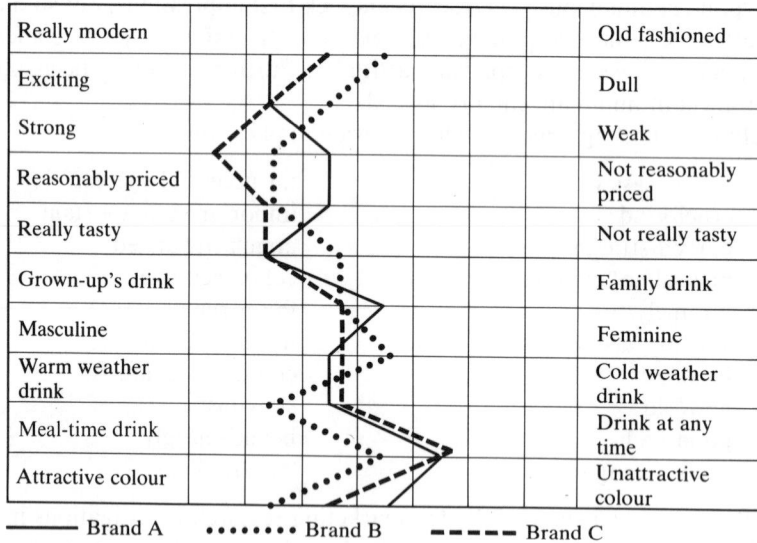

Fig. 8.2   Brand profile – fruit-flavoured soft drink

Cars could be profiled along some of the following dimensions:

Expense account car	Family man's car
Holds the road well	Does not hold the road well
Looks a successful man's car	Looks like anyone's car
Quiet running car	Noisy running car
Sturdy looking	Doesn't look well built

Supermarkets have been surveyed using semantic differential scales designed to give profiles of them as seen by consumers: the following bipolar scales were considered to be most relevant in one study:[43]

good/bad	large/small
friendly/unfriendly	fair/unfair
modern/old fashioned	reliable/unreliable
pleasing/annoying	active/passive
convenient/inconvenient	low prices/high prices
clean/dirty	roomy/crowded
neat/disorderly	

The position of the positive end of the bipolar scale should be randomized when constructing semantic differentials, in order to minimize biasing responses due to regular positioning.

Semantic scaling was used in comparative studies of product images among Japanese businessmen during 1970[44] and 1977.[45] Factors researched covered price and value, service and engineering, advertising and reputation, design and style, and consumers' profile.

The versatility of this measuring device is tempered to some degree by two factors identified by an American researcher:[46]

1. There may be subjective interpretation of the adjectives attached to each end of semantic scales. e.g., a 'fast' car may be one capable of 70 m.p.h. to one respondent, and 150 m.p.h. to another.
2. A 'halo effect' may lead to evaluation along one dimension biasing others.

Semantic differential scales are popular in marketing research because of their simplicity and adaptability. They are used by experienced researchers such as the BBC Audience Research, and they are particularly useful in giving fuller information about aspects of consumer behaviour which are not satisfactorily obtained from direct questioning techniques.

'Thermometer' questions

These are sometimes used to simplify multi-choice questions. The graphic presentation is readily understood, and is particularly valuable in some overseas markets where difficulties may be experienced in understanding qualitative phrases. The 'thermometer' can be scaled with numerical values and simple adjectives, as shown in Fig. 8.3.

Other simple diagrammatic scales may be devised, perhaps with simple cartoons depicting facial expressions ranging from happy to miserable.

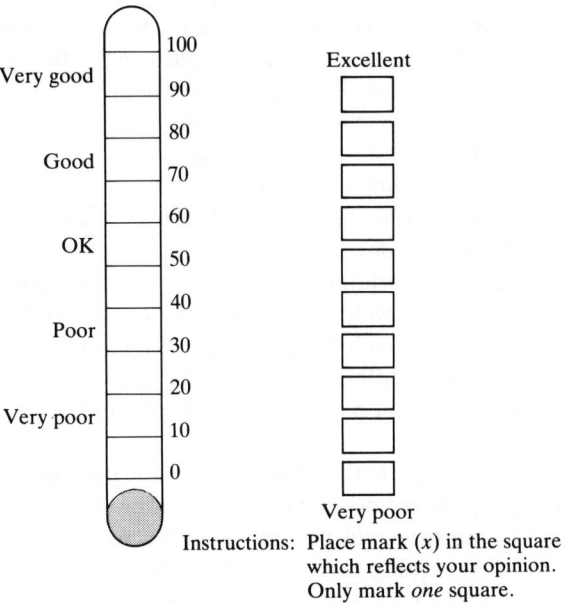

Fig. 8.3 Presentation of questions – the thermometer

8.9 KELLY'S PERSONAL CONSTRUCT THEORY

It is felt by some leading marketing scholars that the study of attitudes limits the overall appreciation of consumers' needs, and that a more comprehensive approach is needed. A better appreciation is needed of 'how an individual's view of the world interacts with messages, their sources, the message setting, the product and its purchase setting, and consumption, so as to lead to improved understanding of the total process'.[47]

This more comprehensive approach rests on personal construct theory, which was a new theory of human behaviour, based on a 'repertory grid' technique of interviewing and classifying subjects, propounded by Professor George A. Kelly in his book *The Psychology of Personal Constructs*. Professor Kelly, who died in 1967, was Professor of Psychology at the Ohio State University, qualifying first as a mathematician and physicist before taking a psychology degree.

Kelly visualized all as scientists: '... each in [a] personal way assumed more of the structure of a scientist, ever seeking to predict and control ... events in which he [or she] is involved'.[48]

Man is active and involved in determining his actions – not a mere pawn in the business game as Vance Packard and other popular writers have suggested. Attempts to understand what is happening and to predict the course of future events use certain criteria in evaluation. The criteria used will be personal to him or her, and these Kelly termed 'constructs'. Within the limitations of these constructs, an individual endeavours to bring some order into the perceptual world. Kelly held that since an individual's behaviour is governed by attempts to predict the future, a detailed study of these constructs will give insight into his or her whole personality and behaviour.

In the course of living, the individual develops a series of constructs to help in dealing with situations which arise. The terms of these constructs may limit, of course, the appreciation of particular situations, but they form, in general, an economical method of dealing with problems and allow the future to be considered within the limits of personal experience and knowledge.

As the individual gains experience of life, some personal constructs may be discarded or modified and new ones developed which will enable a satisfactory relationship with the world about us to be continued. It is conceded that people react differently to events and some, according to Kelly, may exhibit certain inadequacies stemming from deficiencies in their system of personal constructs, of which they may not consciously be aware.

Kelly's personal construct theory is basically concerned with classifying personality along a series of constructs which are bipolar, single dimensional scales. For example, weight is a true construct referring to the bipolar scale light/heavy. But light is not a construct, because it refers only to one extreme of a bipolar scale.

Kelly developed an ingenious technique known as repertory grid analysis which enabled personality to be classified on a scientific basis along a set of constructs. The grid is composed of evaluations made by a respondent of a list of people presented to him in sets of three. He is asked to state in what way any of them differs from the other two. In the case of three men, Smith, Jones, and Robinson, the respondent may use the construct of height, with the bipolar scale of tall/short.

Other names, in groups of three, are then taken systematically from the list and are considered along the same construct. Different constructs will then be developed by the respondent and similarly assessed until a repertory grid has been constructed of certain criteria or constructs used by the respondent in attempting to classify the persons listed. Correlation analysis of the entries on the grid indicates the way in which the respondent's constructs are related to each other.

Table 8.2 shows a possible repertory grid analysis.

Thomas[47] commented that:

> Some relation must exist between polar positioning of an object in a construct system and attitudes

towards it as conventionally measured. Kelly indicates clearly that the concept of bipolar constructs does not oppose scaling concepts, and that several bases exist for deriving attitude scales from construct systems.

Table 8.2   Repertory gird analysis

	Tall/Short	Good/Bad	Fat/Thin	Etc.
Smith	0	1	1	
Jones	1	0	0	
Robinson	0	1	0	

(Score 1 for left-hand pole; 0 for right-hand pole)

He gives a helpful example of an evaluative construct extending the cleavage of three other constructs, as shown in Fig. 8.4.

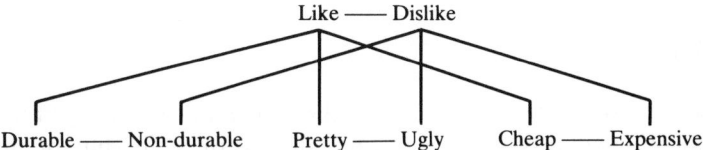

Fig. 8.4   Example of Kelly's Personal Construct Theory

> A product construed as durable, pretty and cheap will be evaluated extremely favourably, and that evaluation would increase in unfavourability as the product was moved, one construct at a time, to the contrast poles. In a system of this nature, the superordinate construct indicates the direction of evaluation, and the degree of polarization is given by the positioning of an object at the poles of subordinate constructs.

The value of Kelly's construct theory to marketing analysis has been given relatively little attention. Thomas has suggested that in the field of marketing communication, particularly advertising, knowledge of how an individual views the world and interacts with persuasive messages is of prime importance.

That Kellian psychology can make a valuable contribution to advertising studies is also acknowledged by Francis Harmar-Brown,[49] who points out:

> Advertisements are today quite an important part of the mass of data that a person has to organise and control in order to predict future events. It would be extremely interesting to know what constructs in this area, different sub-groups of people have in common; and in what way these sub-groups are related to existing media groups, for example. Repertory grid analyses on a group of respondents using as data a series of different advertisements in a related product field, would, I think, yield fascinating results. But as far as I know, this has not yet been done. Instead, the advertising business has ignored, almost completely, Kelly's theories of human behaviour and has rushed to apply repertory grid techniques in areas for which they are totally unsuitable, simply because the techniques are objective, scientific, and statistically respectable.

This carefully qualified approval of Kellian psychological techniques deserves further consideration. Harmar-Brown stresses that Kelly's techniques were designed:

> not to classify the data available to a person but to reveal a person's inadequacies, or successes, in attempting the task for himself. As a marketing tool, all that repertory grid analyses tells us is that the mind of the average housewife is totally inadequate to the task of categorising a product market – not a very surprising result.

The application of Kellian methods is seen as having severe limitations as a tool of marketing analysis: 'I have been concerned with only four cases in which repertory grid analysis has been used to categorise a market. In every case the results were extremely limited, obvious to the point of banality; or downright incomprehensible'.

The valueless nature of some of the responses derived from repertory grid interviews is also noted by Sampson,[12] who categorizes two virtually useless responses:

1. Those which are too descriptive or irrelevant. ('Those two come in bottles; that one comes in a cardboard packet'.)
2. Those which are too evaluative. ('I like those two; I don't like that one'.)

Repertory grids have been used in developing new product concepts, and frequently to obtain attributes for semantic scales.

Further consideration of construct theory in the marketing sphere is called for; the intellectual attractions of Kellian techniques need to be tested at some length before they can be expected to win the support of practical researchers.

8.10 SUMMARY

Qualitative research is essentially diagnostic; it seeks deeper understanding of factors, sometimes covert, which influence buying behaviour. Intrinsically it is subjective but for all its limitations it is able to provide unique insights which direct questioning is unable to obtain.

Qualitative research uses depth interviews (group and individual) and projective techniques; there are several variations of both of these approaches. The former cover synectics, brain-storming, indirect or non-directive interviewing, focus groups, etc. The latter include tests such as: third person, word association, sentence completion, thematic apperception. Rorschach ink blots, story completion, and psychodrama.

Attitude research uses various sealing techniques such as Thurstone's equal-appearing intervals, Likert summated ratings, Guttman's scales (scalogram analysis) and semantic ratings, Guttman's scales (scalogram analysis) and semantic differentials (Osgood, *et al.*) Because some of these scales are versatile and relatively easy to use, care is needed to ensure that the resultant information is valid and reliable.

Kelly's personal construct theory provides a creative approach to understanding better how an individual deals with the many events in his perceptual world. Repertory grid analysis is a technique used to evaluate an individual's constructs, and has been useful in developing bipolar scales.

REFERENCES

1. Lazer, W., 'Marketing research: past accomplishments and potential future developments', *Journal of Market Research Society*, vol. 16, no. 3, 1974.
2. Joyce, Timothy, 'The role of the expert in market research', Market Research Society, Summer School, July 1963.
3. Lunn, J. A., 'Empirical techniques in consumer research', in: *Industrial Society*, Pelican, London, 1968.
4. Chisnall, Peter M., *Marketing: A Behavioural Analysis*, McGraw-Hill, Maidenhead, 1985.
5. Cooper, Peter, 'The new qualitative technology', in: *Qualitative Research: The 'New', the 'Old', and a Question Mark*, Peter Sampson, (ed.), ESOMAR Marketing Research Monograph Series, vol. 2, ESOMAR, Amsterdam, 1987.
6. Market Research Society, 'Qualitative research – A summary of the concepts involved', R&D

Sub-Committee on Qualitative Research, *Journal of Market Research Society*, vol. 21, no. 2, April 1979.

7. McIver, Colin, *The Marketing Mirage: How to make it a reality*, Mandarin, London, 1990.

8. Crespi, Irving, 'Attitude measurement, theory and prediction', *Public Opinion Quarterly*, vol. 41, no. 3, autumn 1977.

9. Cooper, Peter, and Alan Branthwaite, 'Qualitative technology'; New perspectives on measurement and meaning through qualitative research. *Proceedings of the Market Research Society Conference*, 1977.

10. Moser, C. A., and G. Kalton, *Survey Methods in Social Investigation*, Heinemann, London, 1971.

11. Green, Paul E., and Donald S. Tull, *Research for Marketing Decisions*, Prentice-Hall, New York, 1975.

12. Sampson, Peter, 'Qualitative research and motivation research' in *Consumer Market Research Handbook*, Robert Worcester and John Downham (eds.), Van Nostrand Reinhold. Wokingham, 1978.

13. Cooper, Peter, 'Comparison between the UK and US: The qualitative dimension', *Journal of Market Research Society*, vol. 31, no. 4, October 1989.

14. de Groot, Gerald, 'Qualitative research: Deep, dangerous, or just plain dotty?', *European Research*, vol. 14, no. 3, July 1986.

15. Goldman, Alfred, E., 'The group depth interview', *Journal of Marketing*, vol. 26, July 1962.

16. Berelson, W., 'Content analysis' in *Handbook of Social Psychology*, G. Lindsey (ed.), Addison-Wesley, Cambridge, Mass., 1954.

17. Sands, Saul, 'Can business afford the luxury of test marketing?', *University of Michigan Business Review*, vol. 30, no. 2, March 1978.

18. Cooper, Peter, and Giles Lenton, 'Doctor as drug', *Proceeding of BPMRG Symposium*, 1983.

19. Lunn, Tony, Peter Cooper, and Oliver Murphy, 'The fluctuating fortunes of the UK Social Democratic Party: An application of creative qualitative research', 36th ESOMAR Congress, Barcelona, 1983.

20. Churchill, David, 'Marilyn's bait for the boys', *Financial Times*, 30 September 1990.

21. Gildon, Paul, 'Ethnic minorities', MRS Survey, London, Spring 1988.

22. Goodyear, Mary, 'Qualitative research in developing countries', *Journal of Market Research Society*, vol. 24, no. 2, April 1982.

23. Oppenheim, A. N., *Questionnaire Design and Attitude Measurement*, Heinemann, London, 1969.

24. Dichter, Ernest, *The Strategy of Desire*, Doubleday, New York, 1960.

25. Haire, Mason, 'Projective techniques in marketing research', *Journal of Marketing*, April 1950.

26. Arndt, Johan, 'Haire's shopping list revisited', *Journal of Advertising Research*, vol. 13, no. 5, October 1973.

27. Anderson, James C., 'The validity of Haire's shopping list projective technique', *Journal of Marketing Research*, vol. 15, no. 4, November 1978.

28. Sheth, Jagdish N., 'A review of buyer behaviour', *Management Science*, vol. 13, no. 12, August 1967.

29. Vicary, James M., 'How psychiatric methods can be applied to market research', *Printer's Ink*, vol. 235, 11 May 1951.

30. Osborn, Alex F., *Applied Imagination* (3rd Rev. Edn), Charles Scribner's Sons, New York, 1963.

31. Gordon, W. J. J., *Synectics, The Development of Creative Capacity*, Harper & Row, New York, 1961.

32. Kotler, Philip, *Marketing Management: Analysis, Planning and Control*, Prentice-Hall, New Jersey, 1969.

33. Sampson, Peter, 'Can consumers create new products?', *Journal of Market Research Society*, vol. 12, no. 1, 1970.

34. Ferber, Robert, and P. J. Verdoorn, *Research Methods in Economics and Business*, The Macmillan Company, Canada, 1969.

35. Thurstone, L. L., and E. J. Chave, *The Measurement of Attitudes*, University of Chicago Press, 1929.

36. Krech, David, Richard S. Crutchfield, and Egerton L. Ballachey, *Individual in Society*, McGraw-Hill, New York, 1962.

37. Likert, Rensis, 'A technique for the measurement of attitudes', *Archives of Psychology*, no. 140, 1932.

38. Worcester, Robert M., and Timothy R. Burns, 'A statistical examination of the relative precision of verbal scales', *Journal of the Market Research Society*, vol. 17, no. 3, July 1975.

39. Guttman, Louis, 'The basis for scalogram analysis' in *Measurement and Prediction*, Princeton University Press, 1950.

40. Richards, Elizabeth A., 'A commercial application of Guttman attitude scaling techniques', *Journal of Marketing*, vol. 22, no. 2, October 1957.

41. Osgood, Charles E., George J. Suci, and Percy H. Tannenbaum, *The Measurement of Meaning*, University of Illinois Press, Urbana, 1957.

42. Morton-Williams, Jean, 'Questionnaire design' in *Consumer Market Research Handbook*, Robert Worcester and John Downham (eds), Van Nostrand Reinhold, Wokingham, 1978.

43. Anderson, R. C., and E. A. Scott, 'Supermarkets: Are they really alike?', *Journal of Retailing*, autumn 1970.

44. Nagashima, Akira, 'A comparison of Japanese and US attitudes towards foreign products', *Journal of Marketing*, vol. 34, January 1970.

45. Nagashima, Akira, 'A comparative "made in" product, image survey among Japanese businessmen', *Journal of Marketing*, vol. 41, no. 3, July 1977.

46. Hughes, G. David, 'Upgrading the semantic differential', *Journal of the Market Research Society*, vol. 17, no. 1, 1975.

47. Thomas, Robert E., 'Marketing processes and personal construct theory', *Advertising Quarterly*, no. 20, summer 1969.

48. Kelly, G. A., *Psychology of Personal Constructs*, vol. 1, W. W. Horton, New York, 1955.

49. Harmar-Brown, Francis, 'Constructing Kelly – The lure of classification', *Advertising Quarterly*, no. 18, winter 1968–69.

PART
THREE

SPECIFIC RESEARCH APPLICATIONS

CHAPTER NINE

CONTINUOUS MARKETING RESEARCH

9.1 PANELS

A panel or longitudinal survey is a form of sample survey from which comparative data from the sampling units are taken on more than one occasion. Panels can be made up of individuals, households, or firms, and are a convenient method of obtaining continuous information over a period of time.

Regular monitoring of the market for specific products provides two levels of valuable information: (i) general, and (ii) specific.

The first type of data covers broad measurement of the trends in total market expenditure and gives, for example, indications of the impact of some popular news story about diet and health, as has happened in the case of cholesterol content of some foods and the risk of heart disease. The impact of factors 'as much political as social and often occurring with great suddenness and unpredictability',[1] on shopping habits can be checked relatively quickly by companies which subscribe to panel research services.

The second type of data provides continuous purchasing records of individual consumers; these enable changes in shopping preferences, such as brand switching, to be assessed against television viewing habits or some other factor, perhaps family size. Other important uses of continuous data relate to frequency of purchase, established repeat-buying, and repeat-buying pattern of a new brand.

Manufacturers who subscribe to consumer panel surveys can obtain very valuable information about the types of consumer who buy their products, and their buying behaviour. A relatively small number of buyers frequently accounts for a large proportion of the sales of a product. Consumer panel research reveals the frequency of purchase as well as the extent of brand loyalty.

When matched but independent samples are used rather than the panel technique, the degree of sampling error is likely to result in the data being less reliable than those obtained by the latter technique. Because panels are inherently long-term research, data are collected which may reveal significant market segments for certain kinds of products as, for example, has been observed with consumer durables. New homes, newly weds, and recently moved households, were found to represent about 2.5 per cent of the general population in a given quarter but account for 15 per cent of washing machine sales, 20 per cent of refrigerators, 25 per cent of cookers, and 50 per cent of central heating installations.[2]

Panels can be used to evaluate products, advertising themes, advertising viewing, consumer buying patterns, etc. Data are collected from the same sampling units at regular intervals either by mail or personal interview. The method is particularly valuable in studying behavioural and attitudinal changes – which is not possible with single interviews, unless a series of successive but independent samples is taken. The passage of time is always a problem with market investigation, particularly where variables outside the researcher's control may be subject to considerable change over a relatively short period.

Continuous research services demand considerable investment in back-up facilities such as specialized staff, computers, etc., and so retail audits and panels are dominated by the large research organizations – A. C. Nielsen and Pergamon AGB. There are, however, several other research firms running highly successful continuous survey services.

9.2 CONSUMER PURCHASE PANELS

These are the most commonly used panels. Selection of the panel members follows the principles of random sampling used in single surveys. It is generally done by using either a systematic (quasi-random) technique or stratified random sampling. The aim is to achieve a representative membership of an adequately sized panel, which is not easy because people are being asked to supply information of a continuous nature.

The original Attwood Consumer Panel, which started in the UK in 1948, was based on a randomly selected panel of households and experienced some difficulties in recruitment. About 80 per cent of contacts agreed to be enrolled, but by the time the first reporting period arrived, 20 per cent of these failed to cooperate. The remaining 64 per cent of the initial sample did not all stay the course, and a further 16 per cent of the total were lost in the first six weeks, so that 48 per cent of the original sample were left. Those who refused to cooperate or who failed to do so, were replaced by households of similar demographic characteristics; but there remains the problem of bias. It is difficult to know how different those who do not respond are from actual panel members, and how non-response may affect representativeness of the panel.

Another problem of consumer panels is mortality, not just in the conventional sense of the phenomenon, but also because of the drop-out rate, as the Attwood example indicated. To some extent this can be overcome by inflating the size of the original sample, but, of course, this entails extra expense.

Less than one-third of a continuous panel operated by the Market Research Corporation of America were serving as members six months later. In addition, 40 per cent of those contacted had refused to cooperate.[3] The hidden biases, apart from heavy costs, are severe handicaps in developing panel research.

There is some evidence[3] that the stability of American panel membership is influenced by the range and types of products under survey. If only a few products are involved, interest in these products seems to be a prime factor: 40 per cent of cosmetic users withdrew from a panel concerned with cosmetic usage, compared with 59 per cent of non-users.

Other potential weaknesses of panel research may arise from atypical behaviour. New members may suddenly change; for example, their established patterns of television viewing or food buying. To overcome this bias, panel operators may exclude data from new members for a given period. Existing members of a panel may be subject to 'conditioning' and begin to behave in an untypical fashion. They may become self-conscious in their buying habits because they happen to be on a consumer panel, and there is a danger that their reactions in buying situations will become atypical. This danger can be reduced by limiting the time of panel membership and replacing members with others of similar demographic characteristics from a randomly selected 'reserve' list, though it is admittedly difficult to remove from the panel members who have been loyal and reliable. An additional safeguard lies in checking the panel against occasional random samples, taken independently of the population under study.

Yet another source of problems relating to panel research are the heavy costs involved in recruitment and maintenance. This tends to limit the size of a sample, and so affects the extent to which micro-market analyses are feasible.

Further, it is difficult to investigate attitudes or motivations on a continuous or repetitive basis. The first questioning will have alerted respondents and caused them to develop radically different frames of reference which are likely to affect their later responses.[2]

However, a distinct advantage of panel research is the fact that it *is* a long-term operation. This enables considerable investment to be made by research companies into designing high-quality samples and effective methods of ensuring that panels remain representative.

9.3 PANEL METHODOLOGY

Consumer panel data can be gathered at the point-of-sale using bar coding and related electronic systems, or in the home by means of (i) home audits; (ii) diaries, and more recently (iii) electronic scanners used in panel households. Home audits involve research staff visiting panel members' homes and, with their permission, physically checking household stocks of specific products surveyed by the panel. Used packaging is saved by the panel member and stored in a special container, so that these can also be checked ('dustbin check'). Respondents also answer a short questionnaire.

Most panels use some form of 'diary', which members fill in with details of purchases of a range of food and other frequently purchased products, and return to the controlling survey organization. Some organizations operate a weekly system of reporting, which is considered to result in more reliable data than if the time interval is extended. Costs obviously have to be borne in mind.

Diaries should be easy to complete: the layout and terminology should make the task of recording purchases as simple as possible. Completed diaries should be carefully checked by survey staff before processing the data, and any anomalies should be investigated.

It is customary to give panel members some relatively small financial reward for their cooperation. Where products are being tested, members are sometimes allowed to retain or purchase these at a nominal cost.

Useful market experiments can be undertaken with panels by studying the effects of some stimulus, e.g., advertising, to which half of the panel may be exposed. The other half, perhaps in a different part of the country, can be used as a control group. Brand-switching studies can be particularly applicable to panels as individual behaviour can be identified, which is obviously impossible using separate samples.

9.4 AMERICAN CONSUMER PANELS

In the US, consumer panel research is well established and is used in many marketing enquiries covering official, professional, and trade activities. Large consumer panels are run by NPD Research, the Market Research Corporation of America (MRCA), Market Facts, and National Family Opinion (NFO). The NPD Panel covers 13 000 families nationwide; several local market panels are also organized. The MCRA Panel of about 10 000 households dispersed throughout the US operates weekly diaries recording, in detail, the purchases of a wide range of consumer products. Type of product, brand, weight or quantity, package size and style, price, place and time of purchase, also any special promotional offer, are all entered on these weekly sheets.

Diaries are kept on a monthly basis for such items as clothing and photographic equipment, which are bought less frequently than food.

Another well-known American consumer panel with a membership of over 600 families in the metropolitan area of Chicago is operated by the *Chicago Tribune*. The information obtained from this research assists the advertising department of this famous newspaper in selling space.

J. Walter Thompson runs a consumer purchase panel using diary reporting on a monthly basis.

9.5 BRITISH CONSUMER PANELS

Several of the larger research organizations offer continuous research services, and the following examples illustrate the types of panel research which are available. (See also Chapter 11 on advertising research.)

AGB Superpanel

Audits of Great Britain Ltd (AGB), a leading UK-based marketing research organization acquired by Pergamon in 1988, has offered continuous research services for many years. Of these, Attwood Statistics Ltd, which was eventually bought by AGB, was the first marketing research agency to operate a household consumer panel in Great Britain. It started operations in 1948 with a UK-based consumer panel, and extended later to a number of European countries.

AGB's Superpanel replaces its previous Television Consumer Audit (TCA) Toiletries and Cosmetic Purchasing Index (TCPI), and the long-established Attwood Consumer Panel services. AGB has also acquired from the Mars Group, its NMRA Retail Audit service, and has introduced a durable retail auditing service, Lek-Trak, which measures the sales of electrical and electronic products at retail level, by analysis of computerized sales tapes.

The AGB Superpanel is similar to and in direct competition with Nielsen's Homescan (see later notes); it comprises 8500 households – an estimated 28 000 individuals – who are equipped with electronic scanners, similar to those used at supermarket check-out desks, which record price, place of purchase, and selected brand. This enables rapid trend analyses to be supplied to AGB's clients.

Nielsen: Homescan

In the late 1980s, Nielsen launched Homescan, a grocery consumer panel based on 7100 homes, which were derived from the Nielsen establishment survey of 80 000 households. Each panellist involved in the Homescan survey, is provided with a portable bar-code scanner or 'wand', and after each shopping trip purchased items are recorded by means of the 'wand'. When the programmed questions have been completed, the 'wand' is placed in a modem which is linked to the telephone for transfer of the stored data to the production centre. At frequent intervals (e.g., weekly), the automatic dial-up facility at the production centre contacts the panellist's home (a suppressed ring at midnight or later). Data are passed down the line without any panellist's direct involvement. Core data can vary but typical coverage includes: consumer purchases/expenditure and value; penetration – percentage of homes buying; average weight of purchase – average bought by each home buying; average purchase occasions – average number of times each home bought; average price. Other analyses can be designed according to clients' needs.

Taylor Nelson: Family Food Panel

Taylor Nelson and Associates (TNA), which offers a range of special research services, established in 1974 a panel to monitor family eating habits and behaviour. All food and drink, whether home-made or bought from stores, is covered by this continuous survey which operates by means of a two-weekly diary.

The panel covers the whole of Great Britain, and a minimum of 2000 diaries are completed each quarter. Stratification is by constituency/ward spread over 200 sampling points.

Data include types of food and drink consumed, brands, method of preparation, packaging, meal occasions, and demographic profiles of households. The National Dairy Council has used the Family Food Panel to monitor trends in consumption, particularly of home-made foods.

Another TNA service is a continuous survey of social trends and their relationship to consumer opinions and purchasing behaviour. This service, known as *Monitor*, is a multi-sponsored qualitative investigation based on a random sample of 1500 persons aged 16–65. Similar research services are carried out in the US, Canada, France, Japan, Switzerland, Germany, Italy, Scandinavia, and Finland through research institutes which are linked with a central institute in Switzerland entirely dedicated to the international study of social change.

Taylor Nelson Financial (TNF), the specialist financial division of Taylor Nelson, runs the *Insurance Broker's Monitor*, a quarterly survey of opinions of insurance companies' marketing activity; 500 brokers are interviewed each quarter.

A further TNF service is the *City Panel* which consists of 450 'City' decision makers who are interviewed regularly on a wide range of topics of current interest.

Gordon Simmons Research

This research firm offers syndicated studies in the financial, confectionery, retail, and services sectors.

Research International

Formerly known as Research Bureau Ltd (RBL), the company has, since 1962, featured prominently among the leading UK agencies providing information for marketing and social planners. With offices in 30 countries, RI is able to offer a comprehensive marketing research service throughout the world.

Within RI there are nine general *ad hoc* research groups handling a wide variety of client accounts. These include fast-moving consumer goods such as food, drink, and household products, together with more specific market sectors such as finance, retailing, travel, leisure, and consumer durables.

9.6 TELEPHONE PANELS

In Chapter 6, telephone survey techniques were seen to be increasing significantly; CATI and DCI, which are relatively new research methodologies, are attracting considerable interest among survey organizations covering both consumer and industrial markets. Central telephone interviewing facilities were also noted to have expanded markedly over the past few years.

Capital Radio and Marplan (now part of Research International) developed a telephone panel – 'probably the first in Europe'[4] – consisting of 2000 respondents resident in Capital Radio's broadcast area in London. These were recruited to be representative of all adults in the area; all could be contacted at home or work by telephone, thus forming a 'direct access' telephone panel. This service no longer operates.

Capital Radio's direct access telephone panel was set up in 1978 for programme research, and following successful experience, it was decided to expand its scope to both advertising effectiveness and 'recognition' studies (see Chapter 11). In addition, the panel has been used frequently for public opinion polling on a range of topics, from housing to violence and vandalism.

Marplan[4] was convinced that direct access telephone panels would become the major tool of market and social research over the next decade, pointing out that in America the telephone interview is now the most widely used technique of survey. Marplan's prediction is certainly coming true.

Medical survey panels are operated by several marketing research firms, e.g., Facts International which telephones 500 GPs twice a month, and Martin Hamblin Research which operates a monthly telephone panel of 500 GPs.

9.7 USE OF PANELS IN FORECASTING

Panel research data are particularly useful in developing forecasts for the long-term sales of new products which have been subject to test marketing. The cumulative percentage of consumers who have bought a particular brand of product, and the percentage of those making repeat purchases, could be gathered from continuous panel research reports.

A typical set of figures of sales of a new brand of a product over a period of some weeks is shown in Fig. 9.1, while in Fig. 9.2 a typical pattern of repeat purchases is graphed.

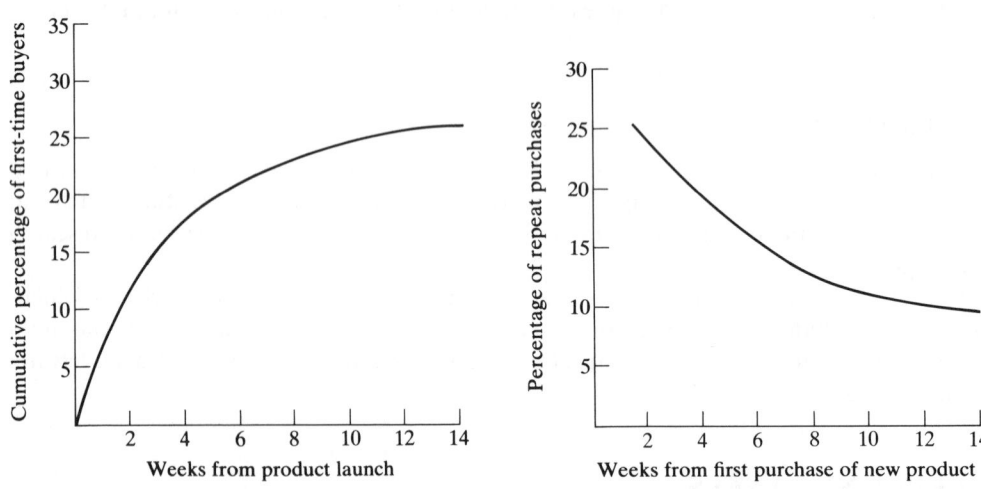

Fig. 9.1   Typical cumulative sales of new product   **Fig. 9.2**   Typical repeat purchase pattern

From the examples displayed in Figs 9.1 and 9.2, the long-term market for the new product could be calculated thus:

Market penetration × Repeat purchase rate = Market share
$$0.25 \times 0.10 = 2.5 \text{ per cent}$$

This forecast could be improved by incorporating a buying-rate index as follows:

Assume that buyers of this new brand represent 40 per cent of all buyers of that kind of product, but account for 45 per cent of the total market purchases. Hence, a buying-rate index would be $\frac{45}{40}$ or 1.125.

Applying this result to the early equation:

$$0.25 \times 0.10 \times 1.125 = 2.8 \text{ per cent.}$$

It will be noted that the second method results in a slightly increased market share being extrapolated. Other refinements have been developed by researchers,[5,6] but it should be remembered that extrapolation assumes that market conditions remain relatively unchanged – which is problematical.

The prediction model has been further developed by Parfitt and Clay,[7] whose researchers enabled them to arrive at these important conclusions:

1. Repeat buying is the most critical of the three factors which make up brand share (see above equation).
2. The later buyers enter a market the lower (on average) their repeat buying is likely to be.

The Electricity Council[8] used panel data, particularly AGB's Home Audit, to measure household ownership and use of electrical appliances, and also to monitor energy usage throughout the year. These data help in load forecasting and in planning future energy supplies.

With AGB, the Electricity Council set up *ad hoc* panels of about 500 households using a diary technique to record use of their cooking, heating, and water heating appliances during half-hour time periods for each day of a four-week recording interval; a specially designed Usage Recording Optimal Mark Reading document is used and respondents are fully briefed about the method of recording, etc.

9.8 SHOP AUDIT VERSION OF PANEL RESEARCH

This was pioneered in the US by A. C. Nielsen in the early 1930s, and came to the UK in 1939. Today, part of the huge Dun and Bradstreet Corporation, Nielsen operates its Retail Index services in 27 countries. In Great Britain, regular audits are operated to cover products sold through grocers, confectioners, toy retailers, tobacconists, and newsagents; off-licences, pharmacies, and drug stores; electrical, DIY, and hardware stores; and cash-and-carry wholesalers. This information is of use to manufactuers.

Nielsen Index Reports, supplied to subscribers, are based on a sample of stores which are audited every two months to provide information on purchases, stocks, sales promotions, and price levels over a range of products. The resulting data are projected from the sample to national population figures, so that estimates of vital movements of merchandise through selected outlets can be studied by manufacturers who subscribe to the Nielsen service. Market size, market share, geographic distribution of market, effectiveness of pricing, and promotional policies, etc., can be evaluated.

Ex-factory sales figures by themselves will not accurately reflect consumer demand for a product, and deliveries from the factory will have been at a high rate during the introductory stages in order to build up stocks in wholesalers' and retailers' stores in anticipation of demand. By the time consumer demand begins to climb to a peak, it is likely that deliveries from the factory will have fallen and this could lead to the wrong assumption, i.e., that consumer demand for the product is falling. Unless some research is undertaken, the real movement of the product in the stores will not be known.

The activities of competitors are likely to affect sales of an individual manufacturer who has launched a new product, and reliable information is needed to guide management. For instance, it could be critical to know whether the new product had expanded the total market for this type of product or if it had merely attracted sales from competing brands. If the total market has not expanded, the market shares of competitive manufacturers will have fallen, and their reactions will be noted by audit research.

The distribution of the total volume of sales of a product type over various kinds of outlet, i.e., where consumers actually buy, is of concern to manufacturers in that market. A relatively small proportion of outlets frequently accounts for a large share of the volume of sales in a market. If a manufacturer plans to be in those outlets where the majority of consumer purchases are made, research is needed to identify these stores.

It is possible for a manufacturer to have high coverage of the distribution points in her market and for her product to be experiencing limited sales because it is largely distributed among small outlets. These may represent over 60 per cent of the stores retailing that product type, although their total volume of sales may be less than 20 per cent of the entire sales made in that market.

This point is reinforced by Nielsen research in the grocery trade which indicated that five major grocery multiples accounted for 61.1 per cent of grocery turnover in Great Britain in 1988. In 1950, 23 per cent of grocery turnover was handled by cooperatives, 20 per cent by multiples (10 or more branches), and 57 per cent by independents. By 1988, cooperatives accounted for 10.9 per cent of total grocery turnover, multiples had risen to 73.9 per cent and independents had dropped to 15.2 per cent (see Table 9.1).

Table 9.1   Grocery stores (GB): number of outlets/turnover (1988)

Outlet	Turnover (£ millions)	Total turnover (%)	Number of outlets	Total outlets (%)
Cooperatives	3 555	10.9	2 704	5.4
Multiples	24 136	73.9	4 251	8.5
Independents	4 977	15.2	42 941	86.1
Total	32 667	100	49 896	100

Source: Nielsen.

Nielsen

Nielsen selects samples of stores for auditing purposes classifying them by type of organization (cooperatives, multiples, large independents, small independents) and by size, in terms of their volume of business. Auditing is concentrated on those stores which sell the most products, and the principle of disproportionate sampling is applied. Stated simply, this means auditing most where most of the sales are made and where variability in store characteristics is greatest (see Chapter 4). The store panel is continually checked to ensure that it is representative of the general pattern of distribution for the particular types of product audited.

From the large multiple chains Nielsen receives data on computer tape. The company also uses a field force of 180 Nielsen auditors (plus 737 part-time auditors) to visit sample stores throughout Great Britain every month. Stocks of specific types of products are carefully checked and recorded by brand and size. Separate counts are taken of stocks in stock rooms and those in selling areas. This methodical approach also involves checking invoices and delivery notes which retailers have received covering the particular products audited. Note is also taken of selling prices, special offers, display material, and other factors affecting sales of audited lines.

From this systematic audit the sales to consumers of various brands (and sizes) of a product type can be accurately given:

$$\text{Past stocks} + \text{Purchases} - \text{Present stocks} = \text{Sales facts}$$

Nielsen indicates that an average audit takes about two man-days to complete. Every month Nielsen audits over 52 000 items. All the information recorded by the auditors and the computer tapes from the major multiple groups are received at Nielsen's Oxford headquarters. Here the data go through an intricate series of validation checks before processing. The heart of the operation is the IBM 30/84Q. In the computer, expansion factors are applied to the 'raw' data before the final chart and table masters are printed out by a laser scanner. Reports are then reproduced in the printing department.

Nielsen clients are given a formal presentation of the report's findings by experienced executives, who discuss market trends indicated by the research. Most Nielsen clients are 'on-line' to their Nielsen data base and can obtain information at any time at the touch of a button.

A typical Nielsen report shows the following:

Consumer sales: value and volume.
Market shares: sales, stocks, deliveries.
Retail deliveries: total, direct or wholesale.
Retail stocks: total and shelf.
Distribution: shop and turnover weighted.
Out of stock: total and shelf.
Average price: to the consumer.
Average sales and stocks: per store handling.
Average expenditure: manufacturer and brand.

Data are shown individually for trade sectors and regions.

This detailed analysis is given for Great Britain as a whole, and shown separately for the nine areas in which Nielsen operates, and by shop type and size. These regions are based approximately on the major television areas, though they can be substituted by clients' own requirements such as sales areas.

Some large organizations do not cooperate with Nielsen, but this is adjusted by suitably weighting final survey figures. Critics in the past have commented on the method of sampling (quota) used, which can introduce bias, but Nielsen declares that its system of continuous checking and updating ensures that the samples it uses accurately reflect changing patterns of distribution in the trades covered. Inevitably, as with all research, there is a delay before the client receives the survey information, though modern systems of data processing have reduced this time-lag considerably.

Retail Audits Ltd

Retail Audits Ltd was formed in 1966 through the merger of Test Marketing Services Ltd and the audit division of the British Market Research Bureau. In 1987 it became part of Nielsen Marketing Research and now specializes in surveys for the tobacco and automotive industries.

The tobacco research is carried out on a monthly basis through a sample representing all possible outlets where tobacco is sold. It comprises 100 vending operators and 1500 retail outlets representing:

Tobacconists
Grocers
Public Houses
Off licences
Clubs
Garages, etc.

Because of the coverage, the company is in the unique situation of providing total retail market research.

Automotive research is carried out on various product fields through garages and accessory shops. In addition, specialist research is provided on automotive spares and accessories within dealer franchises in the UK and this has now been extended into Europe.

9.9 BACK-UP SERVICES

Panel research is also associated with advertising media in order to give advertisers factual information about the effectiveness of campaigns (see Chapter 11). The increasing competition between media owners has resulted in the development of 'back-up' services for their clients.

Stats MR Ltd

This British company, founded in 1963 and bought by Nielsen in 1985, concentrates on providing a specialized range of retail research services, including continuous audits of grocers, chemists, CTNs, off-licences, free trade on-licences, and department stores. Regular distribution and pricing checks are also conducted over several retail sectors.

Gallup: UK record industry trade audit

In the UK, record album charts are based on information provided by Gallup which collects, on a daily basis, sales data from a sample of 850 retailers, each of whom has an Epson computer linked to a light wand. This wand reads bar codes on each item and registers the sale on disk. Gallup gathers this information, at midnight, from the disk via a modem. Because some items still lack bar codes and their sales have to be punched in by hand, Gallup has statistical methods to check errors in entry. Electronically captured data are then compared with information on the top 150 records from a questionnaire sent to shops. From these two sources, Gallup produces a mid-week chart, available on Thursdays and Fridays, for the record companies.

At the end of the week, all the data are processed and result in the chart ratings broadcast on BBC Radio One on Sunday afternoons, and are also distributed to the record companies and retailers on a regional basis as well as by TV area. Sales are analysed by LP, cassette, and CD. Leading record companies find the TV area analyses of special value in evaluating the effectiveness of their television advertisements.

9.10 TECHNOLOGICAL ADVANCES IN STORE AUDITS

Optical mark reading

Store auditing has traditionally relied on human observation linked to basic paper and pencil recording, a slow and often laborious task.

With optical mark reading (OMR), the auditor still uses a humble pencil or pen, but merely enters a simple mark against a selected response or a multi-choice printed form. Special scanning devices convert these marks into computer input; the presence or absence of a mark is detected by sensing reflected by infra-red light. OMR eliminates, therefore, punched cards and key entry, and also the possibility of errors in transcription.

However, OMR appears to be in rather limited use for retail audits, and data tend to be recorded on to computer printed forms which are subject to key punching.

The relatively limited use of electronic scanning in retail distribution in the UK poses certain problems in sampling. As Bloom[9] points out, the number of scanner stores, and hence their profile, will keep changing for some time ahead, so that their unrepresentativeness will continue, but will be dynamic.

Smaller outlets will apparently still need to be audited by 'traditional' methods.

Mintel reports[10] that OMR, used by BMRB in their massive TGI survey, has re-emerged as a cost-effective way of handling data entry.

Bar coding

Bar codes – a series of black lines of varying thicknesses with numbers beneath them – are now printed on many fast-moving packaged grocery products, and, to a very restricted degree, on some other types of consumer products.

Linked to a hand-held computer, data from bar codes can be fed directly into a central computer via a telephone line, using modems (a device which couples a computer with a telephone). An auditor could use a light pen to identify bar codes on the packaging of goods on store shelves. (See Chapter 6, Section 6.13: Hand-held market research terminal.)

Nielsen has developed a special hand-held computer with a light pen auxiliary device with one megabyte of memory. This equipment – the Nielsen International Auditing Terminal (NIAT) – should overcome the disadvantage of limited capacity of other systems.

Bar codes do not appear on packing cases, so auditors still need to do some manual recording. Another problem refers to bar code standardization; this is being tackled by the Article Number Association (ANA). Nielsen has been appointed by ANA to provide manufacturers with sales data from a selected number of retail outlets with scanning installations.

Electronic point of sale scanning (EPOS)

Bar coding, scanning, and computerized information are all part of the new trend in retail auditing. An 'intelligent' terminal (the cash register) records the bar code on a product; this information is then fed to a central computer and used to compute the bill as well as recording the sale for stock-check purposes.

Mintel[10] has observed that an increasing proportion of input data for retail audits is now derived direct from retailers using output from EPOS scanning equipment. EPOS is diffusing rapidly, and about 80 per cent of UK multiples' retail outlets have this equipment. Mintel commented that the increasing penetration of EPOS will result in a rapid decline in traditional manual audits.

In America and Canada, EPOS is widely used. Check-out scanners are now more competitively priced, bar coding is spreading, and the perceived benefits to retailers, such as better control of in-store 'shrinkage', faster check-out of customers, reduced labour costs, and immediate stock-checks, are helping the diffusion of this technology.

Scanner store consumer panels

In the US, Bloom[11] reported that 1100 regular shoppers at four scanned stores, in which they represent about 10 per cent of total sales, have been recruited to a panel. These shoppers show a card to the cashier and a complete record of their purchases is then automatically made.

In France, during 1970, Nielsen developed a range of electronic research services which it called ERIM (electronic research for insights into marketing). These services enable manufacturers to test new products and promotions; a major development occurred with the use of scanners. ERIM TESTSIGHT, for instance, involves the installation of television meters in a sample of panel households who receive individual commercials via a local relay station.

This particular service has been extended to the US; purchases of members of participating households, who use plastic cards to identify themselves, are recorded by store scanners, and their television viewing habits are measured by a Nielsen Telemeter attached to their TV sets.

The Telemeter enables Nielsen to broadcast TV commercials on a special frequency and insert them into regular programming. Software programs within the Telemeter can switch panel TV sets from the channel being watched to the TV commercial being tested and back again without the viewers being aware of this 'planned' intervention.

This sophisticated research methodology allows matched purchase panel testing of advertising copy over different market segments covering both cable, non-cable, and satellite reception of TV signals.

Nielsen intends to extend its electronic research services to other countries such as Germany, Great Britain, Italy, and the Netherlands.

Nielsen: Scantrack

Scantrack is part of Nielsen's integrated data system which provides regular analyses of retail trends. Linked with Nielsen Retail Index and Homescan data bases, Scantrack data are collected electronically from bar codings on packages and reports are delivered every four weeks. The top five UK multiple grocery retailers are covered, viz., Asda, Gateway, Safeway, Sainsbury, and Tesco, accounting for over 60 per cent of grocery trading.

9.11 OMNIBUS SURVEYS

Several research agencies in the UK offer special facilities for clients to obtain data speedily. This is achieved by inserting questions in consumer survey questionnaires which are continuously in operation. This can be a quick and cheap method of collecting information at very short notice.

Basically, an 'omnibus' survey consists of a series of short questionnaires on behalf of different clients who share the cost of interviewing. Interviews may take up to 30 minutes. The method is economical to use provided an individual client's share of the interviewing time does not exceed about 10 minutes, after which diseconomics become evident and it might be cheaper to have an *ad hoc* survey done.

Questions can cover many areas of interest to individual manufacturers, e.g., brand awareness, price awareness, frequency of purchase, place of purchase, media exposure, etc. Advertising effectiveness could be checked by using 'omnibus' surveys before and after an advertising campaign has taken place.

The content of questions has to be kept simple so that they are easily understood and answered quickly. Open-ended questions are generally unsuitable for this type of survey because they usually take longer to answer and to record verbatim. Agencies charge a premium for including questions of this nature. Care is needed in formulating questions so that they are effective; this is customarily the responsibility of clients who are charged on a question basis plus an 'entry fee' to the survey.

Most omnibus surveys are based on national samples of adults or housewives, though there are a few specialist populations also covered, e.g., car owners. Where clients wish to investigate relatively limited markets the omnibus survey method may be expensive because charges per question are based on the number in the initial sample. This is likely to include a very large number of non-users of the product or service. Full value is obtained when questions are related to the general buying behaviour of the population covered.

Standard analyses offered by agencies operating 'omnibus' services cover the usual demographic breakdowns. Additional analyses are usually available at extra cost, and some clients may find it worth while to seek more refined data.

Speed is one of the principal attractions of 'omnibus' surveys. The time involved depends on the length of notice required by agencies to insert questions (some accept questions up to 10 working days before fieldwork starts), the time taken for interviewing, analysis, and preparation of data (up to four weeks), and the frequency of particular 'omnibus' surveys (this varies with individual agencies).

Leading agencies offering 'omnibus' services include British Market Research Bureau (BMRB 'Access' Survey), and Social Surveys (Gallup Poll) Ltd (Consumer Quest Omnibus Service), and NOP. These professional research organizations advise clients on the suitability of this method of research for particular problems, and provide quotations. Unless specifically requested, charges normally cover presentation of the data in computer tables, which can then be processed and interpreted by clients' own research staff.

BMRB runs a telephone omnibus survey (TMRB). NOP runs a random omnibus of 2000 adults weekly, and a fortnightly quota omnibus also of 2000 adults: these are all based on personal interviews. The random sample is drawn from electoral registers and interviewing is in 180 Parliamentary constituencies. The quota sample is carried out at 180 sampling points among a representative quota sample of adults, 15+ years. In addition, NOP organizes a telephone omnibus which covers 1000 adults each weekend; the sampling frame is derived from all the telephone directories in Britain, and a random sample of pages is selected each weekend. CATI facilities provide for rapid feedback of survey data to clients.

Research Surveys of Great Britain, part of the AGB Group, and Marplan, also run well-known omnibus surveys. MAS operates a general weekly omnibus survey (OMNIMAS), and also a telephone omnibus focusing on small businesses (BUSINESS LINE: 2000 small businesses are surveyed every month).

Omnibus survey services are also available in some European countries such as Germany, France, and Italy, and also in the US and Canada.

9.12 SUMMARY

Panel or longitudinal research provides data which enable trends to be identified, panels can be made up of individuals, households, or firms.

Consumer purchase panels use home audits and/or diaries. Several well-known research companies offer panel services; AGB, BMRB, Research International, etc. A new development is telephone panel research which could become a major tool of market research.

Panel research data are useful in developing long-term forecasts of new product sales.

Nielsen offers extensive shop-audit services and operates in 27 countries; another large organization in this specialized field is Retail Audits Ltd.

Technological advances in store audits are: optical mark reading, bar coding, and point of sale scanning. Scanner store consumer panels are now a significant factor in store audit in America; in Great Britain, Nielsen's TOPS service, based on five large multiples, uses scanners to provide manufacturers with detailed analyses.

Smaller outlets will continue to be audited by 'traditional' methods.

Omnibus surveys consist of a series of short questionnaires on behalf of different clients who share the costs of interviewing, etc.: the type and scope of questioning are necessarily limited. Speed is one of the chief attractions of this service.

REFERENCES

1. Bird, Michael, 'Learning about markets: Applications of continuous attitude research'. *Admap*, July 1976.
2. Buck, Stephan, 'Measuring behaviour: Using a panel can measure change very accurately', *AGB 'Audit'*, spring 1976.
3. Tull, Donald S., and Del I. Hawkins, *Marketing Research: Meaning, Measurement and Method*, Macmillan, New York, 1976.
4. Clemens, John, Colin Day, and Debbie Walter, 'Direct access panel: The research mode for the eighties and beyond'. ESOMAR, Monte Carlo, September 1980.
5. Parfitt, J. H., and B. J. K. Collins, 'Use of consumer panels for brand share prediction', *Journal of Marketing Research*, vol. 5, May 1968.
6. McCloughlin, I., and J. H. Parfitt, 'The use of consumer panels in the evaluation of promotion and advertising expenditure', ESOMAR Congress, Opatija, September 1968.
7. Parfitt, John, and Reg Clay, 'Panel prediction techniques – what we have learned and where we are going', ESOMAR, Monte Carlo, September 1980.
8. Clarke, Margaret, and Jonathan Jephcott, 'A fuel usage panel', ESOMAR, Lucerne, October 1982.
9. Bloom, Derek, 'Scanning the horizon: What automated check-outs will do to and for marketing', *Admap*, July 1982.
10. 'Market research', Special Report, Mintel, London, 1990.
11. Bloom, Derek, 'Point of sale scanners and their implications for market research', *Journal of Market Research Society*, vol. 22, no. 4. 1980.

TEN

TEST MARKETING

10.1 INTRODUCTION

Innovation is necessary for business development: no company can exist for long without new products and services; expectations rise and bring pressures on manufacturers and distributors to supply goods and services to satisfy, at least for a while, the needs of people and organizations.

But the manufacturing and marketing of new products inevitably carries risk, particularly if the innovation is radical.

Before a company commits itself to marketing a product on a national scale, it frequently chooses a limited area where the entire marketing programme, in miniature, can be tested in real-life conditions. In some carefully selected test areas, which should be representative of the eventual national market, new products are exposed to the acid test of consumer acceptance or rejection. This experimental marketing is a form of risk control; before substantial resources are used on a national programme, manufacturers can assess the probability of success from data obtained during the test marketing operation.

Test marketing is generally confined to consumer goods, because industrial products, particularly large items of capital equipment, do not lend themselves to concentrated area testing. Some industrial products can, of course, be given experimental runs in certain industries, e.g., arranging with a food manufacturer to pack a selected line in a new type of film packaging, but these individual tests differ from highly organized test marketing as practised by leading consumer product manufacturers.

It is difficult to assess accurately people's likely behaviour. What they may, in good faith, have told an interviewer during a marketing research investigation could be contrasted with their behaviour at some later time when they are in the actual buying situation. The conditions of the market place are dynamic; there are many calls on people's disposable income and there are many factors – political, social, psychological, etc. – which influence their final pattern of expenditure. In addition, the activities of competing suppliers to the market in areas of pricing, packaging, advertising, special promotions, etc., will affect consumers' behaviour at the point of purchase. Test marketing is, therefore, concerned with finding out what people actually do when they are shopping for their families. The facts obtained from this study serve as a guide to future marketing plans.

One of America's dynamic marketing men, Victor A. Bonomo,[1] warned against the dangers of unplanned marketing: 'Don't make a major capital excursion into the unknown without thorough test marketing, for it is only through market test experience that any degree of certainty can be gained'. These timely words of warning and advice from a highly successful businessman indicate the role of test marketing, which is concerned with what happens in the real market place, as opposed to some theoretical concepts or projections of likely consumer behaviour towards a new product.

A leading American marketing analyst has also commented that 'only by the use of actual market experiments is it possible to estimate or predict reliably the effects of changes in marketing expenditures on the sales volume or net profits of each differentiated product, or customer class, or sales territory in a multi-product, multi-functional business organization'.[2]

Test marketing should be designed to identify specific factors which are most likely to make a product a success in the market place. The best combination of marketing factors, i.e., the marketing mix, can be gauged from a study of comparative test markets.

Some years ago, a classic test marketing experiment involving advertising was conducted by Du Pont with cookware coated with 'Teflon'.[3] The non-stick coated cookware market in the US had suffered from inferior products offered by some manufacturers. By June 1962, the stores had marked down 'Teflon' drastically and were refusing to accept further deliveries. Du Pont developed an improved product, but by then the market had virtually disappeared. The company decided to undertake test marketing at three different levels of advertising over 13 cities in an attempt to revive consumer interest in 'Teflon' coated cookware.

'High' advertising was characterized by 10 day-time television spot advertisements per week; 'low' advertising meant five day-time advertisements per week. In four cities, no advertising at all took place. During each test period a random sample (selected from telephone directories) of 1000 female 'heads of households' was interviewed by telephone in each test market. It was subsequently found that there was no significant difference between the sales figures for areas covered by 'low advertising' and 'no advertising', and these two groups were combined in later analysis.

The experiments showed that advertising of the improved 'Teflon' coated cookware was effective at a high level, but that, at a low level, it had no significant effect on sales. The market expanded most where advertising had been maintained at a constant high level. On the other hand, in those areas where there had been a high level of advertising in the autumn of 1962 followed by reduced advertising (or no advertising at all) in the winter of 1963, the total market contracted below that of areas where virtually no advertising had been done.

These market tests indicated to Du Pont that it was possible to revive the 'Teflon' cookware market provided the company was prepared to back its product by continuous and concentrated advertising.

Test marketing is now widely accepted by leading consumer product manufacturers as standard practice, though it has critics whose views are considered later. There is obviously a need to reduce the substantial risks inherent in marketing new products, and this can be done by some form of test marketing. There will, of course, be costs involved in this exercise, and these should be carefully estimated and offset against the risks of failure in a national launch. Where heavy commitments must be made in order to produce for a national marketing operation and the probability of success is no more than 50/50, it is prudent to invest in a test programme. 'Test marketing is warranted if, and only if, it will probably save money for the company ... whenever the financial risk of going with the product or plan is greater than the cost of conducting the test.'[4]

This remark was made by Mr Joseph J. O'Hanlon, manager of the controlled sales test division of Sears Roebuck and Company, the world's largest merchandisers. He claims that less than 20 per cent of products introduced to markets ever meet their sales goals, and that these failures cost the companies involved anywhere from $25 000 in test markets to $20 million or more for a national launch.

10.2 FAILURE OF NEW PRODUCTS

Even highly experienced companies are not immune to failure, as this sobering list by Peter Kraushar, Chairman of KAE Development Ltd, a leading market consultancy specializing in new product research and development, indicates:

Unilever	'Dark Secrets'
	'Close up'
	'Freshmill'
	'Tree Top'
	'Snack Pots'
Colgate Palmolive	'Reveal'
	'Woodleigh Green'
	'Dynamo'
Kellogg's	'Scanda Crisp'
	'Scanda Brod'
	'Extra'
General Foods	'Appeal'
Cadbury Schweppes	'Cresta'
	'Ticket'
	'Appletree'
	'Chillo'
	'Soya Choice'
Mars	'Banjo'
Pedigree Petfoods	'Hap'
Life Savers	'Bubble Yum'

Beecham's, Bristol Myers and other companies all experienced market failures with men's hair sprays; ready meals 'have been a real graveyard for growth potential'.[5] Allied Ironfounders' efforts to market a new bath in the UK ended in frustration; the company had based the planning and product design entirely on experience in the US. Nestlé launched a range of chewy sweets called 'Fruitips', very similar to Mars' 'Opal Fruits', which were marketed at the same time. The Nestlé product was not a market success, probably because Mars was perceived by the trade and the public to be very much more of a sweet company than Nestlé.[5]

American-owned companies seem to be as prone to marketing failures as British companies, and there is some evidence that traders are inclined to be rather more prejudiced when assessing the market performance of the products of American-owned companies. At one time, American-inspired products were launched in the UK with little or no modification to meet British tastes. Not surprisingly, many of them failed, and the hard lesson appears to have been learned that a shared language does not automatically mean similar preferences in consumer products. General Mills' experience with Betty Crocker cake mixes is now part of marketing folklore, and Campbell's soups have never been able to achieve the market position in the UK which they hold in the US. Campbell's type of soup – 'condensed' and, therefore, requiring the addition of water – was unfamiliar to British housewives, who compared its price and flavour to established favourites such as Heinz.

Some years ago, Nielsen[6] analysed new grocery products which had been test-marketed over a period of 14 years. The most frequent causes of failure were faulty products or packaging (53 per cent). Other strong contributory reasons for failure were poor value for money (20 per cent), lack of adequate advertising support (9 per cent), and lack of trade acceptance (18 per cent). Of the 44 products surveyed, 46 per cent were launched on a national scale and of these, 94 per cent were successful. This study was updated in 1973 to cover 30 new product failures (see Table 10.1).

Table 10.1   Nielsen's analyses of new product failure

Reasons cited as most responsible for failure	1965 study (44 new products)	1973 study (30 new products)
Advertising (lack of advertising support)	9%	3%
Trade acceptance (lack of trade acceptance)	19%	15%
Price value (poor value for money)	20%	15%
Product/package (faulty product/packing)	53%	67%

Source: Nielsen.

It will be noted from Table 10.1 that failure is largely attributable to faults in either the product or its packaging. Nielsen comments that more often the fault was simply that the new product had no demonstrable advantage over existing brands; this clearly affected 'trade acceptance'. 'Me-too' products are hardly likely to win the time or favour of busy trade buyers.

Cadbury's[7] analysed 18 of its own new product failures and found the following major reasons accounted for lack of success: recipe: 7; 'conceptual shortcomings': 4; price: 3; package: 2; and low volume: 2. Of these, recipe was a key variable and acknowledged to be the most important factor for success. Conceptual shortcomings related to the overall positioning and advertising of the product.

In the case of a new biscuit product, Cadbury's experienced failure because commercial production could not match product samples prepared for research tests. An instant croquette potato 'Smasher' failed on account of different preparatory techniques in Cadbury's home economics unit and in housewives' kitchens. 'Swiss Dessert', a fresh cream product, was found to be impossible to stack and display in supermarkets. Instant tea – 'Fine Brew' – was of a concentrated strength and needed only half-a-teaspoon per cup. This measure proved to be troublesome for housewives who were, it seems, loyal to the traditional teapot.

Cadbury's underlines the fact that the reasons for new product failure in a test market are usually complex and difficult to identify. Several factors work together to produce either success or failure. The account given above lists the principal reasons, though the contributory effects of other factors should not be dismissed.

In the US, Del Monte decided, after test marketing, not to introduce nationally a shelf-stable yogurt branded 'Little Lunch', after finding that consumers perceived yogurt to be a refrigerated product. It would have been too expensive to 'educate' them to accept a new concept. Similarly, a subsidiary of CPC International withdrew, after market test, a metal tube-packaged mayonnaise, because American consumers, unlike the British, could·not perceive any significant advantages in this type of dispenser pack.[8]

One of the most disastrous marketing failures of recent years was in the UK tobacco industry and related to the loudly heralded tobacco substitute 'New Smoking Mixture' (NSM). In an analysis[9] of this abortive £4 million market launch, which ended in an industry loss of £70 million, it was stated that if the manufacturers had been prepared to phase marketing of this new product and had given themselves time to test market properly, their experiences would have been less traumatic.

10.3 MARKETS CHANGE OVER TIME

Products may, of course, fail because they are before their time; because they require a fairly fundamental alteration to ingrained habits of consumption or traditional ways of behaving. (See ref. 10 for detailed discussion.)

Some years ago, instant mashed potato failed to attract mass market demand, perhaps because it was then associated too closely with wartime 'substitute' foods. Today it is a very successful product, helped no doubt by the changed attitudes of housewives to convenience foods in general. Another example relates to tea bags for domestic use in Britain; they are now widely used and are the growth section of the rather depressed demand for tea in general. Yet, it took nearly 20 years for these 'American' tea-making habits to be adopted by British housewives in any significant numbers.

This market inertia may also be noted with some more durable products, for which the demand has now assumed an exponential curve. Central heating, for example, is now generally thought to be an essential item of equipment in modern homes. But only a few years ago, central heating for 'popular' housing would have been dismissed as an unnecessary fad, and it would probably have been argued that the British climate is far more stable than America's, whose inhabitants needed complete heating systems far more urgently than in this temperate climate. Attitudes have again changed, incomes have risen, and consumers seek to satisfy their growing needs, which include greater comfort in their homes. Other household products are beginning to attract more general interest; deep freezers are following the pattern of refrigerators as 'necessary' household equipment. Diffusion of such products will be increased as the public become more aware of the need for food hygiene; other contributory factors derive from growing affluence, social contacts, great competition which resulted in prices being far keener than formerly, and the tendency for modern houses to be built without the old-style larder.

10.4 SEQUENTIAL APPROACH TO TEST MARKETING

Eight important steps in test marketing can be identified and are considered in some detail in the following sections.

1. Define the objectives

As with other management problems, the first step involves defining clearly the objectives of the operation. Objectives, as noted earlier, will vary according to the specific products under examination and the market conditions which are typically experienced. Statement of the objectives should be in writing, as this ensures that those who propose to undertake the test marketing have marshalled their thoughts in a disciplined manner. Decisions regarding the selection of test areas, control areas, sample sizes, audit frequency, etc., can then be rationally made. Whatever the objectives, care should be taken to ensure that there is complete understanding and agreement by all those taking part in the exercise, and, of course, ratification by top management. Ideally, one variable at a time would be tested in any one market. This could be, as in the case of Du Pont, the study of the effects of different levels of advertising. If too many variables are tested at the same time in one test area, it tends to be difficult to identify their specific influence, although sophisticated methods of statistical analyses have overcome this handicap to some degree.

2. Set criteria of success

Again, modern management techniques demand that performance should be assessed against agreed standards of success; this principle applies equally to test marketing procedures. The criteria set should be realistic and proportionate to the volume of sales, the level of distribution, or share of the market (some of several possible targets) which would be expected at national level. Where advertising is being studied, it would be necessary for researchers to note the degree of increase in sales which would be regarded as significant.

Evaluation must be strictly objective – the enthusiasm of test marketing should not be allowed to influence cool, reasoned assessment of the opportunities which might exist for a new product on a national scale.

3. Integrate test marketing operations

It is vital to ensure that the test marketing campaign fits into the overall marketing plan. For example, the level of selling effort, or the amount spent on advertising, should be consistent with the general marketing policy of the company. Abnormal results are likely to occur if only 'crack' salesmen are used in test areas; likewise, excessive advertising will also distort the natural movements which test marketing is concerned to study. The assessment of an appropriate level of advertising raises special problems for marketing managers. These have been discussed by John Davis[11] in relation to a test area containing a hypothetical 5 per cent of the national population. One approach would be to place 5 per cent of the total advertising appropriation in a test area, but this would ignore the variations in cost per 1000 between, for example, regional television rates. The other approach involves projecting into the test area the schedule of advertising which would apply in the event of a national launch. However, this assumes that a national schedule as such can be compiled, whereas often the total advertising campaign tends to be made up from a series of area schedules. If a national schedule can be prepared (or an approximation to it is feasible), this still does not overcome the additional problem of quite strongly marked differences between television viewing habits over the country. These should, therefore, also be borne in mind when preparing a test campaign advertising schedule. But even then there may be differences in the weight of advertising of competitive brands nationally, and in a test area. The main point is that a very detailed approach to the establishment of the appropriate experimental conditions is needed in *all* test marketing activities.

4. Establish controls

Control areas should be set up in order to provide realistic evaluation of the influence of a particular variable in a test area. It is admittedly very difficult to ascribe to any single factor a causal relationship, and it may be considered desirable to check the effects of a single variable in more than one test market, and over the identical time period. These additional test areas should be comparable in those characteristics likely to affect sales of the product under test. It is good research practice to divide the period of testing into three phases so that valid comparisons can be made of market movements. Planned research is an essential element of market testing. First, it is necessary to know what the market situation is before the test campaign starts; this calls for some survey work to establish the level of competition, competitors' brands, consumer buying habits, attitudes to the product type, brand loyalty, price sensitivity, etc. Shopping habits will affect the types of outlets through which a product can be sold. Trade research is, therefore, advisable. This would cover attitudes to the product type, customary discount structure, quantity discount terms, merchandising practices by competitors, the degree of cooperation which may be expected from the trade, etc. During the test campaign further enquiries will be necessary to monitor market movements so that trends may be identified quickly and also to assess the likely outcome of the campaign. Consumer panels are often organized in test areas by leading research agencies such as AGB or Nielsen's. Auditing of stocks of specific products in stores is another tool of test marketing. This specialized form of research was introduced by Nielsen's in America, and it extended to Britain, where it has now been used by most of the leading food, drug, and related product's manufacturers for over 30 years. (See Chapter 9 for details.)

This systematic auditing of store stocks is also offered by some other research agencies, who have followed the very successful trail blazed by Nielsen's. Nielsen Shop Audits are usually on a monthly basis, though special arrangements can be made. Factory shipments by themselves will not give an accurate reflection of the present state of the market. There may, for instance, be a sudden fall in ex-factory sales because of the build-up of trade stocks. Auditing of trade stocks gives manufacturers a clear picture of the way in which their products are being bought by consumers. After the market test is over, a final survey should be done to confirm the experimental evidence gathered during the operation, and these findings should be compared with the initial survey. Before-and-after studies will assist researchers to obtain a deeper understanding of their markets, and should provide valuable guides for future action. This last phase of research should be extended to dealers, so that an overall appreciation of market influences is gathered. Dealers should be encouraged to give their frank assessments of the test operation – they will not usually suffer inhibitions – and manufacturers should be willing to listen carefully and evaluate these comments. Many valuable clues to guide future marketing activities can be gathered from objectively analysing the reports from trade sources.

5. Select representative areas

Test areas should reflect in miniature the national market, and careful selection is, therefore, of great importance. A survey done by *Printers' Ink*[12] during 1962 found that among the 102 firms investigated, almost half used fewer than four cities as test markets. Certain cities such as Syracuse were popular because of their representative populations, relatively stable economies, and middle class buying strength. In Britain there is also a marked tendency among researchers to concentrate tests in particular regions. It would be unwise, however, to select an area for a test marketing campaign which is too heavily dependent on one industry for its prosperity, because a setback in this industry during the time of test could affect buying habits radically. Areas with diversified industries are, therefore, less likely to be prone to sudden economic upset. Strong seasonal influences should also be borne in mind when choosing test areas; the possibility of prolonged major industrial strikes which would disrupt the normal economy of an area would be another factor to consider.

Of Cadbury's[7] media expenditure, 90 per cent was reported to be on television, and so the TV boundaries in the UK determine the company's test regions. Since the company realizes that none of these regions conforms to the national buying pattern of food and confectionery, they endeavoured to establish how much each region differs from the overall pattern. This knowledge enabled it to develop 'behavioural factor for each region' to be noted when extrapolating national sales.

Kellogg's[8] in the US states that as far as demographic make-up is concerned, almost any of its sales divisions in the Mid-West, because they are representative of the US as a whole, would be suitable for test marketing of cereals.

Test areas should have good publicity services. In Britain the major newspaper groups, such as

Thomson Newspapers and the Westminster Press, have newspapers in several provincial centres which can serve as test marketing areas.

Reader's Digest and the colour supplements of the 'quality' Sunday papers offer special inducements for area advertising of products. Regional advertising facilities are available in *Woman, Woman's Own* and *Woman's Realm* for both ITV and smaller regions. They can be used for a wider range of media or market tests, as well as to give magazine advertising support to regional brands or to up-weight a television campaign in selected areas.

The commercial television companies have built up special facilities for test marketing of a wide range of products. Some companies are particularly active in this field, and many branded products have been tested first in the districts covered by them.

Some marketing people have expressed doubts on the typicality of test areas, but the fact that large national companies continue to use these districts suggests that critics may be generalizing too freely. 'Normally, the most that can be done is to ensure that the areas finally selected for an experiment are not too widely atypical, and then to cope with moderate degrees of atypicality through more sophisticated methods of interpretation and projection.'[11] The essential point is that it is vitally necessary to have a deep and full understanding of the test area it is proposed to use. Results can then be weighted to allow for known variations from national behaviour patterns, media availability, media costs, etc.

The dangers of 'over-testing' are also put forward as a decided disadvantage of using the same test areas, because, it is claimed, the reactions of consumers and the trade tend to become atypical. It is also thought that the sales force may become 'exhausted' by repeated efforts on new lines. These objections may contain some element of fact, but they tend to rather overstate the argument. After all, people are known to like variety and to seek new products; the number of new products on sale at any one time relative to the general run of merchandise offered is usually extremely small.

Another important aspect is the size of test markets; areas should be large enough to contain a reasonable proportion of the various socio-economic groupings of the general population. Areas should preferably have about 100 000–200 000 inhabitants. It may also be significant to note geographical factors. In America[13] the influence of Nielsen on test marketing has resulted in all its test markets being in areas with populations ranging between 75 000 and 115 000. This size range occurs primarily because of the sample size required for Nielsen store audit procedure, and the company is quoted as saying that it prefers test cities of about 50 000–100 000 population. This allows them to maintain a high coverage with a sample of about 50 food stores and 15 to 20 drug stores.

A further factor is advertising economy: most Nielsen clients are relatively heavy advertisers and advertising costs less in terms of total dollar expenditure in small rather than in large cities. This point could be compared with television advertising in Britain, where the smaller television companies are able to offer attractively economic rates to test marketers. This should not, however, delude manufacturers into rather heavier use of advertising than they would be able to afford on a national basis. As already noted, the weight of advertising effort should be assessed so that the extent to which it is used in the marketing mix is in relation to that which could be undertaken in a national campaign.

6. Decide on number of test markets

This problem should be considered in relation to the stated objectives of individual product tests. It is generally accepted practice to have at least two test markets for each variable being tested and, of course, to run control areas in line with these. Sears Roebuck[4] recommended using three rather than two test markets for each variable under test, because if one of these areas is suddenly affected by some unexpected event, such as a large industrial upheaval or some natural catastrophe like a flood, there will still be two areas left to complete the market testing. It also advises that these three areas should be selected so that they represent high, average, and low market penetration for the particular company. The combined results should be quite a good guide to average performance in national markets.

A New York media director[8] comments that for an effective test marketing campaign, a combination of markets with typical 'media' availability and representing 2–3 per cent of the US is needed. In addition, it would be necessary, in the case of a soap product, to test in both hard and soft water areas; and for a soft drink, warm and cold climates might be important variables.

7. Establish duration of tests

The length of time allowed for tests will be largely affected by the nature of the product under survey, the buying frequency, the degree of competition in that particular product market, and the variable being tested. Nielsen[13] declares that 'a test programme is neither sound nor thorough unless enough time is allowed for the answer to develop. This usually involves waiting for customers to use up the product and to come back into the market at least once, preferably twice'. This period of time can stretch from a few months to a year or more. The Nielsen 1968 study, which has already been noted, was updated in 1973 and revealed findings relating to the prediction of results which 'bore considerable similarity' to the earlier enquiry. These are set out in Table 10.2.

Table 10.2   Test results

No. of months after test	Cumulative percentage of 'correct' predictions		
	1968 std. (46 brands)	1973 std. (34 brands)	Combined figs (80 brands)
2	7	6	8
4	15	26	20
6	41	46	44
8	61	61	61
10	80	81	81
12	91	90	91
14	98	96	97
16	99	100	99
18	100	100	100

Source: Nielson.

Examination of the data given in Table 10.2 indicates that 'a reasonable safe prediction may be made after eight to ten months'. However, it should be remembered that these odds are based on average experience and thus provide only an important guide in what must remain a judgement decision.[13] The rate of usage of various products should also be allowed for when assessing the period of test marketing. Consumers should be given time to try out the product, to evaluate it, and to repurchase it if it is found to be of value to them.

The *Printers' Ink*[12] survey mentioned earlier found that 18 per cent of the 102 firms surveyed thought that market tests of one or two months adequate, 16 per cent considered two to four months adequate, 18 per cent – six months, and 24 per cent – one to two years. Judgement and experience are called for in assessing the period of time needed to run a particular test; many market failures have occurred because tests were not run long enough to establish reliable buying habits. Sears Roebuck[4] considers that many frequently purchased food products require about six months' market testing before judgement can be passed, and at least six months is advisable in the case of products infrequently purchased. It also recommends that where tests are concerned with evaluating advertising, the cumulative long-term effects of the campaign may require the tests to be extended rather longer than usual. Victor A. Bonomo,[1] who was responsible for the marketing of 'Maxim' freeze-dried coffee in the United States, has stated that this new type of instant coffee was tested over a period of almost four years before national launch was considered feasible:

> As we look back now, those 43 months were really a god-send. For a while our technical people were striving to solve the problem of producing a freeze-dried coffee at a competitive price, our marketing men were allowed the unusual luxury of thorough testing before we invested in national plant capacity. We were able, first, to test a variety of *different* marketing variables, and second, to allow for those variables to settle out in the market place.

Bonomo stresses the need for testing out a variety of marketing tactics in, for example, promotions, before deciding on the final approach. General Foods learned from local tests the particular marketing weaknesses of this new product, and these were corrected before national launch.

The longer the duration of a test market, the more it will cost. Research activities need to be subjected to the sound management principle of accountability, and some cost-benefit analysis is called for to keep the whole operation on realistic terms. The costs of acquiring further information should be warranted by the value of the data to the decision which has to be taken.

Another important point affecting the time allowed for market tests is the degree of competition existing in that product market. The longer a test runs, the more likely are competitors to become aware of a company's intentions. Several cases have been noted where competitors have 'jumped the gun' and gone national at once, when they have discovered that a test campaign was under way in a market of interest to them. Procter and Gamble launched 'Ariel' bacteriological detergent on a national scale while Lever was still testing its product 'Radiant'. Similarly, Dawnay Foods beat Cadbury's to the national market with 'Dine' instant mashed potato, when it found out that Cadbury's was testing 'Smash'. In America, in 1963, Colgate Palmolive was test marketing a 'home permanent' called 'Lustre Creme', which was considered by the Toni Company to be potentially dangerous to its market situation. As a result of Toni's strong intervention in the test markets, Colgate Palmolive abandoned the project.

Calgon Consumer Products Division, Pittsburgh, is reported[8] to have pre-empted the market for a product designed to be used in clothes driers to eliminate static cling by launching nationally while Procter and Gamble was still test marketing its version of this product. This resulted in cut-throat competition, in which Procter and Gamble developed a massive direct mail sampling campaign.

Market testing is, therefore, subject to many hazards, both accidental and deliberately planned by interested parties.

It is vital to allow market tests to run their full course – this sometimes calls for steady nerves. If the tests are called off because early signs do not appear to be favourable, a good market opportunity may be lost. As already discussed, it may take some time for certain products to work their way into the shopping lists of housewives, and it is these long-term effects which are the real concern of test marketing. As tests progress, it may become evident that modifications may be necessary to the product or to the methods of presentation; these alterations should be made and the tests resumed, after carefully noting sales figures so far achieved.

Occasionally, companies 'go national' at once – and are successful. A notable example was the immediate national marketing by Weetabix of 'Alpen', a breakfast cereal based on the Swiss muesli, with nuts and fruits. After careful pre-testing of the product, Weetabix felt that it was on a winner, and marketed 'Alpen' on a national basis during the spring of 1971. Inevitably, its remarkable success attracted competition: marketers must accept the inevitable risks of launching new products. They have to evaluate the comparative risks of test marketing and a national launch.

When Rowntree Mackintosh launched its highly successful 'Yorkie' chocolate bar, it realized that it could be readily imitated. It was decided, therefore, to market at once throughout the London TV area, and assess market reactions before launching nationally a year later.

A cautious test marketing approach is followed by Cadbury Beverages of North America – the US-based arm of Cadbury Schweppes – which has adopted 'a mass-market niche strategy where we offer Schweppes, Sunkist, Hires root beer, and Canada Dry'[14] through a network of 1100 bottlers across the US. The company is active in test marketing but 'careful not to do something so openly that your competitors can copy you and steal a march'.[14] The company aims for market niches that satisfy its objectives but are not big enough to attract its large competitors.

8. Evaluate the results

This final stage in test marketing needs to be done thoroughly. On expert evaluation of the test results rest important business decisions, involving, perhaps, heavy capital investment and the setting up of volume production lines. Test market results may indicate that a certain percentage market success has been achieved, but merely to project this same percentage to the wider national market would be naïve and likely to be distinctly misleading. More sophisticated evaluation is called for; study should be made of significant factors, such as the demographic structure of the population, types of outlets available, strength of competing brands, and any particular variations among regions in competitors' activities, which may result in variations between the test area and the national market. After this more elaborate analysis, it should be possible to construct a forecast of future likely demand for the new product on a national basis, but always bearing in mind that the data collected are historic, whereas forecasts attempt to estimate the trends of future events.

Various approaches can be made to the projection of test market results; for example, direct market share, proportionate population, buying index, or sales ratio.

John Davis[11] has stressed the critical problem of converting the results observed in an experiment in a limited area into an assessment of what is likely to happen if the project is launched nationally. He differentiates between 'projections' and 'predictions', and between the results of these processes and forecasts.

Straight projection, as in direct market share (x per cent of test market = x per cent of national market) is obviously simple, but highly fallible. As discussed earlier, it ignores the inevitable differences in the multiple variables of market behaviour. It is very unlikely that test markets will be mirror images of national markets.

A prediction, on the other hand, derives from more complex calculations, in the process of which some attempts have been made to obtain a deeper understanding of market behaviour. A model is likely to have developed to act as a basic guide. The simple projection of market share, for example, could be improved by a prediction using a scale-up factor of which Fitzroy[15] gives two examples:

1. Buying index method:

$$I = \frac{\text{Product field national sales}}{\text{Product field test area sales}}$$

2. *Per capita* usage:

$$I = \frac{\text{National population}}{\text{Test area population}}$$

(I = scale-up factor)

These formulae could be further elaborated by incorporating a 'correction factor' to allow for differences in distribution efficiency and other changes which may have taken place between the test marketing operation and the national launch.

It is unlikely that a new product will attract sales equally from existing brands in a test market; product positioning, strength of competition, brand loyalty, etc., will modify the extent of market share erosion. Taking these kinds of factors into account, test market results could be extrapolated if data were available on competitive brand shares before and after a market test.

Fitzroy[15] illustrates this approach with three competing brands and the impact of a new market entrant (see Table 10.3).

Table 10.3   Test market extrapolation based on competitor market shares

Products	Test area market shares		National market shares	
	prior to test	after test	prior to launch	after launch
A	25	20	45	36
B	45	30	15	10
C	30	25	40	33
New product	–	25	–	21

Source: Fitzroy.[15]

In the test market data shown in Table 10.3, product A retained 80 per cent of its market share, product B 66 per cent, and product C 80 per cent, while a new product achieved 25 per cent market share. National market shares are then subject to the percentage variations quoted above, and it will be seen that, after national launch of the new product, product A's market share will fall to 36 per cent, product B's to 10 per cent, and product C's to 33 per cent. The residual share of 21 per cent will fall to the new entrant.

These extrapolations assume, of course, that the conditions applying in the test market will be unchanged when national marketing is undertaken.

A forecast is, or should be, based on a comprehensive examination and evaluation of the data collected during test marketing, and an assessment of the resultant projections or predictions. Calculations are likely at different levels of probability and over short-, medium-, and long-term periods. This demanding task should be the joint responsibility of marketing researchers and marketing management, who would carefully check any changes that might have taken place in the market since the tests were undertaken.

If it is decided to launch the new product nationally, the marketing strategy must be planned to tie in with production facilities. Immediate large-scale production and distribution may not be feasible. Production lines often need a 'warming-up' time before they can cope with a large national demand; management may prefer to sell regionally for a short time to avoid the possibility of a national distribution problem. Furthermore, test market products are frequently made on special pilot plant, and there may be unplanned difficulties arising when production is switched to the regular plant. To avoid this type of trouble, marketing managers should discuss with factory management their test marketing plans and agreement should be reached on the practicability of producing such products on a regular and volume basis.

Regionally phased marketing has advantages, but speed and confidence often pull off prizes. This emphasizes the need for good planning well in advance of the start of test marketing, so that rising public interest may be exploited quickly and profitably.

10.5 NEW APPROACHES TO TEST MARKETING

The conventional approach to test marketing, outlined in this chapter, has been seen[16] to be slow, expensive, and prone to spying and sabotage, so alternative strategies are sought by the mass-market suppliers. In some cases they abandon test marketing altogether, as happened when Procter and Gamble 'put "Folgers" instant decaffeinated coffee on US shelves', or when Pillsbury introduced 'Milk Break Bar'. But in both these cases, the products involved limited risk; 'Folgers' already enjoyed a favourable brand image, and the snack bar market was booming.

Simulated test marketing

Simulated test marketing is beginning to be an attractive alternative to formal test marketing. Typically, a consumer recruited at a shopping centre reads an advertisement for a new product and gets a free sample to take home. Later she – most respondents are women – rates it in a telephone interview. The test-marketing firm plugs her responses and others into a computer to predict potential sales volume.[16] Opinions are mixed about the effectiveness of this method: it is generally agreed, however, to be fine for weeding out failures but not so good at 'predicting the upside potential'.

In the UK, Research Bureau Ltd,[17] now Research International, developed the *'Sensor'* system for predicting the market performance of new products, by simulating advertising expenditure, promotional activity, and the retail purchase situation within a competitive environment. This simulated test market technique is founded upon the Parfitt-Collins[18] model of market share assessment discussed in Chapter 9, viz., market share = penetration × buying index × repeat purchase rate.

The Sensor technique is related to particular product market environments, and 'some are by their nature much easier to simulate than others'. The following various market scenarios are illustrative:

1. New products entering tightly defined markets, e.g., washing powder, dog food, or take-home ice cream, where market size and value are often accurately known, and so if market share can be predicted, likely sales can be calculated. However, while this seems straightforward, it is important to reflect whether the launch of a new product would be likely to increase the frequency of use of existing users, or attract new users; further, a new brand may be used at the *same time* as existing brands merely to augment and not to replace them; to assume simple substitution of one brand for another, could, therefore, lead to misleading projections.
2. New products entering loosely defined markets, perhaps those 'fuzzy around the edges', e.g., some household cleaners, or, at the other extreme, a number of products, most commonly foods, for which the 'potential competition is extremely wide and may vary enormously between individual consumers'. These may, moreover, be competing products in various guises (e.g., tinned, frozen, or chilled), and stocked in different parts of the store. In some cases it may be feasible to treat loosely defined markets as if they were tightly defined and use the Sensor model.

3. Another scenario relates to new products which potentially straddle markets, e.g., deodorant body sprays, which may also be used as perfume substitutes. Research should take account of the minor as well as major market potential.
4. A final category relates to unique new products (rate phenomena); 'in these cases only direct sales estimates are of value'.

The various scenarios discussed are admittedly based on qualitative assessments. As discussed, Sensor is more appropriate for some market conditions than others. In the case of a new dairy product entering a tightly defined product field, the Sensor test was first concerned with showing respondents in central locations a reel of five TV advertisements for the new brand. After viewing, they were asked unprompted recall questions, and prompted purchase intention scores for all the brands advertised. The next stage was a so-called 'simulated shop' (a priced display shelf showing all the major brands, including the new brand). 'Respondents were given a coupon worth slightly more than the price of a pack of the new brand, and were invited to spent it in the shop, change being given, or extra money from the respondent being accepted, as necessary.' Of total respondents 39 per cent bought the new brand – 'a fairly typical figure'.

The researchers[17] state that empirical evidence has shown that the percentage purchasing the new brand in the simulated shop, downweighted for achieved awareness and distribution figures, gives an accurate estimate of penetration of the brand in the market place nine months after launch. In the example quoted, estimates of prompted awareness and value-weighted distribution, supplied by the client, were both high, i.e., 80 per cent. Hence the final estimate of penetration was calculated as follows:

$$34 \text{ per cent} \times 0.80 \times 0.80 = 22 \text{ per cent}$$

In-use tests of the various brands in the experiment were undertaken by respondents, and their experiences were noted in interviews, and after further assessment, a repeat purchasing rate of 20 per cent was established. Taking the trial rate (22 per cent) already noted, and the repeat purchasing rate (20 per cent), the following final estimate of market share of the new brand emerged:

$$22 \text{ per cent (trial)} \times 20 \text{ per cent (repeat purchasing rate)} = 4.4 \text{ per cent}$$

Research International's latest test marketing research service – *Micro Test* – based on a sophisticated computer micro-model, provides: (i) probability that each respondent will *try* the new product; (ii) probability that they will *adopt* it; (iii) *frequency* of purchase; and (iv) *volume* of sales involved. Micro-Tests have been carried out in 25 countries and over 22 major product fields. In many cases, the tested products were not marketed or only after modification, thus saving large investment costs, apart from consumer dissatisfaction and possible loss of goodwill.

Microscope is one of the range of consumer product analyses at retail level which is offered by Retail Marketing Services (RMS). It is specifically designed for regional television test marketing, and is based on the Border TV region, which is taken as a microcosm of the national market. It covers a population broadly made up of one-third Tyne Tees, one-third Lancashire, and one-third Scotland, and spans three Nielsen regions. Test-marketing facilities for new fast-moving consumer products sold in supermarkets include sales and distribution back-up, advertising and other forms of promotion, pricing, stock levels and merchandising, etc. These are evaluated before a client is committed to the further costs entailed in a roll-out or national launch. Border TV collaborates closely in the Microscope research programme, and 'control' stores can be provided to test, on a comparative basis, the effectiveness of particular advertising campaigns.

American study of simulated test marketing

The American Advertising Research Foundation (ARF) published a study of simulated test marketing (STM) in June 1988, based on data from seven research companies, reported to account for 90 per cent of all STM business in the US and covering 42 major marketing companies that have used STMs extensively.

The trend in STM projects indicated a 1985 peak, followed by declines in the following two years. STM predictions 'tended to be correct on a more-or-less chance basis ... with subsequent in-market results confirming the predictions in about 51% of instances, and being either lower (41%) or higher (8%) in 49% of cases (although it must be pointed out that the end result in 45% of STMs was to discontinue the project)'.[19]

Further, the costs of STMs tended to rise significantly; an 'average' STM, as revealed by the ARF study, cost about $47 000. Goodyear takes a distinctly reserved view of the future for STMs in their present form but, nevertheless, is confident that they 'will be developed, modified, repackaged, re-launched and continue to satisfy a genuine – and increasingly complex – client need for some time to come'.[19]

Scanner-based test marketing

This sophisticated method has been outlined in Chapter 9 in the section headed 'Scanner store consumer panels'. Certain supermarket shoppers are given identification cards which they present at check-out points where scanners record their purchases. Consumers are not aware of which products are being tested; the results of the scanning process are fed to computers for analysis. Cable television (in the US) is also used to find out what kinds of advertising attract certain types of buyers. 'For example, it discovered that the audience for TV's *General Hospital* buys about 25 per cent more Granola bars than the average viewer'.[16]

The *Fortune* article[16] comments that traditional test marketing may well be *passé* because Nielsen has taken up scanner-based testing, and after more than half a century in conventional test marketing, is launching 'Testsight', which will measure the impact of commercials on all TV sets, including those wired for cable.

Finally, Nielsen pointed out that, today, successful new grocery products tend to achieve peak market share in a matter of months rather than years; they achieve a 50 per cent distribution level within the first few months; they manage to gain distribution in at least a couple of the top five grocery retailers within two months of launch; and the growth of scanning stores means that a new product can be evaluated as a success or a failure within just a few weeks.

10.6 SUMMARY

Innovation is a risky activity, but essential for business development. Test marketing aims to control risk through conducting area tests before national launch. Products fail for many reasons: bad timing; poor quality; ineffective advertising, etc.

Eight important steps in test marketing have been identified as: define objects; set criteria of success; integrate operations; establish controls; select representative areas; decide on number of test markets; establish duration of tests; evaluate results.

New approaches to test marketing have been introduced: (i) 'simulated test marketing', e.g. Sensor; and (ii) scanner-based test marketing. Test marketing is a remarkably versatile tool of marketing; by intelligently using it, a very wide range of information may be gathered. There is no real substitute for market experimentation: test marketing provides a disciplined approach to marketing many kinds of products. Like other research techniques used in marketing, it does not guarantee success; management must still make decisions, but these can be made with more complete knowledge of real-life reactions to products.

REFERENCES

1. Bonomo, Victor A., '*The do's and don'ts of test marketing*', *Nielsen Researcher*, vol. 2, no. 3, A. C. Nielsen, Oxford, 1968.
2. Sevin, Charles H., *Marketing Productivity and Analysis*, McGraw-Hill, New York, 1965.
3. Becknell, James C., and Robert W. McIsaac, 'Test marketing cookware coated with Teflon', *Journal of Advertising Research*, September 1963.
4. O'Hanlon, Joseph J., 'Experimental marketing – A US businessman puts it to the test', *Marketing*, October 1970, Institute of Marketing, London.
5. Kraushar, Peter M., *New Products and Diversification*, Business Books, London, 1977.
6. Nielsen, A. C., 'Test marketing reduces risks', *Nielsen Researcher*, vol. 14, no. 1, Jan/Feb. 1973.
7. Cadbury, N. D., 'When, where, and how to test market', *Harvard Business Review*, vol. 53, no. 3, May/June 1975.
8. Scanlon, Sally, 'Calling the shots more closely', *Sales and Marketing Management*, 10 May 1976.
9. Rines, Michael, 'Why NSM went up in smoke', *Management Today*, January 1978.
10. Chisnall, Peter M., *Marketing: A Behavioural Analysis*, McGraw-Hill, Maidenhead, 1985.
11. Davis, John, 'Market testing and experimentation', in: *Consumer Market Research Handbook*, Robert Worcester and John Downham (eds), Van Nostrand Reinhold, Wokingham, 1978.
12. *Printers' Ink*, 13 April 1962.
13. Nielsen, A. C.,'How to strengthen your company plan', A. C. Nielsen, Oxford, 1970.
14. Srodes, James, 'It's niche work for Cadbury', *Sunday Telegraph*, 4 March 1990.
15. Fitzroy, Peter T., *Analytical Methods for Marketing Management*, McGraw-Hill, Maidenhead, 1976.
16. Tracy, Eleanor Johnson, 'Testing time for test marketing', *Fortune*, 29 October 1984.
17. Godfrey, Simon, 'The Sensor simulated test market system', *Admap*, October 1983.
18. Parfitt, J. H., and B. J. K. Collins, 'The use of consumer panels for brand share prediction', *Journal of Marketing Research*, vol. 5, May 1968.
19. Goodyear, John R., 'The future development of international research ... the multi-lingual, multi-national, multi-variable', in: Seminar on International Marketing Research, ESOMAR, Amsterdam, November 1988.

ELEVEN

ADVERTISING RESEARCH

Advertising research is concerned with the objective evaluation of advertising as a method of communication and persuasion. This study includes both qualitative and quantitative aspects, and can conveniently be considered under three main headings: advertising content research, advertising media research, and advertising effectiveness research.

11.1 ADVERTISING CONTENT RESEARCH

This focuses on the ability of the advertisement to achieve impact and to project the desired message. Design and layout must be tested in detail, the basic theme – the copy platform – must be closely examined in a series of tests with representative audiences. The purpose of this research is to determine certain facts which will guide copywriters and designers in producing effective advertisements. For example, in advertising a new model of car should the main appeal be that of safety, speed, economy, or prestige? Alternative appeals are evaluated during the course of the research.

Evaluative techniques adopted in 'content' research are used at two stages in advertising: pre-publication and post-publication. With pre-testing, the emphasis is on the development of ideas and methods of presentation, whereas post-testing is designed to measure how effectively these communication concepts were received by the intended audience.

In pre-testing advertisements, groups of individuals, representative of the intended audience, may be invited to view 'mock-up' advertisements (press or television). Afterwards they are asked a series of questions to test their degree of recall ('noting') of specific aspects of these advertisements, e.g., the advertising message, illustration, acceptability, etc. More elaborate techniques involve psychological methods of enquiry, such as depth interviewing and various projective tests. (These are discussed in Chapter 8.) Other tests may be devised to check the spontaneous emotional response to advertisements and include physiological measurements of different kinds, e.g., eye-blink rate, galvanic skin response (popularly called a 'lie detector'), muscle tension, pupil dilation, breathing rate, etc. Machines, such as the tachistoscope, can be used to expose advertisements to viewers for a very brief period. After this measured viewing time is over, the impact is assessed. Eye-blink rate indicates the intensity of interest and is measured on special equipment. These, and other measures of the autonomic nervous system, are costly and are, therefore, more likely to be confined to testing advertisements in relatively expensive media.

Post-testing of advertisements devolves on the basic measurements of recall and recognition. Notable developments in this area were made by Dr George Gallup in the US during the early 1930s; another pioneer was Dr Daniel Starch who founded his advertising research service based on 'Starch Scores'. (Details of these surveys are given later.)

Tests to measure recall (verbal and pictorial) may be either 'aided' (prompted) or 'unaided' (spontaneous). Respondents in aided recall testing may be shown a series of advertisements (press or television). After these have been viewed for a specified period, the respondents are questioned to discover exactly how much of the advertising messages, product brands, etc., they can accurately recall. In unaided recall, respondents are asked if they have seen a particular advertisement and, if so, questioned about its impact on them.

Measuring advertising material by recall and recognition techniques rests on the theory that they are useful in predicting brand purchase. This view appears to be prompted by what might be termed the 'sequential approach' to influencing people to buy products. These stages have been variously described: a popular version is:

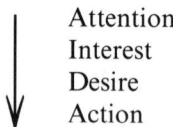

Attention
Interest
Desire
Action

Lavidge and Steiner[1] postulated that people move up a series of steps impelled by the force of advertising. These steps are not necessarily equidistant. Some products are approached slowly; these are likely to have a greater psychological and/or economic commitment. Other products may be regarded as less serious, and it is likely that these will be bought with a relatively low level of conscious decision making. Once brand loyalty has been established, the threat from other brands is considerably less than with ego-involving products.

The six steps of advertising influence in Lavidge and Steiner's approach were related to three phases of psychological model based on the theory that an attitude has three elements, as follows:[2]

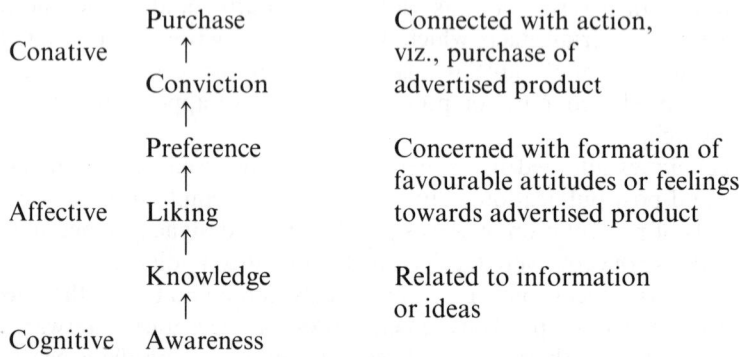

	Purchase	Connected with action,
Conative	↑	viz., purchase of
	Conviction	advertised product
	↑	
	Preference	Concerned with formation of
	↑	favourable attitudes or feelings
Affective	Liking	towards advertised product
	↑	
	Knowledge	Related to information
	↑	or ideas
Cognitive	Awareness	

Another popular flow-model of advertising termed DAGMAR (Defining Advertising Goals for Measured Advertising Results) was developed by Colley,[3] who stated that the ultimate objective of a sale was to carry people through four levels of understanding: awareness → comprehension → conviction → action. Colley perceived the role of advertising as helping to move the consumer 'through one or more levels' to the final act of purchase and to do this with greater economy, speed, and volume than any other methods.

Colley's simple model – which he described as 'applied common sense' – viewed advertising as a persuasive process which took the consumer who had been exposed to some kind of advertising stimulus, by a series of 'logical and comprehensive steps' through to eventual purchase of the advertised products.

The sequential approach ('step-by-step persuasion') has been sharply criticized as being inadequate by several writers, including Kristian Palda,[4] who dismisses it as superficial and unconvincing. Professor Jack Haskins[5] of Indiana University made a spirited attack on what he termed the FIFO process (facts in, facts out) which characterizes so much advertising research. After carefully examining considerable evidence he stated that: 'Learning and recall of factual information does occur. However, recall and retention measures seem, at best, irrelevant to the ultimate effects desired, the changing of attitudes and behaviour'. He commented that it is relatively easy to write factual advertisements and to measure the recall of facts: this rote memorization is indeed encouraged by the prevailing system of education. 'As the products of that system, we consciously or unconsciously build that approach into our efforts at mass communication.'

Leon Festinger,[6] the well-known American psychologist, also criticized the view that changes in attitude are necessarily followed by changes in behaviour. After exhaustive research, he was unable to find any supporting evidence.

More recently, an experienced English advertising practitioner has commented: 'Recall is such a complex process, involving perception, memory suppression and verbalisation, that few psychologists feel happy when using it as a measure of attention, although the depth of their feeling is dependent upon the precise nature of the measurement'.[7]

Anne Wicks[8] has referred to the STARCH, AIDA, and DAGMAR 'classic models of the advertising process', and noted that while there are important differences of emphasis between them, 'they all share a rational, logical orientation and a linear sequential view of the way advertising affects consumers'. They are all, she observed, 'left-hand brain models which elevate the importance of the conscious, verbal, analytic and convergent processes of the human mind over the more intuitive, emotional, diffuse and impressionistic processes'.[8] Because of this, advertising effectiveness testing has tended 'to focus heavily on the measurement of transmission of the rational and functional messages'.[8] Hence, the importance placed on recall in advertising research. However, as already noted, the so-called rational, logical model lacks entire acceptability.

That the various hierarchical models of advertising grossly oversimplify the influence of advertising is evident from this brief review; more detailed discussion is given elsewhere.[2] Subjective perception of advertising messages, and the fact that advertisements compete with other stimuli for the consumer's attention, are two of the many influences which affect their impact. Psychological, sociological, and cultural factors play important roles in buying behaviour; the complex interaction between attitudes and behaviour should be carefully studied.

Valuable practical research into nine different methods of testing advertising copy was undertaken by Lee Adler and colleagues[9] during 1964. This survey, sponsored by the American Association of Advertising Agencies (AAAA), asked the research directors of 40 top-billing American advertising agencies to evaluate certain copy-testing measures.

About five years later, similar research was extended by Harper W. Boyd, Jnr, and Michael L. Ray[10] to the research directors of the 50 largest European agencies, 39 of whom completed the questionnaires. These were distributed as follows:

UK	18
West Germany	13
France	4
Sweden	2
Italy	1
Switzerland	1

The period of research was from late 1968 to mid-1969.

The same questionnaire was used in both surveys and comparative figures for the nine measuring techniques were obtained, as shown in Table 11.1.

It will be seen from Table 11.1 that there is substantial agreement between American and European research directors on copy-testing techniques, the only marked differences occurring in 'recall' and 'buying predisposition'.

Recall was more favoured by American research directors, who tended to prefer unaided recall. The European directors' comparatively low opinion of recall techniques reflected their views on recognition measures, namely that it was, in practice, difficult to isolate an advertisement under test from other influences.

Table 11.1   Comparative figures for the nine measuring techniques

	Highest value or real value	
	(USA 1964) $n = 40$	(Europe 1969) $n = 39$
Recognition	6	6
Recall	25	17
Attitude	25	27
Comprehension	32	32
Believability	15	17
Persuasion	5	7
Buying predisposition	21	16
Ad rating	5	9
Behavioural	25	23

Buying predisposition also attracted more support from American directors, though in both samples some directors thought that highly favourable predisposition measures were a good indicator of purchase decision. More Europeans than Americans doubted the validity of this measure.

Methods relying on recognition, persuasion, and advertising rating received the lowest ratings over both surveys; these were considered to be unreliable, irrelevant, and not predictive. The recognition method was felt to be unsatisfactory because it was not possible to exclude the influence of, for example, previous advertising of the product. Persuasion and ad rating were rejected as useful techniques because the surveys had asked research directors to view 'as seen through the consumer's eyes', and it was thought that consumers were not able to deal adequately with these measures of advertising.

Comprehension (measuring understanding and/or meaning of advertisements) attracted the highest rating in both surveys, and was considered vital to good communication.

Attitude was also rated high by both Americans and Europeans, and this popular measure was valued as a useful predictor of buying behaviour.

Believability measures received moderate support, though nearly half the American directors felt that disbelief or intrigue could sometimes be a highly valuable reaction to advertisements; only a few European directors used this argument. Many directors in both surveys opposed believability measures on the grounds that there was no clear relationship between belief and advertising effectiveness, and that present methods of testing believability tend to be unreliable.

Maloney[11] has commented on the value of 'curious non-belief', which may lead consumers to try the product being advertised. What is believable to some people will not be accepted by others, because advertisements are viewed by consumers against the background of their varying beliefs, experiences, and general attitudes towards promotional activities. Advertising messages, as planned by advertisers, may be unconsciously distorted by consumers so that they fit in with their attitudes and expectations. 'Levelling' may occur, when certain parts of the advertising message are ignored because they are considered disagreeable and likely to upset overall favourable expectations. Messages may also be 'sharpened'; in order to support existing beliefs, consumers may add subjective meanings to advertising messages, which advertisers had not intended should be read into their advertisements. Where existing attitudes are favourable towards a product, 'sharpening' of advertising messages by consumers may be advantageous to advertisers. What people believe from viewing advertisements is not, therefore, easily evaluated.

Attitudes towards the consumption of margarine, for example, have changed considerably over the past decade or so. At one time, margarine was largely perceived to be a substitute for butter and bought by those who could not afford the dairy product. But now it is frequently bought *instead* of butter because of the widely publicized views about the dangers to health of food containing high proportions of animal fat.

Consumption habits are formed in many ways: family tradition, social contagion, peer group influence, etc., all play a part in the formation and restructuring of attitudes (e.g., towards smoking or processed foods) and in the diffusion of products and services. Advertising cannot be productive unless the changing moods, and interests, and attitudes of society are interpreted with skill and understanding. Lannon and Cooper[12] suggest that a 'humanistic view' should be taken of advertising and branding, and their influence on consumers. More appropriate theories are needed, based on language and concepts more in tune with the intuitive and mystical creative process, than the rational, logical organizational process.

Tracking studies

Leading advertisers and large business undertakings are concerned to keep up to date with the perceptions and attitudes of their customers and the public at large.

Tracking studies, as Peter Sampson[13] has observed, are 'methods of continuous measurement in which market research data are collected in a systematic way at intervals, accumulated and summarised periodically'. The time intervals may vary, according to the needs of the company involved.

Tracking studies collect data from matched samples drawn from the same population over a specific period of time, in order to measure, for example, brand awareness, advertising awareness, attitudes to brands, brand preferences, brand usage, corporate image, etc.

Sampson[13] points out that, unlike the continuous panel (see Chapter 9), which collects data from the same sample of respondents over regular periods of time, a tracking study collects data from matched samples of the same population. Tracking studies can be used in conjunction with simulated test marketing (see Chapter 10), and they can be particularly helpful in developing marketing strategies.

General Foods, makers of Maxwell House coffee and other leading grocery products, have tracked the awareness of their brands and advertising campaigns for several years, particularly as the 'acid test for new commercials. Pretesting continues to minimise the investment risk behind production, but tracking is there to minimise the risk of deploying airtime funds against an ad that is failing to achieve the communication objectives in the real world of living rooms'.[14]

As with other forms of market research activities, tracking studies have become more sophisticated and far reaching in their coverage and tend to be fully integrated market studies. Tracking study data covering awareness, repeat purchase, etc., can be used for developing forecasting models, using regression analysis or econometric techniques.

11.2 ADVERTISING MEDIA RESEARCH

This research attempts to eliminate waste in advertising by objectively analysing the media available for promoting products and services. It seeks to make valid comparisons so that advertising expenditure is distributed over media which are most likely to result in achieving the objectives of the advertising campaign. Over the past 30 or so years, a great deal of valuable research has been done by marketing research specialists and professional organizations to improve the standards of expert knowledge about the effectiveness of various advertising media. The development of television advertising has added to the competitiveness of the industry, and has encouraged media owners to produce research data of greater sophistication and reliability.

In the UK, the advertising industry has highly organized systems of research into printed and visual media, and advertisers are offered a wealth of information about the suitability of particular media for specific market segments. The cost of advertising space or time is broadly related to the estimated number of readers or viewers; advertisers want to know the effectiveness of a particular medium in communicating with and influencing existing and potential users of their products.

The principal activities of media research will now be reviewed under the headings of the press, television, radio, cinema, and poster research.

Press research

Readership surveys have been of interest to advertisers and advertising contractors in the UK for many years. Pioneer research was done by the Hulton Readership surveys which were made annually between 1946 and 1955 inclusive.

In 1956 the National Readership Survey was taken over by the Institute of Practitioners in Advertising which published the NRS until 1967. From 1968, the National Readership Survey has been administered by the Joint Industry Committee for National Readership Surveys (JICNARS) under the aegis of a committee representing the Press Research Council, the Institute of Practitioners in Advertising, and the Incorporated Society of British Advertisers.

Since its inception the NRS has classified informants into social grades and this method of socio-economic grouping has been widely adopted by marketing researchers (see Chapter 4). The mechanics of social grading are elaborate, as will be seen from the following quotation from JICNARS:

> **THE MECHANICS OF SOCIAL GRADING**
>
> 1. The social grading of informants is carried out at two stages – by the interviewer at the time of the interview, and by Head Office staff when the questionnaires are returned for editing and coding. At each stage the coding is carried out on the basis of occupational information. Only if the occupational information is refused or is incomplete are other factors taken into account.
> 2. The occupational coding is based on written guides, files kept of decisions taken regarding unusual occupations, and general training. Attempts have been made to have a completely objective system, i.e., a master code book consisting of every possible occupation, but such systems have not found approval. The most recent attempt was that conducted under IPA auspices in 1962 on 8000 informants.
> 3. At the interviewer stage the classification is based on guides to grading given in the interviewers' standard manual. It is on the basis of this manual that interviewers are initially trained. Subsequent education is a continuing process, due to exchanges of information between Head Office coders and individual interviewers when there is a discrepancy between the allocation of individuals. The actual document for the interviewers is reasonably comprehensive and runs to over 19 pages.
> 4. On a study such as the National Readership Survey all questionnaires are checked for social grading by a small group of trained coders. This group of people have a slightly more detailed

guide than the interviewers. They also have files and folders containing previous decisions that have been taken on specific occupations viewed as marginal cases. The Head Office coders are the final arbiters of the allocation of informants to a particular social grade.

5. Except in exceptional cases the grading of informants is based exclusively on occupation information. In the majority of cases the grading is based on the occupation of the head of household. The exceptions to this are: if the head of household is not in full-time employment or is sick (for a period of more than two months), or is retired, widowed, or a pensioner (with a specified minimum income), then the occupation of the chief wage earner determines the status of the household and, therefore, informants living in it. Lodgers, boarders, and resident domestic servants are graded on the basis of their own occupation.

   Definitions of head of household, chief wage earner, etc., are given in Appendix D of the JICNARS publication on social grading.

6. With so much emphasis placed on occupation it is clear the considerable detail of occupation is required. If an informant is the head of household one set of occupational detail is obtained. If an informant is not the head of household then details are obtained for the informant and the head of household. The occupational details obtained may be assessed by looking at the last page of the NRS questionnaire. Schematically, however, the details are as follows:

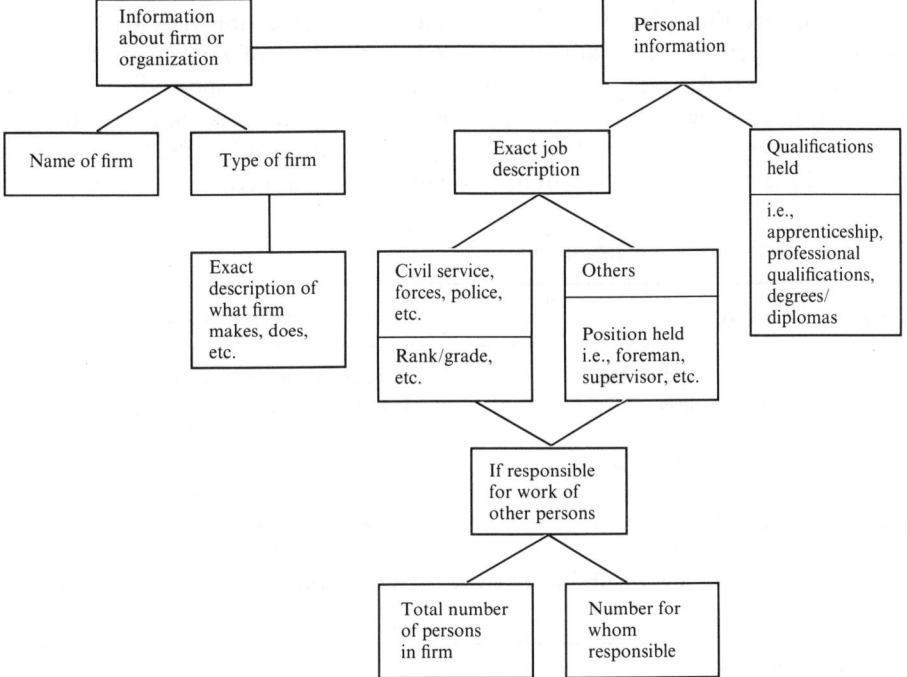

Only when this detail is incomplete, or some very special occupation is involved, is the other information collected and used to supplement the occupation details.

7. It was stated above that irrespective of whether a person was the head of household or chief wage earner, personal details of occupation were obtained. The reason for this is that in addition to allocating people to one of six social grades, informants are also classified in terms of Registrar General categories. There are two such classifications:
   (a) classification of occupation;
   (b) classification of employment status.
   The first is a three digit operational code classification, broadly comparable with the two digit level of International Classification of Occupations. It groups together persons who, on the basis of work done and the nature of the operation performed, are similar. The second classification ('employment status') basically divides the 'employee' from the 'self-employed' and then further subdivides them as follows:

Self-employed

(i) without employees
(ii) with employees (1–24)
(iii) with employees (25 or more)

Employees

(i) managers of large establishments (25 +)
(ii) managers of small establishments (up to 24)
(iii) foreman and supervisors:
  – manual
  – non-manual
(iv) apprentices, articled pupils, trainees
(v) family workers
(iv) other workers

Both sets of data are available by special analyses which may be obtained through any licensed supplier.
Source: JICNARS

Informants are thus placed in a socio-economic classification ranging from A to E which indicates to buyers of press advertising media the types of consumers covered by certain publications. These socio-economic groupings are tabulated, as shown in Table 11.2.

From time to time, criticism of the NRS social grading is made on the grounds that socio-economic groupings based on the occupation of the head of the household are imperfect measures of the propensity of consumers to purchase certain types of products.

Table 11.2 Socio-economic groupings

Social grade	Social status	Head of household's occupation
A	Upper middle class	Higher managerial, administrative or professional
B	Middle class	Intermediate managerial, administrative or professional
C1	Lower middle class	Supervisory or clerical, and junior managerial, administrative or professional
C2	Skilled working class	Skilled manual workers
D	Working class	Semi and unskilled manual workers
E	Those at lowest subsistence levels	State pensioners or widows (no other earner), casual or lowest grade workers

Source: JICNARS.

Critical evaluation The socio-economic groupings in Table 11.2 were devised when, perhaps, society was more stable and consumption patterns were largely class-based. Originally, this grading scheme was intended to reflect the impact of life style, income, and status; but society has been in a state of flux for some years. The old social stratifications based on income have broken down with the emergence of highly organized labour unions, the erosion of differentials, more widespread educational opportunities, and the emergence of 'working wives' as a permanent feature of the labour market.

This misleadingly tidy classification ignores the considerable impact of dual (and even multiple) household incomes. It takes no account of hobby interests, on which sums of money disproportionate to income, may freely be spent. It fails to reflect the dynamic changes in attitudes and behaviour which have affected the consumption of products such as wine.

People are assumed by these groupings to buy directly in relation to the size of their incomes. However, some fairly well-off families may run a small car because of school fees, or on account of strongly held views about the conservation of scarce sources of energy.

A further weakness of the classification is its reliance on the occupation of the head of the household. A printing operative may be as well paid as a barrister; he will almost certainly have more disposable income and his pattern of consumption will be different.

The A–E groupings are highly convenient for marketers and sometimes they relate quite well to actual market behaviour. But they need to be interpreted with sensitive insight and, preferably, used in conjunction with behavioural criteria. To rely exclusively on a system of social classification which originated over a generation ago would be absurd. (See Chapter 4 for discussion of official methods of social classification.)

At the request of JICNARS, Research Services Ltd[15] investigated the NRS social grading system. Among its comments it was stated:

> Although the historical development of social grading based on occupation is well established, the precise reasons for the choice in pre-war studies are not well documented. It would appear that occupations were first used because in the more rigid social order that existed the occupation of the head of the household was a simple and efficient method of deriving income categories. As the relationship between occupation and income has lessened, occupation has remained the background of social grading because no better methods have been found, and because it has still remained a powerful and useful stratification factor, even though the interpretation has become more complex.... Social grading analyses used in published tables of the NRS are to a large degree chosen because:
> (a) From a technical stand-point occupation is relatively stable and reliable at the data collection stage.
> (b) It is a reasonable 'general purpose' classification in that it is useful for most product fields without necessarily being the most ideal for particular product fields.

In 1981, the Market Research Society[16] published the findings of a joint industry working party (IPA; ISBA; ITCA; MRS; and NPA) on social grade validity. The report largely supported the continued use of the present A–E socio-economic grading which provided 'satisfactory discriminatory power' related to product and brand usage; none of the alternative systems studied was found 'to provide consistently better discriminatory power'. The existing method continued to keep its discriminatory power, but there was a need for guidelines to ensure greater consistency in its applications among research suppliers.

It was admitted that while there may be an 'ideal' variable superior to the A–E classification, the 'likely benefit derived would be out of proportion to the substantial expenditure required to investigate this point'. The report admits that the conclusions of the working party may lay them open to criticism of complacency, but it was felt that despite some of its specific shortcomings, the present system of measuring social grade is generally 'perfectly adequate'.

This view is challenged by two experienced marketing researchers[17] who observed that although social grading lacks a degree of reliability, this does not stop it from being a 'consistently powerful discriminator'. Its widespread use should not, however, be allowed to obscure its two distinct weaknesses: it imperfectly represents differences in people's tastes and interests based on cultural and educational dimensions, and it lacks measures of income and wealth. It is suggested that a combined scale which interlaced terminal education age with social grade discriminates more effectively in the consumption of certain products, such as hardback and paperback books. The other perceived drawback to social grading, viz., measures of income and wealth, could be tackled by developing variables known as Total Net Household Income (THI) and Disposable Net Household Income (DHI). It is concluded by these marketing researchers that: 'There are many markets and types of behaviour in which either income or socio-educational grade discriminates more strongly than social grade itself'.[17]

A sub-committee of the Technical and Development Committee of the Market Research Society published a report[18] in 1987 which stated that although the NRS social groupings were widely used, three main problems were encountered: classification by the occupation of head of household/chief wage earner was unpopular with respondents who objected to being classified by someone else's occupation; students and unemployed were variously classified; and certain new technological posts were hard to categorize.

A special tabulation of NRS data showed that about one-half of working women would be classified differently by their own occupation compared with that of the head of household, but the latter still seemed likely to be the best indicator of household life style, and so its continued use was recommended. It was also recommended that all students should be grouped as C1s, and people unemployed for up to six months should be classified according to their previous occupation.

The sub-committee recognized the arbitrary nature of these decisions, but it was felt that they met current needs.

In 1990, the Field Committee of the Market Research Society published *Occupations Groupings: a Job Dictionary*, which lists thousands of jobs in alphabetical order with relevant social gradings.

Methodology   Research Services Ltd currently has the NRS contract. Surveys are based on a stratified random sample involving 27 000 adult interviews over a continuous survey lasting 12 months.

Subscribers receive detailed information covering the major publications researched. Breakdowns by demographic characteristics, regional distribution, television viewing, cinema attendance, commercial radio listening, special interests, etc., are given. Average issue readership for each publication is given with regional analyses. Duplication of readership between two or more publications is also noted.

The NRS is published twice yearly, the reports give main readership tables, readership among special groups, and reading frequency tables and group probability covering the 12 months July to June. This information is updated to cover the calendar year six months later and is published with duplication tables covering the calendar year. Bulletins are circulated to subscribers in advance of the main report to inform them of changes and new developments between the publication of the main reports. Additional services, such as post-survey information service, are available to supplement the main report.

The term 'readership' has been variously defined and this has caused some advertisers to look quizzically at readership figures quoted by larger media owners. As far as NRS research is concerned, it is useful to quote the text of the introduction and the first question in the carefully designed questionnaire:

INTRODUCTION

We want to find out about the newspapers and magazines you have read at all in the past year. I should like you to look through each of these cards in turn. As soon as you see any publication on a card that you remember reading at all in the past year, please put the card on this pile. If you are sure you have not read any of the publications on a card in the past year, please put that card here. If you are not sure about a card, put it aside and we shall come back to it later.

[The interviewer is asked to *explain*, as follows]: It doesn't matter who bought the publication, where you saw it, or how old it was. Just so long as you can remember spending a couple of minutes reading or looking at *any* of the publications on a card in the past year it goes on this pile.

Q.1 Now have you read or looked at any of these newspapers at any time in the past 12 months? (Show cards.)

Respondents' answers are classified as follows:

Almost always	*Quite often*	*Only occasionally*	*Not in the past year*
At least 3 issues out of 4	At least 1 issue out of 4	Less than 1 issue out of 4	

SPECIMEN QUESTIONS – JICNARS MEDIA SURVEY

Cinema

C.1	How often these days do you go to the cinema?	once a week or more often	Y
	Would it be nearer to	two or three times a month	X
		once a month	O
		once every two or three months	1
		two or three times a year	2
		less often	3
		or do you never go these days	4
		OUO	5
C.2(a)	How long ago was the last occasion you went to a cinema?	within last 7 days	Y
		over 7 days up to and including 4 weeks ago	X
		over 4 weeks up to and including 3 months ago	O
		over 3 months up to and including 6 months ago	1
		over 6 months ago/can't remember when	2
		OUO	3

If in last 4 weeks (codes Y or X at C2(a))

C.2(b)	How many times have you been to the cinema in the last 4 weeks?	once	1
		twice	2
		3 times	3
		4 times	4
		5–6 times	5
		7–8 times	7
		more than 8 times	9
		OUO	X

TELEVISION – ASK ALL

			(52)S
TV1	How many television sets in working order are there in your home?	None	0
		One	1
	If none go to next section	Two	2
	If yes ask TV2–TV4	Three or more	3
		OUO	4
			(53)S
TV2(a)	Do you have a video recorder in your home?	Yes	1
	If yes ask (b)	No	2
		OUO	3
			(54)S
(b)	Does it have remote control?	Yes	1
		No	2
	Ask all with TV set		(55)S
(c)	Do you have a video disc player?	Yes	1
		No	2
		OUO	3

		Yes	No
	Show card TV3		
TV3	Does your TV set (do any of your TV sets) have any of these features?	(56)M	
	● a remote control	1	A
	● Teletext: it can receive Oracle or Ceefax	2	A
	● Subscription Cable TV: this gives you different programmes to the ones on the usual BBC & ITV Channels	3	A
	● Satellite dish: giving programmes of Satellite TV companies	4	A
	OUO	5	

			(57)S
	Intro. I would now like to ask about watching television. Please include any time you spend watching programmes or films on TV, whether it was on your own or on somebody else's set; it does not matter which channel it was on or if it was on any sort of video tape (or on cable TV).	7 days	7
		6 days	6
		5 days	5
		3 or 4 days	4
TV4	Firstly, on how many days a week would you say you watch television nowadays?	1 or 2 days	3
	If 'never' go to the next section		
	All others ask TV5–TV7	less often	2
		(never watch TV)	0
		OUO	9

Television (*cont'd.*)

			CC.20 cont'd.		
			TV5	TV6(a)	TV6(b)
TV5	On a day when you watch television, for about how many hours do you view television, on average?		Hrs. TV watched	Channels with Advg	Channel 4
			(58)S	(59)S	(60)S
TV6(a)	Out of every ten hours that	None		0	0
	you watch television, for	½ hour or less	X	X	X
	about how many hours	about 1 hour	1	1	1
	would you say you watch	about 2 hours	2	2	2
	the channels with	about 3 hours	3	3	3
	advertising (that is ITV,	about 4 hours	4	4	4
	Channel 4 and TV-am)?	about 5 hours	5	5	5
		about 6 hours	6	6	6
(b)	Out of every ten hours that	about 7 hours	7	7	7
	you watch the channels	about 8 hours	8	8	8
	with advertising, for about	9 hours or more	9	9	9
	how many hours would	OUO	Y	Y	Y
	you say you watch Channel 4?				

					(63)S
TV7(a)	On how many days a week would you say you watch TV-am, the channel with advertising that transmits up to 9.15 in the morning on weekdays and at weekends?	7 days			7
		6 days			6
		5 days			5
		3 or 4 days			4
		1 or 2 days			3
		less often			2
		never			8
		OUO			9

If not never at TV7(a) show card TV7(b)

			(64)S
(b)	On a day when you watch TV-am, for about how long would you say you view it on average?	less than ¼ hour	Y
		about ¼ hour	0
		about ½ hour	1
		about ¾ hour	2
		about 1 hour	3
		about 1 ¼ hours ..	4
		about 1 ½ hours ..	5
		about 1 ¾ hours ..	6
		about 2 hours	7
		about 2 ¼ hours ..	8
		2 ½ hours or more	9
		OUO	X

In December 1983, JICNARS published[19] a report of a technical study group set up to evaluate the possibility of extending the National Readership Survey to cover 200 or more publications. JICNARS was faced with the problem that every year a number of publications applied for entry into the NRS, but had to be turned away, largely for lack of space and for the unknown effects that their inclusion might have on the validity of the research design.

The extended media list experiment covered 120 national newspapers and magazines which appeared in the NRS publication list, plus 71 extra titles of national magazines (25 weeklies, two fortnightlies, 43 monthlies, and one bi-monthly covering a wide variety of topics). It was established that a total of at least 200 titles could be covered satisfactorily and the research design produced more stable data than the existing NRS limited coverage. JICNARS adopted the recommendations of the working party and the survey system has been changed, partly to include more titles, and partly to improve its stability.

It is perhaps interesting to note the comments of PEP,[20] the independent research organization, concerning readership surveys:

> The basic purpose of a readership survey is to discover who reads what, the 'who' being defined in terms of sex, age, social class, marital status, place of residence, hobbies and interests pursued, and many other characteristics. The statistics thus produced are sometimes closely related to and, also for good reasons, sometimes not so closely related to, the circulation figures published by the journal concerned. The relating factor is, of course, the number of readers per individual copy; this varies from little more than one to a baker's dozen. But this statement is deceptive in its simplicity because there are also many difficulties in determining what shall be the life of an individual copy for the purpose of calculating its readership.... Controversy surrounds readership surveys because the results represent hard cash to the sellers and buyers of advertising space in the journals concerned.

Readership measurement by telephone surveys

After the launch of a new national newspaper and in order to get early estimates of readership, JICNARS has sometimes conducted telephone surveys. From a number of such studies, it was evident that there was a consistent bias: estimates of readerships of the upmarket 'quality' newspapers tended to be higher than those obtained from the main NRS, while readerships of the mass-market 'popular' journals were underestimated.

An experimental telephone study was undertaken by Research Services Ltd[21] for JICNARS in 1988, and new questions were also added to the NRS itself, to try to identify the causes of these biases. Findings revealed that the prime reason lay in the considerable differences between the social grades attributed to respondents in personal and telephone interviews, even when both interviewing methods were conducted by the same research firm.

It was, apparently, 'often difficult to obtain on the telephone the extra information needed to classify a head of household with comparable accuracy to the face-to-face NRS interviewer'.[19,21] There was a 'net tendency' for some of the B social grade people to be classified in the telephone interview as C1s; at the other end of the socio-economic scale, it was easy to classify a pensioner with limited private resources incorrectly as an E from telephone data.

Another, and minor, factor was that 'the use of telephone directories as the source of private telephone numbers introduces a bias towards members of established households and ABs, and, therefore, towards readers of quality newspapers and the range of other AB-oriented products.

The cause of this bias is mainly that households that have acquired a telephone for the first time are excluded from published telephone directories, as are recent movers. ABs tend to be more completely recorded than C1s, and the bias gets worse further down the socio-economic scale.

JICNARS has developed a new telephone survey procedure which entails re-interviewing NRS informants who were interviewed a few months earlier. Since their social grade is known from the first interviews, as also their telephone numbers,[8] the problems of using telephone directories are neatly avoided.

Regional press readership

In August 1990, the Joint Industry Committee for Regional Press Readership Research (JICREG) was launched so that Britain's regional newspapers could be evaluated in common with other media on readership and not just on circulation. JICREG resulted from extensive discussions between advertisers (ISBA), advertising agencies (IPA), and newspaper owners (The Newspaper Society and the Association of Free Newspapers). Initially, JICREG faced significant problems in designing effective research techniques for some 1600 newspapers and newspaper groupings. A pilot study by RSGB was followed by detailed planning of the research methodologies by Telmar. The modelled data are not intended to replace the existing readership research conducted by an increasing number of regional publishers; over 50 of these surveys have proved useful in establishing the parameter of the models.

All the JICREG data are held in the research data base at The Newspaper Society.

Television advertising research

Since its introduction in the UK in September 1955, Independent Television has been dependent on advertising for its revenue. It became apparent that in order to sell advertising time effectively, the programme contractors needed to be able to describe their audiences. In 1957 the Joint Industry Committee for Television Advertising Research (JICTAR) was founded to represent three bodies: the Incorporated Society of British Advertisers Ltd (ISBA), the Institute of Practitioners in Advertising (IPA), and the Independent Television Companies' Association Ltd (ITCA). The first contract for measuring television audiences was held by Television Audience Measurement Ltd (TAM) in 1957. From 30 July 1968, JICTAR appointed Audits of Great Britain Ltd (AGB) to provide a research service based on a television panel of UK households. The costs of the service are borne by the three professional organizations in agreed percentages (programme companies 57.1 per cent, advertising agencies 28.6 per cent, advertisers 14.3 per cent).

Broadcasters' Audience Research Board (BARB) To avoid difficulties arising from different research methods, a joint system for researching both BBC and commercial television audiences was implemented from August 1981.

This new television audience research organization was formed by the BBC and the ITCA which hold equal shares, and its company board consists of directors exclusively from these two organizations. The management committee – for the purposes of audience measurement – is drawn from the IPA, ISBA, ITVA (the successor to ITCA), BBC, Channel 4, S4C, Sky Television, and BSB (these last two having merged since 1990). Members of the management committee for audience appreciation (see Television Opinion Panel below) are from the ITVA, IBA, BBC, Channel 4, and S4C.

These committees are responsible for taking strategic decisions about the data to be collected, the research methodology, and how the data should be deployed. They are supported by technical sub-committees which can give advice on issues of a technical nature; smaller working parties can be set up for specific issues (see Fig. 11.1).

BARB is responsible for commissioning television audience research, both quantitative (audience measurement) and qualitative (audience reaction). The existing system used by JICTAR was adopted for audience measurement and, additionally, adapted to meet the needs of the BBC.

Qualitative research is carried out by the BBC Audience Research Department.

The rationalization of two competing audience measurement research methods was welcomed by the advertising professions.

As noted earlier, AGB was responsible for TV audience research on behalf of JICTAR and this arrangement continued until July 1984, BARB having taken over the contract in 1981. At the beginning of 1982, BARB awarded the contract for TV audience research to AGB after competitive tender. This contract runs for seven years from August 1984 (see below: BARB research developments).

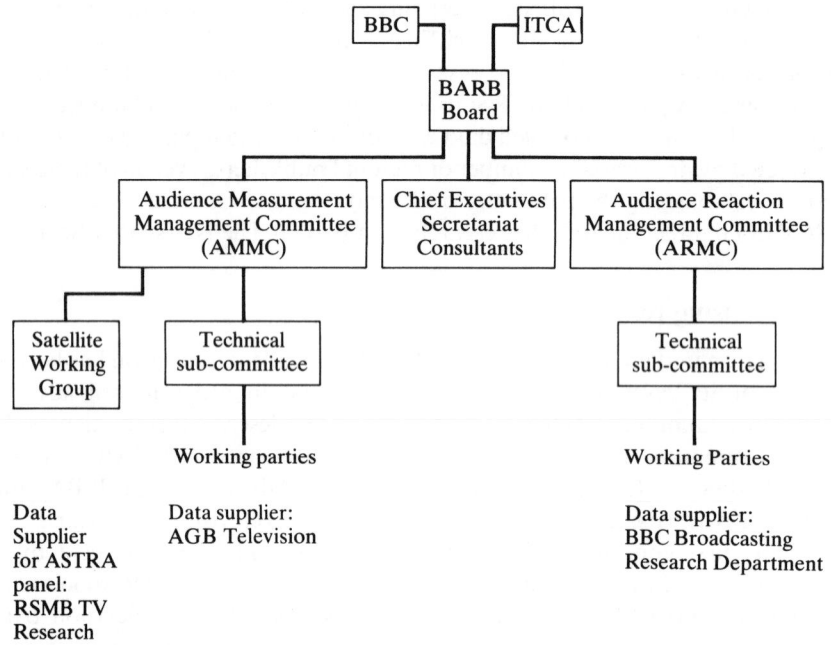

Fig. 11.1 Organization of Broadcasters' Audience Research Board

The old method of measurement based on set meters (electronic meters attached to TV sets) and diaries (personal viewing recorded at quarter-hour intervals) was replaced under the new system of TV audience measurement. Set data are now collected by new on-line meters attached to the TV sets of panel of 3000 private households in the UK. Regional panels vary in size up to 350 households. Each set is monitored by a small RDU (Remote Detection Unit) which passes information through the domestic mains wiring to a central master meter. The central meter acts as a data storage device which is connected to the public telephone network.

At AGB a minicomputer automatically dials each panel home between 2 a.m. and 5 a.m. and retrieves the viewing data contained in the meter store. In this way, a detailed knowledge of the viewing behaviour of the UK population could be made available early on the following day, although reports are, in fact, completed weekly. The new system can easily deal with multiple set ownership. Meters can now be fixed to RDUs attached to portable TVs or a VCR.

Although the meter records accurately when the television is switched on, and the station to which it is tuned, it does not indicate who is actually watching. AGB offered two methods of measuring individual viewing: *push-buttons* and electronic diaries. With the former, all house-hold members aged 4+ are allocated their own personal button on a specially designed handset which they press when they start viewing and again when they stop. In homes with more than one television, a handset is provided for each. Viewing by guests is catered for by additional buttons. When a button is depressed, a signal is picked up by a display unit and passed to the central meter, together with the set data.

The second method – electronic diaries – was intended to be an extension of the original paper diary, but using a light-pen instead of pen and ink. It had the advantage of being able to register out-of-home viewing by panel members, but the disadvantages of being less 'user-friendly' and of only being able to register in 1/4 blocks.

After much deliberation, BARB opted for the use of on-line meters and push-button handsets in all panel homes from December 1984. The possible next stage involving electronic diaries was never introduced.

While the meter system has many advantages and is the preferred method in most countries where TV audience measurement is conducted regularly, there are also some disadvantages.

The main advantage, which is shared with any panel data, is that it enables longitudinal data to be collected (see Chapter 9). However, a significant drawback is defining what viewing really means: a panel member might have the TV set switched on (and the meter recording that a particular programme was being viewed) but he or she could be asleep; reading a book; talking to other members of the family; or even absent from the room (which would not be known unless he or she pressed his personal viewing button). Unlike electronic diaries, push-buttons cannot be used to register out-of-home viewing.

The ratings information provided from BARB TV panel research is used by broadcasters in programme planning and by leading advertising agencies and advertisers in assessing trends in viewing behaviour, so that effective media planning can be done. Crucially, the ratings output of the system are used as the currency for buying and selling commercial air time.

Specific data cover audience sizes over regions and channels, number of hours a week viewed by individuals, and the number of episodes of a series which people have watched.

Television Opinion Panel

In addition to measuring the size of audiences, as described in the preceding section, BARB set up the Audience Reaction Service (ARS) in April 1982 to provide a measure of audience appreciation for BBC, ITV, Channel 4, and S4C programmes. This appreciation service is now entitled Television Opinion Panel, and involves a weekly reporting panel of individuals aged 12 years and over and numbering 3000. This is supported by monthly reporting panels in each ITV area in order to take each ITV regional sub-sample to a minimum size of 500. There is also a supplementary, and again monthly reporting, panel of children between the ages of 4 and 15, which totals 1000 children. There are also arrangements for boosting the Welsh-speaking sample in the Principality of Wales to meet the requirements of S4C.

The research is undertaken by the BBC's Broadcasting Research Department and is linked to its Daily Survey of radio listening (see later section, and also refer to Fig. 11.1). Respondents to the nationally representative sample of 1000 people interviewed every day of the year about their radio listening habits provide the recruiting base for the panels – members of which are (weekly or monthly) posted a booklet which carries details of all TV programmes broadcast in that area, over the seven-day broadcasting week (currently Monday to Sunday). They are asked to continue their normal pattern of viewing, to answer a number of questions and to post back the booklet immediately after the seventh day.

Panellists rate programmes they watched on a six-point scale ranging from 'extremely interesting and/or enjoyable' to 'not at all interesting and/or enjoyable', and from their responses an Audience Appreciation score (AI) is calculated, between 0 and 100. Allowing for refusals, non-return of booklets, etc., the output for each day's programmes nationally is based on a sample of around 3000. A second booklet accompanies the appreciation booklet. Viewpoint provides the facility for the broadcaster/subscriber to the service to ask *ad hoc*, diagnostic, questions of the panel.

Satellite television research

In early 1990, BARB started a special ASTRA panel to monitor viewing behaviour in homes able to receive ASTRA satellite transmissions via cable or DTH. This specialist panel was developed because the initial penetration of ASTRA was not sufficient to form an effective sub-sample within the main BARB panel of 3000 homes (see earlier section). In addition, technical limitations of existing meters did not allow for separate identification of satellite channels.

This new 200-home ASTRA panel is designed to run in parallel with the existing panel and is equipped with meters able to separate satellite channels.

BSB

A sub-sample drawn from the 1991 panel was due to start in 1991, later to be absorbed in the 1991 panel (see BARB research developments below).

BARB research developments

From August 1991, a new system of TV audience research was instigated by BARB and two marketing research companies were awarded seven-year contracts. RSMB (jointly owned by Research Services and Millward Brown) was given a contract for conducting Establishment Surveys, recruiting panel members, monitoring panel balance and operating quality control procedures. Another contract was placed with AGB (which has been responsible for TV audience research for seven years from August 1984 – see page 227) for installing, operating, and polling the meters. A separate contract with AGB covered the processing of data and making it available to BARB subscribers.

The BARB main panel of 3000 homes will be increased to 4435 to provide larger sub-groups for detailed analysis. Significant changes will occur in panel controls to allow, for example, larger sub-samples of the younger and the more upmarket viewers to be developed. The weighting of samples will play a much larger role than formerly, because of this differential sampling. The Establishment Survey, which annually describes the universe and provides a pool for panel recruits, will no longer be an annual event. Instead, it will be the product of interviews conducted continuously throughout the year in order more sensitively to reflect changes in the market, such as the acquisition of satellite dishes, etc. The sample size will increase to over 40 000 per annum, in order to feed the expanded main panel mentioned earlier.

Meters will become more sophisticated, able to discriminate between all the available channels, to monitor a very large number of pieces of equipment in each home, to register some demographic data about guest viewers, and, most importantly, to be able to 'fingerprint', i.e., place an identification mark on a VCR tape so that off-air recording can be identified by date, time, and channel when replayed, in order to identify time-shift viewing.

The vast increase in research data resulting largely from multiple TV channels, longer broadcasting hours and fragmented viewing habits, will be derived from electronic reporting technology supported by some hard copy, rather than, as formerly, vice versa. Sophisticated measurement of TV audiences results in rapid availability of viewing behaviour; costs of such advanced systems of monitoring will, inevitably, increase.

In November 1990, it was announced that Sky Television and BSB were to merge, resulting in a combined channel of 1.35 million subscribers. The new company was called British Sky Television but transmits simply as Sky Television.

Television advertising measurement – overseas

Over the past few years, television audience research methods across the major European countries have largely become standardized and based on the adoption of electronic (peoplemeter) systems which are replacing traditional methods of diary or recall measurements. By 1991 all EC countries and at least three other European markets had adopted the peoplemeter technique.

In Switzerland, which initiated research in 1967, television audiences are measured by the Telecontrol System using electronic meters and based on a randomly selected panel of about 1300 households (distributed proportionately among German-speaking, French-speaking, and Italian-speaking). In addition, random, personal interviews are conducted to survey the whole range of media and persons over 15 years of age are also interviewed every week by telephone on their general and specific media behaviour. Also, selected topics related to TV and radio are subjected to large-scale surveys in two-year cycles. Qualitative studies are also undertaken periodically.

In Austria, ORF–Teletest, through the contractor GFK–Fessel, researches a 600 representative sample of households using the same system as in Switzerland.

In Belgium, a similarly based 600 household panel (Walloon) uses the Telecontrol System, and another panel of 300 Flemish-speaking households uses the AGB 4900 system. This latter system is also used in the Netherlands with a panel of 710 households, in Italy, with a panel of 2300 households, and in the Republic of Ireland, with a panel of 432 households organized by Irish Tam Ltd, a subsidiary of Pergamon AGB.

AGB has developed its peoplemeter technology to include a number of new features required in various markets, including the ability for panel members to vote, i.e., give their degree of appreciation of the programme being viewed. This technique has been adopted in the Netherlands, Belgium, and Ireland.

In France, Mediametric, through Audimedia, researches television networks by a 1000 household panel using Telecontrol VI System, and also another 1000 household panel through Secodip, using the Audimat A2 System.

Spanish viewers are researched by ECOTEL on behalf of RTVE, based on a 1200 household panel (Televimit 100 System), and a 2000 household panel (Telecontrol V1 System); RTVE in Portugal also uses the latter system with a panel of 600 households.

German viewing habits are researched by GFK TV – forschung, based on a representative sample of 3833 households using the Telecontrol System. In Finland, 500 Finnish households are equipped with Finnmeters operated by Finnpanel for YLE/MTV.

Norwegian audience research, covering both radio and television, is organized by Norsk Rikskringkasting, and includes a thrice-weekly telephone survey of 200 people, randomly selected over the age of nine years. Respondents are asked about their radio and TV habits over the previous two days, except on Monday when the interval spans three days. In addition, a sample of 400 people is interviewed each year, and 300 children aged between three and eight years are also surveyed. *Ad hoc* studies related to specific issues may also be conducted from time to time.

In some countries, notably France, there is concern about the possible shortcomings of the peoplemeter system, particularly the extent to which panel members correctly press their button during commercial breaks or other occasions when they may leave the room for a short period of time. Because of this problem, leading research firms, including AGB, have invested in various research methodologies for so-called 'passive sensing'. Particular techniques vary, but most involve some kind of computerized image recognition; they tend to be complex and costly and so commercial implementation in the very near future is unlikely.

The increasingly complicated pattern of TV viewing has led AGB to develop VCR 'fingerprinting' equipment, which allows systems to report what material is recorded and when it is played back.

Over the last few years, peoplemeter measurements have been used in SE Asia, and AGB expects the trend towards this system to become world-wide. In Europe, AGB's extensive organization now conducts peoplemeter panel surveys in 10 countries.

In the US, the Schwerin research organization mails invitations to randomly selected households to see a theatrical presentation of films (general interest films, some commercials). Afterwards, a competitive preference test is organized, and viewers are offered a year's supply of a product, the brand of which they must choose. This test is said to encourage serious judgement, on the lines of everyday shopping, of the relative merits of competing brands. This form of advertising research was tried for a time in the UK, but eventually discontinued.

Television advertising measurement in the US also uses electronic meters (Nielsen 'Audiometer' for national ratings and Arbitron for local); diaries (Nielsen 'Recordometer' and Arbitron); telephone coincidental method (the Trendex service) which involves telephoning people whose names have been selected from the telephone directory, and asking them what television programme or radio programme, if any, they are watching or listening to, and what product or sponsor is being promoted. These enquiries enable researchers to give ratings on programmes within a few hours of transmission, against the inevitable delay of some weeks for a Nielsen rating. The dependence of this system on telephone directories as sampling frames means that bias is bound to occur in sampling. Another method of television research involves personal interviews in the homes of viewers. 'Aided recall' is used to assist respondents in recalling programmes viewed the day before; 7800 homes are visited each day. Inaccurate recall because of poor memory or deliberate falsification together with the relatively high costs of interviewing are significant problems of this methodology.

Radio audience measurement

Measuring radio listening is, in many ways, a more complex task than researching television audiences. Apart from national networks, there are regional and local services (both BBC and commercial stations), and also the BBC's World Service, Radio Luxembourg and many foreign, as well as pirate stations.

Over 90 per cent of radio listening is known to be secondary to activities such as driving a car, reading, preparing a meal, or doing homework, so radio listening is more difficult to define.

As noted in Chapter 1, the BBC has been involved with audience research since 1936, and the BBC's Daily Survey has been the principal source of radio audience data, and remained unchanged until certain important modifications were made to the methodology in April 1982.

As noted already, Daily Survey involves interviewing every day a nationally representative sample of 1000 people aged 4+ (irrespective of whether they have radios or TV sets). Each day's broadcast is the subject of enquiry on the following day. Respondents are also asked about television viewing; although the data supplied by AGB are taken as providing definitive estimates of audience sizes, an important reason for asking questions about television viewing is connected with the Audience Reaction Service (see earlier section).

The sophisticated sampling method used in this extensive survey is worth noting (see Chapters 3–5). At the first stage of sample selection a master sample of 720 Parliamentary constituency selections is uséd; this is then stratified by BBC and ITV regions and ranked in geographical order within. The sample is thus representative of all types of users in different parts of the country. For any particular day's viewing a representative sub-sample of one-twelfth (60) of these constituencies is used.

Radio – the BBC Listening Panel Since November 1941, reactions to BBC radio programmes have been derived from the Radio Listening Panel, of 3000 listeners aged 12 and over, which feeds back listeners' views on selected radio network broadcasts. Panel members, who serve for two years, are sent a questionnaire each week which lists effectively all programmes from the five BBC national networks.

Quotas are set to ensure that different types of listener are represented adequately, and to achieve this a method of classification by listening behaviour is adopted. Results are weighted to correct for over-representation; for example, of Radio 4 listeners (see Chapter 16).

In addition to continuous surveys, the BBC also carries out a large number of *ad hoc* studies as 'special projects' incorporating both quantitative and qualitative research.

Independent local radio research The ILR system of local commercial radio in the UK commenced in October 1973, when LBC and Capital Radio opened. Until then, Radio Luxembourg was the principal commercial station which broadcast regularly to the UK and which, since 1952, has researched its audience by personal interviewing diaries.

Commercial radio stations now cover the principal cities and towns of the UK and have been operated under licence from the Independent Broadcasting Authority (IBA). In January 1991, the Radio Authority took over from the IBA.

A joint ISBA/IPA study group considered the type of radio audience research that would be needed for this developing advertising medium and, in conjunction with the Association of Independent Radio Contractors (AIRC), a joint industry committee (JICRAR – Joint Industry Committee for Radio Audience Research) was founded. This body follows the pattern of the established JICNAR (press) and JICTAR (television) groups. Unlike JICNARS or BARB, the total cost of JICRAR is met by AIRC.

JICRAR survey methodology is based on seven-day diaries distributed among quota samples of persons aged 15 or more living in private households within the radio station's designated area. Samples of from 300 to 1200 adults, according to the size of individual radio station areas, record their radio listening (BBC or commercial) in 15-minute periods in specially printed pocket-sized diaries. The sample is based on one elector per household with procedures to include adult non-electors and children aged 5–14, in order to ensure that research results are representative by size of household. Diaries are placed and collected by interviewers, who also ask respondents about their general media habits.

Surveys are conducted separately in each ILR station's broadcasting area, although not necessarily at the same time, although precisely the same methodology is used.

Teer[22] has observed that the results of this diary-based research confirm, as expected, that those who never listen to the radio or are only casual listeners, are less likely than heavier listeners to complete a diary. However, this bias is not considered to be serious; the nature of over-estimates of the radio audience because of this acknowledged problem would only be assessed by more thoroughly investigating non-respondents' listening behaviour. JICRAR gives no information about those who refused to cooperate, but the data provided appear to be acceptable to the advertising industry.

The research is carried out by Research Services of Great Britain, one of the larger marketing research firms and part of the AGB Group.

In 1985, JICRAR and the industry as a whole, reviewed the long-term needs of radio research, and investigations focused on improving the cost-effectiveness and user value of this survey from 1986 onwards.

The IBA has also carried out about a dozen detailed attitudinal surveys in individual ILR areas, mostly where the contracts of the longest established ILR stations were being re-advertised, in order to check listeners' opinions and expectations. Among the research findings the fund-raising efforts for local charities were acknowledged to be a valuable and attractive aspect of local commercial radio services.

Radio Joint Audience Research (RAJAR) In 1992, the BBC and the Association of Independent Radio Companies (AIRC) plan to set up a joint radio research service – RAJAR – with representatives from the IPA and ISBA. The methodology includes a continuous national radio survey based on a 7-day self-completion diary (UK national sample of 1 000 diarists per week) and also a bi-annual (second and fourth quarters) local radio survey based on 500 diarists per ILR and BBC local radio station.

Cinema audience research

The only continuous marketing research covering cinema attendance is included in the National Readership Survey (NRS): refer to section on press research (page 218) and to the questions extracted from this survey questionnaire (page 223). From these questions, it is possible to calculate the frequency of cinema attendance.

In addition to these data, the Department of Industry publishes cinema admission statistics each month, but these are confined to cinema size analysed over the Standard Regions of the Registrar General; no other data which could be helpful in planning advertising are obtainable from this source.

The General Household Survey gives an analysis of cinema attendances by income group for the UK population 16 years of age and over.

Social Trends published by HMSO, also provides some relatively limited data on cinema attendances with trend diagrams.

In 1980, the Cinema Advertising Association commissioned Carrick James Market Research to undertake an intensive study of cinema patrons. This research, now known as CAVIAR (Cinema and Video Industry Audience Research), has been repeated several times, and covers cinema audience profiles, video films viewing habits and newspaper readership data. A sample of 3027 people aged seven and over is involved.

Poster research

Various attempts[23–26] have been made over the past 30 or so years to research the advertising effectiveness of posters. The classification of poster sites has been one of several problems encountered in developing suitable methods of researching this medium.

JICPAR (Joint Industry Committee for Poster Advertising Research) was established in 1983 as successor to JICPAS (Joint Industry Committee for Poster Audience Surveys). JICPAR comprises representatives of the Outdoor Advertising Association of Great Britain Ltd; the Incorporated Society of British Advertisers Ltd; the Institute of Practitioners in Advertising; and the Council of Outdoor Specialists.

In conjunction with JICPAR, the Outdoor Advertising Association, in April 1985, selected outdoor Research Surveys to provide a computer bureau service for the Outdoor Site Classification and Audience Research – known as OSCAR.

This service will enable estimates to be made of both pedestrian and vehicular audiences for all posters. Posters that are located in low population areas but with a high audience created by traffic passing between major urban centres will now be recognized for their true value. Advertisers will also have access to data related to types of ward, area, shopping, and commercial characteristics, including proximity to named retailers, so that posters can be strategically sited.

JICPAR believes that this new computerized scheme of poster research is probably the most comprehensive and detailed audience estimation system anywhere in the world.

BMRB has conducted surveys related to poster audiences and NOP operates a specialist research service 'Poster Test'.

Research on poster advertising on London Transport buses involving special line-film techniques was described in Chapter 2. This ingenious approach to the measurement of 'opportunities to see' overcame some of the problems of researching the effectiveness of this advertising medium.

Cable televison

In autumn 1982, the Hunt Committee Report opened the way for cable television networks in the UK and following the Cable Bill in 1984, the Cable Authority was set up and awarded franchises. 'Predictions on the future of cable television in the UK tend to be cautious. Much will depend, of course, on the attraction of programmes and the price charged to subscribers.'[2]

JICCAR (Joint Industry Committee for Cable Audience Research) is another research body which is jointly funded and responsible for promoting the development of effective audience research connected with cable television services. JICCAR completed a pilot audience research survey in late 1984, and plans to commission three full sweeps of the cable TV audience. Personal pre-coded diaries will be completed by each respondent in the panel households. Monthly aggregate figures of the total number of homes in the UK passed by cable and the number connected to cable services will be published. BARB is taking over much of the research done by JICCAR.

In 1983, AGB conducted a major study into the market for cable entertainment which was used widely by applicants for interim licences. This research was followed up by the launch of the AGB Cable Monitor, which will trace the progress of cable in selected towns.

AGB Cable and Viewdata Ltd is also, as the title suggests, involved in collecting market research data via the TV screen using Viewdata. (See Chapter 6, Section 6.12: Interactive television polling.)

11.3 ADVERTISING EFFECTIVENESS RESEARCH

This research is concerned with analysing different media (and combinations of media) and evaluating the degree of success with which the advertising objectives have been achieved. It follows that certain criteria should be agreed by which success may be measured, e.g., the rate of growth of sales of a product brand, increase in market share, or, more qualitatively, greater awareness of the company. In some cases, the principal role of advertising may be defensive, i.e., maintaining the present market position of a specific brand of product. Whatever the objective, it should be clearly stated before the advertising plans are devised, so that every detail of the campaign can be carefully worked out to fulfil this.

It is admittedly difficult to make an accurate appraisal of an advertising campaign. Advertising rarely works in isolation – it is one element in the marketing mix, i.e., the amounts and kinds of marketing variables (price, promotion, packaging, distribution, etc.), which a firm may vary from time to time.

In the pithy words of a writer[27] in *Fortune* magazine: 'It has always been one of the charms of the advertising business that, while everybody knows advertising "works", nobody ever knows for sure what makes it work'.

The two complementary studies of advertising measurements,[9,10] which have already been discussed under 'copy research', also considered the evaluation of advertising campaigns. Five measures were rated (awareness, recognition, recall, attitude, buying predisposition). As in individual advertisement testing, 'recognition' was at least favoured while 'attitude' attracted most support. It was felt that because advertising campaigns are concerned with changing consumers' attitudes towards specific products and services, measuring change was a particularly useful method of assessing the effect of advertising.

During these two surveys, research directors were asked if sales should (and could) be the criterion of the effectiveness of an advertising campaign.

American directors were equally divided on this issue, though 27 out of 37 effective responses indicated that sales data could, in fact, be obtained. Many felt, however, that the specific sales influence of advertising cannot be isolated from other variables. Moreover, there appeared to be no generally accepted theory of how advertising works.

About 62 per cent of European directors felt that sales should not be taken as the ultimate standard for measuring the effect of advertising. The remaining 38 per cent agreed that it was possible to use sales data, and many of these said that opportunities to do so were limited to exceptional situations within particular product categories. They were in agreement with the Americans over the difficulty of relating the influence of advertising and sales.

European opinions tended to differ significantly, depending on agency size, extent of American influence, and country of operation. For example, the large, American-influenced, British agencies tended to view sales measures of advertising campaign effectiveness more favourably than techniques of evaluating individual advertisements. Of West German agencies, 92 per cent said that sales should not be the criterion for judging the success of an advertising campaign.

Almost all European directors, expressed concern about the limitations of present methods of measuring and predicting advertising effectiveness; the majority believed that improved techniques would be developed.

More complicated techniques used to check the effectiveness of advertising utilize elaborate statistical models. Classic research in this area was undertaken by Kristian Palda[28] on the effects of advertising on the sales of Lydia Pinkham's Vegetable Compound during the period 1908 to 1960. Because of certain unique features, e.g., the product had no close substitutes and the company regularly spent between 40 per cent and 60 per cent of its sales revenue on advertising, Palda was able to indicate the usefulness of different equations in measuring the carry-over effects of Pinkham's advertising.

An interesting attempt to evaluate advertising effectiveness by applying statistical methodology and model building was published some years ago by the Advertising Association.[29] It covers research by Professor J. M. Samuels of the Graduate Centre for Managment Studies, Birmingham, into the effects of advertising on sales and brand shares. No conclusive claims could be made and many of the studies showed no significant results, though within the limitations of the statistical techniques used some success was achieved. It was possible, for example, to see the influence of price and advertising on the level of brand shares in the household cleanser market.

There is still a great deal of work to be done in measuring advertising's contribution to the success of marketing operations. Controlled marketing experiments should be attempted, using the research techniques of the social sciences in order to acquire a better understanding of consumer behaviour, and implementing developments in statistical analysis.

Coupon research

The most direct way of evaluating an advertising campaign and checking the suitability of the media, occurs in mail-order trading, from which coupon research originated. Coupon research generally relates to printed media, although enquiries are now being invited in response to radio and television advertising. To attract enquiries, some interesting offer is made, e.g., to supply a colour chart or instruction booklet.

Replies are analysed on a cost-per-enquiry basis and the effectiveness of different publications evaluated. This is, of course, a fairly crude measure as the number of enquiries may not accurately reflect the degree of interest in the advertisement or its real effectiveness in winning sales.

Experiments can be made with the relative pulling power of various publications; the degree of variation over regions may be important. 'Split-run' tests, featuring different styles of advertisement for the same product, can be inserted in the same edition of a publication, and an evaluation made of their relative appeal. Several leading publishing houses offer 'split-run' facilities to advertisers. The alternative copies are distributed equally to ensure that the advertisements are viewed by comparable populations.

Many consumer and technical magazines run a 'reader service', which simplifies the task of their readers when asking for information from advertisers. Readers merely tick off manufacturers' names on a blanket enquiry form, printed usually at the back of the magazine. Advertisers then receive a list of enquirers from the magazine's advertising department. When computing the enquiry rate, it would be as well to bear in mind that some people appear to be compulsive coupon-fillers.

Sources of advertising data

British Rate and Data (BRAD) This publication gives detailed information on newspapers, magazines, television, radio, the cinema, outdoor advertising, and other media. Publication is monthly. This comprehensive guide to media facilities, including advertising rates, is valuable to researchers, as well as to advertising executives.

Advertisers Annual (IPC) This contains media, supplies of advertising and promotional services, advertising agencies, and principal advertisers, listed geographically.

The Newspaper Society This society is a national organization which looks after the interests of morning, evening, and weekly papers published in England and Wales. In 1961, it published a comprehensive survey entitled 'Regional readership and markets survey', but this, of course, is no longer up to date. The Society does not now have a research department. JICREG data (see earlier section) are contained in the research data base at the Newspaper Society.

The Audit Bureau of Circulations (ABC) This is a professional body founded by advertisers, advertising agencies, and advertising media owners to secure, by standard and uniform methods of audit, accurate net sales, distribution, audience figures, etc., of advertising media. Audited figures listing average figures are issued at regular six-monthly intervals. ABC certificates give advertisers and agencies a quantitative and objective assessment of media, while media owners are given a 'hallmark' for their product. Rigorous standards of computing the published figures are observed. ABC circulation figures apply to the major part of the British press. Consideration is now being given to the problem of producing qualitative and geographical data, since ABC measurement has been solely quantitative so far.

Publishing houses The larger publishing houses and newspapers produce research data from time to time, frequently using the services of professional research organizations to ensure objectivity and acceptance by clients. Examples are given below.

IPC Magazines, publishers of the mass-market Women's weeklies – *Woman, Woman's Own, Woman's Realm*, and *Woman's Weekly* offers an on-going service for both pre-testing and post-testing advertisements in these magazines. These research studies are designed to evaluate the achievements of an advertisement both qualitatively and quantitatively.

IPC Magazines is also always interested in cooperating with advertisers jointly to sponsor research to trace the achievements of campaigns in the women's weeklies, where there is a possibility of the results being used for case history promotion purposes.

IPC also produces information on particular campaigns associated with its magazines, and publishes a range of booklets. Additionally, IPC publishes, as noted in Chapter 2, *Advertisers' Annual*.

The Radio Times offers a range of services to advertisers and their agencies such as: computer analyses of NRS, TGI, Businessman Survey; market data from on-line text services (Profile, Harvest); ACORN or Town and City targeted inserts; pagination analyses of all major magazines (IMS Medialog data); noting and reading data on *Radio Times* (from Gallup).

Manchester Evening News supplements the standard NRS data – which does not always accurately represent the true readership levels of the major evening newspapers – with *ad hoc* surveys relating to the effectiveness of promotional campaigns for the marketing and circulation departments, specific research for present or potential clients. MEN also publishes a Greater Manchester Media Fact File which provides a major data base for media planners and buyers.

Thomson Regional Newspapers and the Westminster Press Group are also able to provide advertisers with research support.

Birmingham Post and Mail offers specific market research as a back-up to major schedules for selected advertisers. Data include effectiveness of advertising buying behaviour, and readership profile.

Independent television contractors The various independent television programme contractors provide advertisers and agencies with specific market research data and offer *ad hoc* and continuous research services.

Thames Television, for example, offers an 'executive research service', particularly in evaluating the effects of advertising campaigns or awareness of and attitudes to products. TVS Television operats a TVS Survey Research Service particularly designed to serve new or small advertisers and involving pre- and post-campaign awareness testing, for which special economic rates are charged.

Tyne-Tees Television, in common with the other television programme companies, uses ACORN, AGB research data, BMRB TGI data, and Nielsen services in market analyses for its clients and prospective advertisers. Border Television can arrange a comprehensive variety of research and marketing services, including test marketing, shop audits, etc. (see Chapter 10).

Advertising statistics: IPA and AA

Statistical information on advertising is collected by both the Institute of Practitioners in Advertising (IPA) and the Advertising Association (AA). The AA has published statistics of the annual national total of advertising expenditure, analysed by main types of advertising and main types of media, for over 20 years. During the period 1948 to 1968, large-scale surveys were carried out every four years, estimates for the intervening years being projections based upon published material and selected unpublished information. From 1969, full detailed surveys have been carried out annually.

In order to verify their research techniques, the AA appointed Research Services Ltd to undertake a comprehensive survey collating information from advertising media, advertisers, advertising agencies, and from Legion Publishing Co. Ltd and Media Expenditure Analyses Ltd (MEAL).

Postal questionnaires were sent out between the beginning of April and the beginning of June 1969, to which a good response was given. As a result of this research, some slight modifications were made to earlier estimates for total advertising expenditure, and the AA believes that its present techniques produce highly reliable and valid figures.

As already noted in Chapter 2, detailed information on advertising expenditure over media and within product groups is obtainable from MEAL. Monthly analyses are published giving expenditure by brand in press and television with the name of the advertising agency responsible for the account.

The Legion Publishing Co. Ltd also publishes monthly and yearly analyses of advertising expenditure.

The *Advertisers' Annual* published by IPC, gives useful information on media and lists principal advertising agencies and their accounts.

The British Bureau of Television Advertising (BBTA), which was founded in 1966 by the Independent Television Companies, is no longer operating. During its life, a series of specially designed booklets and maps were published as reference guides to advertisers.

Information on advertising expenditure in the US is given in detailed analyses in the publication *Marketing Communications*, known formerly as *Printer's Ink*. Data on advertising are also found in the *Census of Business* and the *Survey of Current Business*.

Advertising research in practice

Starch Continuing Readership Program   This was set up in the US in 1931 by Dr Daniel Starch to investigate magazine readership and the extent to which specific advertisements are read as well as being seen. Starch research is concerned with the 'recognition' of advertisements. Three degrees of readership are noted in Starch reports: *noted* (percentage of readers who remember seeing the ad), *seen/associated* (percentage of readers who saw or read part of ad which indicated brand or advertiser), and *read most* (percentage of readers who read half or more of written material in ad).

Starch inteviewers survey representative cross-sections of the population. Calls are made at homes and people are asked their reading habits. If they mention a specific magazine which Starch is researching, interviewers produce a recent copy and go through it page by page, noting the observations of respondents on articles and advertisements. Probing questions are asked about advertisement readership to establish the impact of various design and layout features.

Leading periodicals are studied by Starch, part of the cost being borne by the media owners who can use Starch readership measurements as a selling aid. Advertisers subscribe to receive an actual copy of the specific magazine in which they advertised, together with 'Starch Scores' shown on paper stickers attached to each advertisement. In addition, Starch supplies statistical summaries relating to the research findings and the cost of advertising.

While the Starch system of continuous research is extremely thorough, high Starch scores themselves do not guarantee that consumers will buy the product advertised. Advertisements may be remembered for many reasons; they may not be those which influence consumers to choose particular brands of products.

Gallup and Robinson   The American research firm of Gallup and Robinson was set up by George Gallup and Claude Robinson in the early 1930s, but neither of the founders has been involved with it for many years. When the company was eventually sold, George Gallup allowed the new owners to continue to use his name. However, the present firm is a separate, independent, totally non-associated company with the American Institute of Public Opinion.

American Gallup operates a research service into advertising readership which attempts to go rather deeper than the Starch enquiries. This system uses 'aided recall', and informants are rigorously questioned about specific magazines they claim to have read. Actual copies of advertisements are now shown, recall being aided by cards on which product brand names are entered. There are some deliberate 'plants'. Informants' remarks are taken down verbatim. The method, called 'Impact', is used also for television advertising research (see Gallup Impact Service below).

Gallup, famous for its Institute of Public Opinion, also has a company, Audience Research Inc., specializing in measuring the likely popularity of publications, films, and television shows not yet released for public viewing. This research centres round special theatrical presentations to invited audiences, who are tested for their reactions to commercials sandwiched between general interest films. The 'Mirror of America', as the theatre is described, is about 10 miles from Princeton. This pre-testing of advertisements also extends to print advertising. Gallup prepares a special magazine, called *Impact*, which has some feature articles plus advertisements for testing purposes. *Impact* is distributed to carefully selected homes, at which interviewers later call to obtain informants' reactions to the advertising features.

The rival attractions of the Starch rating system, based on recognition, and of the Gallup and Robinson recall ratings were the subject of a special investigation by the Printed Advertising Rating Committee (PARM) of the Advertising Research Foundtion in 1955. Their findings were not conclusive; they agreed that both methods had controversial points, but that both contribute usefully, in their own distinctive ways, to print advertising research.

Social Surveys (Gallup Poll) Ltd

This British Gallup organization has no financial or managerial ties with Gallup Poll in America, but the two companies are linked through the Gallup International Research Institute and with other affiliated Gallup companies in over 40 countries throughout the world, including, recently, agencies in Eastern Europe.

Gallup undertakes a large amount of research into advertising in the UK. A lot of this work is conducted using the Noting and Reading technique, the Evaluative Assessment technique, and the Impact 24-hour Recall technique. Each of these involves interviewing a cross-section of readers of a publication a few days after they have read it, asking them about advertising in the particular issue: Noting and Reading covering their readership of the whole publication; Evaluative Assessment covering their thoughts at the time they were looking at specific advertisements; and Impact covering their recall of a number of advertisements in the issue. In addition to these techniques there are placement pre-tests where specific pages are removed and replaced in specially prepared copies. These issues are then given to a representative sample of readers of the publication and a check is made subsequently on the way they read the publication. In this way advertisements can be tested in their natural environment without the reader being aware that the advertisement is under test.

Gallup also undertakes continuous tracking surveys, to measure public awareness and reactions to advertisement through its Omnibus service (through which $c.150\,000$ people are interviewed annually). In addition, the company also operates poster testing and advertisement pre-testing with audiences who are invited to attend special research sessions held in local centres (group discussions and hall tests).

Gallup also runs the record industry trade audit, on which the national pop charts are based – as featured on BBC Radio and *Top of the Pops* (see Chapter 9).

Gallup Noting and Reading Service This was developed by Dr George Gallup in the US as the Field Readership Index, and operates on an *ad hoc* basis in the UK. It measures audience noting and reading of editorial articles and advertisements. Checking over the years has built up a vast store of information relating to factors that influence the attention paid to advertising. Samples of between 200 and 250 people are selected to be representative of the publication readership, as noted in the National Readership Survey. Analysis of readership covers:

1. *Page traffic*: percentage looking at *any* item on each page.
2. *Noting*: percentage *noting* any part of the advertisement.
3. *Noting the name*: percentage noting advertiser's name.
4. *Reading*: percentage reading two or more sentences of advertisement copy.

Gallup Impact Service This research service was also developed in the US and is now undertaken in the UK and major continental countries. Between 200 and 250 respondents at a time are shown a card listing the names of 20 advertisements which appear in the media they claim to have seen. If they then claim that some of the listed advertisements have been seen by them, they are asked to describe them in detail. The verbatim record is then analysed as follows:

1. *Claimed recall*: percentage who recall the advertising.
2. *Proved recall*: percentage who can prove they saw it by accurately describing it.
3. *Action*: percentage who are following up the advertising.
4. *Persuasion*: percentage who find the advertising persuasive.

Print advertisements, television commercials, cinema advertisements and posters can be checked by this technique. Gallup undertakes other special forms of research into the impact of advertising, particularly in specialized areas such as technical and farming publications.

British Market Research Bureau BMRB uses its continuous consumer survey in order to check the effectiveness of advertising. In the belief that advertising works by helping to build in the consumer's mind a pattern of beliefs and attitudes relating to specific products, BMRB seeks to identify, and measure over time, the beliefs and attitudes which affect brand choice.

BMRM also offers small-scale tests of advertising material, e.g., television commercials, to samples of between 20 and 30 people, representative of the target audience. Each respondent is the subject of a non-directive individual interview lasting for up to one hour. This pre-testing measures advertising communication and is also valuable in providing new creative ideas for copywriters.

Target Group Index (TGI) This research service is also operated by BMRB and is available on subscription to advertisers, advertising agencies, and media owners. TGI is designed to increase the effectiveness of marketing operations by identifying and describing in detail specific target group of consumers and their media exposure. TGI identifies heavy, medium, and light users, as well as non-users of a very wide range of product categories and sub-categories.

TGI provides particularly useful information about appliances and consumer durables by establishing who makes the decisions to buy and whether they had a major, or equal, say in purchase. By using TGI, the advertiser will know who uses his products and what they read, watch, and listen to; he will also have the same information regarding his competitors.

TGI is based on a yearly sample of 24 000 adults who have been selected by a random location sampling procedure known as GRID sampling which incorporates ACORN (see Chapter 4). Respondents are personally interviewed in order to collect classification data, and those willing to participate are given a self-completion questionnaire; the effective response rate is consistently 60 per cent of those interviewed.

Fieldwork runs from April of one year to March of the next; the questionnaire is completely revamped every year. Volumes are issued annually in July/August; half-yearly data are available on computer tape.

BMRB can also draw data for monitoring advertised brands of products from its 'omnibus' survey 'Access' (see Chapter 9). It also offers research to assist at any or all stages of planning and evaluating an advertising campaign, such as concept tests, attitude surveys, etc.

TGI 'Outlook' This research system involves a six-variable cluster analysis based on TGI data covering 192 life style statements about people's attitudes and opinions related to products, brands, and media usage. The following distinctive, if slightly bizarre, names have been given to the six 'Outlook' groups:

1. Trendies (15 per cent of sample)
2. The indifferent (18 per cent)
3. Social spenders (14 per cent)

4. Pleasure seekers (15 per cent)
5. Working-class puritans (15 per cent)
6. Moralists (16 per cent).

Life-style research This was developed by the Leo Burnett Agency in Chicago and the University of Chicago. This type of psychographic research is designed to provide insights into attitudes and behaviour. It profiles people in terms of their patterns of work, leisure, living habits, interests, perceptions, etc. It adds qualitative values to the demographic profiles derived from consumer surveys. This research methodology is described in more detail in another text.[30] It has attracted some criticism for its lack of specificity but it has attracted significant support from leading research organizations, such as SRI International, a large Californian think-tank which developed VALS (values and life styles) classification.

Geodemographic analyses

Dissatisfaction with the A–E socio-economic groupings, discussed earlier, inspired the development of a new method of identifying and targeting specific kinds of consumers. Geodemographic, as the name suggests, relates to analysis of the geographical dispersion of the population, as indicated by the Census of Population. Households are classified from multi-variate analysis of census data, and are grouped into several clusters or groups with distinctive types of housing and family behaviour.

In James Rothman's words:[31] 'Geodemographics is based on two simple principles: (i) that people who live in the same neighbourhood, such as a Census Enumeration District, are more likely to have similar characteristics than are two people chosen at random' and (ii) 'that neighbourhoods can be categorized in terms of the characteristics of the population which they contain, and that two neighbourhoods can be placed in the same category, i.e., they contain similar types of people, even though they are widely separated'. Put more simply perhaps: 'Birds of a feather flock together'.

Geodemographic systems have proved valuable in targeting customers for direct mail and mail order campaigns, etc.

Several geodemographic systems have been marketed in the UK over the past few years. They have much in common, for example, data bases are derived from population profiles at the ennumeration district levels of the Census of Population; they are also closely linked with the post code system (see Chapter 3). They differ in some respects, mainly in the number and types of neighbourhood clusters which form their basic framework. The geodemographic analytical approach has existed as Census Tracking in the US for nearly 20 years. In the UK, the system, known as ACORN, was the first to offer this novel approach, and its success was followed by other research firms: some details of these competing systems are now given.

ACORN, originated by Richard Webber at the Centre for Environmental Studies in Liverpool during 1977, classifies people and households according to the types of neighbourhood in which they live. It is based on the theme that neighbourhoods shown by the Census to have similar social and demographic characteristics will share common life-style features and patterns of behaviour. At the invitation of Liverpool Council, Webber's earlier research focused on the incidence of urban deprivation in different sectors of the inner city. He discovered that provided enough different census counts were taken, 25 significantly different types of neighbourhood emerged. From an examination of local authority records of social problems associated with these areas, Webber found a significantly different mix of problems in each. There were not just rich and poor areas in general, but different sorts of poor areas requiring different social policies.

From this pioneering start, Webber, with the cooperation of the Census Office, then extended the methodology to classify each of the 17 000 wards and parishes throughout Great Britain.

From multi-variate analysis related to 40 primary housing, demographic, social, and economic factors, as measured by the 1971 Census, 36 neighbourhood types were identified, each with its own clearly defined characteristics of age, structure, employment, joint income, family structure, type of housing, social status, and even car ownership. Where people live often influences significantly their life-style.

British Market Research Bureau (BMRB) applied this 36 area classification to the 24 000 respondents covered in their annual Target Group Index (TGI) survey. ACORN segmentation was found to be an efficient discriminator for market targeting.

ACORN was further developed by Webber on joining CACI Inc.-International, and this system of segmentation was applied to the UK's 125 000 census enumeration districts, each of about 150 addresses which, because of their limited size, contain basically homogeneous households. The next stage was to match the 1.25 million post codes against the census enumeration districts, and so enable a list of customers' addresses (with post codes) to be readily analysed by ACORN criteria.

Experience indicated that 36 different types of neighbourhood resulted in unnecessarily fine analyses, and an effective 11 Family Group Classification was derived, originally based on 1971 Census data but later modified when 1981 Census information became available; the 36 neighbourhood types were increased to 38.

The 11 ACORN Family Group Classification is shown on Table 11.3. The 11 main groups are subdivided so that 38 neighbourhood types or sub-groups (plus unclassified) result. For example, I Group indicates ACORN Types 30 (high-status area, non-family areas), 31 (multi-let big old houses and flats), and 32 (furnished flats, mostly single people). D Group contains 12 (unmodernized terraced houses with old people), 13 (older terraces, lower income families), and 14 (tenement flats lacking amenities). These and the other types are described in quantitative and qualitative terms by ACORN analysts. Consumption profiles of specific neighbourhoods can be drawn, and areas of high consumption readily identified. For example, ACORN Type J35 'villages with wealthy older commuters' represent 2.9 per cent of the (1981 Census) population; 2.8 per cent of households, 2.4 times the national average of two-car households, and 2.7 times the proportion of those living in seven or more rooms.

ACORN, as already indicated, is used by BMRB TGI analyses, and also by a widening range of stores, mail-order houses, building societies, and car manufacturers. It has particular use in direct marketing, leaflet distribution, and local media selection.

It would be naïve, of course, to conclude that *all* consumers whose residences fall within a specific ACORN neighbourhood group are likely to buy particular products or brands or read certain journals. By linking ACORN with TGI it is possible, however, to measure the varying probabilities of usage and to give guidelines for effective marketing strategies. As just mentioned, it is also feasible to focus mail shots on identified groups of households or businesses in any given television area, county, post town, or post code sector.

CACI offers a comprehensive range of research services linked to ACORN segmentation: among these is 'sample plan' which is a computerized system for sample point selection. The computer selects areas which will provide the most representative set of addresses (sampling frame) for interviewing. It then points out exact instructions to guide interviewers, either to specific addresses or to particular streets, with clear sampling instructions.

'Sample plan' can be used effectively for minority sampling as well as nationally representative samples. The system is widely used by survey organizations.

Another ACORN service is SITE which, as its name suggests, is useful to retailers in planning the location of stores and also in deciding the range of merchandise to stock, SITE reports show the demographic structure of area populations, say within five miles' radius of Solihull, as well as type of household (ACORN 38 types and 11 Groups), and potential buying power for a range of products, including cars, household durables, central heating and travel. (Also see Chapter 13: ACORN analyses in France, Finland, Norway, and Sweden.)

Table 11.3 The ACORN Family Group Classification

ACORN groups	1990 population	(%)	Households (%)
A Agricultural areas	1836	3.4	3.3
B Modern family housing higher incomes	9546	17.5	16.2
C Older housing of intermediate status	9752	17.9	18.8
D Older terraced housing	2281	4.2	4.4
E Council estates – I	7169	13.2	12.6
F Council estates – II	4789	8.8	9.6
G Council estates – III	3812	7.0	6.5
H Mixed inner metropolitan areas	2079	3.8	3.4
I High-status non-family areas	2238	4.1	4.7
J Affluent suburban housing	8623	15.8	15.9
K Better-off retirement areas	2068	3.8	4.6
L Unclassified	294	0.5	0.0

Source: CACI.

CACI provides a similar SITE research service in the US, using census data supplied by the American Bureau of the Census.

Details of ACORN Neighbourhood Types in the UK are given below:

GROUP A

Neighbourhood type 1: agricultural villages – 2.6% Population (1981 Census)

Type 1 consists of villages where farming is still basic to the economy; places too far from larger towns for people to commute to office and factory jobs. Because of this wages are low and there is little chance for married women to supplement household incomes by going out to work.

The poor provision of local shops and services results in very high levels of two-car ownership.

The population is slightly older than the national average. Most people own their own houses but there are still a significant number of farm workers' cottages, many of them in a poor state of repair.

Type 1 is found in all rural counties, but especially in East Anglia, Devon and Cornwall, Central and North Wales and Lincolnshire.

Neighbourhood type 2: areas of farms and smallholdings – 0.8% Population (1981 Census)

Type 2 consists of rural hamlets, scattered farms and smallholdings where over 50% of the workforce is engaged in agriculture.

Socially these areas are divided between the well-off owners of large farms, self-employed farmers running their own farms, and agricultural labourers, many of whom live in tied cottages often in need of improvement.

Because there are so remote from major centres of population, there is barely any provision of shops, public services or public transport. As a result these areas have very high levels of car ownership, very few women at work and very low levels of unemployment.

The falling populations of these areas result in a slightly older than average age profile.

Suffolk, Norfolk, Lincolnshire, Powys, Dyfed, and North Yorkshire have high proportions of population in Type 2.

GROUP B

Neighbourhood type 3: post-war functional private housing – 4.1% Population (1981 Census)

Type 3 consists of post-war private estates of relatively cheap housing, many of which have been built by the large construction companies in recent years. This type of housing is within the financial reach of manual workers involved in routine factory jobs.

These areas tend to be found on the periphery of the industrial conurbations, often on land which has relatively low landscape quality and is hence free of planning restrictions.

Many families in these new estates will be first-time buyers who originate from inner city areas or the better council estates. They will often have few local associations and will travel some distance to work or for family reunions.

With growing families and important mortgage commitments, residents in these areas are likely to make occasional but substantial shopping expeditions to modern supermarkets competing on price.

Places such as Tamworth, Canvey Island, and Wigan have significant amounts of Type 3 housing.

Neighbourhood type 4: modern private housing, young families – 3.1% Population (1981 Census)

This sort of area is characterised by recently built private estates catering for young couples with very young children. Most of this housing has been built since the 1971 Census in counties such as Oxfordshire, Northamptonshire and Cambridgeshire which have allocated most land for new private housing.

People moving into these areas are usually non-manual and managerial workers in services and light industry. Often they may be setting up home for the first time or moving out of older terraced housing now that they are having children. Pre-school age children are relatively very much more numerous than school age children and hardly anyone is over 45.

Many residents are unlikely to have detailed knowledge of the local area or longstanding affinity with it and are likely to shop by car at medium size shopping centres with adequate parking facilities. Not very much of this type of housing is closely accessible to major regional centres.

Neighbourhood type 5: established family housing – 5.8% Population (1981 Census)

This type of area consists of relatively well-established post-war private estates catering for families of above average, though not of the highest, incomes. They are situated mostly in commuter villages and market towns rather than in the suburban areas of large cities.

These are very much family areas. Typically the families will include children who have reached school age, with parents in their 40s. Gardens are now well established and community networks developed. There is a very low amount of population movement.

Houses tend to be larger than in the more modern private estates of Type 4. The housing is also of lower density.

Neighbourhood type 6: new detached houses, young families – 2.6% Population (1981 Census)

Type 6 consists of modern private housing for very well-off families, areas where you would find well-paid young executives in large companies living in detached 3 or 4 bedroom houses with large gardens and double garages. The Camberley, Bracknell, Reading area has a lot of this housing type.

Residents of this type of area are likely to be second- or third-time buyers who have now reached a type of house in which they may be happy for their young children to grow older, provided they are not forced to move jobs.

Wives are relatively unlikely to work, due to high incomes and family responsibilities. Husbands tend to drive long distances to work and to take career demands seriously.

Neighbourhood type 7: military bases – 0.5% Population (1981 Census)

Type 7 consists of those areas populated largely by servicemen's families. What distinguishes these areas are the very large amount of furnished accommodation and the absence of people aged 45+. In addition to young adults, these areas have very high proportions of pre-school children.

Military bases contain a very mobile population which often meets its shopping and leisure needs from within its own resources. Integration into the community is poor and local shops and services weak.

GROUP C

Neighbourhood type 8: mixed owner-occupied and council estates – 3.5% Population (1981 Census)

Grouped into this type are those enumeration districts which contain half council housing and half private housing. Because of its mixed tenure, the type is relatively close to the national average in most respects.

However, many of these areas have a significant number of small flats, many of them for the elderly, and are often situated in small communities or close to town centres. These areas, therefore, represent boundary areas between dissimilar residential categories.

These areas are of below average income but tend not to suffer from serious unemployment.

Neighbourhood type 9: small town centres and flats above shops – 4.0% Population (1981 Census)

This type of area is found mostly in the centres of small country towns and resorts where you find a wide variety of quite different types of housing within a small area. Penzance, Louth, Berwick or Dolgellau are such places. The type is also common in the central areas of wealthy suburbs which were once country towns or villages and which have since been overtaken by inter-war development.

This type of area contains some large, old owner-occupied houses as well as spacious rented flats, many of them above shops. People tend to walk to work locally in shops and offices and be well integrated into the local community.

In their socio-economic profile these areas are close to the national average but with above average proportions of manual and service workers. Generally residents are happy to live in a mixed community with different types of people, including a high proportion of pensioners.

Neighbourhood type 10: villages with non-farm employment – 4.6% Population (1981 Census)

Type 10 consists of housing, outside main urban areas, where residents in older housing commute to work in manual occupations. This housing is often in small-scale developments of different periods that do not necessarily belong to an identifiable community.

These are areas of older than average people, most of them owner-occupiers but some of them in unimproved rented housing. They tend not to work locally but use their cars to drive to work in quarries, power plants, forestry or manual jobs in rural factories.

In this type of area married women are often unable to find a job. However, as in other rural areas, people out of work would seem to leave to search for work in the towns judging from the low level of unemployment.

Much of rural Derbyshire, the Forest of Dean and Somerset falls within this category.

Neighbourhood type 11: older private housing, skilled workers – 5.5% Population (1981 Census)

This neighbourhood type distinguishes the better class of older terraced housing, most of it owner-occupied and situated in smaller towns with a tradition of mining and manufacturing skills. Towns such as Chorley, Mansfield, and Rugby would have many areas of this sort.

Although the housing is often old, most of it has been improved. It is sufficiently attractive to offer an alternative to the cheap modern estates in the outer suburbs.

The population structure of these areas is typical of the country though with somewhat of a bias towards older people. People in these areas are usually married.

Employment is mostly in craft jobs in traditional industries, often in small, local plants. Despite the high proportions of skilled and semi-skilled workers, unemployment is below average with job opportunities for married women.

Geographical horizons in these areas are often rather limited. People know each other well and are used to well-established corner shops.

GROUP D

Neighbourhood type 12: unmodernised terraces, with older people – 2.5% Population (1981 Census)

Type 12 consists of older terraced housing often built before 1914 and most likely to suffer from the absence of a bath or inside w.c. This occurs in town centres, inner city areas, but more especially in traditional industrial areas such as the declining Pennine textile towns.

These areas of older housing have seen relatively little local authority housing improvement. What few houses are not in owner-occupation tend to be privately rented.

In this type of housing there are many pensioners, but also some young married couples with pre-school children. Noticeably absent from these areas are large families, which get rehoused by the local council.

Although the housing in these areas is poor, there are still large numbers of skilled workers living within walking distance of work and unemployment is comparatively low. Household incomes are boosted by married women working, especially in former textile towns.

This type of area is still dependent on the corner store.

Neighbourhood type 13: older terraces, low-income families – 1.4% Population (1981 Census)

Grouped together into Type 13 we find areas where local authorities have been active in purchasing and improving poor quality pre-1914 terraced housing.

This type suffers very seriously from low levels of industrial skill and from high unemployment. It is particularly common in cities such as Liverpool, Hull, Teesside, and Sunderland where docks, steelworks, and chemical plants have often provided well-paid but physically strenuous work for an unskilled labour force. In contrast to Type 12, there is little tradition of married women working. Families are much larger, often containing four or more children. This results in very much higher child populations. In common with other terraced streets, families will often expect to get rehoused by the local authority as their children grow older.

These are 'rough' areas and places where traditional male and female roles tend to be rigorously upheld.

Neighbourhood type 14: tenement flats lacking amenities – 0.4% Population (1981 Census)

This type consists mostly of old, unimproved, privately rented tenement flats. The type is particularly common in Glasgow and in London where it is characterised by Peabody flats and other 19th century blocks of 'model' dwellings for the working classes, built around a central courtyard with communal facilities.

The type is distinguished primarily by the incidence of households lacking a bath (40%), and an inside w.c. (36%), and by levels four times the national average of households in unfurnished rented accommodation and living in one or two rooms.

Compared with older terraced housing, these tenements contain many more single people and very young adults, married or living together, with pre-school children.

GROUP E

Neighbourhood type 15: council estates, well-off older workers – 3.6% Population (1981 Census)

Type 15 consists of early post-war council estates with excellent job opportunities.

Because many of these areas were built as part of a town developments in the late 1950s and 1960s, the young people for whom they were built are now mostly aged between 45 and 64 with their children either in their late teens or having left home. These areas now have very few young children indeed and, during the 1980s, will acquire a rapidly increasing pensioner population.

The early new town estates were developed to serve post-war light industries with advanced technology. As a result these council estates have particularly high proportions of white-collar industrial workers. Car ownership is high and unemployment below average. Crawley, Stevenage, Hemel Hempstead, and Bracknell are particularly well supplied with this sort of housing. Because the infrastructure is relatively modern, there is now relatively little change in these areas, which are characterised by relatively modern pedestrian shopping centres with established multiples.

Neighbourhood type 16: recent council estates – 2.6% Population (1981 Census)

Type 16 contains council housing of very recent origin, most of it low-rise and on green field sites. In contrast to redevelopment estates and new council flats in inner cities, it contains very high numbers of families with young children and relatively few unskilled or unemployed workers.

As would be expected, much of the housing in the more recent new towns such as Milton Keynes, Washington and Runcorn, and the town expansion schemes such as Peterborough, Northampton and Basingstoke, fall within this category.

These are very much family areas with nearly twice the average proportion of pre-school children. Large families are also common.

The young workforce is relatively dependent on its high car ownership to reach work in light industrial estates.

With aspirations raised by a recent move and incomes strained by the need to furnish new houses and bring up families, residents are sensitive to price and needy of credit.

Neighbourhood type 17: better council estates, young workers – 3.9% Population (1981 Census)

Type 17 consists of areas of council housing with a substantial minority of owner-occupiers. Compared with other council estate types they have well above average numbers of car owners and white-collar workers and many fewer unemployed. Many council estates in small service centres and county towns such as Penrith or Salisbury fall into this category.

Most of these areas represent small post-war council estates built to comparatively high standards and accommodating families with large numbers of school age children. These areas are not as socially or physically separated from areas of middle-class housing as the large estates in big cities or towns in traditional manufacturing regions. As a consequence consumer preferences and leisure activities are not distinctively lower income.

Neighbourhood type 18: small council houses, often Scottish – 2.0% Population (1981 Census)

This type comprises the better Scottish council estates. These consist of relatively mature estates with moderate levels of unemployment and comparatively high proportions of white-collar workers in service industries. This type of estate you would find in Perth, Kirkcaldy or Ayr. Compared with better English council housing areas, these estates have much smaller houses and people are very much less likely to own a car.

The predominantly early post-war estates share with English new-town housing high proportions of older couples and a comparative absence of young children. These are not the Scottish estates where you would find large families.

GROUP F

Neighbourhood type 19: low-rise estates in industrial towns – 4.7% Population (1981 Census)

Type 19, which is a large cluster, consists of undistinguished council housing in Northern industrial towns and mining communities.

This type of area is particularly dependent on manufacturing jobs and has low proportions of its workforce in non-manual and professional occupations. In these heavy industrial areas there are relatively fewer married women working. People tend to be able to find work locally and the level of unemployment is not especially high, bearing in mind the large numbers of semi-skilled and unskilled workers.

The age profile of these areas is typical of the country as a whole with a slight bias towards older workers and older children.

Neighbourhood type 20: inter-war council estates, older people – 3.1% Population (1981 Census)

This type consists of inter-war council housing, attractively laid out, where the population has grown old together. These areas are often parts of very large municipal housing schemes and occur in suburbs of very large cities relatively remote from industrial estates. Wythenshawe in Manchester and Hainault in East London are examples of such housing.

Although these estates are relatively attractive environmentally, incomes are low due to the high proportion of pensioners and the absence of grown-up children still at home. A lot of people from these estates commute by bus to work in non-manual and semi-skilled service jobs in city centres.

Houses are smaller than the average for council estates but with the small number of families there is relatively little overcrowding.

Although these estates are attractively laid out at low densities, they are not usually very accessible to shops and workplaces. With low incomes and low car ownership they are particularly dependent on public transport.

Neighbourhood type 21: council housing, elderly people – 1.5% Population (1981 Census)

This type isolates areas characterized both by old people and by local authority housing: 35% of the population are over 65 and 83% rent from the local authority.

The housing takes the form either of high-rise blocks with flats too small for families or of more modern low-rise sheltered blocks.

Besides the elderly, the type also contains many single non-pensioner households, often in the 45–64 age range.

Car ownership levels are very low in this type and people are particularly dependent on public transport to reach work which is often in city centre office jobs.

This neighbourhood type is common both in Scotland and in London.

GROUP G

Neighbourhood type 22: new council estates in inner cities – 2.0% Population (1981 Census)

This type describes modern local authority estates, often in inner cities, that house homeless single people and single parent families in small flats suitable neither for pensioners nor for large families. A number of difficult to let high-rise blocks fall into this type as do more modern low-rise developments which replace demolished Victorian tenements and subdivided large old houses. Much recent housebuilding in Lambeth, Southwark, Hackney, Islington, and Camden falls into this category.

The type is untypical of local authority housing in having many young single people and high proportions of people born in the West Indies.

The inner city location of this type is reflected in high proportions of unemployed and unskilled workers. The decline of manufacturing jobs in the inner city results in dependence on public transport to reach clerical and semi-skilled jobs in service industries.

These areas are often accessible to small corner shops that open late but which charge high prices and lack variety.

Neighbourhood type 23: overspill estates, higher unemployment – 3.2% Population (1981 Census)

This neighbourhood type consists of large local authority schemes on the outskirts of provincial English cities designed in the form of medium-rise flats with walkways, often using industrialised methods. Residents, rehoused from older communities in the inner city, find themselves distant from relatives and familiar shops and pubs, and continue to be dependent upon costly and infrequent buses to reach centres of employment or shopping.

Being now the least desirable estates of cities such as Plymouth or Derby, these areas accumulate residents suffering from lack of jobs and lack of skills. These are the areas within those cities where there are the most large and single parent families, the most overcrowding, and the lowest levels of car ownership.

Neighbourhood type 24: council estates with some overcrowding – 1.6% Population (1981 Census)

Type 24 consists mostly of modern council estates in Scotland containing small houses and flats unsuitable for the large families that live in them.

These estates contain mostly families with children of school age and relatively few single people and pensioners.

The social status of these areas is very low, though not as low as in type 25, nor is unemployment as high. Nevertheless, there is a severe lack of craft skills.

Neighbourhood type 25: council estates with greatest hardship – 0.7% Population (1981 Census)

This type has the highest incidence of any cluster on a wide range of social indicators: 27% of the labour force is unemployed, 18% of workers are in unskilled jobs, 13% of households live at over 1.5 persons per room. Only 22% of households have access to a car.

In this type are combined the low social status and high unemployment of the English overspill council estates and the small flats and serious overcrowding typical of West Central Scottish council housing.

These estates provide some of the most intractable social problems in Western Europe.

GROUP H

Neighbourhood type 26: multi-occupied older housing – 0.4% Population (1981 Census)

A third of the population of this type was born in the Indian sub-continent and much of the remaining population is descended from Asian immigrants.

These immigrants live together at very high occupancies due to the multi-occupation of small older terraced housing. Overcrowding in these areas reaches levels otherwise experienced only in the worst Clydeside overspill estates.

Lack of knowledge of the English language accounts for the exceptionally high proportion of the labour force engaged in manufacturing industry, and for the concentrations of semi-skilled and unskilled workers. Comparatively few married women are at work, very many fewer than in West Indian communities.

The recent arrival of many of these immigrants results in an age profile identical to that of the most recent council estates. The ratio of pre-school children to pensioners, for instance, is five times the national average.

Neighbourhood type 27: cosmopolitan owner-occupied terraces – 1.1% Population (1981 Census)

This type contains 1.1% of the national population, and 22% of these neighbourhood residents were born in the Indian sub-continent. It also provides a home for many Ugandan and Kenyan Asians.

Like Type 26, Type 27 has large numbers of two-family households sharing inadequate space, high levels of unemployment and unskilled labour. Asians in these areas do, however, seem better integrated. There are very many more women at work, more non-manual workers and levels of car ownership equivalent to the average council estate.

Much of Bradford, Birmingham, and Leicester falls into this category.

Neighbourhood type 28: multi-let housing in cosmopolitan areas – 0.7% Population (1981 Census)

In this type 21% of all residents were born in Africa or the Caribbean and probably an equally high percentage are of Afro-Caribbean descent. These, therefore, represent the West Indian communities of Britain, almost all of them in London.

Typical of these areas are Hackney, Harlesden, Tooting, and Lewisham where late Victorian three-storey terraces have been split up into subdivided flats or where Edwardian two-storey terraces have been taken over.

Compared with the main centres of Asians, these areas have very many more people living on their own, more unmarried people living together and more single parent families. There is the same high concentration of pre-school children.

The West Indian communities have very many more working wives and more non-manual and service workers than the Asian communities.

This type of area has been losing population fast in recent years and has, therefore, experienced little public investment in shops, infrastructure, and public services. Shopping centres in these areas have high proportions of off-licences and take-away restaurants.

Neighbourhood type 29: better-off cosmopolitan areas – 1.7% Population (1981 Census)

This type of area is typical of the national average in its age and social structure, but has nine times the average proportion born in the Afro-Caribbean New Commonwealth and five times the average born in Asia.

These communities are found mostly in London, in areas which have experienced considerable gentrification such as Clapham, Fulham, and Haringey. The areas are divided between owner-occupiers and sharers of rented flats.

The London concentration of these areas results in large numbers of non-manual office workers and very high proportions of working wives. Unemployment in these areas is low.

GROUP I

Neighbourhood type 30: high-status non-family areas – 2.1% Population (1981 Census)

This type of area consists mostly of pre-1914 areas of villas and large old houses which have not been as severely subject to subdivision into flats as have Types 31 and 32. However, some of the older houses in these areas have been demolished to make way for privately owned purpose-built flats. This type of area is common in areas such as Richmond and Ealing in London, Edgbaston in Birmingham, and Headingley in Leeds.

This type of area has large numbers of high-status people in their late 20s and 30s, many of them well-educated people with degrees, currently engaged in the arts, advertising, communications, and education.

Many young married couples, where the graduate wife is concerned to pursue a career, may move out to a more suburban location when children are born or reach school age. Older single people live in inter-war and modern private flats travelling by bus or train to city centre service jobs.

These areas tend to be poorly served by local shops.

Neighbourhood type 31: multi-let, big, old houses and flats – 1.5% Population (1981 Census)

This type of area occurs mostly in inner London and contains areas of big, old houses subdivided into small privately rented flats, many of which are one- or two-room furnished bedsits. This type of area has higher proportions of single people than Type 30, moving from flat to flat as opportunities arise. Many of them are in their early 20s. They include students and visitors from overseas as well as immigrant workers in restaurants, hotels, and shops. There are few children in this type of area.

The social composition of these areas is very mixed, with some very affluent professional workers adjacent to semi-skilled service workers. Wives are especially likely to work full-time.

Very much of this type is located close to the centre of London in areas of very high population density.

Neighbourhood type 32: furnished flats, mostly single people – 0.6% Population (1981 Census)

This small type, which is almost exclusively concentrated in London's West End, consists of big, old houses and purpose-built blocks, both providing furnished flats for students, foreigners, and mobile, young, single people. A half of all households are rented furnished and 45% live in one or two rooms. Over 40% of households contain one person only.

There are very high concentrations of single person households in these areas, owing to the availability of suitable, small flats. By no means all of these single people are young – demographically the most distinctive feature of these areas is the absence of children.

Employment is almost exclusively in the service sector, though there is a very high level of apparently voluntary unemployment.

GROUP J

Neighbourhood type 33: inter-war semis, white-collar workers – 5.7% Population (1981 Census)

This type of area consists of owner-occupied inter-war suburban housing, mostly semi-detached housing, often with mock Tudor oriels, gables and leaded windows. It is also found in Northern cities, serving white-collar workers in city centre offices.

These inter-war suburbs are not those of higher status workers but contain now mostly non-manual socio-economic groups. This type of area would be common in Surbiton, Perivale, Bexley, Sale, and Perry Barr.

Like the inter-war council estates, these areas now have ageing populations and relatively few large families or pre-school children. A high proportion of the population in these areas is married and moves house infrequently. People here are unlikely to be highly educated, but they are industrious and seldom unemployed.

Retail outlets in these areas cluster in inter-war parades with medium-sized units and good car-parking facilities.

Neighbourhood type 34: spacious inter-war semis, big gardens – 5.0% Population (1981 Census)

Type 34 consists of high-income, inter-war suburbs, areas of large semi-detached housing with mature gardens, mock Tudor gables, and integral garages.

This type of area is common in outer-London suburbs such as Harrow and Chingford as well as in provincial cities. Smaller towns tend to have less of this type.

In addition to high levels of home ownership we find high proportions of professionals and managers, working in service industries, often commuting by train. There is little local industry for manual workers.

It is not easy for young couples to afford these houses which were built in the 1930s and now have high values. Therefore, most householders are in the 45–64 age range and there are particularly few pre-school children.

Residents choosing to live in these areas buy peace, security, and privacy. They shop by car in suburban centres well supplied with florists, hairdressers, and dry cleaners.

Neighbourhood type 35: villages with wealthy, older commuters – 2.9% Population (1981 Census)

This type of area can be found in attractive countryside which is reasonably accessible to large centres of population. Villages of high amenity value contain substantial numbers of detached inter-war properties providing exclusive retreats for urban professionals. Elsewhere in the village there are some older, smaller houses for agricultural labourers and other providers of services such as postmen, shopkeepers, and publicans. These villages have usually been successful in avoiding the encroachment of 'estates', whether local authority or private.

The rural location of these areas results in very much higher levels of car ownership, especially two-car ownership, than in urban areas of equivalent status. Houses are much more spacious and fewer women work. This is not the sort of area in which clerical workers would live.

People in these areas are keen on country pursuits, tend large gardens, and support the concept of the local community.

Neighbourhood type 36: detached houses, exclusive suburbs – 2.3% Population (1981 Census)

Of all 38 types, this is the one with the highest status, whether measured by car ownership (48% of households have 2 or more) or professional or managerial workers (47%).

These, therefore, are areas of large detached houses in mature grounds in locations of choice landscape value such as Esher, Solihull, Stoke Bishop in Bristol, Ponteland near Newcastle, Bearsden, and so on.

Most of these areas were developed in the 1930s so that this type attracts mostly the older professional with school-age or grown-up children. Younger families with pre-school children are seldom able to afford the house prices and those that can are more likely to prefer more modern executive estates (Type 6).

The employment structure of these areas shows very few married women working, very few jobs in manufacturing and unemployment at 40% of the national average.

GROUP K

Neighbourhood type 37: private houses, well-off older residents – 2.2% Population (1981 Census)

Wealthy, older people have often elected to retire to the coast, especially the South coast. This type defines such areas of the affluent retired.

In these areas 35% of the population are aged over 65 and 60% are over 45. Children aged 0–4, by contrast, form only 3% of the population.

The social class profile of these areas is very up-scale, so that, despite the elderly age structure, disposable incomes and wealth are high.

Inter-war parades and suburban shopping centres are more common than ribbon shopping frontages. Bexhill, Worthing, Lytham, and Paignton have even more of this housing type than Hastings, Brighton, Southport, or Torquay, much of whose population falls into Type 38.

Neighbourhood type 38: private flats, older single people – 1.6% Population (1981 Census)

Typically, this type of area consists of purpose-built private flats and converted flats in big, old houses with high proportions of pensioners and other single people living alone. This would include modern flats in seaside resorts, areas of boarding houses and homes, mansion blocks in metropolitan cities and modern developments of small private flats.

Compared with Type 37, Type 38 is found closer to the central areas of retirement resorts and frequently in town centres and central London. It has much more privately rented accommodation and leasehold property.

As in Type 37, there are very few children. It is an up-market cluster with very few people working in manual occupations or in industry.

Source: CACI.

ACORN Lifestyles List

Associated with ACORN segmentation, CACI has developed the ACORN Lifestyles list (Fig. 11.2) which classifies every UK household into one of 81 Lifestyle segments. These provide marketing management with specific targets for direct marketing strategies.

ACORN Lifestyle definitions are as follows:

HOUSEHOLD COMPOSITION

Singles
Adults living on their own, usually without
young children.

Couples
Two adults, almost certainly married, with or
without young children.

Family
Two adults, almost certainly married. They
have at least one other relation living with
them: child or other adult

Homesharers
Multiple adults living together but not a
couple or family.

AGE STRUCTURE

Younger
Youngest – adults most often between 18 and
24 years of age.
Maturing – adults most often between
25 and 44 years of age.

Older
Established – adults most often between
45 and 64 years of age.
Retired – adults most often over 65 years
of age.

In addition, analyses extend to 24 Lifestyle groups and 81 Lifestyle types which effectively integrate consumer demographic segments and geographic locations as Fig. 11.2 indicates.

Rural areas and villages

LA	*Rural singles*	2.7%

LA01 Younger men
LA02 Younger women
LA03 Older single men
LA04 Older single women
LA05 Affluent singles in commuter villages
LA06 Affluent singles in agricultural villages

LB	*Younger rural couples and families*	2.2%

LB07 Young couples
LB08 Young couples with elderly person
LB09 Maturing couples
LB10 Maturing families

LC	*Older rural couples and families*	1.8%

LC11 Established couples
LC12 Established couples, older children
LC13 Retired couples
LC14 Retired families

LD	*Affluent rural couples and families*	2.4%

LD15 Affluent couples and families in commuter villages
LD16 Affluent couples and families in agricultural villages

Suburbia

LE	*Younger suburban singles*	3.7%

LE17 Younger single males
LE18 Younger single females

LF	*Older suburban singles*	4.0%

LF19 Older single males
LF20 Older single females

LG	*Younger traditional suburban couples and families*	9.7%

LG21 Youngest couples
LG22 Youngest couples with elderly person
LG23 Maturing couples
LG24 Maturing families

LH	*Older traditional suburban couples and families*	5.3%

LH25 Established couples
LH26 Established families with older children
LH27 Retired couples
LH28 Retired families

LI	*Younger very affluent suburban couples and families*	4.2%

LI29 Youngest couples
LI30 Youngest couples with elderly person
LI31 Maturing couples
LI32 Maturing families

LJ	*Older very affluent suburban couples and families*	2.3%

LJ33 Established couples
LJ34 Established families with older children
LJ35 Retired couples
LJ36 Retired families

Council areas

LK	*Younger singles in council areas*	5.1%

LK37 Single men
LK38 Single women

LL	*Older singles in council areas*	5.0%

LL39 Single men
LL40 Single women

LM	*Younger couples in council areas*	6.8%

LM41 Youngest couples
LM42 Maturing couples

LN	*Older couples in council areas*	5.0%

LN43 Established couples
LN44 Retired couples

LO	*Adult families in council areas*	6.2%

LO45 Youngest couples and families with elderly
LO46 Maturing families
LO47 Established families with older children
LO48 Retired families

Fig. 11.2 The ACORN Lifestyle list

Metropolitan and cosmopolitan city

LP	*Affluent single metropolitan dwellers*	3.1%

LP49 Younger men
LP50 Younger women
LP51 Older men
LP52 Older women

LQ	*Affluent couples in metropolitan areas*	4.0%

LQ53 Younger couples
LQ54 Younger families
LQ55 Older couples
LQ56 Older families

LR	*Cosmopolitan inner city dwellers*	2.4%

LR57 Younger singles
LR58 Younger couples and families
LR59 Older singles
LR60 Older couples and families

Traditional urban households

LS	*Younger urban singles*	2.8%

LS61 Men
LS62 Women

LT	*Older urban singles*	3.5%

LT63 Men
LT64 Women

LU	*Younger traditional urban couples and families*	6.8%

LU65 Youngest couples
LU66 Youngest couples with elderly person
LU67 Maturing couples
LU68 Maturing families

LV	*Older traditional urban couples and families*	4.3%

LV69 Established couples
LV70 Established families with older children
LV71 Retired couples
LV72 Retired families

Homesharers

LW	*Homesharers in affluent areas*	3.4%

LW73 Male homesharers in very affluent areas
LW74 Female homesharers in very affluent areas
LW75 Mixed homesharers in very affluent areas
LW76 Male homesharers in tradtnl suburban
LW77 Female homesharers in tradtnl suburban
LW78 Mixed homesharers in tradtnl suburban

LX	*Homesharers in less affluent areas*	3.3%

LX79 Male homesharers
LX80 Female homesharers
LX81 Mixed homesharers

Fig. 11.2 *(cont'd) Source*: CACI

As with ACORN, the Lifestyles analysis is linked to the major market research surveys such as TGI, as well as to CACI's full demographic data base. For example, SITE reports can give area breakdowns by ACORN Lifestyles group in addition to the features mentioned earlier (see ACORN), while the added precision of ACORN Lifestyles is especially useful in direct mail operations. Prospective users can have their mailing lists or data bases analysed across the 81 Lifestyle types, and use the results to target mailing or other marketing or advertising activity with greater accuracy than before.

Pinpoint Analysis

Another research service specializing in the field of computer analyses based on census data and post codes is Pinpoint Analysis Ltd of London, which started trading in 1983. The resultant data are plotted on Ordnance Survey grid maps which, as with ACORN, are related to the census enumeration districts (EDs). Pinpoint claims to offer greater discrimination by focusing on individual postal sectors and so targeting potential customers with particular effectiveness. Sixty different types of neighbourhood are identified which, because they may prove too fine for some purposes, are aggregated to 25, and further to 12 main types.

Specific applications of PiN relate to store location, comparative evaluation of branches, shopping centre development, etc. Retail Potential Reports estimates various retail expenditures analysed by area, nature of merchandise, and type of retail outlet. As with ACORN, other clients are mail order companies, direct marketing businesses, circular distributors, etc.

A specialized system, Finpin, focuses on people's financial characteristics in relation to where they live. It is widely used by banks, building societies, and insurance companies for marketing their financial services.

Pinpoint, with the cooperation of the Ordnance Survey and using the Post Office's Post Code Address File (PAF), has developed a data base called Pinpoint Address Code (PAC) covering England, Wales, and Scotland. Each address on the PAF is located on the appropriate large-scale Ordnance Survey map and allocated a unique 12-digit grid reference which locates it on the National Grid to a notional accuracy of 1 metre. PAC has many applications: direct mail, distribution planning, store location, emergency services, local government services, area health authorities, etc.

A spin-off from PAC was the Pinpoint Road Network (PRN), which is based on detailed digitized maps of Britain's roads – useful, for example, for planning road delivery schedules, or for highway maintenance schemes.

In conjunction with Nielsen Marketing Research, Pinpoint conducted a massive 80 000 interviews of households across Britain; the methodology was as follows: a random sample was taken from the entire PAF for Britain, PiN-coded and names added from the Electoral Register. Finally, the sample was matched with listed telephone numbers. Interviewing was either face-to-face (for households without a telephone or with an unlisted number) or by telephone.

The resultant Shoppin data base gave detailed information on food and non-food purchases, place of purchase, etc., plus demographic and behavioural profiles.

MOSAIC

Richard Webber, pioneer of ACORN for CACI from which he later resigned, has devised CCN Systems and the MOSAIC classification, particularly related to the needs of the large mail order firm, Great Universal Stores (owners of CCN).

The MOSAIC data base contains information at four geographic levels: 22 million residential addresses, 1.3 million full post codes, 170 000 post code groups, and 1000 postal sectors.

Although like ACORN and Pinpoint analysis, it is based on the Census of Population for 1991, MOSAIC also classifies areas on the basis of data from CCN's annually updated data bases, and the new version of MOSAIC uses the latest 1987/88 electoral role information together with county court judgments and credit enquiry data to June 1990, to track changes in demographics.

MOSAIC identifies 58 types of neighbourhood as given in Table 11.4.

Fifty-four variables are used to build the MOSAIC classification system, as shown in Table 11.5.

Table 11.4 The 58 MOSAIC types and their national penetration

		% GB households			% GB households
M1	High status retirement areas with many single pensioners	1.0	M30	Post-1981 extensions to high stress inner city estates	0.4
M2	High status retirement areas, married owner occupiers	0.4	M31	High unemployment estates with worst financial problems	2.4
M3	High status retirement areas, with rented flats for elderly	0.2	M32	Council estates with the highest levels of unemployment	0.3
M4	Boarding houses and lodgings, many in retirement areas	1.9	M33	Council estates, often Scottish flats, with worst overcrowding	1.3
M5	Inter-war O/O housing, commercial and managerial cadres	4.2	M34	Better council estates but with financial problems	2.2
M6	Elite prof/educational suburbs, mostly inner metropolitan	2.1	M35	Low rise council housing, low incomes and serious deprivation	1.7
M7	High status family enclaves in inner city areas	0.5	M36	Areas with some public housing for the elderly	2.7
M8	Highest income and status areas, mostly outer metropolitan	0.9	M37	Council estates, mostly Scottish, middle income small houses	1.9
M9	Inter-war semis, white-collar commuters to urban office jobs	4.7	M38	Council estates in a factory towns with settled older workers	2.1
M10	Inter-war semis, owner occupied by well-paid manual workers	5.0	M39	Quality '30s and '50s overspill estates, now with old people	3.0
M11	Areas of mixed tenure, many old people	3.2	M40	Best quality council housing in areas of low unemployment	5.2
M12	Lower income enclaves in high income suburbs	0.1	M41	New greenfield council estates with many young children	1.8
M13	Older suburbs, young families in Gov't and service emp't	4.6	M42	Post-1981 council housing, higher incomes	0.4
M14	Older terraces, owner occupied by craft manual workers	2.5	M43	Post-1981 council housing, few families	0.8
M15	Lower income older terraced housing	1.5	M44	Post-1981 council housing, with stable families	0.7
M16	Overcrowded older houses, often in areas of housing shortage	1.8	M45	Military accommodation	0.4
M17	Older terraces, young families in very crowded conditions	0.5	M46	Post-1981 housing in areas of highest income and status	0.2
M18	Tenements, caravans and other rented temporary accommodation	0.2	M47	Highest income and status areas, newish family housing	1.1
M19	Town centres and flats above shops	2.9	M48	Post-war private estates with children of school age	3.1
M20	Rented non-family inner city areas with financial problems	0.7	M49	Newly built private estates, high income young families	1.8
M21	Low status inner suburbs with subdivided older housing	1.0	M50	Newly built private estates, factory workers, young families	3.3
M22	Older housing where owner occupiers often share with tenants	0.7	M51	Post-1981 extensions to private estates	1.4
M23	Purpose built private flats, single people in service jobs	2.8	M52	Post-1981 housing in established older suburbs	1.8
M24	Divided houses with mobile single people and few children	0.5	M53	New commuter estates in rural areas	2.1
M25	Smart inner city flats, company lets, very few children	1.5	M54	Villages with some non-agricultural employment	3.1
M26	Post-1981 housing in non-family urban and city centres	0.9	M55	Pretty rural villages with wealthy long-distance commuters	3.7
M27	Post-1981 housing replacing older terraces	0.7	M56	Agricultural villages	2.0
M28	Newly built council housing, mostly high density inner city	1.4	M57	Hamlets and scattered farms	0.7
M29	Newly built inner cities estates with non-family populations	1.0	M58	Unclassified	0.1

Source: CCN.

Table 11.5 The 54 variables used in the MOSAIC classification system

DEMOGRAPHIC	HOUSING	FINANCIAL
Movers in last year	Farm addresses	County court judgments
Average time at address	Flat addresses	High value judgments
Addresses with families	Post-1981 addresses	Low value judgments
Addresses with single persons		Finance house searches
Addresses with pseudo families	**CENSUS: SOCIO-ECONOMIC**	Retail searches
Addresses with mixed household		Credit card searches
Addresses with 17–21 year olds	Professionals	
	Non-manual	
	Skilled manual	**CENSUS: HOUSING**
CENSUS: HOUSEHOLD & AGE	Semi-skilled	
	Unskilled	Dwelling size
Household size	Agricultural employment	Rooms/person
Never married 30 +	Mining and manufacturing	Sharing amenities
Aged 0–4	Services	Lacking a bath
Aged 5–14	Walk to work	Lacking an inside wc
Aged 15–24	Public transport	Owner occupier
Aged 25–44	Students	Council tenant
Aged 45–64	Unemployment	Unfurnished
Aged 65 +	Women in work	Furnished
4-children households	Car ownership	1/2/3 rooms
Single non-pensioners	2-car household	7 rooms
		Acute overcrowding
		Overcrowding

Source: CCN.

The 58 MOSAIC neighbourhood types, listed in Table 11.4, have been divided into 10 'natural' groupings as shown in Table 11.6.

Table 11.6 MOSAIC Lifestyle groupings

L1	Prosperous Pensioners	1–4
L2	Older Couples in Leafy Suburbs	5–8
L3	Families in Inter-War Semis	9–10
L4	Older Communities	11–18
L5	Singles and Flat Dwellers	19–25
L6	Disadvantaged Council Tenants	26–35
L7	Older Council Tenants	36–39
L8	Go-getting Council Tenants	40–45
L9	Young Families with Mortgages	46–53
L10	Country Dwellers	54–57
L99	Unclassified	58

Source: CCN.

Super Profiles is organized by CDMS (Credit Card Data Marketing Services Ltd) of Liverpool, and claims to have the largest number of different neighbourhood types classifications (up to 150). They are linked to the electoral role data base of 22 million households held by Littlewoods Stores mail order division. Other links are with TGI, and the NRS.

SPA (Sales Performance Analysis) is marketed by SPA Marketing Systems of Royal

Leamington Spa. Its social area classification scheme, SET, uses the 1981 Census data to classify postal sectors into 26 different neighbourhood types.

Overview

These competing geodemographic systems, as noted earlier, share much in common, although their powers of discrimination are promoted strongly and, at the same time, evaluated critically by experienced practitioners. 'The general conclusion', James Rothman observes,[31] '... would seem to be that (their) differences are small and the choice between systems varies according to the subject matter and the judgement and other needs of the user'.

'Sagacity' segmentation

In an endeavour to improve the discriminating power of income and demographic classifications, Research Services developed 'Sagacity' in 1981. This consumer classification combines life cycle, income, and socio-economic groups. Using data from JICNARS, Research Services grouped people into 12 easily described and identifiable classifications with markedly different characteristics in terms of media habits and product usage.

The underlying theme of 'Sagacity' is that, as people pass through the various stages of their lives they have different aspirations and patterns of behaviour, including consumption of goods and services.

Four separate types are identified:

Dependant: adults 15–34 who are *not* heads of household or housewives, unless they are childless students in full-time education.
Pre-family: adults 15–34 who *are* heads of households or housewives, but are childless.
Family: adults under 65 who are heads of households or housewives in households with one or more children under 21 years of age.
Late: all other adults whose children have already left home or who are 35 or over and childless.

Cornish states that the cut-off point of 35 between the Pre-family and Late stages is arbitrary, and was chosen in preference to 45, which can be taken as the end of a woman's fertile period, on the grounds that the Pre-family stage should only include households in the relatively early years of household formation.[32]

After life cycle, SAGACITY then considers income and occupational characteristics of the individual or couple forming the household.

Income is defined as 'the net income of the head of the household at constant prices on a 10-point exponential scale, adjusted by the working status of the spouse of the head of the household'.

Income breakdown is applied only to the Family and Late stages, and households are characterized as 'better off' or 'worse off'. For instance, a white-collar adult in the Family stage could be classified as 'better off' if the head of the household's claimed or estimated net income falls within the two highest of 10 income brackets, provided he or she has no working spouse. Adjustments are made to cut-off points where the spouse works full- or part-time.

Dependant and Pre-family stages are not classified into 'better off/worse off' income groups on account of the relatively small sample sizes and also because differences in disposable income are considered to be less marked and therefore less important than in later stages.

Division by income rather than economic activity is stated to be particularly important at the Late stage, since there is a significant minority of retired people who qualify for the 'better off' income grouping, and who might well have consumption habits similar to those who are still working. (See earlier reference to the affluent middle-aged.)

The last element of the SAGACITY groupings refers to the occupation of the head of the household. Individuals are classified as non-manual (white collar) occupations (ABC1s) and manual (blue collar) occupations (C2DEs).

From combination of the three elements (life cycle, income, and occupation) with stages in the family life cycle, the paradigm shown in Fig. 11.3 emerges.

To assist understanding of the SAGACITY system, descriptive notations have been given for each of the 12 groups, together with an indication of their size relative to the total adult population.[33]

Dependent, white (DW) 7 per cent: Mainly under 24s, living at home or full-time student, where head of household is an ABC1 occupation group.

Dependent, blue (DB) 9 per cent: Mainly under 24s, living at home or full-time student, where head of household is in a C2DE occupation group.

Pre-family, white (PFW) 4 per cent: Under 35s who have established their own household but have no children and where the head of household is in an ABC1 occupation group.

Pre-family, blue (PFB) 5 per cent: Under 35s who have established their own household but have no children and where the head of household is in a C2DE occupation group.

Family, better off, white (FW+) 9 per cent: Housewives and heads of household, under 65, with one or more children in the household, in the 'better off' income group and where the head of household is in an ABC1 occupation group.

Family, better off, blue (FB+) 9 per cent: Housewives and heads of household, under 65, with one or more children in the household, in the 'better off' income group and where the head of household is in a C2DE occupation group.

Family, worse off, white (FW−) 5 per cent: Housewives and heads of household, under 65, with one or more children in the household, in the 'worse off' income group and where the head of household is in an ABC1 occupation group.

Family, worse off, blue (FB−) 10 per cent: Housewives and heads of household, under 65, with one or more children in the household, in the 'worse off' income group and where the head of household is in a C2DE occupation group.

Late, better off, white (LW+) 6 per cent: Includes all adults whose children have left home or who are over 35 and childless, are in the 'better off' income group and where the head of household is in an ABC1 occupation group.

Late, better off, blue (LB+) 7 per cent: Includes all adults whose children have left home or who are over 35 and childless, are in the 'better off' income group and where the head of household is in a C2DE occupation group.

Late, worse off, white (LW−) 10 per cent: Includes all adults whose children have left home or who are over 35 and childless, are in the 'worse off' income group and where the head of household is in an ABC1 occupation group.

Late, worse off, blue (LB−) 19 per cent: Includes all adults whose children have left home or who are over 35 and childless, are in the 'worse off' income group and where the head of household is in a C2DE occupation group.

The power of SAGACITY to discriminate both in relation to markets and to media has been demonstrated by Research Sevices. For example, package holidays abroad peak in the Pre-family and Late stages; even among the better off, demand is very much lower in the Family stage. The lower *per capita* disposable incomes of families with children and the problems associated with taking children abroad contribute to this trend. If NRS data showed that 20 per cent of all adults took a package holiday abroad, compared with 30 per cent in one SAGACITY

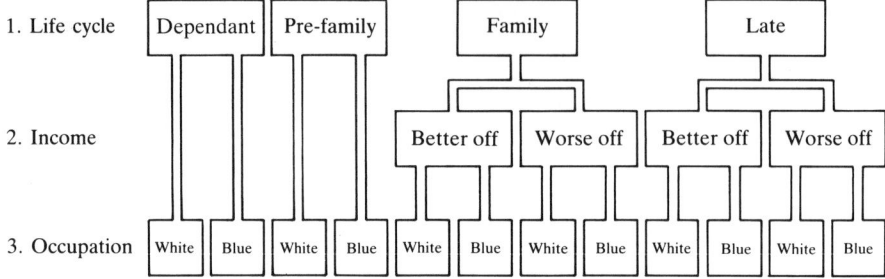

4. Sex

SAGACITY will often be applied to the male and female
populations separately as in the published tables.

Fig. 11.3 SAGACITY consumer segmentation model (*Source:* Research Services)[33]

group and 15 per cent in another, indices for these groups would be calculated thus:
$\frac{30}{20} \times 100 = 150$ and $\frac{15}{20} \times 100 = 75$ (The total population index will always be 100.)

Clearly, the type of package holiday will influence the target market definition. Media can also be selected to cover the SAGACITY groups shown to be the most likely prospects.

Ownership of cheque books contrasts with the pattern of distribution of overseas package holidays in that it is a function of age and social grade rather than income. Joint-stock bank accounts are held by virtually all white-collar workers in the Pre-family and Family stages, but fall off in the Late stage. The index for holding a bank current account by blue-collar workers is below 100 for Dependant, Late, and 'worse-off' groups. However, the Pre-family and 'better off' blue-collar groups have indices of 115 and 111 respectively. These figures may reflect a certain degree of success by the banks in attracting these groups of consumers who, as they enter succeeding life cycle stages, may maintain usage and so change the blue-collar indices.

SAGACITY segmentation is clearly a creative and realistic approach which has generally been 'welcomed by marketing and advertising professionals, although the caveat has been expressed that since it '. . . does, however, presuppose the collection of class and income data . . . it would therefore benefit from any improvements to class and income classifications'.[34]

11.4 SUMMARY

Advertising research covers content, media, and effectiveness.

Content research focuses on the ability of the advertisement to achieve impact and project the desired message.

Media research attempts to eliminate wasteful expenditure by objectively analysing various media. Joint research bodies; JICNAR, JICTAR, JICRAR, JICPAS and JICCAR have been set up to deal with specific media. BARB has direction of TV research in the UK; research is undertaken by research agencies and also by the BBC. JICNAR (press) developed the well-known A–E socio-economic classification. Radio audiences are measured by the BBC, and also by JICRAR.

Effectiveness research is concerned with analysing different media (and combinations of media) and evaluating the degree of success with which specific advertising objectives have been achieved.

Sources of advertising data are: publishing houses, ABC, BRAD, independent TV companies,

IPA and AA. Starch and Gallup have been active for years in reading and noting studies. Target Group Index (TGI) operated by BMRB, offers comprehensive research data on patterns of consumption of wide ranges of goods and services.

Geodemographic systems of consumer segmentation based on census data, neighbourhood types, and life styles, are offered by several research organizations, such as ACORN (CACI), Super Profiles (CDMS), PiNPOINT, MOSAIC, and SPA.

SAGACITY segmentation on life cycle, income, and occupation.

REFERENCES

1. Lavidge, Robert J., and Gary A. Steiner, 'A model for predictive measurement of advertising effectiveness', *Journal of Marketing*, vol.25, no.6, October 1961.
2. Chisnall, Peter M., *Marketing: A Behavioural Analysis*. McGraw-Hill, Maidenhead, 1975.
3. Colley, Russell H., 'Defining advertising goals for measured advertising results', Association of National Advertisers, New York, 1961.
4. Palda, Kristian S., 'The hypothesis of a hierarchy of effects: A partial evaluation', *Journal of Marketing Research*, February 1966.
5. Haskins, Jack B., 'Factual recall as a measure of advertising effectiveness', *Journal of Advertising Research*, March 1964.
6. Festinger, Leon, 'Behavioural support for opinion change', *Public Opinion Quarterly*, autumn 1964.
7. Burdus, A., 'Advertising research', in: *The Effective Use of Market Research*, Staples Press, London, 1971.
8. Wicks, Anne, 'Advertising research: an eclectic view from the UK', *Journal of Market Research Society*, vol.31, no.4, October 1989.
9. Adler, Lee, Allan Greenberg, and Donald B. Lucas, 'What big agency men think of copy testing methods', *Journal of Marketing Research*, November 1965.
10. Boyd, Harper W., Jnr, and Michael L. Ray, 'What big agency men in Europe think of copy testing methods', *Journal of Marketing Research*, May 1971.
11. Maloney, J. C., 'Is advertising believability really important?', *Journal of Marketing*, vol.27, no.5, 1963.
12. Lannon, Judie, and Peter Cooper, 'Humanistic advertising: A holistic cultural perspective', in: *Effective Advertising: Can research help?* ESOMAR, Monte Carlo, January 1983.
13. Sampson, Peter, 'The tracking study in market research', in: *Applied Marketing and Social Research* (2nd Edn), Ute Bradley (ed.), Wiley, Chichester, 1987.
14. Freeman, Paul, 'Continuous surveys and tracking in the UK', *Journal of the Market Research Society*, vol.31, no.4., October 1989.
15. Monk, Donald, 'Social grading on the National Readership Survey', Research Services Ltd, Joint Industry Committee for National Readership Surveys (JICNARS), London, July 1970.
16. Market Research Society, 'An evaluation of social grade validity', January 1981.
17. Cornish, Pym and Mike Denny, 'Demographics are dead – long live demographics', *Journal of Market Research Society*, vol.31, no.3, July 1989.
18. Bound, John, 'The use of socio-economic grading', *MRS Newsletter*, December 1987.
19. Allt, Brian (Chairman), 'The extended media list experiment', Joint Industry Committee for National Readership Surveys (JICNARS), December 1983.
20. Political and Economic Planning, 'Sampling surveys – Part Two', PEP Report, vol.16, no.314, Political and Economic Planning, London, June 1950.
21. Consterdine, Guy, 'Directory and social grading biases', *MRS Newsletter*, November 1989.
22. Teer, Frank, 'Radio, outdoor and cinema research' in *Consumer Market Research Handbook*, Robert M. Worcester and John Downham (eds), Van Nostrand Reinhold, Wokingham, 1978.
23. Copland, B. D., *The Size and Nature of the Poster Audience, Study II*, Mills and Rockley Ltd, London, 1955.
24. Research Services Ltd, 'Bulletin board survey, J.5675/JL', More O'Ferrall Ltd, London, November 1967.

25. Research Services Ltd, 'London and Leeds poster study for Gallaher Ltd and Advertising Agency Poster Bureau', 1974.

26. Research Services Ltd, 'British posters traffic study', 1974.

27. Bernstein, Peter W., 'Psychographics is still an issue on Madison Avenue', *Fortune*, 16 January 1978.

28. Palda, Kristian S., *The Measurement of Cumulative Advertising Effect*, Prentice-Hall, New Jersey, 1964.

29. Samuels, J. M., *The Effect of Advertising on Sales an l Brand Shares*, Advertising Association, 1971.

30. Chisnall, Peter M., '*Marketing: A Behavioural Analysis*', McGraw-Hill, Maidenhead, 1985.

31. Rothman, James, Editorial, special issue on geodemographics, *Journal of Market Research Society*, vol.31, no.1, January 1989.

32. Cornish, Pym, 'Life cycle and income segmentation – SAGACITY', Admap, London, October 1981.

33. Research Services Ltd, 'SAGACITY: A Special Analysis of JICNARS', NRS 1980 Data, London, 1981.

34. Twyman, Tony, 'Re-classifying people', the ADMAP Seminar, Admap, November 1981.

TWELVE

INDUSTRIAL MARKETING RESEARCH

12.1 INTRODUCTION

In Chapter 1, the comparative reluctance of companies making industrial products to research their markets systematically was noted in a study reported[1] in the *Journal of Market Research* in October 1984. Now that markets in general have grown more competitive, industrial companies have begun to take a greater interest in what marketing research might be able to do for them, and in many cases they have discovered for the first time that it can, in fact, give them highly relevant and pragmatic help.

Consumer marketing research has tended to attract attention because of its immediate impact on many members of the public, and industrialists may have been led to believe that the role of marketing research is confined to fast-moving 'supermarket products'. But, as noted in the opening chapters of this text, marketing research has applications over virtually *all* products and services, including the public sector industries and services.

Before considering in some detail the techniques of industrial marketing research, a brief look at some of the fundamental influences in industrial buying behaviour should help in further discussion of this specialized sector of research. It would also be useful to note that the term 'industrial' is used in a wider sense than, for example, industrial capital equipment or technical products; it should be viewed as covering not only those kinds of products, but also technical services, and the many other activities which now characterize industrial production and markets.

12.2 INDUSTRIAL BUYING BEHAVIOUR

A firm seeks its objectives through the medium of profit and, more specifically, through conversion of its resources into goods and/or services and then obtaining a return on these by selling them to customers.[2]

Organizations are interested in survival and development, which the earning of profit allows, and it can reasonably be assumed that all organizations are similarly motivated. In seeking to achieve these organizational goals, buyers will also be influenced by their personal goals – their wish for survival, growth, and personal profit.

It has been commonly assumed that knowledge is widespread and that expert decisions in organizational buying are based firmly on rational and functional grounds. Consumer buying, on the other hand, has been considered to be far less 'scientific', and subject to irrational behaviour, impulse buying, and lack of market knowledge. But these sweeping generalizations overstate the case; the organizational buyer cannot live in a rational vacuum. Feelings can, and often do, intrude into his or her buying behaviour.

Apart from the mixed motivations which influence buyers of industrial products, it is also important to study *how* buying decisions are taken. *Who*, in fact, is the key figure in deciding to buy a particular product and what is the contribution made by other members of the firm? Research has indicated that 'in many cases quite important decisions are influenced by an *ad hoc* committee which meets once a day at lunchtime in the management dining-room'.[3]

Most business executives have had some experience of this type of influence, and some organizations go so far as to construct lunchtime agendas for discussion among senior members of staff.

Complex decision making

Industrial buying processes are generally more complex than consumers' buying decisions; often several executives, from different departments, are involved in buying the many goods and services used by companies in the production of their manufactures. In 1958, for instance, a Dun and Bradstreet study[4] showed that no fewer than nine people influenced the average firm's buying decisions.

Alexander *et al.*[4] reported that a study of 106 industrial firms revealed that three or more persons influenced the buying processes in over 75 per cent of the companies examined.

McGraw-Hill,[5] in a special investigation of British engineering firms, reported that in companies with between 400 and 1000 employees, there were more than five buying influences, and in companies of over 1000 employees, more than six persons influenced the buying decison.

Almost always, industrial buying negotiations are relatively sophisticated, and often highly complex, in the case of very large capital investment or entry into new areas of manufacturing activity, necessitating considerable long-term commitments in production and marketing strategies.

Buying Centre/Decision-Making Unit (DMU)

Over 30 years ago, pioneer investigations into buying behaviour in several industries in America confirmed that many executives were active in the typical buying situation. This original study was updated in 1970 and 1978.[6] The term 'Decision-Making Unit' (DMU) was introduced into British marketing literature[7] in 1967, when it was emphasized that industrial purchasing was essentially a team effort with specific tasks being undertaken by specialists.

Further studies[8,9] have reiterated the importance of understanding the nature of industrial buying decisions, and of identifying, in particular industries and firms, the typical pattern of buying behaviour (see specialist text).[10]

Roles in industrial buying   Five roles have been described[11] as typical of the industrial buying processes: gatekeeper, user, influencer, buyer, and decider, which make up the 'Buying Centre'. There are times when the same person fulfils all of these functions but, more frequently, different people are active in their various roles in particular buying situations.

The degree to which individuals may affect buying decisions is obviously related to their specialist knowledge and to their status in the management hierarchy.

Functional specialists influence the choice of supplier far more than the buyer, who is frequently little more than an approved signature on the order form.

Products of a highly technical nature, e.g., electronic equipment, tend to have buying procedures quite different from those customary in firms having a range of fairly simple, standard items. In the latter case, ordering is largely a matter of routine involving a fairly narrow range of components for which standards of quality, price, and service have been well established. The buyer, in these circumstances, has more real authority, as his decisions are fairly straightforward and based on ascertainable commercial facts. With highly technical products in dynamic market conditions, the buyer is at a disadvantage; he cannot possibly be a specialist in such areas, though there is a tendency to appoint specialist buyers in large organizations who have the opportunity to develop expert knowledge over a narrower field of purchasing activities.

George Strauss, Professor of Business Administration, University of California, Berkeley,[12] made a detailed study of buying agents in 142 firms, biased strongly towards large engineering companies: 'since agents in these firms face the most complex problems'. Suggesting alternatives in specifications, quantities, substitute materials, etc., helps the buyer to keep the initiative; he no longer feels that he is 'at the end of the line'. He experiences conflict with other departmental chiefs, but he can skilfully reduce this by using formal and informal techniques to influence the buying requisitions. This requires an appreciation of the needs of engineering, production, and other functional specialists.

Strauss found that most buyers used a variety of techniques, depending on the problem, to keep their status in the organization. 'Expansionists' favoured informal tactics, and were markedly flexible in their approach: 'They had long-run strategies and sought to influence decisions before they were made'.

As a professional, the industrial buyer regards the limitation of his authority with some disfavour and as a person he feels that he has suffered some loss of status in the organization. His personal feelings may well become more evident in those buying situations where his power as a buyer is unchallenged. In this way, he may feel that he can assert his authority in the competitive structure of the managerial system.

Leonard Sayles, Professor of Business Administration, Columbia University,[13] states that: 'Most managers have stretched or shrunk their jobs to suit their own personalities and the expediencies of the situation'. Buyers must inevitably take an active part in the decision-making processes of the organizations to which they belong, and their success will largely be determined by the way in which they can 'work the organization'.

When the organization is viewed as a complex series of interlocking patterns of human relationships, work-flow patterns and control patterns, the opportunity for the individual to innovate and shape his own environment becomes apparent.

That this view of the buyer is no illusion can be seen in a survey of 47 firms undertaken by PEP[14] and completed in 1964 under the patronage of the Nuffield Foundation. Among a wealth of information, the report states:

> Within the management hierarchy it often appeared that the buyer was a relatively unimportant member of the firm and sometimes he was no more than a senior clerk with direct responsibility to a senior member of management, who might be the accountant, the works director or the commercial manager.

The buyer's status may be further affected by contracts for some strategic supplies being decided at board level. He may, therefore, experience professional dissatisfaction at having large and vital areas of decision making taken from him, apart from those involving highly technical matters. In more progressive organizations, the buyer is encouraged to form close working arrangements with other executives which result in a ready flow of information between the various departmental heads. The buyer refers sellers' representatives to individual technical specialists for appraisal of their particular products. In turn, the technicians provide the buyer with accurate data so that he can obtain competitive quotations and, also, from time to time, discuss with them possible alternative specifications which may affect economies. Strauss's study, already noted, underlines this approach towards 'value analysis'. It was further high-lighted in a report, published in 1964, by the British Productivity Council[15] of 16 case studies which showed clearly that significant advantages were obtained from discussing problems jointly with suppliers' representatives, company technicians, and the buyers.

This type of cooperation will obviously grow with the development of more complex methods of production. The acceptance of risk is inevitable in business; the buyer wishes to minimize the risks while achieving maximum efficiency. It is to his or her professional advantage to bring together all those who are interested in a particular transaction so that the final decision is made with the agreement of all parties involved in the transaction.

Concentrated buying power

Marketing transactions for industrial products tend to be more specialized than for consumer products. There are greater differences between buyers, and the actual number of buyers for specific products is smaller than in consumer markets. Buying power is concentrated in far fewer centres, and industries tend to concentrate in certain geographic areas, e.g, pottery in Stoke-on-Trent, printing and hosiery in Leicester, cutlery in Sheffield, etc.

In 1982, the American professional sales journal, *Sales and Marketing Management*, revealed that 10 states accounted for practically 57 per cent of all US shipments, and 409 industries – almost 50 per cent of the private sector – had a degree of regional concentration that rendered them attractive sales targets.[10]

Apart from geographical concentration, industries are frequently dominated by a small number of firms whose aggregate output covers the majority of the markets in which they operate. For example, over 80 per cent of the capital products turnover of the UK-owned electronics companies is accounted for by five indigenous manufacturers.[10] Buyers for such companies are in a position to place large orders, frequently on a long-term basis, for which competitive terms have to be negotiated. Such orders may, in fact, represent a high proportion of the total output of a supplier, and this may well be distributed over a very small number of customers. Risks inherent in this type of restricted selling need to be carefully assessed, and a marketing policy drawn up which allows the company to retain flexibility in its operations.

Inter-dependence of buyers and sellers

Industrial transactions are often involved and may take many months to complete. The average industrial order is likely to be of much greater value than those booked in consumer markets, and so the capital risks involved are higher. In addition, there may be widespread repercussions in manufacturing processes if industrial goods fail to satisfy standards of quality, or if the delivery promises are not fulfilled. Heavy financial loss may be incurred through the closure (or part working) of a busy production line, owing to the lack of vital raw materials or components. For industrial supplies which are vital to the production process, risk and uncertainty are considerable factors in influencing the buying decision. The buyer seeks to reduce those elements by satisfactory long-term contracts. He or she is reluctant to change suppliers once they have proved reliable and satisfactory in other respects. Price must take its place among the many factors to be considered when placing business.

Price by itself is always a hazardous way of holding business, so suppliers should aim to provide non-product advantages – to build round their products a constellation of buying motives in order to attract interest in their products. There is generally a range of prices for specific products, and the industrial buyer will not necessarily buy the lowest-priced product. With many products, made to BSI or some other standard specification, there is virtually no intrinsic difference between different manufacturers' products. Price is considered, but buying decisions are also strongly affected by reliability and service. Sometimes, buyers make these assessments subjectively, preferring to deal with well-known firms, even though their prices may be marginally higher.

Between industrial buyer and salesman confidence is important, and this may take many months, even years, to establish: it will not be lightly set aside. Industrial buyers become heavily dependent upon their suppliers, and choose them with care. Some specialist products require an efficient maintenance service which suppliers contract to give. Other industrial products of a highly technical nature are dependent upon suppliers maintaining consistently acceptable standards of quality, e.g., the stainless steel used in aircraft engines.

Industrial buyers recognize that the true value of products is made up of many parts, all of which require careful investigation. It is the responsibility of industrial buyers to obtain agreement on what values are necessary in specific products, the relative importance of intrinsic qualities, and the various 'added values' – the services – which surround them. Included in this assessment will be the non-rational factors, the pleasantness (or otherwise) of doing business with particular firms, for buyers tend to be persuaded by a salesman whose personality is acceptable to them provided his product meets their needs.

The building-in of values in industrial products extends to the selling of complete systems, e.g., computers, where companies offer a package deal covering the training of staff, design of the system, installation of the machine, and supply of software. Industrial security firms offer comprehensive services for the protection of factory premises, screening of personnel, and the transportation of cash funds.

Overview

This basic review of the principal characteristics of industrial buying indicates its complexity. Because of its inherent nature, the processes involved in industrial marketing are very different from those experienced in consumer product markets. Without a fundamental appreciation of the factors influencing industrial markets, no effective marketing analysis is possible. The astute and experienced market researcher understands that factors, such as those discussed in this introductory section, are likely to affect both the manner of her approach and the methodology to be used.

12.3 DEFINITION OF INDUSTRIAL MARKETING RESEARCH

In Chapter 1 various definitions of the general function of marketing research were given, including that of the Industrial Marketing Research Association (IMRA),[16] viz.: 'The systematic, objective and exhaustive search for and study of facts relevant to any problem in the field of industrial marketing'. The term 'industrial marketing' has been defined by IMRA[16] as follows: 'All business and activities involving or influencing the movement of industrial products from the manufacturer to the industrial or commercial user'.

As discussed earlier in this chapter, industrial products and services are of many kinds, and many attempts have been made to define them (see ref. 10). Some of these definitions overlap; the uses to which products are put will bias classifications; 'original equipment' sales, although involving the same product, will probably be placed in a different category from replacement sales.

The Industrial Marketing Research Association has given the following definition: 'Materials, machinery and capital equipment used by and services provided for industrial and institutional establishments'.[16] On which basis industrial products were classified as:

1. *Capital goods:* 'sold as an inherent whole to further production, in machines, accessories or components'.
2. *Primary products:* 'basic materials like steel, chemicals, or aluminium bars sold to manufacturers'.
3. *Intermediate products:* 'such as tubes, castings or buildings materials' which have undergone some major change of form.

In addition, services to the above industrial sectors would, of course, be included.

12.4 IMRA RESEARCH

The above classifications, although not, of course, definitive, are particularly useful as they formed the framework of valuable research[17] undertaken by Dr F. T. Pearce, and published by the Industrial Marketing Research Association. Two postal surveys were made among firms in the main industrial areas of the UK, and divided equally among the three main classes of products. These showed that the chemical industry was more active than any other industry in its use of marketing research. Engineering and electrical goods industries were also important users, but only 'marginally compared with the chemical industry'.

Although general interest in marketing research spanned industries, major interest, ranked by importance, was limited to the following industries:

Chemicals and allied industries   Construction
Vehicles   Food, drink, and tobacco
Engineering and electrical goods   Metal manufacture

Ninety per cent of the companies using marketing research had net assets of $£\frac{1}{2}$ million or more compared with 25 per cent as listed by the Department of Trade and Industry (formerly the Board of Trade) in *Company Assets, Income and Finance*, 1963. By number of employees, however, all sizes of company were represented, even down to those employing between 200 and 500. It would appear, therefore, that companies using marketing research are characterized more by financial and capital intensity than by numbers on the payroll.

The top 10 functions of industrial marketing research in the UK companies were 'positively identified' as shown in Table 12.1.

Table 12.1 Top 10 functions of industrial marketing research

Function	Percentage regularly carrying out function
Sales forecasting	76
Analysis of market size	70
Trends in market size	61
Estimating demand for new products	51
Competitive position of company products	48
Determining characteristics of markets	43
Determining present uses of existing products	41
Studying economic factors affecting sales volume	38
General business forecasting	30
Evaluating proposed new products and services	30

Source: IMRA.

This ranking 'turns out to be similar to that of United States marketing research in general', though American companies practise research more consistently, as shown in Fig. 12.1.

There appeared to be little general interest in researching into advertising, media, styling, and motivational work, all areas of considerable interest in consumer marketing research.

The importance attached to desk research is apparent from Table 12.2. 'The Census of Production, where relevant, was assumed to be a major source.' Trade associations, trade directories, non-census government data and industry statistics, and research associations, were most often mentioned.

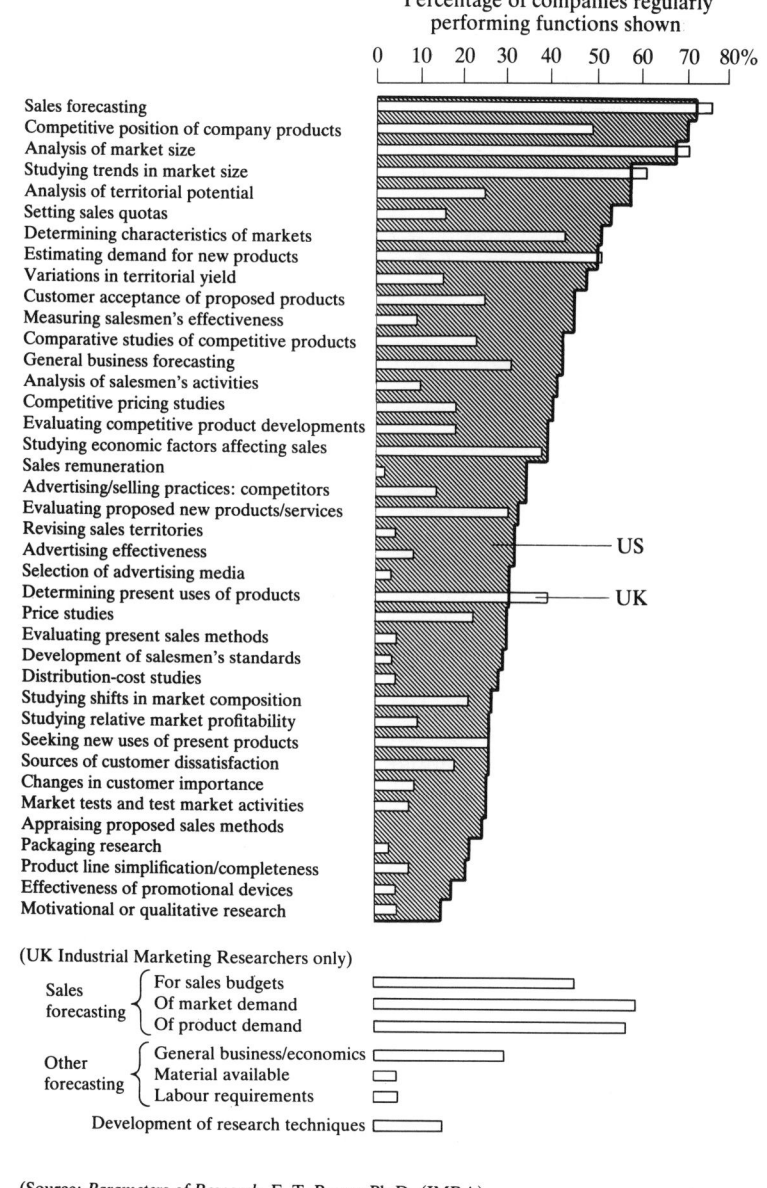

(Source: *Parameters of Research*. F. T. Pearce Ph.D. (IMRA)

Fig. 12.1 Industrial marketing research functions (UK and US practice compared)

Table 12.2 Survey of information-gathering and evaluation methods

Method	Percentage using method	Percentage ranking top
Desk research	88	38
Expert informants	77	23
Own staff and records	79	22
Sample surveys	59	16
Other methods	25	1

Source: IMRA

It was significant that bigger companies stressed the importance of internal records specially developed for research purposes

Information was collected from several types of contacts as shown in Table 12.3.

Table 12.3 Sources of information

Sources	Proportion total contacts made
Direct users	57
End users	22
Competitors	4
Distributors	7
Official bodies	8
Other	2

Source: IMRA

It was found that fieldwork was generally done by personal, unstructured interviews, and the 'overwhelming practice' was to use departmental staff (90 per cent), 'but almost one-third used the sales force on occasions'.

Postal and telephone enquiries were also ranked important, and there was some small interest in group discussion methods. Rarer techniques, such as panels, audits, diaries, etc., were marginally used, possibly by larger companies.

Sampling lists were used by about 75 per cent of respondents and were generally raised internally.

'Formal probability sampling is the exception', and, when used, sampling methods tend to be stratified. It is interesting to note that large companies were much more likely not to use a definite sampling method, and the report suggests that they are likely to have more knowledge about their markets if their market shares are high. They can, therefore, allow their survey to be more flexible and the picture to 'build up' as fieldwork progresses.

12.5 IMRA PROPOSALS FOR EXTENDING THE ROLE OF RESEARCH

Dr Pearce proposes that the role of industrial marketing research should extend beyond mere fact finding, principally for the purposes of sales forecasting. Valuable though this function undoubtedly is, there are other important areas in which marketing research can make a unique and useful contribution. By working closely with related functions such as operational research, and by making research more quantifiable, the difficult and complex task of management decision making can be greatly helped. Marketing research in an industrial organization should be encouraged to evolve into a full-scale operation, collaborating with other functional management to ensure that the company is making full use of its resources. Because marketing goes to the root of a business, and involves fundamental decisions affecting all operational areas, marketing research carries a heavy responsibility. This fact underlines the need for marketing research to become more systematic, quantifiable, and reliable, so that it can be used more fully across a wide span of management decision making.

This critical analysis of industrial marketing research by a highly experienced practitioner clearly indicates that the techniques of scientific management should be firmly based on a systematic flow of reliable information. The risks involved in decision making in a dynamic market environment will be reduced by an objective assessment of all the factors influencing a decision. This is the role of industrial marketing research, an intelligent use of which can aid businesses of all sizes.

12.6 PRINCIPAL CHARACTERISTICS OF INDUSTRIAL MARKETING RESEARCH

In Chapter 2, five sequential stages of marketing research were identified and discussed, principally with reference to consumer product markets. The same general approach is applicable to researching market opportunities for industrial products and services. Although the application of certain techniques may be modified, the essential process of developing an objective and effective research design remains unchanged.

As in consumer marketing research, the first step is to obtain agreement on the nature of the problem to be investigated. This initial stage may take up considerable time and it requires the patience and stamina of both clients and researchers to arrive at a workable brief. But this process of clarification and definition should not be shirked; unless the matters on which the reseach will focus are fully understood and agreed, little productive research is likely later on.

For a client to say: 'We want you to look at our market', is a totally inadequate research brief. Many firms operate in several markets which share, perhaps, general characteristics but which also tend to have distinct features. Also, there are usually particular features of a market which may affect the likelihood of success, and investigation may be needed in some depth in these areas. There may be times when a client is so unwilling to give adequate insight into her problem that no worthwhile marketing research would be feasible. Usually, however, experienced researchers are able to generate an atmosphere of trust and confidence which attracts even hesitant clients to cooperate in delineating their business problems.

12.7 DESK RESEARCH (Secondary Data)

As with consumer research, data collection should start at the secondary level, and full advantage should be taken of available information, both within companies and that published externally, to give a sound base to the whole research programme. There are many sources of published data to which researchers instinctively turn but, usually, there are valuable data to be gathered also from production, accounting, and sales records. Marketing research data may be culled from these internal sources at very low cost and, with a little ingenuity, a regular flow of specific information from the various areas of functional management could be of great value to developing and guiding marketing strategies.

Externally published sources of data include many of those already listed in Chapter 2. Principal sources are:

Census of Production
Business Monitors
Trade Associations
Trade Directories

Stock Exchange Yearbook
Exhibition Catalogues
Research Associations

The Census of Production covers production, which is defined as 'industrial production, including construction, gas, electricity and water supply and mines and quarries'. It covers production by private firms, nationalized industries, and central and local government. Information, under the authority of the Statistics of Trade Act, is collected by postal census of 'establishments', classified according to their main products on the basis of the Standard Industrial Classification.

While this classification is valuable, it may result in the total production of some important firms being included under one classification, whereas they may, in fact, produce considerable quantities of some other products which are important in these particular markets, but represent only a relatively small proportion of total output.

The Census was originally planned on a quinquennial basis: it has now been replaced by an annual one, the first of which took place in 1970. Quarterly enquiries are supplemented by monthly enquiries; in addition, detailed enquiries may also be extended into purchase of materials at three-year intervals. *British Business* publishes summary findings.

In compliance with the requirements of the Statistical Office of the European Communities, certain changes were made in the Census from 1973. Previously, census returns had to be submitted by establishments employing 25 or more people, except that in 13 industries, where small firms made an important contribution to total output, the coverage was extended to establishments with 11 or more employees. In the 1975 Census, all establishments employing 20 or more people were asked to complete a questionnaire.

New questions covered payments for outworkers and the cost of goods bought for merchanting; questions on transport were generally discontinued. Establishments with 100 or more employees were also asked these new questions, and also questions related to value-added tax and the cost of non-industrial services.

To avoid identification of individual companies, census report figures are sometimes amalgamated.

12.8 OFFICIAL INDUSTRY CLASSIFICATION

In Britain, the basic framework for measuring industrial production is known as the *Standard Industrial Classification* (SIC). This originated in 1948 to encourage uniformity in UK official statistics for industry; revisions were made in 1958, 1968, and 1980. These revisions have tended to make study of trends in certain industrial sectors rather difficult. The SIC has been described[18] by the chief statistician of the Central Statistical office as an empirical classification which tries to reflect the existing structure of economic activities in the UK. There is also the problem of keeping a balance between the need to be up to date against the loss in comparability with data. The official view is that a change in industrial classification about once in every 10 years is about right.

The 1980 revised SIC has a decimal structure over four stages as follows:

1. full range of industrial activities
   first divided into 10 broad divisions (single digits)
   ↓
2. subdivided into:
   60 classes (two digits)
   ↓
3. further subdivided into:
   222 groups (three digits)
   ↓
4. then divided into:
   334 activities (four digits)

Overall, this revised system allows more detailed analyses to be available compared with the earlier SICs which were divided into 181 Minimum List Headings (MLHs). However, the full range of potential subdivisions is not followed across the full SIC system; it depends on the diversity of the activities covered by specific classifications. Care is still necessary in interpreting data from sources using the SIC, because, for example, the unit of classification is the establishment which is not necessarily identical with a particular company's overall trading activities. The total production of some important firms may, for instance, be included under one classification, whereas they may produce considerable quantities of some other products which are important in those particular markets but represent only a relatively small proportion of their total output.

The unit of classification in the SIC is the 'establishment', i.e., the whole of the production at a particular address of a farm, mine, factory or shop, classified according to main products on the basis of the SIC. However, care should be exercised when interpreting data from SIC sources.

While the official classifications and sub-headings of industrial activities often provide valuable data for marketing research purposes, specific products tend to be subsumed under fairly broad headings. In some cases, it may be possible, on application to the Business Statistics Office, to obtain more relevant information.

Business Monitors, as noted in Chapter 2, provide detailed information about British industrial production. These series are regularly published so the information is more up to date than that in the Census of Production.

Trade Associations and Chambers of Commerce, as also noted in Chapter 2, should be contacted in the rigorous search for market data. In general, however, the search will not be very fruitful, for apart from a handful of such organizations, they are limited to giving an overall view of particular industries or trades, and economic data are unlikely to be available.

It would be as well to bear in mind that membership is voluntary and some firms, for reasons of policy, may not be members. The collection of information within associations depends largely on goodwill. The complete reliability of the data supplied is a factor to be carefully considered.

Some of the leading trade directories and yearbooks have been listed in Chapter 2; there are others which could be consulted in academic libraries and in the commercial libraries in the cities and larger towns of the UK and many overseas countries.

Trade directories are of variable quality; it is useful to check accuracy and reliability by scrutinizing entries relating to companies which are well known personally. In addition to these publications, there are very many specialist journals, and researchers should acquaint themselves with those covering the markets under survey.

Entries in exhibition catalogues can be used to build up a good general knowledge of particular industries, though it should not be assumed that these necessarily include all companies. Some may have individual methods of promotion which exclude trade exhibitions in some areas.

Some industries have research associations which publish market data; for example, the Furniture Industry Research Association (FIRA).

From this brief review of possible sources of externally published information, it will readily be appreciated that an effective market researcher, particularly when industrial marketing problems are being surveyed, needs to have some of the talents of the sleuth in tracking down relevant and useful data.

12.9 PROBLEMS OF PRIMARY RESEARCH

Sampling frames

One of the salient problems of industrial marketing research is the availability of suitable lists of firms on which a survey could be based. Desk research enquiries, as just outlined, could be instrumental in developing sampling frames; in particular, the Business Statistics Office published *Directories of Business Establishments* which, under SIC headings, listed names and addresses of the majority of firms whose production figures were recorded anonymously in the Census of Production.

The Classified List of Manufacturing Business originates from the Business Statistics Office (BSO) of UK manufacturing businesses and is a result of the cooperation of firms which, from 1970, contributed to the Census of Production. The resultant list gives information about each manufacturing local unit, separate entries are made. Non-manufacturing units, in particular units which are offices, are not included, so the head office of a firm may not be listed. These valuable lists contain about 27 000 business addresses and cover about two-thirds of the employment in the UK manufacturing sector. There are 10 volumes of the Classified List (*Business Monitor* PO 1007), and a separate magnetic tape is also available. Special regional and alphabetical analyses and computer printouts can be obtained from the BSO at reasonable cost.

Sampling frames may also be constructed from telephone enquiries. For example, it may be possible to check the suitability of companies as respondents in a particular survey, whether, in fact, they are significant users of specific kinds of products or services. Further classification can be done by dividing users into some agreed definitions of heavy, medium, and light, so that specified research can be undertaken in these areas. Stratification of the sample can then be designed and final figures can be suitably weighted. During telephone discussions, it may be possible to obtain the names of other significant users and by this personal method to achieve a valid sampling frame, economically and quickly.

Other sources of sampling frames are Yellow Pages, industrial and technical directories, and on-line facilities offered by data firms such as Kompass.(See Section 2.10, Secondary data — internal on p. 40.)

Expert informants

In most industries there are usually people known to be well-informed and to possess sound knowledge of the organization and movements within their particular sphere of interest. Researchers should attempt to identify and contact these experts, who may be recommended to them by trade associations and other helpful sources. An industrial group was reported[19] to subdivide the market into homogeneous sectors, and commence enquiries in each sector with the best-informed sources known. The sample size is not predetermined; successive firms are interviewed until a stable answer pattern emerges.

'Sounding' of expert trade opinion is valuable in forming hypotheses about certain market situations. It is the responsibility of the researcher to evaluate these opinions objectively and to relate them to data obtained by other methods of enquiry.

Well-informed and cooperative respondents are not necessarily in the largest firms in an industry; smaller specialist companies are often staffed by astute and knowledgeable executives who may be willing to give valuable insight to researchers.

The editors and professional journalists attached to the trade and industrial press may also be willing to discuss the market being surveyed, and about which they may have specially relevant knowledge.

12.10 SAMPLING

In Chapters 3, 4 and 5 the basic principles of techniques of sampling were discussed in some detail, particularly with reference to consumer markets. Industrial markets differ considerably from mass consumer product markets in many ways, and so some aspects of the sampling methodologies already covered may not be directly applicable, although, of course, the underlying concepts of representativeness and objectivity remain unchanged. Sometimes, industrial markets, for example, are very limited, and it may be possible to measure consumption, etc., through a complete census. In other cases, the market is widespread, with many different structures and patterns of consumption behaviour, and sampling has to be devised which is both feasible and, of course, valid.

Industrial products are often used in a variety of industries, and where a general survey is required it may be necessary to undertake a series of sample surveys into individual user-industries. Alternatively, it may be possible to apply some method of weighting to the data of a general survey. The problem for the researcher is obtaining reliable information about a well-defined area of investigation. Enquiries should, therefore, be directed specifically to those industries (complete or segmented) which are significant for this purpose.

Constructing a sample for industrial marketing research demands some general knowledge of the particular industry concerned. The more perfect this knowledge, the better the researcher will be able to form a sample which adequately represents the population under survey. Facts about the structure of a particular industry can be obtained from some of the published sources given in Chapter 2, and earlier in this chapter.

As already observed, the total universe to be studied is usually small, from a mere handful of companies to a few hundred and, occasionally, a few thousand. Industrial marketing research typically requires far fewer interviews compared with consumer enquiries.

Industries are often dominated by a small number of companies, whose total output represents a significant share of the market, perhaps as high as 90 per cent. This residual output may be contributed by many comparatively small firms, whose individual market share is relatively unimportant although, of course, they may have a strong position in a specific market sector or niche.

Some companies deal with a very restricted number of customers and, sometimes, two or three of these take almost the entire production.

In cases like these, it would obviously be incorrect to use a random sampling technique, as the survey findings would be unreliable if one of the major companies were not included in the sample taken. To avoid errors of this nature, the whole population would have to be surveyed, i.e., a census would be necessary. In some instances, it may be possible to avoid taking a complete census by carefully weighting a sample.

A leading industrial marketing researcher[20] has commented that when some establishments are very much more important than others, the problem is to identify them, either in advance or by means of a sample design which increases the probability of reaching these important firms without incurring heavy expenses in non-productive interviews.

'Clearly, the most efficient way is to use advance knowledge, preferably from a previous survey'; this desirable short-cut is, however, by no means always available. The problems of sampling incurred in a survey of the reading habits of businessmen were discussed in an article[21] in *IMRA Journal* in 1975.

A survey[22] of the UK market for fork-lift trucks well illustrates some of the problems (and solutions) attached to industrial marketing research. It was known from previous surveys that fork-lift trucks had many industrial applications, and from various official statistics, a matrix of 13 business sectors (groupings of SIC codes) and seven size (employees) classifications was formed. Additional inputs were derived from Dun and Bradstreet, Market Location (a commercial firm specializing in listing, and mapping industrial and commercial firms in the UK), and the survey organization's (Industrial Market Research Ltd) own file.

It was known that the truck ownership was comparatively low generally and varied widely across and within market sectors, and so some type of disproportionate sampling design was considered necessary (see Chapter 4).

From earlier proprietary studies of this market, it was possible to compute an estimated penetration percentage for each cell in the matrix, and by applying these figures to the number of establishments, an estimate was made of the number of 'truck equipped establishments'. Sample quotas were then allocated to each cell in proportion to its relative importance in the total truck-owning market. Each of the 10 Standard Regions was allocated separate quotas.

In order to safeguard the efficiency of the quota sampling scheme, lists of contacts were pre-selected and issued to interviewers on a controlled basis. As a further check, replacement addresses were issued only when the initial set had been fully accounted for. In addition, a sample of addresses from the data base for each business sector size cell was drawn related to 'believed non-users of trucks', and interviews were conducted to identify establishments which had recently acquired trucks. Further amendments to cell penetration levels were also made following enquiries (based on Yellow Pages and other listings) which were largely centered on non-manufacturing firms not covered adequately by the Market Location data.

This relatively complex sampling procedure was followed by structured interviews by a team of 21 mostly home-based telephone interviewers. However, in cases of very large establishments with many trucks, personal interviews were made in order to collect detailed information, including qualitative evaluation.

To build up a satisfactory sampling frame for industrial marketing research, considerable patience and ingenuity are necessary, as the example just quoted illustrates. Comprehensive combing and integration of published data will help in filling in the gaps which are usually to be found in any one source of knowledge. It is obviously important to check such data for their validity and reliability.

12.11 INTERVIEWING AND QUESTIONNAIRES

From the extended discussion in Chapter 7, it will be recognized that interviewing is a critical function of marketing research which, unfortunately, is subject to bias of many kinds. Good research practice aims to eradicate sources of error, and to control, as far as possible, the conditions under which the enquiries are made. Industrial research interviewing should not be regarded as an alternative occupation for members of the sales force; they may be able to produce some information which, at a superficial level, appears satisfactory. There remains, however, the risk of subjectivity, but despite this some organizations tend to rely on their sales staff to provide market information. It is argued that surveys are better undertaken by people who have an intimate knowledge of the product and the industry. But the fact remains, as a PEP Report[14] indicated 'that the man whose job is to sell is often unable to be objective about the reasons for his success or failure, about his competitors, and about many of the factors that contribute to a proper assessment of the firm's prospects in the market'.

Interviewing in industrial marketing research tends to be largely unstructured, i.e., a formal questionnaire is not used and is sometimes replaced by an 'interviewing guide', which lists the main areas of research to be covered by the interviewer. It is more a guide to conversation. Since good 'timing' may sometimes attract the right response, the interviewer is left free to use discretion in the sequence of questioning.

Where questionnaires are used, it is important to ensure that technical terms are correctly handled and that the area of scientific or technical enquiry is clearly understood by both parties. This calls for considerable skill in drafting questions covering specialized fields of knowledge. It also demands interviewers capable of obtaining information, often of a highly technical nature, from management over a representative range of companies. Such interviews need to have expert knowledge of the industries which are being covered by the survey, or they should have the intellectual ability to acquire sufficient information in a short period of intensive training. They should also possess the type of personality which will help them to be accepted by senior management with whom they must necessarily establish confidence, if the interviews are to be successful.

The considerable debate about whether or not industrial marketing research interviewers need to be highly qualified techncially in the specific industries they are surveying is not easily determined. Even in technical markets, factors other than those directly related to product design and manufacture may frequently be involved; for example, delivery time, prices, credit policy, attitudes, or advertising effectiveness. To restrict interviewing to those who are highly trained specialists in engineering and so on, may well affect the findings of specific research surveys because they lack vital business orientation and experience.

Of course, researchers, including interviewers, need to be adequately briefed: this may entail intensive study *before* field research starts. In a comparatively short time, intelligent field researchers can assimilate a surprising amount of background knowledge about particular industrial techniques and applications. Professional interviewing skills are necessarily the most important factor – technical competence alone does not ensure effective interviewing.

It is clearly important to interview whoever is able to provide relevant and accurate information about the subject of the survey, and as discussed earlier, in many industrial buying decisions several executives from different management functions are likely to influence the source of supply. The buyer may not be able to give detailed answers to certain technical enquiries, and it may well be necessary to interview executives in both technical and commercial spheres.

The survey may, therefore, be divided into several parts. Interviewers may have to exercise considerable diplomacy to ensure that the buyer, for instance, gives them the opportunity of meeting other key executives whose opinions on technical matters may be valuable.

On the whole, industrial research is more difficult than consumer research. Fewer calls can be made during the day, and it is advisable to book appointments, as it would be unreasonable to expect executives to lay aside their duties without reasonable advance notification. They may also wish to have a little time in which to obtain specific data. In some cases, a call-back ensures that the information given is reliable.

Frequently, research organizations offer to provide respondent firms with some of the general findings of the survey. This attracts cooperation and helps to ensure that valid and reliable answers are given. With some survey problems, it may be advantageous to institute continuous research at a certain agreed depth, and this could be done by forming a user panel.

12.12 OBSERVATIONAL TECHNIQUES

Industrial marketing research can also adopt observational techniques which can provide very useful information. This may involve checking types of equipment in use, or a study of the way in which certain tools are handled. Patterns of typical behaviour may be established which could prove valuable in the design of workshop equipment.

Observation may also be helpful in checking the validity of data supplied, for instance, about certain characteristics of production.

As observed in Chapter 2, this technique of acquiring knowledge is prone to bias, so observers should be specially trained to maintain, as far as possible, objectivity. Recording of observed behaviour should be systematic, and to encourage this it would be advisable to have standardized report sheets.

12.13 TELEPHONE SURVEYS

In Chapter 6, telephone surveying techniques were seen to be growing in popularity in consumer enquiries, and new computer-based technologies have resulted in almost 'instant information'.

Industrial marketing research has also made increasing use of telephone surveys, although this approach has obvious restrictions. It cannot be used, for example, for very lengthy enquiries involving considerable detail, or where some research would be needed before answers could be given, although it may well be useful where the information sought is of a fairly rudimentary nature. In addition, as already noted, it is often used in forming sampling frames.

In a survey[23] of the market potential for a new, small vending machine suitable only for serving between 6 and 30 employees, telephone interviews effectively filtered out suitably sized firms and institutions and information was collected from them at relatively low cost.

Another example of the effectiveness of telephone interviewing was a readership survey[24] undertaken by Mass Observation on behalf of Morgan Grampian's controlled circulation monthly *Business Administration*. Two hundred and fifty managing directors were interviewed in five weeks, and the response rate was over 50 per cent.

Before telephoning prospective respondents, some planning should be done; for example, researchers should either prepare a well-structured questionnaire so that time is used productively, or write down the main topics of investigation in a logical progression. In addition, make sure that answers can be recorded adequately, perhaps by marking off appropriate codes or entering the information given on relevant data sheets.

It is particularly important to introduce quickly and clearly the nature of the survey and its objectives, to ensure that the person answering the telephone (or those to whom the call is transferred) is knowledgeable and able to give valid information.

Telephone calls may be used to ask for support for a planned mail survey; it was found[25] that a pre-notification telephone call to senior purchasing managers of manufacturing firms in the St Paul, Minneapolis, area to introduce a mail survey containing 40 scale responses related to various buying practices, resulted in 64 out of 66 potential respondents completing and returning the questionnaire. The researchers indicated that the pre-notification request must 'be brief and to the point ... we aimed for businesslike interaction. ... The request by purchasing managers for information about the survey's topic resulted in extremes: some wanted almost no information, while others asked very detailed questions that required specific answers'.[25] Another insight was the influence of the survey sponsors: the Twin City Purchasing Management Association; this established credibility with the executives contacted.

12.14 MAIL SURVEYS

Mail surveys are frequently chosen for research in industrial markets. They are particularly valuable where the population is large and, perhaps, widely dispersed. Superficially, this method of enquiry is attractive in terms of economy, simplicity, and speed. But closer examination of the real costs involved should be made; apart from printing and postage charges, which will be relatively modest, proportionate charges for overheads and salaries should be added. These latter costs should cover the preparatory work, such as drafting the questionnaire, and the subsequent task of analysis and interpretation. Postal questionnaires are not easy to write. Since no interviewer is present to interpret the questions, they must be free from ambiguity. Several pilotings may be necessary; these obviously involve time and cost.

Another aspect to be carefully considered is the real cost of mail surveys, namely, the total cost of the operation spread over the number of effective replies received. The valid reply rate may often result in doubling or trebling the original 'crude' estimate distributed over the total number of questionnaires posted.

In addition, some attempt should be made to compare the values of different methods of survey. This entails studying not merely comparative costs, but also considering the quality of the findings of alternative methods, such as postal surveys and personal interviews. Research[17] had indicated that open-ended questions in postal surveys tended to attract answers mentioning dislikes more frequently than when personal interviewing took place. Admittedly, the initial overall costs of a postal questionnaire may be only half of those involved in a personal interview covering domestic products, and very substantially less than personal interviewing in an industrial survey. But the true costs depend on effective response rates and these vary significantly.

Research by Dr F. T. Pearce[17] indicated that 37 per cent of firms studied expected response rates of up to 20 per cent (31 per cent anticipated a response rate of between 10 and 20 per cent). A seminar organized by IMRA reported[16] that response rates varied widely, and that it was not possible to apply 'any general rule of thumb for calculating response to postal surveys'. It was also commented that low response rates may not necessarily invalidate the findings, provided that sufficient control data are available with which to weight the answers. With simple dichotomous (YES/NO) questions, one large motor manufacturer found that replies tended to stabilize their relationship after a 39 to 47 per cent response rate was achieved. IMRA remarks that 'if this were generally true then high response rates would be less important to the practical industrial researcher'.

Some ways in which mail surveys might be made more productive were examined in Chapter 6; detailed attention to the wording of questions is of paramount importance, since they have to be unambiguous and capable of being answered without too much trouble. Experiments have been conducted to see whether coloured questionnaire forms, attractively drafted accompanying letter, alternative methods of reply-paid facilities, etc., are effective in raising responses. One study[26] involving a stratified random sample of 800 UK textile companies sought information about their marketing strategies in a two-page questionnaire. Four 'treatments' were randomly applied to a sub-sample of 32 large companies: prior letter/white questionnaire, prior letter/blue questionnaire, no prior letter/white questionnaire, and no prior letter/blue questionnaire. The remaining 768 smaller companies were allocated to one of the four treatments.

The questionnaire was accompanied by a covering letter explaining the purpose of the survey, stressing confidentiality, and offering a free copy of the report; a business reply envelope was included in the outward envelope which was white and hand-addressed.

The prior letter had indicated briefly the nature of the survey, a questionnaire would shortly be sent, and offered a free copy of the resultant report.

The use of a prior letter with this particular commercial population appeared to depress the response rate, and the researchers admit that the result is unique and contrary to previous studies of general population studies. Blue questionnaire paper did not increase response over white paper.

While the findings related to the influence of a prior letter are surprising, the overall response rate at 57.2 per cent was 'quite high'. Experience has shown that many factors influence the success of surveys, including sponsorship, which could be more important than the colour of the paper, and these particular survey findings may well not be universally applicable to industrial mail surveys.

In an experimental mail survey[27] of personal computer owners, computer retailers, and computer manufacturers in California, subjects were randomly assigned to receive either a standard cover letter, a cover letter that offered results to respondents, or a standard cover letter with a lift letter that offered results to respondents. Survey findings revealed that offering results to respondents did not increase the rate or speed of response, and had 'only a minor effect' on reducing the number of item omissions. It was reported that offering survey results 'increased the cost of the survey while providing minimal benefits'.

It was suggested that the reasons why offering results failed to have a positive effect were (i) it represented a biased incentive that appealed only to those who had an interest in the survey topic, and (ii) the respondent was not given anything tangible before cooperating in the survey. The study did not reveal any differences among the three sectors involved in their reaction to the offer of survey results, although it was found that manufacturers and retailers were much less likely to be responsive to a survey than PC owners.

How far this particular sectoral survey can be generalized is open to debate.

Non-response is a serious limitation of postal surveys. The greater the response, the more widely costs can be spread, and although this economic aspect is relatively important, the principal concern of researchers is the likelihood that non-respondents are significantly different from respondents in their attitudes towards the products under survey. The reasons for non-response are not known, and these may, in fact, be directly relative to the problem surveyed. It is advisable to make some sort of check on non-respondents, either by telephone or personal interviewing, in order to establish reasons for non-response. Data thus obtained can be compared with those secured from respondents.

Study of response factors in postal surveys covering social investigations has indicated that response is correlated with interest in the subject. This view was shared 'very strongly' by IMRA seminar members, who felt 'lack of identification with the purpose of the survey ... to be the most important single reason for non-response'.[28]

Non-response may also be attributable to ambiguous questions which confuse would-be respondents who eventually discard the questionnaire. Some questionnaires may be unreasonable in the amount of information demanded, either being too lengthy or capable of being answered only after considerable reference to records. Another influencing factor may be the physical presentation of the survey; social survey studies have shown that the letter which accompanies a mail questionnaire can affect the response quite significantly. In general, it would be wise to ensure that the recipient forms a favourable attitude to the survey, and attention to the choice of paper, style of printing, layout, reply-paid facility, and envelope, helps to win his cooperation.

As far as possible, survey questionnaires (with covering letters) should be addressed to those people able to deal with them effectively. This may involve patient enquiry in the course of building sampling frames, so that key personnel are identified. With some complex investigations, it may be helpful to subdivide the questionnaire into specific managerial areas of interest, so that the complete survey can be dealt with more conveniently. Direct posting of questionnaire sections can be done, or it may be possible to distribute these through the chief executive's office.

Some method of following up non-respondents should be devised. Inevitably, this extends the time taken to complete the survey, and, of course, adds to the cost. Two reminder letters are customary, often at 14-day intervals. Replies received as the result of reminders should be carefully scrutinized to see if they differ significantly from early respondents. Dealing with social surveys, Moser[29] has commented that it would appear to be very reasonable to regard respondents to follow-up appeals as representative of all non-respondents rather than of initial respondents. This observation may well be borne in mind in industrial marketing research.

There is some evidence[23] which suggests that the inclusion of a small premium gift, e.g., a pocket knife, with the questionnaire form, encourages response (see Chapter 6).

The popularity of postal surveys with researchers should be balanced by a clear understanding of the problems involved in using them. This appreciation will encourage better research design leading, in turn, to more reliable research findings.

12.15 GROUP DISCUSSIONS

The technique of group discussions was referred to in Chapter 8, and it was seen to have usefulness in generating freer responses to enquiries about particular problems, often connected with household products. This qualitative research technique also has useful applications in industrial marketing investigation.

An example[30] of the value of group discussions in industrial research related to a high-quality food manufacturer, subsidiary of a large international group, who wanted to extend his business in the catering market. A specialist research firm conducted four group discussions among caterers of various sizes and distributed over segments of the catering industry.

Discussants vigorously dealt with the usage of convenience foods, and general problems of catering, and strong views were expressed about the methods used by market leaders to launch new products.

The researchers felt that, through the interaction of knowledgeable respondents exchanging divergent views, more 'usable results' were obtained than through traditional interviewing techniques.

Brainstorming, which Sampson[31] qualifies as a special example of group interviewing, was used as part of a research[32] programme conducted for Post Office Telecommunications during 1979 to generate ideas for the possible uses of a range of visual services that would ultimately result in a full view-phone network, by means of which subscribers would be able both to speak to and see the person at the other end of the line. A sample was generated from the '*Times* Top 1000' companies supplemented by other organizations, such as advertising agencies, energy boards, and government departments which, it was thought, might be interested in this new video phone service, which could be attractive for holding meetings between two or three people per terminal, or for transmitting soft-copy of graphics, documents, etc.

Before the main survey started, two brainstorming sessions were held and resulted in over 200 suggested uses, 'many of which were not business related; but of those that were, very few were new or original'. Following this rather disappointing phase, the research then focused on a survey of 240 organizations; the results indicated that there was a potential market for this novel service.

12.16 CONTINUOUS RESEARCH

There is some evidence of panel research (see Chapter 9) in industrial markets. Some truck firms, for example, operate 'user panels', but this technique is by no means as widely used as in consumer product marketing research. There are opportunities, it would appear, for drawing systematically on the experience of customers, although the generic problems of ensuring representativeness and active participation are likely to discourage experiments.

12.17 OMNIBUS SURVEYS

BMRB operates a monthly telephone omnibus survey of 1000 department heads over various industries. Audience Selection organizes a 'Key Directors Omnibus' survey based on a sample of 400 telephone enquiries each quarter.

12.18 DERIVED DEMAND APPROACH

The nature of demand for industrial products is characteristically derived, i.e., it is significantly affected by end-use and dependent on the rate of usage which may be several stages from the initial buyer. Capital goods suppliers, for example, are ultimately dependent on the demand for the products which their plant is capable of making. Likewise, the demand for raw materials and components will be heavily influenced by the rate of sales in user industries, and eventually the general behaviour of the national economy and also, perhaps, overseas markets. If car sales fall off because of lower consumer demand, the effects will reverberate through many industries; for example, steel, tyres, electrical and electronic components, upholstery fabrics, paint, etc.

The dependent pattern of demand for industrial raw materials and components is illustrated in Fig. 12.2.

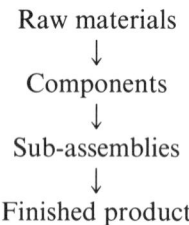

Raw materials
↓
Components
↓
Sub-assemblies
↓
Finished product

Figure 12.2 Demand relevant to industrial raw materials

This inter-dependence among suppliers of a varied assortment of products and services may be used in researching markets. Companies should fully understand their end-use markets and the nature of demand in these, including trends in the final 'consumption market'. The chain of derived demand may have many links, and research may be necessary at several levels.

It may be feasible to develop a consumption indicator for specific suppliers related to the demand experienced by customers for their products. Packaging manufacturers, for instance, study carefully the trends in food consumption: consumer preferences may mean that glass-bottle manufacturers will experience marked variations in demand for their products.

In some cases, it may be difficult to assess the size of a particular industrial market, either because published figures are too general or they do not exist at all. By studying end-use markets, it is often possible to collect some useful data to guide production and marketing decisions. Firms in other industries which supply the same end-use market may be willing to share their market knowledge, and mutual exchange of market data among non-competing companies may be very helpful to all concerned.

End-use analysis offers a very effective approach to industrial market research and can lead to profitable market segmentation strategies. Opportunities across market sectors can be evaluated, and resources targeted on specific end-uses with their distinctive technical and service requirements.

In conclusion, and as stressed in Chapter 2, it is desirable to develop a creative research strategy using a well-balanced mix of methodologies in order to achieve valid and reliable findings.

Industrial marketing research has a long way to go before it is used as extensively as consumer product research. The problems of industry are no less vital than those of manufacturers of consumer products, and in times of difficult trading it is more important than ever to assist the process of decision making by gathering accurate information about the problem in hand.

In general, British industry has neglected marketing and has undertaken comparatively little marketing research, perhaps because of some in-built prejudice about using techniques of management which have become closely associated with supermarket trading.

Technical and industrial marketing enquiries are seldom easy; often they are demanding in their complexity and call for the highest skills in research practice. Over 20 years ago, it was said[33] that British industry suffers from a removable uncertainty – it does not pay sufficient attention to marketing research. While there are signs of a more ready interest in industrial marketing research, there is still a long way to go before there is general acceptance of its vital importance to the successful marketing of industrial and technical goods and services.

12.19 INDUSTRIAL MARKETING RESEARCH ORGANIZATIONS

The Industrial Marketing Research Association

Founded in 1963, IMRA is the principal British organization for those professionally concerned with 'research into the marketing of goods and services to industrial and institutional consumers'.

One of the prime aims of IMRA is 'to create a greater awareness on the part of Industry and the State of the value of marketing research and its needs in the way of information'.

It is now accepted as the representative body for industrial marketing research in the UK. Specialized sectors of IMRA have been developed to study problems of research in specific industries such as construction, electrical engineering, electronics, metals, paper, printing and packaging, and chemical.

Twice a year, IMRA runs residential courses, in the fundamentals of industrial marketing research, at Birmingham University. A list of publications includes *Guide to Industrial Marketing Research Consultancy* which gives useful guidelines on the use and selection of consultants.

The European Association for Industrial Marketing Research (EVAF)

This Association was founded in 1965, with the following aims:

1. To establish the association as the organization representing industrial marketing research in Europe.
2. To carry out the following activities:
   (a) Liaison with:
       European official, professional, or educational bodies or organizations, European marketing research organizations.
   (b) Promotion of national or industry-based marketing research study groups, etc.
   (c) Encouragement and improvement of contact between European researchers.
3. The establishment of ethical standards in industrial marketing research.
4. The improvement of technical standards and quality in industrial marketing research.

The EVAF organizes seminars and encourages researchers to exchange, on an international basis, information and experience of professional interest.

The EVAF and IMRA work very closely together, the former being more concerned with the international aspects of industrial marketing research, whereas the latter is more directly interested in the national aspects.

12.20 SUMMARY

Industrial marketing research and consumer marketing research have a common approach, but the nature and applications of the methodologies will vary; sampling, for instance, is likely to be distinctly different, and interviewing tends to be more difficult and expensive. It may involve considerable technical knowledge about specific industries.

Industrial markets have complex structures; buying behaviour is sophisticated – many may contribute to purchase decisions. Derived demand is a marked feature of industrial markets, and the impact of end-use markets must be fully understood.

A well-formulated research plan should be devised to minimize bias from using just one method of enquiry. Before field research is considered, full value should be obtained from published data.

REFERENCES

1. Hooley, Graham J., and Christopher J. West, 'The untapped markets for marketing research', *Journal of Market Research Society*, vol.26, no.4, 1984.
2. Ansoff, H. Igor, *Corporate Strategy*, Pelican, 1968.
3. Desoutter, Michael, 'Industrial advertising', in: *Marketing of Industrial Products*, Aubrey Wilson (ed.), Hutchinson, London, 1968.
4. Alexander, R. S., J. S. Cross, and R. M. Cunningham, *Industrial Marketing*, Richard D. Irwin, Homewood, Illinois, 1961.
5. McGraw-Hill, 'Special report on the buying and selling techniques in British engineering industry', McGraw-Hill, London, 1963.
6. Erickson, Robert A., 'How industry buys: An update', in: *The Challenge of the Eighties*, ESOMAR, Brussels, September 1979.
7. Buckner, Hugh, *How British Industry Buys*, Hutchinson, London, 1967.
8. Brand, Gordon, *The Industrial Buying Decision*, Cassell, London, 1972.
9. *Financial Times*, 'How British industry buys', *Financial Times*, November 1974.
10. Chisnall, Peter M., *Strategic Industrial Marketing*, Prentice-Hall, Hemel Hempstead, 1985.
11. Webster, Frederick E., Jnr, and Yoram Wind, *Organization Buying Behaviour*, Prentice-Hall, Englewood Cliffs, New Jersey, 1972.
12. Strauss, George, 'Tactics of lateral relationship: The purchasing agents', *Administrative Quarterly*, Cornell University, September 1962.
13. Sayles, Leonard, *Managerial Behaviour*, McGraw-Hill, New York, 1964.
14. Gater, Anthony, David Insull, Harold Lind, and Peter Seglow, 'Attitudes in British management', PEP Report, Pelican, 1965.
15. British Productivity Council, 'Sixteen case studies in value analysis', British Productivity Council, London, 1964.
16. Industrial Marketing Research Association, 'Regulations', IMRA, Lichfield, 1969.
17. Pearce, F. T., *The Parameters of Research*, IMRA, Lichfield, 1966.
18. Green, R. W., 'Statistical classifications – structure and development: The Government's viewpoint', *IMRA Journal* vol.7, no.4, November 1971.
19. Dening, James (ed.), *Marketing Industrial Goods*, Business Publications, 1969.

20. McIntosh, Andrew R., 'Improving the efficiency of sample surveys in industrial markets', *Journal of the Market Research Society*, vol.17, no.4, October 1975.
21. Chisnall, Peter M., 'Problems of sampling the reading habits of businessmen', *IMRA Journal*, vol.10, no.3, August 1975.
22. Atkin, Bryan, and Tore Moritz Larsen, 'Problems of sampling, interviewing and grossing procedures for large-scale representative surveys in industrial markets', in: *Sampling Problems and Data Collection*, ESOMAR, Copenhagen, May 1981.
23. Rubashow, Nicholas, 'The use of telephone interviewing in industrial market research', *IMRA Journal*, vol.8, no.1, March 1973.
24. Ryan, Michael, 'Researching business by telephone', *ADMAP*, August 1976.
25. Hansen, Robert A., Cathie Tinney, and William Rudelius, 'Increase response to industrial surveys', *Industrial Marketing Management*, vol.12, no.3, 1983.
26. Jobber, David, and Stuart Sanderson, 'The effects of a prior letter and a coloured questionnaire paper on mail survey response rates'. *Journal of Market Research Society*, vol.25, no.4, 1983.
27. Dommeyer, Curt J., 'Offering mail survey results in a lift letter', *Journal of Market Research Society*, vol.31, no.3, July 1989.
28. Industrial Marketing Research Association, *Postal Questionnaires*, IMRA, Lichfield, 1967.
29. Moser, C. A., and G. Kalton, *Survey Methods in Social Investigation*, Heinemann, London, 1971.
30. Rayne-Davis, John, 'Interaction can yield more than interviewing', *Industrial Marketing Digest*, vol.3, no.3, 1978.
31. Sampson, Peter, 'Quantitative research and motivation research', in: *Consumer Market Research Handbook*, Robert Worcester and John Downham (eds.), Van Nostrand Reinhold, Wokingham, 1978.
32. Ilsley, Charles, and John Hought, 'Researching new technological products: Visual telecommunications services', Research in the 1980s, Market Research Society Conference Papers, March 1980.
33. Carter, C. F., and B. R. Williams, 'The characteristics of technically progressive firms', *Journal of Industrial Economics*, vol.7, no.2, 1959.

THIRTEEN

INTERNATIONAL MARKETING RESEARCH

13.1 INTRODUCTION

Britain has long been a trading nation and export business is part of our national way of life; in today's competitive environment the value of a large export order is headline news. But this was not always the case, as a 1950 PEP Report[1] once indicated: 'For most exporters overseas trading is a residual interest, of much less importance to the company's progress than the home market. In addition, the standard of export marketing practice is rudimentary'.

This sharp criticism was echoed 25 years later in the BETRO Report,[2] published by the Royal Society of Arts, which focused on the export performance of 122 British companies with annual turnovers ranging from under £5 million to over £50 million, and responsible for about 25 per cent of total UK exports of manufactured goods.

The findings of BETRO are disconcerting: a general lack of a professional approach to overseas markets; a 'curious lack' of managerial logic in planning marketing strategies (one company exported to 164 countries, but 90 per cent of export sales were from only 10 per cent of these countries; general lack of awareness of the dispersion of sales (most companies were surprised to discover that a remarkably high proportion of their exports was spread over very few countries); and the ratios of British export staffs to sales were unrealistically low compared with home market activities. The Japanese appeared to be far better equipped for export selling because their ratios were reversed.

Little appears to have changed in the fundamental attitudes and behaviour of considerable sectors of British industry despite the shock-waves which have passed through the economies of the developed world. Patterns of consumption have changed both at home and abroad; impressions gathered on overseas visits of even a couple of years ago are not likely to be reliable guides in today's markets.

13.2 NEED FOR MARKETING RESEARCH

In competitive world markets, it is more important than ever to identify customers' needs and to supply products which are designed to satisfy these needs as fully as possible. The principles of marketing apply wherever a company seeks business – at home or overseas.

If products are to be accepted by customers, it is necessary, first of all, to find out what they want, and then to make some quantitative estimate of likely demand.

Before attempting to devise a marketing strategy – a method of approaching the market – some form of marketing research should be undertaken so that marketing opportunities can be evaluated and related to overall company policy.

It is likely that less will be known about overseas markets than the home market; there will be greater areas of uncertainty – 'grey' areas of undetermined risk which management should attempt to dissipate. Marketing research helps to clear away some of these uncertainties and provides additional information on which management decisions may be taken.

The type of marketing information required for successful overseas trading is basically similar to that needed for the home market. Often, however, it is more difficult to obtain reliable information about export markets, but the problem should be approached along very similar lines.

Political and Economic Planning undertook a survey,[3] on attitudes to export marketing research, among 47 firms, over a two-year period ending June 1964. Although this report is now some years old, the general behaviour it reflects is still, unfortunately, typical of many firms today.

The report commented that:

> There was a wide spread of attitudes towards the systematic surveying of export markets, just as there was towards market research at home. Only a few of the firms that were visited discounted the value of research into export markets altogether. In more of them there was a realisation that such research had been neglected but that the fault had to be rectified ... A number of the firms visited deployed their export efforts into relatively narrow fields, which were indicated by market research.[3]

For a medium-sized domestic appliance firm taking part in the survey, the first step in marketing a product overseas was a research programme concerned with 'the finding of the market, the discovery of the product that will sell, and then a great deal of discussion back at home here to see if we can produce it economically and at a profit'.

The report quotes another firm, in the wool textile industry, which 'sent a small team of men to six continental countries to make a sample survey. To reinforce the data it commissioned some continental market research agencies to furnish statistics which were not readily available.'

A medium-sized machine tool firm researched its markets thus: 'We try to collect what the potential is, what machines are actually installed in the country, the possibility of replacement, the possibility of expansion in our particular small, narrow market. Those are the figures we try to get at'.

It was reported that some managers regarded export market research as important and specialized enough to warrant their own personal attention. The chairman of a small wool textile firm said that he spent a lot of his time abroad, because in his industry expert knowledge of textiles was necessary in order to do effective market research. With his size of company, personal investigation of the market seemed far preferable to using the services of an outside researcher who would be unlikely to have the necessary technical expertise. This particular viewpoint appears to disregard the danger of bias in estimating market potential, because it would be difficult for a hopeful seller to be entirely objective in assessing the opportunities in a market.

In 1984, Gallup Poll conducted a mail survey[4] among members of the Institute of Export which revealed that of over 650 members (18.5 per cent of all members and over 40 per cent of companies belonging to the Institute) only 4 per cent actually claimed to have bought market research, but 43 per cent relied on 'market research carried out by their own firm' – which could obviously mean many different kinds of activity.

British companies were found to be seriously deficient in foreign language skills; a quarter said that there was only one in their export department who could make sense of a foreign newspaper; only 54 per cent were fluent in French, 42 per cent in German; 30 per cent in Spanish; and 17 per cent in Italian. (The BETRO Report is discussed later in this chapter.)

13.3 PRELIMINARY EVALUATION

Before committing themselves to overseas trading, companies would do well to pose themselves a few questions and to answer these as honestly as possible.

Why export? Is it because:

   (i)   of surplus capacity?
   (ii) the home market is in a no-growth phase or is saturated?
  (iii) of the pressure of home-market competition?
  (vi) of a unique product or service which has attracted substantial business in the home market and enquiries from abroad?
   (v) of special managerial experience and abilities in overseas trading?
  (vi) the grass is always greener elsewhere?
  (vii) export market opportunities are judged to be more promising than the home market?
(viii) the managing director dreams of a world-wide empire over which he can exercise corporate and personal power?

Clearly, some of these motives are less likely than others to lead to business success. Muddled thinking springs from obscure perceptions of the strengths and weaknesses of a company, so it would be constructive to attempt a relatively fundamental corporate audit based on what the company can do this year, next year and, say, in five years' time. Exporting is not an activity to be jumped into and out of; it tends to be a long-haul task before profits are being earned.

13.4 TYPICAL APPROACHES

Exporting is often started accidentally: a chance enquiry lands on the desk of the managing director and, almost reluctantly, the firm is involved in overseas business.

In other cases, companies adopt an experimental attitude, trying out, by a judicious blend of caution and verve, one or two export markets. With luck and some good judgement, their strategy might be successful, but now they are faced with bigger uncertainties as they raise their sights and aim for more difficult targets. Their fortuitous learn-as-you-go strategy will not be able to cope with the increasing complexity of the market environment.

Yet other companies scan the world, the large sectors of it, for suitable business opportunities. Particular areas are 'short-listed' for more detailed appraisal: from the macro-level to the micro-level of investigation. Research projects could be undertaken in several countries simultaneously, sequentially, or independently. 'Superficially, the simultaneous conducting of studies in several countries (or different regions within a country) would seem to be the methodologically preferred technique.'[5] However, it would be necessary to allow for seasonal factors or other special influences, such as political elections, which could distort comparative research of this nature. This carefully phased research in which detailed comparative analyses of markets are made starts with desk research.

13.5 DESK RESEARCH

Desk research is particularly important in export research; this type of research should be fully exploited before considering field research (see Chapter 2). It may well provide sufficient information for the particular decision which has to be made. It saves time and money, and is particularly valuable in giving an in-depth knowledge of markets. A good grasp of statistical data concerning overseas economies is essential; clearly, in some areas there is a shortage of reliable and readily available information. A great deal of desk research can be done in the UK, where extremely valuable information is freely available from governmental and other sources. There is no cause for would-be exporters to say that they do not trade with certain countries because they know little about them. Desk research can be done without leaving this country.

13.6 GOVERNMENT ASSISTANCE IN THE UK

The British Overseas Trade Board (initially known as the British Export Board) was formed in January 1972, to take over the work of the British National Export Council and also some of the activities formerly carried on by the Export Services Branch of the Department of Trade and Industry. It is concerned with giving directions for the development of British export activities and establishing priorities in these areas. Some of its principal ways of helping British exporters are shown below.

Export Market Information Centre*

Resources available include the following:

1. *Foreign statistical publications*: produced by both national statistical offices and international organizations covering a range of topics including trade, production, prices, employment, population and other economic data. EMIC can also undertake some searching of selected trade statistics on-line.
2. *Foreign trade directories*: including telephone directories from most countries and specialized directories covering particular sectors of industry. Please note that UK directories are *not* available.
3. *National development plans*: these are issued by many countries and most are available for loan to exporters.
4. *Mail order catalogues*.
5. *British Overseas Trade Information System* (BOTIS). BOTIS is the DTI's own data base for exporters for information on products and markets, overseas contacts, export opportunities and promotional events. This includes:
   (a) The Product Data Store (PDS) – a computerized microfilm data base of product and industry information on overseas markets. Sources include unique market reports researched by British Embassy staff. Coverage varies from country to country but falls within three broad areas of interest: market size, market structure and market share.

---

* (formerly the Statistics and Market Intelligence Library),
Department of Trade and Industry,
1–19 Victoria Street,
London SW1H 0ET
Tel: 071 215 5444/5445,
Fax: 071 215 4231,
Tlx: 8811074 DTHQ G.

(b)   The Overseas Contacts Service (OCS) – details of potential agents, distributors, importers, retailers and others supplied by British Embassies.

Also available are EMIC publications (PU), Promotional Events (PE), and Export Intelligence (EI).

Services   Coin and cash card operated photocopying and operator services are available for personal visitors to the Centre, subject to copyright regulations. The Centre is open to the public for reference only from 9.30 a.m. to 5.30 p.m. (last admissions at 5 p.m.), Monday to Friday. Students are admitted by appointment only.

The Export Intelligence Service (EIS)

This service sends export-related information to interested subscribing companies, trade associations, and other similar organizations. Its main objective is to secure export orders for British companies by bringing individual export opportunities to their attention. It also supplies market information such as changes in tariff rates and import regulations. Each subscriber is profiled to receive only those notices which are personally relevant – by commodity, overseas market, and type of notice.

Most of the information is provided by the commercial sections of UK diplomatic posts overseas, and is also gathered from the World Bank and the European Community. This information is edited, classified, and checked by the EIS, part of the Department of Trade and Industry.

Under the Government's Export Initiative, the marketing and distribution of the EIS has been contracted out to Export Opportunities Ltd, part of the Export Network Group, which provides a one-stop, dial-up information and trading service. In addition to first-class post, information can also be sent by Telex, Fax, and Electronic Mail via Prestel, One-to-One, Telecom Gold or Mercury 7500.

A modest fee is charged for each notice, according to the method of service used. All charges are payable in advance; full details available from: Export Opportunities Ltd, Export House, 87a Wembley Hill Road, Wembley, Middlesex HA9 8BU (081 900 1313).

Other services

British Business (formerly *Trade and Industry Journal*), published weekly, gives a wealth of information covering overseas markets, tariff changes, import regulations, overseas trade missions. Special market surveys, details of trade fairs and exhibitions, and other vital export data are given. It is a remarkable source of reliable and up-to-date information over world markets.

Hints to Exporters is published by the Department of Trade and Industry. This series of booklets, covering amost every export market, gives a quick overall view of countries, their trading customs, travel facilities, economic conditions, etc.

Economic surveys, published by HMSO on behalf of the Export Credits Guarantee Department, give detailed appraisals of local economic conditions in overseas markets.

Economic surveys and reports published by the United Nations and foreign governments are available through HMSO.

Other useful publications include the *Overseas Trade Bulletin*, issued fortnightly by the Confederation of British Industries. The Overseas Directorate of the CBI is divided into special geographical areas with a network of overseas representatives and contacts.

Valuable information on export markets can also be obtained from: European Community

Information Office, 8 Storey's Gate, London SW1P 3AT. Tel: 071 222 8122; and EC/EFTA Information Unit, Department of Trade and Industry, 1 Victoria Street, London SW1.

Export and import statistics, as summarized in the monthly overseas trade statistics of the UK, can be obtained from: Statistical Office (Bill of Entry Section), HM Customs and Excise, 27 Victoria Avenue, Southend-on-Sea, Essex.

Other sources of data

National Economic Development Office (NEDO)
Central Office of Information (COI), Hercules Road, London SE1.
(Publicity unit working jointly with BOTB to promote British exports.)
Foreign embassies in London
British Export Houses Association
British Standards Institution: 'Technical Help to Exporters' service.
CBI Overseas Reports issued quarterly by Confederation of British Industries.
Institute of Export (publishes *Export*)
Institute of Packaging
Institute of Directors
Chartered Institute of Marketing
Institute of Practitioners in Advertising (IPA)
London World Trade Centre, St Katherine's Dock, London E1
British joint stock banks, merchant banks, and special overseas banks with London offices (e.g.,
    Lloyds Economic Reports: Barclays Overseas Survey).
OECD: *Foreign Trade Statistics Bulletin:*
         (Series A, *Overall Trade by Countries*)
         (Series B, *Trade by Commodities Analytical Abstracts*)
         (Series C, *Trade by Commodities Market Summaries*)
         OECD Economic Outlook
         Main Economic Indicator
         National Accounts of OECD Countries 1960–1970
         OECD Financial Statistics
         Industrial Product – Historical Statistics
IMF: *International Financial Statistics*
The Corporate Intelligence Group
Euromonitor publishes 'Market Research Europe' and other reports.
EIU: *World Outlook*
Press: *The Economist, The Times, Guardian, Financial Times, Daily Telegraph*
         Quality Sunday papers
         Publishing houses, e.g., IPC
Chambers of Commerce, particularly London Chamber of Commerce, 69, Cannon Street, London EC4.
Trade Associations
Academic Institutions
ESOMAR: The European Society for Market and Opinion Research holds annual congresses, as well as special seminars, in European cities at which papers are read on many aspects of marketing and opinion research.
The Market Research Society publishes *Yearbook* giving details of organizations providing overseas (and other) research services; it also publishes *International Directory of Market Research Organizations*, and *Country Notes* offering background information on a wide range of countries in Western Europe, the Far East, and also North America.

International Directory of Published Market Research (BOTB in association with Research and Financial Management Ltd).

UN: *Yearbook of International Trade Statistics*
        World Trade Annual (5 volumes)
        Commodity Trade Statistics
        World Economic Survey
        Yearbook of National Accounts Statistics

On-line services such as *Kompass* and *Key Note* offer extensive coverage of data about overseas companies.

The Patents Office on-line patent search services (see Chapter 2) offers valuable, specific services to exporters.

Export Credits Guarantee Department (ECGD): This government department provides extremely valuable assistance to British exporters through insurance against the major financial risks involved in exporting. Policies are far reaching and give exporters a substantial measure of financial protection against losses arising from insolvency or protracted default of buyers, import licensing and exchange control restrictions, war, and civil war in the buyer's country. Rates vary according to individual markets and the risks involved. Details are obtained from: Export Credits Guarantee Department, Aldermanbury House, Aldermanbury, London EC2, and regional offices.

Research Organizations: Professional advice on export marketing research is obtainable from organizations such as:

1. The European Association for Industrial Marketing Research (EVAF), which can supply a comprehensive list of consultants or companies in Western Europe who are able to undertake industrial marketing research.
2. The Market Research Society, 15 Northburgh Street, London EC1V 0AH.
3. The Industrial Marketing Research Association, 11 Bird Street, Lichfield, WS13 6PW.
4. The British Overseas Trade Board would be prepared to give advice to firms seeking marketing research services.

When the examination of basic data suggests that a particular market may be of value to a marketer, the next step is to make a personal visit to that market. Discussions can be held with potential buyers and distributors, and with embassy officials.

Because marketing is concerned with fitting products to markets, the proposed product should be carefully examined in relation to the special requirements of individual overseas markets. Some factors will have special significance for certain products; the impact of duties and taxes, trade quotas, food and drug legislation, safety regulations, e.g., electrical appliance safety standards, American car safety regulations, labelling and packaging regulations, climatic conditions, etc.

13.7 SCOPE OF INVESTIGATIONS

Investigations into overseas markets should be thorough. As indicated in Fig. 13.1, three principal areas require detailed attention. These are not, of course, watertight, isolated influences: they are interrelated and precise measurement, for example of social trends, is not always feasible or even necessary.

Economic and politico-cultural factors

Economic factors will include the nature and size of market demand. Although population size is obviously of interest, it may not necessarily indicate the potential value of a market. Some

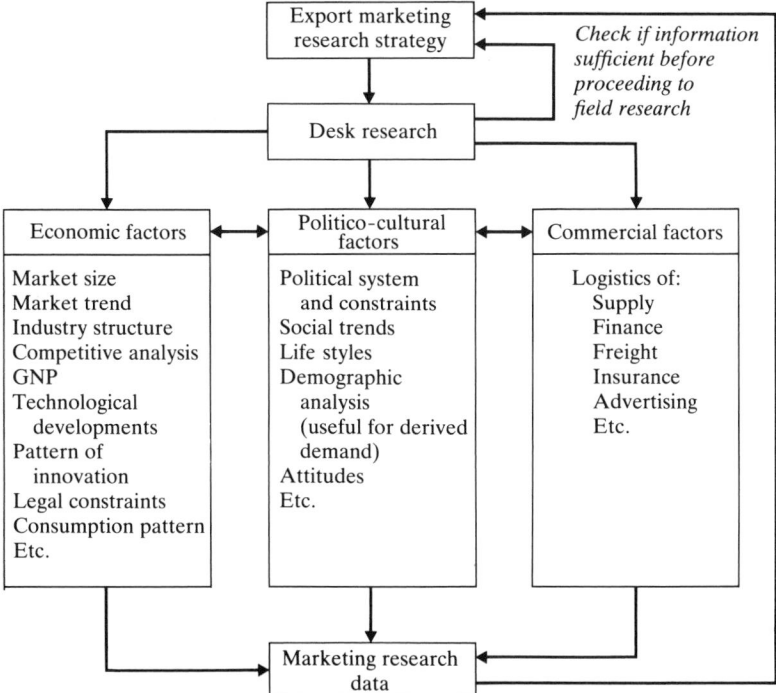

Fig. 13.1   Scope of export marketing research

smaller countries, e.g. Sweden, have high purchasing power and are particularly strong markets for certain types of products, e.g., those having a strong design element.

Enquiries would also be concerned with evaluating the nature of competition which may vary significantly over markets. Exporters sometimes overlook the fact that when they enter an overseas market, they are in competition not just with foreign-based competitors, but are also likely to face stiff competition from indigenous suppliers. Market shares should be analysed to discover what particular segments are of greatest interest. These findings should then be related to marketing proposals.

Countries should be rated for their potential market opportunities based, usually, on gross national product *per capita*. If this criterion is adopted, three main segments of world markets emerge: (i) industrialized countries (ICs); (ii) developing countries (DCs); (iii) less developed countries (LDCs). The DC segment accounts for 19 per cent of the population and 32 per cent of the income of the world, and because growth rates of income are outpacing those of the IC segment, it is suggested[6] that these developing economies present particularly attractive business opportunities.

Politico-cultural factors, like economic factors, also cover a wide spectrum of market influences. Market researchers should endeavour to understand the social and cultural behaviour of consumers in those countries they plan to enter.

> It is important to investigate consumers' attitudes towards the product which it is proposed to market in their country; how frequently they buy: their brand loyalty; their price sensitivity; their spending power and pattern of spending. It is also necessary to know population trends – the birth/death pattern – and also the available education and welfare services. A growing community with increased spending power and rising standards of living will obviously offer valuable opportunities to marketers.

The importance of understanding cultural aspects of consumption is illustrated by a *Reader's Digest* study[5] which shows that French and German customers consume more spaghetti than Italians. This bizarre finding resulted from a survey question which asked about packaged branded spaghetti. In Italy this product is sold loose and unbranded, whereas in Germany and France it is usually sold in branded packs. The survey findings were valid but did not give the information that was needed.

Another example[7] of misleading research occurred in a survey which indicated that *per capita* consumption of bananas in Germany was double that of the UK. Enquiries about this unusual pattern of consumption revealed the more relevant information that in terms of numbers the *per capita* consumption figures were virtually identical; the significant difference lay in the fact that bananas imported from the Caribbean into the UK tended to be much smaller than those sold to Germany.

In the US and the UK hot, milk-based drinks are marketed principally as bedtime drinks, but in much of Latin America a hot milk drink like *chocolate caliente* is a 'morning drink' or perceived as a 'nice way to start the day'. Also, the popularity of Coca-Cola as a 'morning drink' with American college students would sound appalling to a Latin American accustomed to his *café con leche* for breakfast.[8]

Market analysts should beware of broad classifications of countries or regions which may suggest that the economic, political, and social environment is practically identical. For example, it has been stated[9] that the Middle East is not a homogeneous market with similar political philosophies, economic state of development, language, and culture. 'Too often the term "Middle East" is considered to be synonymous with "Arab"', whereas 'Iran is non-Arab and has the Farsi language'. On the other hand, Arab countries penetrate deeply into Africa and now total 20 countries, such as Sudan and Somalia.

Parts of Europe are highly industrialized with large urban populations and substantial spending power. Other parts are still developing, and in some areas the level of economic activity is low. Research into such markets cannot assume that some homogeneous pattern of European buying behaviour exists; broad generalizations about national characteristics are equally misleading. Western Europe has 17 states with 12 major languages which have distinctive differences with national boundaries. The EC cannot be viewed as an entity; it is a fairly loose confederation of nearly 300 million people of several nationalities, languages, cultures, and sub-cultures.

In developing countries, researchers have found that diversity is a singular characteristic:

> Within the same market one may find incredibly rich people with all imaginable luxuries and others so poor they have to pawn their meagre belongings in order to buy the basic essentials. ... Concepts of value for money can be meaningless either if money is inexhaustible or when branded products cost more than the housewife ever has in her pocket.[10]

Latin America has been described[8] as a heterogeneous composite of societies, cultures, and economies, with no particular region in a country representative of that country, let alone the whole of Latin America. With a population totalling about one-tenth of the world's population, and vast stocks of mineral, agricultural, and labour resources, the Latin American markets 'have just started to unleash their enormous growth potential'.[8] Four countries: Brazil, Mexico, Argentina, and Venezuela account for about 65 per cent of Latin America's total population and 75 per cent of its total GNP. Within these communities there are two distinct socio-economic groupings: very high, and very low, with 'no appreciable middle class as yet. Marketing researchers hope to contend with not a single market but with dual markets'.[8]

Cultural differences such as local holidays and other events are also likely to affect marketing research operations ... 'virtually no productive activity transpires in Brazil three weeks before or after the carnival'.[8] Eating habits may change radically during the fasting period of Ramadan in Muslim communities.[10]

The size of population and its distribution are also factors to be checked in a market evaluation. Kuwait, Oman, and the United Arab Emirates, for instance, have large oil assets but small populations so that *per capita* income is extraordinarily high, though their general level of economic and cultural development is unevenly dispersed.

Cultural role differences also affect the pattern of decision making as was found[11] with patent medicines in Saudi Arabia, for which the husband rather than the wife will invariably shop.

In upper-income households in Latin America, daily food purchases are bought by the maids; this fact was belatedly discovered by researchers who originally questioned affluent housewives who were found to know very little about buying food for their families.[8]

Linguistic differences influenced the brand name for household aluminium foil which was researched[12] in Germany, Belgium, and Italy for Alusuisse.

Switzerland has four national languages – French, Italian, German, and Rumantsch, a minority language probably used by about 50 000 inhabitants. However, English is widely adopted in business circles and among young people. 'Indeed, English is being used increasingly as a means of communication between Swiss whose native tongue differs.'[13]

In modern Spain there are many languages and dialects. 'Spain is not one homogeneous, single nation but a political unity created out of four distinct regions: the Basque country, Catalunya, Galicia, and the remainder.'[14] While Spanish ('Castellano', to give it its correct title) is the official language of the nation, three other languages are used, including Catalan which, after being proscribed for years by France, is now experiencing a rapid revival in the prosperous region of Catalunya, of which Barcelona is the thriving capital.

In developing countries, language problems may be particularly difficult, where several languages or dialects may be spoken within one country or area, as in Singapore, where Mandarin, Hokkien, Cantonese, Malay, Tamil, and English are spoken, apart from many dialects. 'India has 16 totally different languages, with 1652 known dialects.'[10]

Education is important in influencing consumers' behaviour; growing literacy will widen the market, and tend to increase the demand for products of better design and appearance. The relative stage of educational development will suggest opportunities for products of differing levels of sophistication. Research should aim to identify the potential market in *qualitative* as well as quantitative terms.

In developing countries the extent of Westernization should be assessed, since this will give impetus to products like fashion clothing and Scotch whisky, which are perceived as reflecting sophisticated life styles.

Ethnic differences, as in the US, may influence patterns of consumption and present opportunities for products with specific appeal to these sub-cultural sectors of the community.

In developing countries, there are often major ethnic divisions which pose problems for researchers. For example, only just over half of the population of Malaysia is racially Malay; 35 per cent are Chinese, who are a majority in urban areas; there is also a sizeable Indian minority. Research designs would need, therefore, to take account of these strata because of significant differences in behaviour and attitudes. While Singapore has the same ethnic groups, 'the Chinese predominate to the extent that research may sometimes confine itself to this one group for reasons of cost effectiveness'.[10]

Another important aspect of ethnic influence in research relates to interviewers who, in some cases, may have to be from the same ethnic groups as respondents in order to avoid racial or tribal antipathies. It would also be important to check that local researchers are really familiar with the consumption habits of consumers in social groups other than their own, which is likely to be superior to many of their respondents.[10]

Cultural norms are vital factors in consumption and religious beliefs and practices cannot be ignored by researchers in, for example, strict Muslim communities. Ingenuity is often needed to overcome the problems of research, for instance, in Saudi Arabia 'where women are needed to interview women, yet females are not permitted to work in situations where they might come into contact with males. Furthermore, men are protective of their womenfolk and suspicious of outsiders – they may try to prevent an interview or insist on being the respondent themselves'.[10] David Aldridge[10] has advised that it is important to use the services of 'a knowledgeable and influential local partner' in this type of research.

Careful examination should be made of the likely impact on trade of political developments in particular countries. (Parts of South America are particularly vulnerable.) Trade is more likely to develop where political stability is evident; this assists future planning. Economic factors are often closely linked with political decisions. Devaluation may be important: the state of the currency may be fluid; rates of exchange may fluctuate considerably, e.g., floating exchanges. The overall politico-economic situation existing in a specific market should be compared with the position in other potential markets, and the risks involved rated accordingly. The general level of trade needs attention: is the economy expanding, contracting, or static? What is the level of trade confidence and the incidence of bad debts?

Commercial factors

Research should endeavour to find out how the overall sales of a specific product or range of products are distributed. What kinds of people buy the product, and what differences exist among the products at present on sale. Is there an identifiable segmentation of the market over age and social groups, and, if so, what are the principal brands in these areas – their market shares? Do products have specific appeals to regional tastes – and how significant are these in developing sales? What is the general trend in that product market, and how is this related to the movement in special segments which may be of interest?

The development of modern methods of retail distribution, for example, hypermarkets in France, has affected significantly standards of negotiation between manufacturers and retailers because of concentrated buying power. The most effective method of distribution should be identified, and costs worked out – discounts, special allowances, transport costs, etc. Speed of movement through distributing channels may be important. Related to this is the type and style of packaging. Feasibility studies of container shipments, roll on–roll off, or air freight, might be advisable. Publicity services should also be investigated. What media are available and at what cost? Commercial television, for example, is not available in every European country, and in some African countries the cinema is an influential method of publicity. France has no actual papers on the British model, while in West Germany only three papers could be classified as national. What methods of publicity are used by existing suppliers to the market? Some study should be made of the principal languages – and the relative importance of these – within specific markets. For example, Belgium, where French and Flemish are in daily use. As far back as 1950, PEP emphasized that:

> The investigator must possess a detailed knowledge of the foreign territory and the social conditions that will govern this work. The size of the area, climate, language, social structure, political conditions, religious prejudices, education, affect his every move from deciding the number of breakdowns in the sample to the number and wording of the questions and, perhaps most of all, the organisation of the fieldwork.
>
> ...A consumer survey in Switzerland involves a threefold racial breakdown and a questionnaire in three languages. In Egypt, it might be necessary to employ Copts, Jews, and Muslems as interviewers and questionnaires in Arabic, French, and English. In India, areas of homogeneous culture are likely to be more significant than administrative boundaries. In South Africa, when it is necessary to use Afrikaans, the wording of questions will be governed by the limitations of that language[1]

Every element in marketing – price, packaging, publicity, distribution, terms of payment, etc. – should be carefully identified and analysed so that a company is in possession of the full facts.

Some form of rating scale could be used as a convenient method of assessing an individual company's position relative to existing suppliers. This should be done as objectively as possible, and a company should be ready to accept that its own product may have features which are less attractive than competitive products. Systematic, objective analysis and comparison form the basic approach to evaluating marketing opportunities, wherever they may occur.

The rate of re-purchase of particular products will also be of vital interest to prospective exporters. Another critical factor is the average life-span of the product which it is proposed to market. Is it, for instance, likely to be affected by some developing technology in the next five years or so? The level of market infiltration of the particular product is also of concern, and some assessment should be made of the possibility of saturation in the next few years.

13.8 BETRO REPORT ON FOREIGN LANGUAGE PROFICIENCY

The critical contribution of foreign language proficiency to export performance was evaluated in another BETRO Report[15] published in September 1979. This survey, undertaken by the PE Consulting Group for the BETRO Trust, interviewed 200 leading British exporters representing the main categories of both manufacturing industry and the services sector of the economy.

The report accepted that many factors are involved in export success, that it was difficult to isolate these, and that strict statistical measurement was not feasible. However, there was evidence that the most successful exporting firms attached great significance to foreign language proficiency. Queen's Award winners, in particular, paid special attention to linguistic coverage, and employed 90 per cent of the language graduates involved in exporting in the sub-sample of manufacturing industries.

However, almost two-thirds of all respondents did not favour language graduates for export sales departments. The general view was that their specific academic training was too theoretical and literature based. Emphasis was placed on recruiting staff with business skills who could acquire a reasonable level of language facility.

About 60 per cent of all companies surveyed regarded foreign language ability as of 'considerable advantage' to their salesforce. Only 62 per cent of export directors and 57 per cent of sales managers in manufacturing industry had 'some linguistic ability', but merely 30 per cent of all export personnel and 42 per cent of export salespeople had some foreign language facility.

Almost 80 per cent of firms used local agents in one or more of their export markets, and although most agents spoke good English, about two-thirds of respondents thought that in certain countries it was essential for export sales staff to speak the local agent's language. About three-quarters of the firms interviewed produced sales literature in foreign languages.

The BETRO Report[15] concluded that some complacency still existed because of the widespread use of English as a commercial langugae. The perceived need for linguistic skills may be obscured because of past business successes. A greater effort by the whole educational system aimed at developing commercial expertise in foreign languages should be made. The outstandingly successful records of Queen's Award winners clearly point the way.

13.9 RESEARCH METHODOLOGY

Desk research, already discussed, will have been the first step before making any other commitments. As indicated in Chapter 2, statistics from some overseas governments and other sources tend to be less reliable than others and discretion is needed when handling them. 'Of the 45 states that make up sub-Saharan Africa, barely a handful have reliable national statistics. Many of the figures about Africa are little better than guesses.'[16] The quality of statistical data varies, therefore, markedly and experienced market researchers evaluate available secondary data for validity and reliability.

Sampling tends to be more complicated in overseas marketing research. It may be difficult, or even impossible, to obtain reliable sampling frames for random sampling techniques. Experienced judgement may have to be the basis for constructing a sample in countries where social and economic data are sparse. The accepted practice of marketing research cannot always be directly transferred to some overseas markets, and data may have to be collected by less formalized methods. Free samples, small gifts, and free lottery tickets have been used to attract cooperation in some economically under-developed countries.

Sampling methods vary from country to country; also, the meaning of 'random' is widely interpreted. 'Whereas in the UK random probability samples are used mainly for quality studies in which a high degree of precision is required, on the continent quota samples are frequently recommended as preferable and/or as accurate.'[17]

The lack of reliable sampling frames in Latin America has led to the widespread adoption of quota or convenience sampling (see Chapter 4). Because quota sampling procedures vary considerably in different Latin American countries, the comparability of the data is severely affected. 'For example, a research agency in one country may select their respondents by a quota sample of housing units, while one agency in another Latin American country may use a quota sample in a shopping area.'[8]

Response rates to mail surveys are also very variable, as an analysis[11] of the 1978, 1980, and 1982 European Businessman Surveys indicated:

Average response rate: UK, Germany, Switzerland.
Better than average: Finland, Sweden, Netherlands, Norway, Denmark, Ireland.
Marginally worse than average: France, Austria, Italy.
Significantly worse than average: Spain, Belgium, Greece.

The opportunities for mail surveys will obviously be restricted by the availability of efficient mail services in particular countries under survey.

Telephone rentals are likely to be inadequate sampling frames in many developing countries. Even in Venezuela, one of the more developed countries of Latin America, average telephone ownership is around 6 per cent of homes. Another problem is that telephone listings 'cannot even be used as an adequate sampling frame for the wealthier segments of the market because in many Latin American countries telephones are listed under the name of the owner but possessed by others'.[8] This applies particularly to Brazil, where a telephone line costs from $2000 for initial service. Hence, the relative scarcity and the investment value of these lines have resulted in a secondary market in which telephones are traded; some individuals may own up to four or five telephones. A further drawback in Latin America to telephone surveys is the high refusal rate (30–50 per cent), because of the marked suspicion of strangers. This is particularly evident with women, and this problem is also experienced in personal interviewing, particularly in affluent homes where the maid tends to act as a 'gatekeeper'. It is observed[18] that in the Middle East, where interviewers are invariably male, interviews with housewives often have to be conducted in the evenings when husbands are present.

Because of the significant problems encountered in contacting representative samples of respondents and of ensuring the consistent quality of interviews in extensive market research enquiries in Europe, an experienced researcher[19] experimented with central location telephone interviewing in Switzerland during 1981. At that time, this agency were already operating a CATI system of interviewing (see Chapter 6). The pilot scheme proved a success, and ' ... at the present time, we are operating in the whole of Europe from two central location units in Morges near Lausanne with 30 work stations'.[19] As a result of this experience, the agency now routinely considers whether each assignment received by it could be carried out by telephone. The interviewers/operators are grouped in seven different teams speaking different languages, covering English, French, German, Swiss-German dialect, Italian, Dutch, Swedish, and Spanish. Interviews vary between 5 and 45 minutes: 'the quantity of information a well-trained telephone operator can collect in 10 minutes is fabulous, since there are almost no pauses in interviewing'.[19]

The Harris Research Centre runs a centralized international telephone system which provides fully controlled and computerized research at a pan-European level and beyond for the leading multi-nationals.

Several research organizations offer continuous marketing research services in overseas markets; these tend to focus on specific groups such as air travellers in Europe and Asia, consumer financial services panel (US), wines and spirits, cosmetics, and branded confectionery. Omnibus surveys (see Chapter 9) are also conducted by several UK-based market research agencies such as Mass Observation which runs a monthly telephone omnibus of consumers and business sectors in Europe.

Gallup also offers a Europe Omnibus survey which, apart from August, is run monthly with 1000 nationally representative respondents in all European countries. Information is gathered by face-to-face interviewing or, where quick results are vital, by 500 telephone interviews each month. The Gallup service can provide tracking studies of international advertising campaigns, brand monitoring, cross-cultural consumption habits, and harmonized demographic data.

Questionnaires, as indicated in Chapter 6, need care in drafting; this is particularly so in the case of overseas surveys. Literal translation would obviously be totally wrong, and expert local knowledge in drafting questionnaires is vital to ensure that they will be acceptable and effective. In some cases, pictorial methods, e.g., the barometer, have been particularly valuable in assessing consumer response, and some ingenuity should be used in designing suitable diagrams. (Details of these methods are given in Chapter 8.)

Multi-country surveys obviously require expert attention to questionnaire construction. Gallup's London office, for example, pilots such enquiries in the UK, and the revised final questionnaire is then sent to the other interested countries for translation and further piloting if this is considered desirable. Translated questionnaires, together with any comments, are returned to London where re-translation into English takes place. These are then checked against the original questionnaire and if any divergencies have occurred, corrections are made. Any changes to take account of local conditions in particular markets are made at this stage, and the translations are then agreed with clients.

The analysis required by clients is compared with the questionnaire to ensure that the correct type of data results.

Coding instructions, to agreed standards, are given by London to affiliate research companies. Punching and tabulation are also controlled by London and processing is by computer in the UK.

The A. C. Nielsen organization operates its well-known research techniques in about 20 countries through a network of locally based companies. These cover the principal European countries, the US, Canada, Australia, New Zealand, and Japan. The Nielsen Retail Indexes are available in many overseas markets, and coordinated programmes can be arranged. (For details of the Nielsen service see Chapter 9.)

The Market Research Bureau develops a master questionnaire in London, local agencies then translate it, and MRB linguist executives visit these to brief agency teams and check translations. Final questionnaires are validated at pilot interviews in each country in the presence of an MRB executive. Local agencies code and edit questionnaires; these are then processed on to punched cards locally or in London; final checks and card clearing are carried out in London. Data are analysed in London to agreed specifications.

MRB also organizes group discussions and industrial surveys on the same basic principles:

survey design and planning in London, fieldwork by MRB executives or by linguist freelance researchers of known competence; all analysis and report preparation by MRB executive staff.

ACORN in Europe

As noted in Chapter 11, ACORN segmentation, based on census data, is widely adopted in the UK and in the US, particularly for direct marketing, financial services, and in the planning of retail outlets – SITE system. This census-based marketing service is now extended to France, Sweden, Norway, and Finland.

The French version is based on 300 000 *Ilots* (census areas) with 12 ACORN groups (A–L) and 90 ACORN types, which include, for instance, major wine growing and fruit farming areas (B5), Algerian ghettos with poor housing conditions (G18), and traditional high-status suburbs for professional people (L38).

At present the lack of cross-reference between the census data and post codes, has tended to retard the development of ACORN in France. However, the extremely detailed nature of French census data has enabled very accurate information to be available for retailers serving local shopping areas.

Swedish ACORN has nine groups and 28 types, based on the 4700 postal districts, and includes small but smart city flats (A1), farming and fishing areas (I28), and divided houses; young and old people (A2). A distinct division of population is observable: the rich live in the big towns and the poor in rural areas.

In developing ACORN in Europe, CACI found that, despite the EC, differences between the member countries remain very marked and considerable care had to be taken to ensure that each national ACORN reflected these differences.

Euro-demographics

Socio-economic classification in the UK, discussed in Chapters 4 and 11, is obviously a complex matter with which market and social researchers are closely involved. The International Committee of the Market Research Society[20] deliberated long on the problems, and possible solutions, of social grading over European countries. It was noted that the French agency ISL had based gradings on cumulative frequency of the ownership of specific household facilities in 1965, as follows:

1965	*1987*
running water (80%)	telephone (90%)
inside toilet	car
hot water	car radio
shower/bath	credit card
telephone (12%)	dishwasher
	2+ cars
	computer (8%)

The 1965 listing makes an interesting comparison with the 1987 listing of durables indicating a family's wealth or standing. Obviously, the dynamic nature of the lists renders comparability over time virtually impossible.

The International Committee reported that the single criterion, 'Occupation of head of household' is unique to the UK; France, Germany, and Italy basing their social grading on three dimensions (differing in all instances) while Spain uses two. In an attempt to clarify European demographic approaches, ESOMAR, in 1980, set up a working party[21] to deal with the harmonization of demographics; a substantial part of their time was devoted to the problem of 'defining, and working with, social class'[20] which was found to have widely different meanings across the countries they studied. Eventually, ESOMAR published a Pan European demographic scale largely based on the level of education and the nature of current employment.

Pan European Survey

Research Services Ltd of Wembley, in conjunction with 11 European research companies, conducted a detailed survey[22] of media habits among high-status professional and business men in Europe; this 1984 Pan European Survey was the third of its kind and was sponsored by *The Economist, International Herald Tribune, Newsweek International, Scientific American*, and *Time*. The following European countries were covered: Belgium, France, Germany, Great Britain, Irish Republic, Italy, Netherlands, Norway, Spain, Sweden, and Switzerland; basic readership figures for 258 publications were collected; 7270 interviews were effected; and a remarkable overall response rate of 55 per cent was achieved.

The population was defined as economically active men aged 25 and over who have achieved high status educationally or professionally, or who have a specified income (income levels were specified for each country).

A two-stage probability sample was used in each country (see Chapter 4); from a representative national sample of all eligible men, the addresses of 30–40 per cent were discarded, since they lived in areas with the lowest concentrations of eligible respondents. The residual (60–70 per cent) addresses generated the first sampling points, and at each point a prescribed constant number of interviews was set for completion with eligible men. They were screened from all men in consecutive addresses on a predetermined route from the starting address.

Face-to-face interviews, lasting about 50 minutes, took place in the homes of eligible respondents; trained interviewers used the mother tongue of the respondents. Questionnaires were translated for use in each country; the publications listed in questionnaires were selected from those with readership profiles of high-status men. The list of titles appeared in the same order on questionnaires, but the order in which groups of publications (daily, weekly, fortnightly, bi-monthly, and monthly) appeared was rotated so as to minimize the general order effects of reduced levels of claimed readership for titles near the end of lists (see Chapter 6).

Income data were grouped into four broad categories as follows:

	Income code position	Approx. $US value during fieldwork
Lower	A,B,C	Up to $17 500
Medium	D,E	$17 500–$25 000
Upper	F,G	$25 000–$35 000
High	H,I,J,K,L	$35 000 or more

The three groups 'Lower', 'Medium', 'Upper and High' divide the sample into three approximately equal groups.

Income was defined as 'your own personal income before tax', and expressed on a showcard in the currency of the survey country. The 12 points of the income scale (A–L) were approximately similar for all countries at the beginning of the fieldwork, allowing for rounding and exchange rate fluctuations.

The administration of this extensive survey and the British fieldwork were undertaken by Research Services Ltd, whose associated companies conducted the fieldwork in the other countries. Editing, coding, and preparation of all materials, including questionnaires, were carried out by Research Services Ltd.

Results were weighted to restore the achieved sample of accepted interviews to the survey design of equal numbers of eligible men at each sampling point; the design called for a constant eight interviews per survey cluster and in a few cases this could not be achieved. The second weighting stage grossed the weighted results for each country to the universe of eligible men in high-status areas within each country.

The new Europe

The dismantlement of internal barriers to trade throughout the European Community by 1992 presents companies with challenging opportunities and, of course, problems. Levels of competition will be raised; home suppliers will have to face increasingly stiff competition from external suppliers of goods and services, as well as finding their overseas markets under potential threat. The impact of a multi-country single market will not be equally felt over industries or countries; it will be particularly important for technologically advanced industries, such as electronics.

Globalization of products already exists in some consumer markets and is increasingly evident: e.g., teenage fashions, jeans, fast-food outlets and sports equipment, but it would be naïve to assume that a 'single European market' will mean identical consumer tastes or habits. These will still need to be researched carefully:

> Shovels, even if the same sort of muck is shovelled with them, are quite differently shaped depending whether you buy them in Italy, Holland, or England. But in all these countries people use the same modern motor diggers. Meat has been butchered differently in different European countries for ages; you couldn't sell an Irish cut of meat in Germany. But the whole of Europe has embraced the Hamburger recently introduced from America.[23]

A study by Hill Samuel for the Confederation of British Industry's 1992 information campaign[24] listed several examples of cultural differences which led to market fragmentation. 'Cultural barriers will persist long after other forms of invisible trade walls have been demolished.' Increased mobility reduces the impact of some cultural inhibitions but it does not destroy the whole intricate structure of cultural and sub-cultural preferences. How soon the French will be willing to load their washing machines from the front (like the British) or demand firmly machines that load from the top is open to speculation.

Food manufacturers, such as Nescafé, are well aware of strong regional tastes; Nescafé, for instance, markets 20 different versions of its product under the same label. A 'single market' by no means implies that a single taste will be acceptable. The prospects for a pan European culture are enthusiastically debated; satellite television networks and radio transmissions will clearly influence consumption habits, but technological innovations are not immune to social and cultural preferences. New electronic-based systems of data collection and retrieval will span the whole community of Europe, but will freezer centres become popular in Germany?

Market knowledge involves knowing about the *reasons* why people buy (or do not) and not just counting what they buy. Professional market research will continue to be a vital function in overseas trading success; markets are made up of people, and their varying needs, personal, professional and organizational, must still be objectively studied and understood.

The future structure of European trade and commerce is shaping up and various, sometimes conflicting, views are being projected. Drucker[25] believes 'almost certainly' that the Europe of tomorrow 'will be both an economy of competing European businesses – in that respect it will look quite different from the "common market" of the United States. But which industry and which market will go which way?'

13.10 PRINCIPAL METHODS OF ORGANIZING RESEARCH

Research for export marketing can be undertaken in various ways, and a brief outline of the principal methods will now be considered:

1. *Using own staff or importing agents*
   (a) The first objection to this method is probably lack of objectivity; sales staff are usually incapable of giving an unbiased estimate of their products' likelihood of success.
   (b) The second objection is that the agents may have other interests which prevent them from giving an objective assessment of the market.
   (c) Research is a specialist's job which requires particular training and experience.
   (d) This method may, perhaps, be the only feasible way of researching in some 'backward' markets.
2. *Using research agencies in overseas markets*
   (a) Selection of these can be difficult and risky.
   (b) Where several markets are involved, multiple agencies may have to be used to cover the whole export programme.
   (c) A big advantage is that national research organizations should possess intimate knowledge of their own home market.
3. *Using a marketing research organization based in the UK plus the services of a locally based research firm*
   (a) This method is rather cumbersome and offers few advantages over method 2.
   (b) It could be useful where manufacturers had no trained research staff (often the case in smaller companies).
4. *Using the services of a consortium of research agencies*
   (a) Superficially attractive, but member firms may vary considerably in the quality of their services.
   (b) Closely related to this method is that of an international research organization linked with advertising agencies over principal markets. This is generally effective.

Several of the larger marketing research organizations, e.g., Gallup, BMRB via its sister company MRBI, and Research Services Ltd, have already been quoted as active in multi-country research. These, and other, highly experienced companies are able to handle complex and far-ranging market investigations.

IFT Research, part of the Gordon Simmons Group, typifies a UK-based marketing research firm which is very active internationally, with research projects covering virtually all Western European countries, North America, the Middle and Far East, Latin America, Southern Africa, and Australia. Some of these projects involve up to 15 countries simultaneously. Planning and questionnaire design are undertaken in the UK and also data processing and report writing, fieldwork for which is carried out by locally based firms. Overseas agencies are also usually responsible for sampling, translation, and interviewing.

Desk research projects are often undertaken direct from the UK; in some cases, telephone interviews may also be done from the UK using the services of interviewers fluent in the leading European languages.

13.11 APPRAISAL OF OPPORTUNITIES

The markets studied in desk and field research should now be related to company resources – finance, production, labour, distribution.

Particular marketing opportunities should be isolated and their implications studied, both long and short term. Following this evaluation, a series of decisions should then be made. Briefly, the areas of decision making cover:

Whether   should we sell overseas?
Where   in what market(s)?
When   at what time should we start?
How   method of operation?

In reviewing opportunities abroad it would be wise for a company to spread its risks, so that it does not become too dependent on one or two large markets, which could, through political or economic circumstances, suddenly decline, e.g., the American protectionist policy of 1971.

13.12 ORGANIZATION OF OVERSEAS OPERATION

The following factors need to be carefully considered:

1. Production:
   (a) Direct export.
   (b) Licensing arrangements.
   (c) Build new factory overseas.
   (d) Joint venture with foreign company.
2. Distribution:
   (a) Direct marketing.
   (b) Stockist–distributor network.
   (c) Agencies:
       (i) exclusive.
       (ii) shared.

The type of product may largely determine its method of sale; capital goods requiring long negotiation and special after-sales service are obviously different from low priced 'quick-repeat' consumer products, and different methods of marketing will apply.

The type of distribution must also be decided. For example, whether sales should be exclusively through selected large stores in major cities and towns by direct selling from the manufacturer's head office, or, alternatively, whether distribution should be via the sales force of the local distributor, who may be expected to hold reasonable stocks for quick delivery. Manufacturers may prefer to set up their own sales offices in major centres and control the marketing operation in this way.

Some large international companies divide their marketing activities into 'zones', with a distribution network controlled by the 'zone' company.

The form of organization adopted will depend upon individual companies, their resources, products, objectives, and the characteristics of the market they plan to enter. As markets develop, new organizational structures may be necessary, to give flexibility to local companies operating in different environments.

Whatever system of overseas organization is adopted, rigidity should be avoided and remote control should not be allowed to frustrate marketing opportunities. Although modern travel encourages head office staff to visit overseas markets regularly, and on special missions, constant intervention will not develop in local marketing staff their personal responsibility for the success of the agreed marketing strategy in their area. Overseas staff should be selected not only for their technical knowledge but also for their commercial abilities. If the right people are appointed, they should be given the opportunity of developing management judgement in their particular sphere of operations. Tactical decisions should largely be left to them within, of course, the framework of the company's policy.

13.13 SUMMARY

Overseas marketing research has grown in importance with the development of export markets which demand expert knowledge of commercial, industrial, economic, political, cultural, and demographic factors affecting buying behaviour, both industrial and consumer.

Exporting is often entered into accidentally; at the other extreme are those companies which deliberately scan the world for growth opportunities.

As with home market research, desk research is the starting point for finding out about overseas markets; there are many sources of information available to prospective exporters.

Research methodology at the primary level will be likely to be more complicated than in Britain; sampling frames, for example, may not be available or may be very unreliable in some countries, so random sampling may be impossible. Telephone and mail surveys obviously depend on the availability of efficient mail and telephone services; many developing countries do not have these.

Interviewing techniques may have to be modified to suit cultural inhibitions. Questionnaires need expert drafting and translation.

Various methods of organizing marketing research can be adopted: from using own staff to sophisticated systems of research agencies in consortia.

Standards of marketing research should always be kept high to ensure that the resultant data are valid and reliable for management decision making.

REFERENCES

1. Political and Economic Planning, 'Sample surveys – Part One', PEP Report, vol. 16, no. 313, May 1950.
2. Royal Society of Arts, 'Concentration on key markets', BETRO Report, 1975.
3. Gater, Anthony, David Insull, Harold Lind, and Peter Seglow, 'Attitudes in British management', PEP Report, Pelican, 1965.
4. Heald, Gordon, and Elizabeth Stodel, 'UK exporters – no use for market research?' *MRS Newsletter*, no. 219, June 1984.
5. Mayer, Charles S., 'Multinational marketing research: The magnifying glass of methodological problems', *European Research*, vol. 6, no. 2, March 1978.
6. Weber, John G., 'Worldwide strategies for market segmentation', *Columbia Journal of World Business*, vol. IX, no. 4, winter 1974.
7. Majaro, Simon, *International Marketing*, Allen & Unwin, London, 1982.
8. Stanton, John L., Rajan Chandran, and Sigfredo A. Hernandez, 'Marketing research problems in Latin America', *Journal of Market Research Society*, vol. 24, no. 2, 1982.
9. Upshaw, Douglas N., 'Organising to sell to Middle East markets', *Conference Board Record*, vol. 13, no. 2, February 1976.
10. Aldridge, David, 'Highly developed research in less-developed countries', ICE/ESOMAR Symposium, Paris, 26/28 November 1984.
11. Dickens, Jackie, and David Aldridge, 'Does co-ordination of international qualitative research bring creativity?', ESOMAR Conference, 1974.
12. Chisnall, Peter M., 'Aluminium foil in the Common Market: Research for an effective brand name', *Journal of Management Studies*, vol. 11, no. 3, October 1974.
13. Baumer-Burton, Helen, Editorial, *Swiss Business*, September/October 1990.
14. Swift, J. S., 'Language as a facet of distance in UK firms' interactions with the Spanish Market', unpublished MSc Dissertation, Manchester School of Management, UMIST, 1989.

15. BETRO Trust, 'Languages and export performance', Royal Society of Arts, September 1979.
16. Holman, Michael, 'An uncharted crisis', *Financial Times*, 14 December 1989.
17. Mitchell, Dawn, 'International research – fieldwork in developed countries', *MRS Newsletter*, no. 204, March 1983.
18. Douglas, Susan P., and C. Samuel Craig, *International Marketing Research*, Prentice-Hall, Englewood Cliffs, New Jersey, 1983.
19. Robert, Paul A., 'International telephone research: An interesting *intermediate* stage between the inefficiency of large-scale personal field research, and the future direct dialogue with the consumer', in: Seminar on International Marketing Research, ESOMAR, Amsterdam, 1988.
20. Booth, Andy, 'Euro-demographics', *MRS Newsletter*, January 1988.
21. Røhme, Nils and Tjarki Veldman, 'Harmonisation of demographics' ESOMAR Congress, Vienna, 1982.
22. Research Services Ltd, 'Pan European Survey 3', Wembley, 1984.
23. Van Mesdag, Martin, 'Multinational, global, international or what?', in: Seminar on International Marketing Research, ESOMAR, Amsterdam, 1988.
24. Martin, Peter, 'Why the single market is a misnomer – and the consequences', *Financial Times*, 21 October 1988.
25. Drucker, Peter F., 'Strategies for survival in Europe in 1993', *Wall Street Journal*, 12 July 1988.

FOURTEEN

MARKETING RESEARCH FOR SERVICES

14.1 INTRODUCTION

The mature economies of the Western world are heavily dependent on the infrastructure provided by the service industries. Without efficient systems of transport or communications, the whole economy grinds inexorably to a halt. Unless power supplies are available, industry and commerce cannot function. For an advanced economy, the services of banking, insurance, and the Stock Exchange are indispensable.

In addition to these commercial services, the health, education, and welfare services of the public sector add immeasurably to the well-being and prosperity of the community. Urban living, in particular, would be intolerable without organized methods of rubbish and sewage disposal, street lighting or street cleaning. Town planning, slum clearance, and recreational facilities are other vital responsibilities of the public administration.

The meteoric rise of the service sector of the economy has been accompanied by a radical restructuring of manufacturing industry, which is undergoing a technological revolution with far-reaching social and economic consequences.

Traditionally, invisible exports, such as banking and insurance, have contributed significantly to Britain's export performance. Sophisticated technical services are now developing and providing new sources of national wealth. The UK is becoming a knowledge-intensive industrial and commercial base from which a new style of world trading is rapidly evolving.

The service industries as a whole have been slow to perceive that marketing is applicable to their activities. Still less have they realized that marketing research is a technique which can be of universal practical help in identifying new opportunities for corporate and personal services.

Worcester[1] has observed that the terms 'marketing' and 'banking' were considered to be mutually exclusive by British bankers. No need was perceived for marketing their services professionally and, because of this, no marketing research was done. The financial services as a whole were distinctly reluctant to use the techniques of marketing and, in particular, marketing research.

Fortunately for the UK economy and for the service industries themselves, this ignorance and indifference have diminished over the past decade or two, and some of the banks, insurance companies, and larger building societies have established marketing departments and developed interest in marketing research. This re-orientation of attitudes towards marketing has often been stimulated by advertising agencies, which have sought to know more about the customers, present and potential, to whom publicity was being directed. Fundamental, almost elementary, knowledge of their customers, was lacked by the clearing banks as late as 1967. 'The general managers with responsibility for marketing [such as it was] had no effective means of detecting shifts in brand share, much less of explaining why they had occurred.'[1]

But of recent years, the fastest growing sectors of the marketing research industry have included the financial services,[2] and public sector services. AMSO statistics indicate that the research turnover of its members related to financial services in 1988 was £11.8 million and rose to £13.3 million the following year. In 1982, financial services research accounted for only 2 per cent of AMSO members' turnover; by 1989 this figure had increased threefold. Mintel[3] expects further development of this sector.

There has been considerable activity in financial marketing research by such groups as NOP Market Research which has a special division – Whitmore's Financial Research Services – which has run a mammoth syndicated Financial Research Survey since 1977; this involves 65 000 interviews every year, and covers all aspects of personal financial arrangements such as banking, credit cards, insurance, etc. NOP adopts a high-quality, systematic random sample methodology; interviewing is carried out by over 1000 trained interviewers. Each month, on average, three surveys are made of about 1900 adults aged 16 and over spread throughout 180 Parliamentary constituencies. The large sample and demographic controls allow for statistically reliable analysis of small minority groups.

Another syndicated service covering financial matters is offered by AGB Index, with data drawn from a panel of 10 000 consumers for their banking, building society, and other financial clients. BMRB's Target Group Index (TGI: see Chapter 9) includes the use of personal financial services among the major areas covered by this extensive panel research which has been operating for almost 20 years. Another research company – Taylor Nelson – has a specialist financial division, Taylor Nelson Financial (TNF), which runs the *Insurance Brokers' Monitor*, a quarterly survey of opinions: 500 brokers are interviewed each quarter. Another TNF service is the City Panel which consists of 450 'City' decision makers who are interviewed regularly on a wide range of topics of current interest.

IFT Marketing Research (see Chapter 13) also has marketing research activities covering financial services and has published detailed reports on specific topics, such as pensions, marketing finance to women and finance for the under 35s.

From this brief review of some pragmatic research undertaken in financial service markets, it will be apparent that UK-based market research companies have extended their professional interests and are able to offer banks, building societies, and others, valuable insight into the needs of their corporate and private clients.

14.2 CLASSIFICATION OF SERVICES

Services may be classified in two generic ways: commercial services (corporate clients), and consumer services (private clients), but these are not mutually exclusive. The first type is provided to enable organizations to achieve their corporate objectives which are generally related to profit targets. However, identical services are frequently consumed by non-profit organizations such as national and international charities. While the service needs of commercial firms, public-sector organizations or charities are largely similar, the primary objectives of those who buy such services will differ.

The second general classification of services refers to consumer services provided to satisfy particular personal needs which, in developed economies like the UK, represent an increasing proportion of consumer expenditure over the past 20 or so years.

Another method of classifying services identifies them according to the degree of their complexity, along a continuum with simple services such as milk delivery at one pole to complex services like international financial transactions at the other extreme. But with improved technology and experience, complexity may be reduced and the simplified service will then open up new marketing opportunities, as with 'over-the-counter' share dealings or package-deal holidays.

Services could also be typified according to the time they are given: pre-sales → during sales → post-sales. After-sales service is an increasingly important element of many transactions, and the more sophisticated products become, the more vital is the contribution paid by the service side of the selling organization. 'In several industrial product markets, "package deals" involving the supply, installation, and servicing of equipment help to overcome buyers' legitimate anxieties and confirm their judgement in selection of particular suppliers.'[4]

As with products, markets for services are dynamic, so marketing professionalism is needed to identify and keep in time with the changing needs of companies and of individuals. The diffusion of services such as life-assurance or joint-stock banking would have been far more effective 'downmarket' if the methods of acquisition could be simplified. With considerable panache, the Trustee Savings Banks have captured the patronage of the wage-earners of the UK whose increased economic power was not generally matched by their money-handling skills. They lacked the family tradition and experience of dealing with the 'high street' banks which, in turn, seemed unable to communicate effectively with this new and lucrative market segment. This gap was filled by the TSBs whose range of banking services now parallels those of the joint-stock banks.

On the other hand, the old-established banks like Barclays were quick to seize the profitable opportunities offered by the growth of the credit culture in the UK. Bank credit cards have proliferated and offer customers a relatively easy way of acquiring a financial loan to buy almost every imaginable kind of product and service at stores and other sources of supply.

The underlying philosophy of marketing – that customers' needs are the starting point from which business firms and other organizations should logically plan their activities – is as relevant to 'non-tangible' products, i.e., services, as it is to physical products. Yet, until fairly recently there has been a curious, if not stubborn, unwillingness by providers of services to acknowledge the value of this basic guide to successful operations. It is perhaps significant that this set of attitudes has also characterized many firms selling industrial and technical equipment.[5] Technology-oriented selling has impeded the progress of many companies which have tended to regard marketing and marketing research as irrelevant accretions. British industry, as Chapter 12 has shown, is still reluctant to use effectively modern marketing techniques.

14.3 FINANCIAL MARKETING RESEARCH

Banks offer their clients many kinds of financial services ranging over current accounts, deposit accounts, trusteeship, investment advice and new venture advice and, sometimes, funding. Marketing research data would be helpful in directing promotional and other resources into the most likely areas of profitable development.

Banks are both lenders and borrowers of funds: it would again be useful to have 'profiles' of investors and borrowers, both corporate and private. Analyses would include appraisals of competitive activities, not only from other banks but also from institutions such as unit trusts and the building societies. Regional and local demographic analyses would provide management with guidelines to future development opportunities. Corporate image research would indicate how various sectors of their customers and the community in general viewed banks; it could be specifically directed to evaluation of advertising effectiveness and to the design of alternative forms of promotion, such as sponsorship of national or local cultural events.

Some of these types of information could be gathered from internal records; desk research (see Chapter 2) is the first step in marketing research whether concerned with products or with services. The wealth of information already held by banks about their customers and their businesses would provide valuable and essential background data for planning the growth of banking services. One British clearing bank found[1] that basic data about advances, deposits, and number and type of customers when computerized and 'matched' with official administrative areas such as economic planning regions, local autnority administrative areas, etc., gave the bank a much better appreciation of the regions covered by its services.

Marketing research can contribute valuably in the evaluation of new financial or investment ventures. This particular contribution was evident in a decision to open a new bank in London[6] – American Express Bank – providing a number of new services, pre-tested in the research, to key market segments identified in the initial research.

The first stage of this carefully planned research was concerned with identifying and developing a profile of bank customers who could be attracted by specialized services not provided by the existing banks.

This research revealed the following facts:

1. Almost all bank customers had current/cheque accounts with an average (1974) balance of over £300 and nearly two-thirds had deposit or savings accounts with an average (1974) balance of over £500.
2. Three-quarters were middle class, and of these over 40 per cent were AB.
3. An average of three visits per month were made to the bank and an average of 11 cheques were written.
4. Virtually all customers rated their bank good on arithmetic accuracy of account handling, but a quarter did not view favourably the problem of queuing time.
5. Over one-third would have liked to visit their bank outside current banking hours – one-quarter mentioned either Saturday or one of the general working days of the week.

These findings, bearing in mind the known inertia of bank customers to change banks, confirmed that a new bank offering 'me-too' services would be unlikely to be successful. However, the balances on current and deposit accounts, particularly of AB customers, suggested that this segment might be attracted by special services.

The target market was, therefore, defined as higher income AB customers for whom the following services were specifically designed:

1. Interest-bearing current accounts.
2. MLR linked savings account with rates related to amount and duration of deposit.
3. Telephone service for arranging withdrawal without queuing.
4. Cashier's window on street to provide out-of-hours service.
5. Monthly statements.
6. Dual currency accounts (for travellers).
7. 'Gold' American Express Card with instant credit/travel cheque facilities.
8. Automatic issue of £30 cheque guarantee card, with availability of £100 cheque card on application.
9. Cheques returned with statements.

The second stage of the research measured the reactions of the projected customers to the strategic and tactical plans of the bank.

Nearly half of the target market sample expressed some interest, 10 per cent said they would be likely to open an account, and another 30 per cent said they were fairly likely to open an account if such a bank opened in the vicinity. In addition, the research evaluated the corporate image of American Express and its impact on attitudes to the new bank.

After evaluating the research, American Express decided to convert part of its London travel centre in Haymarket into a new bank. As a result of the success of this venture, American Express Bank later moved to larger, purpose-built premises nearby.

Another example of the effective use of marketing research in banking services related to a survey[7] about the perceptions, attitudes, levels of satisfaction, motivations, etc., of local users of a German banking group.

The basic costs of the research were met by the Federal Association of the Co-operative Banks. Information gathered was of two main kinds: (i) standardized, and (ii) specific. The first type related to the local bank's market share, broad demographic profile of its customers, services used by different sections of bank customers, image profile of the bank and its competitors, motives for choosing a bank, degree of bank loyalty, and attractiveness of the cooperative concept of banking. Specific data referred usually to the reactions of customers to new banking services such as travel agency activities; to various opening hours; to ways of presenting information; and to visits by bank clerks to customers' homes; ways in which services might be improved were also surveyed.

The results of this research were presented against 27 criteria covering 'emotional as well as rational components'. Among the findings was the fact that in towns with a population of half-a-million and over there is more likelihood of customers changing their banks, perhaps because of the more marked competition between banks in those areas. But, in general, there was a strong tendency to remain faithful to the bank originally chosen, 'even with the critical young set and the upper class' who usually adopt 'a more rational attitude' towards their banking arrangements.

Marketing research in the specialized area of corporate banking at both domestic and international levels indicated[8] that while the financial needs and problems of industry are shared across national frontiers, international banking is still made up of national markets. Hence, the need to understand differences in attitudes and priorities within national boundaries is of paramount importance to success in international banking.

Corporate banking research assists the development of international banking policies and the design of services which can benefit banks in the highly competitive nature of their global operations. It was observed[8] that in the US, where both consumer and corporate banking have traditionally been more competitive, survey techniques in marketing banking services to corporate customers have been well used. In Europe and across the world, American banks also habitually adopt this research-based approach in developing their corporate banking business. But it was noted that in order to derive full value from research, banks 'must be prepared to devote a substantial amount of high-level executive time to the evaluation of marketing problems and opportunities thrown up by the research'.

When Hill Samuel wanted to expand sales of unit trusts and to develop new financial services, a small-scale programme of qualitative research[9] was designed which gave insight into investment behaviour and attitudes among relatively wealthy shareholders. Researchers accompanied selected members of Hill Samuel's team of insurance consultants who, at pre-arranged visits, presented a hypothetical new Hill Samuel investment management service. During the early part of the discussions, researchers confined their activities to observation, only later asking some probing questions. There was, however, little probing needed because of the flow of information generated by the effective negotiations.

As a result of this limited research, a new service was launched on a trial basis – the Personal Financial Service – and after six months in 'test market', which involved no advertising but direct selling, the scheme was marketed nationally.

Hill Samuel then tackled the problem of improving the effectiveness of its advertising for unit trusts. Little was known about the buying decisions in this segment of the financial market; for example, what caused investors to choose a particular unit trust?

A series of individual depth interviews with investors who had bought unit trusts within the past six weeks were conducted by two psychologist researchers. Three important significant factors were found to influence buyers of unit trusts; two of these factors could not be disclosed by the researchers in their account of this survey, but the third crucial factor was the name of the investment house offering the units. 'No matter how attractive the actual offer might be, the majority of respondents tended to ignore it or discount it unless it was backed by a name they felt they knew and could trust.'[9]

This highly relevant reaction led to Hill Samuel's name being featured more boldly in their advertisements for unit trusts. Other trading changes were also made as a result of this survey.

Doyle[10] has suggested that the building society market could usefully be segmented into three main types of customers: bankers, savers, and investors. The first type appears to be particularly evident in the North of England, and uses the building society just like a bank, paying in wages and withdrawing to pay current expenses. Working classes, in particular, tend to deal with building societies rather than banks which are not open on Saturdays and which are perceived to have a rather forbidding appearance. The second group, 'savers', are regular depositors with some express objective in mind, such as the purchase of a colour television. Their needs are unsophisticated and the operation of a building society account is readily understood by them.

The third group, 'investors', consists of customers who respond 'consistently and decisively' to changes in interest rates.

Although these segments – like all market segments – are not entirely discrete, they contain sufficiently different kinds of customers that special marketing approaches should be considered in order to build up overall market share. Doyle[10] has stressed that, as a whole, building societies have made themselves unnecessarily vulnerable because they have followed an undifferentiated marketing strategy. This criticism, though valid at the time of the comment, i.e., 1976, is no longer so apt, as the building society movement has come to grips with the rising expectations of investors and borrowers, and several leading societies, such as Halifax and Abbey National, have now adopted proactive marketing strategies.

Over the past decade or so, building societies in the UK have taken on ambitious new roles in the field of financial services. From their strong grass-roots in local and regional communities, building societies have challenged the joint-stock banks, and with the advantage of new legislation, they have now entered into direct competition in the tradition-bound consumer banking sector. Imaginative advertising campaigns have helped to popularize some of the leading building societies, several of whom have undertaken marketing research in order to evaluate, for example, the specific role of branding in financial decision making.

'The Pru' – the long-established and popular name for the Prudential Assurance Co.[11] – commissioned Research International, in mid-1989, to undertake qualitative research concerned with branding and personal financial services; the 'not unsurprising conclusion' was that branding was the key means of discriminating between companies. In fact, as the company's own market research team commented, branding as a tool appears to be under-used in the financial services sector. While the Prudential had over years built up a strong image of security there were also negative perceptions of its being 'old-fashioned, staid and unexciting'. A new corporate identity was designed, linked with an aggressive advertising campaign, resulting in a transformed corporate image. Various qualitative studies revealed the Pru had successfully shaken off its 'stick-in-the-mud' image, and was now perceived as a modern organization.

A well-designed research programme could help building societies to meet competition from other kinds of financial institutions by providing them with better information about people's behaviour and their attitudes towards the handling of money.

Life-cycle analyses (refer to Chapter 11) are of particular relevance to building societies: early saving schemes, mortgage arrangements, deposit accounts, etc., are all related to stages in an individual's life and to family needs.

14.4 TRAVEL AND LEISURE RESEARCH

The travel and leisure industries, as observed earlier in this chapter, take an increasingly large share of consumers' expenditure in a developed country like Britain. Tourism and sport attract vast sums of money which are competed for by hotel chains, restauranteurs, air, sea, and land travel organizations, insurance companies, 'special activity' holiday centres, etc. These leisure markets are highly segmented with distinctive patterns of buying behaviour, expectations, and attitudes.

Several leading market research agencies are very active in offering tailored research facilities to tourist boards, hotel groups, motoring organizations, and the myriad other firms eager to secure a share of the growing leisure market.

Gallup, for instance, markets a comprehensive study of the package holiday market, *Travel Counter*, which publishes data weekly, monthly, and end of season, collected from a representative sample of 300 ABTA travel agents, each of whom has been equipped with a 'simple-to-operate' computer. Details include resorts, type of holiday, type of accommodation, mode of travel, length of holiday, numbers of adults/children/infants, value (£) of bookings, etc. In addition, Gallup offers a consumer survey of 10 000 adults per month, available as a monthly supplement to the *Travel Counter* reports.

NOP Travel and Leisure is responsible for the conduct of the *British National Travel Survey* (BNTS) on behalf of the British Tourist Authority. This survey is the travel industry's major measuring instrument for long (4+ nights) holidays both at home (GB) and abroad, and provides incidence, volume estimates, and detailed characteristics of such holidays. The survey is conducted annually (in November) among a probability sample of adults throughout Great Britain. Personal in-home interviews in 240 Parliamentary constituencies generate a sample base of 3000 adults and – via probability booster samples added to the core survey – details of 2000 GB holidays and 2000 holidays abroad. NOP has conducted this work for the statutory authority every year since 1970.

NOP Travel and Leisure is also responsible for the *United Kingdom Tourism Survey* (UKTS), on behalf of the four statutory tourist boards of the UK home nations (English Tourist Board/ Northern Ireland Tourist Board/Scottish Tourist Board/Wales Tourist Board). This continuous survey accumulates around 75 000 adult interviews, conducted face-to-face with a probability sample, in home, in 564 sampling points, over the course of each year. This massive sample generates measurements of the volume (trips/nights) and value (pounds sterling) of tourism undertaken anywhere, for any purpose, of any duration of one night or more, by the UK population. This survey was undertaken for the first time in 1989, replacing earlier smaller surveys undertaken individually by the statutory tourist boards of each country.

NOP Travel and Leisure is also well known for a syndicated hotel visitors survey (jointly undertaken with ARC Ltd) and a wide variety of tailor-made *ad hoc* research at and about resorts, visitor attractions, garden festivals, exhibitions and shows, shopping centres, and sports/entertainment facilities.

The Harris Research Centre specializes in motoring, transportation, and local authority leisure surveys. Public Attitude Surveys have undertaken research for the English Tourist Board on visitors to historical monuments, and on users of swimming pools for the English Sports Council and the Scottish Sports Council.

14.5 PUBLIC SECTOR SERVICES

The public services should make wider use of the techniques of marketing research. Objective enquiry should be used in order to assess the effectiveness of existing services and to identify the changing needs of society. Research may identify an emerging social need; this could require careful evaluation and study in relation to existing and planned resources.

The optimum allocation of scarce resources concerns not only commercial firms but should also be the direct interest of those who formulate policies in the public service.

At the 1970 Conference of the Market Research Society, Mr Anthony Wedgwood Benn urged that research techniques which had been perfected in commercial investigations should now be applied to problems of community welfare. Six years earlier, Mr Harold Wilson had also appealed for marketing research resources to be diverted to high-priority social objectives for the benefit of the community. Professional marketing researchers responded[12] by referring back these appeals to those who are able to influence the allocation of funds: these 'paymasters' may be in the public service or political life. There is no shortage of professional research skills: there has been a marked disinclination to hire some of these skills in the development of social policies.

From hard experience, if not enlightened business management, commercial firms make and market products that will satisfy their customers' needs. Increasingly, they are using marketing research to give them more valid and reliable knowledge about their customers' needs and preferences. It has been said by a leading marketing researcher[13] that government and social planners have not been motivated to study the factors affecting demand 'because they have so often been in a monopolistic situation. They have not had to attract people to use their schools rather than other schools, their hospitals rather than other hospitals, their roads rather than other roads'. However, there is growing interest by the public in the services which are offered to them; organized and articulate groups are challenging some of the policies and practices of the health, education, and welfare services. If objective information is lacking, subjective judgement will impose itself, and services may become over-elaborated and wastefully administered.

The widening horizons of marketing research may be noted from the variety of welfare problems with which professional marketing research firms have been involved over the past few years.[14] The Harris Research Centre, for example, has surveyed the problems of hypothermia among the elderly, black unemployment in a London borough, and the relationships between Asian young people and their parents as they grow up in Western society. Public Attitude Surveys Research has also contributed significantly to the study of community problems, such as Youth Opportunities Special Programme Participants (for the Manpower Services Commission), Improvement Grants (for the Department of the Environment), and Possible Racial Discrimination (for the Commission for Racial Equality).

BMRB has had many years' experience of social research which has become a major source of business and has increased so much overall that the National Surveys Consortium (NSC) has been formed with four other leading research agencies. The NSC has successfully completed very large-scale projects for government departments which would be beyond the resources of any one company to handle on its own.

Further examples of social research applications are given later in this chapter; the wheel has, in a way, turned full circle, since marketing research, as noted in Chapter 1, has significant roots in social research.

Although the techniques of marketing and social research are general, there is 'something unique about the way we, as market researchers, analyse a problem or pose a research proposition. ... Press together planning and social research of the kind that is conventionally practised and nothing happens. But press together the wires of planning and market research and the sparks begin to fly'.[12] The dynamic nature of commercial investigations has bred in marketing researchers a sense of urgency, allied with professional commitment to objectivity in all aspects of research designs. This blend of attitudes and expertise should not be left solely at the disposal of industry and commerce. The 'paymasters' should encourage policy makers to use the highly developed skills of marketing researchers by placing funds at their disposal for the essential tasks. It was heartening, some 10 years ago, to note that 'Governments now seem open-minded about using research skills to obtain public opinion and more inclined than previously to discuss the possibilities offered by consumer research'.[15]

The reluctance to adopt a research-oriented approach to policy decisions is not so marked at the national level. Many surveys, as discussed, have been sponsored by government departments, but there still often appears to be a distinct reluctance to adopt a research-oriented approach to policy decisions at regional and local levels. At these levels, which are necessarily much nearer to individuals and households, objective and up-to-date information about people's health and social needs appear often to be lacking. The role of research tends to be misunderstood by officials and is often perceived as not relevant. Frequently, their professional experience had precluded them from acquiring a more sophisticated appreciation of the versatile applications of managerial techniques like marketing research. Added to this problem is the fact that a community's needs are fragmented and dealt with by distinct departments such as housing, public health, or social services. On the other hand, it would be naïve to assume that national policies are based firmly on objective survey data; the realities suggest rather different determinants.

A senior British official statistician, Muriel Nissel, who was editor of *Social Trends* for some years, has observed that 'broad decisions about policies are based neither on statistics nor perhaps on any systematic information, but more on the subjective hunches of politicians who have for their antennae the press, television and radio, pressure groups, constituency parties, etc.'.[16]

Policy making is inspired by political creeds; the philosophies of the ruling party are likely to be dominant influences. Objective survey data, if collected at all, may play a limited role in the development of policies.

One local authority recognized the value of marketing research which enabled it to understand better the perceptions, attitudes, and expectations of its electors. Strathkelvin District Council was formed in 1975 through merging two town councils and adjacent rural areas in the Strathclyde region of Scotland. For some years the Council had striven to overcome the usual problems of its residents failing to identify with the new area. A new logo was introduced and a survey[17] commissioned to find out public awareness of the Council's present and planned activities. A representative sample of 1000 residents, profiled by ACORN criteria (see Chapter 11), was interviewed and questions covered housing services, leisure and recreational facilities, environmental services, and planning and development issues. In addition, 50 local businesses were surveyed by telephone.

The Council derived valuable insights into the perceived quality of the services it offered, and of people's preferences and expectations. Within the limited resources available, not all demands could, of course, be satisfied, but policy makers have acquired a fund of objective knowledge to guide their decision making.

14.6 'PASSIVE' VERSUS 'INSTRUMENTAL' ROLE OF SOCIAL RESEARCH

Social researchers must be able to argue the case for objective research based on well-defined objectives that are operational. Conflict between the professional planners and social researchers is to be expected. Social researchers may adopt what has been described[18] as a passive or descriptive role or, alternatively, become active and 'instrumentalist'. In the former case, the social researcher will be welcomed by the planner because there will be no challenge to established planning procedures. 'Indeed, social research becomes the hand-maiden of the planner in offering him information with an ease and accuracy which can only add strength to the planner's purposes.'[18]

On the other hand, the active and instrumentalist mode of social research is concerned 'not with finding out what people want, but of finding out what they *might* want or be *persuaded* to want, that is, if they are given a lead and direction'.[18] This type of research is more probing and compels planners to come face to face with new dimensions in their planning proposals. It forces planners to think again about the nature of the problems confronting them, and to be prepared to consider new approaches. Instead of seeking data to support value-judgements, the planner should be willing to 'recognize the political nature of planning',[18] and through the techniques of 'active' social research to learn about society's emerging needs, some of which may not fit neatly into the framework of his or her presuppositions.

Two Canadian researchers[19] have stressed that because government products and services are 'often highly innovative and at the frontier of social changes, both positive and negative', there is a great need for exploratory consumer research to aid the policy maker in evaluating alternative approaches for the design of public services. They feel that in the field of health and welfare services there is particular need for the application of survey techniques to guide policy makers. Suchman[20] has observed that in many cases, community health surveys have successfully uncovered unmet needs, particularly those referring to those health conditions and sub-groups of the population that escape the attention of established medical channels. Moreover, surveys may be able to highlight inefficiencies in the existing system of health care. 'Too often, these services are either over-utilized or under-utilized, fragmented, lacking in continuity and comprehensiveness, and of low quality'.[20]

14.7 THREE GENERAL CONTRIBUTIONS OF SURVEY DATA

Teer[16] has identified three general types of contributions which survey data may offer:

1. Commissions of enquiry.
2. Non-contentious policy making.
3. Research in support of policy.

In the first area of policy making, survey data are 'increasingly common' as one of the methods of opinion and fact gathering, though the actual effects of such data on the Commissions' recommendations seem to be small, as with the Royal Commission on Local Government. Survey findings had indicated concern about remoteness and a wish for greater participation in local affairs, whereas the report subsequently recommended greater responsibility should be given to much larger and more remote forms of local government.

Another example of the apparently limited influence of survey findings occurred in the research commissioned by the Committee on the Age of Majority set up by the Labour Government of 1966–70.[21] The findings – that young people between 18 and 21 had little interest in becoming full adults at 18 and were in no way dissatisfied with their existing legal status – were, in fact, ignored by the Committee which recommended that the age of majority should be reduced to 18.

With the second category – non-contentious policy making, party politics are less dominant and the role of research data is, therefore, stronger.

In these circumstances, decision makers are interested in collecting and analysing survey data to enable them to evaluate alternative strategies, such as new methods of shopping, e.g., hypermarkets.

Teer's third category – research in support of policy – relates to what may be termed the defensive role of research. Official policies may have been devised without, or with little, anterior research and have become the foci of attacks by pressure groups from either within government, or government departments, trades unions, recreational groups, etc. Survey research was able to demonstrate, for example, that, contrary to the motoring organizations' demands, there was considerable public support (including a majority of motorists) for the motoring legislation which, in the late 1960s, introduced the 70 m.p.h. speed limit and the breathalyser.

Teer concluded that while the influence of survey research into the formulation of the broad direction of government policy is, therefore, both limited and variable, 'it is nevertheless significant and growing'.[16] He stressed that politicians are suspicious of survey data and tend readily to reject opinions research findings which contradict their own entrenched beliefs, as typified by the late Richard Crossman who is reputed to have said that he was only completely convinced of the findings of the Gallup Poll when they confirmed his impressions of what the public are thinking.

14.8 SOCIAL RESEARCH ACTIVITIES

It would not, of course, be equitable to assume that research into societal needs has received scant attention for, as discussed in Chapter 1, the Government Social Survey has been responsible for conducting a very wide range of surveys covering trade, health, housing, social welfare, etc. The excellence of the Social Survey's reports has helped significantly to raise the general level of research standards and practices.

In addition, there are official censuses and surveys conducted by various ministries dealing with demographic analyses, family expenditure patterns, employment, etc. (see Chapter 1). Several surveys have researched specific population trends, birth control practices, and education; for example, the Crowther Report,[22] the Robbins Committee[23] on Higher Education, and the Plowden Committee on Primary Education.[24]

The Health Education Council has acknowledged the value of marketing research in evaluating, for example, the effectiveness of poster campaigns against smoking, and also in investigating knowledge of and attitudes to venereal diseases, before mounting a public information campaign.[12] Social surveys are strongly urged by the Health Education Council in order to determine whether a need exists for specific health education or, where this clearly exists, to give guidance in planning health education programmes and also in monitoring their effectiveness.

Research sponsored by the Department of the Environment evaluated road safety publicity, particularly related to the use of car seat belts. The survey data enabled 'some significant steps to be taken in the direction of a scientific approach to decision making affecting road safety publicity campaigns'.[25] A series of controlled area experiments with media advertising were continuously monitored. The results showed both a direct and positive relationship between advertising exposure and the extent of seat belt wearing. Alternative advertising themes were evaluated for their influence on motorists' attitudes towards road safety practices, especially the regular use of seat belts. Of all the themes used, the catch-phrase 'clunk click' appears to have been the most memorable and to have been effective in 'converting' non-wearers to wearers. This verbal device was also seen as making the wearing of seat belts into something of a community game – thus rendering wearing easier because, by implication, it really *was* socially accepted and approved.[25]

Following the 1973 'energy crisis', several energy conservation measures were introduced into the UK, including an official publicity campaign aimed at industrial and personal consumers to encourage the economical use of energy. To check the effectiveness of these efforts, a series of surveys between 1974 and 1976 was undertaken by three leading marketing research agencies on behalf of the Department of Energy.[26] The general conclusions were as follows:

1. Price *alone* will not lead directly to efficient energy saving.
2. Paid advertising needs to be supported by other publicity activity.
3. The fuel industries must support the economy campaign.
4. The advertising campaign needs to be followed through to the point of purchase of heating equipment.
5. Different households have different priorities in interpreting the energy-saving message.

'These differences will be partly subjective (such as council house tenants' rejection of the relevance of loft insulation) and partly objective according to type of property, space heating needs, etc.'[26]

This research has been quoted at some length because it illustrates the complexity of consumption behaviour, as revealed by research; attitudes and traditional types of behaviour, household composition, occupational groupings, and age of housewife were some significant factors influencing dispositions to cut personal consumption of scarce energy fuels. Energy saving was found to be highest among owner-occupiers, owners of central heating, detached house owners and those with newer properties, the high social grades, and younger households.

In 1964 the Housing Development Division of the Ministry of the Environment initiated a study of the housing needs and living conditions of single working people, concentrating on the low-paid, middle-aged, and the relatively better off younger and more mobile sectors of the population.[27] By 1973, a 21-storey tower block in Leicester had been constructed as a result of the study which clearly had substantial 'operational' value. The tower block contained five different types of accommodation, embodying the main characteristics of 'independence' and 'sociability' which the research survey had identified.

The Building Research Establishment was asked by the Department of the Environment to suggest appropriate housing standards for the 1980s. National Opinion Polls undertook a national survey of people's expectations and preferences in housing standards.[28] Housing amenities were classified as 'basic necessities' (things you couldn't possibly live without); 'desirable' (things which help make life run smoothly and pleasantly); and 'unnecessary' (things you are not bothered about). This research-based evaluation of prospective housing amenities provided guidelines for setting new minimum standards of housing for England and Wales to replace those based on public health criteria of the early part of this century.

Community preferences in housing and environmental variables such as traffic noise, pedestrian safety, journey time to work, parking restrictions at shops, etc., have been researched by Hoinville,[29] and by Shostak,[30] whose study was specifically concerned with the new city of Milton Keynes. Hoinville[29] underlines the responsibility of planners to understand the *values* of the people who form the communities for whom they plan. He points out that the planning process generally seems to be most effectively geared to learning about the views and wants of pressure groups. However, it has not been able to extend much beyond this to learn more about the complex preferences of the community at large. It should not be assumed that the so-called silent majority do not have preferences, although for various reasons, they may fail to articulate these.

Shostak[30] states that the criterion which governs research at Milton Keynes is simple: if it assists decision making it is valuable; but if it is too late, misses the relevant issues, or is unintelligible to a non-researcher, then it is worthless for their purposes. The survey into the development proposals for Milton Keynes had five main uses:

1. It provided basic information for future planning.
2. It reinforced intuitive perceptions.
3. It refuted some elements of conventional wisdom (patronage of a new leisure centre was low not because people didn't know about it but because of apathy and costs of transport).

4. New issues originating from the survey results were placed on the Corporation's decision-making agenda.

5. Data provided for future internal and external policy debates on issues known to be important but which could not be tackled immediately because of staff resources.

The Chronically Sick and Disabled Persons Act 1970, placed upon local authorities the special responsibility for meeting the accommodation needs of the disabled. The Department of the Environment briefed a commercial marketing research firm to survey the housing needs and preferences of disabled persons living in either purpose-built accommodation or in adapted dwellings. The study [31] was conducted from June 1972 to May 1973, and focused on two major areas of enquiry:

1. What special design features are required by people with different types of disability?
2. What are the most important social factors affecting the housing of the disabled?

The preliminary results of the survey 'suggest that in many cases the accommodation immediately prior to the purpose-built dwellings was unsuitable and probably not amenable to adaptation'. However, 'there was a considerable amount of dissension and uncertainty about living next door to other disabled people. Less than half the sample liked this aspect and even some of these people qualified their approval by saying that this applied only if the scheme was small.[31] The researchers commented that in areas such as physical handicap, strong emotions are aroused, and strong beliefs are held as to ideal solutions.

Another example of the application of commercial survey techniques to socio-medical problems relates to a study of hypothermia among the elderly in Britain.[32] The researchers observed that 'although several distinguished medical researchers have done detailed work on hypothermia it has tended to be fragmentary and small scale in nature. Surveys concerned with the incidence of hypothermia have been neither national nor representative and usually relied on mouth temperature measurements'.[32] Such surveys, although acceptable within their context, failed to 'provide the impetus needed to alter radically the thinking of a cautious medical establishment, and an even more cautious Civil Service'.[32] This research indicated that in Britain there may be up to half-a-million old people living at home who suffer from cold; moreover, these are more likely to be among the poorest of their age group. In addition, 'there are several million old people who are living in temperatures below the advised level'.

The researchers suggested that housing authorities should evaluate better systems of house insulation and the feasibility of introducing district heating schemes in new housing developments. At the same time, they admit that one of the more difficult aspects of a research project such as theirs, which was not undertaken 'with a direct view to investment decisions', is the education of policy makers so that action is seen to be necessary. In such a case, research may have a relatively long-term effect and it may be difficult to trace its contribution to decisions taken even a generation later. Changes in attitudes and behaviour are seldom affected merely by one piece of research. But information from objective surveys is difficult to avoid entirely: even official inertia has its limits.

14.9 SURVEYS SHOULD NOT DETERIORATE INTO 'BOOKKEEPING'

Suchman[20] has warned against the dangers of survey practice deteriorating into some kind of 'bookkeeping' which is concerned with presenting statistical reports of very little use for determining policy: 'the data become ends in themselves instead of means toward programme improvement'. Professionals in the areas of medicine and public health 'have turned to the social scientists with mixed feelings of need and suspicion'.[20] It is now the responsibility of social researchers to work with these other professionals as a team in developing new insights into human needs. Suchman[20] underlines that research in the area of health entails the study of man: this cannot be done effectively without finding out about all those environmental factors which influence his life. This more comprehensive and enlightened approach is the special contribution which marketing research is able to make to health and social welfare. Modern diseases and modern health problems are complex; social and psychological factors influence the incidence of disease, and also determine the ways in which people respond to illnesses. Further, social and cultural differences inhibit communication between those who need medical attention and those who are able to offer it. The illness cannot be considered as clinically separate from the person, that person's life style, social habits, and psychological characteristics.

14.10 NEW HORIZONS OF MARKETING RESEARCH

The diversity of research studies outlined in this chapter reflects the new horizons of marketing research. These increasingly involve the service industries and extend into medical and social areas of human activity where, in a comparatively short period of time, positive contributions have been made. Commercial research agencies like the Louis Harris Medical Survey Division of the Harris Centre provide comprehensive market research into all aspects of health care on a world-wide basis. Their enquiries cover medical specialists, general practitioners, dentists, paramedical staff, the general public, and health authorities. With surveys abroad, overseas agencies are responsible for fieldwork only, using questionnaires and interviewing guides provided by the Harris organization, which also carries out all the data processing. To some extent, the old prejudices about using marketing research for investigating the market for services, both commercial and public sector welfare, may have become less marked, but there is still a long way to go before there is whole-hearted acceptance of the value of objective field surveys. Practitioners of a relatively new discipline like marketing research cannot expect to have easy access to professions such as medicine and banking which are characteristically 'closed'. But the increasingly articulate and informed criticism from the users of services should motivate top management to become more responsive to consumers. This new orientation should be based on objective data obtained through systematic surveys; without this guidance, the gap between policy makers and the public can only widen.

It is sometimes argued that modern industrial communities such as the UK are in danger of being 'over-surveyed'. But it should be borne in mind that human needs have increased in complexity and in scale; vast programmes of health and social welfare should not be undertaken merely at the whim of politicians, at whatever level they may exercise influence in public affairs.

The elderly have been found[33] to be generally cooperative when surveyed; they are seen to identify themselves as part of a group more readily than other sections of the population, and they generally welcome contact with other people once they have been reassured about the nature of the enquiries. However, in general population surveys on topics that are not of direct interest to the elderly, they tend to be less cooperative, often feeling that they have little to contribute and that their contribution would, anyway, not be welcomed. To overcome the inherent problems of surveying the elderly, interviewers should receive special training. They need to be able 'to handle long, stressful interviews which require more intervention on their part, more social skills and yet great care to avoid biasing the responses'.[33] (Also see Chapters 6 and 7.) A survey[34] sponsored by the Market Research Society into the general population's awareness of, knowledge of, and attitudes to marketing research was reported in 1979. Overall response rate was 66 per cent and 876 effective interviews were conducted.

The conclusions of this research were briefly:

1. General attitudes to marketing research were 'really very favourable'.
2. There is considerable, but restricted, understanding of what research is and why it is undertaken. Two-thirds agreed that more research should be done to find out the public's attitudes and needs.
3. There is comparatively little understanding of the more technical aspects of research.
4. Small minority believed that research can help to combat price increases.
5. Marketing research is not perceived to be an invasion of privacy.

However, 'three points of concern' arose from the survey findings:

1. Refusers may be very much more 'anti' research.
2. 'Sugging' (selling under the guise of marketing research) seems to be at a high level.
3. Research and selling seem to be connected in some way – as noted above.

The researchers concluded that a general publicity campaign could usefully combat 'sugging', give reassurance on how marketing research actually works, and explain, to some extent, government survey activities.

Among specific findings of this survey, it is interesting to note that nearly half of all respondents preferred being interviewed at home for marketing enquiries, 28 per cent said they liked street interviewing the least, and telephone interviewing was liked least by 41 per cent. The main reasons for liking home interviews were that respondents felt more at ease and able to give more balanced views, apart from being a more convenient method for them. Telephone interviewing was disliked because the callers could not be seen and their authenticity checked; further, the method is perceived to be impersonal, while almost one-fifth of respondents said they disliked speaking on the telephone.

In general, however, the evidence from this professional research indicates that the public as a whole are really quite favourable to marketing surveys and recognize that these methods generally benefit them.

In Chapter 6, it was observed that the public had generally favourable views about marketing research, according to Mintel's special report, published in 1990.[1] The findings of the MRS (1979) report seem, therefore, largely to be relevant today.

Although 'sugging' had been perceived in the 1979 survey to be at 'a high level', Mintel had found it less threatening, but two experienced researchers stated[35] in 1989 that the expansion of market research in the UK had been accompanied by 'a parasitic growth in sugging' (20 per cent in 1978 but 30 per cent in 1989). But their concern was somewhat lessened by also noting research that the British public's overall good opinion of market research had increased from 59 per cent in 1978 to 76 per cent in 1989.

The MRS Code of Conduct (Chapter 16), the Interviewer Identity Card (Chapter 7) and the Interviewer Quality Control Scheme (Chapter 7) discuss further aspects of these professional issues.

Researching the arts

In advanced, prosperous communities the arts flourish, even though some manifestations of the so-called pop culture may certainly lack universal appeal. Market segmentation strategies are obviously relevant and have been practised, deliberately or accidentally, for generations.

Marketing research techniques can (and should) be applied effectively in identifying patrons, their preferences, living styles, media habits, travelling arrangements, etc. Theatres, music, concerts, cultural exhibitions, museums, art galleries, etc., can all benefit from specific information to enable them to provide programmes and facilities which are likely to win the favour of their customers.

In autumn 1987, the Market Research Society dedicated a whole issue of *Survey*[36] to case histories illustrating the applications of marketing research to a wide range of artistic enterprises. The adoption of marketing research methodologies in the management development of cultural activities in no way debases cultural and aesthetic standards – it should enlarge them and assume that reputations for quality and diversity are maintained.

Social forecasting

As economic forecasting is almost entirely concerned with the collection and interpretation of economic data, so social forecasting focuses on identifying and interpreting trends in social and cultural attitudes and behaviour which may, eventually if not immediately, affect the consumption of goods and services. Consumption is surrounded by an intricate web of influential factors: these are not always easily discerned or defined, but that does not mean that they do not exist or that their existence should be denied. Such factors include the impact of female emancipation – popularly termed the feminist movement – on social and economic activities; the changed pattern of family structure and life; changing attitudes towards the consumption of scarce natural resources; articulate and original public criticism of political and corporate behaviour; the rise of an indulgent, hedonistic society; concern with security, safety, freedom, social and ethnic equality, and the adoption of new life styles.

Economic and social forces interact; modern markets are volatile and information about habits and trends is incomplete if it depends solely on economic data. However, social forecasting is not meant to usurp economic forecasting: it should be accepted as a legitimate partner. Unless organizations include an appreciation of social trends when, for example, market forecasts are being prepared or management development programmes are being designed, there is an inherent instability in such plans.

Social forecasting research has been conducted in the US for several years. In the UK, Taylor Nelson conducted an annual survey of social change based on seven social value groups derived from the Monitor survey, now operated by Applied Futures Ltd. The seven groups: self-explorers; social resisters; experimentalists; conspicuous consumers/achievers; belongers; survivors; and 'aimless' have been studied closely for over 10 years, using market and social research techniques. (Further discussion of life style classification and TGI services occurred in Chapter 11.) While some of the labels given to life style groups may cause a wry smile, and critics have commented unfavourably on the generalized nature of these classifications, there is also professional support for typologies which, like those of the International Research Institute on Social Change, seem capable of more specific application.

14.11 SUMMARY

Developed communities depend significantly on the service industries which, as a whole, have been slow to use marketing research. However, there are now signs of much greater awareness and interest in adopting marketing research in the financial services, travel and leisure industries, and, to a growing extent, in the public sector health, education, and welfare services.

Several leading marketing research agencies offer tailor-made research facilities for the service industries.

Services can be classified in two generic ways: commercial (corporate) and consumer (personal), but these are not mutually exclusive. Services can also be typified according to the time they are given: pre-sales; during sales; post-sales. Services may also be simple or complex; the latter tend to become simplified with the growth of package deals.

Social research, from whose roots marketing research has grown, has become widely developed by the marketing research profession. Social research may be passive or descriptive or, alternatively, active and 'instrumentalist', when public sector planners will then be faced with data-based challenges to their proposals.

In general, the public have really quite favourable attitudes to marketing surveys and recognize that, on the whole, systematic enquiries are useful activities.

REFERENCES

1. Worcester, R. M. and R. Stubbs, 'Marketing research for financial services', ESOMAR, Versailles, 1975.
2. Brennan, John, 'Banking on research', *Marketing*, 14 March 1985.
3. Market Research, Special Report, Mintel, London, 1990.
4. Chisnall, Peter M., *Marketing: A Behavioural Analysis*, McGraw-Hill, Maidenhead, 1985.
5. Chisnall, Peter M., *Strategic Industrial Marketing*, Prentice-Hall, Hemel Hempstead, 1985.
6. Flack, Mervyn, 'Research for financial and investment marketing decisions', ESOMAR, Oslo, August/September 1978.
7. Geiger, H., 'Standard surveys for analysing local bank competition', ESOMAR, Versailles, 1975.
8. Flack, M., N. Spencer, and P. Bartram, 'The corporate banking customer', ESOMAR, Versailles, 1975.
9. Cockavne, J. H. M., 'The Hill Samuel case background', ESOMAR, Versailles, 1975.
10. Doyle, Peter, and Gerard D. Newbould, 'New marketing and advertising policies for building societies', ADMAP, February 1976.
11. Churchill, David, 'Fresh face from the Pru', *Financial Times*, 30 September 1990.
12. Corlett, Tom, and Michael Barnes, 'Publicity on social issues: The need for research', *Journal of Market Research Society*, vol. 13, no. 3, 1971.
13. Tuck, Mary, 'How methods of commercial research can help social planners', ESOMAR, Wapor Congress Budapest, September 1973.
14. Jameson, Conrad, 'Notes on a revolution in urban planning', Market Research Society Conference Papers, 1973.
15. Horne, Annette, Judith Morgan, and Joanna Page, 'Where do we go from here?', *Journal of Market Research Society*, vol. 16, no. 3, 1974.
16. Teer, Frank, 'The contribution of survey research in government policy making', in: *Planning for Social Change: The Contribution of Opinion Research Worldwide*, ESOMAR, Montreux, August/September 1975.
17. Windle, Richard, 'The public good', *Survey*, MRS, spring 1988.
18. Jameson, Conrad, 'The impact of social research on planning procedures', in: *The Application of Market and Social Research for more Efficient Planning*, ESOMAR, Wapor Congress, Budapest, September 1973.
19. Ritchie, J. R. Brent, and Roger J. La Breque, 'Marketing research and public policy: A functional perspective', *Journal of Marketing*, vol. 69, July 1975.
20. Suchman, Edward A., 'The survey method applied to public health and medicine' in *Survey Research in the Social Sciences*, Charles Y. Glock (ed.), Russell Sage Foundation, New York, 1967.
21. 'The Report of the Committee on the Age of Majority', Command Paper 3342, HMSO, 1967.
22. Central Advisory Council for Education – England, 'Research and surveys', 15–18, A Report, vol. I, The Report, vol. II, HMSO, London, 1959–60.
23. UK Committee on Higher Education, 'Higher Education: Report of the Committee Appointed by the Prime Minister under the Chairmanship of Lord Robbins', Command Paper 2154, DES, HMSO, London, 1964.
24. Central Advisory Council for Education – England, 'Children and Their Primary Schools' (2 volumes), HMSO, London 1967.
25. Levens, G. E., and E. Rodnight, 'The application of research in the planning and evaluation of road safety publicity', in: *The Application of Market and Social Research for more Efficient Planning, ESOMAR, Wapor Congress, Budapest, September 1973.*

26. Philips, Nicholas, and Elizabeth Nelson, 'Energy savings in private households – An integrated research programme', *Journal of Market Research Society*, vol. 18, no. 4, October 1976.

27. Eastaugh, Tony, and Stephen Porter, 'A place of one's own: Development and appraisal of single person housing', in: *Planning for Change: The Contribution of Opinion Research Worldwide*, ESOMAR, Montreux, August/September 1975.

28. Macey, Frank, 'Housing standards: The application of research techniques in planning for future needs' in *Research that Works for Today's Marketing Problems*, ESOMAR, Venice, September 1976.

29. Hoinville, G., 'Evaluating community preferences', *Journal of Market Research Society*, vol. 15, no. 1, January 1973.

30. Shostak, Lee A., 'Research and policy planning', in: *Planning for Change: The Contribution of Opinion Research Worldwide*, ESOMAR, Montreux, August/September 1975.

31. Fernando, E., 'Housing for disabled people', in: *The Application of Market and Social Research for more Efficient Planning*, ESOMAR, Wapor Congress Budapest, September 1973.

32. Taylor, H. J., and J. T. Harvey, 'Socio-medical research into hypothermia among the elderly', in: *The Application of Market and Social Research for more Efficient Planning*, ESOMAR, Wapor Congress Budapest, September 1973.

33. Hoinville, Gerald, 'Carrying out surveys among the elderly', *Journal of Market Research Society*, vol. 25, no. 3, 1983.

34. Bowen, Jennifer, 'A survey of the general public's attitudes to market research', *Journal of Market Research Society*, vol. 21, no. 2, 1979.

35. Bartram, Mary, and Peter Bartram, 'Maintaining public acceptance of market research: the way forward', *Journal of Market Research Society*, vol. 31, no. 4, October 1989.

36. 'Researching the Arts', Survey, MRS, autumn 1987.

FOUR

DATA HANDLING AND INTERPRETATION

FIFTEEN

STATISTICAL ANALYSIS

In the vast field of data analysis there are many analytical techniques and their applicability is governed by the number of variables involved which may range from one to several.

Data may be classified as follows:

1. *Uni-variate*: where a single variable is analysed alone, e.g., sample statistic such as the mean, which might refer to the age of a certain type of consumer, or to the consumption of a particular kind of food.
2. *Bi-variate*: where some association is measured between two variables simultaneously, e.g., cross-classification of age group and consumption of a product. This extends the amount of information which is severely restricted in uni-variate analysis.
3. *Multi-variate*: where simultaneous relationships between more than two variables are involved. Such analysis extends further the analyses feasible by uni-variate and bi-variate methods; most multi-variable statistical techniques require the use of a computer. Such analyses might be concerned with identifying consumption habits in terms of age, sex, socio-economic group, geographical location, etc.

Examples of data analyses and the application of statistical tests of significance are given later in this chapter.

15.1 TESTS OF HYPOTHESES AND SIGNIFICANCE

Apart from the estimation of population parameters, sampling theory is also concerned with the testing of statistical hypotheses. Decisions have frequently to be taken on the basis of information obtained in sampling, and in the process of reaching such decisions certain assumptions have to be made about the population under survey. These tentative theories or guesses are termed 'statistical hypotheses'. They are statements àbout the probability distribution of the population.

Typical hypotheses could be concerned with deciding whether one method of advertising was more effective than another, or whether consumption of a particular food product was significantly different in certain selected areas of the country. On the basis of a stated hypothesis, characteristics of a population are explored and the information obtained compared with the supposition contained in the hypothesis which will then be accepted or rejected according to the probability that it is true.

Hypotheses which have a very good chance of being accepted or found true are termed 'probably true'; those with a very poor chance of acceptance are called 'probably false'. For example, the probability of getting 15 heads in 20 tosses of a fair coin would be very small, and so any hypothesis based on this event would be improbable.

Often, a statistical hypothesis is formed for the sole purpose of rejecting or nullifying it, and it is then termed a 'null hypothesis' (NH). For example, if the relative efficiency of two different mailing shots was being investigated, a null hypothesis would state that there was no real difference between them, and that any difference that did occur was merely the result of chance sampling fluctuations. In effect, the assumption in a null hypothesis is directly opposite to what it is hoped to prove.

Tests of significance enable statistical hypotheses to be accepted or rejected. They provide evidence which must then be evaluated by statisticians; they do not provide absolute or final reasons for accepting or rejecting a particular hypothesis. The fact that sample size improves the precision of sample findings means that the results of significance tests will be valid for particular samples. Moser[1] warns that although a test may produce a negative result, i.e., not statistically significant, it cannot be automatically assumed that the effect does not exist in the population under survey. The results of significance tests indicate merely that particular samples have failed to indicate a significant relationship.

Two types of error may occur in dealing with hypotheses. Type 1 error occurs when a hypothesis is rejected when it should have been accepted as true. Type 2 error occurs when a hypothesis is accepted which should be rejected as false (see Table 15.1).

Table 15.1 Types of error

	Accept hypothesis	Reject hypothesis
Hypothesis is true	Correct decision	Type 1 error
Hypothesis is false	Type 2 error	Correct decision

For a specified hypothesis which is being tested, the level of significance of the test refers to the maximum probability with which a Type 1 error would be an acceptable risk. In statistics, it is customary to use the Greek letters α and β (alpha and beta) to denote the probabilities of committing Type 1 and Type 2 errors respectively.

The probability value of α is often specified before the samples are drawn to avoid any possible bias which might arise when the results of the survey are known.

Although the choice of an actual level of significance is purely arbitrary, in practice the levels

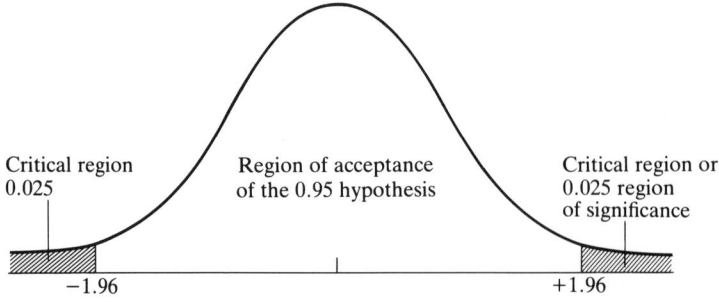

Fig. 15.1 Example of 95% confidence level

most commonly used are 0.05 (5 per cent) and 0.01 (1 per cent). The former means there are 5 chances in 100 that the hypothesis would be rejected when it should actually have been accepted; in other words, the confidence level of the decision is 95 per cent. In the latter case, there is only 1 chance in 100 that the hypothesis would be rejected when it should have been accepted, and the resulting confidence level of the decision is 99 per cent.

Where a sampling distribution is distributed normally with a given hypothesis that is true, it can be stated with 95 per cent confidence that the Z score of an actual sample statistic will lie between -1.96 and 1.96 (see Fig. 15.1).

If a sample statistic, e.g., $\bar{x}$, selected at random, were found to be outside the limits (± 1.96), it would be concluded that such an event would be likely to occur in only 5 per cent samples drawn from populations. It could then be stated that this statistic differed significantly from μ, and the hypothesis would be rejected at the 5 per cent (0.05) level of significance.

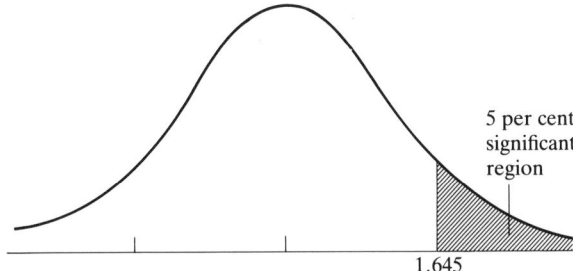

Fig. 15.2 Levels of significance

Other levels of significance can, of course, be used. For example, 1 per cent (0.01) could be used where more stringent testing of an estimate was thought to be desirable. In this case, the Z value would be ± 2.58 (refer to Fig. 5.5 on p. 107).

As already noted, the researcher must decide beforehand at what level of significance her hypothesis will be tested. She must accept the risk that she cannot expect to make the right decision *every* time; she may accept where she should have rejected or reject where she should have been accepted. Whatever level of significance is used, the researcher must eventually use her judgement based on the statistical evidence which has become available. She may, in fact, conclude that the results of experimental surveys so far achieved have not provided her with sufficiently reliable grounds on which to base some critical decision. Further research may be warranted in such cases.

So far the extreme values occurring on both sides of the mean have been considered, e.g., $\mu \pm 2.58\sigma$, and the tests of significance involved are known as two-tailed (or two-sided) tests. This concerns tests to discover whether one process (or product) is different from another. Sometimes, however, the hypothesis may be concerned only with testing whether one product is better than another. In this case, the test is referred to as a one-tailed test (or one-sided), and only one extreme of the distribution curve is considered (see Fig. 15.2).

The significant region (critical region) of a one-tailed test is based on the *total* area of the curve, as Table 15.2 indicates.

Table 15.2 The significant region

Significant level α	0.10	0.05	0.01	0.005	0.002
Critical region values of Z for one-tailed tests	-1.28 or 1.28	-1.645 or 1.645	-2.33 or 2.33	-2.58 or 2.58	-2.88 or 2.88
Critical region values of Z for two-tailed tests	-1.645 and 1.645	-1.96 and 1.96	-2.58 and 2.58	-2.81 and 2.81	-3.08 and 3.08

Systematic approach to making hypotheses

1. State the hypotheses that are to be tested:
    e.g., NH (null hypothesis):
    The mean number of pints of milk consumed per family in Stoke-on-Trent in one week is 12 pints.
    AH (alternative hypothesis): the family milk consumption does not equal 12 pints.
    The null hypothesis can be either true or false. If it is rejected after test the alternative hypothesis must be accepted.
2. State the significance level for the value below which the hypothesis would be rejected.
3. By sampling the population under survey, using an appropriate method and analysing the resultant data, determine the sample statistic relevant to the hypothesis.
4. Accept or reject the hypothesis after comparing it with the statistic obtained in (3).

Example

1. NH = 12 pints.
    AH $\neq$ 12 pints.
2. Reject null hypothesis if probability that it is true < 0.05.
3. Sample data reveal that probability of hypothesis being untrue is 0.09.
4. Because of the information obtained in (3) the NH is *not* rejected.

Testing the sample mean

Assuming the distribution to be normal with a mean μ and variance σ^2, it follows that any sample chosen from this distribution will have a mean of $\bar{x}$. Hence, the sampling distribution of $\bar{x}$ will be normal and have a mean μ and variance σ^2/n under the hypothesis that $\bar{x}$ is, in fact, an estimate of μ. It will then have a standardized normal distribution as follows:

$$z = \frac{\bar{x} - \mu}{(\sigma/\sqrt{n})}$$

i.e., $\dfrac{\bar{x} - \mu}{(\sigma/\sqrt{n})} \sim N(0,1)$ or $\dfrac{\bar{x} - \mu}{(s/\sqrt{n})}$ (if σ^2 is unknown)

Example Family consumption of a certain food product in the UK is normally distributed with a mean of 200 half-pound packs p.a. and a variance of 32 400.

A sample of 144 families taken in the Manchester area revealed a mean consumption of 245 packs p.a. Do Manchester consumers seem to be significantly different from the country as a whole?
NH:$\bar{x}_1$ is good estimate of μ ($\bar{x}_1 = 245$)
AH:$\bar{x}_1$ is not a good estimate of μ

$$\bar{x} \sim N\left(\mu, \frac{\sigma^2}{n}\right)$$

$$\text{i.e., } \bar{x} \sim N\left(200, \frac{32\,400}{144}\right)$$

$$z = \frac{\bar{x} - \mu}{(\sigma/\sqrt{n})} \frac{245 - 200}{(180/12)} = \frac{45}{15} = 3 \text{ (which is } > 2.58)$$

Thus $\bar{x}_1$ (245) is significantly different from μ at the 1 per cent (2.58) level.
NH = null hypothesis which states there is no difference between the sample and the population with regard to the mean.

AH = alternative hypothesis which must be accepted if the test indicates that the NH should be rejected.

Testing the difference between two means

Given two random samples of size n_1 and n_2, with sample means of $\bar{x}_1$ and $\bar{x}_2$, drawn from populations with means of μ_1 and μ_2 respectively, the null hypothesis is that there is no difference between the population means, i.e., $\mu_1 = \mu_2$ or $\mu_1 - \mu_2 = 0$.

It is, therefore, necessary to test whether the difference between $\bar{x}_1$ and $\bar{x}_2$ is significant or whether it may reasonably be attributed to chance sampling variation.

The first step is to calculate the standard error of the difference between the means by the formula:

$$\sqrt{[(\sigma_1^2/n_1) + (\sigma_2^2/n_2)]}$$

But the population variances are usually not known, and it is necessary to approximate by using s_1^2 and s_2^2, given sample values.

The formula for testing the difference between two means then becomes:

$$Z = \frac{|\bar{x}_1 - \bar{x}_2|}{\sqrt{[(s_1^2/n_1) + (s_2^2/n_2)]}} \sim N(0,1)$$

The numerical value obtained from this equation is compared with the Z value of the level of confidence of the test. If, for example, a two-tailed test at the 5 per cent (0.05) level of significance is being used, and if the equation value is more than 1.96, the difference between the two means can be considered as significant at 95 per cent confidence level. In this case, the null hypothesis ($\mu_1 = \mu_2$) would be rejected.

Example A research organization surveyed the food buying habits of housewives in two cities. A random sample of 300 housewives in supermarket A in one city showed that the average weekly expenditure on food was £10, with a standard deviation of £3. Another random sample of 300 housewives in supermarket B in the other city showed that the average weekly expenditure on food was £8, with a standard deviation of £2.

Test at 5 per cent level of significance whether the average weekly food expenditures of the two populations from which the random samples were drawn are, in fact, equal.

NH: $\mu_1 = \mu_2$ $\alpha = 0.05$
AH: $\mu_1 \neq \mu_2$
(Estimate variances from sample values, s_1^2 and s_2^2)

$$\text{Therefore, } Z = \frac{|\bar{x}_1 - \bar{x}_2|}{\sqrt{[(s_1^2/n_1) + (s_2^2/n_2)]}} \sim N(0,1)$$

$$= \frac{10 - 8}{\sqrt{[(3^2/300) + (2^2/300)]}}$$

$$= \frac{2}{\sqrt{(13/300)}} \text{ i.e., } 9.6$$

Since $9.6 > 1.96$, the hypothesis is rejected (i.e., the difference is significant).

Example Two areas of the UK were surveyed and it was found that a random sample of 500 households in the North East of England had an average annual consumption of 26 lb of tea, with a standard deviation of 6 lb. A random sample of 400 households in southern counties revealed an average annual consumption of 20 lb of tea, with a standard deviation of 4 lb.

Can the difference between these samples be attributed to sampling variation, or is it significant?

NH: $\mu_1 = \mu_2$ Test at 1 per cent level ($\alpha = 0.01$)
AH: $\mu_1 \neq \mu_2$

$$\text{By formula, } Z = \frac{|\bar{x}_1 - \bar{x}_2|}{\sqrt{[(s_1^2 + s_2^2)/(n_1 + n_2)]}}$$

$$= \frac{26 - 20}{\sqrt{[(6^2/500) + (4^2/400)]}}$$

$$= \frac{6}{\sqrt{(224/2000)}}$$

$$= \frac{6}{0.334} \text{ i.e., } 17.6$$

Since $17.6 \gg 2.58$, the hypothesis is rejected.

Example Two random sample surveys were undertaken to study the consumption of a certain brand of instant coffee in different communities.

Four hundred households were samples in a dormitory town and the average annual consumption was found to be 33.0 oz, with a standard deviation of 15.0.

Eight hundred households were sampled from a manufacturing town and the average annual consumption was about 31.6 oz., with a standard deviation of 12.0.

Can the difference between these samples be attributed to sampling variations, or is it significant:

NH: $\mu_1 = \mu_2$ (Test at 5 per cent level ($\alpha = 0.05$))
AH: $\mu_1 \neq \mu_2$

$$\text{Hence, } n_1 = 400 \quad \bar{x}_1 = 33.0 \quad s = 15$$
$$n_2 = 800 \quad \bar{x}_2 = 31.6 \quad s = 12$$

$$\text{By formula, } Z = \frac{|\bar{x}_1 - \bar{x}_2|}{\sqrt{[(s_1^2/n_1) + (s_2^2/n_2)]}}$$

$$= \frac{33.0 - 31.6}{\sqrt{[(15^2/400) + (12^2/800)]}}$$

$$= \frac{1.4}{\sqrt{0.7425}}$$

$$= 1.63$$

Since $1.63 < 1.96$, the null hypothesis should be accepted at the 5 per cent level (i.e., the difference in consumption is the result of sampling variation).

Testing attributes

In many cases the proportions in which an event occurs (or does not occur) are of special interest, particularly in the area of marketing. For example, the proportion of ownership of some consumer durables such as colour television sets. This gives rise to the use of the Binomial

Distribution, where for large samples the Central Limit Theorem permits the use of the normal approximation to the Binomial Distribution, thus simplifying the calculation of the probabilities.

Test of significance of difference between $\hat{p}$ and expected value p

$$p = \text{true proportion of success}$$
$$\hat{p} = \text{estimate of proportion of successes from sample } n$$

Therefore, $z = \dfrac{\hat{p} - p}{\sqrt{(pq/n)}}$ i.e., $\dfrac{actual\ number\ of\ successes - expected\ number\ of\ successes}{\sqrt{(pq/n)}}$

If $z > 1.96$, then difference between $\hat{p}$ and p will be significant at the 5 per cent level and the hypothesis will be rejected.

If $z > 2.58$, then difference between $\hat{p}$ and p will be significant at the 1 per cent level and the hypothesis will be rejected.

Example It was stated by a pharmaceutical firm that a new formula cold cure, if taken to their instructions, would be effective in 75 out of 100 cases in getting rid of colds within hours. This claim was tested independently on a random sample of 120 people. The results showed that 80 people were cured of their colds as promised by the manufacturers of the cold cure, while 40 people actually received no such benefit.

NH: $p = 0.75$ (+ 'one-tail' test at 0.01 level)
AH: $p < 0.75$

$$Z = \frac{\hat{p} - p}{\sqrt{(pq/n)}} = \frac{(80/120) - (75/100)}{\sqrt{[(0.75 \times 0.25)/120]}}$$

$$= \frac{-0.083}{\sqrt{0.00156}}$$

$$= \frac{-0.083}{0.039}$$

$$= -2.13, \text{ which is} > -2.33$$

The claim is therefore legitimate, i.e., the null hypothesis is accepted.

The one-tail test has been selected because we are interested in determining whether the proportion of people cured of their colds is too low.

Example A well-known car manufacturer claimed that 40 per cent of the cars made by the firm in 1960 were still in running order after 10 years, i.e., 1970. Test this claim at 0.05 level of significance against a sample, drawn at random of 1000 cars made by this manufacturer which revealed that 360 were still in a good usable condition in 1970.

NH: $p = 0.4$
AH: $p < 0.4$

$$Z = \frac{\hat{p} - p}{\sqrt{(pq/n)}} = \frac{(360/1000) - (40/100)}{\sqrt{(0.4 \times 0.6/1000)}}$$

$$= \frac{-(40/1000)}{\sqrt{(0.24/1000)}} \text{ i.e. } \frac{-0.04}{\sqrt{0.024}}$$

$$= \frac{-0.04}{0.155}$$

$$= -0.26, \text{ which is} \ll 1.645$$

Therefore, the null hypothesis must be accepted at the 0.05 level (note: 'one-tail' test).

Example A certain branded food product claimed to have a 40 per cent share of the UK market. A random sample of 1000 consumers in the North West revealed that 450 people actually used the product. Is there a significant difference between the regional brand share and the national brand share?

NH: $p = 0.4$
AH: $p \neq 0.4$

$$|Z| = \frac{\hat{p} - p}{\sqrt{(pq/n)}} = \frac{(450/1000) - (40/100)}{\sqrt{[(0.4 \times 0.6/1000)]}}$$

$$= \frac{0.05}{\sqrt{0.000\,24}}$$

$$= 3.3$$

Since $3.3 > 2.58$ (1 per cent level) there is a significant difference between the North West and the national pattern of buying of this product. The null hypothesis is, therefore, rejected at the 1 per cent level.

Comparing two sample proportions

In this case, two random samples of sizes n_1 and n_2, having proportions of success of p_1 and p_2 respectively, are considered. The problem is to test whether they come from the same population. The test is similar to that used to test the significance of difference between two sample means:

NH: $p_1 = p_2$ or $p_1 - p_2 = 0$
AH: $p_1 \neq p_2$

$$|Z| = \frac{\hat{p}_1 - \hat{p}_2}{\text{SE}(\hat{p}_1 - \hat{p}_2)}$$

$$\text{SE}(\hat{p}_1 - \hat{p}_2) = \sqrt{\frac{(n_1 \hat{p}_1 + n_2 \hat{p}_2)\,[n_1(1 - \hat{p}_1) + n_2(1 - \hat{p}_2)]}{n_1 \times n_2(n_1 + n_2)}}$$

The calculation of the standard error is less difficult than the equation suggests at first sight.

If $|Z| > 1.96$, there will be a 5 per cent significant difference between the proportions p_1 and p_2 and the null hypothesis will be rejected at this level.

A similar procedure applies for the 0.01 level.

Example The findings of a sample survey, which used random sampling techniques, were that of 200 households in the Birmingham area, 80 per cent had a family car, whereas a sample of 300 taken in the Manchester area showed a comparable figure of 75 per cent. Is there any significant difference between these two proportions at the 0.01 level?

NH: $p_1 = p_2$ or $p_2 = 0$
AH: $p_1 \neq p_2$

$$\alpha = 0.01 \quad \hat{p}_1 = 0.8 \quad \hat{p}_2 = 0.75 \quad n_1 = 200 \quad n_2 = 300$$

$$\text{SE}(\hat{p}_1 - \hat{p}_2) = \sqrt{\frac{(n_1 \hat{p}_1 + n_2 \hat{p}_2)\,[n_1(1 - \hat{p}_1) + n_2(1 - \hat{p}_2)]}{n_1 \times n_2(n_1 + n_2)}}$$

$$= \sqrt{\frac{[(200 \times 0.8 + 300 \times 0.75)]\,[(200 \times 0.2) + (300 \times 0.25)]}{200 \times 300\,(200 + 300)}}$$

$$= \sqrt{\frac{385 \times 115}{60\ 000 \times 500}} = \sqrt{0.001\ 476}$$

$$\text{Therefore,}\ \frac{\hat{p}_1 - \hat{p}_2}{\text{SE}(\hat{p}_1 - \hat{p}_2)} = \frac{0.8 - 0.75}{\sqrt{0.001\ 476}} = \frac{0.05}{0.038} = 1.32$$

$1.32 < 2.58$. The null hypothesis is accepted because there is no significant difference.

Example A random sample of 100 people in a certain rural area showed that 54 per cent favoured five-day shopping in the local market town, while a sample of 200 townspeople revealed that 48 per cent were in favour of shopping being restricted to five days per week. Is there any significant difference between these proportions? Test at 0.05 level.

NH: $p_1 = p_2\ np_1 - p_2 = 0$
AH: $p_1 \neq p_2$

$$\alpha = 0.05\ \hat{p}_1 = 0.54\quad \hat{p}_2 = 0.48\quad n_1 = 100\quad n_2 = 200$$

$$\text{SE}(\hat{p}_1 - \hat{p}_2) = \sqrt{\frac{[(100 \times 0.54) + (200 \times 0.48)]\,[(100 \times 0.46) + (200 \times 0.52)]}{100 \times 200\,(100 + 200)}}$$

$$= \sqrt{\frac{150 \times 150}{6\ 000\ 000}}$$

$$\text{Therefore,}\ \frac{\hat{p}_1 - \hat{p}_2}{\text{SE}(\hat{p}_1 - \hat{p}_2)} = \frac{0.54 - 0.48}{\sqrt{(22\ 500/6\ 000\ 000)}} = \frac{0.06}{\sqrt{0.003\ 75}} = \frac{0.06}{0.062} = 0.97$$

$0.97 < 1.96$. Therefore, the null hypothesis cannot be rejected and there is no significant difference between the proportions at 0.05 level.

Example A research agency undertook two random surveys of 1000 families before and during a test campaign for a consumer food product. The first test showed that 26 per cent were aware of the product and bought it regularly; the second sampling revealed that 28 per cent were aware of the product and bought it on a regular basis. Is this 2 per cent increase significant? Test at both 0.01 and 0.05 levels.

NH: $p_1 = p_2$ or $p_1 - p_2 = 0$
AH: $p_1 \neq p_2$

$$\alpha = 0.01 \text{ and } 0.05\ \hat{p}_1 = 0.26\quad \hat{p}_2 = 0.28\quad n_1 = 1000\quad n_2 = 1000$$

$$\text{SE}(\hat{p}_1 - \hat{p}_2) = \sqrt{\frac{[(1000 \times 0.26) + (1000 \times 0.28)]\,[(1000 \times 0.74) + (1000 \times 0.72)]}{1000 \times 1000\,(1000 + 1000)}}$$

$$= \sqrt{\frac{540 \times 1460}{2\ 000\ 000\ 000}}$$

$$= \sqrt{0.000\ 39} = 0.0198$$

$$\text{Therefore,}\ \frac{\hat{p}_1 - \hat{p}_2}{\text{SE}(\hat{p}_1 - \hat{p}_2)} = \frac{0.26 - 0.28}{0.0198} = -\frac{0.02}{0.0198} = 1.01$$

$$(-1.01 < 1.96;\ -1.01 \ll 2.58)$$

Therefore, the increase in the use of the product is not significant, and the null hypothesis cannot be rejected at either level.

Value of standard error in testing hypothesis

From the examples just given, it will be evident that the standard error is the key to the whole process. Any hypothesis which involves a sample statistic can be tested provided the standard error is known: the median, the mode, the variance, the standard deviation, the semi-interquartile range, etc., can all be tested. In actual practice, the sample mean and the proportion are the most commonly used statistics. Table 15.3 summarizes their standard error equations.

Table 15.3 Summary of standard error equations

	Θ (Parameter)	Θ (Estimator)	SE (Θ) (Estimate)
Mean	μ	$\bar{x}$	$\dfrac{s}{\sqrt{n}}$
Difference between the two means	$\mu_1 - \mu_2$	$\bar{x}_1 - \bar{x}_2$	$\sqrt{\dfrac{s_1^2}{n_1} + \dfrac{s_2^2}{n_2}}$
Proportion	p	$\hat{p}$	$\sqrt{\dfrac{p\,(1-p)}{n}}$
Difference between the two proportions	$p_1 - p_2$	$\hat{p}_1 - \hat{p}_2$	$\sqrt{\dfrac{(n_1\,\hat{p}_1 + n_2\,\hat{p}_2)\,[n_1(1-\hat{p}_1) + n_2(1-\hat{p}_2)]}{n_1 \times n_2(n_1 + n_2)}}$

't' Distribution (also known as 'Student's' 't' distribution)

This distribution enables tests to be performed upon the mean of small samples, i.e., $n < 30$, drawn from a normal distribution. Where σ^2 (population variance) is unknown, the sample estimate s^2 must be used.

$$'t' = \frac{\bar{x} - \mu}{(s/\sqrt{n})} \text{ with } (n - 1) \text{ degree of freedom (d.f.)}$$

The 't' distribution is more dispersed than the normal distribution. This dispersion will be greater the smaller the size of the sample, because $S_{\bar{x}}$ tends to vary more markedly from sample to sample the smaller the sample size (see Fig. 15.3).

As n becomes larger, the t distribution approaches the normal distribution. For $n > 30$ it is practically identical to the normal distribution. (This can be checked by reference to statistical tables of these distributions.)

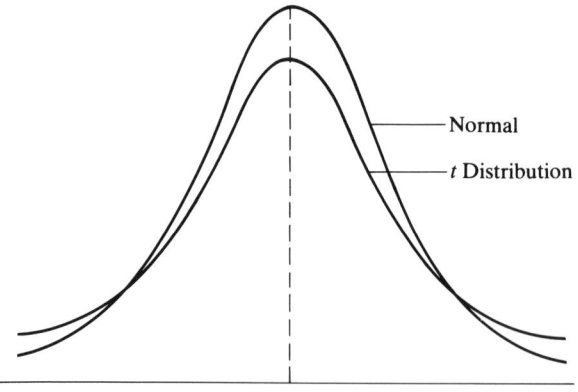

Fig. 15.3 Graph showing distribution

Testing using 't' distribution

$$\text{Mean, '}t\text{'} = \frac{\bar{x} - \mu}{(s/\sqrt{n})} \text{ distribution on } n - 1 \text{ d.f.}$$

NH is rejected at either 5 per cent or 1 per cent, if the result of the test allows.

Example Samples of six observations taken from a normal distribution were: 6.5, 8.6, 7.4, 5.7, 8.3, and 7.2. Is it reasonable to assume $\mu = 7$?

NH: $\mu = 7$
AH: $\mu \neq 7$

$$\bar{x} = \sum \frac{x_1}{n} = \frac{43.7}{6} = 7.28$$

$$s^2 = \frac{1}{n-1} \sum (x_1 - \bar{x})^2 = 1.0870$$

$$\text{Therefore, } s = 0.992 \quad \frac{s}{\sqrt{n}} = \frac{0.0992}{2.449} = 0.426$$

$$\text{Now, '}t\text{'} \quad = \frac{\bar{x} - \mu}{(s/\sqrt{n})} = \frac{7.28 - 7}{0.405} = 0.658$$

From tables the 5 per cent value for 't' on $(6 - 1)$ d.f. $= 2.57$. As $0.691 \ll 2.57$, the null hypothesis that $\mu = 7$ cannot be rejected.

Example A census of retail stores in a certain year showed that the average turnover of privately owned food stores was £15 000. A sample of 16 of these stores (taken at random) in the following year revealed an average turnover of £16 500 and a standard deviation of £1900. Has there been any significant change in average sales?

NH: That the sample comes from a population having a mean £15 000, i.e., $\mu = £15\ 000$.
AH: $\mu \neq £15\ 000$.

$$\text{'}t\text{'} = \frac{\bar{x} - \mu}{(s/\sqrt{n})} n = 16 \; s = £1900$$

$$\bar{x} = £16\ 500 \; s_{\bar{x}} = \frac{s}{\sqrt{n}} = \frac{1900}{\sqrt{16}} = 475$$

$$\mu = £15\ 000$$

$$= \frac{£16\ 500 - £15\ 000}{475} = 3.16$$

From 't' tables 't'$(n - 1)$ d.f. at 5 per cent level, i.e., 't' 15 d.f. at 5 per cent level $= 2.13$.

Since $3.16 \gg 2.13$, the null hypothesis is rejected since there has been a significant change in the average turnover of food stores since the census was taken.

Testing the difference between two means

$$t = \frac{|x_1 - \bar{x}_2|}{\sqrt{[(n_1 s^2 + n_2 s_2^2)/n_1 n_2]}} \text{(Note similarity to ND test)}$$

NH: $\mu_1 = \mu_2$
AH: $\mu_1 \neq \mu_2$

Example
$$n_1 = 10 \quad \bar{x}_1 = 54 \quad s_1^2 = 3.2$$
$$n_2 = 12 \quad \bar{x}_2 = 56 \quad s_2^2 = 3.6$$

$$t = \frac{|54 - 56|}{\sqrt{\{[(10 \times 3.2) + (12 \times 3.6)]/(10 \times 12)\}}} = \frac{2}{\sqrt{0.6276}} = \frac{2}{0.79} = 2.53$$

5 per cent for 't' distribution with $(n_1 + n_2 - 2)$ d.f., i.e., $(10 + 12 - 2) = 20$, is t_{19} (5 per cent) $= 2.09$.

As $2.53 > 2.09$, the null hypothesis, that the samples are drawn from normal distributions having the same mean, can be rejected.

Special note on 't' test examples

To simplify the examples illustrating the 't' test applied to testing the difference between two means, the formula used has been:

$$'t' = \frac{|\bar{x}_1 - \bar{x}_2|}{\sqrt{[(n_1 s_1^2 + n_2 s_2^2)/n_1 n_2]}}$$

on the assumption that the variances can be estimated from the given standard deviations and that the variances are equal (or approximately so).

It is advisable, however, to submit the variances to a special test known as the Fisher 'F' test for which the formula is:

$$F = \frac{s_1^2}{s_2^2}$$

This indicates whether or not variances are equal. (Special 'F' distribution tables for calculating the values are to be found in statistical textbooks.)

Example (refer to example at top of page.)

$$F = \frac{s_1^2}{s_2^2} = \frac{3.2}{3.6} = 0.889$$

Upper F value $2\frac{1}{2}$ per cent (0.05) point $F_{v_1}, F_{v_2} = F_{9,11} = 3.595$

Lower F value $2\frac{1}{2}$ per cent (0.05) point $\dfrac{1}{F_{v_2}, F_{v_1}} = F\dfrac{1}{11.9}$

$$= \frac{1}{3.915} = 0.255$$

Therefore, the value of F of 0.889 lies between the acceptance region of 0.255 and 3.595. (The 't' test can now be proceeded with in the usual manner.)

Example (refer to next example and calculate Upper and Lower F values)

$$F = \frac{s_1^2}{s_2^2} = \frac{(2.8)^2}{(4.6)^2} = \frac{7.84}{21.16} = 0.37$$

Therefore, the value F of 0.37 lies within the acceptance region of 0.255 and 3.595. (Proceed to do 't' test as shown below.)

Example A food product was tested in two areas, A and B, and average sales for 10 and 12 weeks respectively were 50.2 cases and 54.2 cases, with standard deviations of 2.8 and 4.6. Have the two areas the same mean level of sales? Check at 5 per cent level.

NH: That there is no difference between the average sales in the two areas.
AH: That there is a significant difference between the average sales in the two areas.

$$'t' = \frac{|\bar{x}_1 - \bar{x}_2|}{\sqrt{[(n_1 s_1^2 + n_2 s_2^2)/n_1 n_2]}}$$

$$= \frac{4.0}{\{[(10 \times 2.8^2) + (12 \times 4.6^2)]/(10 \times 12)\}}$$

$$= \frac{4.0}{\sqrt{2.77}} = 2.4$$

$'t'$ distribution at 5 per cent level with $(10 + 12 - 2)$, i.e., 19 d.f. = 2.09.

Since $2.4 > 2.09$, the null hypothesis, that the two samples are drawn from the same mean, can be rejected. There is a significant difference between the two areas.

Example Two independent samples were taken of eight and ten salesmen, the former having been assisted during the quarter under the review by supervisors, whereas the latter had received no field training. Their respective increases in sales over the quarter are shown in Table 15.4.

Table 15.4   Increases in sales

Salesmen	Increases in sales(£000's)									
A Assisted by supervisors	12	8	15	16	14	12	8	15	—	—
B No field training	6	10	7	15	20	14	8	2	21	10

Are the average increases in the two samples significantly different?

NH: $\mu_1 = \mu_2$
AH: $\mu_1 \neq \mu_2$

$$\bar{x}_A = \frac{100}{8} = 12.5 \quad \bar{x}_B = \frac{113}{10} = 11.3$$

$$s_A^2 = \frac{1}{n-1} \Sigma(x - \bar{x})^2 = \tfrac{1}{7}$$

$$\Sigma(0.5^2 + 4.5^2 + 2.5^2 + 3.5^2 + 1.5^2 + 0.5^2 + 4.5^2 + 2.5^2) = 9.7$$

$$s_B^2 = \frac{1}{n-1} \Sigma(x - \bar{x})^2 = \tfrac{1}{9}$$

$$\Sigma(5.3^2 + 1.3^2 + 4.3^2 + 3.7^2 + 8.7^2 + 2.7^2 + 3.3^2 + 9.3^2 + 9.7^2 + 1.3^2) = 37.6$$

$$'t' = \frac{|\bar{x}_1 - \bar{x}_2|}{\sqrt{[(n_1 s_1^2 + n_2 s_2^2)/n_1 n_2]}} = \frac{|12.5 - 11.3|}{\sqrt{[(8 \times 9.7) + (10 \times 37.6)/8 \times 10]}}$$

$$= \frac{1.2}{\sqrt{5.6}} = \frac{1.2}{2.386} = 0.507$$

$'t'$ test with $(8 + 10 - 2)$ d.f. at 5 per cent level = 2.12

Since $0.507 < 2.12$, the null hypothesis cannot be rejected. The observed difference between the two groups of salesmen is not significant.

Example (paired comparison) A company has eight sales areas, and from each area one salesman's performance is checked *before* and after an intensive sales training course. The results are shown in Table 15.5.

NH: That the course has not resulted in a significant increase in sales.
AH: That the course has resulted in a significant increase in sales.
Let 'd' = difference between values of x and y, i.e. $(x - y = d)$

Therefore, $d - 10 - 10 - 3 - 2 - 6 - 12 - 12 - 12$

$$\Sigma\frac{d}{n} = \frac{-67}{8} = -8.375 \ (n = \text{no. of pairs})$$

$$s_d^2 = \frac{1}{n-1}(\Sigma d_1^2 - nd^2)$$

$$= \tfrac{1}{7}[(100 + 100 + 9 + 4 + 36 + 144 + 144 + 144) - 8(-8.375)^2]$$

$$= \tfrac{1}{7}(681 - 561.12) = 17.12$$

Therefore, $s_d = 4.14$

$$`t' = \frac{-d}{(S_d/\sqrt{n})} = \frac{-8.375}{(4.14/\sqrt{8})} = \frac{-8.375 \times 2.828}{4.14} - 5.72$$

't' at $(8-1)$ d.f. at 5 per cent level = 2.36

Hence, we can say that there was a significant increase in sales, and the null hypothesis is rejected.

Table 15.5 Performance before and after sales training course

	Salesmen	A	B	C	D	E	F	G	H
					Sales (£000's)				
(x)	Before training	55	30	45	44	52	55	56	60
(y)	After training	65	40	48	46	58	67	68	72

15.2 BI-VARIATE ANALYSIS

Bi-variate analysis uses statistical techniques such as chi-square, simple correlation and simple regression, cross-classification and analysis of variance to give insight into why there are differences or variations in a dependent variable. It will be recalled that a dependent variable is one which, as the name suggests, is dependent upon the action taken; for example, by a marketing manager. His or her activities will affect sales volume, brand preferences, etc. The independent variable is the one the marketing researcher believes may account for the observed differences or variations in the dependent variable, e.g., changes in price, packaging, methods of distribution, etc.

Changes in the independent variable are carefully studied to see in what way they influence the dependent variable. To illustrate bi-variate analysis, some examples of chi-square applications are based on the data given in Tables 15.6–15.10.

Chi-square (pronounced ki and denoted by χ^2)

Chi-square distribution has many applications and is particularly useful in testing whether observed frequencies in a sample distribution differ significantly from frequencies which could be expected to arise from some hypothesis. Chi-square tests are concerned with establishing whether the discrepancies between observed frequencies and expected frequencies are, in fact, statistically significant or whether they may be attributed to chance sampling errors or variations in the data.

Chi-square tests are particularly useful in studying the relationship between attributes which is frequently of interest in marketing. Data can be arranged conveniently in cross-classification or matrix form. The number of frequencies in each cell should not be fewer than five – it may be necessary to combine cells in order to achieve this figure, though this may lead to some loss of precision in definition. At least 50 observations should be included in the total sample, and these must be randomly selected. Chi-square data are always stated in terms of original units and not percentages.

Basically, the χ^2 test procedure is quite simple: an hypothesis is set up – frequently a null hypothesis. Observed frequencies are then compared with data based on some assumed frequencies. The χ^2 statistic is computed from special statistical tables (found in most statistical textbooks), at some agreed level of significance, usually either 5 per cent or 1 per cent. The resultant figure is compared with that obtained from the equation involving observed and expected frequencies. The hypothesis is then accepted or rejected on the basis of this statistical evidence of probability.

The equation to compare observed and expected frequencies is:

$$\chi^2 = \sum \frac{(O_i - E_i)^2}{E_i}$$

Where: O_i = observed frequencies in a distribution.
E_i = expected frequencies under the hypothesis that the data have a particular distribution.

The larger the value of χ^2, the greater the difference between observed and expected frequencies. Note also that since the right-hand side of the formula represents a sum of squared quantities, χ^2 is always positive.

If data are originally expressed in percentage or proportional form, they should be converted to *absolute* numbers. For example, if 40 per cent of people in a sample size of 200, is female, then computations for calculating χ^2 should be based on 80 females (and *not* on 40 per cent of a sample being female).

Example

Table 15.6 Packaging test for instant coffee

	Tin	Glass bottle	Total
Favoured	45 (50)	55 (50)	100
Not favoured	55	45	100
Total	100	100	200

A random sample of 100 customers revealed that 45 favoured tins, whereas 55 favoured glass bottle packaging, as shown in Table 15.6. Is the difference between these sample estimates significant?

NH: $p_1 = p_2$

By formula, $\chi^2 = \sum \dfrac{(O - E)^2}{E}$

$E = \dfrac{\text{Product of the marginal totals pertaining to the cell under consideration}}{\text{Total observations in sample}}$

$$= \frac{100 \times 100}{50} = 50 \text{ (shown in parentheses in matrix)}$$

Therefore, $\chi^2 = \dfrac{(45 - 50)^2}{50} + \dfrac{(55 - 50)^2}{50} + \dfrac{(55 - 50)^2}{50} + \dfrac{(45 - 50)^2}{50}$

$$= 0.5 + 0.5 + 0.5 + 0.5 = 2$$

χ^2 at one degree of freedom* is χ^2 $(2 - 1)$ $(2 - 1)$ d.f. at 5 per cent level $= 3.84$. Because, $2 < 3.84$, the hypothesis cannot be rejected. The difference noted in the sample is due to sampling errors and it is not statistically significant.

Example Data in this example are cross-classified on a two-way basis, as shown in Table 15.7, which is particularly useful in marketing studies. This enables associations between variables to be tested; often referred to as contingency tables.

Table 15.7   Consumer food product

Socio-economic group	Brand loyalty			Total
	High	Medium	Low	
A – B	20 (17.5)	20 (20)	10 (12.5)	50
C	20 (31.5)	40 (36)	30 (22.5)	90
D – E	30 (21.0)	20 (24)	10 (15)	60
Total	70	80	50	200

NH: Membership of social group and brand loyalty are independent.
Calculate expected frequencies, e.g.:

$$\text{A} - \text{B} \frac{50}{200} \times 70 = 17.5 \frac{50}{200} \times 80 = 20 \frac{50}{200} \times 50 = 12.5$$

(Enter these in parentheses against observed frequencies in matrix.)

$$\text{C} \frac{90}{200} \times 70 = 31.5 \frac{90}{200} \times 80 = 36 \frac{90}{200} \times 50 = 22.5$$

$$\text{D} - \text{E} \frac{60}{200} \times 70 = 17.5 \frac{60}{200} \times 80 = 20 \frac{60}{200} \times 50 = 15$$

* Computed by deducting one from number of cells (both horizontal and vertical) and calculating their product, i.e., $(r - 1)\,(s - 1)$ d.f.

(The last line can, of course, be obtained by deducting the other expectancies from the total cell figure.)

$$\text{Therefore, } \chi^2 = \frac{(20 - 17.5)^2}{17.5} + \frac{(20 - 20)^2}{20} + \frac{(10 - 12.5)^2}{12.5}$$

$$+ \frac{(20 - 31.5)^2}{31.5} + \frac{(40 - 36)^2}{36}$$

$$+ \frac{(30 - 22.5)^2}{22.5} + \frac{(30 - 21)^2}{21}$$

$$+ \frac{(20 - 24)^2}{24} + \frac{(10 - 15)^2}{15}$$

$$= \frac{(2.5)^2}{17.5} + \frac{(2.5)^2}{12.5} + \frac{(11.5)^2}{31.5} + \frac{(4)^2}{36} + \frac{(7.5)^2}{22.5}$$

$$= 0.36 + 0.5 + 4.2 + 0.44 + 2.5 + 3.9 + 0.66 + 1.66$$

$$= 14.2$$

$\chi^2 (3 - 1)(3 - 1)$ d.f. at 5 per cent level $= 9.49$

at 1 per cent level $= 13.28$

Since $14.2 > 9.49$, the null hypothesis can be rejected at the 0.05 level. It appears, therefore, that brand loyalty is significantly affected by social group membership. Likewise, since $14.2 > 13.28$, the null hypothesis can also be rejected at the 0.01 level.

Example

Table 15.8   Consumer food product

Brand preference	A	B	C	Total
Bought	30 (33)	25 (33)	45 (33)	100
Did not buy	70 (67)	75 (67)	55 (67)	200
Total	100	100	100	300

NH: $p_1 = p_2 = p_3$

The expected frequencies have been calculated in the usual manner and are shown in parentheses in Table 15.8

$$\chi^2 = \Sigma \frac{(O - E)^2}{E}$$

$$= 0.27 + 1.94 + 4.36 + 0.134 + 0.96 + 0.96$$

$$= 8.624$$

$\chi^2 (3 - 1)(2 - 1)$ d.f. at 5 per cent level $= 5.99$

Since $8.624 > 5.99$, the null hypothesis, that probabilities of selection are equal over the various brands, can be rejected.

However, χ^2 with 2 d.f. at 1 per cent level $= 9.21$ and $8.624 < 9.21$; the null hypothesis *cannot* be rejected at this level.

This example illustrates that a statistical hypothesis cannot be rejected or accepted absolutely; it depends on the probability level which the researcher chooses as a measure of significance.

Example In a quality check, four outer cartons of different brands of tinned peaches were chosen at random. Each carton contained 12 tins, and several tins were found to be below the acceptable standard. These were distributed (see Table 15.9) over the four brands involved as follows:

$$3 \quad 9 \quad 5 \quad 2$$

From these data, is it reasonable to conclude that the four brands were of comparable quality?
NH: $p_1 = p_2 = p_3 = p_4$

$$\chi^2 = \sum \frac{(O - E)^2}{E}$$

$$= \frac{(9 - 7.25)^2}{7.25} + \frac{(3 - 7.25)^2}{7.25} + \frac{(7 - 7.25)^2}{7.25} + \frac{(10 - 7.25)^2}{7.25}$$

$$+ \frac{(3 - 4.75)^2}{4.75} + \frac{(9 - 4.75)^2}{4.75} + \frac{(5 - 4.75)^2}{4.75} + \frac{(2 - 4.75)^2}{4.75}$$

$$= 0.42 + 2.49 + 0.009 + 1.04 + 0.65 + 3.8 + 0.013 + 1.6$$
$$= 10.022$$
$$\chi^2 \ (2 - 1) \ (4 - 1) \ \text{d.f. at 5 per cent level} = 7.81,$$
$$\chi^2 \ (2 - 1) \ (4 - 1) \ \text{d.f. at 1 per cent level} = 11.34.$$

Therefore, the null hypothesis can be rejected at the 5 per cent level, but *not* at the 1 per cent level.

Table 15.9   Cartons of peaches

	Brand A	Brand B	Brand C	Brand D	Total
OK	9 (7.25)	3 (7.25)	7 (7.25)	10 (7.25)	29
Below standard	3 (4.75)	9 (4.75)	5 (4.75)	2 (4.75)	19
Total	12	12	12	12	48

Example A random sample of television viewers showed that television sets were either owned or rented in the proportions given in the contingency table, Table 15.10.

Table 15.10   Television sets

Television sets	Area			Total
	Midlands	North West	North East	
Owners	100 (110.7)	40 (43.1)	100 (86.2)	240
Renters	80 (69.3)	30 (26.9)	40 (53.8)	150
Total	180	70	140	390

NH: That owning and renting television sets are independent, i.e., are now associated with the area of residence of the viewer.

$$\chi^2 = \sum \frac{(O - E)^2}{E}$$

Calculate expected frequencies, e.g. first cell (Midlands) $\frac{240}{390} \times 180 = 110.7$

$$\chi^2 = \frac{(100 - 110.7)^2}{2} + \frac{(40 - 43.1)^2}{43.1} + \frac{(100 - 86.2)^2}{86.2}$$

$$+ \frac{(80 - 69.3)^2}{69.3} + \frac{(30 - 26.9)^2}{26.9} + \frac{(40 - 53.8)^2}{53.8}$$

$$= 1.03 + 0.22 + 0.16 + 0.015 + 0.36 + 0.26$$
$$= 2.045$$

$\chi^2 (3 - 1) (2 - 1)$ d.f. at 5 per cent level = 5.99

Since 2.045 < 5.99, the null hypothesis, that there is no relationship between the distribution of ownership and rental of television sets, is accepted.

15.3 MULTI-VARIATE ANALYSIS

Multi-variate analysis involves complex and sophisticated statistical methods which 'focus upon and bring out in bold relief, the structure of *simultaneous* relationships among three or more phenomena'.[2] Unlike simple uni-variate methods which deal with averages and variances, and bi-variate techniques which deal with pairwise relationships, multi-variate methods concentrate on the more complex relationships among several variables in a set of data.

Sheth[2] typifies multi-variate methods as either functional or structural. The former are 'most appropriate for building predictive models and for explaining one or more phenomena based on their relationships'. Multiple regression is a widely used technique; also used are multiple discriminant analysis, multi-variate analysis of variance, canonical correlation analysis, and conjoint or trade-off analysis. The latter type is more descriptive than predictive, and includes factor analysis, cluster analysis, and multi-dimensional scaling.

Factor analysis

Factor analysis, not to be confused with factorial design (see Chapter 2), has grown in popularity, although it has also attracted criticism because certain aspects, it is alleged, lack mathematical rigour. It is a form of multi-variate analysis based on the hypothesis that buying behaviour, for example, is rarely attributable merely to one cause or influence. Therefore, enquiry should endeavour to identify the multiple factors which are influential in certain buying conditions.

In a brand image study[3] related to consumers' life styles in America, a factor analysis program was used to identify 25 factors which were significant in establishing life styles. Beer drinkers and non-beer drinkers were compared and distinct brand loyalties emerged.

> Brand Y drinkers are Outdoorsmen, and thus more inclined to be Hard Drinkers; whereas the Brand W drinkers are more associated with the Cosmopolitan Traveller, the Dress-Conscious Man, the Well-Groomed Man, the Cocktail Drinker, and the Car-Conscious Man. Brand W drinkers seem to

seek more oral satisfaction, being associated with the Candy Consumer, and the Cigar and Pipe Smoker. Among light beer drinkers, approximately the same type of pattern can be discerned, though with less extreme differences between the brands.[3]

Douglas and Craig[4] indicate that factor analysis is useful in international marketing research because, for example, it can be used 'to reduce the number of variables to be analysed, and to identify comparable constructs in subsequent phases of the analysis'. For instance, in a comparative survey of magazine readership in the United States and France, the frequency of reading different magazines in each country was the first factor analysed, and divergent behaviour was established. In the United States, family, news, and housemaker magazines were the most frequently read groups, whereas in France, readership was more diverse; the most frequently read were those magazines focusing on women's interests, fashion, business, and televison.

Factor analysis[4] was also used in a study of women's life style patterns in the United States, the UK, and France. Five factors were highly similar in all countries, of which four: home; social; frustration; and innovation were extracted.

Harper[5] used factor analysis techniques to study the relationships between Cheshire and Cheddar cheeses. Over a period of time, five Cheshire cheeses from each day's production at a cheese factory 'were subjected to light mechanical tests and six types of subjective assessment'. Product moment correlation coefficients were finally calculated between all pairs of variables, and it was possible to identify 'at least three dimensions' which differentiate Cheshire cheeses. Comparative tests were then made with Cheddar cheeses. 'In the study on Cheshire cheeses, firmness and springiness emerge effectively indistinguishable in spite of the fact that two forms of assessment are not perfectly correlated. In the Cheddar cheese studies, the qualitative distinction between firmness and springiness is well substantiated.'

Factor analysis was also used in a study[6] of the qualitative attributes of coffee. Fourteen attributes of coffee were developed from open discussion with a group of consumers; these attributes were rated on a 10-point semantic differential scale (see Chapter 8). Ninety-four consumers, randomly selected, rated each of the 14 attributes after drinking a cup of coffee, the brand of which was unknown to them. In fact, only one brand was tested. The data were processed by an appropriate computer program, and the findings revealed that four factors were significant influences in coffee preferences: 'comforting taste', 'heartiness of flavour', 'genuineness of product', 'freshness'. Other attributes such as 'alive taste' and 'tastes like real coffee' appeared related to the last mentioned significant factor. The researcher concluded that this could imply 'that a major factor behind coffee preference may be the distinction between pure coffee and artificial coffee'; advertisements could profitably accentuate the 'genuineness' of their product.

Doyle[7] has reported a study of eight beverages: tea-bags, coffee-instant, fruit juice, soft drinks, coffee-fresh, tea-packet, drinking chocolate, and milk, in which factor analysis techniques were successfully used.

Cluster analysis, as Fitzroy[8] emphasizes, is not an analytical technique or single method, but a set of numerical methods in which there are large areas of subjectivity, so researchers should proceed cautiously. The scepticism with which the uninhibited use of cluster analysis has sometimes been greeted is also referred to in a review paper by Punj and Stewart.[9]

Cluster analysis examines people, products or brands, and attempts, often through factor analysis, to evaluate them in terms of clusters or comparative profiles. As a result of this cluster analysis, gaps may be found in the market where new products might be introduced. But none of the problems of cluster analysis has been that of definition: what determines the boundaries of clusters – 'the criterion for admission to a cluster is rather arbitrary', and clusters tend to be defined in various ways, according to the 'discipline and purpose of the reseacher'. It has been suggested[10] that clusters should have two properties: external isolation (objects in a cluster should be separated from those in another cluster by well-defined 'space'); and, internal cohesion (objects within the same cluster should be similar).

In other words, for clustering to be a valid and reliable method of analysis, it is of paramount importance that the objects or individuals within a cluster should be more similar to each other than to those in another cluster. In overseas research, for example, it may be possible to develop groups of countries that share significant life styles, stages of economic development, etc. (see Chapter 13).

Morgan and Purnell[11] designed 10 clusters in a study of electors' attitudes to political issues as follows: High Tory; Me first; Whig; Labour (little England); Meritocrat; Me first (anti-Europe); One-nation Tories; Left-wing labour; Meritocrat (pro-Europe); and right-wing Labour.

Marketing segmentation for a new drink was derived from cluster analysis,[11] from which three 'clusters' of existing drinks were apparent: hot health drinks, cold drinks, and hot non-health drinks (see Fig. 15.4).

Between these three clusters point NEW 1 was calculated, equidistant from Chocolate 1, Hot Lemon Barley, and Ideal Hot Drink. Further product suggestions resulted from reclustering until finally a total of five new products resulted. Thus, an area was highlighted 'where a product perhaps, Hot Fruit Juice: as healthy as Lemon Juice and as hot as Hot Lemon Barley might be marketed'.

Discretion is needed in handling this method of researching new products. Market gaps might be identified which are clearly nonsensical; for example, a product cheaper than existing brands but of the highest quality. Such meaningless concepts would, of course, be eliminated immediately.

Conjoint analysis ('trade-off' approach?)

When people buy products and services they tend to compare alternative suppliers and make some evaluation (which will vary in depth, according to the nature of the purchase) of the advantages and disadvantages which they perceive as attached to certain sources of supply and/or brands. What marketers need to have is some way of measuring and understanding the 'trade-offs' which specific people make when comparing kinds of products and eventually, perhaps, deciding on a particular brand.

A basic assumption of conjoint analysis is that products and services are made up of features or 'attributes': these may be varied according to the identified preferences of consumers. The more dominant the interest in a particular attribute of a product, the higher will be the 'utility' value given to it by actual or potential purchasers. The word 'conjoint' as Johnson[12] points out, refers to 'the fact that we can measure relative values of things considered jointly which might be unmeasurable taken one at a time.... The greatest strength of the procedure seems to be its ability to generate rather refined predictions from quite primitive data.

A new paper tissue, for example, may be available in three different colours, several sizes, and various thicknesses, with some price differentials. 'The trade-off approach would not only predict the winning combination of these attributes but would also estimate how much consumers value changes in one attribute against changes in the others – in other words, to what extent they are prepared to "trade-off" size against thickness, colour against size, and all of these against price.'[13]

Green and Wind[14] refer to the difficult problem facing marketing managers when the nature of the product under consideration has several disparate qualities, each attractive to a diverse number of consumers with different interests. For example, when considering replacement radial tyres for his two-year-old car, a motorist might be faced with three options: 'Goodyear's, with a tread life of 30 000 miles at $40 per tyre, and available at a store 10 minutes drive from his home;

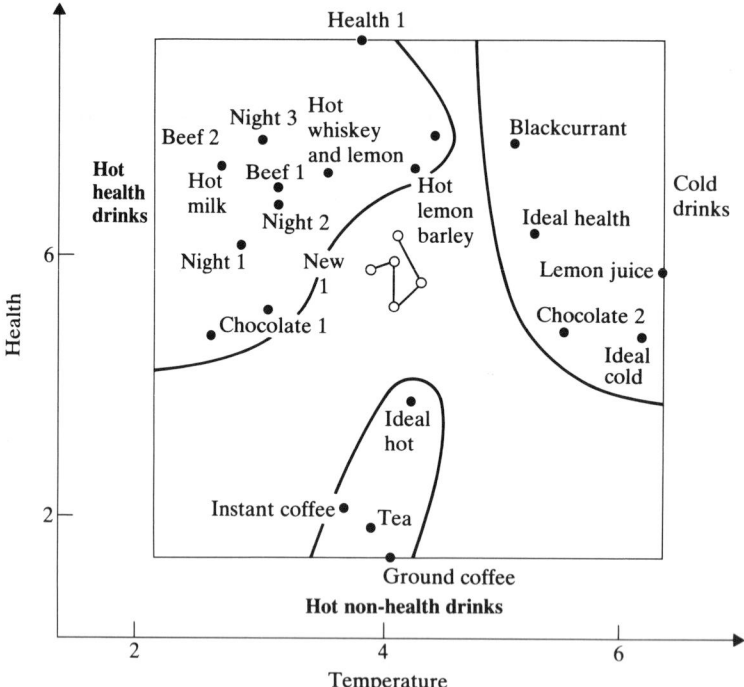

Fig. 15.4 Development of a new drink (*Source*: Morgan and Purnell)

Firestone's, with a tread life of 50 000 miles, at $85 per tyre, and available after 20 minutes drive; or Sears, with a tread life of 40 000 miles, at $55 per tyre, and available within 10 minutes drive from home.

To tackle this kind of problem, Green and Wind[14] noted that the conjoint measurement, which starts with the consumer's overall judgement about a set of complex alternatives, can help 'in sorting out the relative importance of a product's multi-dimensional attributes'. The relative utilities of each attribute are worked out from ranked order responses by various computer programs.

With some products, such as cars, houses, or office machinery, the possible design factors are virtually unlimited and it could be expensive, if not impossible, to offer physical specimens across all possible variations. In such cases, 'the researcher usually resorts to verbalized descriptions of the principal factors of interest'.[14] A study among car owners in the United States to identify preferences for new vehicles, focused on the relative influences of mileage per gallon, price, country of manufacture, maximum speed, roominess, and length. Consumers evaluated these factor levels on a two-at-a-time basis. It was found that evaluations of attributes desired in a new car were highly associated with the type of car currently used.

Two approaches to the application of conjoint analysis have been identified[15] as: the profile or scenario approach, and the pairwise or trade-off method.

With the former, a respondent could be asked to choose between all the attributes of a product at the one time; for example, a red cubic scented soap versus a blue cubic unscented soap, and so forth. This method is often thought to reflect realistically the decisions facing buyers; the problem is that survey data covering five attributes each at three levels, result in 243 possible combinations of product (i.e., 3^5), an unmanageable number.

The alternative method – pairwise or trade-off – allows a respondent to consider possible alternatives in a simpler way; first of all, for example, trading colour against shape, and then colour against aroma, and shape against aroma. Compared with the profile or scenario approach, this method merely handles nine sets of stimuli (3^2) (see Fig. 15.5).

Aroma \ Colour	Red	Blue	Yellow
Scented			
Unscented			

Fig. 15.5   Soap: aroma/colour matrix

A respondent could give ranked preferences for the attribute combinations; or a seven-point scale, for instance, could be used to indicate reactions to photographs or sketches of the alternative versions of the product.

An interesting application[16] of the 'trade-off' approach to customer service in industrial markets in Germany and Benelux was used in a mail survey of UK exporters and their European customers who were asked to choose between a number of alternative customer service 'packages'. Utility values were calculated for each factor/level for each respondent; the results showed that exporters' perceptions differed quite significantly from prospective customers' in many cases; for example, delivery promise reliability was ranked first with UK exporters, third with German customers, but was considered of paramount importance by Benelux customers; after-sales service was ranked second by UK firms, first by German customers, and third by Benelux customers; multi-language literature was particularly important to Benelux customers, less so to German customers, but it was not thought important by UK exporters.

With the development of computer programs, the complexity of multi-variate analysis has expanded considerably. A detailed knowledge of these and other statistical methodologies should be obtained from statistical textbooks, specialist books, and professional journals.[17-23]

Finally, sophisticated techniques should not be applied indiscriminately. Sheth[2] has observed that it is not uncommon to come across researchers who are familiar with a particular multi-variate method and who try to use that technique across all research problems. 'They seem to be literally in search of problems which will fit the technique rather than the other way round.'

Non-metric multi-dimensional scaling (MDS) or mapping

In the 1970s, an interesting method of presenting a comparative evaluation of products and brands was introduced and adopted the rather awesome title of 'non-metric multi-dimensional scaling', or the more understandable description: 'mapping'. A 'perceptual map' is drawn of how consumers perceive comparative products along certain dimensions or attributes. A perceptual map of four brands of a given product may be shown, as in Fig. 15.6. Where products or brands are mapped close to one another, it may be presumed that they are in fairly direct competition. 'It should be emphasized, however, that ... it is only the relative location of the points representing the stimuli that has meaning – the axes are arbitrary.'[8] To name the axes, additional information could be obtained from Kelly's Repertory Grid or, perhaps, semantic differential scales (see Chapter 8).

Basically, respondents are asked to rank order pairs of brands in terms of their perceived similarities, so that eventually some insight will be gained of people's choice criteria. Hence, ordinal data underlie this technique which has developed with specially devised computer programs. Doyle[17] has observed that the purpose of a spatial representation is to find out how brands or products in a class are perceived in comparative terms, so that strategic guides may be obtained for the development or improvement of new brands or products.

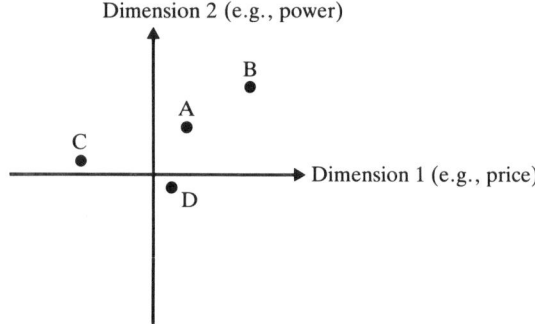

Fig. 15.6 Perceptual map of four brands

Because of the degree of subjectivity involved in this technique and its relatively limited applications, researchers need to use it with care.

15.4 SUMMARY

There are many analytical techniques in the field of data analysis; their applicability is governed by the number of variables involved which may range from one to several: uni-variate, bi-variate, and multi-variate.

Uni-variate data are concerned with a single variable, e.g., the mean; bi-variate data occur where some association is measured between two variables simultaneously, e.g., age group and consumption; multi-variate data occur where more than two variables are concerned, e.g., simultaneous analyses involving age, sex, and social group.

Bi-variate analysis uses chi-square, simple correlation and regression, analysis of variance, etc. Changes in the independent variable are carefully studied to see how they influence the dependent variable.

Multi-variate analysis involves complex statistical techniques and computer programs. Multi-regression, multi-variate analysis of variance, conjoint or trade-off analysis, factor analysis, cluster analysis, and multi-dimensional scaling, are some of the sophisticated techniques used. While multi-variate analysis has expanded considerably, the application of specific statistical techniques should be approached cautiously.

As well as being used for estimating population parameters, sampling theory is also concerned with testing statistical hypotheses. Often, a statistical hypothesis is found for the sole purpose of rejecting or nullifying it, if test results allow; it is then termed a 'null hypothesis'.

The standard error is the key to the whole process of hypothesis testing.

REFERENCES

1. Moser, C. A., and G. Kalton, *Survey Methods in Social Investigation*, Heinemann, London, 1971.
2. Sheth, Jagdish N., 'How to get the most out of multivariate methods', *Combined Proceedings*, no.37, American Marketing Association, 1975.
3. Alpert, Lewis, and Ronald Getty, 'Product positioning by behavioural life-styles', *Journal of Marketing*, April 1969.
4. Douglas, Susan P., and C. Samuel Craig, *International Marketing Research*, Prentice-Hall, Englewood Cliffs, New Jersey, 1983.

5. Harper, Roland, 'Factor analysis as a technique for examining complex data on foodstuffs', *Applied Statistics*, vol.1, no.1, March 1956.

6. Mukherjee, Bishwa Nath, 'A factor analysis of some qualitative attributes of coffee', *Journal of Advertising Research*, vol.5, no.1, March 1965.

7. Doyle, P. M., 'Market segmentation by factor analysis', *European Journal of Marketing*, vol.6, no.1, spring 1972.

8. Fitzroy, Peter T., *Analytical Methods for Marketing Management*, McGraw-Hill, Maidenhead, 1976.

9. Punj, Girish, and David W. Stewart, 'Cluster analysis in marketing research: Review and suggestions for application', *Journal of Marketing Research*, vol.20, May 1983.

10. Cormack, R. M., 'A review of classifications', *Journal of the Royal Statistical Society (Series A)*, vol.134, 1971.

11. Morgan, N., and J. Purnell, 'Isolating openings for new products in a multi-dimensional space', *Journal of the Market Research Society*, vol.11, no.3, July 1969.

12. Johnson, Richard M., 'Trade-off analysis of consumer values', *Journal of Marketing Research*, vol.11, May 1974.

13. Greenhalgh, Colin, 'Research for new product development', in: *Consumer Market Research Handbook*, Robert M. Worcester and John Downham (eds), Van Nostrand Reinhold, Wokingham, 1978.

14. Green, Paul E., and Yoram Wind, 'New way to measure consumers' judgements', *Harvard Business Review*, July–August 1975.

15. Mullett, Gary M., 'Using customer preferences to design products', *Business*, vol.27, Oct./Dec. 1983.

16. Marr, Norman E., 'The impact of customer service in international markets', *International Marketing Review*, vol.1, no.4, autumn/winter 1984.

17. Doyle, Peter, 'Non-metric multi-dimensional scaling: A user's guide', *European Journal of Marketing*, vol.7, no.2, 1973.

18. Harris, Paul, 'Statistics and significance testing', in: *Consumer Market Research Handbook*, Robert M. Worcester and John Downham (eds), Van Nostrand Reinhold, Wokingham, 1978.

19. Holmes, C., 'Multivariate analysis of market research data', in: *Consumer Market Research Handbook*, Robert M. Worcester and John Downham (eds), Van Nostrand Reinhold, Wokingham, 1978.

20. Green, Paul E., and Donald S. Tull, *Research for Marketing Decisions*, Prentice-Hall, Englewood Cliffs, New Jersey, 1975.

21. Ferber, Robert, *Market Research*, McGraw-Hill, New York, 1949.

22. Gatty, Ronald, 'Multivariate analysis for marketing research: An evaluation', *Applied Statistics, Series C*, vol.15, no.3, 1966.

23. Lunn, J. A., and R. P. Morgan, 'Some applications of the trade-off approach', in: *Consumer Market Research Handbook*, Robert M. Worcester and John Downham (eds), Van Nostrand Reinhold, Wokingham, 1978.

SIXTEEN

FINAL STAGES OF THE SURVEY

The field research has been completed and now there is the task of dealing with the wealth of data that has been collected.

The first step is to process these data so that they are in a usable form for the purposes of analysis and interpretation. Processing must be done systematically over a sequence of operations; these will include the editing of survey forms, the coding of answers, and tabulation. This work should be carried out with scrupulous care and attention to detail because it produces the raw material of research findings. The whole research programme needs to be under the control of an experienced and professional researcher, who will work closely with those in charge of processing the data.

16.1 EDITING

Editing ensures that the information on questionnaire forms is complete, accurate, and consistent. This is inclined to be rather dull, repetitive work, but it is a vital task which cannot be shirked. It is a responsibility to be accepted by experienced staff who recognize the importance of this phase of research. Every question must be checked to see either that it has been answered, or, if omitted, that it is not applicable to the particular circumstances of the respondent. Where answers have been omitted, it may be possible for the researcher to deduce the correct responses from other data given, or the interviewer may be able to recollect what was told. If the missing information is vitally important, interviewers can be asked to call back and collect it. Alternatively, and certainly attractive economically, respondents may be contacted by post or telephone. In view of the likelihood of 'missing' answers, it would be advisable to check survey forms at very short intervals, so that any call-backs can be made conveniently by field staff, who would probably still be working in the same area. Guessing at answers is not good research practice, because there are several possible reasons why responses are not recorded: the interviewer may have forgotten to ask a certain question, or asked it but omitted to record it; some respondents may have objected to answering certain questions, and the interviewer may have failed to note their refusal. Even experienced interviewers lapse occasionally, so editing calls for vigilance and patience.

Accuracy is another important aspect of editing. Obvious inaccuracies in answers should be rejected; some may be facetious or extremely doubtful, and these can be checked against other sections of the questionnaire. Frequently, surveys contain 'check' questions to test the validity of other responses. Arithmetical answers should be checked; for example, 'number in family' could be compared with individual information concerning marital status, number of children, etc. Where daily consumption figures have been requested, has the respondent, by chance, given weekly consumption?

Consistency and accuracy are closely bound together. Such details as a respondent's personal qualifications for inclusion in the survey should be checked. Is he or she living in the specified district under survey? Do the occupations given seem compatible with the type of housing reported, or the income level? Inconsistent answers must be rejected or changed. If some serious doubt arises, then interviewers may have to call back to clarify apparent inconsistencies. Inconsistencies might also suggest that some interviewers have been insufficiently trained to spot such responses during the course of field enquiries, and retraining or better supervision should be considered.

Editing is, therefore, a slow, laborious task, perhaps unexciting compared with other activities in research. It must largely be done by personal scrutiny. Good organizational work helps to reduce the load by ensuring a regular flow of survey forms throughout the course of the investigation. Particular sections of the questionnaire could be audited by specialists who will be able to complete the task speedily.

16.2 CODING

When editing has been completed, the next stage is the coding of answers for analysis purposes. Coding is usually printed on questionnaire forms to enable interviewers to pre-code responses during the course of interviewing. This cuts down considerably the final coding task and speeds up the whole operation. The codes entered on questionnaires are based on work carried out at the pilot stage of the survey. The amount of detailed breakdown (classification of data) is largely a matter of judgement, but as the pilot survey progresses it may well be necessary to amend certain classifications as more general data become available. Only after further testing should researchers accept coding frames for inclusion in the final survey. Investigators indicate responses by encircling or ticking the appropriate coded answers. Open questions require coding by experienced research staff who, after an examination of a representative selection of completed survey forms, draw up certain categories into which answers can be allocated and coded. It will readily be understood that the coding of answers is a delicate matter, calling for considerable attention to the needs of particular surveys. Experience at the pilot stage is reinforced by later examination of a selected number of completed surveys; this is the general practice of the Government Social Survey which takes 10 per cent of schedules in order to construct the final coding frame. In 1983, the Market Research Society published the findings[1] of a special study group on coding practice and the way in which it should be integrated into good survey operations.

> It is easy for the researcher to ignore the processes that occur between finalising a questionnaire and receiving tabulated responses. Efficient field and data processing departments encourage the researcher to think of tasks as mechanical routines. In fact, of course, they involve as much judgement and skill as the process of survey design, and they can influence profoundly the data upon which a survey report is based.[1]

In Chapter 6 it has already been noted that numerical values should be allocated to various responses of a questionnaire; these are usually ringed for easy identification; for example:

How long have you lived in your present house?

	Code
Up to one year	1
Over one year up to two years	2
Over two years up to four years	3
Over four years up to six years	4
Over six years up to ten years	5
Over ten years	6

Pre-coded questions similar to the quoted example are often referred to as 'multi-choice' or 'cafeteria' questions.

The layout of the questions should enable coding to be done easily by the interviewers, often while working in difficult conditions. Where street interviewing is concerned, the interviewer must be able to complete the questionnaire fairly quickly. Interviewing may frequently involve calling at houses in the evening. In some cases, the questionnaire may have to be filled in by the interviewer while standing on the doorstep.

In the cases of CATI and DCI techniques (see Chapter 6), direct input of coded responses is made by telephone interviewers with the former system or by respondents in the latter instance.

16.3 TABULATION

After editing and coding, the next stage in processing data is tabulation, the objective of which is to prepare quantitative data so that they are readily understandable and their significance is appreciated. This entails counting the frequency of certain cases within classifications relevant to particular surveys. Tabulation can be either manual, mechanical or electronic; the method will be determined by the nature of the survey, namely size, complexity, and also speed with which the findings are needed by management. Generally speaking, a simple survey involving fewer than 500 questionnaires could be hand processed. This would also be advisable where the qualitative aspects are greater than the quantitative elements.

Hand tabulation is easy and, provided a little organizing ability is present, convenient. Summary tables are designed to show the various characteristics being measured, and simple tally marks are then entered and added together. These are often entered in sets of five tally marks thus: ⊥⊦⊦⊦, which simple device makes the process of totalling easy.

Admittedly, hand processing gets difficult when cross-tabulations become complex or lengthy. On the other hand, manual processing is flexible – there is no time wasted waiting for machine availability – and it can be done by relatively junior staff under supervision. Machine tabulation is a complex operation, particularly suited to extensive surveys where large quantities of data are to be handled or intricate analysis is required. Before this method can be used, data have to be transferred to punch cards by means of punching equipment. The Hollerith system was widely used in marketing research data processing for many years, but has now largely been replaced by mainframe and micro computers. However, this system is not entirely abandoned, and BMRB, for instance, has a full-time analysis staff of around 30, who are responsible for editing, coding, detailed response analysis, and tabulations. The preparation of the editing and coding manuals is the responsibility of research teams headed by an analysis officer. Conventional punch cards are sometimes used, and BMRB has about six in-house punch operators supported by a few selected punching agencies.

Punch cards, measuring about $7\frac{3}{8}$in $\times$ $3\frac{1}{4}$in, are generally printed with 80 columns and in each column there are 12 positions. One or more columns of a card are allocated to each question, and the various answers to that question are represented by a punched hole in that column. Reference to any position on a card can easily be given by quoting column and hole numbers.

Key punch operators punch codes on to the cards direct from questionnaires, and the possibility of error is minimized, therefore, by a well-designed questionnaire. It is advisable for key punching to be checked, if possible by a different operator, to ensure accuracy at this stage of analysis.

Hence, when the cards have been punched, they are verified, i.e., if the re-punch does not agree with the original punching on the card, the verifier locks the machine and thus enables the discrepancy to be checked. The next step is to place the cards in a sorter. A particularly useful version of this machine is called a counter-sorter which is popular for the tabulation of surveys. It counts the number of cards in each answer classification and records the total on a dial. Another piece of vital equipment is the tabulator, which extracts cards with numbers punched in given columns, totals these, and prints the total on special forms. It will also reproduce, direct from the cards, the coded information.

Machine tabulation requires skilled operators and is fairly expensive. From the efficiency angle it is very attractive, but there is a danger that this may encourage researchers to accumulate an enormous amount of classified data, some of which may never be used or even read. Researchers should be guided by the agreed objectives of the survey, and resist the temptation to expand the research area unreasonably. This does not mean to say that researchers should not remain sensitive to the experiences gathered during the survey, which may sometimes lead them to discuss with management the original objectives and modifications that circumstances now suggest to be desirable.

An alternative to punch cards is specially designed paper tape which, unlike cards, can accommodate as many columns as a questionnaire may need. This flexibility is somewhat diminished by the fact that subsequent analysis is confined to computer processing. Alternatively, data may be punched directly on to magnetic tape one reel of which (usually about 2400 feet) can contain a very considerable volume of data. The 'total elimination' of the 80-column card was forecast[2] as computers became fully integrated into a 'total systems approach' in data collection and analysis.

16.4 COMPUTERS

As noted earlier, computers are now widely used in the analysis of marketing research data. Complex data can be handled extremely rapidly, and developments in computer processing are still taking place.

The accessibility of computers and the 'almost science-fiction faith in their usefulness'[3] should not mislead researchers; 'the fact is that computers are basically simple things unable to do more than they are told to do'. Or, in Drucker's more pungent phrase: 'The computer is a moron'.[4]

The immense ease with which complex calculations can be handled by computers may itself be counterproductive for effective management. Discretion should be exercised as to the quality and the quantity of data inputs to avoid what has been popularly termed 'the GIGO syndrome' (garbage in-garbage out). Computers enable sophisticated multi-variate statistical analyses to be applied to research data – and these, unless used with skill and understanding, may merely clog up a research report with impressive but never-to-be-read data. Sheth[5] has warned against the dangers of misapplying advanced statistical analyses. 'It is not at all uncommon to find a brilliant researcher totally competent in multi-variate analysis whom the management or even others in the research department simply cannot understand.'[5]

Data have to be organized systematically before they can be processed by computer. Computer 'software packages' enable data to be organized into 'language' which is 'understood' by the computer. In other words, a set of data is fed into the computer which is instructed to handle it in specific ways, e.g., calculating correlations.

Computer 'software packages' involve 'programs' which provide complete printed instructions on carrying out a series of operations designed to achieve certain kinds of data outputs. There are many computer programs available; the researcher should refer to the respective manuals and establish the suitability of a particular program for the survey. 'No matter how sophisticated a [mini] computer is, the system is only as good as the programs that run upon it.'[6]

Of the many programs in use, the Statistical Package for the Social Sciences (SPSS) offers marketing researchers and other analysts a very considerable and flexible means of analysing data. The Economic and Social Research Council (ESRC) keeps a register of software packages applicable to market and social surveys. Specialist agencies offer data-processing services in most cities and large towns.

There are special market research packages for micros; spreadsheets of varying levels of sophistication are widely adopted. Several research firms offer specialized services related to coding and tabulation of data from clients' questionnaires. Their services can extend to multi-variable analyses, if desired. Companies such as Demotab are listed in the *Market Research Society Yearbook*.

16.5 USE OF WEIGHTS

Some data derived from a sample may need to be corrected for differences in the composition of the sample and the known characteristics of the population from which it was drawn. Weights are needed, for example, when unequal probability is used in sampling (see Chapter 4: Variable sampling fraction, and Chapter 13: Pan European Survey). Where, for example, too many males were present in a sample of the general population, most cross-tabulation packages can correct this by applying fractions weights to male and female respondents, so that the sample data reflect the population composition. However, it is not easy to do this with hand or mechanical methods.

16.6 ANALYSIS AND INTERPRETATION

After the data have been tabulated, the processes of analysis and interpretation play their part in the development of the final survey.

Analysis and interpretation are closely linked and depend largely on the objectives of individual surveys. Analysis aims to organize and clarify data so that they become more comprehensible. It is influenced and largely controlled by the type of information which was sought in the objectives of the survey. This demands, therefore, thorough planning of every stage of the survey to ensure that the critical task of analysis will be supported by the right kinds of tabulation. Last-minute arrangements should be avoided; market researchers must think well ahead and work to a soundly conceived research design.

Analysis of data may cover simple statistical descriptions such as averages, percentages, distributions, and measures of dispersion, to be found in most surveys. Data are examined to detect possible relationships and their significance. It is customary, for example, to discover either a positive or negative correlation between product use and income level or social group, e.g., telephones in the UK are predominantly found in middle- and upper-class homes. Correlation indicates the degree of movement between two variables; it gives a measure of the association but the existence of correlation does not imply that the relationship is causal. The relationship may have occurred by chance and have nothing to do with cause and effect. In some cases, however, the relationship is causal as in the cases of the birth rate and the sale of perambulators.

An example of wrongly inferring a relationship between x and y because a set of observations on x and y gave a high measure of correlation was illustrated by a study[7] of the proportion of Church of England marriages to all marriages in England and Wales during the period 1866 to 1911 compared with the standardized mortality rate for the same period. This resulted in a correlation coefficient of .95. (It is generally agreed that correlations above .8 represent a very high degree of relationship.) To conclude from this study that the greater the proportion of marriages solemnized by the Church of England the higher the death rate would, of course, be absurd. In fact, the trend in both sets of statistics showed a steady fall over the years 1866 to 1911 for quite unconnected reasons, but because of this common movement their values over the period followed each other.

With many marketing problems, for example the volume of sales, several variables have to be considered, which involve the use of more sophisticated statistical methods such as multiple regression. A third factor might, in fact, be the cause of the association noted between two other factors. The cold weather might have been the cause of reduced sales of ice-cream in a holiday resort, although analysis of the number of visitors showed that they were increasing while sales of ice-cream were falling, and a negative correlation appeared to exist between these two variables. It would be incorrect to assume that increased numbers of visitors caused the sales of ice-cream to fall over a certain period.

It will be apparent that correlation analysis has to be handled with care and common sense. Correlation indicates that certain variables appear to be associated, but it does not state that they are connected in a cause-and-effect relationship. The task of skilled interpretation lies in studying the nature of the association and its significance. Data should be scrutinized carefully for likely relationships, though the intrusion of sampling errors must never be overlooked. Tests of significance (see Chapter 15) can be applied, but it should be remembered that the findings are relevant to the particular samples taken during the survey. Other samples (of different size) may reveal data that react differently to a test of significance.

This point should be clearly appreciated by researchers who should not be misled into making sweeping assertions based on tests of significance. Moser[8] has directed attention to the fact that an effect shown to be statistically significant may yet be of such small magnitude that it is of no substantive interest to researchers. These two aspects of the outcome of significance tests should be carefully borne in mind by marketing researchers.

Interpretation of survey findings is a matter on which experts express strongly conflicting views. Some would have researchers give their own interpretation of the findings of surveys, while others, equally dogmatic, believe that researchers should limit themselves to reporting the facts discovered through the survey. The comments of leading experts are worth careful reading; what is acceptable practice would seem to depend largely on the brief given to individual researchers.

Moser[8] states categorically that 'whatever the nature of data, the task of interpretation falls squarely on the shoulders of the researcher'. During the course of research, he will have obtained valuable experience in dealing with raw data, and 'while every reader is entitled to draw his own conclusions, the writer of the survey report should not shirk the duty of giving his own'. Furthermore, the researcher would fail to make his own full contribution to the survey if he did not include his 'own ideas and speculations, even if he cannot offer chapter and verse to substantiate them'.

This controversial view is supported by a paper by Ehrenberg[9] who feels that 'The proposition that the researcher should restrict himself in his report to "describing the facts" conflicts implicitly with his duties as a researcher'. He pleads that the proposition is impossible, or, alternatively, that it would inhibit good research and not be in the public interest. It would seem impossible to avoid the researcher's opinions and conclusions – implicitly if not explicitly – from entering the report. At the same time, there is the danger that 'the researcher's opinions might be [wrongly] thought to be as incontrovertible as his reporting of "facts"'. While the responsibility for acting on a marketing research report belongs to the marketing man, the researcher should not be precluded from offering his opinions.

The case against the researcher involving himself in interpretation of survey findings is strongly advanced by another experienced researcher[10] whose views are 'that findings should always be confined to factual reporting, unembellished by the opinions of the researcher or by his conclusions, however pertinent in his opinion these might be. It is essential that marketing people should look upon and rely upon research reports as unbiased findings and this confidence can only be established when the personal opinions of the researcher are not in evidence'.

It is felt that marketing people and marketing researchers should be encouraged to work closely together making full use of their special expertise and not attempting 'to usurp each other's functions'. In this way, good research will develop 'based on unimpeachable techniques and speedily reported in order not to lose actuality'.

Dr John Treasure[11] feels that the researcher 'must do more than report on the facts he has found'. He would prefer that recommendations should *not* be added – 'these tend to be distressingly naïve' – but he would expect questions to be put to the data and some attempt made to answer them:

> For example, what are the main reasons why the repurchase rate is low? how important is the heavy user? is social class of any importance in determining consumer demand? This means asking the right questions, assembling all the data available (not necessarily all taken from the current survey) and producing coherent, reasoned, well-written answers.

Experts, such as those quoted, differ sharply in their views on the interpretation of research findings, and it is surely only reasonable to expect that they should do so. Marketing research is still developing and improving its techniques, and it is increasingly able to make a valid contribution to the marketing strategy of companies over a wide range of industries. The skill and knowledge of professional researchers should be used fully by their clients. Their professionalism ensures that the findings of surveys are the result of objective research, while, at the same time, from the wealth of their experience, they are able to indicate to clients particular developments in their markets. Skilled and sensitive handling of data brings with it valuable insight, which it would seem bad business practice to ignore.

As suggested in the introduction to this aspect of research, the question of interpretation by marketing researchers when presenting their reports rests on the brief given to them. No experienced researcher would wish to accept an assignment that contained conditions which, in his opinion, would inhibit good research practice.

16.7 PRESENTATION OF THE SURVEY REPORT

The final step in marketing research is to report the survey findings to those who authorized the investigation. Preparation of the research report deserves, therefore, special consideration.

The American Marketing Association appointed a committee to study this aspect of the research programme, and reported that 'The findings in marketing research remain valueless until they are communicated accurately and effectively to the persons who are responsible for policy decisions'.[12]

The report must communicate to management, clearly and concisely, knowledge about its specific marketing problems as defined in the objectives of the research.

The AMA committee named the following factors as influencing the form of the research report:

1. The instructions from the authority or client may indicate a purely statistical report on the one extreme or a fully elaborated recommendation on the other.

2. The nature and complexity of the problem will certainly dictate the manner in which the report must be presented.
3. The nature and variety of readers for whom the report is intended will vitally affect its form and content. If a report on the habits of buyers and users of a product is intended for the company's salesmen, it must certainly be less formal and technical, and perhaps briefer and more pictorialized than if it is solely for the use of the sales manager.
4. The size of the report will influence its format, binding, and even the nature of the exposition of the findings.
5. The number of copies to be made will determine the method of reproduction and, therefore, the nature of the illustrative material.
6. The length of the useful life of the report may influence the amount of money and effort to be invested in presentation.

When preparing a research report, the researcher should keep in mind those who will read it. He or she should form an opinion of their needs and make sure that the report is drafted in language that will be fully understood by those particular readers. As in the preparation of any type of report, words should be carefully chosen so that they convey the findings of the survey clearly. This calls for a good command of English, but it does not mean that literary effects should be the ambition of report writers. Good, clear, grammatical English, free of jargon, and organized in a logical flow to assist readers to assimilate without difficulty the evidence collected as a result of the research, should be the aim of professional researchers.

Some years ago a small book on the use of English for official purposes was published by the Treasury.[13] It approached the problem of report writing with refreshing candour, and its influence went far beyond the Civil Service. Marketing researchers will find in this manual some very helpful guides to the art of good report writing and also questionnaire wording (see Chapter 6); they should not neglect the critical task of communication, which is an inherent part of an effective survey report. The technical skills involved in planning and executing a research programme are different from those required to write a clearly understandable report. Report writing requires a thorough knowledge of the survey, and the ability to synthesize and transmit that knowledge so that it is perfectly understood. Professional writers cannot hope to influence their readers precisely as they wish without care and practice in the use of words.

Researchers should, therefore, always bear in mind that a report is a method of *communication*. This essential process cannot be successful if too little emphasis is placed on the art and science of display and communication while too much attention is given to the elegant techniques which were involved in gathering and analysing the data.[5] Many years ago, Edgar Allan Poe wrote scathingly of 'donkeys who bray, using inordinate language which no man has ever understood, and which any well-educated baboon would blush in being accused of understanding'.

If technical terms are used in the survey report, they should be defined to prevent possible misunderstanding. Researchers should not presume that their readers will automatically understand technical jargon, and, at first appearance, it is advisable to qualify it. Where the report is to be read exclusively by technical specialists, the general level of writing can be more specialized. In practice, most survey reports are the subject of discussion between commercial and technical management, and unless two separate editions are planned, it is advisable to write the report in a style comprehensible to both areas of management. A summary report, covering the main features of a highly technical survey, is a useful means of ensuring that commercial management knows the facts which research has established.

16.8 COMPOSITION OF THE REPORT

Research reports should present survey findings within a logical framework. Although particular reports will obviously cover different subjects of enquiry, three main elements form the general construction: introduction, main body, and appendices. These will now be considered in some detail.

Introduction

The introduction starts with a title page giving a simple description of the research, e.g., 'National Consumer Survey into Supermarket Shopping'. It also contains the name of the client, the organization which undertook the research, and the date.

The title page is followed by a table of contents, giving a detailed guide to the report. This should be designed to facilitate easy reference by systematically numbering sections (and sub-sections) of the main areas of the report. A list of graphs and statistical tables should also be given. Following this reference list is the preface, which outlines the purpose, method, and scope of the research. The objectives should be clearly stated, and a brief description given of the methodology used. The characteristics and size of samples should be recorded here.

The introductory material in a report sometimes includes a summary of conclusions, though these are also to be found at the end of some reports. It is useful to place them at the beginning of a report for easy reference by clients, who may read the full report at some later date. The conclusions should be clear, succinct, and objective. They should reflect accurately the research findings, and statements should be supported by references to appropriate sections of the main report.

In some reports, the summary of conclusions is followed by recommendations but this practice is not generally accepted as being within the scope of marketing research. It is felt by some experienced researchers that the objectivity of research could be doubted by some clients if they are given recommendations in the survey report. Where recommendations are included in a report – at the request of the client – it should be understood that they represent the considered *opinion* of the researcher and are not part of the objective findings of the survey. In many cases it would be unfair to researchers to ask them to give recommendations on policy, since there are so many other factors involved in management decisions about which they may know nothing. Experienced researchers will not wish to extend their responsibilities without full knowledge of all the relevant facts, and clients should not expect them to do so.

A survey of marketing research practice in the UK undertaken by the British Institute of Management,[14] some years ago, revealed that only 74 per cent of survey reports included actual recommendations. Of these, only about 50 per cent were acted upon by management. The BIM survey covered 86 actual investigations out of a total of 265 companies contacted. In view of the small sample, it would be unwise to read too much into the finding quoted.

Where market researchers have been invited to present their recommendations in the survey report, they might well consider offering these to be effective over a period of time. A phased plan of operation is more likely to attract management interest than a wholesale change of policy which could be more disruptive than beneficial. Researchers should form an opinion of the 'management climate' in which their clients are accustomed to work and design recommendations that will have a good chance of being heard favourably. These recommendations follow a logical progression, management feels more willing to accept them.

Main body

The next part of the report contains the main body which presents the survey findings in some considerable detail. The material should be presented systematically, and there should be some framework outlined beforehand to control the development of the report. The actual contents of this section of the report depend largely on the nature of the survey. Where quantitative measures are involved, the text and statistical extracts from the main body of the report will be almost completely textual.

Data used should be relevant to the objectives of the survey and the report should present these so that they are readily understood. Major relationships should be adequately discussed and compared, where available, with published facts from other sources.

Strict standards of professional research should always be maintained, and clients should never be encouraged to read into reports more than researchers can legitimately support by their survey findings. Marketing research has limitations as well as great values, and management should not expect researchers to provide them with information outside the scope of the survey. To avoid any possible confusion at a later date, the objectives of research should, as noted earlier, always be fully discussed and agreed by both parties before the survey is undertaken.

Ehrenberg[15] has emphasized the importance of presenting numerical data in an intelligible way. He has drawn attention to the fact that numeracy has two facets – *extracting* numerical information and *presenting* it. Tabulated data should be so laid out that the overall patterns and exceptions should be 'obvious at a glance'. Simplification of data, e.g., rounding to two significant or effective digits, may get rid of a bewildering array of top-heavy data. Cluttered tables do not aid mental digestion. Spurious accuracy in the presentation of data should also be avoided.

Appendices

The last section of the report is in the form of appendices giving supplementary information, sometimes of a fairly extensive type. A detailed description of the sample design used is given; the questionnaire used in the survey is also included, and so are the instructions given to interviewers. Full statistical tables are given for reference (extracts from these will have appeared in the main body of the report). Where survey information has been drawn from official or other sources, full details of these are listed. In the case of motivation research, it is customary to include one or two typical interviews verbatim. Photographs or other illustrative material might also be included featuring, perhaps, packaging or advertising which was of interest to the survey.

A typical marketing research report might have the general format shown in Fig. 16.1.

16.9 FINAL STAGES OF PREPARING AND PRESENTING THE REPORT

The type of printing and binding of survey reports should be carefully considered by researchers.

The method of printing the report depends largely on the number required for distribution. Modern electric typewriters used in conjunction with off-set litho machines can produce extremely well-presented reports. Good-quality paper should always be used, and the binding should be serviceable. Laminated boards are particularly suitable. The research title, etc., should be entered clearly on the outside covers.

With most research projects, time is a critical factor, so everything possible must be done to avoid delays at the many different stages of the survey. The whole operation should be programmed, and a continuous check kept on the progress of office staff, interviewers, printers, etc. It may be advisable to prepare a distillation of the research findings and to submit to clients a preliminary report if some urgent decision has to be taken within a limited period of time.

Clients often find it helpful for researchers to make a formal presentation of the main findings of a survey at a meeting of senior executives. This matter should be checked with clients before the research project is accepted. Copies of the research report should preferably be distributed before such a meeting, so that executives have the opportunity of raising matters arising from scrutiny of research findings.

Researchers should plan carefully a report presentation, making sure that they have suitably designed visual aids which project clearly salient findings. Clients canot be expected to digest a range of quantitative and qualitative data merely given verbally.

Management will be particularly concerned with the *meanings* and *applications* of the research findings; the actual process involved in the research process will be of secondary interest. In presenting their findings, researchers should aim to help their audience by a balanced, logical exposition that avoids pretentious jargon and, at the same time, results in a better understanding of the problems facing management and of the decisions which have to be taken.

The task of the market research statistician should not be confined to techniques; he or she must increasingly become a better communicator and skilled in presenting complicated technical data to non-technical audience in language which they can understand.[16] This is a challenging, new and expanded role for statisticians, who are often dealing today with arcane concepts and methodologies that are more likely to confuse rather than enlighten their clients.

TITLE PAGE
CONTENTS PAGE
LIST OF APPENDICES
TEXT OF REPORT

    Introduction (purpose of report)
    Main Conclusions (series of short statements)
    Methodology (outline of research)
    Details of Survey Methodology
    Survey Findings (text plus tables and diagrams)
        Definition of Product Market
        Domestic Production
        Imports
        Market Trends
    Target Market Size
    Planned Market Share
        Nature of Buying Behaviour
        Nature of Competition
        Prices
        Promotion
        Distribution
        Packaging
        After-Sales Service
        Delivery
    Summary of Survey Findings
    General Conclusions and Recommendations

LIST OF TABLES
LIST OF DIAGRAMS
REFERENCES
APPENDICES

Fig. 16.1 Essential elements of market report

This skilful exposition should encourage management to read the report in full and, as Worcester has observed,[17] reduce the likelihood that it will 'moulder in desk drawers or on bookshelves and never see the light of day'. Scarce research skills and talents should not be so wastefully expended.

16.10 BUYING MARKETING RESEARCH

In industry, management often has to consider the problem of whether to produce, in its own plant, specific components needed in the assembly of a final product or, alternatively, whether to buy these parts from an outside supplier, possibly more advantageously. 'Make-or-buy' decisions are largely accepted as routine administration.

With professional services, the principle of 'make or buy' may also be applied. Many companies rely on specialist advice from outside consultants in complex areas such as the law, taxation, design, and similar activities. At the same time, some of these companies may have members of their staff, qualified in these professions, acting as general practitioners. When expert knowledge is required at some depth, companies may well call in the services of specialists, who are able to contribute valuably to the quality of management decisions. To employ talent of this nature on a staff basis would generally be outside the resources and needs of most companies. However, Mintel[18] stated that almost two-thirds of market research projects in the UK are commissioned by specialist market research buyers, and most large companies involved in consumer goods and services employ professional staff for this purpose.

Marketing information, both quantitative and qualitative, is necessary in companies of all sizes. This information may be available, to some extent, inside the company or from external published sources. Whether to 'make', i.e., rely on existing company resources, or to 'buy', i.e., use the services of professional marketing research organizations, will depend on several factors. These will include assessing the present state of knowledge related to the particular decision which has to be taken. For example, what data can be obtained from company records and published sources on the present and potential market for a specific type of product? Available information may be sufficient for a decision to be taken at an acceptable level of risk. Where this is not the case, gaps in information should be identified by careful analysis of the situation, and an evaluation made of the benefits which further data would be likely to bring to the process of decision making. An estimate of the costs involved should, of course, be included in the assessment. Management must then decide what further research is justified, bearing in mind that this will inevitably delay the final decision.

Where and how to buy this extra marketing information cause concern to many companies, which are considering, perhaps for the first time, the need for more specialized research into their marketing problems. It will be a matter of company policy whether to build up research facilities within the organization or to rely entirely on outside experts: the degree of urgency of the research will need to be borne in mind.

As in other areas of professional expertise, it is advisable for companies to decide whether their research needs warrant special research appointments. Where new markets are under consideration and the organization is expanding its other resources, a staff researcher would be likely to be fully and usefully occupied. But even then, some outside assistance may be sought in connection with surveys involving, for example, psychological methods of investigation. In such cases, the staff researcher would control the research programme and collaborate closely with experts handling specific aspects of the survey. Dr John Treasure has drawn attention to the growth during the 1960s of research departments in large companies, usually staffed by ex-research practitioners and charged with the job of writing research briefs, buying research, interpreting the results and spelling out the implications for their companies'.[19]

Those companies preferring to buy their marketing research externally are faced with the problem of seeking the best source of supply. Buying research is admittedly more difficult than ordering tangible products, the physical characteristics of which can be fairly easily assessed.

Before the search for suitable marketing investigators commences, companies should spend some time in analysing their marketing problem, forming objectives, and specifying the type of data which they are seeking. This exercise provides a sound base for discussions with prospective research agencies.

Marketing research organizations fall into two main categories:

1. Independent market research companies.
2. Market research departments of advertising agencies.

Independent marketing research companies tend to be of two kinds: those offering a comprehensive range of services, and those specializing by function or by type of research undertaken. The larger agencies, such as AGB or BMRB, are able to give clients the benefit of broadly based experience in all aspects of survey practice. Smaller agencies often specialize in providing useful services such as questionnaire construction or interviewing, and in investigations into specific markets. Large specialist agencies like Nielsen's undertake a continuous audit of selected retail outlets.

In addition to commercial research organizations, several academic institutions have been notably successful in practical research projects over a wide range of industries. Universities, polytechnics, and business schools are usually willing to offer professional assistance with the marketing problems of companies of all sizes.

A few of the larger advertising agencies have marketing research departments. These tend to have particular expertise in advertising research techniques, though they also cover other types of research.

Professional organizations like the British Institute of Management, the Chartered Institute of Marketing, the Market Research Society, and the Industrial Marketing Research Association, provide companies interested in marketing research with lists of their members who are able to offer suitable services.

Guidance in selecting a research agency may also be forthcoming from trade associations and from business associates who have commissioned research in the past.

A short list of agencies who appear to be suitable should be drawn up and invited to submit details of their services. These should include information on the experience and qualifications of their research staff, the type of research customarily undertaken, the principal industries they have covered. A list of past and present clients is often a valuable clue to the standing of the agency. Some of these clients may be willing to offer an assessment of the capabilities of the agency they employed.

The next stage in selecting an agency consists of selecting two or three firms whose background and experience suggest they could be of particular value in solving the present marketing problem.

The activities of professional marketing researchers who belong to the Market Research Society the leading professional body in the UK, are subject to a detailed and extensive Code of Conduct. This covers professional ethics, standard conditions for conducting scientific sample surveys, and the presentation of survey findings.

The January 1989 edition of the Code of Conduct is an amended version of a self-regulatory code that has existed since 1954.[20] Supported by both the MRS and IMRA, the code is stated to be broadly compatible with the codes of AMSO, ESOMAR and the ICC (International Chamber of Commerce). The two latter organizations have drawn up an International Code of Practice. MRS members responsible for research overseas are exhorted to take the provisions of the MRS Code or those of the ESOMAR Code as minimum requirements and fulfil any other responsibilities set down in law or by nationally agreed standards.

Codes of Conduct cannot, of course, avoid every possible problem that might materialize in survey practice, but they do provide clients with stated standards of marketing research practice which should reassure, in particular, those who are seeking to commission marketing research surveys for the first time.

Mary and Peter Bartram[21] have reflected on the 'ethical dilemmas' facing marketing researchers in today's highly competitive conditions. They argue that there is a 'pressing need' to define the boundaries of market research which, over the past 40 years or so, have extended considerably into areas not envisaged by its early practitioners. It is, these experienced researchers state, essential that the core values of the market research industry 'should not be undermined by any temptation to accommodate the wishes of other bodies, or of individual members, with conflicting "objectives"'. These core values should be fully recognized; they embrace: (i) total respect for the respondent; (ii) professional competence in data collection and analysis; (iii) use of information for research and not directly for selling purposes; and, (iv) independent objectivity in the interpretation of survey findings.

16.11 BRIEFING RESEARCH ORGANIZATIONS

From the outset, a company seeking marketing research assistance should be prepared to discuss fully with prospective agencies its marketing problem. Unless there is good communication between the parties, research cannot be planned on a sound basis. While the client company may have formed some opinions about the research needed – and there should be some serious attempt to define marketing problems before approaching an agency – it would be unwise to allow preconceived ideas to preclude objective discussion with independent researchers, who may suggest additional or alternative analyses.

Agencies need to know the type of data required and the degree of accuracy which will be adequate for the particular problem to be researched.

Briefing of the agency must be thorough. It may include visits by agency staff to the production plants of clients, and also to trade outlets. Companies proposing to use the services of research organizations should ensure that close cooperation is maintained throughout the period of survey.

Selected research agencies should now be in a position to submit formal research proposals specifying the research to be undertaken, methods of enquiry, sample design, and the data to be collected. Estimates of the period of time involved should also be given. If the original briefing is modified in any way, the reasons should be clearly stated and the client company should check these carefully. Costs of the survey will also be given.

The competitive research proposals require careful study, and a comparative evaluation should be made, Bearing in mind that an important management decision may rest on the research findings, the cost of the research should be viewed as an investment in marketing information.

When the final selection has been made, another meeting should take place between the client company and the research agency to check any outstanding points arising from the comparative analysis. After satisfactorily clearing these matters, the agency should be instructed to undertake the survey. By now a close relationship between the two organizations should be developing, and every endeavour should be made to improve this exchange of confidences as the research progresses.

The client company should appoint an executive member of staff to liaise closely with the agency. If there is no functional specialist on the staff, this duty should be given to a marketing executive well versed in the subject of research. Occasionally it may be advisable to modify the research brief after the early stages of research have been completed. Regular meetings between client and agency should be held to assess the progress of the survey and check on the success with which the original objectives are being achieved.

16.12 INTERPRETING AND USING MARKETING RESEARCH FINDINGS

When the survey has been completed the agency will be busy analysing and processing the data collected. Interpretation of the research findings, discussed earlier in this chapter, will be of prime importance to the client company. Whether or not the research agency's responsibilities extend to the interpretation of the data and recommendations for future policy is a matter to be agreed when the original briefing is given. The insight which researchers have gained into the clients' activities and the market in which they operate, would appear to qualify them to offer unique guidance based on objective findings.

The Mintel survey[18] on market research, quoted earlier, found that of the key features which research buyers looked for in their research suppliers, the ability to interpret survey findings was rated high, equal with the ability to meet deadlines, and only slightly lower than technical competence.

Finally, *ad hoc* research can soon lose its value through the passage of time. Delay in dealing with survey findings may reduce the effectiveness of research, especially when the pace of change in a market is quickening.

16.13 MANAGERIAL ATTITUDES TO MARKETING RESEARCH

In the opening chapter, the role of marketing research in management decision making was recognized. It was seen that while managerial experience and judgement are vital elements of decision making – and these are particularly applicable to daily decisions which are largely of a routine nature – there are times when the existing fund of knowledge is inadequate. It is on such occasions, in particular, that marketing researchers may be called in to lend their expertise to the decision makers.

Three typical managerial attitudes towards marketing researchers have been listed as follows. The first set of attitudes was held by a manager called the 'plumber' who thought that marketing research could be turned on and off like a tap. The two other sets of attitudes were held by managers termed the 'oriental potentate' or the 'feudal lord' who, in their characteristic ways, expected marketing researchers 'to jump when they said jump' and 'at the drop of a hat to provide immediate answers to sometimes lunatic questions'.[22]

These portrayals may seem to be almost caricatures, but experienced marketing researchers will probably have little difficulty in recognizing some of the managerial attitudes described. The 'plumber' appears to be a 'crisis-shooter' who does not realize that a regular flow of information, in addition to *ad hoc* research, would help marketing decisions. The 'oriental potentate' and the 'feudal lord' suggest an authoritarian and not very intelligent use of managerial power in the naïve belief that marketing research can provide answers to problems which they have not really thought about sufficiently.

As a professional in his own right, the marketing researcher is unlikely to be either dazzled or dismayed when encountering such restrictive attitudes. He will endeavour to get to the heart of the problem and, after securing agreement, then proceed to apply his analytical skills in objective research. Uncertainty in decision making will remain, but with valid and reliable data it should be possible to reduce its level significantly.

In Mintel's opinion,[18] stress may sometimes be detected in the relationship between research and marketing specialists, the latter feeling that it is their prerogative to initiate changes to marketing strategy; marketing researchers, on the other hand, may feel that their experience and knowledge are not really being used fully by their clients.

16.14 COSTING MARKETING RESEARCH

Management information costs money and involves the use of scarce resources. It is important, therefore, to check that the value of the information will be greater than the costs involved in its collection and processing.

Alternative methods of acquiring marketing research expertise have been outlined already; attention will now be given to alternative methods of evaluating expenditure on marketing research.

The ways in which this problem can be tackled range from subjective estimates to sophisticated decision theory based on Bayesian statistics.

The simplest method of deciding whether or not to enter a particular market would be to toss a coin; the chances of a correct decision would be 50:50, so on the basis of a £500 000 market launch the estimated possible loss would be £250 000.

But this simplistic approach is likely to be modified by the fund of knowledge and experience which management may already possess. This 'background knowledge' is, as observed earlier, a necessary constituent of management decision making and, in some cases, it may be adequate. The more novel the product and the more dynamic the marketing environments, the greater risk in making decisions on this basis.

To continue the example given above and assuming that present information is judged to be sufficient for management to make a correct decision on a 60:40 basis, the estimated cost of making a wrong decision could be calculated thus: £500 000 × 40 per cent = £200 000.

Management may then consider the increased chances of a successful decision being taken if it had access to extra information about the proposed market. An estimate might be made that more information would be likely to increase the probability of success to 80:20. On the basis of a £500 000 market launch, the estimated loss could then total £100 000 if the market entry failed. In this case, the value of marketing research would be computed thus:

£200 000 (wrong decision taken — £100 000 (wrong decision with = £100 000
with present information) extra information)

Hence, management could usefully spend up to £100 000 on marketing research to improve the chances of market success.

Managers who seek a more sophisticated method of evaluating expenditure on marketing research could apply formal Bayesian decision rules.

In dealing with day-to-day problems, managers may be accustomed to making three levels of estimates of the outcome of decisions: an expected, an optimistic, and a pessimistic one. They may, in a relatively informal way, attach probabilities to these projections. Bayesian decision theory offers a formal procedure for enabling management to make an efficient choice from among various alternatives.

The processes involved in the Bayesian approach are detailed in statistical textbooks.[23] Essentially, the process makes use of the concepts of utility, subjective probabilities, and Bayes's theorem for revision of prior judgements or hypotheses.

The Bayesian decision process involves four stages: (i) definition of problem; (ii) prior analysis; (iii) posterior analysis; and (iv) preposterior analysis.

So that mathematical calculations can be projected, the problem must be defined in quantitative terms. Prior analysis refers to the existing state of knowledge relative to the problem which will enable prior probabilities to be applied. Posterior analysis occurs after the management decision has been taken and when feedback may be available about the outcome of the action. Preposterior analysis is the intermediate stage which may occur if management decides that more information is needed before a final decision can be taken. At this stage, a marketing research survey, for example, may be considered.

The following simplified example will indicate the essential nature of Bayesian analysis applied to the evaluation of marketing research.

A company wishing to expand into a new market has been told that detailed marketing research investigation would cost about £50 000.

Prior analysis of this marketing venture allows the company to estimate the probability of attaining a market share of at least 15 per cent at 0.6.

	Market share Probability	≥ 15 per cent Pay-off	Market share Probability	< 15 per cent Pay-off
Enter market	.6	£300 000	.4	(£50 000)
Do not enter market	.6	0	.4	0

Expected Monetary Value (EMV) is one of the most suitable criteria which could be adopted for evaluating this project, although there are others which might also be applied. Hence, EMV = 0.6 (£300 000) + 0.4 (−£50 000) = £160 000.

If posterior analysis is now applied, it may be assumed that this product is already on sale in another market. Information on existing sales performance indicates that earlier predictions of 75 per cent success were actually realized.

Taking this increased probability into account, the revised EMV can be calculated as follows:

$EMV_2 = 0.75$ (£300 000) + 0.25 (−£50 000) = £212 500
The value of the additional information is calculated thus:
$EMV_2 - EMV_1$
= £212 500 − £160 000
= £52 500

A marketing survey costing £30 000 could, therefore, be afforded. It would appear worth while to reduce the level of uncertainty regarding market entry, provided that research findings could be available without a long delay.

It should be borne in mind, however, that although Bayesian decision theory applies probabilities and results in fairly imposing mathematical equations, the probabilities are derived from estimates and are subjective in nature. The elegance of the theory should not be allowed to obscure its inherent fragility. So far this technique does not appear to be widely used in evaluating marketing research estimates.[19, 24, 25]

16.15 DATA PROTECTION ACT

Following signature by the UK of the European Convention for the Protection of Individuals with regard to Automatic Processing of Personal Data, implementation was effected by passing the Data Protection Act, which became law on 12 July 1984. Its purpose is 'to regulate the use of automatically processed information relating to individuals and the provision of services in respect of such information'. Personal data refer to data related to a living person who can be identified from that information. The Act is concerned, therefore, with individuals not corporate bodies; it does not refer to the processing of personal data by manual means. The types of equipment which might be described as 'automatic processes' are not closely defined. However, the Data Protection Registrar, who was appointed in October 1984, has issued a very helpful booklet: *Guideline No. 1: An Introduction and Guide to the Act* (published February 1985, and available from the Office of the Data Protection Registrar, Springfield House, Water Lane, Wilmslow, Cheshire SK9 5AX), which explains the general philosophy of the Act, and provides some basic definitions, explanatory material and 'rules of thumb'. Formal decisions will be made known later, as particular cases arise.

The UK was comparatively late in adopting data protection legislation; such laws had already existed for some time in, for example, Sweden, Germany, Austria, and France. This lag was advantageous because it enabled UK legislators to benefit from the earlier experiences, and attempt to avoid the serious problems for industry in general and for market researchers in particular, which had arisen in certain countries, such as Germany. Close contact with Government and legislators was maintained by the UK market research industry, so as to ensure that its special needs and attitudes towards the collection and storage of personal data were appreciated.

Generally speaking, the market research industry has favoured some form of data protection legislation, and it has well-established ethical standards of professional behaviour, best expressed through Codes of Practice, originally developed by the Market Research Society and more recently by the Association of Market Survey Organisations. The UK Code has existed for 30 years and has been a model for the codes of most European countries and many others across the world. The Market Research Society's Interviewer Card Scheme also exemplified the self-regulation procedures which are designed to protect the good image of professional marketing research.

The MRS Code of Practice is still stronger with regard to protecting personal data than the Data Protection Act: hence, there is no need to update or improve this section of the Code which, in particular, lays upon researchers the strict obligation to keep personal information confidential in manual as well as automated form and not to release information about who has been inter-viewed or to release data in a form which might allow it to be identified. Some organizations operate, of course, outside of the MRS and AMSO and do not follow these codes, but similar codes have now been established for ESOMAR and the International Chamber of Commerce.

To date, most of the controls and checks on those doing research have been of a self-regula-tory nature: the Data Protection Act changes this emphasis and, to some extent at least, places more responsibility and obligations on *all* who carry out survey research.

Most market research organizations which have observed the professional Codes of Practice will have little need to change their mode of operations in order to comply with the Act. In fact, they will obtain certain exemptions and have the support of legislation in a number of aspects of their research.

However, those in industries and organizations that have abused survey research as a means of obtaining personal, often confidential, data are now more vulnerable under the Act and in some cases their previous practices, such as 'sugging' (selling under the guise of research) are illegal.

The Data Protection Act establishes a register on which all users of personal data covered by the Act must be entered. From September 1985, the register entry will show: (i) the data user's name and address; (ii) a description of the personal data held; (iii) the purposes for which the personal data are held; (iv) a description of the sources from which data are derived; (v) a description of people to whom the data may be disclosed; (vi) names or descriptions of places outside the UK to which the data may be transferred; (vii) an address for the receipt of requests from data subjects who wish to have access to the data. It will be illegal to hold or use data in any way inconsistent with the Register entry; any changes will have to be recorded officially. Registration entries will be valid for three years unless the data user opts for a shorter period of one or two years. Two years from the date of the introduction of data registration, the Act will come fully into force and it will then be an offence to hold unregistered personal data. Certain exemptions may be made, but these are very narrowly defined and users are advised to register unless they can find an exemption that exactly fits their case.

Under the Act, eight data protection principles will be affected; all eight apply to all data users, only the eighth applies to computer bureaux. These general principles are briefly as follows:

1. The personal data shall be obtained and processed fairly and lawfully.
2. Personal data shall be kept only for the purposes specified in the Register.
3. Personal data shall not be used or disclosed in any manner inconsistent with the purposes registered.
4. Personal data held should be adequate, relevant, and not excessive for the registered purpose.
5. Personal data shall be accurate and, where necessary, kept up to date.
6. Personal data shall not be kept longer than necessary for the specified purposes.
7. Individuals shall be entitled to reasonable access to personal data and to have such data corrected or erased, where appropriate.
8. Appropriate measures shall be taken to protect the security of the data.

The Registrar is empowered to serve notice on any data user who may be found in breach of any of these principles; failure to comply with the terms of such a notice will be an offence.

A data subject, i.e., a person to whom specific data relate, is to be compensated if he/she suffers damage because the data are inaccurate, lost or disclosed without authority.

A number of these general principles are particularly relevant to market research companies and other organizations, such as universities or colleges, which undertake field surveys. The first principle – fair and lawful collection and processing – mirrors the long-standing objection by professional market researchers to those organizations or individuals who deliberately mislead respondents and attempt selling under the pretext of doing research. As noted earlier, 'sugging' is a disreputable commercial practice which has tended to bring legitimate research into disfavour. The second and third principles state that data collected for one purpose should not be used for another purpose and that such data should not be used or disclosed in a way incompatible with the registration. Clearly these stipulations emphasize that all who hold research survey material on computer must ensure that it should only be accessible to authorized personnel. While reputable organizations already observe this practice, it now becomes a legal requirement, and it may prove particularly difficult for some academic institutions to maintain strict security where so many people may have access to a computer file.

The seventh principle – subject access – is also of particular interest to the research industry, which has gained a special exemption from subject access, where the survey data user abides by the obligation not to release the data at a personal level. In exchange for keeping the information confidential, the researcher user is not obliged to comply with a request to provide a member of the public with any information he may hold about him or her. As may well be imagined, to do so could prove particularly difficult for major users of research who hold massive volumes of personal data on computer, most of which cannot easily be traced by means of an individual's name and address. Hence, if a member of the public asks for information about him/herself which is held by a research organization it could prove very difficult to find it, yet under the general law a data user has this obligation. It appears, as indicated earlier, that organizations following the MRS/AMSO Code of Practice with regard to respondent confidentiality will benefit under the Act, while other organizations, not subscribing to these ethical standards, will have to respond to such requests and keep their data in a way which allows them to do so economically.

The eighth principle – security of data – is already observed in the professional Codes of Practice, and benefits such organizations in two other ways under the Act, namely:

1. They do not have to keep the personal information up to date (which can be a considerable operation with people moving, change in their personal circumstances, etc.).

2. They can hold the data as long as they wish.

In summary the UK market research industry appears to have to deal with a Data Protection Act that is more understanding and less strict than its counterparts in other European countries. The needs of researchers to have free access to data, as long as they have responsible attitudes towards holding and using those data, have been understood. The professional research bodies' Codes of Conduct have stood them in good stead.

Mintel[18] feels that the data protection legislation to date has actually reinforced the position of market researchers in their professional dedication to protecting respondents' interests.

16.16 SUMMARY

Survey data have to be processed before they are useful for management decision making: the processing stages cover editing, coding, and tabulation. All these activities must be expertly done to ensure that the processed data are valid and reliable.

Computers have revolutionized the handling of data and enabled complex analyses to be made: various programs are available; it is important to remember that sophisticated computer printouts are only as good as the programs from which they are derived.

Analysis and interpretation of processed data are closely linked and depend largely on the objectives of the survey. Statistical measures may range from the relatively simple, e.g., average, to sophisticated multi-variate analyses involving, perhaps, factor analysis, cluster analysis, etc.

It is largely a matter of opinion, plus the expressed wishes of clients, whether research reports should not only present survey data but also comment on such findings and offer specific strategic recommendations. Survey reports should be carefully planned in every detail: wording, format, printing, binding, etc.

Buying marketing research may be approached on the 'make-or-buy' principle common to other professional services to management. Evaluating the costs of marketing research can range from subjective estimates to sophisticated decision-tree theory based on Bayesian statistics.

REFERENCES

1. Market Research Society, *Guide to Good Coding Practice*, July 1983.
2. Katz, Mark, 'Advances in data editing techniques', Market Research Society Conference Papers, March 1980.
3. Joyce, Timothy, 'The role of the expert in market research', *Market Research Society Abstracts*, 1963.
4. Drucker, Peter, *The Practice of Management*, Heinemann, London, 1961.
5. Sheth, Jagdish N., 'How to get the most out of multivariate methods', *AMA Combined Proceedings*, no. 37, 1975.
6. Wills, P. A., 'Market research and the computer', Market Research Society Conference Papers, March 1980.
7. Yule, G. A., 'Why do we get sometimes nonsense correlations between times series?', *Journal of Royal Statistical Society*, vol. 89, January 1926.
8. Moser, C. A., and G. Kalton, *Survey Methods in Social Investigation*, Heinemann, London, 1971.
9. Ehrenberg, A. S. C., 'What research for what problem?', in: *Research in Marketing*, Market Research Society, London, 1964.
10. Nowik, Henry, 'The role of market research in a marketing orientated company', in: *Research in Marketing*, Market Research Society, London, 1964.
11. Treasure, John, 'Discussion opener', in: *Research in Marketing*, Market Research Society, London, 1964.
12. American Marketing Association, 'Preparation and presentation of the research report', *Journal of Marketing*, American Marketing Association, July 1948.

13. Gowers, Ernest, *Plain Words: A Guide to the Use of English*, HMSO, London, 1948.
14. British Institute of Management, 'Survey of marketing research in Great Britain', Information Summary no. 97, January 1962, British Institute of Management, London.
15. Ehrenberg, A. S. C., 'Rudiments of numeracy', *Journal of the Royal Statistical Society*, vol. 140, part 3, 1977.
16. Holmes, Cliff, 'The role of the market research statistician in the 1980s', Market Research Conference Papers, March 1980.
17. Worcester, Robert M., 'Improving the communications of research findings', ESOMAR Conference: 'Quality in Research', Montreux, August/September 1975.
18. Market Research, Special Report, Mintel, London, 1990.
19. Treasure, John, 'Market research in the sixties', *Market Research Society Yearbook*, 1970, Market Research Society, London.
20. Code of Conduct, Market Research Society and the Industrial Market Research Association, January 1989.
21. Bartram, Mary and Peter Bartram, 'Ethical dilemmas of the market researcher: Where do we now draw the line?', *European Research*, vol. 16, no. 4, November 1988.
22. Methven, Sir John, 'The use, mis-use, and non-use of market research in business and industry', *Journal of Market Research Society*, vol. 20, no. 3, July 1978.
23. Schlaifer, Robert, *Probability and Statistics for Business Decisions*, McGraw-Hill, New York, 1959.
24. Downham, John, 'Use of consumer market research: Introduction', in: *Consumer Market Research Handbook*, Robert Worcester and John Downham (eds), Van Nostrand Reinhold, Wokingham, 1978.
25. Green, Paul E., and Ronald E. Frank, 'Bayesian statistics and marketing research', *Applied Statistics*, vol. 15, 1966.

INDEX